# Parasitic Gaps

Parasitic Gaps

edited by Peter W. Culicover
and Paul M. Postal

The MIT Press
Cambridge, Massachusetts
London, England

This book was set in Times New Roman in '3B2' by Asco Typesetters, Hong Kong and was printed and bound in the United States of America.

Library of Congress Cataloging-in-Publication Data

Parasitic gaps / edited by Peter W. Culicover and Paul M. Postal.
    p.   cm. — (Current studies in linguistics; 35)
    Includes bibliographical references and index.
    ISBN 0-262-03284-8 (alk. paper)
    1. Grammar, Comparative and general—Syntax. 2. Parasitic gaps (Linguistics)
I. Culicover, Peter W. II. Postal, Paul Martin, 1936–   III. Current studies in linguistics series; 35.
P291.P374   2000
415—dc21                                         00-055043

# Contents

Preface    vii

**PART I**
**Some Historical Background**    1

**Chapter 1**
**Parasitic Gaps: A History**    3        Peter W. Culicover

**Chapter 2**
**Parasitic Gaps**    69        Elisabet Engdahl

**Chapter 3**
**Parasitic Chains Revisited**    99        Katalin É. Kiss

**PART II**
**What Is a Parasitic Gap?**    125

**Chapter 4**
**Versatile Parasitic Gaps**    127        Elisabet Engdahl

**Chapter 5**
**Parasitic Gaps and Resumptive**        Jamal Ouhalla
**Pronouns**    147

**Chapter 6**
**Parasitic Gaps in English: Some**        Robert D. Levine, Thomas E. Hukari,
**Overlooked Cases and Their**        and Michael Calcagno
**Theoretical Implications**    181

**Chapter 7**
**Further Lacunae in the English**        Paul M. Postal
**Parasitic Gap Paradigm**    223

**PART III**
**What Is Not a Parasitic Gap?**    251

**Chapter 8**
**Parasitic and Pseudoparasitic**          Paul M. Postal
**Gaps**    253

**Chapter 9**
**On the Nonexistence of True Parasitic**    Andreas Kathol
**Gaps in Standard German**    315

**PART IV**
**Restrictions on Parasitic Gaps**    339

**Chapter 10**
**On Some Distinctive Properties of**      Christine Tellier
**Parasitic Gaps in French**    341

**Chapter 11**
**Explaining Parasitic Gap**              Alan Munn
**Restrictions**    369

**Chapter 12**
**VP-Deletion and "Nonparasitic**         Christopher Kennedy
**Gaps"**    393

**Chapter 13**
**Missing Parasitic Gaps**    403          Paul M. Postal

References    419
Author Index    439
Subject Index    441

# Preface

Parasitic gaps (P-gaps), represented by the underlined gaps subscripted $p$ in example (1), have been an intensely studied subdomain of natural language syntax for almost twenty years.

(1) a. It was Ernest who pictures of _____$_p$ tended to depress _____.
    b. No matter which candidate the reporter criticized _____
       immediately after meeting _____$_p$, he won't vote for you.

An enormous body of research in several different frameworks has focused on the topic. As in other areas, as more work has been done and more learned, the complexity and mystery of the phenomenon have, perhaps unexpectedly, seemed to grow. This is even true if one focuses on a single language like English. Despite such growth, there seems to have been no full-scale work devoted exclusively to P-gaps. We hope to partially fill this lacunae in the present volume. In making available in one volume a range of diverse works, some new but a few drawn from early stages of work in the above cited period, we intend for the present collection to help researchers at all levels, both students and established professionals, better understand the current state of work on the topic.

In our view, this understanding should involve minimally six elements. First, one needs to have a good overall view of both the documented factual uniformity and diversity of P-gaps. Second, it is important to establish an idea of the boundary conditions that divide P-gaps from non-P-gaps, especially those non-P-gaps which have been taken to be P-gaps on occasion. Third, it is necessary to grasp the relation that exists between P-gaps and the diverse theoretical proposals that have been claimed either to illuminate their nature or to be supported/disconfirmed by P-gap properties. Fourth, one should establish clear generalizations as to how P-gaps relate to a variety of other syntactic properties including grammatical category, grammatical agreement, word order, command relations, grammatical case, distinctions between extraction gaps and other types of gaps, differences between pronominal and nonpronominal forms, control constructions, conditions on extraction (e.g., islands), conditions on the distribution of pronominal forms, and so on. Fifth, one should establish an understanding of the history of research on P-gaps. Sixth and finally, one should have available as complete an account as possible of the literature on the topic. We believe the present volume contributes to our understanding with respect to all these elements.

The volume contains four major sections. Section I, which is broadly historical, begins with a newly written study by Culicover that traces in great detail the history of work on P-gaps during the last few decades. Section I continues with a reprinted version of Engdahl 1983, widely, and we believe correctly, considered to be the work that initiated the modern study of P-gaps. Finally, section I contains an updated version of Kiss 1985, which focuses on the role of case properties in P-gap distribution and which considers in detail the P-gap facts in Hungarian and their parallels to those of English.

Section II considers broadly the identifying characteristics of P-gaps. It contains four new papers. The contribution from Engdahl appeals heavily to Swedish data to deal with a range of questions that have been widely discussed since her initial paper. These include the relation between P-gaps and category restrictions, anaphoric elements, referentiality, and island facts. A study by Ouhalla focuses on claimed P-gaps in Moroccan Arabic and their relation to resumptive pronouns. In their contribution, Levine, Hukari, and Calcagno, using English evidence, dispute the often-made claims that P-gaps are all of the category NP and that P-gaps have inherently pronominal properties. Finally, Postal considers putative evidence for pronominal characteristics of the P-gap phenomenon in a new area—that of their licensing gaps.

Section III contains two papers addressing the boundaries of the P-gap domain. Kathol's new paper argues that Standard German lacks true P-gaps; rather, he takes claimed P-gaps in German to instantiate the distinct pseudo P-gap phenomenon discussed in Postal 1994a, which is reprinted here. The latter paper questions the existence of P-gaps whose licensing gaps involve right extractions. It proposes to treat a range of putative P-gaps as being instead right-node raising gaps.

Finally, section IV contains four papers, three published here for the first time, dealing in detail with a variety of factors that limit the occurrence of genuine P-gaps. Tellier considers four major contrasts between French P-gaps and their English counterparts and relates the differences to distinctions in tense and agreement systems. Munn treats the relation between P-gaps and logical concepts such as individual variable as well as the link between P-gaps and coordination and pronouns. This section reprints Kennedy's (1997) argument that contrary to an earlier claim, a certain class of cases do not involve P-gaps "inside" elided VPs or indeed any P-gaps at all but rather ordinary pronouns as an instance of what Fiengo and May (1994) call "vehicle change." Finally, Postal extends Kennedy's argumentation and argues that although Kennedy's claim is essentially correct for the class of cases he treated, application of the same and related argumentation to a different range of data supports the claim that English has P-gaps "inside" of verbal ellipsis structures.

We believe that this book gives a valid overview of the current state of the art with respect to P-gap study at the end of the twentieth century. Most if not all issues of relevance that have been discussed since 1983 are either treated directly or referred to somewhere within the body of included studies. Thus we believe that the work included here provides a useful basis for further efforts to understand the fascinating puzzles of P-gaps and their relations to broader issues in syntactic theory.

# PART I

Some Historical Background

# Chapter 1

Parasitic Gaps: A History     Peter W. Culicover

The parasitic gap (henceforth P-gap) construction is exemplified by the following examples. The first gap, marked *t*, is called a "true gap" because it is in a position that normally permits extraction; for example, *which articles did John file t.*[1] The second gap, marked *pg* for "parasitic gap," appears in a location that normally does not permit extraction.[2]

(1) a. Which articles did John file *t* without reading *pg*? [E83:5,(1)]

    b. This is the kind of food you must cook *t* before you eat *pg*. [E83:5,(2)]

The key property of the P-gap construction is that a single filler (e.g., *which articles*), is the antecedent of more than one gap. Engdahl (1983) notes the following examples in support of this point.

(2) a. Here is the paper that John read *t* before filing *pg*. [E83:14,(35a)]

    b. ?Here is the paper that John read his mail before filing *t*. [E83:14,(35b)]

    c. Here is the paper that John read *t* before filing his mail. [E83:14,(35c)]

(3) a. Who did John's talking to *pg* bother *t* most? [E83:14,(36a)]

    b. ?Who did John's talking to *t* bother you most? [E83:14,(36b)]

    c. Who did John's talking to Mary bother *t* most? [E83:14,(36c)]

The ungrammatical examples are typical violations of extraction constraints (Chomsky 1973, 1981, 1986b).

The first section of this introductory chapter summarizes and gives examples to illustrate what I will call the Current Consensus Position (CCP) on P-gaps, much of it based on Engdahl's seminal work. Not surprisingly, almost everything that has been claimed about P-gaps has been challenged in the literature at one time or another, and the central sections of this chapter explore the variety of factual and theoretical issues that have been touched on since Engdahl 1983.

## 1.1 In the Beginning: Engdahl 1983

The study of P-gaps was effectively initiated by the publication of Engdahl 1983, although the phenomenon had been noted previously (Ross 1967, Bresnan 1977,[3] Taraldsen 1981). We reprint Engdahl's paper in this collection because it not only describes the phenomenon of P-gaps in some detail, but it systematically identifies the majority of the important questions that have attracted the attention of researchers since its publication. I highlight the essential points here.

The canonical P-gap examples are given in (1). Engdahl observes that even where a P-gap is licensed, native speaker judgments vary according to the precise configuration in which the P-gap appears. For example, she notes that although P-gaps in subordinate clauses are often quite acceptable (cf. (1a) and (2a)), acceptability declines for English P-gaps when the subordinate clause is tensed.

(4) a. Who did you tell $t$ that we were going to vote for $pg$?
   [E83:11,(18)]
   b. Which colleague did John slander $t$ because he despised $pg$?
   [E83:11,(19)]

The question of precisely where a P-gap may appear, and what properties of its local domain might affect its acceptability, concern what I will call the "domain of the P-gap." As far as I know there is no consensus position on this question.

A second question discussed by Engdahl concerns the configurational properties of the antecedent. The examples that we have already considered show that a P-gap is licensed by an antecedent in an Ā-position. The following show that a P-gap is (apparently) also licensed by Heavy NP Shift (see (5)), Object Raising (see (6)), and object deletion (see (7)).

(5) John offended $t$ by not recognizing $pg$ immediately [NP his favorite uncle from Cleveland]. [E83:12,(26)]

(6) These papers were hard for us to file $t$ without reading $pg$.
   [E83:12,(28)]

(7) This book is too interesting to put $t$ down without having finished $pg$. [E83:13,(29)]

Engdahl suggests (p. 13) that the key factor determining the appropriateness of a constituent as an antecedent of a P-gap is that it participates in an unbounded dependency, although this generalization is made somewhat problematic by the inclusion of Heavy NP Shift (p. 30, n. 3). Suppose, following Chomsky (1977), that all unbounded dependencies are produced by Ā-movements, either overt as in the case of *wh*-questions, or involving empty operators, as in the case of Object Raising. Crucially, NP movement, as in Passive and Raising to Subject, does not license P-gaps.

(8) a. *John was killed *t* by a tree falling on *pg*. [E83:13,(31)]
    b. *Mary seemed *t* to disapprove of John's talking to *pg*.
       [E83:13,(32)]

It appears that only Ā-movements, and not A-movements, license P-gaps. This forms a crucial part of the CCP.

CCP1. The antecedent of a P-gap must be in an Ā-position.

A possible corollary of CCP1 is that the antecedent of a P-gap forms a chain with a trace. For languages in which an operator in Ā-position appears to form a chain with a resumptive pronoun, it is an open question whether such an operator can be the antecedent of a P-gap (see section 1.3.5.1 for discussion). Moreover, a *wh*-phrase in situ does not license a P-gap, which suggests that it is S-structure where P-gaps are licensed, and not LF.

(9) a. *John filed which articles without reading *e*. [E83:14,(33)]
    b. *I forget who filed which articles without reading *e*. [E83:14,(34)]

This observation forms another important part of the CCP.

CCP2. A P-gap is licensed only at S-structure.

Engdahl also observes in her discussion of Swedish P-gaps that not only NPs but also PPs and APs can serve as the antecedent of P-gaps.[4]

(10) a. [PP Till himlen] är det inte säkert  att [NP alla [S′   som
           to  heaven  is it   not certain that     everyone that
        längtar [PP *pg*]]] kommer [PP *t*]
        longs            gets
        'To heaven, it is not certain that everyone who longs (there)
        gets.' [E83:17,(47a)]
     b. [AP Fattig] vill [NP ingen [S′ som någonsin varit [AP *pg*]]] bli [AP *t*]
           poor   want  no one  that has ever been            become
        igen.
        again

'Poor, no one who has ever been (it) wants to become again.'
[E83:17,(47b)]

These data point to the parallel question for any language that has P-gaps: what is the category of a possible P-gap, and what is the category of the antecedent of a P-gap? If the antecedent/gap pair is taken to form a (uniform) chain, then one would expect that the answer to both questions would be the same. Whether there is in fact a chain containing the antecedent and the P-gap is an independent question. It is logically possible, however, that the category of the antecedent can differ from that of the P-gap.

Although Engdahl provided examples of non-NP antecedents, the CCP position on category is that only NPs can be the antecedents of P-gaps, as discussed in more detail in the next section.

CCP3. The antecedent of a P-gap must be an NP.

Naturally it is incumbent on someone who holds this position to account for the apparent counterexamples in Swedish and other languages. Levine, Hukari, and Calagno, this volume, propose that CCP3 is false, on the basis of a number of robust English counterexamples. They do not, however, provide a complete account of why CCP3 is such a strong generalization. On the other hand, Engdahl ("Versatile P-gaps", this volume) suggests that languages with non-NP proforms may have non-NP P-gaps. She thus extends Postal's (1993b) proposal that the English P-gap is a null pronoun, a point to which I return below.

Another persistent claim in the literature is that subjects cannot license P-gaps, because of the ungrammaticality of sentences like those in (11).

(11)  a.  *Which articles $t$ got filed by John without him reading $pg$?
          [E83:20,(53)]
      b.  *Who $t$ sent a picture of $pg$? [E83:20,(54)]
      c.  *Who $t$ remembered talking to $pg$? [E83:20,(55)]
      d.  *Who $t$ remembered that John talked to $pg$? [E83:20,(56)]
      e.  *Which articles did you say $t$ got filed by John without him
          reading $pg$? [E83:20,(57)]

But Engdahl notes that a subject can be the antecedent of a P-gap in other configurations.

(12)  a.  Which caesar did Brutus imply $t$ was no good while ostensibly
          praising $pg$? [E83:21,(60)]

b. Who did you say John's criticism of *pg* would make us think *t* was stupid? [E83:22,(61′)]

Hence a plausible hypothesis is that what rules out the examples in (11) is that the true gap c-commands the P-gap. This forms another important part of the CCP.

CCP4. The true gap cannot c-command the P-gap.

As Engdahl points out, there are actually (at least) two types of P-gap constructions. In one, the P-gap appears to the left of the true gap.

(13) Kim$_i$ is a person that everyone who knows *pg*$_i$ really likes *t*$_i$ a lot.

In the other, the P-gap appears in a constituent to the right of the true gap.

(14) These are the reports that I filed *t*$_i$ without reading *pg*$_i$.

These two types of P-gaps are distinguished by the fact that the left P-gap is obligatory, in the sense that it cannot be replaced by a pronoun. The right P-gap, on the other hand, is optional.

(15) a. *Kim$_i$ is a person that everyone who knows her$_i$ really likes *t*$_i$ a lot.
     b. These are the reports that I filed *t*$_i$ without reading them$_i$.

When the pronoun appears to the left of the true gap, as in (15a), a WCO violation typically occurs, which may account for the apparent obligatoriness of the P-gap.

Engdahl also discusses the question of what kind of gap a P-gap might be. She argues that a P-gap is not an extraction gap of the sort found in cases of coordinate extraction, by noting simply that the contexts that allow P-gaps are not coordinate structures. The possibility remains open that a P-gap is the trace of movement of some kind of empty operator, in which case it would not actually be the trace of its apparent antecedent in an "across-the-board" extraction configuration.

Finally, Engdahl proposes that there is an "accessibility hierarchy" for P-gaps, similar to the extraction hierarchy of Keenan and Comrie (1977). I repeat her formulation here and add the numbers (i) etc. to the groupings for convenience of reference.

(16) *Accessibility hierarchy for occurrence of P-gaps [E83:9,(7)]*

manner adverbs $\qquad$ $\vee$ = more accessible than

$\vee$

temporal adverbs $\quad$ (i) $\quad$ untensed domains

$\vee$

purpose clauses

$\vee$ $\qquad\qquad$ $\vee$

$\left.\begin{array}{l} that \\ than \end{array}\right\}$ clauses $\quad$ (ii)

$\vee$

$\left.\begin{array}{l} when \\ because \\ cond.\ if \end{array}\right\}$ clauses $\quad$ (iii) tensed domains

$\vee$

$\left.\begin{array}{l} \text{relative clauses} \\ \text{indirect questions} \end{array}\right\}$ (iv)

Briefly, the best cases of P-gaps involve manner adverbs, whereas the worst involve relative clauses and indirect questions. As already noted, untensed domains are in general preferable to tensed domains. Some examples are given below.

(17) a. $\quad$ Which articles$_i$ did John file $t_i$ without reading $pg_i$?
$\qquad$ [E83:5,(1)] [manner adverb, untensed]

$\quad$ b. $\quad$ (?)?Who$_i$ did you talk to $t_i$ when you first met $pg_i$?
$\qquad$ [*when* clause, tensed]

$\quad$ c. $\quad$ *This book$_i$, it would be stupid to give $t_i$ to [$_{NP}$ someone
$\qquad$ [$_{S'}$ who has already read $pg_i$]] [E83:11,(22)]
$\qquad$ [relative clause, tensed]

But note that tensed domains have overt subjects, while the untensed subordinate clauses are typically subjectless gerunds or infinitives, or have PRO subjects. Hence the possibility cannot be ruled out that the presence of an overt, uncontrolled subject plays a role in determining the acceptability of a P-gap in a given context.

In summary, Engdahl's seminal paper either directly identifies or immediately suggests the key issues about P-gaps: the *location of the antecedent* (A- or Ā-position), the *level* at which the P-gap is licensed, the *character of the P-gap* (trace or pronominal or otherwise), the *anti-c-command condition*, the *obligatory/optional distinction*, and the *domain of the P-gap*.[5] Questions have also been raised as to whether the antecedent is actually the antecedent of the true gap, or whether the antecedent is rather some empty element that is linked to the antecedent of the true gap—the *character of the antecedent*.

## 1.2   The Common Consensus Position

Here I trace briefly the development of the CCP from the original observations of Engdahl to the work of Kayne (1983) and Chomsky (1986b).

### 1.2.1   Connectedness

Kayne (1983) observes that P-gaps within islands embedded in other islands produce ungrammaticality comparable to movement.

(18) a.   the books that it became difficult to talk about *t*
     b.   *the books that talking about *t* became difficult
          [movement] [K83:166,(5)]

(19) a.   ?the books you should read *t* before it becomes difficult to talk
          about *pg*
     b.   *the books you read *t* before [talking about *pg*] becomes difficult
          [P-gaps] [K83:166,(3a,b)]

If there is no movement involved in the P-gap, (19b) and comparable cases are not ruled out by Subjacency (which is a constraint on movement), nor by the ECP, since the P-gap is properly governed. But the generalization with the overt movement cases seems very strong.

Kayne therefore proposes an extension of the ECP to account for these recalcitrant P-gap cases.[6] The key idea is that in all of these cases, as well as in the standard ECP cases, the problematic empty category is on a left branch. On Kayne's proposal, an empty category is licensed if it and its antecedent are contained in the same "g-projection," defined informally as follows: Let $\gamma$ be a structural governor of XP. Then the immediate projection of $\gamma$ will be a g-projection of $\gamma$. If there is a sequence of structural governors in a configuration of uniform canonical government, then the g-projection of $\gamma$ will extend to the projection of the highest structural governor. The notion "configuration of canonical government" is a precedence relation that correlates with the relative linear order of verb and direct object in a language. The set of all g-projections constitutes the g-projection set. Kayne proposes an extension of the ECP such that the entire set of g-projections of all of the gaps in a tree must constitute a subtree that is locally c-commanded by the antecedent. A gap in a left branch is licensed just in case the g-projection of this gap meets this condition.

There are four basic cases. First of all, consider the case where $\alpha$ c-commands a gap on a right branch to the right of it.

(20) $[_{\gamma''} \, \alpha_i \, [_{\gamma'} \, [ \ldots [ \ldots [ \, \gamma \, e_i \, ]]]]]$

Here, $\gamma$ structurally governs $e_i$, and $\gamma'$ is a projection of $\gamma$. $\gamma''$ is a g-projection of $\gamma$ because it is a projection of $\gamma$. Hence $\alpha$ and $e_i$ are contained in the same g-projection set.

Second, suppose that $\alpha$ c-commands a gap on a left branch, where canonical government is to the right.

(21) $[ \, \alpha_i \, [_{\gamma'} \, [ \, \gamma \, e_i \, ] \ldots ]]$

In this case, $\gamma'$ is the largest g-projection of $\gamma$ that contains $e_i$. There is no g-projection of $\gamma$ that also contains $\alpha_i$, and so the empty category is not licensed. Although $\gamma'$ may be governed, it will not be canonically governed, because its governor will be to the right of it.

But suppose that there is another empty category on the right branch, in the configuration of (20).

(22) $[ \, \alpha_i \, [_{\gamma'} \, [ \, \gamma \, e_i \, ] \ldots t_i \, ]]$

In this case, the g-projection of $t_i$ contains the g-projection of $e_i$. So the g-projection set that contains $t_i$ and $e_i$ forms a subtree, namely $\gamma'$, that is c-commanded by $\alpha$. This is the configuration of a P-gap in a subject, for example.

Finally, consider a gap that is itself a left branch, say a subject, but in a configuration where there is no g-projection to a subtree locally c-commanded by the antecedent.

(23) $\alpha_i \, [ \ldots C \, [_{IP} \, t_i \ldots ]]$

By assumption, the complementizer C is not a structural governor. Hence the projection of C is not a g-projection of $t_i$. Thus there is an ECP violation. The maximal g-projection of $t_i$ is IP, which excludes $\alpha$.

The force of Kayne's analysis is that the antecedent of the true gap forms a chain with the P-gap that is subject to the same locality conditions that govern all chains. Moreover, the P-gap is a variable in the same sense that the true gap is a variable. There is no formal difference, on this analysis, between the chain that contains the P-gap and the chain that contains the true gap. This view has become a central part of the CCP.

CCP5. The P-gap is in a chain with the antecedent of the true gap.

Such a view is argued for by Levine, Hukari, and Calagno (this volume), although in a much different framework.

**1.2.2 Barriers**

Chomsky (1986b), taking into account the observations of Kayne (1983), proposes a view of P-gaps having its roots in the proposal of Contreras (1984) that there is a null operator that binds the P-gap. The P-gap, on this analysis, is the trace of the null operator, and the chain produced by movement of the null operator is subject to the usual locality conditions on movement.

In order to relate the antecedent of the true gap and the P-gap, Chomsky proposes that the chain of the true gap and the chain of the P-gap are "composed"; Chomsky (1986b:56) gives the following characterization of a composed chain:

(24) If $C = (\alpha_1, \ldots, \alpha_n)$ is the chain of the real gap, and $C' = (\beta_1, \ldots, \beta_m)$ is the chain of the P-gap, then the "composed chain"

$$(C, C') = (\alpha_1, \ldots, \alpha_n, \beta_1, \ldots, \beta_m)$$

is the chain associated with the P-gap construction and yields its interpretation.

It is clear that this is a stipulative solution, since there is no independent requirement that chain composition exist. Moreover, (24) is inexplicit regarding the formal operation that produces a composed chain given two primary chains.

Nevertheless, this approach suggests an account of the anti-c-command condition in terms of the binding theory. The P-gap is c-commanded and A-bound by the true gap, a situation that leads to a Condition C violation. The P-gap (or its chain) must be understood to be an r-expression. Similarly, an antecedent in an A-position A-binds the P-gap and produces a Condition C violation. This view forms part of the CCP, already noted. It is also part of the CCP that anti-c-command is due to Condition C of the binding theory.

CCP6. Anti-c-command is due to Condition C of the binding theory.

**1.2.3 Categorial Properties**

As noted, the consensus in the literature on P-gaps is that the antecedent of the P-gap must be an NP. This restriction may be related to the pronominal character of the gap; see for example Cinque (1990:115). Cinque cites the following examples from Italian to support this generalization.

(25) a. *[AP Quanto importanti] si    può diventare *t* [senza    sentirsi *pg*]
        how    important   REFL can become    without to-feel
     'How important can one become without feeling?'

b. *[$_{PP}$ A chi] hai        lasciato la  lettera *t* [dopo esserti
     to who you-have left     the letter    after to-be-REFL
   rivolto *pg*]
   returned
   'To whom did you leave the letter after having returned?'
c. *[$_{QP}$ Quanti]    ne        hai         presi *t* [senza
          how-much of-them you-have gotten  without
   pagarne *pg*]
   to-pay-for-of-them
   'How many of them did you get without paying for?'
d. *[$_{VP}$ VENUTO A CASA] era *t*   [senza    che fosse *pg* suo
          came         home       he-was without that he-was  his
   padre]
   father
   'He had come home without his father having (done so).'
e. *[$_{AdvP}$ Quanto gentilmente] si    è comportato *t* con  te
             how    nicely      REFL is behaved          with you
   [senza     comportarsi *pg* coi   tuoi  amici]?
   without to-behave-REFL with your friends
   'How nicely did he behave with you without behaving with
   your friends?'
[Ci90:102,(15a–e)]

These Italian facts and the comparable English examples appear to contrast with the situation in Swedish. Engdahl (1983) cites Swedish examples
in which the antecedent of the P-gap is not an NP; I repeat here the
examples in (10).

(10) a. [$_{PP}$ Till himlen] är det inte säkert  att [$_{NP}$ alla [$_{S'}$   som
            to   heaven is it   not certain that    everyone that
       längtar [$_{PP}$ *pg*]]] kommer [$_{PP}$ *t*]
       longs              gets
       'To heaven, it is not certain that everyone who longs (there)
       gets.' [E83:17,(47)]
   b. [$_{AP}$ Fattig] vill [$_{NP}$ ingen [$_{S'}$ som någonsin varit [$_{AP}$ *pg*]]] bli [$_{AP}$ *t*]
          poor    want  no-one   that has ever been             become
       igen.
       again.
       'Poor, no one who has ever been (it) wants to become again.'
       [E83:17,(47b)]

Cinque points out (p. 187, n. 9) that in these examples the P-gap is in a subject, and notes that the comparable examples in Italian, while not acceptable, are better than those in which the P-gap appears in an adjunct, as in (25). Cinque speculates that these are cases where extraction from the subject is itself almost acceptable.

Postal 1994a (reprinted in this volume) summarizes the arguments for taking P-gaps to be null pronouns. Cinque's examples, and the more general claim that P-gaps must be NPs, are examined by Engdahl in her paper in this volume. She argues that in Swedish the set of proforms is broader than that in English. If P-gaps are in fact proforms, and not simply pronominals, then this difference could be used to explain the fact that Swedish allows for non-NP P-gaps whereas English (arguably) does not. Levine, Hukari, and Calagno (this volume) make the stronger claim that a non-NP P-gap may occur even when there is no suitable overt proform in the language.

### 1.2.4 Summary of the CCP

In summary, the CCP is as in (26):

(26) CCP1. The antecedent of a P-gap must be in an $\bar{\text{A}}$-position.
 CCP2. A P-gap is licensed only at S-structure.
 CCP3. The antecedent of a P-gap must be an NP.
 CCP4. The true gap cannot c-command the P-gap.
 CCP5. The P-gap is in a chain with the antecedent of the true gap.
 CCP6. Anti-c-command is a consequence of Condition C of the binding theory.

I take up the primary factual challenges to the CCP in section 1.3. I summarize in section 1.4 the major theoretical proposals concerning the licensing of P-gaps, in particular those that seek to derive the existence of P-gaps from general principles of Universal Grammar and the specific properties of individual languages.

### 1.3 Challenges to the CCP

### 1.3.1 Location of the Antecedent

Concerning the location of the antecedent (or the operator that forms part of the antecedent chain), the CCP holds that the antecedent, whatever it is, must be in an $\bar{\text{A}}$-position. There is a crucial relationship between this view and the CCP view that the P-gap is in a chain with the antecedent. But observations about apparent P-gap constructions involving clitic movement in the Romance languages, Heavy NP Shift in English and scrambling in languages such as German, Hindi, and Persian have raised the possibility that the antecedent of a P-gap could also be in an A-position. On the other hand, it is possible that such apparent A-movements are actually Ā-movements, and a number of researchers have taken this position. There is a substantial literature, which I do not have space to review here, in which the possibility of P-gaps with scrambling is taken as evidence that scrambling is a type of Ā-movement (see for example the papers in Corver and van Riemsdijk 1994).

In this section I review the evidence for apparent A-movement P-gaps.

**1.3.1.1  Clitic Movement**  Since Kayne 1975 it has been standard to treat the relationship between an argument clitic and an argument position as involving A-movement.[7] It would then follow that if CCP1 is correct, clitics cannot license P-gaps.

1.3.1.1.1  FRENCH  Tellier (1991) notes, however, that the following examples in French are not totally unacceptable [Te91:136,(17)–(19)].[8]

(27) a.  C'est un livre dont$_i$ la critique $t_i$ a été publiée par les
         détracteurs $pg_i$.
         'It is a book of-which the critique has been published by the
         detractors.'
     b.  ??La critique $t_i$ en$_i$ a été publiée par les détracteurs $pg_i$.
         'The critique of-it has been published by the detractors.'

(28) a.  Voilà une idée dont$_i$ on attribue le charme $t_i$, au caractére
         subversif $pg_i$.
         'Here-is an idea of-which one attributes the charm to-the
         subversive character.'
     b.  ??On en$_i$ attribue le charme $t_i$, au caractère subversif $pg_i$.
         'One of-it attributes the charm to-the subversive character.'

(29) a.  C'est là un sentiment dont$_i$ on peut attribuer la pérennité $t_i$ à
         la manifestation assidue $pg_i$.
         'This-is a sentiment of-which the perenniality is attributable to
         the constant manifestation.'
     b.  ??On peut en$_i$ attribuer la perennité $t_i$ à la manifestation assidue
         $pg_i$.
         'One can of-it attribute the perenniality to the constant
         manifestation.'

Noting that P-gaps are not possible in French with object clitics,[9] Tellier leaves open the question of why the cases with *en* allow variation in judgments. One possibility is that *en* is adjoined to an Ā-position, whereas object clitics are in A-positions.[10]

It is clearly not an accident that well-formed P-gap constructions occur in French not only with Ā-binding antecedents, as in (30), but with *dont* 'of-which/whom', as in (27)–(29).

(30) Voilà le livre$_i$ que vous avez rangé $t_i$ sans avoir lu $pg_i$.
here-is the book that you have put-away without to-have read
'Here is the book that you put away without having read.'
[Te91:135,(16a)]

I discuss the "double *dont*" type of P-gap construction in section 1.3.6.3.

1.3.1.1.2 SPANISH   Campos (1991) argues that Spanish P-gaps have the following distinctive properties: (i) they can be licensed by clitics, and (ii) they can be licensed by *wh*-in-situ. Some relevant examples are the following:

(31) a. Lo archivaron $t_i$ sin leer $pg_i$.
   it they-filed without to-read
   'They filed it without reading (it).'
   b. Conozco a un muchacho que los archivó $t$ sin leer $pg$.
   I-know a boy that them filed without to-read
   'I know a boy that filed them without reading (them).'
   [Ca91:119,(6a)]
   c. No sé quién preguntó por qué José los archivó sin
   NEG know who asked why Jose them filed without
   leer $pg$.
   to-read
   'I don't know who asked why Jose filed them without reading
   (them).' [Ca91:119,(6b)]

(32) a. ¿Tú archivaste cuál artículo sin leer $pg$?
   you filed which article without to-read
   [Ca91:120,(9a)]
   b. ¿Tú mandate cuál artículo sin revisar $pg$?
   you sent which article without to-proofread
   [Ca91:120,(9b)]

Campos ties the possibility of P-gaps in (32) to the fact that *wh*-in-situ in Spanish can be used as a direct question, which he takes to mean that in

Spanish it is generally possible to have an operator in situ at S-structure. To account for the P-gap with clitics, Campos suggests that the true gap is a null operator-in-situ that is bound by a null topic that also binds the clitic.[11] The structure is thus the following:

(33) TOPIC$_i$ lo$_i$ archivaron $Op_i$ [sin leer $pg_i$]

The P-gap is then licensed by the operator-in-situ. The question naturally arises as to why the same construction is impossible in French, which also permits *wh*-in-situ in direct questions.

Suñer and Yépez (1988) note the following in Quiteño.[12]

(34) a. Te      permitirán      entregar [e] sin      terminar [e]
        to-you they-would-allow to-hand-in  without to-finish
        'Would they allow you to hand it in without finishing it?'
     b. La carta de   ese  idiota, ahí   dejé *t* sin       siquiera abrir *pg*.
        the letter from that idiot   there I-left without even        to-open
        'That idiot's letter, I left it there without even opening it.'

Suñer and Yépez suggest that there are null object pronominals in both clauses in (34a) that happen to have the same referent. Campos proposes that the empty argument of *entregar* could be a null operator that licenses the P-gap in the same way that the *wh*-in-situ does in (32).

Campos also discusses examples in which a null subject appears to license a P-gap, an apparent counterexample to the anti-c-command condition (CCP4).

(35) Qué pasó      con el   avión? —Explotó      antes de hacer
     what happened with the plane      it-exploded before of to-make
     revisar *pg*.
     to-check
     'What happened with the plane? —It exploded before they checked (it).' [Ca92:135,(35a)]

Campos proposes that there is a null operator (not *pro*) in the subject position in such cases. An empty pronominal does not license the P-gap.

(36) *Los restos   del    avión muestrán que      explotó antes de
      the  remains of-the plane show        that *pro* exploded before of
      hacer    revisar *pg*.
      to-make to-check
      [Ca92:135,(36)]

Nor does an overt subject.

(37) *El avion explotó   antes  de hacer    revisar *pg*.
the plane exploded before of to-make to-check
[Ca92:135,(35b)]

It is particularly striking that a null operator in subject position could license a P-gap, in view of the general tendency for overt operators in situ and in subject position not to do so.

The factual claim that P-gaps are licensed by clitics in Spanish is independently attested by García-Mayo (1992:17), who also notes that this stands in sharp contrast with French (Tellier 1991:135). Rizzi (1986) and García-Mayo (1992:17) note that only [–animate] clitics may license P-gaps in Spanish. Catalan and Italian also allow for the licensing of P-gaps by clitics, as in the following examples [G-M92:22,(23)–(24)].

(38) a. *Catalan*
El$_i$ vaig enviar $t_i$ [sense signar *pg*$_i$ com indicavan les instrucciones]

b. *Italian*
L$_i$'ho   spedito $t_i$ senza   firmare *pg*$_i$ come indicato  nelle
it I-have sent        without to-sign   as      indicated (in) the
istruzione.
instructions

(39) a. *Catalan*
El$_i$ vaig cuinar $t_i$ sense posar *pg*$_i$ al forn.

b. *Italian*
L'ho   cucinato $t_i$ senza   mettere *pg*$_i$ al    forno.
it I-have cooked      without to-put      in-the oven

García-Mayo proposes that the structure in these cases is one that has a null operator binding *pro* in the position of the gap in the clause that contains the P-gap. The null operator forms a chain directly with the clitic, which is assumed to be adjoined to IP, and is thus in an Ā-position. These observations are consistent with the proposal of Rizzi (1986) that Italian allows for object *pro* in certain cases and with the proposal of Cinque (1990) that P-gaps are in fact *pro*.

An important question that arises in this case is the adjunction site of the clitic such that it can be an antecedent of the P-gap. The difference between Spanish, Italian, and Catalan on the one hand and French on the other follows if the clitic is adjoined to IP in the first case, but to V in the second case. García-Mayo points out that this is precisely the difference proposed by Kayne (1991) to account for the fact that French clitics adjoin to the left of infinitives, whereas clitics adjoin to the right of infinitives in the other languages.[13]

Contrasting with the Italian data given by García-Mayo is the claim by Haverkort (1993), who cites Sportiche (1983) and Chomsky (1982), that Romance clitics cannot license P-gaps. Haverkort gives the following example from Italian, due originally to Rizzi (see Chomsky 1982:65).

(40) *Italian*

    \*Glie-li$_i$      dobbiamo far      mettere $t_i$ nello  scaffale invece

    to-him-them we-must  to-make to-put     on-the shelf    instead

    di lasciare $pg_i$ sul     tavola.

    of to-leave     on-the table

    'We must make him put them on the shelf, instead of leaving (them) on the table.' [H93:137,(14a)]

Moreover, as discussed in the next section, Haverkort makes the same proposal for Germanic that García-Mayo suggests for those Romance languages in which clitics license P-gaps, and he rules out such an analysis for the Romance languages in which they do not.

1.3.1.1.3 GERMANIC Haverkort (1993) cites the following data in support of the claim that Germanic clitics license P-gaps [H93:137–138,(15)–(16)].

(41) a. *German*

    Der Peter hat'n$_i$  [ohne $pg_i$ anzusehen] $t_i$ zusammengeschlagen.

    the Peter has-him  without to-look-at    beaten-up

    'Peter beat him up without looking at (him).'

  b. *Swiss German*

    Der Peter het'ne$_i$  [ooni $pg$  aaz'luege] $t_i$ zämegschlage.

    the Peter has-him  without to-look-at    beaten-up

    'Peter beat him up without looking at (him).'

  c. *Dutch*

    Dat ik't$_i$    [zonder $pg_i$ uitgelezen te hebben] $t_i$ opgestuurd

    that I-it/them without    read       to have     sent

    heb.

    have

    'That I sent it/them away without reading (it/them).'

  d. *West Flemish*

    Dan-k ze$_i$    [zunder $pg$ gelezen t'een] $t_i$ opgestierd een.

    that-I it/them without    read    to-have sent      have

    'That I sent it/them away without reading (it/them).'

The explanation that Haverkort gives for the Germanic data is that a clitic is a maximal projection in an $\bar{A}$-position. Specifically, the clitic adjoins to IP (p. 131). The Germanic clitic is thus distinguished from the Romance clitic, which is a head, and the adjunction of the Germanic clitic is distinguished from scrambling, which is typically viewed as an A-movement. (For discussion of Romance clitics that license P-gaps, see sections 1.3.1.1.1 and 1.3.1.1.2, and for discussion of cases in which scrambling licenses P-gaps, see section 1.3.1.2.)

**1.3.1.2 Scrambling** The literature on the configuration of the antecedent has generally taken one of two positions on the position of the antecedent of the P-gap. Some researchers have held to the CCP that the antecedent of the P-gap is in an $\bar{A}$-position, thus drawing the conclusion that scrambling to various positions is $\bar{A}$-movement. This is the conclusion of Browning and Karimi (1994) for Persian, Felix (1985) for German, and Bennis and Hoekstra (1985a,b) for Dutch. Webelhuth (1989) suggests that there can be "mixed" $A/\bar{A}$-positions in order to accommodate the fact that scrambling in German also shows A-properties, as it does in Persian. But Bayer and Kornfilt (1994) note that there are differences in judgments in German P-gap examples depending on whether an antecedent NP is moved to [Spec,CP] or adjoined to IP under scrambling. In the latter case, only a pronominal clitic and not a full NP allows for an apparent P-gap.

(42) *Da hat diesen Mann$_i$ der Polizist [ohne $pg_i$ verwarnt zu
there has this man the policeman without warned to
haben] $t_i$ ins Gefängnis gesteckt.
have in-the prison put
'The policeman has put this man into jail without having warned
him.' [B&K94:25,(11e)]

(43) Da hat ihn$_i$ der Polizist [ohne $pg_i$ verwarnt zu haben] $t_i$ ins
there has him the policeman without warned to have in-the
Gefängnis gesteckt.
prison put
'The policeman has put him into jail without having warned him.'
[B&K94:25,(11d)]

Bayer and Kornfilt appear to suggest that these cases are not true P-gaps and that they are therefore not evidence for the $\bar{A}$-character of scrambling. There is an alternative, which is that the movement of clitics is different from scrambling, a position taken by Haverkort (1993).

Huybregts and van Riemsdijk (1985) note that although scrambling appears to be an Ā-movement that licenses P-gaps in Dutch, there are problems with this view. Example (44) shows the apparent P-gap in Dutch, while (45) shows the same configuration with a pronoun in place of the gap.

(44) Hij heeft deze  artikelen [zonder PRO *ec* te lezen] opgeborgen.
     he  has  these articles    without        to read  filed

(45) Hij heeft deze  artikelen [zonder ze    te lezen] opgeborgen.
     he  has  these articles    without them to read  filed

If the NP *deze artikelen* were in an Ā-position, then we would expect a WCO violation, as in the case of topicalization. Huybregts and van Riemsdijk (1985) propose that the construction in (44) is not in fact a P-gap construction but an instance of the leftward counterpart of Right Node Raising. I return to this interpretation of this class of P-gaps in section 1.3.1.3; see also Kathol (this volume), who argues that the (apparent) P-gaps in German are pseudo-P-gaps.

Müller and Sternefeld (1994:373–375) argue that scrambling is an Ā-movement that licenses P-gaps in German, and that there is no need to assign scrambling a mixed status, as proposed by Webelhuth (1989). Compare the following examples.

(46) ?weil      Fritz jeden Gast$_i$      [ohne $e_i$ anzuschauen] seinem$_i$
     because Fritz every guest-ACC without to-look-at    his
     Nachbarn      vorgestellt     hat
     neighbor-DAT introduced-to has

(47) *?weil      Fritz jeden Gast$_i$      seinem$_i$ Nachbarn      [ohne $e_i$
     because Fritz every guest-ACC his       neighbor-DAT without
     anzuschauen] vorgestellt     hat
     to-look-at    introduced-to has

(48) *?weil      Fritz jeden Gast$_i$      der   Maria      [ohne $e_i$
     because Fritz every guest-ACC ART Maria-DAT without
     anzuschauen] vorgestellt     hat
     to-look-at    introduced-to has

According to Mahajan (1990), the P-gap in (47) is bound by *jeden Gast$_i$*, which renders it ungrammatical. But Müller and Sternefeld note that (48) is equally ungrammatical without the bound pronoun. Hence, they argue, there is no need to consider the scrambled antecedent of the P-gap in the grammatical case to be in a mixed or A-position. Lee and Santorini (1994) make the same point.

Neeleman (1994) claims that P-gaps in Dutch are much less acceptable than they are in English and cites the Bayer/Kornfilt claim for German. But Neeleman goes on to suggest that the P-gap is in a null operator chain that is licensed by an antecedent in an A-position. In the following example, the P-gap is licensed by an NP that is also the antecedent of an anaphor.

(49) dat Jan [de  rivalen]$_i$ namens      elkaar$_i$ [$Op_i$ [zonder $t_i$ aan
     that Jan  the rivals    on-behalf-of each-other  without  at
     te  kijken]] feliciteert
     to look      congratulates
     [N94:403,(30)]

Neeleman notes the same P-gap pattern in passives—

(50) dat [de  boeken]$_i$ door Jan [$Op_i$ [zonder $pg_i$ in te  kijken]] $t_i$
     that the books     by   Jan          without     in to look
     afgekraakt worden
     slated     are

—as well as in nominalizations.

(51) het [$Op_i$ [zonder $t_i$ in te  kijken]] afkraken van boeken$_i$
     the       without     in to look      slating  of  books

In (51) there is no basis for a movement analysis. Neeleman concludes that in Dutch (but not in English), P-gaps can be A-bound. The mechanism that produces this result is a difference in the status of the null operator: in Dutch it is governed, while in English it is not. By stipulation, adjuncts in Dutch are in the governing domain of the verb, while in English they are not.

Mahajan (1994:317–323) argues that Hindi has P-gaps on the basis of examples such as the following:

(52) kOn sii kitaab (mohan soctaa hE ki) raam-ne  [binaa PRO $e_2$
     which book    Mohan thinks that    Ram-ERG   without
     paRhe] $e_1$ pheNk dii
     reading    threw away
     'Which book (does Mohan think that) Ram threw away without reading?'

The issue for Mahajan is whether a constituent that is in a scrambled argument position can also be the antecedent of a P-gap. In the following example, the reflexive cannot be in an argument position because it must reconstruct in order to be bound.

(53) apnii$_i$ kOn sii kitaab$_j$ binaa PRO $e_2$ paRhe us   aadmii ne$_i$ $e_1$
     self's which book   without     reading that man-ERG
     pheNk dii
     threw away
     lit. 'Self's which book without reading the man threw away.'

However, in the following example the *wh*-phrase binds the pronoun from an argument position and hence cannot be the antecedent of the P-gap.

(54) *kOn sii kitaab$_i$ [us   aadmii ne jis-ne use$_i$ dekhaa  thaa]
      which book   that man-ERG who it   saw     be-PST
      [binaa PRO $e_2$paRhe] $e_1$ pheNk dii
      without    reading  threw away
      'Which book did that man who saw it throw away without reading?'

But if there is no pronoun, the *wh*-phrase can be analyzed as being in an Ā-position.

(55) kOn sii kitaab$_i$ [us   aadmii ne jis-ne mohan-ko dekhaa thaa]
     which book   that man-ERG who Mohan   saw    be-PST
     [binaa PRO $e_2$ paRhe] $e_1$ pheNk dii
     without    reading  threw away
     'Which book did that man who saw Mohan throw away without reading?'

Taking a somewhat different perspective, Browning and Karimi (1994) in their study of Persian suggest that the classical A/Ā dichotomy is not the correct one for characterizing the licensing of P-gaps. Rather, they suggest, the key property of the antecedent of the P-gap is that it is in an adjoined, not an argument position, but it is also in a Case position and in virtue of this can be the antecedent of a reflexive.

Déprez (1994) contrasts the German/Dutch scrambling with object movement (O-M) in Icelandic and Danish, which does not appear to license P-gaps.

(56) *Icelandic ( Déprez 1989)*
     a. *Eg las    baekunar$_i$ alltaf/ekki $t_i$ [an tehss adh kaupa $pg_i$]
        I   read book      always/not  without      buying
        [D94:108,(16a)]
     b. *Eg bothadhi petta granmeti$_i$ ekki/aldreai $t_i$ [an thess adh
        I   eat      this vegetable not/never      without
        sjodha $pg_i$]
        cooking
        [D94:108,(16b)]

(57) *Danish (Vikner 1990)*
  *Han inviterede dem$_i$ [uden    at kende $pg_i$ pa forhand] $t_i$
  he   invited    them without to know    beforehand
  [D94:108,(17)]

But both Icelandic and Danish license P-gaps with *wh*-antecedents.

(58) *Icelandic*
  Hvadha granmeti$_i$ bortar thu $t_i$ [an thess ath sjotha $pg_i$]
  which   vegetable eat    you    without    cooking
  [De94:108,(18a)]

(59) *Danish (Vikner 1990)*
  Hvor mange gaester$_i$ har han invitered $t_i$ [uden    at kende $pg_i$
  how   many   guests   has he   invited    without to know
  pa forhand]
  beforehand
  [De94:109,(18b)]

Icelandic also allows O-M of a *wh*-phrase. Example (60) suggests that it is the particular configuration of the landing site that determines whether a P-gap is licensed, not the character of the antecedent as an operator (e.g., at LF).

(60) *Hver etur hvadah granmetti$_i$ ekki/aldrei $t_i$ [an thess adh sjodha $t_i$]
  who eats which   vegetable not/never    without    cooking

   Déprez proposes that the landing site of O-M is different in those languages where P-gaps are licensed and in those where they are not. She suggests that where O-M licenses a P-gap, its landing site is a Caseless position, while it is a Case position when it does not. The Ā-properties of the antecedent of a P-gap in the case of O-M are attributed to the absence of Case; however, a Caseless position may be an argument position in other respects, which accounts for the A-properties of O-M noted by Webelhuth (1989).

**1.3.1.3 Apparent VP-adjoined Antecedents**   Heavy NP Shift is generally viewed as adjunction within VP, produced by local movement. A similar approach is taken to VP-scrambling in languages like German and Dutch. It is an open question whether these are A- or Ā-movements. There is evidence that both Heavy NP Shift and scrambling license P-gaps, a property that is typically reserved for Ā-movements.

   The possibility of P-gaps with Heavy NP Shift in English is illustrated by Engdahl (1983) with examples such as (61).

(61)  John offended *t* by not recognizing *pg* immediately [$_{NP}$ his favorite
      uncle from Cleveland]. [E83:12,(26)]

The independent claim by Engdahl (1983) that P-gaps are only licensed
by an antecedent in an S-structure Ā-position is called into question if
the heavy NP can be shown to be in an A-position. But another variable
at play here is whether or not there is actually a P-gap in this type of
sentence. Postal (1994a, reprinted in this volume) denies that these cases
involve P-gaps; if this is correct, then they do not bear on the analysis of
P-gaps.

Briefly, on Postal's analysis, the structure of (5) is derived not by Heavy
NP Shift from the object position of *offended*, but by applying RNR to
the direct object of *offended* and the direct object of *recognizing*. This
produces the following structure, parallel to that of (5).

(62)  John offended [*e*] by not recognizing [*e*] [$_{NP}$ his favorite uncle from
      Cleveland]

This analysis has a range of potentially very dramatic consequences for
the analysis of P-gaps themselves. It raises the possibility that cases of apparent P-gaps produced by any instance of Ā-movement are actually produced by RNR or an equivalent construction. So, in the case of scrambling
for example, it is possible that what has been claimed to be the P-gap
configuration in (63a) is actually the mirror image of the RNR configuration, shown in (63b), suggested by Huybregts and van Riemsdijk (1985).

(63)  a.  ... NP$_i$ PP [$_{Adjunct}$ *pg*$_i$ V] *t*$_i$ V
      b.  ... NP$_i$ PP [$_{Adjunct}$ [*e*] V] [*e*] V

Of course, the soundness of any proposal along these lines depends on
independently motivating such a left mirror image counterpart of RNR in
these languages. See Bennis and Hoekstra (1985a) and Postal (1994a) for
additional discussion of this point.

A proposal along related lines for German is due to Kathol (1995) for
cases such as (64), due to Felix (1985:190). Note that the antecedent is the
scrambled direct object.

(64)  a.  Hans hat Maria$_i$ [ohne *pg*$_i$ anzusehen] geküßt.
          Hans has Maria   without to-look-at   kissed
      b.  Man hat Hans$_i$ [ohne *pg*$_i$ zu verständigen] entlassen.
          one   has Hans  without  to notify        laid off

Kathol proposes an HPSG analysis in which the PP headed by *ohne* and
the V′ share the same COMPS (complements) list. Such an approach is

motivated by the fact that at least in German the P-gap construction with scrambling has a quasi-coordinate character.

A crucial property of this analysis is that it cannot accommodate subject P-gaps, owing to the branching structure of the subject and the VP. Interestingly, in contrast to English, German and Dutch lack subject P-gaps.

(65) a. *Dit is een vraag$_i$ waar [iedereen [die $pg_i$ over dent]] een
       this is a question which everyone who about thinks an
       antwoord $t_i$ op weet
       answer to knows

     b. *Dies ist ein Umstand$_i$ wo/welcher [jeder [der $pg_i$
       this is an understanding where/which everyone who
       von gehört hat]] $t_i$ mit rechnen muß.
       heard has with count must
       [K94:367,(11)]

P-gaps are possible only with *ohne* ('without'), *(an)statt* ('instead of'), and *um* ('in order to') (p. 308f).[14]

An additional piece of evidence for the shared COMP analysis is that the shared antecedent can be dative—

(66) Maurice hat seiner Tochter [ohne Geld zu geben]
     Maurice has his daughter-DAT without money to give
     helfen können.
     help could
     'Maurice was able to help his daughter without giving her money.'
     [K94: 313,(22a)]

—but only when the dative is assigned by both V's, as in (67).

(67) a. *Hans hat seine Tochter [ohne Geld zu geben] unterstützen
       Hans has his daughter without money to give support
       können.
       could

     b. ?Peter hat jeden Gast seinem Nachbarn ohne anzuschauen
       Peter has every guest his neighbor without to-look-at
       vorgestellt.
       introduced

     c. Peter hat jeden Gast ohne anzuschauen seinem Nachbarn
       vorgestellt.
       [K94:313f:(23b),(26a,b)]

Kathol (this volume) extends his analysis to argue that there are no P-gaps in German. He argues that the cases of putative German P-gaps actually represent Left Node Raising; that is, German only has pseudo P-gaps.

Another potential consequence of Postal's proposal is that even standard P-gap constructions may turn out to be pseudoparasitic. Such a possibility arises if the constituent that is separated from the rest of the sentence in the RNR construction in a language like English can itself move to another position. Under such circumstances, the configuration in (68a) would actually be that in (68b).

(68) a. $XP_i \ldots V \; t_i \; [_{\text{Adjunct}} \ldots pg_i]$

    b. $XP_i \ldots V \; [e] \; [_{\text{Adjunct}} \ldots [e]] \; t_i$

Again, the soundness of such a proposal rests on independent motivation for the properties of RNR, as well as the theoretical status of the notion that a construction such as RNR can be completely neutralized by a subsequent movement.

In part Postal's argument for the existence of pseudo-P-gaps rests on the observation that non-NPs may undergo RNR, producing the appearance of P-gaps with non-NP antecedents.

(69) a. John seemed $t_i$ to everyone $[_{\text{AP}}$ very pleased with the outcome$]_i$.

    b. John seemed $[e]$ to everyone and Mary certainly was $[e]$ when I last saw her $[_{\text{AP}}$ very pleased with the outcome$]_i$.

    c. John seemed $[e]$ to everyone without actually being $[e]$ $[_{\text{AP}}$ very pleased with the outcome$]_i$.

If leftward movement of an RNR constituent is permitted, it follows that there should be pseudo-P-gap constructions with non-NP antecedents to the left as well. If such cases exist, they would be consistent with the CCP in a strict sense, although they would produce apparent counterexamples. If these non-NPs in fact fail to produce P-gaps, then we would have to rule out the possibility that movement could apply to the RNR structure.

This last possibility is explored by Steedman (1987), who applies Dowty's (1988) device for handling nonconstituent conjunction to P-gaps. Dowty (1988) showed that it is possible in a categorial grammar to conjoin nonconstituents, each of which must be combined with a particular category in order to form a complete phrase. This device can be applied to RNR. For example, if *John saw* requires an NP for completion and *Bill insulted* also requires an NP for completion, then the conjunction *John saw and Bill insulted* is a coordinate that can be completed with an NP: *[[John saw and Bill insulted] Mary]*. The application to pseudo-P-gaps is evident. Extending this device to P-gaps is conceptually straightforward; in these cases the expression that completes the phrase is to the left, not to the right, as in the case of RNR. What remains unclear in such an approach is why non-NPs cannot freely be the antecedent of a P-gap, given that non-NPs can freely undergo RNR. Moreover, Steedman's approach does not account in any obvious way for the evidence that a P-gap is pronominal. See section 1.3.2 for further discussion.

### 1.3.2 The Character of the Gap

CCP5 holds that a P-gap forms a chain with some antecedent, and hence is a trace. The literature also contains arguments that it is pronominal. There are two variants of both approaches. On one variant of the trace analysis, T1, the empty category forms a chain with the antecedent of the true gap. On the second variant, T2, the empty category forms a chain with a null operator which in turn is linked to the chain that contains the antecedent and the true gap.[15] On one variant of the pronoun analysis, P1, the parasitic gap is an empty pronoun.[16] On the other variant, P2, the parasitic gap is an anaphor, related to a reflexive or the trace of NP movement.

**1.3.2.1  P-gaps as Traces**  T1 was proposed originally by Chomsky (1982), within a framework in which there is only one empty category [*e*]. This is assigned values of the features [pronoun] and [anaphor] on the basis of its contextual distribution. A trace, which is [−pronoun, −anaphor], occurs when [*e*] is $\bar{\text{A}}$-bound by an operator. This is the case for both the true gap and the P-gap, as can be seen in (70), on the assumption that the relative pronoun is an operator.

(70)  which$_i$ [we filed $t_i$ [without reading $pg_i$]]

This theory was undermined in two ways. First, as Kayne (1983) observed, the P-gap shows Subjacency effects. While the P-gap is not subjacent to the antecedent in either (70) or the following example, only the latter is ungrammatical.

(71)  *which$_i$ [we filed $t_i$ [without meeting [$_\alpha$ the person who wrote $pg_i$]]]

The Subjacency violation suggests that there is an extraction from the constituent labeled $\alpha$, but application of the contextual determination of empty categories to P-gaps does not involve extraction from the P-gap position.[17]

Second, Brody (1984) showed that Chomsky's theory of the contextual definition of empty categories was in part factually incorrect, and in part

followed from independent grammatical principles such as the ECP and
the θ-Criterion.

A different version of T1 is the proposal of Frampton (1990). Here the
traces are base-generated and Subjacency is a condition on the well-
formedness of chains. On his analysis there are two chains, one containing
the true gap and one containing the P-gap. The head of the P-gap chain is
replaced by a trace, allowing this chain to be linked to the higher chain.
Movement of the antecedent of the true gap introduces an intermediate
trace that locally c-commands the trace that heads the P-gap chain. As a
consequence, a chain is formed between the P-gap and the antecedent.[18]
The tree in (72) illustrates.

(72) a. Alex, who friends of *pg* admire *t* [F90:49,(1b)]

b. Alex,

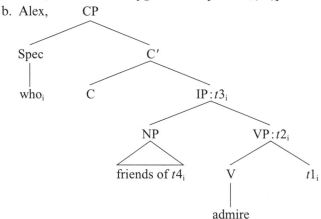

Here, the traces *t1*, *t2*, and *t3* are produced by movement of *who* from the
VP into [Spec,CP]. The trace *t4*, on the other hand, is not produced by
movement at all; it is the trace of the deleted *wh*-phrase.

A consequence of Frampton's analysis is that extraction from an adjunct produces a Subjacency violation, while the links of a parasitic chain
obey Subjacency. Tellier (1991:182f) notes that Frampton's analysis does
not work for French P-gaps involving double-*dont* (see section 1.3.6.3),
because the true gap in this case is in the subject, while the P-gap is in the
VP. There is thus no intermediate trace in the true chain that is attached
to VP that can be used to link to the parasitic chain without a Subjacency
violation.

Apparent evidence that the P-gap is a trace is the fact that it appears to
produce ECP violations. The following are due to Munn (1992:22).

(73) the man
    a. *who John suspected $t$ after $pg$ had committed the crime
    b. *who Bill said $t$ was innocent after $pg$ had committed the crime
    c. *who Bill believed $t$ to be innocent (even) after $pg$ had been
       convicted of the crime

These cases can be analyzed as similar to *that-t* violations, where the conjunction *after* blocks proper government of the P-gap by the null operator, for example:

(74) $[_{PP}\ Op_i\ [\ \text{after}\ [_{IP}\ t_i\ \ldots ]]]$

In contrast, it has been argued (Perlmutter 1971) that languages that permit empty subject pronominals lack *that-t* violations. If this proposal is correct, then it might constitute a difficulty for the anti-CCP view discussed in section 1.3.2.2 that the P-gap is a pronominal. Complicating the situation is the fact that the two types of pronominals are not necessarily the same, since the putative pronominal in the P-gap construction would have an $\bar{\text{A}}$-antecedent, while the empty subject pronominal is either free or A-bound.

**1.3.2.2  P-gaps as Pronominals**  An important proposal of type P1 is due to Cinque (1990). Cinque argues that there is a class of apparent extractions that are the consequence not of movement, but of binding of an empty pronominal by an operator. In certain cases where extraction is impossible, which Cinque calls "weak islands," the empty pronominal can be bound. This difference makes it appear that only NPs can be extracted from such islands.

(75) a.  Who did you leave the party without talking to $t$?
     b.  *To whom did you leave the party without talking $t$?

P-gaps appear to display the same behavior with respect to weak islands, a result that follows if the P-gap is in fact a pronominal. See Levine, Hukari, and Calagno, this volume, for a critique of Cinque's proposal.

    In support of P1 is the following observation, attributed by Chomsky (1986) to Kearney (1983).

(76) a.  [Which books about himself$_i$]$_j$ did John$_i$ file $t_j$ before Mary
        read $t_j$
     b.  *[Which books about herself$_i$]$_j$ did John file $t_j$ before Mary$_i$
        read $t_j$

The striking fact here is that reconstruction of the NP containing the reflexive into the true gap in (76b) produces an agreement violation, but no such agreement violation arises in the case of a putative reconstruction into the position of the P-gap, as in (76a). If the P-gap is a variable whose antecedent is the fronted *wh*-phrase, this difference is puzzling, given the lack of agreement in *before Mary$_i$ read (which) books about himself$_i$*. But if the P-gap is a pronominal of some type, an example like (76b) patterns just like (77).

(77) [Which books about himself$_i$]$_j$ did John$_i$ file $t_j$ before Mary read them$_j$.

On the other hand, a similar phenomenon occurs in the case of extraction from coordinate structure.

(78) a.  [Which books about himself$_i$]$_j$ did John$_i$ file $t_j$ and Mary read $t_j$?

 b.  *[Which books about herself$_i$]$_j$ did John file $t_j$ and Mary$_i$ read $t_j$?

There are a number of possible approaches to the similarity, including taking into account linear precedence in the processing of the reflexive, and taking coordination to have essentially the same structure as P-gaps. For discussion, see Munn, this volume.

Additional evidence that a P-gap is pronominal is adduced by Postal (1993b), who argues that P-gaps do not appear in contexts that are "anti-pronominal." One particularly robust example involves *there*.

(79) a.  *There are them in the soup. [Po93b:744,(29a)]

 b.  What kind of spiders are there $t$ in the soup? [Po93b:744,(29b)]

 c.  *What kind of spiders did he praise $t$ before learning there were *pg* in the soup? [Po93b:744,(29d)]

 d.  The kind of spiders that he found $t$ in the chicken soup yesterday and there will be $t$ in the bean soup today are hairy ones. [Po93b:744,(31)]

Postal expands on his earlier work in his paper in this volume ("Further lacunae in the parasite gap paradigm"). He presents evidence that shows that the true gap may not occur in a class of contexts that exclude weak pronominals.

(80) a.  What color did she paint her house $t$?

 b.  She painted her house yellow/*it.

 c.  What book did she buy $t$ after discussing *pg* with Abigail?

 d.  *What color did she paint her house $t$ after discussing *pg* with Abigail? (= Postal's (22b))

See Postal's paper for his proposal about why both true gaps and P-gaps should display antipronominal properties.

Finally, Hornstein (1995:172) observes the following data.

(81) a. What did everyone review *t*?
     b. What did everyone review *t* before I read *pg*?

According to Hornstein, (81a) is ambiguous, but (81b) is not. The first has the individual or the pair-list reading, whereas the latter has only the individual reading. Only the individual reading is possible when a pronoun is substituted for the P-gap.

(82) What did everyone review before I read it?

The absence of ambiguity in (81b) would follow if the P-gap were an empty pronominal, on the assumption that such pronominals have the same properties as overt pronominals.

Additional support for P1 is given by Ouhalla (this volume), who shows that the behavior of P-gaps in Moroccan Arabic can be given an elegant explanation if they are taken to be null presumptive pronouns.

P2 is proposed by Bordelois (1986:12), who observes that P-gaps can appear in questions. On this basis she concludes that it is "implausible to analyze both P-gaps and adverbial gaps as silent resumptive pronouns...." The reasoning here is that typically questions do not allow resumptive pronouns, as in:

(83) Who did you see (*him)?

even in languages that allow resumptive pronouns in relative clauses.

(84) the man who I saw (him)

(However, in Vata there are resumptive pronouns in certain *wh*-questions according to Koopman and Sportiche 1986.) But the logic is complicated by the fact that the resumptive pronouns on the Cinque/Postal approach are empty, and thus may fall outside of any universal prohibition against *overt* resumptive pronouns in *wh*-questions. Furthermore, even if the P-gap is pronominal, the presence of the true gap may obviate the restriction against resumptives in *wh*-questions. So, for example, while (83) is ungrammatical with a resumptive pronoun, there is no problem with (85).

(85) Who did you see *t* after you called him?

Any general restriction against pronouns bound by an interrogative would appear to hold, if at all, only if there is no true gap.

Bordelois's counterproposal is that the P-gap is actually an empty anaphor. The basic evidence is that in Spanish, P-gaps occur only when the adjunct is infinitival, while clitics cannot occur unless the adjunct is tensed.

(86) a. los articulos que archivaste sin       leer (*los)
        the articles   that you-filed   without to-read (them)
     b. los articulos que archivaste sin       que *(los)    liste
        the articles   that you-filed   without that (them) you-read

The distinction between these two types of cases is gotten by restructuring the infinitival adjunct with the main clause so that there is a single binding domain for the binding theory; the anaphor is bound in this domain and the pronoun is not free, a violation of Condition B of the binding theory. On the other hand, no such restructuring occurs when the adjunct is tensed; here, the anaphor cannot be bound, a violation of Condition A of the binding theory results, and the pronoun is free, as required. However, as pointed out by Huckabay (1989), the same distinctions do not hold in English, requiring a parametrization of the restructuring rule. Moreover, the presence of tense and an overt subject nevertheless produce degraded acceptability judgments for comparable English examples.

Evidence that the P-gap is pronominal constitutes a challenge to the CCP view that the P-gap forms a chain with the antecedent of the true gap, as in the connectedness approach of Kayne (1983) (see section 1.2.1) and the composed chain proposal of Chomsky (1986b) (see also Frampton 1990). Locality effects do not in themselves constitute conclusive evidence for the trace approach, given Cinque's (1990) observations that "strong island" effects hold occur even when the empty constituent is pronominal.

**1.3.2.3   Other Views**   Lasnik and Stowell (1991) address the fact that P-gap constructions in general do not appear to yield weak crossover (WCO) effects, in violation of the Bijection Principle of Koopman and Sportiche (1982). The problem is partly solved under the CCP, following Contreras (1984) and Chomsky (1986b), if the P-gap is bound by a null operator. Hence there is not a configuration in which there are two variables bound by one operator. But they point out that if the Bijection Principle is accepted, then the question arises as to why there is no WCO effect in examples like the following:

(87) Who$_i$ did you gossip about $t_i$ [despite his$_i$ teacher's having vouched for $pg_i$]? [L&S92:695,(23a)]

There would be a null operator in the adjunct containing the P-gap, which should produce the WCO violation.

(88)  [$Op_i$ [despite his$_i$ teacher's having vouched for $pg_i$]

Their solution is that the WCO effect occurs only when the operator is a "true Quantifier Phrase" (pp. 703–704). They argue that the trace of a non-QP null operator is not a variable, but a null epithet. In the P-gap construction the null epithet is an r-expression, and hence a Condition C violation is produced when it is c-commanded by the true gap. Postal (1997:34) cites the following data from Barss (1986) and Cinque (1990) to illustrate that P-gaps produce strong crossover effects when they are c-commanded by pronouns, consistent with the view that they are r-expressions.

(89)  a.  *It's John who$_i$ Mary voted for $t_i$ after he$_i$ asked someone to nominate $pg_i$. [Barss 1986:378]
      b.  *Who$_i$ did they find $t_i$ hostile before he$_i$ realized they wanted to help $pg_i$?
      c.  *What woman$_i$ did Joe discuss $t_i$ while she$_i$ tried to persuade Mike to hire $pg_i$? [Cinque 1990:150]

However, as also pointed out by Postal, the proposal that the P-gap is an r-expression is clearly at odds with the evidence cited earlier in this section that it is a pronominal.

**1.3.2.4  Chomsky 1982**   The P-gap analysis of Chomsky (1982) is based on the theory of functional determination of empty categories. On this theory, an empty category acquires the properties of being a pronoun, an NP trace (and hence an anaphor), PRO or a variable as a function of the context in which it appears. An empty category is a variable if it is in an A-position and is locally Ā-bound (p. 34). On this view, the two empty categories in the following example are both variables.

(90)  Who$_i$ did you give a picture of $e_i$ to $e_i$?

Since there are two variables bound by a single operator, this example formally violates the Bijection Principle (Koopman and Sportiche 1982), as discussed in section 1.3.4.3.[19] Chomsky also considers examples such as the following.

(91)  a.  a man whom everyone who meets $e$ knows someone who likes $e$ [Ch82:57,(79a)][20]
      b.  a man whom to know $e$ is to like $e$ [Ch82:57,(79d)]

He suggests that these are preferred because of the parallelism that is not found in the WCO cases with one gap and one pronoun. This suggestion is developed in some detail by Safir (1984).

For the case where the P-gap is in an adjunct, Chomsky proposes that the empty category is an empty pronominal that alternates with the overt pronominal that is possible in the same position.

(92) a. Which articles did John file *t* without reading *pg*/them.
   b. This is the kind of food you must cook *t* before you eat *pg*/it.
   c. Here is the influential professor that John sent his book to *t* in order to impress *pg*/him.
   [Ch82:38,(54)]

A pronoun is licensed in this position because by assumption it is not locally A-bound. However, what needs to be explained is why the empty pronominal can *only* appear when there is a true gap in the particular configuration of the P-gap construction. If the true gap c-commands the P-gap, then there will be a chain that contains the two, hence two θ-roles, in violation of the θ-Criterion. An operator in situ cannot c-command the P-gap, for the same reason. The only possibility that is admitted is one in which the antecedent of the true gap c-commands and Ā-binds the P-gap.

Consider the case where there is a *wh*-phrase generated in Comp that Ā-binds an empty pronominal. Chomsky proposes that only a phrase in an A-position at S-structure has an index; thus the base-generated *wh*-phrase cannot bind the pronominal.

Chomsky points out that P-gaps are possible without overt movement, a fact that is consistent with the assumption that null operators can license P-gaps.

(93) this book is too interesting [*Op* [PRO to put down *t* without PRO having finished *pg*]] [Ch82:45,(64b)]

Since movement does not produce the P-gap on this analysis, there need not be intermediate traces in Comp. On the view that a trace in Comp permits a trace in subject position while an overt Comp does not, it is predicted that the familiar alternation associated with *that-t* will not occur with a P-gap; neither *[CP that pg ... ]* nor *[[CP e][pg ... ]* will be acceptable. This prediction assumes, of course, that intermediate traces cannot be freely generated in Comp. Chomsky (1982:53) cites the following examples as evidence that supports the prediction.

(94) a. someone who John expected *t* would be successful though believing *pg* is incompetent

    b. this is the student everyone thinks *t* is intelligent because John said *pg* was intelligent

    c. a woman who *t* called John an idiot as often as *pg* called him a cretin [Ch82:53,(71)]

For Chomsky these examples are ungrammatical, in contrast to cases where the P-gap is in a governed position.

(95) a. someone who John expected *t* to be successful though believing *pg* to be incompetent

    b. *This is the student everyone expected *t* to be intelligent because John believed *pg* to be intelligent.[21]

    c. a man who Mary called *t* an idiot as often as Jane called *pg* a cretin[22]

[Ch82:54,(72)]

    Compare examples (94a) and (94b) with the following:

(96) a. someone who John expected *t* would be successful though believing that *pg* is incompetent

    b. This is the student everyone thinks *t* is intelligent because John said that *pg* was intelligent.

Chomsky (1982:55) notes that these examples with *that pg* are worse than those without *that*, suggesting a problem with either the analysis of P-gaps or of the *that-t* effect.

    In summary, on the analysis of Chomsky (1982) P-gaps in adjuncts are empty pronominals, while in multiple gap constructions (as in (90) *Who did you give a picture of to?*) the two gaps are variables both bound by the operator.

### 1.3.3 Case Properties

Related to the question of whether the P-gap is a trace or a pronominal is the question of the compatibility of Case assignment to the P-gap and the true gap. On the assumption that there are two chains in the P-gap construction with a common head, it would follow that the true gap and the P-gap would have to have the same Case, the Case of the head. However, if we take the position that the P-gap is a pronominal, then it does not form a chain with the antecedent of the true gap, and hence there is a possibility that its Case may be different from that of the true gap.

**1.3.3.1 Kiss 1985** The relevance of Case compatibility was first noted by Kiss (1985), reprinted in this volume. In Hungarian, the cases of the

P-gap and the true gap must be identical, in the sense that the overt case marking on the antecedent must be compatible with the chain that it forms with the true gap and with the chain that it forms with the P-gap. Case compatibility may hold even if the Cases associated with the two gap positions are different, since extraction though the Comp position of a complement of a transitive verb changes a nominative Case to an accusative Case (p. 55). Kiss's condition on Case identity is the following, generalized to all features.

(97)  In a parasitic gap construction, the syntactic features of both the real gap and the parasitic gap are properly transmitted to the phonologically realized operator. [K85:62,(48)]

For cases in which the true gap c-commands the P-gap, condition (97) holds even though the P-gap is not grammatical.

(98)  *Which man$_i$ do you think [$t_i'$ $t_i$ warned the police [$t_i$ they should arrest $pg_i$]] [K85:63,(50)]

Kiss proposes (p. 63) that the two chains must have the same Case at the point in the tree at which they meet. In (98) the accusative Case of the P-gap and the nominative Case of the subject are in conflict at the lowest node that dominates both, and the nominative case only gets changed to accusative in the Comp of the complement of *think*. However, Horvath (1992) argues that even when case compatibility is observed, there are examples where c-command must be invoked in order to account for ungrammaticality; see section 1.3.3.2. Furthermore, Kiss herself notes (p. 68) that (97) will not account for the following cases, which fall under the anti-c-command condition.

(99)  a.  *Who did you introduce *t* to *pg*? [K85:68,(63)]
      b.  *Which man do you expect *t* to warn the police that they should not arrest *pg*. [K85:68,(64)]
      c.  *This is the student that we consider *t* sure that we can help *pg*. [K85:68,(65)]

**1.3.3.2  Nakajima, Horvath**  Nakajima (1985–1986) notes a number of problems with the formal apparatus proposed by Kiss for transmitting case to a chain. Nakajima also considers another type of P-gap construction (see (100)), noted originally by Haegeman (1984).

(100) a.  a man who [whenever I meet *pg*] *t* looks old
      b.  This is a note which [unless we send *pg* back] *t* will ruin our relationship.

The key property of these examples for Kiss's proposal is that there cannot be Case identity between the two chains, yet they are grammatical. The examples are also of broader interest because they show that a subject of a clause that contains the adjunct in which the P-gap appears can be the antecedent for a P-gap. I discuss this point at greater length in section 1.3.4. For further discussion of Kiss's proposal, see also Kiss 1988, Nakajima 1990, and Kiss, this volume.

Horvath (1992) argues against Kiss's proposal that Case identity is sufficient to account for the distribution of P-gaps in Hungarian without considering configurational properties. Horvath shows that even if there is Case compatibility, it is also necessary to incorporate an anti-c-command condition between the true gap and the P-gap. Horvath cites the following examples to support her argument.

(101) a. *A férfiak akiket hallotunk, [$t'$ hogy [szeretnek $t$
the man-PL who-PL-ACC we-heard that like
[mindenkit aki ismeri $pg$]]]
everyone-ACC who-NOM knows
'The men who we heard $t$ like everyone who knows $pg$'

b. *Kiket gonodlsz, [$t'$ hogy [figyelmeztették $t$ a
who-PL-ACC you-think think warned-DEF.do the
rendőrséget [hogy [le ne tartóztasson $pg$]]]]
police that V.PREFIX not it-should-arrest
'Who do you think $t$ warned the police that they should not arrest $pg$?'

In both of these examples the subject trace is linked to an accusative operator, because of the phenomenon of "Case switch" in Hungarian. Hence Case compatibility is maintained, yet the examples are ungrammatical.

**1.3.3.3 Franks 1992** Franks (1992) discusses the function of Case agreement in Slavic, particularly Polish and Russian. He argues that there are two sorts of Case conditions on ATB extractions, where two (or more) chains share a single head. First, the morphological form of the Case marking on the head of the chains must be consistent with the Case assignment on the tail of the chain. So, for example, an accusative chain and a genitive chain can be joined at a single head if the form of the accusative and of the genitive are identical. This occurs when a masculine animate NP is in the accusative, which has the same form as the genitive. Second, the gaps must be thematically parallel, in the sense that the θ-roles associated with the two gaps must be the most prominent ones in their individual clauses.

Similar conditions hold in P-gap constructions in Russian.[23] The Case condition is illustrated in the following examples.

(102) mal'čik, *kotoromu/*kotorogo Maša          davala den'gi *t*
      boy     who-DAT/-GEN          Masha-NOM gave   money
      do togo, kak (ona) stala    izbegat' *pg*, ...
      until           she started to-avoid
      'the boy who Masha gave money to until she started to avoid him'
      [F.92:15,(30)]

(103) devuška, kotoroj        Ivan        daval den'gi *t* do togo, kak (on)
      girl       who(DAT-GEN) Ivan-NOM gave   money until          he
      stal    izbegat' *pg*, ...
      started to-avoid
      'the girl who Ivan gave money to until he started to avoid her'
      [F.92:13,(27a)]

The verb *davit'* ('give') governs the dative Case, while *izbegat'* ('avoid') governs the genitive. The masculine dative and genitive forms of the relative pronoun are morphologically distinct, whereas the feminine dative and genitive forms are identical. Thus (103) is grammatical but (102) is not.

The following example illustrates the role of thematic prominence when Case forms agree.

(104) *devuška, kotoroj *t*        bylo veselo do togo, kak
      girl       who(DAT-GEN) was merry    until
      Ivan      stal    izbegat' *pg*, ...
      Ivan-NOM started to-avoid
      'the girl who was merry until Ivan started to avoid her'
      [F.92:13,(28a)]

In this example, the subject of *bylo veselo* is thematically most prominent in its clause, while the object of *izbegat'* is not. But an argument can be made that the subject of *bylo veselo* c-commands the P-gap in this example, as in the following.

(105) *okno,   kotoroe    razbilo *t* vetrom     do togo, kak my
      window which-ACC broke      wind-INST before      we
      uvideli *pg* na zemle, ...
      saw          on ground
      'the window which the wind broke before we saw it on the ground' [F.92:14,(28b)]

Case identity appears to display the same pattern in Polish, as discussed by Kardela (1990), except that Kardela does not discuss whether nominative Case can be changed to accusative as a consequence of extraction through Comp.

### 1.3.4 The Anti-c-command Condition on the True Gap

**1.3.4.1 Anti-c-command, Not Anti-subject**   The original observation that a subject cannot license a P-gap if it c-commands it is due to Engdahl (1983). Various proposals have been made in the literature to account for this generalization, and some apparent counterexamples have been discussed as well. As pointed out in section 1.1, the generalization cannot be simply that subjects do not licence P-gaps, because an embedded subject that does not c-command a P-gap can license it, as illustrated by the examples in (12), repeated here.

(12)   a.   Which caesar did Brutus imply *t* was no good while ostensibly praising *pg*? [E83:21,(60)]
       b.   Who did you say John's criticism of *pg* would make us think *t* was stupid?

Moreover, as noted by Haegeman (1984) (see also Nakajima (1985–1986)), there are cases where a main subject does not c-command the P-gap, in which case the construction is grammatical.

(106) a note which [unless we send back *pg*] *t* will ruin our relationship [Ha84:231,(9)]

But when the same adjunct follows the true gap in subject position, ungrammaticality results.

(107) *a note which *t* will ruin our relationship unless we send back *pg*

So the relevant property would appear to indeed be that of c-command.[24]

**1.3.4.2 Accounting for the Condition**   A natural approach to accounting for the anti-c-command condition is to relate it to binding theory, which in its classical form crucially invokes the relation of c-command. Failure to license a P-gap could in principle be related to any of the three standard conditions: Condition A, which requires an anaphor to be locally bound, Condition B, which requires a pronoun to be locally free, and Condition C, which requires a referring expression to be free.[25] The approach that one takes is thus tied to arguments for the character of the P-gap, as outlined in section 1.3.2.

Engdahl (1984) considers the properties of P-gaps whose antecedents are subjects and those whose antecedents are nonsubjects, as in (108) (the judgments are Engdahl's).

(108)  a. *Which candidate did you say [$t$ shook hands for 7 hours to make people vote for $pg$]? [E84:92,(2)]
       b. ?Which candidate did you [$_{VP}$ convince $t$ that you were going to vote for $pg$]? [E84:93,(8)]

Example (108a) is ruled out in a phrase structure approach such as GPSG because there is no subject gap in the complement at all. The complement, which is a VP, lacks a SLASH feature that corresponds to the initial *wh*-phrase, and hence the P-gap is not licensed. Cases such as (108b) are allowed because the SLASH feature is on the VP headed by *convince* and therefore licenses both the true gap and the P-gap.

Engdahl points out that the same type of difference does not follow from an account based on (anti-)c-command. Crucially, it is not possible to get around the problem by assuming a non-c-command structure for examples like (108b) given the standard small clause analysis for the following examples, in which the subject and the predicate are sisters.

(109)  a. ?Which famous linguists do you consider [$t$ smarter than most friends of $pg$]?
       b. ?Which painter did John regard [$t$ as more promising than most contemporaries of $pg$]?
       [En84:96,(15)–(16)]

The same conclusion also follows if the structure is [V NP Pred], but not if it is the nonstandard [[V NP] Pred]. On the GPSG analysis, the feature SLASH may appear both on the subject and the predicate of the small clause.

The crucial quality of the GPSG analysis that produces the effect of an anti-c-command condition is that just in the tensed sentence the extracted subject is not a trace.[26] Engdahl suggests that a counterpart to this analysis can be constructed in GB terms, using the notion of antecedent government.[27]

(110)  Parasitic gaps may not be bound by an antecedent governed empty category.

A trace that is the subject of a tensed S is only antecedent governed, whereas traces that are the subject of a small clause, a direct object, the object of a preposition, and so on are lexically governed. (As Engdahl (p. 103) notes, they are also antecedent governed, hence requirement (110) must be understood in terms of "antecedent but not lexically governed".)

Another approach is that of Aoun and Clark (1985), who propose that "the non-overt operator in P-gap constructions is treated as an $\bar{A}$-anaphor which is subject to a generalized binding theory." (See Contreras 1987 for a similar proposal.) On this view, the P-gap is an anaphor with an $\bar{A}$-antecedent. The overt operator is an $\bar{A}$-anaphor in an $\bar{A}$-position. There is a general condition on S-structure that the anaphor must be bound in its governing category, which is the matrix S'. The local antecedent is a null operator, which is itself an $\bar{A}$-anaphor whose antecedent is the antecedent of the true gap. This null operator is subject to principle A of Generalized Binding Theory. The anti-c-command condition follows from the requirement that an $\bar{A}$-anaphor cannot be A-bound (at S-structure). The c-commanding trace is the A-binder.

But as Kiss (1985) among others points out, if a direct object c-commands a sentential complement then Condition C of the binding theory correctly rules out examples such as the following:

(111)  *The police warned him$_i$ that they would arrest John$_i$. [K85:45,(9)]

and a quantifier can bind a pronoun to its right—

(112)  The police warned everybody$_i$ that they would arrest him$_i$
       [K84:45,(10)]

but then surprisingly, the following is a grammatical P-gap construction:

(113)  Which man did the police warn $t$ that they would arrest $pg$?

Hence the Aoun and Clark proposal runs into a problem, as does any account of anti-c-command, given cases such as (113) where the direct object is taken to c-command the sentential complement and the c-command theory of binding is assumed. Moreover, assuming the proposal of Kiss (1985) that Hungarian has a flat structure, the anti-c-command condition should rule out grammatical P-gap constructions in Hungarian, which show essentially the same subject-object asymmetry as do the P-gap constructions of English.

In the connectedness account of Kayne (1983) and Longobardi (1984), the anti-c-command condition is a consequence of the definition of the Connectedness Condition.

(114) *Connectedness Condition*
Given a maximal set of empty categories $\beta_1, \ldots, \beta_n$, each locally bound by the same antecedent $\alpha$ in a tree T, the union formed by the g-projection sets of every $\beta$ and by the antecedent $\alpha$ must form a subtree of T.

Since the P-gap is a variable it is an r-expression, and hence falls under Condition C of the binding theory. If the true gap binds the P-gap, the antecedent is not a local binder of the P-gap. Hence the Connectedness Condition does not apply, and Condition C rules out the P-gap.

**1.3.4.3 Counterexamples to the Anti-c-command Condition**  Contreras (1984) observes that there is an apparent conflict between the anti-c-command condition and the fact that direct objects appear to bind into adjuncts to their right.

(115) a.  Which articles did John file *t* without reading *pg*.
          [C84:698,(2)]
      b.  *John filed them$_i$ without reading Mary's articles$_i$.
          [C84:698,(4)]

The sentence in (115b) appears to be a Condition C violation, in which *them* c-commands and therefore binds *Mary's articles*. But then it would appear that the true gap in the a-example also c-commands the P-gap. It would then follow that there is a single chain that contains the true gap and the P-gap, leading to a violation of the $\theta$-Criterion. Contreras also argues that under the theory of Chomsky (1982), the P-gap cannot be an anaphor (NP trace or PRO), since it is not locally bound but is governed, nor a pronominal, since it is not properly identified.[28] The solution that Contreras proposes anticipates the approach of Chomsky (1986b): there is a null operator in the clause that contains the P-gap that $\bar{\text{A}}$-binds it. On this view, the P-gap is a variable, and the chain is parasitic on the true chain. See also Stowell 1986.

Contreras (1984) (see also Contreras 1987) considers the difference in acceptability between examples like (115a) and those like (116) (a type of example originally noted by Engdahl (1983)).

(116) Who$_i$ did you give pictures of $e_i$ to $e_i$? [C87:61,(1)]

Contreras suggests that the clausal adjunct that contains the P-gap in the acceptable P-gap construction permits the null operator analysis, which is ruled out in the case of (116).

The following examples suggest that the binding evidence is equivocal.

(117) a. We admitted them$_i$ without those students$_i$ meeting even the most minimal standards.]

   b. You can't even try to help them$_i$ without the twins$_i$ getting very upset.[29]

   c. John filed them$_i$ without even *reading* Mary's articles$_i$. [C84:85,fn.1,(i)]

One plausible conclusion, given the grammaticality of the examples in (117), is that the direct object does not c-command the adjunct, and that other factors are responsible for the marginal status of (115b). But this will not help with other problematic examples such as:

(118) Who did you warn $t$ that the police were going to arrest $pg$?

Here it appears that the true gap c-commands the P-gap because of the ungrammaticality of—

(119) *I warned him that the police were going to arrest Bill.

—which appears to be a Condition C violation. It does not appear to be possible to ameliorate this violation using intonation and context, as in the case of binding into adjuncts.

   Safir (1987) argues that there is no c-command of the P-gap by the true gap in a case such as (118), because the sentential complement is adjoined higher than VP, in an extraposed position; however, the judgments used to support the argument are not entirely sharp. Saito (1991) also argues that these examples in fact involve extraposition; he attributes the ungrammaticality of (119) to a condition distinct from Condition C which has the same effect in spite of the extraposition.

   Koopman and Sportiche (1982:148–149) offer an account of (116) in terms of the Bijection Principle, claiming that it has the same grammatical status as:

(120) a. *Who$_i$ did you give a picture of him$_i$ to $e_i$? [K&S.87:149,(25a)]

   b. *Who$_i$ did you give a picture of $e_i$ to him$_i$? [K&S.87:149,(25b)]

By definition, the empty category that is not produced by movement is a variable in virtue of being locally $\bar{A}$-bound. It is not clear that this is the correct approach, however, in view of the greater unacceptability of the examples with overt pronominals, which are also variables. In fact, for some speakers (including the editors of this volume), example (116) is completely unobjectionable. It is therefore far from clear that the Bijection Principle is relevant here.

The picture is further confused by the observation (see Contreras 1993), that various binding relations do not always appear to observe the same configurational conditions. An anaphor must be "strongly" c-commanded by its antecedent (in the sense of Chomsky (1986)), whereas an r-expression may not be "weakly" c-commanded (or m-commanded) by a pronominal. Contreras (1993) stipulates that Condition C violations such as

(121) *We accepted them$_i$ without interviewing those students$_i$.

are due to a condition on backwards pronominalization (citing Chomsky (1986b:62) and Cinque (1990:190–191); see also Lasnik and Stowell 1991:713), so that it is not necessary to hold either that the r-expression is "strongly" c-commanded by the pronoun, or that there are two notions of "bound," one for Condition A and one for Condition C.

A perhaps more serious class of counterexamples to the CCP was first noted by Horvath (1992).[30]

(122) a. Which papers do you think $t$ got published without the editor having read $pg$? [H92:201,(23)]
   b. Who do you expect [$t$ to disappear without anyone having met $pg$/before anyone could talk to $pg$]? [H92:210,(31)]
   c. Who do you expect [$t$ to withdraw his candidacy before the Committee has a chance to interview $pg$]? [H92:210,(32)]

(123) *Hungarian*
   a. Kiket          mondtál $t'$ hogy sosem panaszkodnak $t$
      who-PL-ACC you-said    that  never  complain
      [azután hogy a   tanító          megbüntet $pg$]
      it-after that the teacher-NOM punishes
      'Who did you say $t$ never complains after the teacher punishes $pg$?' [H92:199,(17a)]
   b. Milyen iratokat      hittetek $t'$   hogy el      fognak veszni $t$ [ha
      what    papers-ACC you-believed that away will     get-lost if
      nem rakunk       el $e$]?
      not we-put-PRES away
      'What papers did you believe $t$ will get lost unless we put away $pg$?' [H92:199,(18a)]
   c. Kiket          szeretnél $t'$  ha anélkül     távoznának $t$ [hogy
      who-PL-ACC you-would-like if without-it left                that
      Mari          megismert volna $pg$]
      Mary-NOM had-met
      'Who would you like if $t$ left without Mary having met $pg$?' [H92:199,(19a)]

Horvath observes that the grammatical P-gaps that do not obey the anti-c-command condition are in adjuncts; those in complements are ill formed.

(124) a. *Who do you expect [$t$ to warn the police that they should not arrest $pg$]? [H92:209,(29a)]
     b. *Who do you expect [$t$ to convince the boss that he should not fire $pg$]? [H92:209,(30a)]

Horvath proposes that the ungrammatical examples are Condition C violations. In the grammatical examples, the P-gap is c-commanded by the subject trace, and so they should be Condition C violations too, but they are not. The reason, she suggests, is that the null operator that heads the chain containing the P-gap in the adjunct is not evaluated with respect to Condition C at S-structure. Hence the P-gap is licensed at S-structure. Extending a proposal of Lasnik and Saito (1984), this null operator can be deleted at LF and so avoids the Condition C violation at that level as well.

Brody (1995) offers a different explanation for the different status of c-commanded P-gaps in adjuncts and complements. Let the underlying subject position be VP-internal, as suggested originally by Manzini (1983) and argued for by Kitagawa (1986) and Koopman and Sportiche (1991), among others. An adjunct will be adjoined higher than the VP, so the subject position will not in fact c-command it. However, this solution does not avoid the problem that the subject position does c-command into the adjunct from the perspective of Condition C. Hence Brody must allow for two types of c-command and two types of binding—a consequence ruled out by Contreras (1984), for example.

A different type of challenge to the anti-c-command condition is of a more technical nature.[31] Consider a case such as the following in which the P-gap is ostensibly in a complement and c-commanded by the true gap.

(125) *Who$_i$ [$t_i$ bought [$_{NP}$ a picture of $pg_i$]]

The NP in this case allows extraction.

(126) Who$_i$ did you buy a picture of $t_i$?

Therefore, the following derivation must also be ruled out.

(127) *Who$_i$ [$pg_i$ bought [$_{NP}$ a picture of $t_i$]]

One might pursue the idea that (125) is ruled out by the anti-c-command condition, whereas (127) is ruled out by the impossibility of having both the *wh*-operator and the empty operator corresponding to the P-gap in the same position, as in the following analysis.

(128) [who$_i$ $Op_i$] [$pg_i$ bought [$_{NP}$ a picture of $t_i$]]

For longer movements of the *wh*-operator, such a condition would have to extend to intermediate traces.

(129) [who$_i$ [you think [[$t_i'$ $Op_i$] [$pg_i$ bought a picture of $t_i$]]]]

### 1.3.5  Licensing

**1.3.5.1  Resumptive Pronouns**  As noted earlier, it is an open question whether a P-gap can be licensed by an Ā-antecedent that forms a chain with a resumptive pronoun. Engdahl (1985) shows that resumptive pronouns can occur in Swedish where otherwise an extraction violation would arise. Where resumptive pronouns can occur, they license P-gaps.

(130) Det var den fången$_i$   som läkarna     inte kunde avgöra [om
      it   was that prisoner that the-doctors not   could  decide   whether
      han$_i$ verligen var syk] [utan      att tala    med $pg_i$ personligen.
      he   really   was ill    without to speak with      personally
      'This is the prisoner that the doctors couldn't determine if he
      really was ill without talking to in person.' [E85:7,(8)]

The licensing property of resumptive pronouns in Swedish is accounted for if the resumptive pronoun is the spelling out of a syntactic variable (essentially a visible trace), and if the licensing of the P-gap depends on its antecedent forming a chain with such a variable (Engdahl 1985:7; see also Rizzi 1990:61f). (The use of resumptive pronouns as variables is systematic in Swedish only in the subject position of tensed S; Engdahl 1985:11.) However, it is quite clear that resumptive pronouns in English, which are at least marginal when extractions are disallowed, do not permit P-gaps, as noted by Chomsky (1982).

(131) a. *a man whom everyone who meets him knows someone who
         likes *pg*.
      b. *a man whom everyone who meets *pg* knows someone who
         likes him
      [Ch82:57,(79b,c)]

Chomsky also cites evidence from Spanish due to Torrego that suggests that resumptive pronouns in Spanish cannot license a P-gap.

Sells (1986) appears to have been the first to point out that Hebrew resumptive pronouns do license P-gaps.

(132) ha'iša    še  [[ha-anašim še  šixnati    levaker *pg*]
 the-woman who  the-people that I-convinced to-visit
 [te'aru    ota]]
 described her
 [Se86:63,(8)]

The resumptive pronoun is not simply an overt trace since, as Sells points out, it does not produce the Subjacency effects that are found when there is a gap produced by extraction (examples from Borer 1981).[32]

(133) a. *ha'iša$_i$    še  pagašti et ha'iš$_j$  še $t_j$ ra'a $t_i$
 the-woman who I-met    the-man who saw
 b. ha'iša$_i$    še  pagašti et ha'iš$_j$  še $t_j$ ra'a ota$_i$
 the-woman who I-met    the-man who saw her

Shlonsky (1986) proposes to account for this fact, and for P-gaps in general, by adapting the mechanism of scope-indexing of Haïk (1984). Shlonsky argues, first, that there is no operator movement in the case of resumption, which accounts for the absence of Subjacency effects, among other things. Hence the binding relation between the P-gap and the resumptive pronoun is not mediated by chains, but is a function of the indices on them. For Haïk, an NP headed by a quantifier phrase receives the index of an NP that it contains; this second index can bind a variable in the scope of the first NP. Haïk originally applied this mechanism to so-called donkey sentences.

(134) [Every farmer [who owns [a donkey]$_i$]$_{j/i}$ beats it$_i$

Here, the index $i$ of *a donkey* transfers to *[Every farmer who beats a donkey]*, which binds *it*. Hence *a donkey* can bind *it*. In the P-gap construction in (132) the index of the P-gap transfers to the NP that contains it, which in turn binds the resumptive pronoun. Interestingly, Shlonsky points out (p. 575) that where this indexing mechanism cannot apply, the P-gap cannot be licensed by a resumptive pronoun—for example, where the P-gap is inside of an adjunct.

(135) a. *Ze  ha-baxur še-nišakti    oto mibli  lehakir.
 this the-guy  that-kissed+1MS him without to-know
 'This is the guy that I kissed without knowing.'
 b. Ze  ha-baxur $t$ še-nišakti    mibli  lehakir.
 this the-guy  that-kissed+1MS without to-know
 'This is the guy that I kissed without knowing.'
 [Sh86:575,(15)]

Tellier (1989) observes that in Mooré, P-gaps are licensed by apparent relative *wh*-in-situ. Mooré relative clauses can have a gap or can be "internally headed"; that is, the head of the relative clause is in the argument position in the clause itself.

(136) a. m   yaa [biig   ninga]$_i$ rawa sen seg $t_i$ wa
           1SG see   child NINGA   man   REL meet   DET
           'I saw the child that the man met.' [Te89:300,(4)]

     b. m   mii    [rawa sen seg   biig   ninga wa]
           1SG know   man   REL meet child   NINGA DET
           'I know the child that the man met.' [Te89:301,(5)]

Tellier argues that *ninga* marks the head of the relative clause.

Strikingly, both types of relative clauses license P-gaps, as does *wh*-movement in questions.

(137) a. m   mii   neb$_i$   [fo   sen tɔ $t_i$] n yaol n ka ya *pg*$_i$ ye
           1SG know people 2SG REL insult after   NEG see       NEG
           'I know the people that you insulted without having seen.'
           [Te89:301,(6a)]

     b. m   mii   [fo   sen tɔ    neb   ninga$_j$ n yaol n ka pogl *pg* wa]
           1SG know 2SG REL insult people NINGA after   NEG hurt       DET
           'I know the people that you insulted without having hurt.'
           [Te89:302,(7)]

     c. kom   bɔs$_i$   la   [fo   tɔ $t_i$] n yaol n ka ya *pg*$_i$
           which children WH 2SG insult after   NEG see
           'Which children did you insult without having seen?'
           [Te89:301,(6b)]

But *wh*-in-situ does not license P-gaps.

(138) *fo   tɔɔ   kom   bɔse$_i$   n yaol n ka ya
      2SG insult which children after   NEG see
      'You insulted which children after having seen?' [Te89:301,(6c)]

Nor do resumptive pronouns.

(139) *ad   neb   nins$_i$   yamb sen wɔm t'a   Maari pab əb$_i$ la
      here people NINGA 2PL   REL claim COMP Mary hit   3PL DECL
      zaame n   yaol   n ka pogl *pg*.
      yesterday before NEG hurt
      'These are the people that you heard the claim that Mary hit
      them without hurting.'

Furthermore, a P-gap with the internal relative is not possible when the verb takes two arguments unless the head of the relative precedes the second argument (p. 313). Tellier argues that this is because the NP that licenses the P-gap actually undergoes leftward "focus movement" to the left in the VP. The V then raises to Infl, and appears to the left of the arguments. *Ninga* is a focus marker, on this analysis. The focused constituent is in an Ā-position and thus licenses the P-gap in the usual way.

**1.3.5.2  *Wh*-in-situ in Jeddah Arabic**   An additional fundamental point in the analysis of P-gaps is that they do not appear to be licensed by LF movements. The following examples are repeated from section 1.1.

(9) a. *John filed which articles without reading *t/pg*. [E83:14,(33)]
    b. *I forget who filed which articles without reading *t/pg*.
        [E83:14,(34)]

Hence the CCP is that P-gaps are licensed by an antecedent that c-commands it and the true gap at S-structure.

The CCP can be challenged on this point by showing that there are examples of P-gaps where the *wh*-phrase is in situ. This has been argued for Jeddah Arabic as summarized in this section. It can also be challenged, although more weakly, by showing that the antecedent of the P-gap and the antecedent of the true gap are not the same (see section 1.3.5.3), or by showing that the P-gap appears in LF but not S-structure (see section 1.3.5.4).

Wahba (1995) provides evidence that *wh*-movement and resumptive pronouns license P-gaps in Standard Arabic, and that *wh*-in-situ does as well in Jeddah Arabic. The last observation constitutes a counterexample to the CCP that P-gaps are licensed only at surface structure, because the gap associated with *wh*-in-situ is present only at LF, if at all. The following examples illustrate the trace and resumptive pronoun constructions in *wh*-questions.

(140) *Standard Arabic*
    a. maða$_i$ ?aʕṭayta $e_i$ li-l-walad-i?
        what   gave-you   to-the-boy-GEN
    b. ma-allað$_i$ ?aʕṭayta-hu$_i$ li-l-walad-i?
        what-that gave-you-him to-the-boy-GEN
        'What did you give to the boy?' [W93:61,(3)]

It is impossible to have a resumptive pronoun in an island—

(141) $\left\{ \begin{array}{l} \text{*maða}_i \\ \text{*ma-allað}_i \end{array} \right\}$ qaabala omar al-raǰul-a$_j$   allað$_{ij}$ $e_j$ ištaraa-hu$_i$

        what(that)   meet   Omar the-man-ACC who     brought-him
        'What did Omar meet the man who brought?' [W93:61,(4)]

—which suggests that the resumptive in the case of *wh*-movement is a visible trace. There are also resumptive pronouns in relative clauses, but these do not produce Subjacency violations.

The following show that *t* and *pro* both license P-gaps.

(142) *Standard Arabic*
    a.  ʕomar$_j$ faqada al-kitaab-a$_i$ qabla ann PRO$_j$ yaqrʔa-hu$_i$
        Omar lose    the-book    before that       to-read-it
    b.  *ʕomar$_j$ faqada al-kitaab-a$_i$ qabla ann PRO$_j$ yaqrʔa $e_i$
    c.  Maaða$_i$ faqada $t_i$ omar qabal ann PRO$_j$ yaqraʔa $pg_i$
    d.  Ma-allaði$_i$ faqada-hu$_i$ omar qabala ann PRO$_j$ yaqraʔa $pg_i$
        'What did Omar lose before he read?'
    [W93:62,(5)]

The two sentences in (143) show that *wh*-in-situ licenses P-gaps in Jeddah Arabic as well.

(143) a.  Gabal-t miin   il-yoom
        met-you whom yesterday
        'Whom did you meet *t* yesterday?' [W93:64,(10c)]
    b.  Mona ɣaarat      min miin$_i$ ʕašaan [ʕomar$_j$ yebɣa [PRO$_j$
        Mona was-jealous of  whom because Omar  wants
        yetjawwaz $pg_i$]]
        to-marry
        'Whom was Mona jealous of *t* because Omar wants to marry *pg*?' [W93:64,(11c)]

Curiously, the example (144) is ungrammatical.

(144) *ʕali xabbar miin$_i$ inn-u   biyekrah $pg_i$.
      Ali told    whom that-he hates
      [W93:(12a)]

Wahba argues that this is because *miin* c-commands the P-gap, but note that the comparable sentence is grammatical in English.

(145) Who did John tell *t* [that he hates *pg*]

**1.3.5.3  Weak P-gaps**    Safir (1984) notes the following contrast.

(146) a.   the report which$_i$ Mary read $t_i$ without filing $pg_i$
      b.  the report [the author of which$_i$]$_j$ Mary married $t_j$ without meeting $pg_j$
      c.  *the report [the author of which$_i$]$_j$ Mary married $t_j$ without filing $pg_j$

d. *the report [the author of which$_i$]$_j$ Mary filed $t_i$ without reading $pg_i$

[Sa84:665,(12)]

These examples confirm that the antecedent of the P-gap must c-command and $\bar{\text{A}}$-bind it at S-structure. Seely (1991) notes, however, that the examples in (147) are possible.

(147) a. ?a report [before filing which$_i$]$_j$ one must be sure to label $pg_i$ correctly $t_j$

b. ?a comment [immediately after making which$_i$]$_j$ the president had to apologize for $pg_i$ $t_j$

(148) a. ?Woody Allen, whose$_j$ movies$_i$ I always send reviews of $t_i$ to $pg_j$

b. ?the patient whose$_j$ fears$_i$ we discussed possible sources of $t_i$ with $pg_j$

The two groups of examples have a slightly different character. In (147) the preposed constituent is an adjunct which contains the relative pronoun in situ. In (148) the preposed constituent is a piedpiped argument that moves as a consequence of the relative pronoun in specifier position. But both groups have the characteristic that the antecedent of the P-gap does not c-command it at S-structure.

**1.3.5.4 Multiple *Wh*-questions**   Kim and Lyle (1996) argue that P-gaps are licensed at LF and argue against S-structure licensing. One key observation is that P-gaps are not compatible with multiple *wh*-questions.

(149) a. *Which parcel$_i$ did you give $t_i$ to whom without opening $pg_i$?

b. Which parcel$_i$ did you give $t_i$ to Susan without opening $pg_i$?

[K&L96:288,(3)]

(150) *¿Que articulos$_i$ asignaste $t_i$ a que estudiantes sin leer $pg_i$?

[K&L96:288,(4)]

They propose that multiple *wh*-questions undergo absorption at LF, by the following rule.

(151) $(Q_1x{:}\Phi_1)(Q_2y{:}\Phi_2)\ \Phi(x,y) \rightarrow (Q_1x\ Q_2y{:}\Phi_1\ \&\ \Phi_2)\ \Phi(x,y)$

where $\Phi(x_1 \ldots x_n)$ stands for an open sentence.

[Higginbotham and May 1981:61]

Assume chain composition as in Chomsky (1986b). If there is a multiple *wh*-question, the *wh*-chains and the P-gap chains are different in character (the first is binary, the second is unary) and there is a violation of homogeneity (p. 291), a subcase of Chomsky's (1995) Uniformity Condition, reducible to Full Interpretation. The LF object is therefore illegitimate.

There is an obvious problem with this analysis (p. 291): Why doesn't QR, which raises a quantifier to an Ā-position at LF, license P-gaps? The answer proposed by Kim and Lyle is that a chain produced by QR is not homogeneous with a chain for a P-gap, the first being a chain involving an adjunction to IP, and the latter, a CP chain.

Kim and Lyle do not consider the fact that an overt pronoun cannot appear in place of the P-gap in (148a).

(152) *Which parcel$_i$ did you give $t_i$ to whom without opening it$_i$?

Hence the problem may be not that the P-gap is not licensed, but that the operators in a multiple *wh*-question cannot serve as the antecedents of unbound pronominal elements, taking a P-gap to be a member of this category. The following suggests that this is the correct explanation.

(153) *Which parcel$_i$ did you give to whom$_j$ without warning her$_j$?

It may be turn out to be possible, of course, to characterize the problem in terms of absorption.

Kim and Lyle also note the following interesting cases with ellipsis.

(154) Which article did John file $t$ without meaning to [*e*]?

(155) a.  *Which article did you file $t$ without asking who had read *pg*?
      b.  ?Which article did you file $t$ without asking who else had [*e*]?
      c.  **Who did you meet the people who didn't know where there would be an opportunity to see $t$.
      d.  Chomsky, who everyone met $t$ except the people who didn't know when there would be an opportunity to [*e*], ...
      [K&L96:295,(23)–(24)]

Example (154) shows that it is possible for an elliptical VP to contain a P-gap. Arguably, the interpretation of the sentence must "reconstruct" the P-gap and interpret it at LF, because it is not present in the S-structure representation, as Kim and Lyle suggest.

The examples in (155) illustrate more complex cases of ellipsis. Example (155a) shows that a P-gap is not licensed in an embedded *wh*-question, which is an extraction island. When the P-gap does not appear in S-structure, as in (155b), the sentence is far more acceptable. Similar differences hold for complex NPs, as shown in (155c,d). Kim and Lyle argue that these examples support the view that P-gaps are licensed at LF. Again, there is an alternative view in which the reconstructed VP, *met Chomsky* in (155d), is itself reconstructed into the empty VP position at LF.[33]

In his paper in this volume, Kennedy invokes the notion of "vehicle change" from Fiengo and May (1994), arguing that the counterpart of a P-gap in a elliptical VP may be pronominal. Kennedy provides evidence in support of this proposal, by showing that in the elliptical VP the counterpart to the P-gap behaves like a pronoun—for example, it produces Condition B effects, not strong crossover effects. Kennedy's conclusion of course brings to mind the arguments that the P-gaps themselves are pronominal; see section 1.3.2.2 as well as Postal (1994a, reprinted in this volume).

Finally, Kim and Lyle discuss cases involving multiple gaps:

(156) a. *What$_i$ did you show $t_i$ to whom$_j$ [without $Op_i/Op_j$ giving $pg_i$ (to) $pg_j$]

   b. *Which package$_i$ did you send $t_i$ to which student$_j$ [without PRO wrapping $pg_i$ sufficiently to satisfy $pg_j$]]

   c. What grades did you give to which students without really meaning to?

   [K&L96:298,(34)]

On their analysis, (155a,b) have two binary operators formed by absorption and therefore satisfy homogeneity, but these sentences are ruled out by the doubly-filled Comp filter applying to the empty operators in the *without*-clause. Example (155c) also has two binary operators, but at LF, and thus satisfies the homogeneity condition without also violating the doubly filled Comp filter.

As in the case of the simpler examples discussed earlier, it should be noted that examples like (155a,b) are ungrammatical when the P-gaps are replaced by overt pronouns.

(157) a. *What$_i$ did you show $t_i$ to whom$_j$ [without giving it$_i$ to her$_j$]

   b. *Which package$_i$ did you send $t_i$ to which student$_j$ [without PRO wrapping it$_j$ sufficiently to satisfy her$_i$]]

It thus appears that the ungrammaticality of these cases may be due to the impossibility of nonbound pronominal reference in the case of multiple *wh*-questions.

### 1.3.6 The Character of the Antecedent

**1.3.6.1 CP Antecedents** Perhaps the most robust challenge to CCP3—that the antecedent of a P-gap must be an NP—consists of examples like (158) where the antecedent is a CP.

(158) [CP That parasitic gaps don't really exist]ᵢ, I believed $t_i$ even before proving $pg_i$.

The argument is of course weakened if one assumes that the topicalized CP is actually a member of the category NP (see Rosenbaum 1967), but this view is currently not widely held.

Notice that CP antecedents also license subject P-gaps.

(159) [CP That parasitic gaps don't really exist]ᵢ, no one who believed $pg_i$ could prove $t_i$.

These cases are parallel to those involving NP antecedents.

(160) a. That proposalᵢ, I believed $t_i$ even before proving $pg_i$.
      b. That proposalᵢ, no one who believed $pg_i$ could prove $t_i$.

Crucially, it may not be possible to argue that the subject P-gaps are pseudo-P-gaps, if applying RNR in cases like (161) produces ungrammaticality.

(161) *No one who really believed [e] could manage to prove [e] [CP that parasitic gaps don't really exist].

**1.3.6.2  Non-CPs in English**  In section 1.1, I noted Engdahl's (1983) Swedish data suggesting that PPs and APs can be the antecedent of P-gaps (see example (10)). Along similar lines, Steedman (1996:98, note 41) judges the following example "impeccable"—

(162) the table on which I placed the book $t$ before carefully positioning the glass $pg$

Here, the gap is a PP. Note that examples such as these are potentially problematic for the anti-CCP view that a P-gap is an empty pronominal, if it can be shown that there are non-NP P-gaps for which no plausible proform exists. Levine, Hukari, and Calagno, this volume, pursue this question in some detail.

**1.3.6.3  French Double *Dont***  Another clear case in the literature of non-NP antecedents of P-gaps is that cited by Tellier (1991) for French. Some examples were given in (27)–(29) and are repeated here.

(27) a. C'est un livre dontᵢ la critique $t_i$ a été publiée par les détracteurs $pg_i$.
         'It is a book of which the critique has been published by the detractors.'

(28) a. Voilà une idée dont$_i$ on attribue le charme $t_i$ au caractére
        subversif $pg_i$.
        'Here is an idea of which one attributes the charm to the
        subversive character.'

(29) a. C'est là un sentiment dont$_i$ on peut attribuer la pérennité $t_i$ à la
        manifestation assidue $pg_i$.
        'This is a sentiment of which the perenniality is attributable to
        the constant manifestation.'

Tellier presents substantial evidence that there are in fact two gaps in
this construction, that is, that the argument marked $pg_i$ is syntactic and
not determined by pragmatic operations at the level of interpretation.
Accepting this conclusion, it is then plausible that the antecedent *dont* is a
PP, if *de* is a preposition in expressions such as *la manifestation de la
perennité* ('the manifestation of the perenniality'). If, on the other hand,
*de* is a genitive Case marker, then the double *dont* construction is not a
counterexample to the claim of CCP3.

### 1.3.7 The Domain of the P-gap

Comparative considerations suggest a certain degree of variability in the
domain restrictions on P-gaps, as well as the contribution of subjects to
restricting their appearance.

**1.3.7.1 Spanish** Bordelois (1985) shows that in Spanish P-gaps occur
only in untensed adverbial clauses (p. 2), a stronger restriction than we
find in English, where untensed adverbials are in general preferred.
Moreover, there are no P-gaps in Spanish in domains that have an overt
subject in the adjunct (p. 3), in contrast to English, in which the presence
of a subject is dispreferred but not a guarantee of ungrammaticality.
Compare:

(163) a. the man that the police arrested $t$ without speaking to *pg*
      b. ?the man that the police arrested $t$ without the officer in charge
         even speaking to *pg*

(164) *Spanish*
      a. el    poema que todos admiramos al    leer
         the poem  that all    we-admired when reading
         'the poem that we all admired when PRO reading'
      b. *el    poema que todos admiramos al    leer    el    autor
         the poem  that all    we-admired when reading the author
         'the poem that we all admired when the author read'

   c. Todos admiramos el  poema al    leerlo    el autor.
      all     we-admired the poem  when reading-it the author
      'We all admired the poem when the author read it.'
   [B86:3,(9),(10),(8)]

According to Bordelois, P-gaps in Spanish are illicit when there is an adjunct to the main VP that is unselected and intervenes between the main VP and the adjunct containing the P-gap (p. 3f). And clitic climbing shows the same distribution as P-gaps, in the sense that it cannot occur when the clause is tensed or has a subject (p. 6). Bordelois points out that this restriction on the domain of P-gaps is reminiscent of the characterization of Opacity in terms of "governing category" in the classical binding theory (Chomsky 1981). She argues that the domain restriction on P-gaps in Spanish would follow if P-gaps are anaphors, and therefore subject to Condition A of the binding theory: "an anaphor must be bound in its governing category." But note that this approach requires that the P-gap be taken to be an anaphoric variable. This point is discussed in greater detail in the discussion of the character of the P-gap in section 1.3.6.

A different view of the restriction on Spanish P-gaps is taken by García-Mayo and Kempchinsky (1993). They propose that the fundamental difference between English and Spanish P-gaps is that in English the null operator that binds the P-gap is moved into an $\bar{\text{A}}$-position and binds a trace, whereas in Spanish the null operator is generated in initial position and binds a *pro* (see section 1.3.5). Considering now temporal adjuncts, they recall the proposal of Geis (1970) that these clauses contain a null temporal operator, which binds a tense variable. In English tensed CP, there is an ambiguity depending on where this operator originates, as noted by Larson (1990).

(165) John left after he said he would.

This ambiguity does not occur in untensed adjuncts, since there is only one tense variable that the operator can bind.

(166) John left after saying he would.

García-Mayo and Kempchinsky (1993) propose the following account for the English/Spanish difference. In Spanish adjuncts, the [Spec,CP] position is occupied by the operator that binds the P-gap *pro*. In a tensed adjunct, the temporal operator must adjoin higher than this operator; hence it is not maximal in the adjunct and cannot be linked to the true gap, producing a Subjacency violation.[34] In English, on the other hand, the operator that binds the P-gap can move to a position higher than the temporal operator, avoiding the violation.

**1.3.7.2 German** Felix (1985) argues that P-gap constructions in German occur and are subject to the same principles that govern English P-gaps. The following examples are from Bavarian German.

(167) Das ist der Kerl$_i$ den$_i$ wenn ich $e_i$ erwisch, erschlag ich $e_i$.
   that is the guy who if I catch, beat I
   'This is the guy who I will beat (up) if I catch him.'

(168) Das ist das Buch$_i$ das$_i$ wenn ich $e_i$ finde, kauf ich $e_i$ auch.
   this is the book which if I find, buy I also
   'This is the book which I will buy if I can find it.'

(169) Ich bin ein Typ$_i$ der$_i$ wenn $e_i$ gefordert wird, leistet $e_i$ auch
   I am a type who if challenged is, accomplishes also
   etwas.
   something
   'I am the kind of person who accomplishes something if he is challenged.'

(170) Das ist eine Frau$_i$ die$_i$ wenn $e_i$ etwas verspricht hält $e_i$ es
   this is a woman who if something promises, keeps it
   auch.
   also
   'She is a woman who keeps her promises if she promises something.'

First, Felix notes that the embedded *wenn*-clause immediately follows the *wh*-pronoun and precedes the final clause. In Standard German the *wenn*-clause would appear finally and there could be no P-gap.

(171) Das ist der Kerl$_i$ den$_i$ ich $e_i$ erschlag, wenn ich $\left\{ \begin{array}{l} *e_i \\ \text{ihn}_i \end{array} \right\}$ erwisch.

   this is the guy who I beat if I him catch

Second, the V precedes the subject in the final clause; this is not the normal order.

(172) a. Das ist der Kerl$_i$ den$_i$ ich $e_i$ erschlag.
   b. *Das ist der Kerl$_i$ den$_i$ erschlag ich $e_i$.

Felix's analysis is that the *wenn*-phrase is in the Comp of the relative clause, that the relative pronoun moves to the front of the *wenn*-clause and then up into the higher clause, and licenses the gap in the relative clause. That is, it is the relative gap that is parasitic, and the gap in the adjunct that is the true gap. The evidence that supports this analysis is threefold: (i) the inversion of verb over subject is V2, triggered by the fronted *wenn*-clause, (ii) doubly filled Comp is possible only in Bavarian German but not in Standard German, and (iii) the case depends on the first gap, not the second gap (p. 177).

(173) Das ist der Kerl$_i$ den$_i$        wenn ich $e_i$ treff, werd ich $e_i$ helfen
       this is the guy  whom-ACC if   I      meet will I       help

Here, *helfen* governs the dative Case, while *treffen* governs accusative.

(174) *das ist der Kerl$_i$ dem$_i$ (DAT) wenn ich $e_i$ treff, werd ich $e_i$ helfen

Felix notes (p. 175, note 2) that this construction is possible only with *wenn*, not with *weil* ('because'), *obwohl* ('although'), *nachdem* ('after'), and so on.

**1.3.7.3 Dutch**  According to some accounts, Dutch lacks P-gaps of the English type. Huybregts and van Riemsdijk (1985) attribute the difference between English and Dutch to a difference in the government properties of prepositions that serve as subordinate conjunctions. They assume the chain composition account of P-gaps of Chomsky (1986b), where the operator that forms a chain with the P-gap is subjacent to the true gap. In English the preposition *without* governs the subject of a clausal complement, as does the preposition *for* in the *for-to* infinitive. The complement is not a barrier, and the operator is subjacent to the true gap, allowing chain composition to occur. In Dutch, however, the preposition lacks this property, so that the clausal complement is a barrier, and chain composition is blocked.

**1.3.7.4 French**  In her paper in this volume, Tellier discusses three main differences between English and French P-gaps, all of which have to do with the domain of the P-gap. Unlike English, French disallows P-gaps in adjuncts and in relative clauses. And French permits P-gaps in definite NPs whereas English does not. Tellier attributes the observed differences to differences in the agreement properties of the functional categories C and D in the two languages, with interesting and somewhat surprising consequences.

**1.4   Theories of P-gap Licensing**

**1.4.1   Subordinate P-gaps**
Theories of P-gap licensing can be viewed as combining the values of certain features in different ways. Theories differ on whether the anteced-

ent of the P-gap is the antecedent of the true gap, or an empty operator. For those that do not assume an empty operator, there is the question of whether the domain that contains the P-gap is subordinate to that which contains the true gap, or coordinate. The groupings in this section roughly reflect these features of various proposals.

**1.4.1.1  Contreras 1987**  Contreras (1987) proposes an extension of the approach of Chomsky 1982, assuming as with Chomsky (1986b) that the P-gap construction is a null operator construction. He proposes that the null operator that binds the P-gap is assigned values for the features [anaphor] and [pronominal] on the basis of where it appears in S-structure. According to Contreras, the null operator in a P-gap construction is governed, and is therefore [−anaphor, −pronominal]. The governor in an expression like *without reading pg* is the preposition (p. 12).

(175) [PP without [CP $Op_i$ [IP ... reading $pg_i$]]]

The null operator must be free, which accounts immediately for the anti-c-command condition without chain composition. If the null operator is c-commanded by the true gap then Condition C is violated.

**1.4.1.2  Longobardi**  Longobardi (1984) (see also Longobardi, 1985a,b) considers the case in which there is a gap in an adjunct on a right branch, as illustrated in (176).

(176)

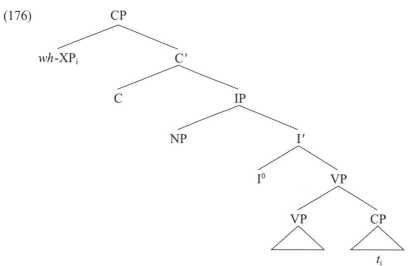

The question that arises is whether C′ is a g-projection (in the sense of Kayne 1983b) of the governor of $t_i$, which we will call α. Suppose that the lower CP is such a g-projection. The lower VP does not govern this CP but is in the configuration of canonical government with respect to CP, because it precedes it and canonical government in English is left-to-right. The higher VP immediately dominates the lower VP and CP, and CP is a g-projection of α. Thus the higher VP is a g-projection of α. Hence the higher CP is a g-projection of α and, because it contains α, the gap should be licensed. However, it is not; this is the configuration of a standard CED violation.

Longobardi proposes to tighten up the definition of configuration of canonical government so that it includes government. Under such a tightening, the lower VP would not be in such a configuration with CP, since it does not actually govern the CP. Thus the empty category would not be licensed. The requirement for government here anticipates Chomsky's later use of L-marking as a means of accounting for the ungrammaticality of extractions from adjunct islands in Chomsky (1986b). As Longobardi demonstrates (1985b:176), the approach extends directly to cases where the empty category is in an adjunct within another adjunct. When the containing adjunct contains an empty category, if it is a licensed P-gap, the lower adjunct may also contain a P-gap.

(177)  ?Which article should I study *t* thoroughly before I send *pg* back
       to the author without reviewing *pg*? ((22c))

But if there is no P-gap in the higher adjunct, the P-gap in the lower adjunct is not licensed.

(178)  *Which article should I study *t* thoroughly before I call the author
       without reviewing *pg*? ((22a))

### 1.4.2  ATB Extractions

**1.4.2.1  Sag 1983**  Grosu (1980) appears to have been the first to suggest that P-gap constructions are an extension of across-the-board (ATB) extraction from a coordinate structure. Sag (1983) (see also Sag 1982a,b) was the first to point out that the SLASH feature of a PSG approach can be generalized to all phrasal daughters of a phrase, producing multiple gaps with a single antecedent. It is not necessary to claim that the daughters are coordinate, simply that the gap appears in all of them. Sag's schema—

(179) *P-gap Metarule ( PGM )*
$(\sigma \rightarrow \alpha/N'', \beta) \Rightarrow$
$(\sigma \rightarrow \alpha/N'', \beta/N'')$
[Sa82:39,(11)]

—yields a multiple gap structure involving the sisters in any phrase that can itself contain a gap. Sag shows that this approach yields P-gap configurations such as those in (180).

(180)  a. [$_S$ [$_{NP}$ ...*e*... ] [$_{VP}$ ...*e*... ]]
     b. [$_{VP}$ V [$_{NP}$ *e* ] [$_{PP}$ P *e* ]]
     c. [$_{VP}$ V [$_{PP}$ P *e* ] [$_{PP}$ P *e* ]]
     d. [$_{VP}$ [$_{VP}$ V *e* ] [$_{PP}$ P ...*e*... ]]

A point not discussed by Sag is whether there are languages that allow for ATB extraction from coordinate structures but do not allow P-gaps; it would appear that the formalism introduced here would predict that the two would always go together. (Such a question arises generally for ATB type approaches.) It is also unclear how to account for cases where the true gap appears in one sister, the P-gap appears in another sister, but there is a third sister that lacks a P-gap.

(181)  a. the person who John sold [a picture of *t*] [to a friend of *pg*]
       [for a nickel]
     b. the person who Mary put *t* [in the most expensive hotel room]
       [without warning *pg*]

If strict binary branching is assumed in the VP in (181a) then *for a nickel* can be taken to be outside of the slashed category; however, it does not appear that such an approach will work for (181b) without additional stipulations, because *in the most expensive hotel room* is between the two constituents containing gaps. If binary branching is not assumed then the status of the nongapped PPs arises in both examples.

For refinements of this general approach, see Gazdar, Klein, Pullum, and Sag 1985 and Hukari and Levine 1987, as well as Levine, Hukari, and Calagno, this volume. Pollard and Sag (1994) update the proposal in the framework of HPSG. Hukari and Levine point out that using the PSG formalism, the anti-c-command condition follows directly. The c-commanding empty category is immediately dominated by a projection that dominates the P-gap. This projection inherits the SLASH feature from the P-gap, but not from the empty category, which instantiates the feature. Hence there is a mismatch, which is not licensed by the formalism.

**1.4.2.2   Cowper 1985**   Cowper (1985) argues that there are similarities in P-gap and ATB constructions. She notes first the relative acceptability of the following, due to Chomsky (1982), noted earlier as (91a).

(182)  George is a man who everyone who meets *e* knows someone who
       likes *e*. [Co85:76,(2)]

In this case, neither gap is subjacent to the leftmost *who* and so there should be dual Subjacency violations. Cowper argues that in coordinate structures, Subjacency fails to rule out ATB extractions just in case the antecedent is higher than the branching point and the gaps are lower than the branching point.

(183)  Which students did they decide [[to expel *e*] and [give raises to
       everyone who taught *e*]] [C85:76,(5a)]

Cowper claims that this sentence is more acceptable than the corresponding example with one gap.

(184)  *Which buildings did they give raises to everyone who taught in *t*.
       [C85:76,(5b)]

In the editors' view, this conclusion is not sustainable, our judgment being that (183) is on a par with (184).

Cowper raises the technical question of whether the coordinate structure shares with (182) the crucial properties that will produce a violation. Suppose for the sake of exposition that in long extractions there are intermediate traces in the Comp position of each CP. The intermediate trace associated with *which students* is in the Comp position of the CP containing *expel*. There is no intermediate trace in *give raises to everyone who taught e* that forms a chain with *e* that violates Subjacency. Similar observations hold for the expressions *everyone who meets e* and *someone who likes e* in the P-gap construction in (182). Cowper goes on to suggest that if there is an additional barrier (in the form of a bounding node) on one of the branches, a Subjacency violation arises.[35]

(185)  *George is a man who everyone who meets *e* has read a book
       about someone who likes *e*. [C85:78,(10a)]

Here, the problem is with *a book about someone who likes e*. Cowper's account of the phenomenon is that Subjacency is due to syntactic processing (p. 78). A filler such as a fronted *wh*-phrase forms a chain with its gap or gaps, which must be identified in the course of processing. In case there is a branching chain, as in a P-gap construction or ATB extraction, the portion of the structure containing the multiple gaps is processed first. Processing involves creating an existential quantifier at the branch point. This quantifier is then linked to the fronted *wh*-phrase as though it was a variable. If there are no Subjacency violations between the created quantifier and the gaps, or between the fronted *wh*-phrase and the quantifier, then the sentence is judged to be well-formed.

The well-formedness of (182) also appears to depend on the presence of a quantifier, such as *everyone, no one,* or *someone.* Cowper suggests that this is due to the consolidation of the created quantifier and the overt quantifier, eliminating a bounding node. It is not clear precisely what formal mechanisms are entailed by such a proposal.

**1.4.2.3  Williams 1990**  Williams (1990) suggests that a P-gap construction may be analyzed as follows.

(186)  Who [[would you warn *t*] [before striking *pg*]]

where the two bracketed expressions are taken to be in a coordinate structure.

(187)  Who [[would you warn *t*] COORD [before striking *t*]] [W90:265,(3)]

The nature of such coordination is somewhat obscure, especially given that it is necessary to invoke it for cases where the P-gap is in a subject.

(188)  Which stars do [pictures of *t*] COORD [annoy *t*]] [W90:270,(27)]

Postal (1993b) criticizes Williams's proposal on on both conceptual and factual grounds. First, it is generally agreed that P-gaps can only have NP antecedents, while ATB extraction can involve any category (but see section 1.2.3). Second, ATB extractions can apply to the subjects of embedded clauses, while P-gaps cannot be the subjects of embedded clauses, according to Postal.[36]

(189)  a.  *Which patient did he convince *t pg* should visit him?
            [Po93b:737,(8b)]
       b.  Which patients did he convince you *t* were already doctors
            and *t* were going to become psychiatrists? [Po93b,737,(10a)]

Third, P-gaps are disallowed in contexts that also disallow passive (see Postal 1990); ATB extraction does not observe this constraint.

(190)  a.  Diptheria can be caught/*gotten by anyone. [Po93b:738,(11b)]
       b.  Which disease did everyone who caught/*got *pg* want Dr.
            Jones to study *t*. [Po93b:738,(11d)]

    c. Which disease did Dr. Johns study *t* but Dr. Kline deny that he
       had ever caught/gotten *t*? [Po93b:738,(12a)]

A set of additional restrictions on passive also appear to hold for
P-gaps but not for ATB extraction.

(191)  a.  Abigail felt the rocks move. [Po93b:741,(20a)]
      b.  *The rocks were felt move by Abigail. [Po93b:741,(20b)]
      c.  *Which rocks did the gorilla sit on *t* after feeling *pg* move?
         [Po93b:741,(20e)]
      d.  the rock which Ted sat on *t* but only Joyce felt move *t*
         [Po93b:741,(20f)]

(192)  a.  It amused Sonia to tickle alligators. [Po93b:743,(25a)]
      b.  *Sonia was amused by it to tickle alligators. [Po93b:743,(25b)]
      c.  *It was Ida that Bob contacted *t* immediately after concluding
         that it would amuse *pg* to tickle alligators. [Po93b:743,(25e)]
      d.  The kind of people who Bob might warn *t* but it would
         nonetheless amuse *t* to tickle alligators [Po93b:743,(25f)]

Furthermore, as already noted, Postal presents evidence that P-gaps are
excluded in positions that cannot contain overt pronouns, a restriction
that is not shared by ATB extractions (see section 1.3.2.2 for a summary).
Postal notes that these properties of P-gaps, and others not mentioned
here, appear to be shared by other "empty operator" constructions, such
as Object Raising, complement object deletion (Lasnik and Fiengo 1974),
purposives (Bach 1982), and infinitival relatives; see Cinque 1990, as well
as Browning 1987 and Jones 1987.

**1.4.2.4 Munn 1992** Munn (1992) assumes that P-gaps are produced by
across-the-board (ATB) movement. His approach differs from earlier
treatments in that for him, coordinate ATB constructions are a subtype of
P-gap construction. The P-gap is produced by null operator movement
(along the lines of Contreras 1984 and Chomsky 1986b), as is the gap in
an ATB construction. Munn notes that P-gap constructions are similar to
ATB constructions in restricting the category of the antecedent; some of
the evidence is summarized in section 1.2.3. However, note that Munn's
proposal is incompatible with the evidence of Postal (1993b) cited in section 1.3.2 that the P-gap is pronominal. Munn develops his ideas further
in his contribution to this volume, arguing for some striking parallels
between P-gap and coordinate constructions.

## 1.5 Summary

In summary, let us recall the CCP of (26).

(26) CCP1. The antecedent of a P-gap must be in an $\bar{\text{A}}$-position.
  CCP2. A P-gap is licensed only at S-structure.
  CCP3. The antecedent of a P-gap must be an NP.
  CCP4. The true gap cannot c-command the P-gap.
  CCP5. The P-gap is in a chain with the antecedent of the true gap.
  CCP6. Anti-c-command is a consequence of Condition C of the
     binding theory.

It is striking that although there is support for all of these clauses of the CCP, none has gone without serious challenge. CCP1 has been challenged primarily by the evidence that scrambling and clitics license P-gaps in some languages. CCP2 has received a limited challenge from Jeddah Arabic but otherwise seems fairly robust. Perhaps the most contentious issue is CCP3. There is overwhelming empirical evidence in support of this position, although it has also been challenged by Levine, Hukari, and Calagno (this volume) for English. The striking contrast between the extended evidence in support of CCP3 and the robust counterexamples is an intriguing puzzle that merits further study.

The anti-c-command position of CCP4 appears to be substantially correct and without serious challenge in the literature, although CCP6 is not yet firmly established as the basis for CCP4. Finally, CCP5 is very much at issue, regardless of the status of CCP3.

So, although much has been learned about P-gaps since Engdahl's original paper, most of the central questions remain open. We hope that the papers in the current volume will provide a useful perspective on the key issues, that they will bring together the essential factual material that must be accounted for in any treatment of the subject, that they will offer new insights into the nature of P-gaps in a range of languages, and that they will stimulate new research on the basis of which our understanding of these issues may be advanced.

## Notes

I am indebted to Paul Postal for numerous comments, suggestions, and corrections. Any errors are my responsibility.

1. For consistency I have replaced cited authors' use of *e* in examples with *t* and *pg* where their intention is clear.

2. "E83 refers to Engdahl (1983), "5:" to page 5, and "(1)" to example (1) of her paper. A similar notational scheme is used throughout for references to the literature.

3. See note 5 for a discussion of Bresnan's observations.

4. Current terminology calls a noun phrase "DP," on the view that the determiner (D) is the head of the phrase. This issue is not relevant here and for accessibility I will use the more classical terminology.

5. As pointed out to me by Paul Postal (personal communication), a number of Engdahl's observations were anticipated by Bresnan (1977). Postal observes that in section 1.3.4 ("Across-the-board" deletions) Bresnan discussed cases such as her (55) (see also her (56)–(58) and (81)–(84).)

(55) ... a man who Mary called _____ an idiot as often as June called _____ a cretin

Bresnan took these to be analogous to ATB extractions. (This was, of course, before the early 1980s papers on P-gaps by Engdahl, Sag, Chomsky, etc., and recognition of the special properties did not yet exist.) Bresnan explicitly noted several key properties now taken to be standard (e.g., that the second gap depends on the first), as expressed in the following observation (p. 189): "Notice also that removal of the second object depends upon the relativization of the first object":

(84) *The French cook one food in the same way that the Italians cook _____.
       (cf. The French cook one food in the same way that the Italians cook it.)"

and that the second "deletion" in effect permits extractions from (comparative clause) islands without violation (p. 182): "In these cases, we can extract elements from comparative clauses without creating the ungrammatical effects of violations of 'island' constraints."

Strikingly, Bresnan also gave as well formed the following:

(58a) ... someone that I believe _____ hates me as much as you believe _____ hates you

In this example, *both* the true gap and the P-gap are embedded subjects. Postal (personal communication) notes that the phenomenon is of course far from free:

(i) *Who$_i$ did she believe _____$_i$ had proved _____$_i$ was innocent?

This example would be ruled out by an anti-c-command condition.

Bresnan's cases were noted by Engdahl (1983), who took them to be P-gaps. Besides that, the only discussion we know of is by Chomsky and Lasnik (1977). They claimed that the examples were hypermarginal, but did propose a special pronoun deletion rule to cover some of them.

6. The original proposal to account for P-gaps in terms of "connectedness"—that is, the relative configuration of paths in the tree between antecedent and gap— is due to Kayne (1983). A refinement is due to Longobardi (1984, 1985a, 1985b). I summarize Kayne's proposal here and Longobardi's in section 1.4.1.2.

7. See Sportiche 1996 for a review of the literature.

8. "... it is worth pointing out that the relevant constructions give rise to a range of diverging judgments among native speakers. While some find the contrast between *dont* and *en* quasi-inexistent [sic], others reject the *en* cases on the PG interpretation. The diacritics given below reflect my own judgments, which are situated somewhere in between" (Tellier 1991:136).

9. However, compare with:

(i) *Vous l$_i$'avez rangé     sans     avoir   lu $e_i$
    you   it-have put-away without to-have read
    'You put it away without having read.' [Te91:135,(16b)]

10. "Either *en* and other clitics differ in their manner of derivation (the former undergoes movement while the latter are base-generated), or else *en* and other clitics differ with respect to their projection level (*en* is a maximal projection while other clitics are heads)." (Tellier 1991:136)

11. A similar proposal for Dutch clitics is made by Zwart (1992). See Haverkort (1993) for some problems with this approach for West Flemish.

12. Cited by Campos (1992:122, ex. 14).

13. As suggested by Tellier (1991), French *en* could be a phrasal clitic, perhaps adjoining to IP, but keep in mind that *en* adjoins to the left of infinitives like the other clitics in French.

14. Subordinate clauses headed by these elements are extraposable in German.

15. A somewhat different trace proposal is due to Mahajan (1991:93), who suggests that the P-gap is an NP trace that forms an A chain with an antecedent in [Spec,VP]. This antecedent is the trace of a null operator that ultimately moves to an Ā-position in the adjunct that contains the P-gap. Hence the scrambled NP can Ā-bind the P-gap while its trace in A-position A-binds the pronoun, avoiding Webelhuth's paradox. Lee and Santorini (1994) argue against Mahajan's approach on the grounds that scrambling the constituent containing the pronoun does not produce ungrammaticality even though the P-gap is then A-bound.

16. Ross (1967) appears to be the first to have suggested this possibility.

17. Similarly, where extraction out of a relative clause is marginally possible, the corresponding P-gap construction is more acceptable.

(i) a. a book which I didn't meet [anyone [who had read $t$]]
    b. which$_i$ we filed $t_i$ without meeting [anyone [who had read $pg_i$]]

18. A variant of the Frampton proposal, under somewhat different formal assumptions, and particularly with a different implementation of the locality restrictions on chains, is made by Manzini (1994).

19. However, contrary to the claim of Chomsky and of Koopman and Sportiche, such examples are more acceptable than true WCO violations (cf. (77)).

20. Strikingly, there is no true gap in this example, yet it appears to be a genuine case of a P-gap construction. Compare with

(i) a. *a man whom everyone who meets Mary knows someone who likes $e$
    b. *a man whom everyone who meets $e$ knows someone who likes Mary

both of which are significantly less acceptable.

21. The ungrammaticality of (95b) may be due to other factors, such as the presence of the subject and Tense:

(i) This is the student everyone expected $t$ to be intelligent without believing $pg$
    to be worthy of promotion.

22. This type of example was noted originally by Bresnan (1977); see note 5 for discussion.

23. Franks (p. 13, n. 13) says that Polish lacks P-gaps, and instead uses a resumptive pronoun where the P-gap would be.

24. Haegeman also notes (p. 232) that this construction is attested at least as far back as Shakespeare.

25. However, it is open to question whether c-command is either a necessary or sufficient condition for Condition C effects; see Postal 1997.

26. This property is also found in some HPSG analyses, such as Pollard and Sag (1994).

27. $\alpha$ antecedent governs $\beta$ if

(i)    $\alpha$ and $\beta$ are coindexed
(ii)   $\alpha$ c-commands $\beta$
(iii)  there is no $\gamma$ ($\gamma$ an NP or $\bar{S}$) such that $\alpha$ c-commands $\gamma$ and dominates $\beta$, unless $\beta$ is the head of $\gamma$
        (Lasnik and Saito 1984)

28. Hence the option that the P-gap is *pro* is ruled out on this approach, but not on others. See section 1.3.2.

29. An example due to Robert Levine (personal communication).

30. The judgments here are delicate. Example (a) is clearly not as acceptable as (b,c), which are themselves less than perfect.

31. Pointed out by Paul Postal (personal communication).

32. The assumption here, of course, is that an overt trace will behave in all respects like an empty trace with respect to islands. This is not a necessary assumption.

33. The data here is reminiscent of the cases discussed by Ross (1969). Ross showed that island violations are mitigated when the actual gap is not present in the S-structure, as in the following:

(i) a. *Mary met a woman who wrote a famous book, but I don't know which book Mary met a woman who wrote *t*.
    b. Mary met a woman who wrote a famous book, but I don't know which book.

These data are consistent with the widely held view that Subjacency does not hold at LF.

34. In a Relativized Minimality framework, the P-gap operator blocks the temporal operator from binding the tense variable.

35. Curiously, I find example (185) to be no worse than (182), and possibly better.

36. This example strikes me as unobjectionable. Consider, along similar lines, the following:

(i) a. The student who I convinced *t pg* should run for class president was Otto.
    b. Which prisioners did you warn *t pg* would be searched after lunch?

# Chapter 2

Parasitic Gaps          Elisabet Engdahl

In this paper, I will discuss a phenomenon that I will refer to as "parasitic gaps."[1] Tentatively, we can define a parasitic gap as a gap that is dependent on the existence of another gap, which I will henceforth refer to as the "real gap," in the same sentence. By a gap, I understand an empty node that is necessarily controlled by a lexical phrase somewhere in the sentence. It follows from this definition that a parasitic gap will only occur if there is a filler-gap dependency elsewhere in the sentence and the parasitic gap is interpreted as controlled by that filler. The characterization of parasitic gaps rules out gaps that arise as the result of a pronoun deletion rule. In languages like Japanese and Turkish, which have rules of optional *pro* drop, a gap may act just like a deictic pronoun and be interpreted as referring to something salient in the context. In languages like English and Swedish, from which I will draw the data for this discussion, optional *pro* drop does not occur and gaps are controlled sentence internally. Here are some examples of sentences with parasitic gaps. For perspicuousness, I will, when possible, indicate the parasitic gap by *pg*.

(1) Which articles did John file *t* without reading *pg*?

(2) This is the kind of food you must cook *t* before you eat *pg*.

(3) Which girl did you send a picture of *t* to *t*?

(4) Which boy did Mary's talking to *pg* bother *t* most?

Some of these examples have been previously noted in the literature, but I'm not aware of any systematic attempt at assessing the relevance of parasitic gaps to grammatical theory. This will be the main purpose of this paper.

Sentences with parasitic gaps show that one filler may control more than one gap. The same is true for sentences with simultaneous extractions out of coordinate structures. In section 2.1, I will discuss some reasons for not subsuming parasitic gaps under coordinated extractions and point to a general parsing problem posed both by parasitic gaps and by gaps in coordinate structures. The distribution of parasitic gaps is shown in section 2.2, and in section 2.3, I address the question of what the licensing conditions for parasitic gaps are. In section 2.4, I illustrate the nature of these gaps. I further argue that they fall naturally into an optional and an obligatory class (section 2.5) and show how obligatory parasitic gaps interact with Postal's crossover constraint (section 2.6). Certain interesting restrictions on parasitic gaps are discussed in section 2.7. In section 2.8, I discuss a proposal by Chomsky and Lasnik (1977) for similar cases. Some implications for sentence processing are drawn out in the final section.

## 2.1  Parasitic Gaps and "Coordinate Gaps"

First some terminological clarifications. In talking about long distance dependencies, I will use the terms "filler" and "displaced constituent" to refer to topicalized constituents, heads of relative clauses, and preposed interrogative phrases, i.e., constituents which according to a transformational analysis would have been "moved" from their deep structure position. The surface position of such fillers, viz., as leftmost sisters of S, is not a possible deep structure position, a fact that presumably is recognized and utilized by the parser (Fodor 1978).

In general there is a one-to-one correspondence between fillers and gaps. One notable exception is when a gap occurs in a coordinate structure, as in (5)

(5) Who$_i$ did you say [$_S$[$_S$ John liked $t_i$] and [$_S$ Mary hated $t_i$]]?

(5) illustrates what I will call "coordinate gaps." Williams (1978) shows that such sentences can be derived by one single application of a transformation given a factorization of the string into parallel structures where the conjunction and Comp nodes play a crucial role. Gazdar (1981) shows how the same facts can be handled in a nontransformational grammar and uses the coordination facts as an argument for using "slashed categories" in the grammar.

The question is now whether parasitic gaps are amenable to similar analyses. We note that in (1) and (2), the parasitic gap occurs in an adverbial clause. It is irrelevant to the present argument exactly where in the tree the adverb is attached. In fact, different types of adverbial clauses are probably attached at different heights in the tree and all three structures in (6) are motivated. (See Reinhart 1976 and Williams 1978 for discussion.)

(6) a.

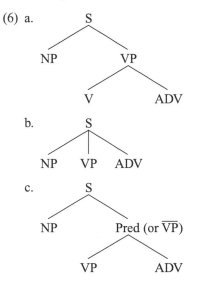

b.
```
        S
      / | \
    NP  VP  ADV
```

c.
```
        S
       /  \
     NP   Pred (or V̄P̄)
          /  \
        VP    ADV
```

In none of the structures illustrated in (6) does the attachment of the adverbial clause involve coordination of two constituents of the same syntactic category. Consequently, there is little syntactic motivation for analyzing sentences (1) and (2) in a similar fashion to (5).

Semantically the adverbial clauses act as modifiers on VP or S. It follows that they will be of a different type than the argument they apply to, and hence cannot be coordinated with these. Rather they are often analyzed, as for instance in Montague grammar, as functions that take either VP meanings or S meanings as arguments and yield results of the same type. The examples in (3) and (4) provide even less ground for a coordination analysis. In (3), there are two gaps in two distinct argument positions of the verb *send*. Since *send* subcategorizes for both a direct and an indirect object, it is not possible to analyze the arguments as a conjoined structure. Example (4) shows that a parasitic gap may in fact precede the real gap. In this case, the parasitic gap occurs inside the subject NP and the real gap in the direct object NP. One will be hard put to analyze such a structure as an instance of coordination. Further evidence that (1)–(4) do not involve across-the-board dependencies comes from the fact that sentences formed by replacing the parasitic gaps with full NPs are grammatical, as illustrated in (1′) and (4′),

(1′)  Which articles did John file *t* without reading more than their titles?

(4′)  Which boy did Mary's talking to the policeman bother *t* most?

If these sentences involved dependencies into coordinate structures, replacing a gap with a full NP would lead to a violation of the coordinate structure constraint and the sentence would be ungrammatical, as in the case of (5′).

(5′)  *Who did you say John liked *t* and Mary hated Bill?

There thus seem to be good grounds not to assume that the examples in (1)–(4) involve underlying conjunctions. I take it then that Williams' and Gazdar's across-the-board approaches will not be applicable to these cases.

There is one respect, however, in which parasitic gaps and coordinate gaps are alike, namely in the demand of increased flexibility that they put on the parser. Examples like (1)–(5), where one filler must be linked with more than one gap, show that a theory of gap filling cannot consist simply of the assumption that a recognized filler is put in some special location, call it HOLD, until a gap of matching category is detected. When a gap has been identified, the filler is retrieved from HOLD and "plugged into" the gap. The examples given above show that the filler must in some sense be "available" across conjunctions and also into a variety of non-conjoined domains.

## 2.2    The Distribution of Parasitic Gaps

When I started to collect judgments on sentences with parasitic gaps, it became painfully clear to me that there is a lot of variation among speakers. Some speakers are very restrictive about which positions they accept parasitic gaps in, others are much more permissive. This makes indicating the status of the example sentences rather problematic. Rather than marking the sentences with some combination of stars and/or question marks, I will continue to just give the examples and leave it up to the reader to supply the judgments. All example sentences, except when the parasitic gap is explicitly marked as ungrammatical, are acceptable to some speakers.

The interesting fact about the variation in judgments is that it is not at random but seems to follow a relative ordering. That is, given two sentences with parasitic gaps in different types of domains, people in general agree on which sentence is more acceptable. This suggests that we can order the domains in which parasitic gaps can occur into an accessibility hierarchy.[2] People who accept parasitic gaps in one type of domain, generally accept gaps in any domain higher up on the hierarchy, but there is a lot of individual variation as to how far down the hierarchy parasitic gaps may occur. A tentative, incomplete formulation of the hierarchy is given in (7).

(7) *Accessibility hierarchy for occurrences of parasitic gaps*

manner adverbs  ∨ = more accessible than
∨
temporal adverbs    untensed domains
∨
purpose clauses

∨      ∨

*that* / *than* } clauses
∨
*when* / *because* / cond. *if* } clauses } tensed domains
∨
relative clauses
indirect questions

The ordering in (7) is based on a relatively small sample of ranked examples and is in no way intended to be exhaustive, only suggestive. Most likely the category of "*that* clauses" should be broken down further depending on properties of the embedding verbs such as factivity and [±emotive], cf. Ross's notion of "variable strength" (Ross 1971). Certain factors cut across the categories in the hierarchy. For instance, temporal clauses appear to be pretty accessible parasitic gap domains, regardless of whether they are tensed or not. No one seems to find a significant contrast in acceptability between (2), repeated here, and its untensed counterpart (8).

(2) This is the kind of food you must cook *t* before you eat *pg*.

(8) This is the kind of food you must cook *t* before eating *pg*.

The hierarchy bears a certain similarity to the accessibility charts developed by Keenan (1975) and Keenan and Comrie (1977) but differs in that we are here primarily interested in different types of subordinate clauses, not in NP positions. One question that is brought up both by

Keenan and Comrie's work on accessibility to relativization and the hierarchy in (7) is to what extent there is a correlation between the accessibility hierarchies and experimental findings that different types of clauses vary both in processing load and processing depth (cf. Bever and Townsend 1979). A somewhat related question is whether real gaps and parasitic gaps are handled by the same processing strategies. In a later section we will discuss examples which seem to show that the parser recognizes both the occurrence of a gap and its "status," i.e., whether it is a possible real gap or not. Before addressing these issues, let me present some more examples to give some justification for the hierarchy in (7).

The contrast between different types of adverbial clauses and complements is illustrated in the examples in (9)–(11), taken from Ross 1967:chap. 4. Ross observes that the acceptability of a gap in a certain context is inversely correlated with the goodness of a pronoun, interpreted as coreferent with the filler, in the same position. The judgments on the examples are Ross's, the gap indications are mine.

(9)   The curtain which Fred tore *t* in rolling *pg*/?it up was the kind gift of my maternal Aunt Priscilla.

(10)  I suspect that the contract which I wanted to peruse *t* before filing ?*t*/?it away may have had loopholes.

(11)  The blintzes which Sasha is gobbling *t* down faster than I can reheat ?*t*/them are extremely tasty, if I do say so.

Ross suggests that these kinds of examples can be derived by a pronoun deletion rule. The difference in acceptability of the gaps in (9)–(11) can then be accounted for by assuming that the rule is obligatory in (9), optional in (10) and not applicable in (11). Note that the proposed deletion rule must make reference to intended interpretation of the pronouns since a pronoun can only be deleted if it is understood to refer to whatever the filler refers to. Ross also notes that "it is theoretically possible to relativize any number of NPs at once, although the resulting sentences are somewhat less than felicitous" (Ross 1967:105). He gives the following sentence:

(12)  The contract which I want to peruse *t* before damaging *pg* while filing *pg* is written on Peruvian papyrus (Ross, 4.156b).

Another example illustrating the possibility of multiplying parasitic gaps was brought to my attention by B. Partee and given here in (13).

(13)  Here is the man who meeting *t* convinced Mary that beginning to love *t* would make her end up hating *t*.

Further examples, which I believe illustrate the decreasing degree of acceptability, are given in (14)–(17). (15) was suggested by B. Partee.

(14) Here is the influential professor that John sent his book to *t* in order to impress *pg*.

(15) Which professor did you persuade the students of *t* to nominate *t* for the Distinguished Teacher's Award?

(16) Which students did you persuade some friends of *t* to write to *t*?

(17) Which students did you persuade *t* to invite us to come and see *pg*?

Sentences where the parasitic gaps occur in tensed subordinate clauses are even more marginal, which might indicate that, at least for English, the distinction between untensed and tensed domain is important for determining the likelihood that a parasitic gap will be acceptable.

(18) Who did you tell *t* that we were going to vote for *pg*?

(19) Which colleague did John slander *t* because he despised *pg*?

(20) This is the professor that you must say hello to *t* if you run into *pg*.

(21) How many students did John inform *t* whether we had accepted ???*pg*/them or not?

(22) This book, it would be stupid to give *t* to [NP someone [s̄ who already has read *\*t*/it]].

If the ordering in the accessibility hierarchy in (7) reflects facts about processing, we would expect it to hold across languages, at least across languages with similar structures. Indeed, relevant parts of the hierarchy apply to Swedish and Norwegian as well, but in these languages the major break between acceptable and unacceptable domains does not fall between tensed and untensed structures, as in English, but somewhere further down.

**2.3 What Licenses Parasitic Gaps?**

We now turn to the question: What factors can trigger the occurrence of a parasitic gap? First, I want to reemphasize a point made in the introduction, namely that parasitic gaps do not arise through some optional pronoun deletion rule of the type that applies in languages like Japanese, Portugese, and Turkish. In these languages, a pronoun may delete if the referent is highly salient in the context. In languages like English and Swedish, however, subcategorization restrictions may not be violated even if the argument is totally predictable from the preceding context. Consider the English and Swedish dialogues in (23).

(23)  Q: What happened to John?    Vad hände med John?
      A: Someone hit *$t$/him.      Någon slog *$t$/honom.

Although the context uniquely determines the referent of the pronoun *him*, it cannot be left out. This shows that gaps must be controlled sentence internally. However, not any sentence internal phrase will qualify as a controller, as the following examples illustrate.

(24)  John filed a bunch of articles without reading *$t$/them.

(25)  Mary's talking to *$t$/him bothered John a lot.

Even if there is a plausible antecedent for the gap in the same sentence, the subcategorization requirements cannot be violated. It appears that the good examples of parasitic gaps all occur in sentences where there is another gap, due to a filler-gap dependency in the same sentence, and the parasitic gap is interpreted as controlled by the filler. So far all good examples have involved constituent questions, relativizations, or topicalizations, i.e., constructions where the filler occurs as leftmost sister of a sentential node. A first hypothesis might be that only fillers in the designated location, leftmost sister of S, license parasitic gaps. When we look at other dependencies besides leftward dependencies, this hypothesis turns out not to be correct, for instance, parasitic gaps may also be triggered by Heavy NP Shift,[3] as illustrated in the following examples, suggested by Tom Wasow.

(26)  John offended $t_i$ by not recognizing $t_i$/him$_i$ immediately, [$_{NP_i}$ his favorite uncle from Cleveland].

(27)  Susan always files $t_i$ without reading $t_i$/them$_i$ properly, [$_{NP_i}$ all the memos from the low-level administration].

A number of speakers find these sentences approximately as acceptable as some of the leftward dependency sentences. Similar sentences in Swedish are better with a parasitic gap than with a pronoun that is understood as coreferent with the rightward moved phrase, and some speakers apparently get the same contrast in English. It seems that the possibility of having a coreferent pronoun in the intervening position increases if the adverbial clause is taken to be a parenthetical and set off from the rest of the sentence by heavy intonation breaks. Furthermore, leftward dependencies involving *tough* movement and *too/enough* constructions also license parasitic gaps, a fact first noticed by A. Zaenen. In these cases, the controller for the gap occurs in subject position.

(28) These papers were hard for us to file $t$ without reading $pg$.

(29) This book is too interesting to put $t$ down without having finished $pg$.

Examples (26)–(29) show that it is not the position or the nature of the filler that determines the possibility of having a parasitic gap. The filler may be to the right or to the left, attached as leftmost sister of S or occurring in an argument position inside S. Rather, what seems to be relevant is that there is a controlled gap in the sentence, i.e., an obligatory consistuent that is not lexically realized, but which is interpreted as controlled by a lexically realized phrase in the sentence. However, it's not sufficient to say that there has to be another control relation in the sentence. In recent proposals within trace theory (Chomsky 1975, 1977; Chomsky and Lasnik 1977) constructions like Passive, Equi, and Raising are analyzed as involving movement of a NP which leaves an empty position, coindexed with the moved constituent. If in fact the gap left behind by any movement rule could act as a trigger for parasitic gaps, then we would expect parasitic gaps in sentences with Passive, etc. But as can be seen in (30)–(32), the traces left behind by NP movement do not license parasitic gaps.

(30) $\text{John}_i$ was killed $t_i$ by a tree falling on $*pg$/him.

(31) $\text{Mary}_i$ tried $t_i$ to leave without John's hearing $*pg$/her.

(32) $\text{Mary}_i$ seemed $t_i$ to disapprove of John's talking to $*pg$/her.

It appears that the relevant property which distinguishes between sentences like (1)–(4) and (26)–(29) where parasitic gaps are allowed, and sentences like (30)–(32), where they are not, is that the real gaps in the former sentences arise through nonlocal dependencies, whereas the traces in (30)–(32) involve local dependencies. By a nonlocal or unbounded dependency I mean a dependency that holds over an arbitrary domain and whose description requires the use of an essential variable.

To summarize briefly the theoretical significance of this contrast, we can say that the parasitic gap phenomenon shows that there is at least one process in the grammar which is sensitive to a distinction between local and nonlocal dependencies. Consequently, the parasitic gap facts provide an argument against subsuming wh-type movement and NP-type movement under one and the same rule and for making a systematic distinction in the grammar between bounded and unbounded processes.[4] Ideally, for languages that have parasitic gaps we might want to be able to refer to the property of licensing parasitic gaps as a diagnostic for unbounded phenomena. In the theoretical framework of Chomsky (1981), apparent unbounded phenomena like *wh*-movement, are analyzed as resulting from iteretive applications of cyclic movements. However, one could claim that parasitic gaps are sensitive not to the distinction between local and nonlocal dependencies, but to the distinction between caseless and case-marked traces.

It is also worth noting that it appears to be the actual presence of a real gap that licenses a parasitic gap and not just the presence of a *wh*-phrase. In sentences where there is no gap because the *wh*-phrase occurs in situ, as in an echo-question, (33), or in a multiple question (34), no parasitic gaps are allowed.[5]

(33) John filed which articles, without reading *$t$/them?

(34) I forget who filed which articles, without reading *$t$/them.

## 2.4 The Parasitic Nature of Certain Gaps

I now want to turn to some properties of parasitic gaps which may give some justification for talking about "real" and "parasitic" gaps. In several of the examples given above, the parasitic gaps appear in domains that are considered to be extraction islands in the language. Although some of these domains may not be absolute islands, it is clear that the extraction site indicated by the parasitic gap is in some sense less accessible or more marked than the site of the real gap. One way of establishing this ranking of accessibility between a real gap and a parasitic gap in a given sentence is to look at what happens when each of the gaps is plugged up. Consider the following triples of sentences. In the (b) version, the real gap has been filled with a lexical NP, and in the (c) version the parasitic gap has been plugged up.

(35) a.   Here is the paper that John read $t$ before filing *pg*.
     b.   ?Here is the paper that John read his mail before filing $t$.
     c.   Here is the paper that John read $t$ before filing his mail.

(36) a.   Who did John's talking to *pg* bother $t$ most?
     b.   ?Who did John's talking to $t$ bother you most?
     c.   Who did John's talking to Mary bother $t$ most?

It is generally agreed that the (b) versions are considerably worse; that is, sentences where what I have indicated as the parasitic gap in the (a) version must be understood as the real gap, because this is the only gap in the sentence, are quite bad. This shows that a parasitic gap does not survive easily as an independent gap.[6] Instead of plugging up each of the gaps, we can establish the same point by substituting an intransitive verb in the clause with the real gap, thereby eliminating the possibility of a gap there and forcing the parasitic gap to be reanalyzed as a real gap. In trying out examples to test this point, I noticed an interesting feature which might provide some impressionistic evidence for what the gap searching strategies of the parser look like. Consider a sentence like (37).

(37) Who did you sneeze, after meeting *t*?

Tom Wasow reports that when he first heard this sentence, he found himself reanalyzing *sneeze* as a transitive verb which would allow for a real gap immediately after it. Similarly, in cases where the main verb is optionally transitive, as in the case with *leave*, listeners say that they tend to take the transitive reading, for instance in (38)

(38) Who did you leave (*t*), before seeing *t*?

although this makes the sentence semantically implausible.

The processes illustrated by the ways (37) and (38) are understood, may be indicative of how the parser uses knowledge about what syntactic domains are possible extraction domains on line during comprehension. It seems that the parser's expectation to find a matching gap within a certain domain sometimes leads it to choose a particular syntactic analysis which turns out to be incompatible with the interpretation of the sentence as a whole. But some of the previous examples show that the parser is not limited to gap detection in expected domains, a point we will return to in section 2.9.

### 2.5  Optional and Obligatory Parasitic Gaps

So far in our discussion we have treated all occurrences of parasitic gaps in a similar fashion. However, they seem to fall naturally into two types, both on structural grounds and in terms of their relative obligatoriness. The two types can be distinguished by the properties summarized in (39), for "optional" parasitic gaps, and in (40), for "obligatory" parasitic gaps.

(39) *"Optional" parasitic gaps*
   a. follow the real gap
   b. primarily occur in (untensed) adverbial and complement clauses
   c. are in almost free variation with unstressed personal pronouns, which are understood to be coreferential to or bound by the filler.

(40) *"Obligatory" parasitic gaps*
   a. precede the real gap
   b. primarily occur in gerunds and noun complements
   c. can normally not be replaced by a coreferential pronoun without
      significant loss of acceptability.

The fact that not all occurrences of parasitic gaps have the same status,
but that certain gaps are perceived as more obligatory was demonstrated
in a small survey that was carried out at Stanford University during January 1981.[7] Twenty-eight subjects were presented with five pairs of sentences, differing only in that one version had a parasitic gap where the
other had a pronoun. The subjects were asked to decide which of the
sentences sounded "most natural" for them. I will here give the sentences
used in the survey, indicating next to them the number of subjects that
preferred that version.

(41) a.  This is the kind of food$_i$ you must cook $t$ before you eat *pg*   (15)
     b.  before you eat it$_i$                                                (13)

(42) a.  Which girl$_i$ did you send a picture of $t$ to $t$?                 (19)
     b.                  a picture of her$_i$ to $t$?                         (13)
     c.                  a picture of $t$ to her$_i$?                          (2)

(43) a.  Susan always files $t$ without reading $t$ properly, [$_{NP_i}$ all the
         memos from the lowlevel administration.]                            (12)
     b.  Susan always files $t$ without reading them$_i$ properly, [$_{NP_i}$ all the
         memos from the lowlevel administration.]                            (16)

(44) a.  Which boy$_i$ did Mary's talking to *pg* bother $t$ most?           (15)
     b.                               to him$_i$ bother $t$ most?             (8)

(45) a.  Which student$_i$ did your attempt to talk to *pg* scare $t$ to
         death?                                                              (17)
     b.  talk to him$_i$ scare $t$ to death?                                  (8)

Notice that in examples (41)–(43), which according to the proposed classification illustrate optional parasitic gaps, the subjects are almost equally
divided between preferring gaps and preferring pronouns. This distribution should be contrasted with the results in (44) and (45), where the
responses show a strong tendency to prefer the version with a parasitic
gap. Although the sample of constructions investigated was small, the
trend seems quite clear. I expect that in a larger experiment, we would
find a significant effect of the position of the parasitic gap with respect to
the real gap.

In English, the obligatory type of parasitic gaps arises primarily inside complex subjects e.g., in PP complements, noun complements, and gerunds. In Scandinavian languages, the range of constructions that allow for parasitic gaps is broader. For instance, parasitic gaps occur quite frequently in relative clauses that modify a NP that precedes the real gap, as can be seen in (46).

(46) a. Räkna upp de filmer som [$_{NP}$ alla [$_{\bar{S}}$ som sett *pg*/?dem]] tyckte bra om *t*.
       List those films that everyone who has seen *t*/?them liked *t* a lot.
   b. Kalle är en kille som [$_{NP}$ ingen [$_{\bar{S}}$ som träffat *pg*/?honom]] kan tåla *t*.[8]
       Kalle is a guy who no one who (has) met *t*/?him can stand *t*.

(47) a. [$_{PP}$ Till himlen] är det inte säkert att [$_{NP}$ alla [$_{\bar{S}}$ som längtar [$_{PP}$ *pg*/dit]]] kommer [$_{PP}$ *t*].
       To heaven it is not certain that everyone who longs *t*/there get *t*.
   b. [$_{AP}$ Fattig] vill [$_{NP}$ ingen [$_{\bar{S}}$ som någonsin varit [$_{AP}$ *pg*/?det]]] bli [$_{AP}$ *t*] igen.
       Poor no one who has even been *t*/?it wants to become *t* again.

(47) illustrates that the parasitic gap phenomenon is not limited to NP gaps but extends to PP and AP gaps as well. For certain speakers of English, similar examples are not totally excluded. Wynn Chao provided me with (48) and Janet Fodor with (49). Note that in both cases the head NP is nonspecific.

(48) This is the type of book that [$_{NP}$ no one [$_{\bar{S}}$ who has read *pg*]] would give *t* to his mother.

(49) Here is the boy who [$_{NP}$ everyone [$_{\bar{S}}$ who has met *pg*]] thinks *t* is clever.

## 2.6  Obligatory Parasitic Gaps and the Crossover Constraint

At this point, the obvious question to ask is: Why is it that the second type of parasitic gaps doesn't seem to allow free alternation with a personal pronoun? One interesting point about examples like (44)–(45) and (48)–(49) in English and (46)–(47) in Swedish is that a pronoun in the position of the parasitic gap would violate Postal's crossover constraint (Postal 1971) and Jacobson's leftmost constraint (Jacobson 1977). According to this constraint, a pronoun cannot be understood as bound

by a *wh*-phrase that has crossed over it. In a question like (50), *he* cannot
be understood as bound by *who*,

(50)  Who$_i$ did he$_{*i/j}$ claim $t_i$ had won?

but must be taken to refer freely. In the examples we have been dealing
with here, the pronoun would occur inside a NP, not as an argument of
the main verb directly, and would hence be an instance of so-called weak
crossover. Nevertheless, many speakers do not like pronouns in these
contexts. In fact, a majority prefer a gap, as shown by the scores indicated
in (44) and (45). The subject's tendency to avoid the version with a coreferential pronoun seems to indicate that to some extent the crossover
constraint has been grammaticized and is operative among speakers of
English. By using the option of a parasitic gap, the speaker gets around
violating the constraint. We can contrast this way of avoiding the utterance of an ungrammatical sentence with the use of resumptive pronouns.
It is often assumed that inserting a resumptive pronoun may "save" a
sentence which would otherwise violate an extraction island. Sentences
like (44) and (45) show that the opposite strategy is also available. A
sentence that would violate a constraint is "saved" or at least considerably improved, if the pronoun is replaced with a gap.

I proposed earlier that the position of the parasitic gap with respect to
the real gap might be an important variable for determining its relative
obligatoriness. This suggests one line of explanation for the distribution of
parasitic gaps which ties in quite straightforwardly with the way people
interpret pronouns and gaps during speech processing. Tentatively, I
would like to suggest that the alternation between pronouns and parasitic
gaps is closely connected with the fact that personal pronouns are inherently ambiguous between a deictic reading and a bound reading on which
the pronoun is bound by some other NP in the sentence. As soon as a
listener hears a pronoun, he presumably searches his discourse model for
a likely referent or enters a new referent. A gap, on the other hand, must
be interpreted as controlled by a displaced constituent in the same sentence and the listener must not go outside the sentence to find a referent.
In most cases, the filler-gap assignment is uniquely determined by the
syntactic rules of the language, perhaps augmented by parsing-motivated
no-ambiguity constraints (cf. the discussion of nested and intersecting
assignments in Fodor 1978 and Engdahl 1979, 1981). By not pronouncing
a pronoun, the speaker in effect makes sure that the listener does not go
outside the sentence to supply a referent, hence he prevents the hearer
from computing a possible but unintended interpretation for the sen-

tence.[9] If this argument holds up, we would expect pronouns that are likely to be affected by the noncoreference rules of the language to drop out more often than pronouns in contexts where the noncoreference requirements don't apply. Consequently in a sentence with an unbounded filler-gap dependency, plausible candidates for being deleted would be those pronouns that are most likely to be understood as disjoint in reference from the filler according to restrictions on anaphora such as the crossover constraint. In order to turn this suggestion into a more convincing argument we need to investigate to what extent the constraints on crossover and the appearances of parasitic gaps are correlated for individual speakers. We also need to look at contexts where a pronoun cannot be deleted for some other reason. For instance, it appears that many speakers who find a referent pronoun in (51a) impossible accept a coreferent possessive pronoun in a similar sentence.

(51) a. Which student$_i$ did your attempt to talk to him$_{*i/j}$ scare $t_i$ to death?
     b. Which student$_i$ did your threat to talk to his$_i$ parents scare $t_i$ to death?

In (51b) where a deletion is impossible because of the general condition on recoverability (loss of possessive case) and where there is no alternative way of expressing the desired meaning, a pronoun is accepted. The contrast between (51a) and (51b) illustrates in my opinion the trade-off between the expressor's needs and the precise formulation of grammatical constraints discussed by J. Fodor (Fodor 1980).

It follows from this way of looking at the interaction between the crossover constraint and the expressor's needs that the parasitic gap strategy would not be used to avoid violations of strong crossover. In these cases, there is another, more straightforward way of expressing the same message or asking the intended question, in the latter case by questioning the first position directly. The reason (52a) does not have the reading marked by the coindexing is that there is a simpler way of asking

(52) a. *Who$_i$ did he$_i$ claim $t_i$ had won?
     b. Who$_i$ claimed he$_i$ had won?

that question, viz. as in (52b).

Another factor that might lie behind the tendency to "not pronounce" a coreferent pronoun inside a constituent in a main clause preceding the real gap is the fact that the referent of a pronoun in a main clause tends to be resolved immediately. Bever and Townsend (1979) report on a series of experiments which show that main clauses in general are completely interpreted, whereas subordinate clauses receive a more shallow interpretation. Bever and Townsend take a full interpretation of a clause to involve, among other things, assignment of referents to all referring expressions in the clause, including pronouns. Although none of the experiments bear directly on pronoun interpretation, Bever and Townsend suggest that the fact that subordinate clauses are only incompletely interpreted would account for the tendency to postpone assignments of referents to pronouns occurring in them. On the basis of Bever and Townsend's findings, we would expect listeners to be more likely to defer reference assignments to pronouns in explicit subordinate clauses such as those introduced by complementizers and subordinating connectives. This observation is consistent with the fact that in all languages, backwards anaphora is possible in subordinate clauses, if at all.[10] In general, this way of looking at pronoun resolution ties in quite straightforwardly with the formulations of the noncoreference facts given by Lasnik (1976) and Reinhart (1976, 1983). A pronoun that precedes and commands or c-commands other NPs is likely to occur in an initial main clause, and hence tends to be interpreted immediately.

### 2.7 Restrictions on Parasitic Gaps

We now turn to constructions where parasitic gaps are excluded, although the preconditions seem fulfilled. Consider (53)–(56):

(53) Which articles *t* got filed by John without him reading *pg/them?

(54) Who *t* sent a picture of *pg/himself?

(55) Who *t* remembered talking to *pg/himself?

(56) Who *t* remembered that John talked to *pg/him?

In none of these sentences are parasitic gaps allowed. A pronoun, personal or reflexive, is required. In these examples, the real gap occurs in subject position. A first hypothesis would be that questioned matrix subjects are not "moved" and consequently don't leave gaps, in which case there would be no reason to expect a parasitic gap. However, if we question a nonmatrix subject, which would give rise to a nonlocal filler-gap dependency, a parasitic gap still is not possible.

(57) Which articles did you say *t* got filed by John without him reading *pg/them?

(58)  Who did you say *t* was bothered by John's talking to *\*pg*/him?

It is interesting that there is no doubt about the unavailability of parasitic gaps in examples (53) through (58). Similarly, Swedish counterparts with parasitic gaps are completely impossible. The clear judgments on these examples show that, even if the acceptability range for parasitic gaps varies a lot, the phenomenon is not hopelessly fuzzy. On the contrary, people have quite strong intuitions about where parasitic gaps may not occur. These intuitions, together with the overlap in intuitions about possible parasitic gaps, provide evidence that we are here dealing with a systematical grammatical principle.

How, then, can we explain the unavailability of parasitic gaps in (53) through (58)? One possible explanation, suggested by Janet Fodor, is that parasitic gaps require some kind of parallelism is grammatical function, that is, a real object gap only licenses a parasitic object gap, etc. Hence, we would only expect subject gaps to licence subject parasitic gaps, and a relevant example would be a sentence like (59), proposed by J. Fodor.

(59)  This is the student everyone thinks *t* is clever because John said ?*pg*/he was clever.

Although making the gaps parallel in function might improve the examples somewhat, most people reject the parasitic gap in (59). Furthermore it turns out that there are good examples where a real subject gap licenses a parasitic object gap. The following example was suggested by Alan Prince.

(60)  Which caesar did Brutus imply *t* was no good while ostensibly praising *pg*?

A real subject gap may also license a parasitic gap in an oblique position, as in (61), following a suggestion by Janet Fodor.

(61)  Who did you say John's criticism of *pg* would make us think *t* was stupid?

These examples show that it is not the case that there is a subject-object asymmetry with respect to parasitic gaps.[11] What, then, is the relevant difference between a sentence like (57) which is clearly out, and (60) which is quite good? In both types, the relative position of the filler with respect to the real gap remains the same, but the structural relations between the real gap and the parasitic gap differ, as we can see by looking at a partially bracketed representation.

(57′)  Which articles did you say [s $t$ got filed by John [AdvP without him reading *$pg$/them?]]

(60′)  Which caesar did Brutus imply [s $t$ was no good] [AdvP while ostensibly praising $pg$?]

In (57′) the real subject gap c-commands everything that is in the embedded S, including the adverbial phrase which contains the parasitic gap. In (60′) on the other hand, the real gap does not c-command the parasitic gap since the *while* clause is attached at a higher VP. The unacceptable (58) differs from the acceptable (61) in the same respect:

(58′)  Who did you say [s $t$ was bothered by John's talking to *$pg$/him?]

(61′)  Who did you say John's criticism of $pg$ would make us think [s $t$ was stupid?]

It turns out that the configurations where parasitic gaps are disallowed are exactly the configurations which have been taken to require non-coreference (cf. Lasnik 1976 and Reinhart 1976). If NP$_1$ c-commands NP$_2$ and NP$_2$ is not a pronoun, then NP$_1$ and NP$_2$ are noncoreferent. Such a restriction would rule out coreference between *he* and *John* in (62), given a normal use of this sentence, as well as binding of *he* by *every man* in (63).

(62)  He talked to John.

(63)  He thinks every man will win.

If we assume that the relation between the real gap and the parasitic gap is some form of anaphoric linking, and furthermore parasitic gaps are understood to be necessarily coreferent with the real gap (i.e., with the filler that controls the real gap) then it would not be surprising if parasitic gaps were excluded just in those contexts where the anaphora rules of the language assign disjoint reference. We can summarize this restriction as in (64).

(64)  A parasitic gap may not be c-commanded by the real gap.[12]

It is at present an open issue whether non-coreference should be handled by rules in the grammar or not. T. Reinhart in an extremely interesting restatement of the anaphora question (Reinhart 1983) proposes that the noncoreference facts follow from Gricean requirements on rational use of language, and suggests that the noncoreference rules be replaced by pragmatic strategies which govern decisions about intended coreference.[13] If a speaker avoids using the options of expressing coreference in a context where bound anaphora is possible, then he didn't intend his expressions to corefer. Reinhart summarizes the rules for bound anaphora as in (65), ignoring certain requirements.

(65) Bound anaphora is possible if a given NP c-commands a pronoun
     (Reinhart 1983:(66a))

Using Reinhart's notion of bound anaphora, it turns out that we can account for the cases where parasitic gaps are excluded if we apply (65) strictly, i.e., if we assume that only pronouns can be interpreted as bound anaphors in her sense. If you don't take the option of using a pronoun in a context like (62) or (63), but instead use a full NP, you get a non-coreferential reading. Similarly, in sentences like (53)–(56), if we don't take the option of using a pronoun, but instead use a gap, we should get a noncoreferent interpretation of the gap. However, since gaps must be controlled sentence-internally in languages like English and Swedish, this is not a viable option. This would explain why these sentences are no good with parasitic gaps.

It follows from Reinhart's principle in (65) that anaphora is not possible if neither NP c-commands the other and in those contexts, non-coreference is not excluded. This is for instance the case in (66) and (67) which are parallel to (60) and (61), which permit parasitic gaps.

(66) Brutus managed to imply that he$_i$ was no good while ostensibly praising Julius Caesar$_i$

(67) They said that John's criticism of her$_i$ would make us think Mary$_i$ was stupid.

There thus appears to be a correlation between the positions where bound anaphora can occur and the positions where parasitic gaps are excluded. Following Reinhart, we can account for this correlation by appealing ot general principles for the interpretation of intended non-coreference. If this is in fact the case, we would expect the correlation between subject extractions and the impossibility of parasitic gaps which we noted above in connection with examples (53)–(56) to be just an instance of this more general principle. We would expect parasitic gaps to be excluded also in other context where bound anaphora is possible. This prediction turns out to be correct, as can be seen in the following examples.

(68) Which slave did Cleopatra give $t$ to *$pg$/himself?

(69) Which slave did Cleopatra give $t$ *$pg$/himself?

It turns out that this inverse correlation between the unavailability of bound anaphora and the possibility of parasitic gaps is very close. We now turn to further cases where they pattern together. As Reinhart notes in Appendix II, there are exceptions to the generalization in (65). For instance, NPs in certain types of PPs behave as if they c-command a pronoun outside it.

(70)  I talked to John$_i$ about himself$_i$.

(71)  I talked to every boy$_i$ about his$_i$ result.

The availability of bound anaphora here leads us to expect that parasitic gaps should be impossible, and this turns out to be correct.

(72)  Who did you talk to $t$ about *$pg$/himself?

If the PP is embedded inside a NP, however, bound anaphora is excluded, as seen in (73).

(73)  I sent a picture of Mary$_i$ to her$_i$/*herself.

Since noncoreference is possible, we expect a parasitic gap also to be possible; this is in fact the case as already illustrated in (3), repeated here as (74).

(74)  Which girl did you send a picture of $t$ to $pg$?

It appears that in exactly those configurations where (65) does not seem to be a necessary condition for bound anaphora, (64) is insufficient to rule out unacceptable parasitic gaps. It is interesting to note that in a language like Swedish where object control of reflexives is more limited than in English, and hence bound anaphora in a context like (70) is impossible, a parasitic gap is quite good.

(70′)  Jag talade med Johan$_i$ om      *sig/honom$_i$.
       I    talked to   Johan about   REFL/him

(72′)  Vem brukar du sällan tala med $t$ om $pg$?
       Who do you seldom talk   to $t$ about $t$?

However, in those contexts where object controlled reflexives are possible, parasitic gaps are avoided (see Hellan 1980 for a characterization of the domain for object control of reflexives in Norwegian which also applies to Swedish).

(75)  Jag såg dig köra Johan$_i$ hem   till sig$_i$.
       I    saw you take Johan home to REFL

(76) Johan$_i$ har jag ofta sett dig köra $t_i$ hem till *$pg$/sig$_i$.

Johan, I have often seen you take $t$ to $t$/SELF

Rather than taking (64) literally, we should understand it as an abbreviation for those contexts where bound anaphora is excluded in the language in question.[14] It makes the correct predictions in a number of cases which differ only minimally, as we will now see. For the generalization in (64) to hold for examples involving adverbial clauses as in (1) and (2), we must assume that the VP has the structure illustrated in (77).

(77) [$_{VP'}$[$_{VP}$ V $X$] [$_{AdvP}$]]

We assume that the minimal VP contains only direct arguments of the verb. For instance, an agentive $by$-phrase will count as an argument of the verb and will attach inside the minimal VP, whereas an adverbial $by$-phrase will attach at VP'. Since a direct object real gap only c-commands a parasitic gap inside the minimal VP, we would expect to find a contrast in sentences with parasitic gaps in $by$-phrases depending on how these are interpreted. This prediction seems to be borne out in view of the examples in (78) and (79).

(78) Which caesar did Cleopatra say [$_S$ $t$ [$_{VP}$ was impressed [$_{PP}$ by her singing to *$pg$/him]]]

(79) Which caesar did Brutus imply [$_S$ $t$ [$_{VP}$ was senile]] [$_{PP}$ by mimicking $pg$ in public?]

In (78), where the parasitic gap occurs within the minimal VP, and hence is c-commanded by the real gap, a parasitic gap is impossible. In (79), where the adverbial $by$-phrase modifies a higher VP, a parasitic gap seems pretty good.[15] The reader is invited to verify that bound anaphora is indeed possible in (78) but not in (79) as predicted by the inverse correlation we found between bound anaphora and parasitic gaps.[16]

## 2.8 Comparatives

Comparative constructions provide another context where it is possible to get more than one gap depending on a single filler. These facts were brought up in Bresnan 1977 and were further discussed in Chomsky and Lasnik 1977. Some examples are given below:

(80) A man who Mary called $t$ an idiot as often as June called $t$ a cretin. (Bresnan 1977:55)

(81) The books that Mary read $t$ as often as Bill read $t$/them. (Chomsky and Lasnik 1977:191d)

First we note that these cases, just like some of the previously discussed cases, cannot be analyzed a resulting from an across-the-board application of *wh*-movement. It is possible to extract from only one of the constituents involved in the comparative construction, as shown in (82).

(82) A man who Mary called $t$ an idiot as often as June called Bill a cretin.

Extraction out of the second conjunct only is less acceptable, which shows that that domain probably constitues a fairly strong extraction island. Chomsky and Lasnik observe that the phenomenon of across-the-board deletion does not bear on these types of examples and suggest that they arise through a stylistic pronoun deletion rule which they formulate as in (83).

(83) In "paired structures" ... optionally delete a pronoun in the second member of the pair if trace appears in the corresponding position in the first member; acceptability of the result varies from high to low as the position of the deleted item ranges from the end to the beginning of the clause. (Chomsky and Lasnik 1977:492)

The principle in (83) would apply to a structure like (84) and delete the pronoun *him*.

(84) A man$_i$ who Mary called $t_i$ an idiot as often as June called him a cretin.

However, the principle in (84) is insufficient in several respects. We note that the deletion is made contingent upon the presence of a trace in a corresponding position. But, as we showed earlier, not all traces qualify to license parasitic gaps. On Chomsky and Lasnik's formulation we would expect a sentence like (85) to be good.

(85) John$_i$ was called $t_i$ an idiot as often as Mary called *$t$/him a cretin.

The fact that the deletion in (85) is impossible follows according to our analysis from the fact that only nonlocal dependencies can license parasitic gaps. As mentioned above in section 2.3, this could be captured in the framework of government-binding theory (Chomsky 1981) by making parasitic gaps sensitive only to case-marked traces. We note furthermore that the principle specifically refers to the output of a movement rule. We have found that parasitic gaps can occur in constructions that are normally not analyzed as involving any movement, such as the *too*-deletion case in (29).[17]

A more serious objection to Chomsky and Lasnik's principle (83), is that it relies on a notion of "paired structures" and can thus not account for those occurrences of parasitic gaps where there is no parallelism involved, in particular occurrences of what I have called obligatory parasitic gaps in positions preceding the real gap, such as in (4), repeated here as (86) and in (87).

(86)  Which boy$_i$ did Harry's talking to *pg*/??him$_i$ bother $t_i$ most?

(87)  Which city$_i$ do the people from *pg*/??it$_i$ always talk about $t_i$?

(83) also fails to account for examples like (3), repeated here as (88) where the real gap and the parasitic gap occur inside the same VP.

(88)  Which girl did you send a picture of $t$ to $t$?

Chomsky and Lasnik note that deletions that occur at the end of the clause are better than deletions earlier in the clause. With respect to positions inside the VP, it is not clear that there is any systematic difference. Chomsky and Lasnik find a deletion of the direct object in (89) unacceptable. However, in a structurally similar sentence, (90), the deletion is less offensive.

(89)  the books that you gave $t$ to Mary as often as Bill gave ?$t$/them to Sue (Chomsky and Lasnik, 191b).

(90)  the children that you take $t$ to school as often as I take $t$ to church.

However, when we look at gaps in subject position, most examples sound quite bad, as for instance (91) and (92).

(91)  Who do you think [$_S$ $t$ hates John as much as ??$t$/he hates Mary?]

(92)  Who would you say [$_S$ $t$ would drive to work more often than ??$t$/he would take the bus?]]

Note that in (91) and (92) the first gap c-commands the second gap, a condition that we have previously found to block a parasitic gap. In order to test whether this condition is applicable in comparative constructions as well, I tried to construct examples where the second conjunct is attached higher up where it would not be c-commanded by the first gap. (94) was suggested to me by M. Kay.

(93)  Who are you more convinced [$_S$ $t$ would show up] than $t$ would fail to come?

(94)  Who are you more concerned [$_S$ $t$ would do the job] than $t$ would benefit from the proceedings?

A number of speakers perceive a contrast between (91) and (92) on the one hand and (93) and (94) on the other. Notice furthermore that bound anaphora is possible in (91), but not in (93), as we would expect from the inverse correlation between parasitic gaps and bound anaphora.

(91')  I don't think any boy$_i$ hates Anne as much as he$_i$ hates Mary.

(93')  I am more convinced that no boy$_i$ would show up than that he$_{*i}$ would try to come.

## 2.9   Implications for Sentence Processing

In this section, I want to spell out what the existence and distribution of parasitic gaps can tell us about the strategies the human parser might employ during the processing of sentences with filler-gap dependencies. We noted earlier that the existence of coordinate gaps, as well as parasitic gaps, shows that the parser cannot simply remove a filler from HOLD and plug it into the first gap it encounters. Rather, it appears that a recognized filler has a special salience which obtains even after a gap has been found. This special status seems reserved for long distance fillers, which is not surprising in view of the fact, recently emphasized by Fodor (1980) that it would be in the parser's interest to limit the number of positions where gap-controlling fillers may occur, since this would make the task of distinguishing fillers from illegitimate extra constituents simpler.

We also noted above that parasitic gaps often occur in domains that are more or less inaccessible to ordinary extractions in the language. This shows that the parser's gap detecting strategies are not turned off inside an extraction island. Whereas adverbial clauses are generally considered to be extraction islands in English, examples like (1) and (2) show that parasitic gaps in these domains are accepted. Similarly, extractions out of subjects of tensed sentences usually result in ungrammatical sentences (cf. (36b)), but sentences where the subjects contain parasitic gaps, such as (36a) and (45) are surprisingly good. From looking at sentences with a parasitic gap preceding a real gap, as in (44) and (45), it becomes clear that one possible functional explanation for why there should be extraction islands in languages does not fit the facts. On such a theory, it would be useful for a parser that is trying to come up with a valid parse for a sentence to be able to distinguish between accessible and inaccessible extraction domains, because if the parser is faced with the possibility of postulating a gap inside such a domain, it can immediately discard that parse and try a different one. But the facts seem to be that the parser detects the gap inside the island and proceeds to parse the rest of the sentence. Note, however, that the parser presumably also registers that the gap it has detected, is not a real or legitimate gap, and consequently that the filler cannot be assigned to it directly. Evidence for this comes from the contrasts between the (b) and (c) versions in (35) and (36). If no real gap in an accessible domain is found, which is the case in the (b) version, the parser apparently recognizes that it has an unmatched filler and the whole sentence is rejected.

Finally, we note that since both leftward and rightward dependencies seem to license parasitic gaps, it appears that whatever strategies the parser uses for identifying and matching fillers and gaps, they can be extended to parasitic gaps.

## 2.10 Conclusions

In this article I have given an overview of the distribution of a certain type of null anaphors which seem to be *parasitic* on the presence of a syntactic gap in the sentence. Before we can draw any definite conclusions about the implications of this phenomenon for the analysis of particular languages as well as for grammatical theory, more research is needed in order to find out what types of languages allow parasitic gaps, in what contexts they occur, etc. Nevertheless, even in the absence of a more complete overview, it is clear that the phenomenon bears more or less directly on several issues that are central to grammatical theory and to the study of sentence processing. One of these issues is the distinction between local and non-local processes. Since parasitic gaps are licensed only by gaps arising in unbounded dependencies, we have an indication that local and nonlocal processes need to be distinguished at some level of the grammar. It also seems plausible that this distinction is correlated with different types of parsing principles.

I have argued in the paper that the appearance of parasitic gaps is not an inherently fuzzy phenomenon but that it lends itself naturally to a characterization along certain grammatical dimensions. Furthermore, we have seen that it is subject to systematic restrictions which pattern together with general principles for anaphora in the language. Consequently, an explicit formulation of the conditions on parasitic gaps might shed new light on how restrictions on regular extractions should be stated in the grammar. In this respect the parasitic gap facts will be directly relevant to evaluating the ways of formulating constraints that are available within current grammatical theories such as the government-binding theory, Generalized Phrase Structure Grammar, Lexical-Functional Grammar, and semantically based versions of Montague grammar. The parasitic gap facts may also provide some evidence for constituent structure, compare the contrasts between (78) and (79) above.

The characterization of parasitic gaps is also relevant to attempts at formulating and testing hypotheses about how the human parser operates when it parses a sentence with filler-gap dependencies. The existence of parasitic gaps shows that the parser must be assumed to have a great deal of flexibility in how it applies its filler-gap matching strategies. The difference in status between real gaps and parasitic gaps, as witnessed by the contrasts in (35) and (36), can be taken as an indication that the parser is sensitive to accessible and inaccessible gap domains, but that it is able to put off judgments of unacceptability until more of the sentence is available for processing. In addition, the existence of what I have called obligatory parasitic gaps might reflect the degree to which speakers are sensitive to a grammatical constraint like the crossover condition. It will presumably be worthwhile to look more deeply into the interaction between non-coreference, crossover, and parasitic gaps.

**Notes**

This is a revised version of a paper presented at the Sloan workshop on Processing of Unbounded Dependencies at the University of Massachusetts/Amherst, January 20–23, 1981. I want to thank the participants of the workshop, in particular Emmon Bach, Joan Bresnan, Charles Clifton, Janet Fodor, Lyn Frazier, Lauri Karttunen, Ron Kaplan, Barbara Partee, Alan Prince, and Annie Zaenen, for several valuable suggestions and comments. I have also benefited from discussions with and comments from the following persons: Herbert Clark, Robin Cooper, Mürvet Enç, Nomi Erstschik-Shir, Charles Fillmore, Lars Hellan, Martin Kay, Christer Platzack, Ivan Sag, Tarald Taraldsen, Tom Wasow, and two anonymous *L&P* reviewers.

The initial research for this paper was done while the author held a Sloan Foundation Post-doctoral Fellowship at Stanford University. The final version was completed while the author was Visiting Research Fellow at the Max-Planck-Institut für Psycholinguistik, Nijmegen.

1. Taraldsen (1981) independently introduces the same term for this phenomenon. David Perlmutter coined the term "sympathetic deletion" for similar cases.

2. Following a suggestion made by Herb Clark.

3. It is not totally clear that Heavy NP Shift is an unbounded rule but see Gazdar 1981 for an argument that the apparent boundedness of rightward movement rules follows from parsing considerations.

4. Compare Postal's distinction between cyclic and postcyclic rules and van Riemsdijk and Williams's (1980) recent separation of NP movement from *wh*-movement.

5. These facts were pointed out to me by Jane Robinson and David Evans.

6. As one reviewer points out, this test does not distinguish between the gaps in the Heavy NP Shift cases in (26) and (27).

7. I am grateful to John Rickford and his sociolinguistic field methods class at Stanford for carrying out the survey.

8. In Scandinavian languages, there is a clear contrast in acceptability of parasitic gaps inside relative clauses depending on whether they precede or follow the real gap, that is, depending on whether the gap is obligatory or optional according to (39) and (40). Whereas the parasitic gaps in (46) and (47) are good, in fact, clearly better than a pronoun in that position, a parasitic gap in (i) where the relative clauses modifies a NP that follows the real gap, is marginal at best.

(i) Den här boken vore det dumt att ge *t* till [NP någon [s̄ som redan har läst ?*t*/den]]
This book, it would be stupid to give *t* to someone who already has read ?*t*/it.

If a relative clause with a parasitic gap is extraposed to the right of the real gap, the result is good as illustrated in (ii).

(ii) Räkna upp de filmer (som) [NP alla] tyckte bra om *t* [s̄ som såg *pg*/?dem]
List those movies everyone liked *t* a lot who saw *pg*.

This shows that the relevant ordering between the parasitic gap and the real gap must be determined with respect to surface structure. Note that the relative clauses in (46) and (47) are all restrictive. Parasitic gaps in nonrestrictive relatives are unacceptable, even if the relative clause precedes the real gap, as illustrated below.

(iii) Maja brukar Kalle, som ju känner *\*t*/henne väl, ofta gå på bio med *t*.
Maja, Kalle, who knows *\*t*/her well, often goes to the movies with *t*.

(iv) Här är boken som alla flickorna, ingendera av vilka hade läst ut *\*t*/den, tyckte *t* var urdålig.
Here is the book that all the girls, none of which had finished *\*t*/it, thought was very bad.

9. This tendency applies quite generally, as was pointed out at the workshop by Larry Solan. Whereas (i) is ambiguous, with the noncoreferent reading being the preferred reading, (ii) is not.

(i) John$_i$ likes his$_{j,i}$ writing books

(ii) John$_i$ likes writing books.

The implicit subject of the gerund must be interpreted as John. In the Pisa lectures, Chomsky refers to the same tendency as the "avoid pronouns" principle.

10. For further discussion of the correlation between crossover and backwards anaphora, see Cole 1974. Cole claims that there are (at least) five different dialects in English with respect to these facts.

11. At the workshop, Joan Bresnan pointed out that the unavailability of parasitic gaps in (53)–(58) would follow automatically if we assume that parasitic gaps

are derived via Right Node Raising; i.e., a sentence like (i) would be derived via (ii).

(i)  Which articles did John file $t$ without reading $pg$?

(ii) John filed $t$, without reading $t$, which articles?

Since Right Node Raising cannot apply to subjects, this predicts that none of the sentences in (53)–(58) could be derived. However, this account would rule out the good examples (60) and (61), as well as earlier examples like (3) and (4), since none of them can be analyzed as involving Right Node Raising.

12. The more general formulation that neither gap may c-command the other, (cf. Taraldsen 1981) is equally correct. However, the situation where the parasitic gap asymmetrically c-commands the real gap will not arise, since in that case the parasitic gap would presumably occur in a more accessible extraction domain than in the real gap, and would, by the substitution test used above, be understood as the real gap.

13. This much too brief summary does not do justice to Reinhart's careful argument. The reader is referred to her article for a full presentation. A very similar approach to the noncoreference issue is taken in Dowty 1980.

14. At this point, it might be illustrative to compare this approach to accounting for restrictions on parasitic gaps with an account phrased in government-binding theory terms. N. Chomsky and T. Taraldsen (personal communications) suggest that the nonoccurrence of parasitic gaps in sentences like (53)–(58) in the text follow from the principles of binding theory. If you assume that parasitic gaps are *variables* in the technical sense of the term, defined in Chomsky (1981), and furthermore, it is assumed that variables cannot be coindexed with any term or variable in a c-commanding argument position then (53)–(58) are excluded. The latter assumption serves to exclude cases of strong cross-over as well. Because of its reliance on c-command, this account fails in exactly the same cases as (64) and (65) and consequently must be revised in a similar fashion, a fact also acknowledged by N. Chomsky.

15. This contrast obviates a possible objection that could be raised against a claim that was made earlier in connection with examples (30)–(32). We claimed there that local dependencies, such as Passive, Equi, and Raising don't allow parasitic gaps. However, in these examples, it is also the case that the trace, which would presumably act as the real gap, c-commands the parasitic gap. Hence, one could argue that (30)–(32) are out by the principle stated in (64). But note that a parasitic gap is also impossible in (i) where it is not c-commanded by the trace.

(i)  Brutus announced [$_{\bar{S}}$ that Caesar$_i$ had been killed $t_i$] by showing *$pg$/him$_i$ in a coffin.

Furthermore, in a sentence like (ii) the *without* phrase may attach either to *try* or to *leave*.

(ii) Mary$_i$ tried $t_i$ to leave without John's helping *$pg$/her.

On the reading where the *without* clause modifies Mary's trying, the trace does not c-command the parasitic gap. However, a parasitic gap is still not possible.

16. Nomi Erteschik-Shir (personal communication) has suggested an alternative way of looking at the distribution and characterization of parasitic gaps which makes use of the notion of *dominant position* (cf. Erteschik and Lappin 1979). According to this proposal, extractions, i.e., real gaps, are only allowed out of positions, marked [+DOM] (by a rule of dominance interpretation that belongs to a set of interpretive rules). Erteschik-Shir suggests that cases where both gaps are in dominant positions should be best and consequently acceptable to most speakers and that cases where only the real gap is in a dominant position come next in acceptability. Provided we have an independent characterization of [±DOM] positions, this would allow for a general characterization of a parasitic gap as the non-dominating of two gaps, or when both gaps are dominant, the second one. Given the close correlation between extraction possibilities and [+DOM] domains, this account seems quite plausible. It makes an interesting prediction in the case of dative shifted sentences. Erteschik-Shir claims that the indirect object position after Dative Movement must be [−DOM], hence they should not allow for a real gap but only for a parasitic gap. This prediction seems to be borne out.

(i) a.   Who did Mary send *pg* her book in order to impress *t*?
    b.   ?Who did Mary send *t* her book in order to impress her colleagues?
    c.   Who did Mary send the publisher her book in order to impress *t*?

We can contrast (i) with the nonshifted version (ii), where the same order of plugging up the gaps leads to opposite results.

(ii) a.   Who did Mary send her book to *t* in order to impress *pg*?
     b.   Who did Mary send her book to *t* in order to impress you?
     c.   ?Who did Mary send her book to the publisher in order to impress *t*?

One slight problem with Erteschik-Shir's account is that she assumes that untensed domains are usually dominant, which would account for the goodness of (35a). This does not fit with the fact that adverbial clauses are usually extraction islands (cf. 35b). It is also not clear to me how the apparently real distinction between optional and obligatory parasitic gaps would follow from this approach. It remains to be investigated whether the generalization captured in (64) can be recast using the notion of dominance.

17. I owe this observation to Paul Postal.

18. The same remarks apply to the account for similar data given in Grosu 1980. I did not become aware of Grosu's analysis until after I had finished the manuscript for this article. Grosu takes occurrences of parasitic gaps (without using this terminology) to come from analogical extensions of across-the-board type rules to "coordinate-like noncoordinate structures" (Grosu 1980:22). His article contains several valuable observations but he does not consider such cases of parasitic gaps which do not lend themselves to an analysis based on coordination-like properties, nor does he address the issue of where parasitic gaps are systematically excluded which is discussed in section 2.7.

19. See Frazier, Clifton, and Randall 1981 for an extensive discussion of the "salient filler hypothesis" and for some very interesting experimental results.

# Chapter 3

## Parasitic Chains Revisited   Katalin É. Kiss

### 3.1   Introduction

This chapter argues that the parasitic gap construction involves two chains that share the same top section, including the antecedent. If the parasitic chain is analyzed as an Ā-chain sharing the top section of the licensing chain, all properties of the parasitic gap construction attested in English and Hungarian fall out from general properties of Ā-chain formation.

Section 3.2 will discuss the most widely accepted licensing conditions on parasitic gaps. It will argue—on the basis of Hungarian and English data—that the anti-c-command constraint is a necessary but insufficient condition on the formation of parasitic gap structures. In section 3.3 the analysis of Hungarian data will lead to the formulation of a case-matching condition on parasitic gap constructions, which is a manifestation of the requirement that case be transmitted in a regular way from root to head in both the licensing branch and the parasitic branch of the forking Ā-chain that parasitic gap constructions represent. Section 3.4 will generalize the requirement of proper case transmittance to the requirement of proper feature transmittance in both branches of the parasitic gap structure. Section 3.5 will examine the locality features of forking Ā-chains.

### 3.2   Preliminaries

#### 3.2.1   The Facts
Observe the distribution of grammaticality in the English parasitic gap constructions (1a–c) and in the corresponding Hungarian parasitic gap constructions (2a–c).

(1) a.   Which papers did you file *t* without reading *pg*?
    b.   *Which papers *t* fell off the table without John reading *pg*?

   c.  Which papers did John decide before PRO reading *pg* to tell his
secretary *t* were unavailable?[1]

(2) a.  Milyen iratokat tettél   el *t*,  mielőtt elolvastál-volna *pg*?[2]
      what   papers  you-put away before  you-had-read
      'What papers did you put away before you had read?'
   b.  *Milyen iratok vesztek el *t*,  mielőtt elolvastál-volna *pg*?
      what   papers got-lost away before  you-had-read
      'What papers were lost before you had read?'
   c.  Milyen iratokat     gondoltál,   mielőtt elolvastál-volna *pg*,
      what   papers-PL-ACC you-thought before  you-had-read
      hogy nem szeretnél,     ha elvesznének *t*?
      that not you-would-like if got-lost
      'What papers did you think, before reading, that you would not
      like if were lost?'

The various theories of parasitic gap constructions all agree that parasitic
gaps (marked by *pg* in (1)–(2)) are gaps licensed by an operator-variable
chain at S-structure. Paranthetically, in Hungarian, a definition along
these lines yields a wider variety of parasitic gap constructions than it
does in English. In Hungarian, not only the *wh*-operator, but also the
focus and the quantifiers, among others, are preposed into Ā-positions at
S-structure (see Kiss 1994). Thus the focus and the quantifiers are also
potential licensers for parasitic gaps. For example:

(3) a.  [$_{QP}$ Minden iratot [$_{VP}$ [$_{VP}$ el-   veszített *t*] még mielőtt
          every   paper-ACC   away he-lost    still  before
          elolvasott-volna *pg*]]
          he-had-read
          'He lost every paper before he had read.'
   b.  [$_{FP}$ FONTOS IRATOKAT veszített [$_{VP}$ [$_{VP}$ el *t*]  még mielőtt
          important papers-ACC   he-lost       away still  before
          elolvasott-volna *pg*]][3]
          he-had-read
          'It was important papers that he lost before he had read.'
but:
   c.  *[$_{VP}$ [$_{VP}$ El-   veszített fontos   iratokat] még mielőtt
            away he-lost  important papers   still  before
          elolvasott-volna *pg*]
          he-had-read
          'He lost important papers before he had read.'

The defining property of parasitic gaps is satisfied in every sentence under (1) and (2). The question is what additional licensing condition(s) are observed in (1a,c) and (2a,c), while being violated in (1b) and (2b).

### 3.2.2 The Anti-c-command Condition on Parasitic Gap Constructions
In the most widely accepted parasitic gap theories, the ungrammaticality of the starred English example in (1b) is attributed to the violation of the following licensing condition (first proposed in Engdahl 1983):

(4) A parasitic gap cannot be c-commanded by the licensing variable.[4]

The most obvious way to account for condition (6) is to derive it from binding Condition C.

In the Connectedness theory of Kayne (1983, 1984) and in its slightly modified version proposed by Longobardi (1985), parasitic gap constructions are regarded as structures in which one and the same operator binds two or more variables bearing identical indices. The operator and the g-projections of the variables must be connected—that is, they must form a subtree of the syntactic tree. The anti-c-command constraint is built into the definition of the Connectedness Condition by means of the qualification *locally bound*:

(5) *Connectedness Condition*
    Given a maximal set of empty categories $\beta_1, \ldots, \beta_n$, each locally bound by the same antecedent $\alpha$ in a tree T, the union formed by the g-projection sets of every $\beta$ by the antecedent $\alpha$ must form a subtree of T.[5]

If the parasitic variable is c-commanded (i.e., bound) by the licensing variable, then the operator binding the licensing variable is a nonlocal binder for the parasitic variable. Because the licensing variable and the parasitic variable bear identical indices, Condition C is violated, and the Connectedness Condition does not apply.

In the theory of Chomsky (1986b), parasitic gap constructions are composed of two chains: the chain binding the real gap to the overt operator, and a chain linking the parasitic gap to a null operator.

If $\mathscr{C} = (\alpha_1, \ldots, \alpha_n)$ is the chain of the real gap, and $\mathscr{C}' = (\beta_1, \ldots, \beta_m)$ is the chain of the parasitic gap, then the "composed chain" $(\mathscr{C}, \mathscr{C}') = (\alpha_1, \ldots, \alpha_n, \beta_1, \ldots, \beta_m)$ is the chain associated with the parasitic gap construction and yields its interpretation. (Chomsky 1986b:63)

The anti-c-command condition (which Chomsky somewhat hesitates to accept) can be derived either from binding Condition C, or from the following Chain Condition:

(6) A maximal A-chain $(\alpha_1, \ldots, \alpha_n)$ has exactly one case-marked
    position $(\alpha_1)$ and exactly one $\theta$-marked position $(\alpha_n)$.

Condition (6) holds of any chain $(\alpha_1, \ldots, \alpha_n)$ where the links meet the c-command condition, hence uniformly for noncompound chains and for a subchain of a composed chain satisfying the c-command requirement for links. If in a composed chain the real gap c-commands the parasitic gap, they form an A-chain headed by the real gap and violating the Chain Condition.

Whereas the parasitic gap theories of both Kayne (1983, 1984) and Chomsky (1986b) correctly predict the distribution of grammaticality in the English examples discussed, they fail to make correct predictions about the Hungarian examples (2a–c). The subject-object asymmetry attested in Hungarian parasitic gap constructions cannot be derived from the anti-c-command condition, as in Hungarian there is every reason to assume that the subject is generated in a flat VP, as a sister to the V and the object. It only leaves the VP when it undergoes topicalization, Q-raising, or focusing, which are operations also open to the object and the other arguments. As demonstrated in Kiss 1987a, Hungarian lacks the usual manifestations of a structural subject-object asymmetry; thus it has no movement and deletion rules involving the verb+object sequence and excluding the subject; it has not only verb+object but also verb+subject idioms; it shows no ECP effects in subject position; and it displays neither superiority effects, nor weak crossover phenomena. The Hungarian sentence shows no subject/object asymmetry with respect to Condition C, either. Thus both an object pronoun is in disjoint reference with the genitive specifier of the subject, and a subject pronoun is in disjoint reference with the genitive specifier of the object, obviously because the subject and object mutually c-command each other. (Surface order does not affect the judgments, as the (b) examples will testify.)

(7) a. *Meglátogatták őket$_i$ a   diákok$_i$  szülei.
       visited         them the students' parents-NOM
       'The students' parents visited them.'

    b. *A  diákok$_i$  szülei          meglátogatták őket$_i$.
       the students' parents-NOM visited              them

(8) a. *Meglátogatták ők/*pro*ᵢ a diákokᵢ szüleit.
visited they the students' parents-ACC
'They visited the students' parents.'
b. *A diákokᵢ szüleit meglátogatták ők/*pro*ᵢ.
the students' parents-ACC visited they

If we assume that adjunct clauses are adjoined to the VP (or some higher clausal projection), in Hungarian parasitic gap constructions a parasitic gap is not c-commanded by the licensing gap whether the licensing gap is in subject or object position; that is, the sentence is never ruled out as a Condition C violation, with the parasitic variable bound by an argument. Consider the structures we attribute to (2a) and (2b):

(9) a.

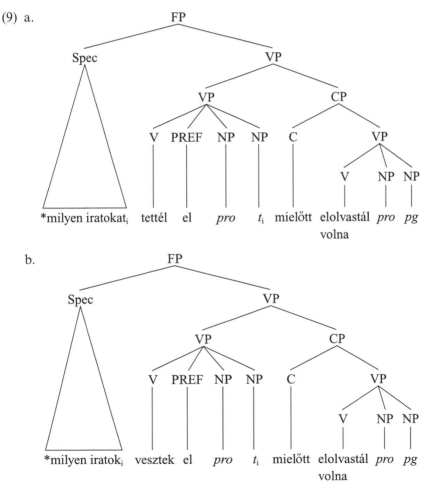

b.

The anti-c-command condition is not only insufficient to account for the Hungarian data; it cannot rule out various English constructions, either. Thus it cannot explain the grammaticality difference between the following sentences:

(10) a. *the book from which,$_j$ I copied $t_i$ without buying $pg$
     b. the book which,$_j$ I copied from $t_i$ without buying $pg$

The parasitic gap is not c-commanded by the real gap either in the grammatical (10b) or in the ungrammatical (10a). (A further apparent problem for the anti-c-command constraint will be discussed in section 3.5.)

**3.3   An Additional Proposal: The Case Matching Condition on Parasitic Gap Constructions**

The clue to the formulation of an additional licensing condition for parasitic gaps, which makes the right predictions for both English and Hungarian, will be provided by the analysis of the Hungarian examples. The strategy will be to focus first on (2a–c), rewritten here as (11a–c).

(11) a. [$_{FP}$ Milyen iratokat    tettél    el $t$ [$_{CP}$ mielőtt
            what    papers-ACC you-put away    before
         elolvastál volna $pg$]]
         you-had-read
         'What papers did you put away before you had read?'
     b. *[$_{FP}$ Milyen iratok  vesztek el $t$ [$_{CP}$ mielőtt elolvastál volna $pg$]]
             what    papers got-lost away    before  you-had-read
         'What papers were lost before you had read?'
     c. [$_{FP}$ Milyen iratokat    gondoltál [$_{CP}$ mielőtt
            what    papers-ACC you-thought  before
         elolvastál-volna $pg$] [$_{CP}$ hogy nem szeretnél
         you-had-read          that not you-would-like
         [$_{CP}$ ha elvesznének $t$]]]
            if got-lost
         'Which papers did you think before reading that you would not like if were lost?'

The initial hypothesis, to be qualified below, is that the ungrammaticality of (11b) arises from the fact that in this sentence the Case of the parasitic gap differs from the Case of the antecedent of the real gap: the parasitic gap is in the accusative, whereas the antecedent of the real gap is in the nominative. In the grammatical (11a), on the other hand, both the parasitic gap and the antecedent of the real gap (as well as the real gap itself) are in the accusative. Although in (11c) the case of the real gap (nominative) is different from the case of the parasitic gap (accusative), the sentence is saved by the fact that the antecedent of the real gap acquires accusative in the course of the derivation. If in such sentences the optional process of Case change does not take place—that is, if the nominative complement extracted out of the object clause is not assigned accusative—then the nominative operator will not license an accusative parasitic gap (see (12c)).

(12) a.  *Kik$_i$       jöttek el $t_i$  anélkül,   hogy meghívtál-volna $pg$?[6]
         who-PL-NOM came  away without-it that  you-had-invited
         'Who came without you having invited?'

    b.  Kiket$_i$      szeretnél,     ha eljönnének $t_i$, anélkül,   hogy
        who-PL-ACC you-would-like if came            without-it that
        meghívtál-volna $pg$?
        you-had-invited
        'Whom would you like if came without you having invited?'

    c.  *Kik$_i$      szeretnéd,     ha eljönnének $t_i$, anélkül,   hogy
        who-PL you-would-like if came            without-it that
        meghívtál-volna $pg$?
        you-had-invited
        'Who [NOM] would you like if came without you having invited?'

The accusative marking taking place in (12b) is presumably a variant of the process of Case marking into Comp described in French by Kayne (1980, 1981). As Kayne showed, the French *believe*-type verbs (e.g., *croire*) are not capable of deleting the CP node of their infinitival complement; consequently, the CP and IP boundaries, forming a barrier that blocks government, prevent them from assigning Case to the subject of the infinitival clause. Thus (13a) is excluded by the Case Filter. If, however, the subject of the infinitival complement is preposed through the embedded [Spec,CP] into the matrix [Spec,CP] slot, the Ā-chain headed by it will receive accusative Case, and the sentence will be grammatical, as in (13b).

(13) a.  *Je crois [$_{CP}$ [$_{IP}$ Jean être  le   plus intelligent]]
         I believe       Jean to-be the most intelligent

    b.  [$_{CP}$ Quel garçon$_i$ [$_{IP}$ crois-tu [$_{CP}$ $t_i{}'$ [$_{IP}$ $t_i$ être  le   plus
              which boy           believe-you              to-be the most
         intelligent]]]]
         intelligent

Of the elements of the chain *quel garçon*$_i$ $t_i'$ $t_i$, it is obviously $t_i'$ (i.e., the trace in the embedded [Spec,CP]) that is marked accusative by the matrix verb, since $t_i'$ is the only element of the chain that is governed by a Case assigner.

The Case-assigning process taking place in the Hungarian (12b) may appear to be somewhat more problematic, given that it involves multiple Case assignment to a chain, in other words, a Case conflict. However, multiple Case assignment—that is, the phenomenon of a Case assigned to a lower element of a chain being overridden by a Case assigned to a higher element of the chain—is such a well-documented fact for various languages (e.g., for Classical Greek) (see Groos and van Riemsdijk 1981), or, for that matter, for Hungarian (see Zolnay 1926; Kiss 1987a, 1991; Chomsky 1981:174) that Case theory must in all probability be relaxed so as to accommodate it.

Let us attempt to identify the properties of multiple Case marking by analyzing the Case-assigning process taking place in (14), for example.

(14) [$_{FP}$ Kiket$_i$        szeretnél [$_{CP}$ $t_i'$ ha eljönnének $t_i$]]
       who-PL-ACC you-would-like if   came
       'Whom would you like if came?'

In (14) $t_i$ is a variable assigned nominative case. On the other hand, $t_i'$, separated from the matrix V only by a single, nonblocking CP boundary is marked accusative by the matrix V. The accusative case of $t_i'$ is transmitted to the head of the chain. Case marking into [Spec,CP] is optional (unlike in French, it is not forced by the Case Filter). Thus, (14) is also acceptable to many speakers if the nominative case of $t_i$ is transmitted to the head of the chain:

(15) ?[$_{FP}$ Kik$_i$        szeretnéd [$_{CP}$ $t_i'$ ha eljönnének $t_i$]]
       who-PL-NOM you-would-like if   came
       'Who would you like if came?'

(In (14) the matrix V bears the $-l$ 2-SG indefinite suffix because it agrees with the indefinite object *kiket* ('whom'); in (15), on the other hand, it bears the $-d$ 2-SG definite suffix because it agrees with the object clause, which always counts as a definite object.)

In Hungarian, the only type of verbs that allow long operator movement out of their sentential complement are transitive verbs; consequently, the only types of Case conflict that arise are accusative versus nominative, accusative versus accusative, and accusative versus oblique. The conflict between two accusatives (assigned by two different verbs) is obviously invisible. In the case of a variable marked accusative, and inheriting nominative from the next lower member of the chain, it is the accusative that gets the upper hand (see (14)). In the case of a variable marked accusative and inheriting an oblique Case, on the other hand, it is the oblique Case that prevails. For example:

(16) a. Kitől$_i$      szeretnéd,      hogy $t_i{}'$ ajándékot kapj $t_i$?
        who-ABL you-would-like that      gift-ACC you-receive
        'From whom would you like that you should receive a gift?'
     b. *Kit$_i$       szeretnél,      hogy $t_i{}'$ ajándékot kapj $t_i$?
        who-ACC you-would-like that      gift-ACC you-receive
        'Whom would you like that you should receive a gift?'

In the Classical Greek Case conflicts quoted by Groos and van Riemsdijk (1981), an accusative assigned to a variable is overridden by a dative or a genitive assigned to the relative pronoun binding the variable. Generalizing from the Hungarian and the Classical Greek data, it can be tentatively hypothesized that in Case conflicts it is always the more marked Case that wins.

The phenomenon of the multiple Case marking of an Ā-chain may seem to be problematic not only for Case theory, but for theta theory, too. Namely, in Kiss 1987b it is claimed that nominative and accusative in Hungarian are thematically based, inherent Cases assigned by the verb in observance of the Uniformity Condition of Chomsky (1986a), according to which a Case assigner α can assign an inherent Case to β if and only if α also assigns a θ-role to β. Thus, at least in Hungarian, multiple Case marking appears to involve multiple θ-role assignment, too. In fact, when an intermediate element of an Ā-chain, occupying the [Spec,CP] of an object clause, is Case marked by the verb governing it across the CP boundary, the real target of Case assignment and θ-role assignment is the whole object clause. It seems that if the primary target of accusative assignment cannot bear case (i.e., if in Hungarian, it is a CP without a nominal head), the Case assigned to CP is allowed to be realized on an NP in the specifier of CP.

The possibility of the multiple Case marking of an Ā-chain arises from the fact that the elements of an Ā-chain can receive Case in two ways: by Case marking, and by Case inheritance. (Of course, for the lowest elements of the chain only the former possibility is open.) Case inheritance, in all probability, proceeds successive cyclically; that is, an element of a chain can only inherit the Case of the next lower element of the chain. Evidence for this claim is provided by (17).

(17) *[FP Kik$_i$         mondtad [CP $t_i''$ hogy szeretnél [CP $t_i'$
      who-PL-NOM you-said              that  you-would-like
      ha eljönnének $t_i$]]]
      if came
      'Who did you say that you would like if came?'

In the chain consisting of kik$_i$ $t_i''$ $t_i'$ $t_i$, $t_i$ is in the nominative, whereas $t_i'$ is in the accusative (given that the verb szeretnél, governing $t_i'$, bears an Agr marker showing the presence of an indefinite object). $t_i''$ is in the nominative (the matrix verb governing it does not agree with an indefinite object), and the head kik ('who') is in the nominative, too. $t_i$, the subject of the lowest clause, is assigned nominative Case. $t_i'$ both inherits nominative from $t_i$ and is marked accusative by the intermediate verb, and of the two Cases, accusative wins. $t_i''$ is neither marked accusative by the governing verb nor does it inherit the accusative of $t_i'$ (the next lower trace), but it illegitimately receives the nominative of $t_i$. The head legitimately inherits nominative from $t_i''$; nevertheless, the illegitimate step renders the sentence ungrammatical.

The observed properties of the multiple Case marking process can be summarized as follows:

(18) *Case marking in Ā-chains*
   a. A transitive V Case-marks its noun phrase object, or the noun phrase occupying the specifier of its sentential object, whether the target noun phrase is empty or lexically filled. (Case marking is optional, unless forced by the Case Filter.)
   b. In an Ā-chain, Case is inherited successive cyclically.
   c. If an element of an Ā-chain is both Case marked by a Case assigner and inherits a Case, the more marked one of the two Cases is realized.

Having examined the process of multiple Case marking in some detail, let us return to the original objective: the identification of the property of parasitic gap constructions that is responsible for the distribution of grammaticality, for example, in (2a–c) or (10a,b). The data observed in Hungarian suggest that the condition licensing parasitic gaps involves some kind of a Case identity requirement. As (11c) and (12b) make clear, this requirement cannot be the Case identity of the real gap and the parasitic gap—parasitic gap constructions are also grammatical if the real gap differs in Case from the parasitic gap, but its antecedent assumes a Case identical with the Case of the parasitic gap in the course of the derivation. Therefore, I tentatively hypothesized that the parasitic gap must bear the same case as the antecedent binding the real gap. However, as (19) shows, this hypothesis is false, too.

(19) [$_{FP}$ Kiket$_i$      hívtál      meg $t_i$ [$_{PP}$ anélkül [$_{CP}$ $pg''$
      who-PL-ACC you-invited PREF      without-it
      hogy szerettél-volna [$_{CP}$ $pg'$ hogy eljöjjenek $pg$]]]]
      that you-would-have-liked   that come
      'Whom did you invite without wishing that come?'

In (19) the Case of the antecedent of the real gap differs from that of the parasitic gap: the former is in the accusative, whereas the parasitic gap is in the nominative. The chain containing the parasitic gap, however, undergoes a Case change; $pg'$, the trace binding the parasitic gap, is marked accusative.

In fact, the antecedent of the real gap can differ in Case from both the real gap and the parasitic gap at the same time:

(20) [$_{FP}$ Kiket$_i$      szeretnél [$_{CP}$ $t_i'$ hogy írjanak $t_i$ neked
      who-PL-ACC you-would-like that   write       you
      [$_{PP}$ anélkül [$_{CP}$ $pg''$ hogy akarnál [$_{CP}$ $pg'$ hogy
      without-it       that you-would-want that
      meglátogassanak $pg$]]]]]
      visit-you
      'Whom would you like that write to you without wanting that visit you?'

In view of (19) and (20), what distinguishes the grammatical parasitic gap constructions in (11a), (11c), and (12b) from the ungrammatical parasitic gap constructions in (11b) and (12a) is the fact that in the former both the real gap and the parasitic gap form a chain with the phonologically realized operator, wheras in the latter no chain link can be established between the element(s) binding the parasitic gap and the phonologically realized operator, because the conditions of Case marking in Ā-chains (see (18)) are not satisfied. So I propose the following licensing condition for parasitic gaps:

(21) In a parasitic gap construction, the Case of both the real gap and the parasitic gap must be properly transmitted to the phonologically realized operator.[7]

If a parasitic gap construction is assumed to involve two chains that share the same antecedent (more precisely, the same top section), then (21) falls out without being stipulated.

Let us check how condition (21) is observed in (20), rewritten as (22):

(22) [FP Kiket$_{i,j}$      szeretnél [CP      hogy $t_i'$ írjanak $t_i$ neked
     who-PL-ACC you-would-like that      write        to-you
     [PP anélkül [CP $t_j''$ hogy akarnál [CP $t_j'$      hogy meglátogassanak $t_j$]]]]]
     without-it      that you-would-want that  visit-you

In the chain kiket$_i$ $t_i'$ $t_i$, $t_i$ is assigned nominative, $t_i'$ is marked accusative
by the V szeretnél, and the operator inherits its Case from $t_i'$—all in accordance with the requirements of (18). Similarly, in the chain kiket$_j$ $t_j''$ $t_j'$
$t_j$, $t_j$ is in the nominative, $t_j'$ is marked accusative, $t_j''$ inherits accusative
from $t_j'$, and the operator inherits accusative from $t_j''$.

Let us also examine how condition (21) predicts that (12a), rewritten
here as (23), is ungrammatical.

(23) *[FP Kik$_{i,j}$        jöttek el $t_i$ [PP anélkül [CP $t_j'$ hogy
        who-PL-NOM came   away   without-it     that
     meghívtál-volna $t_j$]]]
     you-had-invited
     'Who came without you having invited?'

In (23) the chain kik$_i$ $t_i$ is legitimate; kik ('who') inherits its nominative
from $t_i$. The chain kik$_j$ $t_j'$ $t_j$, on the other hand, is not permissible, because
both $t_j$ and $t_j'$ are in the accusative, and the antecedent kik does not inherit their Case.

Condition (21) will correctly predict the distribution of grammaticality
also in the English (1a–c) and (10a,b), if the properties of Case assignment
to Ā-chains summarized in (18) can also be shown to hold in English.
As is stated in (18), an element of an Ā-chain can receive Case in two
ways: through inheritance, and through Case marking by the governing
verb. There is evidence that this is what happens in English Ā-chains, for
example in (24).

(24) [CP Who$_i$/Whom$_i$ did [IP you suggest [CP $t_i'$ [IP $t_i$ should be the
     chairman]]]]

According to (18), $t_i$ is assigned nominative Case by Agr. $t_i'$, on the other
hand, is optionally marked accusative by the verb suggest. If it is marked
accusative, the more marked of the two conflicting Cases (i.e., accusative)
wins, and the head of the chain inherits the accusative of $t_i'$. As is noted
by Mark Steedman, a British English native speaker, in structures like
(24) whom is not only possible but is the preferred morphological variant
for many speakers, including himself. According to Kayne (1980), and
various other native speakers of American English consulted, whom in

constructions of type (24) also exists in American English. It is associated with a somewhat archaic, pompous, hypercorrect style; that is, it has the same stylistic value, albeit in a stronger form, as *whom* has when functioning as a simple object. If the process of multiple Case assignment to Ā-chains did not exist in English, then it would be impossible to account for the *whom* form occurring in (24). In other words, if (18) were not operative, then (25a) ought to be as ungrammatical as (25b).

(25) a.  ?Whom did you suggest should be the chairman?
     b.  **Whom should be the chairman?

If, as I hope to have shown, the multiple Case marking process in (18) can be maintained in English, then condition (21) correctly predicts the distribution of grammaticality in, for example, (1a–c), rewritten here as (26a–c).

(26) a.  [$_{CP}$ Which papers$_{i,j}$ did [$_{IP}$ you file $t_i$ [without $t_j'$ [PRO reading $t_j$]]]]
     b.  *[$_{CP}$ Which papers$_{i,j}$ [$_{IP}$ $t_i$ fell off the table [without $t_j'$ [John reading $t_j$]]]]
     c.  [$_{CP}$ Which papers$_{i,j}$ did [$_{IP}$ John decide [before $t_j'$ [PRO reading $t_j$]] [$_{CP}$ $t_i''$ [$_{IP}$ PRO to tell his secretary [$_{CP}$ $t_i'$ [$_{IP}$ $t_i$ were unavailable]]]]]]

Example (26a) is grammatical because both $t_i$ and $t_j$ can legitimately be Case-linked to the antecedent *which papers* (i.e., all three elements have accusative Case). Example (26b), on the other hand, is ruled out not only by the anti-c-command constraint but also by the Case-matching condition—because no chain link can be established between the antecedent *which papers* and the parasitic gap $t_j$, owing to the fact that the antecedent has nominative Case (through inheritance from $t_i$), whereas the parasitic gap is in the accusative. Example (26c) is, again, grammatical because both the chain *which papers$_i$ $t_i''$ $t_i'$ $t_i$* and the chain *which papers$_j$ $t_j'$ $t_j$* are legitimate. In the latter chain, *which papers* simply inherits the accusative Case assigned to $t_j$. In the former chain, $t_i$ is marked nominative; $t_i'$ both inherits the nominative Case of $t_i$ and is marked accusative by the V *tell*; $t_i''$ inherits accusative (i.e., the more marked one of the two conflicting Cases received by $t_i'$); and the antecedent *which papers* inherits the accusative of $t_i''$.[8]

The proposed licensing condition for parasitic gaps also explains the difference between the grammaticality of (10a) and (10b), rewritten here as (27a,b) (the so-called Pesetsky problem mentioned in Chomsky 1982:55).

(27) a. *the book from which$_{i,j}$ I copied $t_i$ without buying $t_j$
     b. the book which$_{i,j}$ I copied from $t_i$ without buying $t_j$

In (27a) the parasitic gap, having the category NP and being marked accusative, cannot transmit its features to the non-Case-marked PP antecedent. In (27b), on the other hand, the accusative NP variable can legitimately transmit its syntactic features to the antecedent *which* (see Pesetsky 1982).[9]

Along the same lines, the difference in grammaticality between (28a) and (28b) can also be explained (A. Belletti's examples, discussed in Chomsky 1986b under (63i,ii)).

(28) a. *He is the person to whom [they left [before [speaking]]]
     b. He is the person who [they left [before [speaking to/meeting]]]

Chomsky (1986b) analyzes both sentences as involving movement out of an adjunct, and attributes the ungrammaticality of (28a) to the violation of Subjacency. What is unclear is why (28b) is acceptable. In my view, (28b) is saved by the fact that it can be interpreted as a parasitic gap construction with the gap in the adjunct being parasitic on an object gap governed by *left*, as shown in (29).

(29) He is the person who$_{i,j}$ [they left $t_i$ [before [speaking to/meeting $t_j$]]]

Example (28a) cannot be saved by a parasitic gap interpretation because no chain link can be established between an empty NP governed by *left*, and the operator *to whom*.[10]

### 3.4 The Feature Matching Condition on Parasitic Gap Constructions

It is not only the failure of Case inheritance in either of the two chains that can render a parasitic gap construction ungrammatical; the sentence will also be out if any of the other syntactic features that are passed on in an Ā-chain from root to head are not transmitted to the overt operator properly (i.e., successively, from trace to trace) in either of the two chains.

The set of syntactic features to be transmitted in an Ā-chain is to some extent language-specific. It obviously includes Case, person, and number, both in English and in Hungarian. The feature [±definite], on the other hand, may be relevant only in Hungarian, where [+definite] objects and [–definite] objects trigger different Agr markers on the V. Example (30), for instance, is ungrammatical because the feature [+definite] of the parasitic gap is not transmitted to the head *kiket* ('whom').

(30) *[$_{FP}$ Kiket$_{i,j}$      szeretnél [$_{CP}$ $t_i{}'$ ha eljönnének $t_i$
      who-PL-ACC you-would-like if  came
      [$_{PP}$ anélkül [$_{CP}$ $t_j{}'$ hogy meghívod            $t_j$]]]]
      without-it    that you-invite[+DEF ]
      'Whom would you like if came without you having invited?'

In (30) the V governing the parasitic gap agrees with a definite object (i.e., $t_j$ and $t_j{}'$ are [+definite]). The operator *kiket* ('whom'), however, has the feature [−definite]; therefore, no chain link can be established between *kiket* and $t_j{}'$.

In languages where Ns and the Agr element on the V are marked for gender, gender is presumably also among the features that have to be transmitted to the head in an Ā-chain.

Examples (31a,b) (both from Kearney 1983, discussed as (140i,ii) in Chomsky 1986b) also raise questions about the transmittance of the feature [±bound].

(31) a.   [$_{CP}$ Which books about himself$_{i,j}$ did [$_{IP}$ John file $t_i$ [before $t_j{}'$
          [Mary read $t_j$]]]]
     b. *[$_{CP}$ Which books about herself$_{i,j}$ did [$_{IP}$ John file $t_i$ [before $t_j{}'$
          [Mary read $t_j$]]]]

The ungrammaticality of (31b) is intepreted by Chomsky (1986a) as evidence demonstrating that in parasitic gap constructions the operator can only be extracted from the position of the real gap, not from the position of the parasitic gap; in other words, parasitic gap constructions are not multiple gap structures. In fact, the grammaticality of (31a) and the ungrammaticality of (31b) also follow if we interpret parasitic gap structures as involving two Ā-chains sharing the same antecedent. The key to the correct analysis of (31a,b) is provided by the independently motivated principle in (32), the first versions of which were proposed by Koster (1982) and Barss (1986).

(32) If an element bears a relation R to a chain link, it bears the same relation to the lexical content of the Ā-chain, too.

Principle (32) was abstracted from sentences like (33).

(33) Which books about himself$_i$ does John think $t_i{}'$ that Bill likes $t_i$?

In (33) *himself* can be coreferent either with *Bill* or with *John*, because both *Bill* and *John* c-command a link of the chain *which books about himself$_i$ $t_i{}'$ $t_i$*.

As for the parasitic gap constructions in (31), (31a) is grammatical because *himself* is bound both in the licensing chain and in the parasitic chain. In the licensing chain *which books about himself*$_i$ $t_i$, the chain link c-commanded by *John* is $t_i$, whereas in the parasitic chain *which books about himself*$_j$ $t_j''$ $t_j'$ $t_j$, it is $t_j'$. If $t_i$ and $t_j'$ are regarded as layered traces, then the empty element corresponding to *himself* has *John* in its governing category both in the case of $t_i$ and in the case of $t_j'$; consequently, binding Condition A of Chomsky (1981) is satisfied in both chains.

The sentence in (31b), on the other hand, is ungrammatical because *herself* can only be bound in the parasitic chain, where the lowest chain link is c-commanded by the antecedent of *herself*. Because no chain link is c-commanded by *Mary* in the licensing chain, *herself* has no binder, in violation of Condition A.

In fact, Condition A requires that an anaphor be bound, and principle (32) allows that an anaphor in an Ā-chain assume this feature at any point of the derivation. The effects of principle (32) for anaphora fall out from the properties of Ā-chain formation—if we generalize the mechanism established for Case marking in Ā-chains under (18a,b) as the mechanism determining in Ā-chains the transmittance of all noninherent, context-dependent syntactic features. Then, an element of an Ā-chain can assume the feature [+bound] in two ways: by being c-commanded by a coindexed antecedent in its governing category, or through inheritance. For the root of the chain, naturally, only the former option is available. If in this way a chain link acquires both the feature [+bound] and the feature [−bound], the marked feature (i.e., [+bound]) prevails. Consider now (31a). In the chain *which books about himself*$_i$ $t_i$, the trace of *himself* in the chain link $t_i$ is [+bound] because it is c-commanded by *John* in its governing category; and the antecedent, *himself*, inherits this feature. In the chain *which books about himself*$_j$ $t_j'$ $t_j$, the trace of *himself* in the chain link $t_j$ is free, therefore [−bound]. The corresponding element of $t_j'$ both inherits the feature [−bound] and acquires the feature [+bound], by being c-commanded in its governing category by *John*. Of the two conflicting features, [+bound] wins and is transmitted to the antecedent *himself*. Thus, the feature [+bound] is transmitted to the anaphor in both chains—that is, Condition A is satisfied.

In (31b), on the other hand, the anaphor *herself* assumes the feature [+bound] only in the parasitic chain, that is, *in which books about herself*$_j$ $t_j'$ $t_j$. In this chain the trace of *herself* in the chain link $t_j$ is c-commanded by *Mary* in its governing category; it is [+bound], and this feature is properly transmitted first to the corresponding element of $t_j'$ and then to the antecedent *herself*. In the licensing chain *which books about herself*$_i$ $t_i$, on the other hand, the trace of *herself* in the chain link $t_i$ receives the feature [−bound], because, owing to the fact that it is [+feminine], it has no potential binder in its governing category. So it is the feature [−bound] that is passed on to the antecedent *herself*; consequently, the chain *which books about herself*$_i$ $t_i$ violates Condition A.

In sum: in a parasitic chain, similar to Ā-chains proper, the inherent (i.e., non-context-dependent) features of the NP such as person, number, gender, [±definite] are passed on from root to head through inheritance, from chain link to chain link, whereas the properties that are conditional on an outer element (e.g., Case and the feature [±bound]) cannot only be inherited but can also be reassigned to each chain link; see (18).

In view of these observations, the licensing condition proposed for parasitic gaps in (21) has to be modified as follows:

(34) In a parasitic gap construction, the syntactic features of both the real gap and the parasitic gap are properly transmitted to the phonologically realized operator.

Let me emphasize again that (34) need not be stipulated as a primitive of grammar; if the parasitic gap construction is analyzed to consist of two Ā-chains that share the same top section, condition (34) falls out.

### 3.5   An Apparent Problem

Neither the c-command condition nor the feature-matching condition on parasitic gap constructions seems to be able to predict the distribution of grammaticality in the following examples of Engdahl (1985) and their Hungarian equivalents:

(35) a.   Which man$_{i,j}$ did the police warn $t_i$ that they would arrest $t_j$?
   b.   *Which man$_{i,j}$ $t_i$ warned the police that they should not arrest $t_j$?
   c.   *Which man$_{i,j}$ did you think $t_i$ warned the police that they should not arrest $t_j$?

(36) a.   Kiket$_{i,j}$      figyelmeztetett a   rendőrség $t_i$, hogy letartóztat $t_j$?
      who-PL-ACC warned        the police-NOM   that they-arrest
      'Whom did the police warn that they would arrest?'
   b.   *Kik$_{i,j}$        figyelmeztették $t_i$ a   rendőrséget, hogy le     ne
      who-PL-NOM warned        the police-ACC   that PREF not
      tartóztasson $t_j$?
      they-arrest
      'Who warned the police that they should not arrest?'

c. *Kiket<sub>i,j</sub>     gondolsz, hogy figyelmeztették *t*<sub>i</sub> a   rendőrséget,
   who-PL-ACC you-think that   warned                  the police-ACC
   hogy le     ne   tartóztasson *t*<sub>j</sub>?
   that  PREF not they-arrest
   'Whom do you think that warned the police that they should
   not arrest?'

The problem is how to exempt from the anti-c-command condition the
grammatical (35a) and (36a), in which the licensing object gap is believed
to c-command the parasitic gap.[11] Chomsky (1986b) raises the possibility
that the complement clause of *warn* is actually adjoined to the VP node
dominating the object of *warn*; hence it is outside the c-command domain
of *warn*. That is how Kayne (1982, 1983) represents the structural position
of the clausal complement of *warn*, as well. Hungarian data also support
this view; they show the *that*-clause accompanying *warn* to be an adjunct
ungoverned by *warn*. In Hungarian, argument clauses are always associated with a pronominal head bearing a Case corresponding to the θ-role
of the clause. (The pronominal head of an object clause can also be represented by a *pro*; however, the presence of *pro*, too, is clearly indicated
by the fact that the verb bears a morpheme agreeing with a definite
object.) *That*-clauses without a nominal head—for example, the *that*-clause
of *dicsekszik* ('brag'), *szól* ('send word'), *üzenetet küld* ('send message'),
*csenget* ('ring'), or *integet* ('wave'), specifying the content of the communication denoted by the verb—are adjunct clauses, presumably adjoined
to the VP (see Kenesei (1992:612–615)). Their adjunct status is confirmed
by the fact that they are islands:

(37) *Kinek<sub>i</sub>   figyelmeztette Pétert    a   rendőrség, hogy
     to-whom warned          Peter-ACC the police-NOM that
     idézést         küld  *t*<sub>i</sub>?
     summons-ACC sends
     'To whom did the police warn Peter that they would send
     summons?'

If the clausal complement of *warn* is not an argument, then the object
of *warn* does not c-command the content of the *that*-clause, hence the
ungrammatical (35c) does not violate the anti-c-command condition. The
same holds of the Hungarian (36b,c), as well. Whereas (36b) is correctly
ruled out by the feature-matching condition, and (35b) is ruled out by
both the feature-matching condition and the anti-c-command condition,

(35c) and (36c) still remain to be explained. It is the Hungarian data, again, that provide the clue to their ungrammaticality. Notice that the verb *figyelmeztet*—just like *warn*—has two variants with different argument structures. Compare:

(38) a. A  rendőr      figyelmeztette Jánost,    hogy engedje
        the policeman warned         John-ACC that release-SUBJ-3SG
        el       *pro*-NOM *pro*-ACC.
        PREF
        'The policeman warned John that he should release him.'
     b. A  rendőr      figyelmeztette Jánost,    hogy el-engedi
        the policeman warn-PAST-3SG John-ACC that  releases
        *pro*-NOM *pro*-ACC.
        'The policeman warned John that he would release him.'

In (38a), in which the clausal complement of *warn* is in the subjunctive, the embedded pro subject is obligatorily controlled by the matrix object.

(39) *A  rendőr      figyelmeztette Jánost,    hogy Mari menjen
       the policeman warned         John-ACC that  Mary go-SUBJ-3SG
       haza.
       home
       'The policeman warned John that Mary go home.'

Owing to object control, the disjoint reference triggered by binding Condition B between the embedded subject and the embedded object leads to disjoint reference also between the matrix object and the embedded object. This explains why (35c) and (36c) are out: if the matrix object and the embedded object are obligatorily disjoint in reference, they cannot be bound by the same antecedent.

In the (38b) case, in which the embedded clause is in the indicative, on the other hand, the situation is the reverse. There is a default subject control: the matrix subject controls the nonlexical subject of the embedded clause. Given that the embedded *pro* subject is in disjoint reference with the embedded *pro* object (owing to Condition B), the embedded *pro* object is also in disjoint reference with the matrix subject. Examples (35a) and (36a), in which the matrix object is coreferent with the embedded object, do not violate any referential restriction. Example (40), however, in which the subject of *warn* is bound by the same antecedent as the object of the embedded indicative clause, while they are also required to be disjoint, is ungrammatical.

(40) *Kiket$_{i,j}$       gondolsz [$_{CP}$ $t_i$ hogy figyelmeztették $t_i$ a
who-PL-ACC think-you          that warned                    the
rendőrséget [$_{CP}$ $t_j$ hogy valaki       letartóztat $t_j$]]?
police-ACC           that  somebody arrests
'Whom do you think warned the police that somebody would
arrest?'

### 3.6   Parasitic Chains and Locality

In sections 3.3 and 3.4, I identified the following properties of parasitic
gaps:
   (a) In parasitic gap constructions, the syntactic features of both the
licensing gap and the parasitic gap are transmitted to the overt operator
(see (34)). The syntactic features inherently associated with an NP (e.g.,
person, number, gender, [±definiteness]) are passed on from the variables
to the operator unchanged. The contextually determined features (e.g.,
Case, [±bound]), on the other hand, when transmitted successive cyclically, from chain link to chain link, are subject to reassignment on each
cycle.
   (b) The path between the licensing gap and the overt operator, and the
path between the parasitic gap and the overt operator merge at some
point. The shared section of the paths transmits identical features from
the two variables to the operator.
   As has been suggested, properties (a) and (b) follow without stipulation
if it can be maintained that the parasitic gap is linked to the antecedent
through a proper Ā-chain—that is, if it can be demonstrated that parasitic gap constructions involve two or more proper Ā-chains that share the
same top section.
   For a string of coindexed elements to count as an Ā-chain, certain
locality requirements must also be met; namely, each chain link must be
subjacent to the next higher link coindexed with it.
   The locality relations among the links of the parasitic chain, in fact,
have been thoroughly examined in the literature. As Chomsky (1986b)
has shown, the independent section of the parasitic chain observes
Subjacency—for example, in (41a,b) (Chomsky's (126)–(127)) we find
exactly the same degree of grammaticality as in the corresponding simple
*wh*-movement cases.

(41) This is the man$_{i,j}$ John interviewed $t_i$ before ...
       a.   [$t_j$ [expecting us [$t_j$ [to tell you [$t_j$ [to give the job to $t_j$]]]]]]
       b.   *[$t_j$ [asking you [which job [to give to $t_j$]]]]

(42) a.   Who$_j$ did they [$t_j$ [expect us [$t_j$ [to tell you [$t_j$ [to give the job to
          $t_j$]]]]]]

    b.   *Who$_j$ did they [$t_j$ [expect us [$t_j$ [to ask you [which job [to give to
          $t_j$]]]]]]

Subjacency is obviously also observed in the section of the parasitic chain
that is shared with the licensing chain.

(43)  This is the man [0$_{i,j}$ [John proposed [$t_{i,j}$ [to interview $t_i$ [before $t_j$
      [expecting us [$t_j$ [to tell you [$t_j$ [to give the job to $t_j$]]]]]]]]]]]

At the same time, however, it has also been known since Engdahl 1983
that parasitic gaps most typically occur in islands (e.g., in adjunct clauses)
from which nonparasitic extraction is barred by Subjacency. The extra
barrier that blocks nonparasitic extraction occurs in the parasitic chain
between the highest link of the independent section and the lowest link of
the shared section. So a typical parasitic gap construction—for example,
that in (43)—can be represented by the following diagram, with the dotted
lines marking possible barriers to Subjacency:

(44)

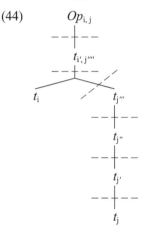

As pointed out by Barss (1984) and Chomsky (1986b), the top link of the
independent section of the parasitic chain ($t_j$′′′) can be dominated by at
most one barrier that does not dominate the licensing variable ($t_i$). Thus,
what the top link of the independent section of the parasitic chain must
be close to is not the bottom link of the licensing chain but the licensing
chain itself. In other words, (45) is also a possible parasitic gap configuration (cf. e.g. (1c)).

(45)

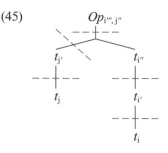

The observations of the literature concerning the locality relations in the parasitic chain all fall out as properties of $\bar{\text{A}}$-chains under the following minimal relaxation of the locality constraint on $\bar{\text{A}}$-chain formation:

(46) In an $\bar{\text{A}}$-chain $\alpha_1, \ldots, \alpha_n$
    i.   $\alpha_i$ is subjacent to $\alpha_{i-1}$, or
    ii.   $\alpha_i$ is subjacent to chain $\beta_1, \ldots, \beta_n$, where $\beta_1 = \alpha_1$

(47) $\alpha_i$ is subjacent to chain $\beta_1, \ldots, \beta_n$ if it is subjacent to a node of the path between $\beta_1$ and $\beta_n$.

In the present analysis of parasitic gap constructions, parasitic chains differ from "normal" $\bar{\text{A}}$-chains only in the respect that, on the one hand, they may contain an extra barrier for Subjacency; and, on the other hand, they cannot be independent; they must be parasitic on a host chain. In fact, both of these properties follow from (46ii); that is, if the locality constraint on $\bar{\text{A}}$-chain formation is extended by (46ii), then every property of parasitic chains can be derived from the properties of $\bar{\text{A}}$-chains.

### 3.7 Conclusion

This chapter has argued for a theory of parasitic gaps which is based on the assumption that a parasitic gap construction involves a forking $\bar{\text{A}}$-chain in which both the real gap and the parasitic gap are bound by the same antecedent. Because the features of both the real gap and the parasitic gap must be properly transmitted to the shared antecedent, it follows that the parasitic chain and the licensing chain must have matching features. If parasitic gap constructions are seen as forking $\bar{\text{A}}$-chains, then their locality features can also be accounted for: whereas a link of the licensing chain must be subjacent to the next higher link of the licensing chain, a link of the parasitic chain must be subjacent to the next higher link of the parasitic chain, or to a link of the licensing chain.

    The question naturally arises whether the results of the proposed approach could not also be made to follow from the null operator theory of parasitic gaps proposed by Chomsky (1986a,b). In this framework, parasitic gap constructions involve two separate chains: a licensing chain headed by the overt operator, and a parasitic chain headed by an empty operator. In the (1986a) version of the theory, the empty operator is linked to the overt operator through strong binding—namely, it is claimed that the value of a variable bound by an empty operator must be determined by an antecedent that binds the empty operator, (i.e., in this case, by the overt *wh*-operator). A binding relation between $\alpha$ and $\beta$, however, only requires that $\alpha$ and $\beta$ be coindexed, and $\alpha$ c-command $\beta$; but it does not require that $\alpha$ and $\beta$ share all their syntactic features. $\alpha$ and $\beta$ can differ, for instance, with respect to Case and [$\pm$definiteness]; for example, in the sentence *Egy kisfiú megütötte magát* ('A little boy hurt himself'), the antecedent is nominative and [−definite] whereas the element bound by it is accusative and [+definite]. That is, the requirement of strong binding is not restrictive enough; it cannot ensure the transmittance of all the relevant syntactic features between the parasitic gap and a phonologically realized operator. It is not clear, either, how the locality requirements could be built into the notion of "strong binding."[12]

In the framework of Chomsky (1986b), the two chains involved in a parasitic gap construction are associated not by strong binding but via chain composition. Chain composition, however, is not an independently motivated mechanism of Universal Grammar, so the properties of parasitic gap constructions identified above, instead of falling out from the properties of chain composition, are to be stipulated as conditions on chain composition. Therefore, this approach is less consistent with the general assumption that the parasitic gap construction is the direct output of independently existing principles of Universal Grammar than the approach proposed in this paper, in which the properties of parasitic gap constructions are derived from the properties of Ā-chain formation.

**Notes**

This paper is a revised version of Kiss (1985–1986). The permission of Mouton de Gruyter to reprint parts of that paper from *The Linguistic Review* is thankfully acknowledged. My original paper elicited reactions from Heizo Nakajima (see Nakajima (1985–1986)), and Julia Horvath (see Horvath 1990, 1992). My answer to Nakajima's comments appeared in *The Linguistic Review*; see Kiss (1986–1987). My reactions to Julia Horvath's criticism are included in the present paper, particularly in section 3.5. I have revised some of my original assumptions so as to account for the facts brought to light by her.

1. Examples (1a–c) are taken from Barss 1984; they are also discussed in Chomsky 1986b.

2. Hungarian is a *pro*-drop language: subject pronouns and singular object pronouns can be phonologically empty. So as to avoid mistaking *pro* objects for parasitic gaps, I will always use accusative parasitic gaps bound by a plural antecedent (as in (iii)), because a plural object cannot be represented by a *pro*. Compare:

(i)    Eltetted       a  könyvet,   bár    nem olvastad *pro*-ACC.
       you-put-away the book-ACC  though not  you-read
       'You put away the book though you have not read [it].'

(ii)   *Eltetted      a  könyveket, bár   nem olvastad *pro*-ACC.
       you-put-away the books-ACC though not  you-read
       'You put away the books though you have not read [them].'

(iii)  Milyen könyveket tettél   el      anélkül,  hogy olvastál-volna *pg*?
       what   books-ACC you-put away without-it that  you-had-read
       'What books did you put away without reading?'

Parasitic object gaps can also be distinguished from pro objects on the basis that they can be [±definite] depending on the specificity of the operator—that is, they can trigger either the [+definite] or the [−definite] conjugation of the V. (In Hungarian, every verbal paradigm has two variants: one used in the presence of a definite object, and one used in the absence of a definite object.) A third-person *pro* object, on the other hand, is always [+definite]. Hence the empty element in the embedded clause of (iv) must be *pro*, as it does not agree in definiteness with the [−definite] operator.

(iv)  Milyen könyvet tettél        el      anélkül,  hogy olvastad-volna *pro*-ACC?
      what   book   you-put[−DEF] away without-it that  you-had-read[+DEF]
      'What book did you put away without reading[+DEF] (it)?'

3. Brody (1990) argues that the filling of [Spec,FP] with a focus constituent triggers verb movement into the empty F head. This assumption, among others, is made plausible by the fact that in the presence of a focus the verb precedes the verbal prefix, whereas in neutral sentences it follows it, as is also demonstrated by the examples in (3). Nevertheless, I will not represent V-to-F movement in the examples to come, partly because it does not bear on the problems discussed in this paper.

4. Following Chomsky (1986b), I assume that the *without*-adjunct is adjoined to the VP, as follows:

(i)

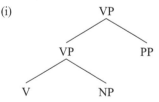

This assumption is confirmed by the fact that the *without*-adjunct can either undergo VP-preposing or remain stranded:

(ii)  He asked me to pay for those papers without taking them, and pay for them without taking them I did.

(iii) ... and pay for them I did, without taking them.

The fairly strong disjoint-reference effect between the object of the V and the material in the PP in (iv), for example, must be due to the fact that the direction of pronominalization is backward. That is, the disjoint reference attested is not necessarily a Condition C effect, but is comparable to that in (v).

(iv) ??I paid for them$_i$ without taking those papers$_i$.

(v) ??I paid for them$_i$ but I did not take those papers$_i$.

5. (i) The g-projection set of a category $\beta$, governed by $\alpha$, is constituted by $\beta$, by every g-projection of $\alpha$, and every category dominating $\beta$ and not dominating $\alpha$.

(ii) Y is a projection of X iff:
   a. Y is a projection of X or of a g-projection of X
   b. Y immediately dominates W and Z, Z is a g-projection of X, and W and Z are in a canonical government configuration

(iii) W and Z are in a canonical government configuration if and only if:
   a. in a language with basic VO order, W precedes Z
   b. in a language with basic OV order, Z precedes W

6. Both (12a) and (12c) are grammatical if $t_j$ is interpreted as a first-person-singular *pro* object. However, this is not their intended interpretation; $t_j$ is supposed to be coreferent with *kik* ('who-PL').

7. Taraldsen (1982) claims that in Finnish parasitic-gap constructions the Case of the real gap and the Case of the parasitic gap need not be related. It is not clear, however, that the phenomenon he describes indeed involves parasitic gaps. Taraldsen says that there are only two Cases—the accusative and the partitive—that can freely cooccur in parasitic gap constructions. Given that in Finnish the object can be represented by *pro*, the constructions claimed to involve an accusative gap and a partitive gap certainly contain only one variable and one *pro*. Taraldsen claims that parasitic gaps can be distinguished from *pro*s in Finnish, because the latter are necessarily singular; a parasitic gap, on the other hand, can also take a plural secondary predicate. The example proving this point, however, involves two gaps in identical Cases.

Taraldsen found only three examples in which one or both of the two gaps bear an oblique Case. The limited number of examples suggests that the sentences involve, instead of a parasitic gap (which can, after all, be generated fairly freely), an implicit argument.

8. A *TLR* reviewer pointed out to me that

(i) Which papers$_{i,j}$ was John sure even before reading $t_j$ $t_i{}'$ $t_i$ were so bad?

is not appreciably different in grammaticality from (26c), even though *sure*, being an adjective, cannot assign accusative to the trace in [Spec,CP].

A convenient explanation for this problem would be to say that *be sure* can be reanalyzed as a verb and can thereby assign Case. This possibility is raised by Kayne (1980:note 5), who notices that *be sure* behaves like verbs that can assign Case into [Spec,CP], in allowing the extraction of the subject of its sentential complement:

(ii) John I'm not sure has any friends.

Kayne (1980) also notes, however, that the assumption that *be sure* can be re-analyzed as a V would wrongly predict (iii) to be grammatical.

(iii) *I am not sure John to have any friends.

9. Condition (21) in itself cannot account for the ungrammaticality of (i), too.

(i) *About whom$_{i,j}$ did you think $t_i$ after talking $t_j$?

10. Principle (21) also correctly predicts the distribution of grammaticality in the following Italian sentence pair (examples by L. Rizzi, discussed by Chomsky (1986b) as (152i,ii)):

(i)  Che studente hai      convinto *t* che puoi      aiutare *pg*?
     which student did-you convince   that you-would help

(ii) *Che studente è    stato convinto *t* che puoi      aiutare *pg*?
     which student was convinced           that you-would help

In (i) both the licensing gap and the parasitic gap are assigned accusative Case, which is properly transmitted to the antecedent in both chains. In (ii), on the other hand, the licensing chain transmits nominative Case to the operator, but the parasitic gap transmits accusative Case; consequently, the operator cannot head both chains at the same time.

11. In the previous version of this paper published as Kiss (1985–1986) I proposed an incorrect explanation of these facts, the inadequacy of which was pointed out by Horvath (1990, 1992). See also Brody 1994 for a different analysis of the data in question.

12. The notion of strong binding is not intended to be more restrictive, because it is also employed to characterize the relation of the empty operator and its antecedent in *tough*-constructions:

(i) John$_i$ is easy [$\emptyset_i$ [PRO to get on with $t_i$]]

# PART II
## What Is a Parasitic Gap?

# Chapter 4

Versatile Parasitic Gaps      Elisabet Engdahl

## 4.1 Introduction

On November 28, 1660, Samuel Pepys wrote in his diary:[1]

(1) This morning I went to White-hall to my Lord's where Major Hart did pay me 23.14.09, due to me upon my pay in my Lord's troop, at the time of our disbanding—which is a great blessing to have $t$ without taking any care in the world for $pg$.

Parasitic gaps have thus been around for some time. Linguistic analyses of this construction are more recent, but since 1980 quite a few analyses have been published for different languages.[2] This chapter discusses three claims that seem to have become part of the standard analysis. The first is that parasitic gaps are limited to NPs, the second is that parasitic gaps must be "referential" or "specific" in some sense, and the third pertains to the island sensitivity of parasitic gaps. The point I want to make in this paper is that when we look at more languages, these claims are not particularly well founded. Instead parasitic gaps appear to be more variable, or versatile, than has been hitherto recognized. However, the versatility of parasitic gaps should be seen in connection with other properties of the languages in question. The chapter is organized as follows. In section 4.2, I discuss some evidence from Swedish which shows that some languages allow non-NP parasitic gaps. A correlation between the availability of parasitic gaps and pronominals, discussed by Cinque and Postal, will be particularly relevant. In section 4.3, I look at restrictions on the types of NPs that license parasitic gaps, and in section 4.4, I suggest that the notion "island" needs to be understood in a relativized fashion.

## 4.2 Are All Parasitic Gaps NPs?

I believe that the claim that only NP extraction licenses parasitic gaps was first made by G. Cinque around 1983–1984 and published in Cinque 1990 (chap. 3). Following some ideas of Chomsky (1982), Cinque argues that parasitic gaps should not be analyzed as traces left behind by *wh*-movement. Rather they should be seen as empty pronominals *(pro)* identified through coindexation with an empty operator. Support for this analysis comes from Italian, where NP extraction licenses parasitic gaps but PP and AP extractions do not. Cinque assumes that NP is the only category that has an empty pronominal form *(pro* or PRO) and this explains why the PP, AP, and VP extractions with parasitic gaps are ill formed; there are no empty pronominals corresponding to those categories.

### 4.2.1 PP, Adverbial, and AP Gaps

We start by looking at non-NP complements, PPs, predicative APs, and locative adverbials. A couple of Cinque's examples are given here in (2) (Cinque 1990, chap. 3:(15)).

(2) a. *[$_{AP}$ Quanto importanti] si può   diventare *t* [senza    sentirsi *pg*]
         how       important  can-one become      without feeling

    b. *[$_{PP}$ A chi]     hai      lasciato la   lettera *t* [dopo esserti rivolto *pg*]
         to whom did-you leave     the letter      after turning

The question whether non-NP parasitic gaps are possible was taken up in Engdahl 1983, where the following examples were used as evidence that Swedish has non-NP parasitic gaps (chap. 2:(47a,b)).

(3) a. [$_{PP}$ Till himlen] är det inte säkert  att [$_{NP}$ alla [$_{S'}$ som längtar
         to   heaven is it   not certain that      all       that long
       [$_{PP}$ *pg*/dit]]] kommer [$_{PP}$ *t*]
             there come
       'It is not certain that everyone who longs to (go to) heaven gets to go there.'

    b. [$_{AP}$ Fattig] vill [$_{NP}$ ingen [$_{S'}$ som någonsin varit [$_{AP}$ *pg*/?det]]]
         poor     wants no-one    who ever       been          it
       bli [$_{AP}$ *t*] igen.
       become again
       'No one who has ever been poor wants to become poor again.'

Cinque (1990) remarks in a footnote that all the examples I cite of non-NP parasitic gaps are of the subject type (i.e., the parasitic gap occurs in a relative clause modifying the subject of the sentence) and adds, "In Italian, too, examples of the subject type tend to sound better than those of the adjunct type, though they are not really acceptable. Perhaps, in the subject case, real movement ... can be involved" (p. 187). Cinque does not pursue this issue further but takes the examples in (2) to show that non-NP parasitic gaps are impossible in Italian. However, the facts are different in Swedish, where PP and AP parasitic gaps in adjunct clauses are also possible. Let us first look at some examples of PP and adverbial parasitic gaps in adjuncts.

(4) a. Till San Francisco längtar många *t* utan     att kunna resa *pg*.
       to  San Francisco long    many    without be-able to travel
    b. Där  måste du lägga skyddsplast *t*  innan  du  ställer något *pg*.
       there you must lay   a-plastic-sheet before you put    anything
    c. Dit      gav sig många av *t* utan    att hitta *pg*.
       to-there many took off      without finding the way
    d. Var   kan man arbeta *t* utan    att bosätta sig *pg*?
       where can one  work      without settling

In (4a) a fronted PP is interpreted as an argument of both *längta* ('long') and *resa* ('travel'). (4b) involves a fronted locative proform *där* ('*there*'), (4c) has a fronted directional proform *dit* (roughly 'to there'), and (4d) has an interrogative locative adverb.[3] In all the examples, the adverbials are complements of the verb, not modifiers.

Turning now to English, Postal (1993, 1994) maintains that the contrast Cinque finds in Italian also holds in this language. An NP gap, as in (5a), is fine, but adverbial gaps are impossible.

(5) a. What city did Elaine work in *t* without ever living in *pg*? (Postal 1994:(7))
    b. *Where did Elaine work *t* without ever living *pg*?

Postal (1994:note 23) observes that parasitic gaps cannot occur in positions where *there* is possible but where a pronominal NP is impossible. However, the ungrammaticality of (5b) cannot be due to an inherent incompatibility between parastic gaps and adverbials, as the Swedish data in (4) show.

Two examples of adjective parasitic gaps in adjuncts are given in (6).[4]

(6) a. Hjälpsam kan han visst verka *t* utan att vara *pg*.
       helpful  he can  sure seem    without being
    b. Sjuk känner jag mig ofta *t* utan att egentligen vara *pg*.
       ill   I often feel          without really        being

**4.2.2   VP Gaps**

Cinque's example of an impossible VP parasitic gap is given here in (7a). The capitals indicate Focus Movement (Cinque 1990:10). The corresponding Swedish example in (7b) is clearly impossible as well.

(7) a. *[vp VENUTO A CASA] era *t*    [sensa    che fosse *pg* suo padre]
        come      home      he-had   without that had      his father
    b. *[vp Kommit hem] hade han *t* [utan      att   hans pappa hade *pg*]
        come      home had   he      without that his   father had

VP-fronting in Swedish usually requires a form of *do*-support; a form of the verb *göra* ('do') that agrees with the fronted VP appears in the sentence (Källgren and Prince 1989).

(8) a. Talat        dialekt i   radio har han ofta   gjort.
        talk-PERF dialect on radio has he   often do-PERF
        'Talked dialect on the radio he has often done.'
    b. Talar        dialekt gör        han *t* ofta.
        talk-PRES dialect do-PRES he       often
        'Talks dialect he often does.'

Provided *göra*-support, examples with parasitic tensed VP-gaps seem possible, although I have never heard an actual example.[5]

(9) a. Talar        dialekt ska   inga       som gör *pg* behöva skämmas
        talk-PRES dialect shall nobody who do-PRES need      be-ashamed
        för att   de     gör *t*.
        for that they do-PRES
        'Nobody who speaks dialect need be ashamed of doing so.'
    b. Talar        dialekt gör        vi  ofta *t* utan      att tänka på
        talk-PRES dialect do-PRES we often    without to think about
        att   vi   gör *pg*.
        that we do-PRES
        'We often talk dialect without thinking about doing it.'
    c. Vi talar ofta   dialekt utan      att tänka på   att   vi   gör *e*/det.
        we talk  often dialect without to think about that we do       it
        'We often talk dialect without thinking about doing (it).'

There is a noticeable contrast between (9a,b) with fronted VPs and (9c) with no fronting and a gap. Nevertheless these sound like constructed examples. The preferred way of conveying the meaning of (9b) is as in (10).

(10) Talar    dialekt gör    vi ofta *t* utan    att tänka på *e*.
     talk-PRES dialect do-PRES we often without to think about
     'We often talk dialect witout being aware (of it).'

The missing complement of *tänka på* ('be aware of') is interpreted as referring to something like the proposition 'that we talk dialect' and is not a simple parasitic gap, because it is of a different syntactic category and type from the fronted constituent. This looks rather like the kind of missing definite object that one can find with optionally transitive verbs such as *notice* (Fodor and Fodor 1980).

### 4.2.3  Predicate Nominals

Postal (1993, 1994) discusses several further restrictions on parasitic gaps and formulates a number of conditions. One condition that is particularly relevant to this discussion is given in (11) (from Postal 1994:(64)).

(11) *Postal's Pronominal Condition*
     P-gaps cannot occur in positions incompatible with definite pronouns.

Postal uses this condition to account for, among other things, the fact that predicate nominal (PN) constructions in English don't license parasitic gaps, as also noted by Lasnik and Saito (1992). Two of Postal's examples, given here in (12) and (13), show that PN complements of *turn into* and *become* cannot be replaced by definite pronouns. They are of course well formed on an NP interpretation.

(12) a. *[What kind of derelicts]$_1$ did they analyze $t_1$ after their children turned into $pg_1$? Postal (1994:(73d))
     b. *What people who want to be *pg* are often unable to become *t* is doctors. Postal (1993:(38d))

(13) a. The children turned into *them.
     b. Many people wanted to become *them.

As (13) shows, definite pronouns are impossible in place of a PN. The only way you can pronominalize a PN in English is with the generic pronoun *one*, as shown in (14a). The preferred option seems to be to use VP deletion and leave out the whole predicate as in (14b). For superlative antecedents, this is the only option, as shown in (14c).

(14) a. John wanted to become a doctor but he never did become one/*him/*it.
     b. John wanted to become a doctor but he never did.

    c. John wanted to become the best doctor but he never did
      (become *one/*him/*it).

The correlation behind the condition in (11) leads Postal to the conclusion
that parasitic gaps are essentially pronominals which are interpreted via
control. I will not here be able to discuss the full crosslinguistic ramifica-
tions of Postal's alternative analysis. I will limit myself to the PN cases
where I think the correlation he notes is correct and provides some insight
into the variation we find between English and Swedish.

In Swedish, the proform used for PN is not the generic *en* or *ett* (i.e.,
one marked for ±NEUT gender) but the definite singular neuter pronoun
*det* ('it'). The same pronoun is used to refer to VPs and events.

(15) a. Johan ville    bli      läkare        men han blev      aldrig
        Johan wanted become doctor[−NEUT] but   he   became never
        det/*den/*en.
        it[+NEUT]/it[−NEUT]/one[−NEUT]
    b. Johan ville    bli      den skickligaste läkaren      men han
        Johan wanted become the best        doctor[−NEUT] but  he
        blev      aldrig det/*den/*en.
        became never it
    c. men det/*den/*en blev     han aldrig.
        but  it            became he   never

As can be seen from the examples in (15), Swedish systematically uses the
neuter definite pronoun *det* where English uses *one* or VP deletion. Note
that this pronoun does not agree with the PN antecedent, which is non-
neuter. Example (15b) illustrates the the fact that unstressed pronouns are
often fronted in Swedish.[6] Given Postal's assumption that parasitic gaps
can occur in positions where definite pronouns occur, we now expect
Swedish PN extractions to license parasitic gaps, and they do.

(16) Läkare är det inte säkert  att   alla som vill   bli *pg*       verkligen
     doctor is it   not certain that all   that want to-become really
     borde bli *t*.
     ought to-become
     'Doctor it is not certain that everyone who wants to become (one)
     really ought to (become one).'

### 4.2.4 Manner Adverbials
Given the assumption that only NP parasitic gaps exist, manner adverbial
parasitic gaps are clearly expected to be impossible, as they have been
argued to be by Tellier (1991), who gives the following example:

(17) *This is the way you presented it *t* without having read it *pg*.

Furthermore, manner phrases in English cannot be replaced by definite pronouns, as Postal notes (1994, fn. 24), so the ungrammaticalty of (17) is correlated with the ungrammaticality of (18).

(18) *He told me to read them in that way, but I didn't read them (in) it.

Note that Postal uses the nominal pronoun *it*. Swedish has a distinct proform for manner adverbials, namely *så* (so). It is used both deictically and anaphorically, just like a definite proform. Consequently the Swedish version of (18) is fine. *så* either occurs in the manner adverb position, or fronted.

(19) a. Han sade till mig att läsa  dem  på det  sättet,
        he   told to me  to  read them in  this manner
     b. men jag läste dem  inte så.
        but I   read them not  so
     c. men så läste jag dem  inte.
        but so read I    them not

As expected, Swedish also allows parasitic manner adverbial gaps, at least in principle. I have not come across any actual examples.

(20) Så blir alla som säger *pg* tillsagda att inte säga *t*.
     so get all  that say       told  to  not say
     'All who say it that way are told not to do so.'

## 4.2.5 Summary

I will round off this section by making a few comments on Postal's Pronominal Condition in (11). According to this condition, we should only expect to find parasitic gaps in positions that allow definite pronouns. The condition is successful in excluding a number of potential cases which are ungrammatical in English. From a crosslinguistic perspective, it is highly interesting that if we reformulate the condition slightly and replace *pronoun* with *proform*, it correctly predicts a wider range of parasitic gaps in Swedish. Given that Swedish has proforms for PNs and manner adverbials, it is not surprising that parasitic gaps in those categories are also possible in this language. We noticed that English uses indefinite proforms for PNs, whereas Swedish uses a definite proform (*det*). In the case of manner adverbials, English lacks a proform but Swedish has one that is clearly not nominal. Differences also show up in the ways that VPs can be omitted and/or referred to anaphorically in the two languages. Thus slight differences in the proform systems between languages can have consequences elsewhere in the grammar.

## 4.3    Are All Parasitic Gaps Referential?

### 4.3.1    Amounts and Durations
Cinque also noted some restrictions on what kinds of NPs license parasitic gaps when extracted. In particular, he noted that amount NPs and duration NPs didn't allow parasitic gaps. Let us first look at the example he gives of amounts (Cinque 1990:104).

(21) *Quanti    chili pesa $t$         [senza    credere    di pesare $pg$]?
      how many kilos does-he-weigh  without believing he weighs

According to Cinque, the property that makes (21) unacceptable is the fact that they are nonreferential in the sense introduced in Rizzi (1990). Rizzi makes a distinction between *referential* θ-roles used for participants in an event such as *agent, theme,* or *goal.* Nonreferential θ-roles are *measure* and *manner.* Cinque also notes that such nonreferential phrases cannot be referred to by pronouns, as shown in (22) (= Cinque 1990, chap. 3:(60a)).

(22) *Lui vorrebbe    pesare    cento chili perché *li*      pesa    il suo
      he   would-like to-weigh 100   kilos since   *them* weighs his
      attore preferito.
      actor favorite (i.e., since his favorite actor weighs them)

In fact, Cinque claims that being nonreferential is incompatible with being referred to by a pronominal form.[7] However, it is worth looking carefully at precisely which pronominal form is unavailable. The plural pronoun *li* presumably is intended to refer back to the referent of the plural NP *cento chili* ('100 kilos'). But on the relevant reading of *pesare* ('to weigh'), the object denotes an amount and the question arises whether an amount can be referred to by a plural pronoun like *li.* Consider the following dialogue in Swedish.

(23) a. Du har    väl        aldrig vägt      70 kilo?
         you have PARTICLE never weighed 70 kilos
         'You have never weighted 70 kilos, have you?'
      b. Jo, det/*dem           vägde    jag när    jag väntade barn.
         yes it[+NEUT]/*them weighed I    when I    expected child
         'Yes, that (much) I weighed when I was pregnant.'

Note that the speaker of (23b) refers to the amount by using the singular neuter pronoun *det* ('it'). If she had used the plural form *dem* ('them'), which agrees in number with the antecedent *70 kilo* ('70 kilos'), she would have made a very strange claim. I think the only way this could be interpreted is that the two people were talking about some specific 70 kilos that more than one person could weigh. That is, we get an individual interpretation for the kilos, not the amount interpretation. The demonstrative form that corresponds to the amount reading is *så mycket* ('that much'). Some but not all speakers accept examples like (24) with a parasitic gap interpreted as an amount phrase, where the fronted phrase is a contrastive topic and carries stress.

(24) SÅ mycket vill    ingen   som väger *pg* erkänna att   hon väger *t*.
     that much  wants no-one who weighs    to-admit that she  weighs
     'That much, no one who weighs (that) wants to admit to weighing.'

Let us now turn to measure phrases used in expressing duration, as in (25) (= Cinque 1990, chap. 3:(21a)).

(25) *Quante    settimane ha       passato *t* a  Berlino
     how-many weeks       did-he spend      in Berlin
     [senza aver voluto passare *pg* a   Londra]?
     without wanting   to-spend   in London

Note that the verb *passare*, which requires a duration phrase, is used in both clauses, thereby forcing the unavailable parasitic gap interpretation in the adjunct clause.[8] Swedish examples with duration phrases are unacceptable as well.

(26) *Längre än    tre    timmar får    man inte tillbringa *t* i   labbet
     longer than three hours    may  one  not  spend         in the-lab
     utan att också tillbringa *pg* på tjänsterummet.
     without also    spending    in the-office

I have deliberately added *längre än* ('longer than') to the duration phrase to force the measure reading and prevent an interpretation where one is talking about the same three hours. Still the result is unacceptable. It is tempting at this point to link this to the fact that Swedish does not have a simple proform for durations. Whereas *det* ('it') can be used to refer to weights (see (23b)), it cannot be used for durations or speeds. Instead, you have to use a compound form.[9]

(27) a. En disputation    kan väl       inte vara fem timmar?
        a  thesis-defense can PARTICLE not last  five hours
        'A thesis defense cannot last five hours, can it?'

    b. Jo, så   länge/*det varade min.
      yes, that long/*it    lasted  mine
      'Yes, mine did.'

(28) a. Körde du   över 90?
      drive  you above 90
    b. Nej, så   fort/*det körde jag inte.
      no,  that fast/*it   drove I   not

Cinque uses the thematically based nonreferentiality condition on parasitic gaps to exclude parasitic manner adverbials as well. We have already
looked at manner adverbials in section 4.2.4, where it was noted that
some languages do in fact have proforms for manners.

### 4.3.2  Referentiality and Quantifiers

Cinque also discusses another notion of (non)referentiality that is linked
to the type of quantifier involved. He shows that in order to make the
right predictions concerning which phrases can be extracted in Italian, it
is necessary to distinguish between phrases that are used *strictly referentially* in the sense that they refer to members of a preestablished set (see
Cinque 1990:8, who notes the similarity with Pesetsky's (1987) notion of
"D-linking"). Definite NPs, proper names, and interrogative quantifiers
with *qual-* ('which') are strictly referential phrases whereas quantifiers like
*every* and *no* and bare interrogatives like *che* ('what') are said to be nonreferential. This distinction is relevant to parasitic gaps, he argues, because only the strictly referential type clearly licenses parasitic gaps and
can be resumed by pronominals. Two of his examples are given in (29)
(= Cinque 1990, chap. 3:(92), (96), (98)).

(29) a. (?)Quali libri   hai       presto *t* senza   pagare *pg*/pagarli?
        which books have-you taken    without paying    paying-it
    b.  *Che  posso fare *t* stasera per cena   senza
       what can-I do     tonight for dinner without
       esser in obbligo di mangiare *pg*?
       having-to-eat

Example (29a) shows that the D-linked *wh*-phrase can either license a
parasitic gap in the adjunct clause or be referred back to by a pronoun.
The bare *wh*-word *che* apparently allows neither. Cinque comments
(p. 126) that "parasitic gaps appear to display here a property more
typical of pronominals than of pure variables (they cannot be linked to a
nonreferential operator)." If this is indeed a characteristic property of

parasitic gaps—that they are pronominal and coreferential with a referential phrase or quantifier—we would expect similar facts to hold in other languages as well. Let us look at some data from English, discussed by Chao and Sells (1983).

The main topic of their article is the interpretation of resumptive pronouns. Chao and Sells argue that languages differ in whether or not they make use of resumptive pronouns that are interpreted as bound variables. According to them, English doesn't have resumptive pronouns (i.e., pronouns that have to be interpreted as bound). This would explain the data in (30) (= Chao and Sells 1983, (34, 35)).

(30) a.   I met {every, each, no} influential professor that John sent his book to *t* in order to impress *pg*.

   b.   *I met {every, each, no} influential professor that John sent his book to *t* in order to impress *him*.

They note that in order to get the reading where the nonreferential quantifier *every*, *each*, or *no* binds the argument after *impress*, it is necessary to use a parasitic gap. Inserting a pronoun decreases the availability of this interpretation, according to the authors. It is interesting to compare Chao and Sells's analysis with Cinque's. On the one hand, Chao and Sells make a claim that is similar to Cinque's—namely, that languages that don't use resumptive pronouns avoid using pronouns to refer back to nonreferential antecedents. On the other hand, they show that to get the bound variable reading in English, it is necessary to use a parasitic gap, which is not what we would expect given Cinque's assumption that parasitic gaps are essentially pronominal. Chao and Sells further argue that the choice between a pronoun and a parasitic gap affects the interpretation of sentences like (31) (their (36, 37)).

(31) a.   John owns *some sheep* that Harry keeps healthy *t* by vaccinating *pg* in the spring.

   b.   John owns *some sheep* that Harry keeps healthy *t* by vaccinating *them* in the spring.

Example (31a) with the parasitic-gap/bound-variable interpretation is compatible with a situation in which John owns other sheep that Harry doesn't deal with, whereas (31b) is understood to convey that Harry vaccinates all of John's sheep—that is, the pronoun gets an E-type reading in Evans's (1980) sense.

Cinque's correlation between pronominal status and referential antecedents in Italian cannot be seen in isolation from the way overt and empty pronouns work in Romance languages, as discussed for example by Montalbetti (1984). Chao and Sells take the English data to show that in English, a language that does not have real resumptive pronouns, the preferred interpretation of a pronoun is as an independently referring phrase, not as a bound variable. The differences in judgment concerning the Italian and English data and the differences in the theoretical conclusions reached by Cinque and by Chao and Sells convince me that we need to look more carefully at a range of data from different languages before we can make any general claims about the correlation between referentiality and parasitic gaps. The following section looks at some relevant data from Persian.

### 4.3.3   Referentiality and Specificity

Karimi (1999) argues that there is in fact an even stricter condition that governs the availability of parasitic gaps in Persian. She discusses data like that in (32) (her (3)) where an object NP has been scrambled out of the VP and licenses a parasitic gap. This is apparently only possible if the object is interpreted as specific.

(32)   Kimea [$_{NP}$ *ye kârgar* \*(*ro*)]$_i$ [$_{CP}$ ghablaz inke *pro pg*$_i$ estexdâm
        Kimea      a worker    RÂ       before    that              hiring
        be-kon-e]   be kâr   vâdâsht.
        SUBJ-do-3SG   to work   forced
        'Kimea forced a (specific) worker to work before hiring (her).'

Example (32) is grammatical if the scrambled object is followed by the specificity marker *ro* but not if the marker is absent.[10] An indefinite NP without *ro* is interpreted nonspecifically, by which Karimi understands that it gets either a kind level interpretation or that it is interpreted as part of an event without being individuated. Nonspecific object NPs tend to be placed immediately before the verb and "constitute a semantic unit with the verb" (Karimi 1999:709). The specific object, on the other hand, exists independently of the event, can enter into coreference relations, and can license a parasitic gap.

   The Persian data are interesting and prompt us to look at whether this distinction is relevant in other languages as well. In Swedish, singular NPs are either definite, indefinite, or "bare," in which case they are interpreted nonspecifically in a way that seems quite similar to Persian.

(33)   a.  Kalle köpte   bil-en.
            Kalle bought car-the
            'Kalle bought the car.'

b. Kalle köpte   en bil.
   Kalle bought a   car
   'Kalle bought a car.'
c. Kalle köpte   bil.
   Kalle bought car
   'Kalle became a car owner.'

Utterances like (33c) are used to convey that Kalle has changed his status; he has gone from being carless to being a car owner. Although you can infer the existence of a car, it is not important which car he has bought. Contrary to the case in Persian, however, this kind of nonspecific NP also licenses parasitic gaps when fronted.

(34) a. Dator      ville     alla som hade råd med *pg* köpa *t* med en gång.
        computer wanted all  that could afford     buy    at once
        'All that could afford a computer wanted to buy one at once.'
     b. Bil bör       man inte köpa *t* utan att ha råd med *pg*.
        car should you  not buy      without to afford
        'You shouldn't buy a car if you can't afford it.'

Interestingly enough, the proform used for these bare NPs is the singular definite neuter pronoun *det*. The utterance in (34a) could also be conveyed using the contrastive dislocation form in (35).

(35) Dator,              det         ville      alla som hade hade råd med *pg*
     computer[−NEUT] it[+NEUT] wanted all  that could afford
     köpa *t* med en gång.
     buy    at once
     'All that could afford a computer wanted to buy one at once.'

Consider also the example in (36) which is most naturally uttered with stress on the adjective (*bra*).

(36) En BRA student vill    alla som träffar *pg* gärna   handleda *t*.
     a  good student want all  that meet        rather supervise
     'Everyone who meets a GOOD student would like to supervise him or her.'

The fronted indefinite NP doesn't refer to a particular student; rather it refers to a kind of student. It is interesting that the natural English paraphrase takes the form of a so-called donkey sentence. *Him* or *her* is interpreted as bound by the indefinite *a good student* inside the relative clause.

   Both Cinque and Karimi assume in their analyses that good antecedents for parasitic gaps must be D-linked—that is, interpreted as referring to some specific referent available in the discourse context. If this was a universally valid restriction, we would only expect to find parasitic gaps with those NPs that assert or presuppose the existence of referents; for instance, monotone increasing quantifiers in Barwise and Cooper's (1981) sense. When we look more closely at the range of NPs that allow parasitic gaps in Swedish, it turns out that monotone decreasing quantifiers also allow parasitic gaps. A few examples are given below.

(37) a.  Nuförtiden är det få böcker     som jag skulle våga ge *t*
         nowadays there are few books that I would dare give
         till min dotter   utan att själv ha läst *pg*.
         to my daughter without having read myself
     b.  Det finns inga fakturor som jag skulle våga skriva på *t*
         there are no bills        that I would dare sign
         utan att granska *pg* först.
         without checking first

Even if *få* ('few') in (37a) doesn't introduce any referents, one might nevertheless argue that it is a cardinality predicate that presupposes a non-empty set of appropriate books.[11] But *inga* ('no') in (37b) denies the existence of a particular kind of bill. The examples in (36) and (37) show that it cannot be a universally valid constraint that parasitic gaps must have referential or specific antecedents. Rather, one needs to look at what types of NPs can be fronted, or scrambled, in the language in question, as this seems to determine what types of parasitic gaps are possible.

## 4.4   Island Sensitivity

In the preceding sections, I discussed the considerable variation among languages regarding the contexts where parasitic gaps are felicitous and the types of antecedents they can take. As a final example, let us look at a claim made by Kayne (1984: chap. 8), Cinque (1990: chap. 3), Postal (1994), and others. The claim is that although parasitic gaps can occur in phrases that are normally islands, they are nevertheless island sensitive. As Cinque puts it, "In general, they seem to be able to violate one, but not more than one, island at the time" (1990:133). As evidence, he gives examples like the following (Cinque's (119a) and (123a)). Example (38a) involves a parasitic gap in a relative clause modifying the subject and is fairly acceptable. However, if the parasitic gap is embedded inside another relative clause as in (38b), the result is apparently strongly ungrammatical.

(38) a.  ?E′  un uomo che [chiunque  incontri *pg* una volta]
          he-is a  man   that those-who meet        once
          non può dimenticare *t*.
          cannot  forget

  b.  **E′  una donna  che [chiunque conosca [qualcuno che
          she-is a   woman that  whoever knows    someone who
          ama *pg*]] non può non considerare *t* fortunata.
          likes     cannot but consider       lucky

Postal (1994) formulates an explicit condition as in (39) (= Postal's (59))

(39) *Postal's Island Condition*
     A P-gap "licensed" by a gap G cannot occur internal to an island Σ
     not containing G unless Σ is coextensive with the entire parasitic
     domain.

Both Cinque and Postal use the term "island" in a rather general way.
However, what is an island in one language is not necessarily an island in
other languages. For instance, certain extractions out of complex NPs
such as relative clauses are not only acceptable but quite productive in
Swedish (Engdahl 1982, 1997).

(40) a.  Engelska finns det   många som förstår *t*.
          English   exist there many  that understand
          'There are many who understand English.'

  b.  Det där låset är det bara Pelle som kan låsa upp *t*.
          that    lock is it  only Pelle who can unlock
          'It is only Pelle that can unlock that lock.'

Example (40a) is a presentational construction, and (40b) is a cleft. These
two types are the most common in my corpus of extractions out of relative clauses in Swedish, but other constructions are also possible. In Engdahl (1997) I concluded that it is not so much the structural properties of
the utterance as certain pragmatic conditions that are relevant for determining when an extraction is possible in Swedish. Given that relative
clauses don't act as islands in some contexts in Swedish, it is not surprising that we don't find the sharp difference in acceptability that Cinque
and Postal report for Italian and English, respectively. Consider the pairs
of examples in (41) and (42).

(41) a.  Det är en kvinna  som var och en [som hör talas om *pg*] vill
          it  is a  woman that everyone    that hears    about   wants
          dansa med *t*.
          dance with

'It is a woman that everyone that hears about (her) wants to dance with.'

b. Det är en kvinna  som var och en [som hör talas om
   it  is a  woman that everyone     that hears     about
   någon   [som fått dansa  med *pg*]] också vill    dansa med *t*.
   someone that has danced with      also   wants dance with
   'It is a woman that everone that hears about someone who has
   danced with (her) also wants to dance with.'

(42) a. Här är en artikel som jag lade undan *t* [utan     att läsa *pg*].
        here is an article that I   put away      without to read
     b. Här är en artikel som jag lade undan *t* [utan     att hitta
        here is an article that I   put away      without to find
        [någon   som ville    läsa *pg*]]
        anyone who wanted to-read
        'Here is an article that I put away without finding anyone who
        wanted to read.'

The sentences in (41a) and (42a) are familiar examples of parasitic gaps in relativized subjects and adjunct clauses. In (41b) and (42b), the parasitic gap is further embedded inside a relative clause, but this has very little (if any) effect on the acceptability. I believe that the lack of contrast in these cases is due to the fact that these relative clauses don't function as islands in Swedish. In fact, one of the most common type of parasitic gap construction in this language is shown in (43).

(43) a. Engelska finns det   många [som förstår *t*    utan     att kunna
        English   exist there many   that understand without to be-able
        tala *pg* särskilt     bra].
        to-talk particularly well
        'There are many who understand English without being able to
        speak it particularly well.'
     b. Det där låset är det bara Pelle [som kan låsa upp *t* utan     att
        that    lock, is it only Pelle that can unlock     without to
        förstöra *pg*].
        damage
        'That lock, Pelle is the only one who can unlock (it) without
        damaging (it).'

Here the "real gap" is inside a relative clause and the parasitic gap is inside an adjunct clause that is part of the relative clause. If we don't have a relativized notion of "island," both gaps would be inside islands and hence the sentences should be unacceptable.

Given a relativized notion of extraction possibilities, we should look for positions in Swedish where extractions are impossible and check what happens with parasitic gaps. One strong structurally based constraint that doesn't seem to be affected by pragmatic factors is the constraint against extracting the highest subject in a relative clause, as shown in (44).

(44) a. Den filmen$_j$ var   det   många$_i$ som $t_i$ blev imponerade av $t_j$.
        that film   were there many   that   were impressed   by
        'There were many that were impressed by that film.'
     b. *Den filmen$_j$ var   det   många$_i$ som $t_j$ imponerade på $t_i$.
        that film   were there many   that   impressed
        'There were many that that film impressed.'

The same contrast shows up with parasitic gaps. Example (45a) with a parasitic gap in the object position of a relative clause is acceptable, but (45b) where the subject gap is parasitic is clearly impossible.

(45) a. Den här filmen$_i$ rekommenderade alla$_j$ [som $t_j$ blev imponerade
        this     film   recommended     all   that   were impressed
        av $pg_i$] sina vänner att se $t_i$.
        by       their friends to see
        'All that were impressed by this film recommended their friends to see it.'
     b. *Den här filmen$_i$ rekommenderade alla$_j$ [som $pg_i$
        this     film   recommended     all   that
        imponerade på $t_j$] sina vänner att se $t_i$.
        impressed       their friends to see
        'All that this film impressed recommended their friends to see it.'

## 4.5  Conclusion

In some languages it appears that the distinction between NPs and non-NPs is important for predicting the distribution of parasitic gaps, but this is not always the case as the Swedish data discussed here show.[12] Some languages require specific antecedents for parasitic gaps, but we have seen that this is also not a universal restriction. I have suggested that there is indeed a correlation with the availability of proforms in the language, as suggested by Cinque and Postal, but that the existing patterns are not as restricted as was previously thought. Instead, the pattern that emerges suggests that parasitic gaps are very versatile devices, both crosslinguistically and within a particular language. Consequently, we cannot analyze

parasitic gaps as an isolated phenomenon but need to look at the way
they interact with, for example, the proform system and the NP denotation types in various languages.

One question that remains to be resolved is whether what we call parasitic gaps is a uniform phenomenon. Engdahl (1983) made a distinction
between *obligatory* parasitic gaps preceding the real gap (essentially those
inside subjects) and *optional* parasitic gaps following the real gap (essentially those in adjuncts). This distinction reflected judgments that it is
harder to replace gaps inside subjects with proforms than gaps inside
adjuncts.[13] The same difference showed up in the extended survey I con-
ducted to gather data for this article. If a person gave different judgments
on pairs of examples, it was always in the same direction: parasitic gaps
inside subjects were more acceptable than parasitic gaps inside adjuncts.
Clearly there is more to find out about parasitic gaps.

**Notes**

I presented some of the crosslinguistic differences discussed in this chapter in the
Parametric Variation workshop at the Centre for Cognitive Science, Edinburgh, in
1992. I am grateful to the editors of this volume for prompting me to write this
chapter and for helpful comments. For the present version, I have benefited from
discussing the data with friends and colleagues in Göteborg. Klaus von Bremen,
Benjamin Lyngfelt, Joakim Nivre, and Torbjørn Nordgård have given me helpful
comments on a previous draft.

1. This example was brought to my attention by Roger Higgins. For clarity, I
indicate parasitic gaps with *pg* and real gaps with *t*.

2. To my knowledge, the first theoretical discussion of the construction can be
found in Ross 1967 (chap. 4). The term "parasitic gap" was suggested independently in Engdahl 1980 and by T. Taraldsen in a GLOW talk in 1980 (published
1981).

3. The directional-locative distinction is maintained in the relative and interrogative pronoun system in Swedish as well.

4. I have come across one Swedish speaker who does not like AP parasitic gaps at
all. More work is needed in order to establish how common this is.

5. For clarity I have indicated the source location of the fronted VP even when
the proform *göra* is present. There is still a contrast between (9) and (7b) even
when this example is amended with *göra*-support as in (i).

(i) Kommit hem  hade han gjort *t* utan     att  hans pappa hade gjort *\*pg*/det.
    come      home had  he  done   without that his   father  had done
    'He had come home without his father having (done so).'

Example (i) is grammatical if a proform (*det*) is inserted. I suspect that the ill-
formedness has to do with the fact that the fronted VP and the VP in the adjunct
clause have different subjects, but more research is clearly needed.

6. Andersson (1974, 1982) coined the term "topic movement" for this kind of fronting. It is often combined with a stressed initial phrase, as in (i), in which case the result is often called "contrastive dislocation."

(i) Läkare, det$_i$ skulle jag aldrig vilja bli $t_i$.
doctor  it   would I   never want become
'Doctor, I would never like to become (one).'

7. This is quite similar to Postal's Pronominal Condition in (11), but Cinque's claim is based on a different class of examples.

8. Not all examples in the literature observe this. For instance, in (i), taken from Emonds 1991 (p. 91), the duration phrase is an optional modifier in both clauses.

(i) *How long does John drink $t$ before lecturing $pg$?

9. As expected, both examples are acceptable with the proform $det$ ('it') if it can be interpreted as referring to the whole VP.

(i)  Jo, det gjorde min.
yes it   did    mine
'Yes, mine did.'

(ii) Nej, det gjorde jag inte.
no   it   did    I   not
'No, I didn't.'

10. Karimi also discusses examples with specific definite NPs.

11. This was suggested to me by Helen de Hoop (personal communication). See also example (27) from Chao and Sells.

12. According to Torbjørn Nordgård (personal communication), parasitic gaps in Norwegian are similar to the Swedish cases, with the same provisos regarding speaker variation.

13. Engdahl (1993) suggested that there might be a connection with crossover facts. See also Cinque 1990 (pp. 150–151).

# Chapter 5

| Parasitic Gaps and Resumptive Pronouns | Jamal Ouhalla |
|---|---|

## 5.1 Introduction

Parasitic gaps have been claimed to take the form of a null pronoun (Cinque 1990, Postal 1993b). The fact that parasitic gaps have an obligatory bound reading with respect to the *wh*-operator in the root clause makes them superficially similar to resumptive pronouns, both null and overt. This chapter explores the question whether parasitic gaps, insofar as they are null pronouns, are or are not instances of resumptive pronouns. It does so by comparing the properties of parasitic gap constructions (PG-constructions) with those of parallel constructions from Moroccan Arabic (MA) which include an overt pronoun in the position corresponding to the parasitic gap, as well as with classic examples of resumption. The conclusion reached is that parasitic gaps are indeed instances of resumptive pronouns. Moreover, some of their peculiar properties arguably make better sense in the context of an analysis that treats them as null resumptive pronouns.

Section 5.2 introduces PG-constructions, the corresponding constructions in MA, as well as classic contexts of resumption. The three constructions are compared to each other, and certain initial differences between them are explained. Section 5.3 provides a definition of resumptive pronouns and the contexts in which they are licensed, and shows that the null pronoun in PG-constructions and the overt pronoun in the corresponding MA constructions are both consistent with this definition of resumptive pronouns. This section also shows how the conclusion that parasitic gaps are null resumptive pronouns explains some properties of PG-constructions, including the "anti-c-command requirement." Section 5.4 discusses some properties of resumptive pronouns which show that their interpretation cannot be said to involve the mechanism of (free) indexing. These properties are more consistent with the view that the interpretation of resumptive pronouns involves movement of the resumptive pronoun to its *wh*-antecedent. The movement analysis of resumptive pronouns, including the null pronoun in PG-constructions, is shown to account for additional properties of PG-constructions. Finally, section 5.5 addresses the issue relating to the S-structure effects in the licensing of parasitic gaps. These effects are shown to follow from the null property of the pronoun in PG-constructions that requires it to undergo movement in overt syntax. Section 5.5 also addresses the question why MA, unlike English, lacks PG-constructions.

## 5.2   Parasitic Gaps and Pronouns

Examples (1a,b) show adjunct PG-constructions from English. Their MA counterparts (2a,b) include a clitic pronoun in the position of the parasitic gap:[1]

(1)  a.  Which article did he criticize before reading?
     b.  This is the article he criticized before reading?

(2)  a.  Shmen maqal ntaqd        qblma yqra     h?
         which  article he-criticized before reading it
         'Which article did he criticize before reading?'
     b.  Hada huwwa l-maqal   lli    ntaqd        qblma yqra     h.
         this   is       the-article that he-criticized before reading it
         'This is the article he criticized before reading.'

As is well known, there is evidence suggesting that parasitic gaps are null pronouns (Cinque 1990, Postal 1993b). Part of the evidence relates to the fact that parasitic gaps are restricted to DPs (Aoun and Clark 1985, Cinque 1990). This is shown in (3a,b), which are cited by Postal (1993b:736) and attributed to Emonds (1985:91):

(3)  a.  *How sick did John look without actually feeling?
     b.  *How long does John drink before lecturing?

   In the rest of this chapter, I will take the conclusion that parasitic gaps are null pronouns to be basically correct and proceed to compare them with the corresponding constructions in MA (with overt pronouns).

   The idea that parasitic gaps are null pronouns obviously brings PG-constructions closer to the MA constructions illustrated in (2a,b). Both include a pronoun inside the adjunct phrase which is somehow linked to the *wh*-operator in the root clause. They appear to differ only in that the pronoun is null in PG-constructions and overt in the corresponding MA constructions. Whether the two constructions are indeed similar is an empirical question that is one of the major concerns of this paper. To the extent that the two constructions are similar, any differences between them are expected to be reducible to the difference in the null versus overt property of the pronoun in the adjunct phrase. In this section, I discuss one major difference that appears to be reducible to the difference in the null versus overt property of the pronoun. Other differences are discussed in various sections below.

The difference in question relates to the interpretation of the pronoun. In PG-constructions, the null pronoun has an obligatory bound reading whereby it is bound by the *wh*-operator in the root clause. The sentence in (4a), for example, cannot have a reading whereby the null pronoun refers to a discourse antecedent, such as "the pupil's teacher" (4c).

(4) a.   Which pupil did they expel without interviewing?
    b.   Which pupil$_i$ did they expel $e_i$ [without interviewing $pro_i$]
    c.   *Which pupil$_i$ did they expel $e_i$ [without interviewing $pro_j$]

In contrast, the corresponding overt pronoun in the MA example (5a) can have a nonbound reading (5c), in addition to a bound reading (5b). In an appropriate context, (5a) can have a reading whereby the pronoun refers to "the pupil's teacher."

(5) a. Shmen tlmid Terdu        blama   yshufu h?
       which  pupil they-expelled without seeing him
       'Which pupil did they expel without interviewing?'
    b. Shmen tlmid$_i$ Terdu        $e_i$ [blama    yshufu h$_i$]
       which  pupil they-expelled     without seeing him
    c. Shmen tlmid$_i$ Terdu        $e_i$ [blama    yshufu h$_j$]
       which  pupil they-expelled     without seeing him

The overt pronoun in the MA example (5a) has the interpretive properties usually associated with pronouns. It can take its antecedent either from the sentence that includes it (bound reading) or from the context (nonbound reading). In contrast, the null pronoun in PG-constructions, at least initially, does not appear to have the interpretive properties of pronouns. The obligatory bound reading it has is more akin to that of variable traces of *wh*-movement. However, the fact that parasitic gaps can only correspond to DPs excludes the possibility that they are variable traces of a null *wh*-operator. This is because null operators are not restricted to DPs (Postal 1993b). Postal (1993b) suggests that parasitic gaps are null pronouns that undergo movement. Movement of the null pronoun by itself does not explain the obligatory bound reading. The latter is assumed to be the consequence of an obligatory Control relation that holds between the null pronoun and the overt *wh*-operator.

On the assumption that Control is a property of null pronouns and does not apply to overt pronouns, Postal's analysis is consistent with the observation above that any differences between PG-constructions and the corresponding MA constructions with an overt pronoun must reduce to the null versus overt property of the pronoun in the adjunct phrase. The analysis of parasitic gaps defended here borrows from Postal's analysis the idea that parasitic gaps are null pronouns that undergo movement. However, it does away with an additional mechanism of interpretation to explain the obligatory bound reading of the null pronoun on the ground that it is unnecessary.[2]

Another explanation for the obligatory bound reading of the null pronoun in PG-constructions is outlined by Cinque (1990). The explanation is based on two independently motivated ideas. First, the null pronoun, like all empty categories, is subject to an identification requirement. Secondly, Ā-binding is a form of identification (see also Rizzi 1990). According to this analysis, the nonbound reading for the null pronoun in PG-constructions is excluded by whatever condition requires null categories to be identified. It is not due to some inherent interpretive feature of the pronoun that requires it to be bound. The pronoun in the corresponding MA constructions is not subject to identification because it is overt. Consequently, it can have a nonbound reading. It should be clear that this analysis also reduces the difference between PG-constructions and the corresponding MA constructions with an overt pronoun to the null versus overt property of the pronoun.

Although the obligatory bound reading of the pronoun in PG-constructions appears to be a consequence of its null property, the obligatory bound reading is not an exclusive property of null pronouns. Overt pronouns too can be found in contexts where they have an obligatory bound reading, in particular the classic contexts of resumption illustrated in (6a,b).

(6) a. Shmen maqal nsiti       fin      qriti      h?
        which  article you-forgot where you-read it
        'Which article have you forgotten where you read?'
    b. Shmen maqal saferti       l Casablanca blama  tqra      h?
        which  article you-traveled to Casablanca without reading it
        'Which article did you travel to Casablanca without reading?'

If it is indeed the case that pronouns generally never have interpretive features that require them to be bound, the obligatory bound reading of the resumptive pronouns in (6) must be due to some other factor. I would like to suggest that it is due to the resumption context in which the pronoun is included.

The examples in (6) are best compared to (5a). Recall that the overt pronoun in (5a) can either have a bound reading (5b) or a nonbound reading (5c). Identifying the property that distinguishes this context from the ones in (6a,b) will provide an explanation for why the overt pronoun in (6a,b) can only have a bound reading. Example (5a) includes a variable trace in the root clause bound by the *wh*-operator. Consequently, even if the pronoun inside the adjunct phrase is assigned a different index, the *wh*-operator in the root clause still has a variable to bind. However, if the resumptive pronoun in (6a,b) is assigned an index different from that of the *wh*-operator, the operator will not have a variable to bind, in violation of the ban on vacuous quantification (Chomsky 1986a). Thus, the obligatory bound reading is excluded in (6a,b) not because the resumptive pronoun has a special property that requires it to be bound. Rather, it is excluded because it leads to a representation where the *wh*-operator does not have a variable to bind.[3]

If the explanation just provided for the obligatory bound reading of resumptive pronouns is plausible, it is possible to maintain the generalization that pure pronouns, including resumptive pronouns, never carry an interpretive feature that requires them to be bound. In PG-constructions, the obligatory bound reading of the null pronoun is due to its null property, which requires that it be identified by a related overt category in the sentence. In the classic contexts of resumption such as (6a,b), the obligatory bound reading of the overt pronoun is due to the ban on vacuous quantification. If the resumptive pronoun is assigned an index that is different from that of the *wh*-operator, the *wh*-operator will not have a variable to bind.

Although this conclusion makes it clear that the null pronoun in PG-constructions and the overt resumptive pronoun in the classic contexts of resumption have an obligatory bound reading for entirely different reasons, it does not necessarily have any implications for the question whether the null pronoun in PG-constructions is or is not an instance of a resumptive pronoun. Whether the null pronoun in PG-constructions is an instance of a resumptive pronoun is an empirical question that must be settled on the basis of clear ideas about the properties of resumptive pronouns and their licensing. This question is the main topic of discussion in the next section.

To summarize, this section prepared the ground for a comparison between parasitic gaps and resumptive pronouns in the subsequent sections by spelling out three ideas on which the comparison is based. First, parasitic gaps are null pronouns (Cinque 1990, Postal 1993b). Second, the obligatory bound reading of the null pronoun in PG-constructions is due to its null property rather than to some inherent interpretive feature that requires it to be bound. And third, the obligatory bound reading of overt resumptive pronouns in classic contexts of resumption is due to properties of the context in which they are included rather than to the interpretive properties of the pronoun.

### 5.3   Parasitic Gaps and Resumptive Pronouns

This section addresses the question whether the null pronoun in PG-constructions shares any properties with resumptive pronouns. As pointed out in section 5.2, a proper discussion of this issue must be based on a clear definition of resumptive pronouns.

Sells (1984) defines resumptive pronouns as pronouns that are "operator-bound." Operator-binding is in turn defined as binding by an operator that occupies an $\bar{\text{A}}$-position at S-structure. Situations involving binding by an operator situated in an A-position at S-structure, such as *Every pupil thinks that the teacher likes him (best),* do not involve operator-binding. Instead, they involve a relation called "anaphoric binding." Contexts that involve a genuine operator-binding relation are classic contexts of resumption, illustrated by the MA examples in (6), repeated here as (7).

(7) a.  Shmen maqal nsiti        fin      qriti        h?
         which  article you-forgot where you-read it
         'Which article have you forgotten where you read?'
    b.  Shmen maqal saferti        l Casablanca  blama  tqra      h?
         which  article you-traveled to Casablanca without reading it
         'Which article did you travel to Casablanca without reading?'

According to Sells, genuine cases of resumption do not exist in English. For some reason, English pronouns can never have a resumptive function. It follows from this observation that the pronoun in examples such as *Which pupil thinks (that) the teacher likes him (best)?* is not an instance of resumption even though the *wh*-antecedent of the pronoun occupies an

$\bar{A}$-position at S-structure (at least on the vacuous movement hypothesis). According to Sells (1984), the pronoun in such constructions is an E-type pronoun rather than a resumptive pronoun, although he does not provide a definition of resumptive pronouns that explicitly excludes such cases. To exclude such cases, I would like to introduce the notion "direct ($\bar{A}$-) binding" defined as in (8).

(8) $\alpha$ directly $\bar{A}$-binds $\beta$ iff $\alpha$ $\bar{A}$-binds $\beta$, and there is no $\gamma$, $\gamma$ a trace of $\alpha$ that c-commands $\beta$.

In contexts where $\alpha$ is a moved *wh*-operator, $\beta$ a pronoun coindexed with the *wh*-operator, and $\gamma$ the trace of the *wh*-operator, (8) basically says that the *wh*-operator does not directly $\bar{A}$-bind the pronoun if the trace of the *wh*-operator c-commands the pronoun. In such contexts, the trace of the *wh*-operator blocks the *wh*-operator from directly $\bar{A}$-binding the pronoun. In sections 5.4 and 5.5, I show that the blocking effect by a c-commanding trace described in (8) is not very different from the interception effects familiar from the core cases of Relativized Minimality. Incorporating (8) into Sells's definition of resumptive pronouns and adapting ideas from Aoun and Li (1990) and Montalbetti (1984), we obtain the definition stated in (9).

(9) A pronoun P is resumptive iff there exists an operator O such that O directly $\bar{A}$-binds P at S-structure.

Classic contexts of resumption such as (7a,b) do not include a trace of the *wh*-operator that c-commands the pronoun. Thus, the pronoun they include qualifies as a resumptive pronoun, consistent with (9). In contrast, the English example *Which pupil thinks that the teacher likes him (best)?* includes a trace of the *wh*-operator (in the subject position) that c-commands the pronoun. Therefore, the pronoun it includes does not qualify as a resumptive pronoun.

The relationship of direct $\bar{A}$-binding defined in (8) and included in (9) is to be understood, for the moment, as a narrow form of (mere) $\bar{A}$-binding. In section 5.4, a different interpretation is given to the notion "direct $\bar{A}$-binding." Crucially, the notion of direct $\bar{A}$-binding is not intended to replace the notion of mere $\bar{A}$-binding. Although the *wh*-operator does not directly $\bar{A}$-bind the pronoun in *Which pupil thinks that the teacher likes him (best)?,* the *wh*-operator does (merely) $\bar{A}$-bind the pronoun.

The definition of resumptive pronouns in (9) needs further refinement having to do with strong pronouns. In MA, it is possible for a strong pronoun to cooccur with a weak pronoun in the direct object position in contexts such as (10):[4]

(10) a. Shmen tlmid kayDen belli l-mu'allima katbghi h (huwwa)?
which pupil believes that the-teacher likes him (HIM)
'Which pupil believes that the teacher likes him?'
   b. Shmen mu'allima qalt belli l-mudir      tehm    a (hiyya)?
which teacher    said that the-headmaster accused her (HER)
'Which teacher said that the headmaster accused her?'

The strong pronoun in (10a,b) is not directly Ā-bound by the *wh*-operator
as the sentence includes a trace of the *wh*-operator (in the root subject
position) that c-commands the position of the pronoun. Interestingly, a
strong pronoun cannot cooccur with a clitic pronoun in a position that is
directly Ā-bound by a *wh*-operator. Thus, the strong pronoun is excluded
from genuine contexts of resumption such as (11a,b).

(11) a. Shmen Talib    nsiti      fin     tlaqiti    h (*huwwa)?
which student you-forgot where you-met him (HIM)
'Which student have you forgotten where you met?'
   b. Shmen Talib    saferti     qblma yTerdu    h (*huwwa)?
which student you-traveled before they-expelled him (HIM)
'Which student did you travel before they expelled?'

The sentences in (10a,b) and (11a,b) together lead to the descriptive generalization in (12). In view of the definition of resumptive pronouns in (9),
the generalization in (12) amounts to saying that strong pronouns cannot
function as resumptive pronouns in MA. Only weak pronouns can. Understood as such, (12) turns out to be a language-specific generalization
that is part of a broader generalization stated by Postal (1994b) on independent grounds and reproduced in (12') (see also Aoun and Li 1990,
McCloskey 1990, and Montalbetti 1984, among others).

(12)  A strong pronoun cannot be directly Ā-bound in MA.

(12')  "All RPs are weak definite pronouns." (Postal 1994b, p. 178)

For the moment, the notions "weak pronoun" and "strong pronoun"
remain undefined, and the reason why weak pronouns are compatible
with the resumptive function but strong pronouns are not remains unexplained. These issues are dealt with in section 5.4.

We are now in a position to provide a more accurate working definition
of resumptive pronouns: (13) is the definition of resumptive pronouns that
will be adopted in the rest of this paper. The class of weak pronouns referred to in (13) includes clitic pronouns as well as null pronouns.

(13)  A pronoun P is resumptive iff P is weak and there exists an
operator O such that O directly Ā-binds P at S-structure.

The definition in (13) raises some obvious questions that a proper analysis of resumption must address. For example, why are resumptive pronouns licensed by the narrow relation of direct $\bar{A}$-binding instead of the broader relation of $\bar{A}$-binding? Why can't strong pronouns be directly $\bar{A}$-bound? Why are resumptive pronouns licensed at S-structure and not at the later level of LF? These questions, among others, are addressed in various sections to come. The rest of this section is devoted to finding out if the null pronoun in PG-constructions and its overt counterpart in the corresponding MA constructions are or are not members of the class of resumptive pronouns as defined in (13).

Starting with PG-constructions, it turns out that the null pronoun they include is consistent with (13) in a fairly straightforward way. The null pronoun belongs to the weak class and, moreover, is directly $\bar{A}$-bound by the *wh*-operator at S-structure. As is well known, the trace of the *wh*-operator in the root clause does not c-command the position of the parasitic gap. Therefore, the trace of the *wh*-operator does not prevent the *wh*-operator from directly $\bar{A}$-binding the null pronoun in the parasitic gap:

(14) a. Which article did he criticize before reading?
   b. Which article did [he criticize $t_{\text{which article}}$ [before reading *pro*]]?

The null pronoun in (14) also satisfies the identification requirement via direct $\bar{A}$-binding by the *wh*-operator. This is basically the view outlined by Cinque (1990), except that in the present context the relationship between the null pronoun and the *wh*-operator takes the narrow form of direct $\bar{A}$-binding instead of the broader form of mere $\bar{A}$-binding. The narrow relationship of $\bar{A}$-binding works just as well for examples such as (15), which Cinque (1990) analyzes as involving a null resumptive pronoun inside the adjunct phrase. As in (14), the null pronoun in (15) is identified by the *wh*-operator in the root clause which directly $\bar{A}$-binds it.

(15) a. Which article did you travel to London without reading?
   b. Which article did you travel to London [without reading *pro*]?

The sentences in (15) and (14) show two different contexts where the null pronoun is licensed via direct $\bar{A}$-binding by a *wh*-operator. As is well known, null pronouns can also be licensed via rich agreement inflection (Rizzi 1986). However, because English lacks rich agreement inflection, null pronouns can only be licensed via direct $\bar{A}$-binding. When considered in relation to the definition of resumption in terms of direct $\bar{A}$-binding by a *wh*-operator, this conclusion amounts to saying that null pronouns can only be found in resumption contexts in English. This property of English will be clarified at a later point.

The conclusion that the null pronoun in PG-constructions is resumptive turns out to be compatible with well-known properties of PG-constructions. One such property, known as the "anti c-command requirement," can be seen in examples such as (16) adapted from Chomsky (1986b:54).

(16)  a.  *Who saw you before you recognized?
      b.  *Who [$t_{who}$ saw you [before you recognized *pro*]?

In (16) the trace of the *wh*-operator c-commands the position of the parasitic gap. Compared to (14), example (16) is said to show that parasitic gaps are licensed by *wh*-traces that do not c-command them. It is widely recognized that this licensing relationship is at best mysterious, because licensing in dependency relations in general holds under the c-command requirement and fails to hold when the c-command requirement is not met. According to the analysis outlined for (14), the parasitic gap is licensed by the *wh*-operator that directly Ā-binds it rather than by the variable trace of the *wh*-operator that does not c-command it. The variable trace of the *wh*-operator plays no role in the licensing of the parasitic gap. According to this analysis, (16) is excluded because the null pronoun in the parasitic gap fails to be licensed via direct Ā-binding by the *wh*-operator. The variable trace of the *wh*-operator in the subject position c-commands the null pronoun and consequently prevents the *wh*-operator from directly Ā-binding the pronoun.[5]

The anti-c-command requirement, which is probably the most mysterious property of parasitic gaps, turns out to be their most revealing. It indicates that parasitic gaps must be null resumptive pronouns—as it is, resumptive pronouns that must (by definition) be directly Ā-bound. Parasitic gaps are licensed in contexts where they are directly Ā-bound by a *wh*-operator (i.e., resumption contexts). Example (14) is a resumption context, but (16) is not.

Another property of PG-constructions that also falls out from the analysis outlined here is illustrated in (17) (Chomsky 1982:44). Example (17) is said to show that parasitic gaps are licensed at S-structure and cannot be licensed at the later level of LF. Assuming that *wh*-in-situ raise at LF, leaving a variable trace behind, this process does not lead to the licensing of the parasitic gap in (17).

(17)  a.  *I forgot who filed which article without reading.
      b.  *I forgot who filed [which article] [without reading *pro*]

The property of parasitic gaps illustrated in (17) is also revealing of their nature as null resumptive pronouns because it is resumptive pronouns that are licensed at S-structure (by definition). Example (17) is excluded on the ground that it does not constitute a resumption context in which the null pronoun can be licensed. Although (17) includes a *wh*-operator, the *wh*-operator does not c-command the null pronoun at S-structure and therefore does not directly $\bar{\text{A}}$-bind the null pronoun at S-structure.

Other well-known properties of PG-constructions are shown in later sections to receive equally plausible explanations on the view that parasitic gaps are null resumptive pronouns that can only be licensed via direct $\bar{\text{A}}$-binding by a *wh*-operator at S-structure. For the moment, I will turn to the overt pronoun in corresponding MA constructions with the purpose of finding out if it too is consistent with the definition of resumptive pronouns adopted.

The overt pronoun in the corresponding MA constructions is also trivially consistent with (14). The pronoun belongs to the weak class and is directly $\bar{\text{A}}$-bound by the *wh*-operator at S-structure. As in PG-constructions, the trace of the *wh*-operator in the root clause does not c-command the pronoun.

(18) a.  Shmen Talib    ntaqdu        qblma ytlaqaw h (*huwwa)?
         which  student they-criticized before meeting him (HIM)
         'Which student did they criticize before meeting?'
     b.  Shmen Talib    ntaqdu        $t_{\text{shmen Talib}}$ [qblma ytlaqaw [h]]?
         which  student they-criticized            before meeting him

As shown in (18a), a strong pronoun is excluded from cooccurring with the clitic pronoun. This fact confirms that the position of the pronoun inside the adjunct phrase is indeed $\bar{\text{A}}$-bound, and that the MA constructions are legitimate resumption contexts for the pronoun.

So far, the parallelism with PG-constructions appears to hold. However, the parallelism breaks down in relation to examples such as (19) with a subject *wh*-operator instead of an object *wh*-operator. Unlike (16), examples (19a,b) are perfectly acceptable with a bound reading for the pronoun.

(19) a.  Shmen Talib    xrj qblma tshuf    u?
         which  student left before you-see him
         'Which student left before you could see him?'
     b.  Shmen maqal tnshar        blama yqra    h?
         which  article got-published without he-read it
         'Which article appeared without him reading it?'

If (19a,b) include a trace of the *wh*-operator in the root subject position, they do not constitute legitimate resumption contexts for the pronoun.

The trace of the *wh*-operator, which c-commands the pronoun, blocks direct Ā-binding of the pronoun by the *wh*-operator. One could perhaps argue that the pronoun in this particular context is licensed as a non-resumptive pronoun and its relationship with the *wh*-operator is one of mere Ā-binding instead of direct Ā-binding. Given that the pronoun is overt, and therefore not dependent on direct Ā-binding for identification, this view is consistent with the claim that any differences between PG-constructions and the corresponding MA construction with an overt pronoun reduce to the null versus overt property of the pronoun inside the adjunct phrase.[6]

However, the view that the pronoun in (19a,b) is not directly Ā-bound by the *wh*-operator is inconsistent with another property of these constructions, illustrated in (20). A strong pronoun cannot cooccur with the clitic pronoun in this particular context:

(20) a. Shmen Talib    xrj qblma tshuf    u (*huwwa)?
        which  student left before you-see him (HIM)
        'Which student left before you could see him?'

    b. Shmen mu'allim xda l-taqa'ud    qblma yTerdu
        which  teacher    took-retirement before they-expelled
        h (*huwwa)?
        him (HIM)
        'Which teacher retired before they expelled him?'

Earlier, we saw that strong pronouns are excluded from positions that are directly Ā-bound by a *wh*-operator. It follows that, contrary to appearances, the position of the pronoun in (19a,b) and (20a,b) is indeed directly Ā-bound by the *wh*-operator. To see why, we need first to consider example (21a), which differs from its version discussed so far in that it includes an overt resumptive pronoun instead of a gap in the root direct object position. In (21a), the *wh*-operator is linked to two overt pronouns instead of to a gap and a pronoun, both patterns being equally acceptable:

(21) a. Shmen maqal ntaqd        u qblma yqra      h?
        which  article he-criticized it before reading it
        'Which article did he criticize before reading?'

    b. [CP shmen maqal [IP ntaqd        [u] [qblma yqra      [h]]?
        which article      he-criticized it   before reading it

If we assume that resumption implies lack of movement (see Shlonsky 1992, among others), (21a) has the representation shown in (21b), which does not include a trace of the *wh*-antecedent. The *wh*-operator is base-generated in the root [Spec,CP] and linked to the two pronouns in the sentence.

Example (21) shows that it is possible for the MA construction under discussion not to include a trace of the *wh*-operator in the root clause. Suppose that this is also the case in (19a,b) and (20a,b). The resumptive pronoun in the subject position is a null pronoun locally identified by the rich subject agreement inflection, MA being a null subject language. According to this particular analysis, (19a/20a) has the representation shown in (22b). The *wh*-operator is base-generated in the root [Spec,CP] and linked to the two pronouns in the argument positions:

(22) a. Shmen Talib   xrj qblma tshuf   u?
       which  student left before you-see him
       'Which student left before you could see him?'

    b. [CP shmen Talib   [IP *pro* xrj [qblma tshuf   [u]]]
        which student          left before you-see  him

The crucial property of (22) holding the key to an explanation for why it is possible is that it does not include a trace of the *wh*-operator. Because only the trace of the *wh*-operator can block direct Ā-binding by the *wh*-operator, the *wh*-operator directly Ā-binds the pronoun in the adjunct phrase in (22). This is the reason a strong pronoun is excluded from this position, and the reason why this particular context is a legitimate resumption context for the pronoun inside the adjunct phrase. Example (22) is also a legitimate resumption context for the null resumptive pronoun in the subject position, which is directly Ā-bound by the *wh*-operator.

The analysis outlined in (22b) does not extend to the English example (16) because English does not license null pronouns in the subject position of finite clauses (Rizzi 1986).

To summarize, the aim of this section was to provide a working definition of resumptive pronouns and to find out if the null pronoun in PG-constructions and the overt pronoun in the corresponding MA constructions are consistent with it. It turned out that the two pronouns are indeed consistent with the definition of resumptive pronouns adopted, with the consequence that the constructions that include them are legitimate resumption contexts. As far as PG-constructions are concerned, it also turned out that some of their properties, including the anti-c-command requirement, make sense in the context of an analysis that treats the null pronoun in the parasitic gap position as a resumptive pronoun. The key relationship that licenses resumptive pronouns is direct Ā-binding, which only holds in contexts that do not include a trace of the *wh*-antecedent that c-commands the position of the resumptive pronoun.

## 5.4   A Derivational Analysis of Resumption

This section addresses some of the questions that arise from our current working definition of resumptive pronouns. In particular, why are resumptive pronouns licensed by the narrow relation of direct Ā-binding instead of the broader relation of Ā-binding? and why can't strong pronouns be directly Ā-bound?

The typology of pronouns adopted here on the basis of the resumptive function divides them into two classes—the weak class and the strong class. The weak class includes clitic pronouns and the null pronoun *pro*, and the strong class includes strong pronouns. In accordance with recent work (see, for example, Hestvik 1992 and Cardinaletti and Starke 1994), I assume that there is a structural difference between the various classes of pronouns. The structure I adopt for weak pronouns is the one suggested by Chomsky (1995:249) for clitic pronouns in the context of bare phrase structure (BPS). The structure in question has the form roughly shown in (23), which incorporates Postal's (1966) suggestion that pronouns are D(eterminer) elements:

(23)   D/DP
       |
       CL *pro*

According to (23), weak pronouns are ambiguous between heads and maximal projections, owing to the fact that they have a nonbranching structure. A consequence of this categorial ambiguity of weak pronouns, crucial for the analysis outlined below, is that they can move either as maximal projections, to a specifier position, or as heads, to another head position.

The structure of strong pronouns differs from that of weak pronouns in that it is internally branching. The empirical basis for this claim can be seen by comparing MA strong pronouns to their clitic counterparts, illustrated in (24a–d) with the third-person members of the two paradigms.

(24)   a. -h/-u     'him'
       b. hu-wwa  'HIM'
       c. -(h)um   'them'
       d. hum-a   'THEM'

Strong pronouns (24b,d) include clitic pronouns (24a,c) and additional morphology, the exact nature of which is not easily transparent and probably requires delving into the history of the language. It is not implausible to take the extra morphology, whatever its exact nature, to imply extra internal structure. For the purposes of this paper, I assume that strong pronouns have the structure shown in (25), where X is an unspecified functional or lexical category:[7]

(25)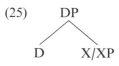

According to (25), strong pronouns are unambiguously maximal projections, by virtue of having a branching structure. A consequence of this property of strong pronouns, crucial for the analysis outlined below, is that they can only move as maximal projections to a specifier position. They cannot move as heads to another head position.[8]

If the proposed distinction between strong and weak pronouns is all that separates them, it is hard to see how resumption can distinguish between them such that it can involve a weak pronoun but not a strong pronoun. The problem arises if the interpretive mechanism that underlies resumption is assumed to take the form of free indexing (see, for example, Cinque 1990). According to this view, resumption arises when a pronoun is assigned the same index as a c-commanding $wh$-operator, resulting in the $\bar{\text{A}}$-binding of the pronoun by the $wh$-operator. It is not clear how such a mechanism can be made sensitive to whether the pronoun is weak or strong. The fact that resumption distinguishes between weak and strong pronouns implies an interpretive mechanism that involves more than the mere assignment of indices. It must involve a mechanism that makes a natural distinction between weak and strong pronouns, presumably quite independently of the issue of resumption.

The process that is known to make a natural distinction between weak and strong pronouns is cliticization, responsible for placement of the direct-object clitic pronoun in the preverbal position in French examples such as (26a,b).

(26) a. Marie l'a   vu.
        Marie him has-seen
        'Marie has seen him.'
     b. Marie se      lave.
        Marie herself washes
        'Marie washes herself.'

Kayne (1989, 1994) argues that clitic pronouns are head categories and that cliticization is a head movement process. Kayne outlines numerous arguments for this claim, among them the fact that clitic pronouns move to head positions. Here, I adopt the less rigid view, suggested by Chomsky (1995) in the context of BPS, that clitic pronouns are ambiguous between heads and maximal projections. As noted above, this view of clitic pronouns is compatible with the fact that they move to head positions.

Although cliticization does not appear to have an interpretive role in (26a), it arguably has an interpretive role in (26b). Movement of the clitic to Infl results in linking the direct object position to the subject of the sentence located in [Spec,IP], thereby deriving the reflexive reading. Exploiting this particular property of cliticization in Romance, Lebeaux (1983) suggested that English reflexives can be interpretive along similar derivational lines, except that the process of cliticization they involve applies at LF instead of overt syntax. An example such as *Mary washes herself* undergoes cliticization of the morpheme *self* to Infl, deriving the LF representation *Mary self washes*. Cliticization establishes a derivational link between the direct object position and the subject in [Spec,IP], which forms the basis for the reflexive reading. Chomsky (1986a, 1995) dubs the process involved in the interpretation of (English) reflexives as cliticization$_{LF}$ and extends it to other contexts, including contexts of long distance reflexives (e.g., *The children thought that pictures of each other were on sale*) and contexts of ambiguous binding (e.g., *John wondered which picture of himself Bill saw*).

An interesting consequence of the analysis of reflexives in terms of cliticization$_{LF}$, which reduces their interpretation to movement, is that "indexing can be abandoned" (Chomsky 1995:211). Although Chomsky does not extend cliticization$_{LF}$ to the interpretation of pronouns, there is a sense in which this particular observation is consistent with our conclusion that the interpretation of resumptive pronouns is unlikely to involve (free) indexing.

An attempt to extend cliticization$_{LF}$ to pronouns is outlined by Hestvik (1992), who shows that it is necessary to explain certain differences in interpretation between Norwegian and English pronouns. Norwegian pronouns are head categories that undergo cliticization$_{LF}$ to the head position associated with their antecedent. English pronouns, in contrast, are maximal projections and therefore do not feed cliticization$_{LF}$. Although the details of Hestvik's analysis and the facts motivating it cannot be included here for lack of space, it is important to highlight two major ideas on which the analysis is based. First, pronouns fall into two classes, heads and maximal projections. Secondly, pronouns that are heads are interpreted via cliticization$_{LF}$, which moves them to the head associated with their antecedent. Underlying these two ideas is the assumption that because overt cliticization (cliticization$_{SYN}$) affects both pronominal clitics, as in (26a), and reflexive clitics, as in (26b), its covert counterpart cliticization$_{LF}$ may also affect both pronominal and reflexive head categories.

We are now in a position to outline an analysis for resumption that explains why the licensing of resumptive pronouns must take the form of direct $\bar{\text{A}}$-binding instead of just mere $\bar{\text{A}}$-binding, and why only weak pronouns are compatible with the relationship of direct $\bar{\text{A}}$-binding. To start with, direct $\bar{\text{A}}$-binding is actually cliticization$_{LF}$, a movement process subject to a particular interception effect by a c-commanding trace of the *wh*-antecedent (which we will return to below). Direct $\bar{\text{A}}$-binding is not a special, narrow case of $\bar{\text{A}}$-binding but an entirely different relation. Moreover, cliticization$_{LF}$ only affects head categories, by virtue of the fact that it is a head movement process that targets a head category as host —namely, the C associated with the *wh*-antecedent. It follows that only pronouns that are heads (i.e., that can feed cliticization) can function as resumptive pronouns. However, because weak pronouns are head categories by virtue of having a nonbranching structure, they are compatible with the resumptive function. In contrast, strong pronouns are unambiguously maximal projections by virtue of having a branching structure and therefore cannot feed cliticization, either overtly or covertly. This is the reason strong pronouns are incompatible with the resumptive function.

According to the proposed analysis, classic contexts of resumption such as (27a) and (28a) have the LF representations roughly shown in (27b) and (28b) subsequent to cliticization$_{LF}$. The resumptive pronoun is attached to the C associated with the *wh*-antecedent in the root clause. Cliticization$_{LF}$ establishes a derivational link between the *wh*-operator and the original position of the resumptive pronoun, enabling the *wh*-operator to $\bar{\text{A}}$-bind the variable in that position:

(27) a. Shmen maqal nsiti          fin     qriti      h?
        which  article you-forgot where you-read it
     b. [$_{CP}$ shmen maqal [$_{C'}$ [h]-C [$_{IP}$ nsiti        [$_{wh\text{-}CP}$ fin
           which article    it        you-forgot          where
        qriti      $t_h$] ...?
        you-read

(28) a. Shmen maqal saferti        (l Casablanca)   blama   tqra    h?
       which  article you-traveled (to Casablanca) without reading it

   b. [CP shmen maqal [C′ [h]-C [IP saferti         [Adjunct blama
         which article       it       you-traveled             without
      tqra    $t_h$] . . . ?
      reading

The same analysis applies to the English example (29a), which was said
previously, following Cinque (1990), to include a null resumptive pronoun
inside the adjunct island.[9]

(29) a. Which article did you go to London without reading?

   b. [CP which article [C′ *pro*-did [IP you go to London
      [Adjunct without reading $t_{pro}$] . . . ?

Extending the analysis in terms of cliticization$_{LF}$ to PG-constructions
yields the LF representation roughly shown in (30b) for (30a). The null
resumptive pronoun is attached to the C associated with the *wh*-operator
in the root clause. Cliticization$_{LF}$ establishes a derivational link between
the parasitic gap and the *wh*-operator in the root clause, which enables the
*wh*-operator to Ā-bind the parasitic gap:

(30) a. Which article did he criticize before reading?

   b. [CP which article [C′ *pro*-did [IP he criticize $t_{which\ article}$
      [Adjunct before reading $t_{pro}$] . . . ?

The corresponding MA example with an overt clitic pronoun (31a) has
basically the same representation at LF, roughly shown in (31b). The
clitic pronoun is moved to C by cliticization$_{LF}$:

(31) a. Shmen maqal ntaqd        qblma yqra     h?
       which  article he-criticized before reading it

   b. [CP shmen maqal [C′ [h]-C [IP ntaqd         $t_{shmen\ maqal}$ [Adjunct qblma
         which article       it       criticized                        before
      yqra    $t_h$] . . . ?
      reading

Recall that the MA example (31a) can have an alternative reading
whereby the clitic pronoun has an antecedent in discourse. The LF representation underlying this particular reading differs from (31b) in that
the pronoun does not undergo cliticization$_{LF}$. The nonbound reading,
therefore, reduces to absence of cliticization$_{LF}$. No indexing is required
for the interpretation of the pronoun in this particular context. The explanation for why the null pronoun in the PG example (30a) cannot have a

similar nonbound reading remains as before: The null pronoun remains in its position inside the adjunct phrase where it fails to be identified. The difference is that now there is a local and more familiar relation of identification in (30), namely identification via spec-head agreement, instead of the comparatively bizarre relation of identification via direct $\bar{\text{A}}$-binding. In any case, with the relation of direct $\bar{\text{A}}$-binding reduced to cliticization$_{\text{LF}}$, it can no longer be maintained that the null pronoun in (30) is identified via direct $\bar{\text{A}}$-binding by the *wh*-operator. As shown in (30b), the null pronoun is locally identified via spec-head agreement with the *wh*-operator.

Let us now turn to the question why resumptive pronouns are licensed by the relation of direct $\bar{\text{A}}$-binding and not the relation of mere $\bar{\text{A}}$-binding. According to the analysis outlined earlier, the relation of direct $\bar{\text{A}}$-binding reduces to cliticization$_{\text{LF}}$ of the resumptive pronoun, a movement process. In view of this, the question needs to be restated in terms of movement —namely, why does a c-commanding trace of the *wh*-antecedent of a resumptive pronoun block movement of the resumptive pronoun across it, but a non-c-commanding trace does not? Recall that an answer to this question is necessary to explain the contrast between PG examples with an object *wh*-antecedent such as (30) and PG-examples with a subject *wh*-antecedent such as (32).

(32) a. *Which student saw you before you could recognize?
   b. *[$_{\text{CP}}$ which student [$_{\text{C}'}$ C [$_{\text{IP}}$ $t_{\text{which student}}$ saw you [$_{\text{Adjunct}}$ before you could recognize *pro*] ...?

In (30), the trace of the *wh*-antecedent does not c-command the pronoun and therefore does not block movement of the pronoun in terms of cliticization$_{\text{LF}}$. In (32), however, the trace of the *wh*-antecedent c-commands the pronoun and consequently blocks its movement.

The blocking/interception effect by a c-commanding trace of the *wh*-antecedent described is not dissimilar to the interception effects familiar from relativized minimality cases, except that it implies a finer-grained distinction in relation to blocking categories. In the familiar cases of relativized minimality, any A-specifier blocks movement of another A-specifier—for example, *John seems it is likely to win the race* (super-raising)—and any $\bar{\text{A}}$-specifier blocks movement of another $\bar{\text{A}}$-specifier— for example, *How do you wonder whether John fixed the car?* (adjunct extraction out of a *wh*-island). Cliticization$_{\text{LF}}$ appears to differ in that only the trace of the targeted *wh*-antecedent blocks it. A different intervening *wh*-operator does not block cliticization$_{\text{LF}}$. This can be trivially seen in resumption contexts involving a *wh*-island such as (27) above. In that example, the resumptive pronoun moves out of the *wh*-island across the intervening *wh*-phrase in the embedded [Spec,CP]. The reason cliticization$_{LF}$ differs in this particular way is that cliticization$_{LF}$ is fundamentally an interpretive rule that has the function of linking a pronoun to its *wh*-antecedent. It does so by looking for the intended *wh*-antecedent and attaching the pronoun to the head associated with it. As such, cliticization$_{LF}$ is blind to other *wh*-operators that may intervene between the pronoun and the targeted *wh*-antecedent, except for the trace of the targeted *wh*-antecedent.

To see exactly how cliticization$_{LF}$ operates, let us assume LF representations for (30) and (32) that exploit the copy theory of movement as outlined by Chomsky (1995). According to this theory, the LF representations of (30) and (32) each includes two copies of the moved *wh*-operator at LF. One copy is located in the operator position, the root [Spec,CP], and another located in the argument position of the trace. Cliticization$_{LF}$ looks for the first c-commanding occurrence of the targeted *wh*-operator and attaches the pronoun to the head associated with it. In (30), the first c-commanding occurrence of the targeted *wh*-antecedent is the copy in the operator position, the root [Spec,CP]. The copy in the position of the trace does not c-command the pronoun and therefore is ignored. In (32), however, the first c-commanding copy of the targeted *wh*-antecedent is the one in the subject position rather than the one in the operator position. Cliticization$_{LF}$ therefore attaches the pronoun to the Infl associated with the copy in the subject position. However, this representation does not derive the required operator-variable link necessary for the interpretation of the variable in the parasitic gap. Once the LF rules of interpretation apply, they convert the copy in the subject position into a variable, not an operator.

One of the advantages of the analysis in terms of cliticization$_{LF}$ is that the generalization that only a c-commanding trace or copy of the targeted *wh*-antecedent blocks the link with the resumptive pronoun does not need to be stated. It follows from the nature of cliticization$_{LF}$ as a movement rule that can only apply upwards. The non-c-commanding trace or copy of the *wh*-antecedent in (30) is ignored precisely because it does not fall within the movement path of cliticization$_{LF}$. The trace or copy of the *wh*-antecedent in (32) falls within the movement path of cliticization$_{LF}$ and therefore cannot be ignored. The relationship of direct Ā-binding as defined above turns out to be a statement of the condition that the movement path between the pronoun and its *wh*-antecedent should be clear of a blocking category, in particular the trace or copy of the *wh*-antecedent.

The LF representation of the MA example (31a), shown in (31b), is consistent with the explanation of the blocking effect on cliticization$_{LF}$. The trace or copy of the *wh*-antecedent in the root direct-object position does not c-command the pronoun and therefore does not fall within the movement path of the pronoun. More interestingly, the analysis of example (33a) outlined in section 5.3 is also consistent with the proposed explanation of the blocking effect on cliticization$_{LF}$.

(33) a.  Shmen Talib   xrj qblma tshuf   u?
         which student left before you-see him
     b.  [$_{CP}$ shmen Talib   [$_{C'}$ C [$_{IP}$ *pro* xrj [$_{Adjunct}$ qblma tshuf   [u]]?
         which student            left       before you-see him

Recall that (33a) was assigned the S-structure representation shown in (33b), which does not include a trace or copy of the *wh*-antecedent in the subject position. The subject position is filled with a null resumptive pronoun and the *wh*-operator is base generated in the root [Spec,CP]. Like the clitic pronoun inside the adjunct phrase of the same sentence, the null resumptive pronoun in the subject position also undergoes cliticization$_{LF}$ to C. Thus, (33a) has the LF representation roughly shown in (34), with both pronouns attached to the root C.[10]

(34) [$_{CP}$ shmen Talib   [$_{C'}$ [u] + *pro*-C [$_{IP}$ $t_{pro}$ xrj [$_{Adjunct}$ qblma
         which student       him           left        before
     tshuf   $t_u$] ... ?
     you-see

The S-structure representation (33b) was partly motivated on the basis of examples such as (35a) which include a resumptive clitic pronoun instead of a gap in the root direct-object position.

(35) a.  Shmen maqal ntaqd       u qblma yqra   h?
         which article he-criticized it before reading it
     b.  [$_{CP}$ shmen maqal [$_{C'}$ C [$_{IP}$ ntaqd       [u] [$_{Adjunct}$ qblma
         which article             criticized it         before
     yqra   [h]] ...
     reading it
     c.  [$_{CP}$ shmen maqal [$_{C'}$ [u] + [h]-C [$_{IP}$ ntaqd       $t_u$ [$_{Adjunct}$ qblma
         which article       [it] + [it]       criticized       before
     yqra   $t$[h]]
     reading ...

As in (33) and (34), the *wh*-antecedent is base-generated in the root [Spec,CP] and linked to the two pronouns via cliticization$_{LF}$. The latter applies to both instances of resumptive pronouns and attaches them to the C associated with the *wh*-antecedent, deriving the LF representation roughly shown in (35c).

The blocking effect that a c-commanding trace or copy of the *wh*-antecedent has on cliticization$_{LF}$ shows that cliticization$_{LF}$ is not as unrestricted as it appears initially. It is subject to a Relativized Minimality–like effect, although one that discriminates more closely between potential blocking categories. The next section shows that the rule that moves resumptive pronouns to their antecedent is even more constrained than stated so far.

To summarize, this section addressed two major questions that arose from the working definition of resumptive pronouns adopted: why are resumptive pronouns licensed by the narrow relationship of direct Ā-binding instead of the broader relationship of Ā-binding? and why can't strong pronouns be directly Ā-bound? Direct Ā-binding was argued to be fundamentally a movement process rather than a narrow relation of Ā-binding. The movement process, cliticization$_{LF}$, applies at LF and places the resumptive pronoun in the head position associated with its *wh*-antecedent. This movement establishes a derivational link between the original position of the resumptive pronoun and the *wh*-antecedent. Cliticization$_{LF}$ is subject to a locality restriction such that it is blocked by a c-commanding trace or copy of the targeted *wh*-antecedent. As a head movement process that targets a head category as host, cliticization$_{LF}$ only applies to pronouns that are heads, in particular weak pronouns. Strong pronouns are unambiguously maximal projections and consequently cannot feed cliticization in general. This is the reason strong pronouns cannot be directly Ā-bound, unlike weak pronouns.

### 5.5   Null versus Overt Resumptive Pronouns

This section addresses the remaining question raised by our definition of resumptive pronouns: why are resumptive pronouns licensed at S-structure and not at the later level of LF?[11] The answer to this question will make it possible to address another question that has been obvious all along but has not been explicitly stated: why does MA, unlike English, lack PG-constructions?

As far as PG-constructions are concerned, the question why parasitic gaps are licensed at S-structure but not at LF arises in relation to examples with a direct object *wh*-antecedent in-situ such as (36).

(36) a. *I forgot who filed which article without reading.

   b. *I forgot who filed [which article] [$_{Adjunct}$ without reading $pro$]

In section 5.3, (36) was said to be excluded because the *wh*-antecedent of
the null pronoun does not c-command the pronoun at S-structure and
therefore does not directly Ā-bind the null pronoun at S-structure. In
other words, (36) is not a legitimate resumption context in which the
null pronoun can be licensed. Extending the analysis of direct Ā-binding
as cliticization$_{LF}$ to (36), and assuming that *wh*-in-situ undergo covert
raising at LF, (36) has the LF representation roughly shown in (37). The
*wh*-phrase in the subject position is ignored, as it is not directly relevant to
the discussion:

(37) *I forgot [$_{CP}$ [which article] [$_{C'}$ [$pro$]-C [$_{IP}$ who filed $t_{\text{which article}}$
    [$_{Adjunct}$ without reading $t_{\text{pro}}$] . . .

To the extent that (37) is the right LF representation of (36), it is identical to the representation of acceptable PG-examples with an overtly
moved direct object *wh*-antecedent (e.g., *I forgot which article John filed
without reading*). Movement of the null pronoun to the C associated with
the *wh*-antecedent derives a legitimate operator-variable link between the
*wh*-operator and the position of the parasitic gap. Moreover, the null
pronoun is locally identified by the *wh*-operator. Consequently, on the
scenario outlined, the reason why (37) is excluded remains a mystery.

The situation becomes more complicated when corresponding MA
examples with an overt pronoun are brought into the picture. One property of these constructions not mentioned so far is that examples corresponding to (37) are possible insofar as they have the same status as
multiple *wh*-questions in the language. Thus, (38) is possible with the
reading whereby the pronoun inside the adjunct phrase has the root direct
object *wh*-phrase in situ as the antecedent.

(38) a. Nsit     shkun ntaqd     shmen maqal qblma yqra     h.
       I-forgot who   criticized which article before reading it
       'I have forgotten who criticized which article before reading it.'

   b. . . . [$_{CP}$ [shmen maqal] [$_{C'}$ [h]-C [$_{IP}$ shkun ntaqd     $t_{\text{shmen maqal}}$
           which article     it       who   criticized
       [$_{Adjunct}$ qblma yqra     $t_h$] . . .
           before reading

The sentence in (38a) has the LF representation roughly shown in
(38b), which is identical in relevant respects to the LF representation of
the PG-example (37). Yet, the PG-example (37) is excluded, but the MA

example (38) is not. This difference is likely to be due to the null versus overt property of the pronoun in the two constructions.

Although the MA example (38) complicates the situation, it also points toward the source of the problem and eventually the solution to it. Example (38) is clearly inconsistent with our definition of resumptive pronouns. The *wh*-antecedent of the pronoun does not c-command and therefore does not directly Ā-bind the pronoun at S-structure. Also, (38) shows that the claim that resumptive pronouns are licensed at S-structure does not hold of overt resumptive pronouns. Overt resumptive pronouns are licensed at LF and, given (38), cannot be said to be licensed at S-structure. This conclusion is consistent not only with (38), but with all MA examples discussed so far.[12]

Just as (38) shows that resumptive pronouns are licensed at LF and not at S-structure, the PG-example shows that null resumptive pronouns are licensed at S-structure and not at LF. Example (37) is excluded because the *wh*-antecedent does not c-command the null pronoun at S-structure. This difference between overt and null resumptive pronouns is stated in (39).

(39)  Overt resumptive pronouns are licensed at LF. Null resumptive pronouns are licensed at S-structure.

The mechanism that interprets resumptive pronouns, by linking them to their *wh*-antecedent, must therefore reflect the distinction between overt and null resumptive pronouns stated in (39). To the extent that the mechanism in question takes the form of cliticization of the pronoun to the head associated with the *wh*-antecedent, it does not apply to both overt and null resumptive pronouns at LF. Although overt resumptive pronouns undergo cliticization at LF (i.e., cliticization$_{LF}$), null resumptive pronouns undergo cliticization in overt syntax (i.e., cliticization$_{SYN}$). Null resumptive pronouns must undergo cliticization$_{SYN}$ because they are subject to identification. On the assumption that the identification of null pronouns is part of the more general condition of Recoverability, it is a property of overt syntax and not of LF. Overt resumptive pronouns are not subject to identification, hence their cliticization is delayed to LF. At LF, all resumptive pronouns must be attached to the head associated with their *wh*-antecedent for reasons of interpretation.

The revision introduced obviously does not affect the analysis of the MA examples outlined above, including (38). The idea that the overt resumptive pronoun they include undergoes movement at LF remains as presented. The analysis of PG-constructions is affected only insofar as movement of the null pronoun is now assumed to take place in overt syntax instead of LF. This change has no further implications for examples with an overtly moved direct object *wh*-antecedent (e.g., *Which article did he criticize before reading?*). The change has no further implications either for examples with a subject *wh*-antecedent (e.g., *\*Who did you meet without recognizing?*). The trace or copy of the subject *wh*-antecedent blocks overt movement of the pronoun across it in technically the same way as explained in section 5.4. However, the change introduced has a major implication for (37) in that we now have a plausible explanation for why it is excluded. Because the intended *wh*-antecedent of the null pronoun is in situ instead of in the root [Spec,CP], overt movement of the null pronoun to the root C does not result in the identification of the null pronoun in overt syntax. The null pronoun fails to satisfy the identification requirement in overt syntax regardless of whether it moves to C or remains in situ.

The conclusion that the null pronoun in PG-constructions undergoes overt movement is basically the conclusion reached by Postal (1993b). Where the present analysis differs is in assuming that movement of the null pronoun takes the form of cliticization. However, there is evidence suggesting that the path of pronoun movement is not fully determined by cliticization. Rather, pronoun movement applies in at least two stages (legs), only one of which takes the form of cliticization. The evidence relates to another property of PG-constructions noted by Chomsky (1986b), namely the fact that parasitic gaps appear to be sensitive to islands. Chomsky (1986b:55–56) remarks in relation to the examples in (40a,b) and others that their "relative acceptability ... matches that of the corresponding examples with *wh*-movement":

(40) This is the man John interviewed before
    a. asking you which job to give to.
    b. hearing about the plans to speak to.

Chomsky concludes that PG-constructions involve local movement of a null operator and therefore form part of the larger class of null operator constructions. As noted earlier, Postal (1993) argues that this conclusion is inconsistent with the fact that parasitic gaps are restricted to DPs. Postal concludes that PG-constructions involve movement but that the moved category is a pronoun.

The property of PG-constructions illustrated in (40a,b) can be incorporated into our analysis of resumptive pronouns in a way that is consistent with the widely held view that Subjacency effects are a property of overt movement but not covert movement (Huang 1982). Overt movement of the null pronoun in PG examples such as (41a) takes place in two separate and distinct steps. The first step, shown in (41b), takes the form of local Ā-movement of the null pronoun to an appropriate specifier position in the left edge of the adjunct phrase. This is the movement process assumed in Chomsky's analysis and presumably also Postal's analysis. The second step, shown in (41c), takes the form of cliticization$_{SYN}$, which places the null pronoun in the root C. The instance of the null pronoun attached to C bears the categorial label D to indicate that it is a head category. The other instances of the null pronoun are identified with the categorial label DP:

(41) a. Which article did he criticize before reading?
     b. Which article did he criticize $t_{\text{which article}}$ [Adjunct [DP *pro*] before reading [DP $t_{\text{pro}}$]]?
     c. [CP [which article] [C′ [D *pro*]-did [IP he criticize [$t_{\text{which article}}$] [Adjunct [DP $t_{\text{pro}}$] before reading [DP $t_{\text{pro}}$]] …?

The first step (i.e., Ā-movement of the null pronoun), can be said to have the effect of placing the null pronoun in a position from which it can undergo cliticization to the root C.[13] If Ā-movement of the pronoun to the left edge of the adjunct phrase is indeed necessary for the pronoun to escape out of the adjunct phrase via cliticization, the derivation of the corresponding MA constructions with an overt pronoun must involve the same scenario.

Contrary to PG-constructions, the corresponding MA constructions with an overt pronoun do not show any signs of being sensitive to islands. The complex NP island in (42a) and the *wh*-island in (42b) have no discernible effect on the status of the construction.

(42) Shmen maqal ntaqd      qblma
     which  article he-criticized before
     'Which article did he criticize before
     a. ytkellem m'a l-talib      lli   ktb        u?
        talking  with the-student who had-written it
        talking to the student who had written it?'
     b. yteddekker   wash qra         h?
        remembering if   he-had-read it
        before remembering if he had read it?'

It follows that the derivation of the corresponding MA examples with an overt pronoun does not involve local Ā-movement of the resumptive pronoun in overt syntax, a fact that is already obvious from the position of the resumptive pronoun. However, (42a,b) do not necessarily exclude the possibility that their derivation involves $\bar{\text{A}}$-movement of the overt pronoun at LF, assuming that Subjacency effects are a property of overt but not covert $\bar{\text{A}}$-movement. To the extent that the ability of the pronoun inside the adjunct phrase to undergo cliticization to the root C depends on its placement at the edge of the adjunct phrase by $\bar{\text{A}}$-movement, the derivation of the MA constructions in question must also involve two movement steps, both of which take place at LF. The first step is $\bar{\text{A}}$-movement of the pronoun to the edge of the adjunct phrase, and the second step is cliticization$_{LF}$ of the pronoun to the root C. This particular derivation is outlined in (43b,c) for (43a).

(43) a. Shmen maqal ntaqd      qblma yqra    h?
      which article he-criticized before reading it

    b. Shmen maqal ntaqd      [$_{Adjunct}$ [$_{DP}$ h] qblma yqra    [$_{DP}$ $t_h$]]
      which article he-criticized              before reading

    c. [$_{CP}$ [shmen maqal] [$_{C'}$ [$_D$ h]-C [$_{IP}$ ntaqd         $t_{shmen\ maqal}$
      which article    it        he-criticized
      [$_{Adjunct}$ [$_{DP}$ $t_h$] qblma yqra    [$_{DP}$ $t_h$]] ...?
      before reading

The conclusion that movement of the pronoun in the adjunct phrase operates in two steps, one of which is an instance of $\bar{\text{A}}$-movement and the other an instance of cliticization, is consistent with the idea pointed out in section 5.4 that weak pronouns are ambiguous between heads and maximal projections, and therefore can either move as heads or as maximal projections. The conclusion that movement of the pronouns operates in two steps, which at least in PG-constructions is empirically motivated by the need to account for the fact that parasitic gaps are sensitive to islands, also shows that movement of the pronoun is not as unbounded as it initially appears. Recall that movement of the pronoun is also subject to a Relativized Minimality–like effect such that it is blocked by a c-commanding trace or copy of the targeted *wh*-antecedent.

The last question I would like to address can be stated as follows: Why is the scenario that takes place in (English) PG-constructions excluded in MA? The scenario in question is one whereby the parasitic gap takes the form of a null pronoun that undergoes overt movement to the root C instead of an overt pronoun that undergoes covert movement to the root C. If this scenario were possible in MA, examples (44a,b), with a gap instead of a clitic pronoun inside the adjunct phrase, should be possible. However, (44a,b) and similar examples have a very marginal status at best.

(44) a. *Shmen maqal ntaqd        qblma yqra?
       which article he-criticized before reading
       'Which article did he criticize before reading?'
     b. *Hada huwwa l-maqal    lli   ntaqd          qblma yqra.
       this   is      the-article that he-criticized before reading
       'This is the article he criticized before reading.'

Clearly, the answer to this question will amount to an explanation for why MA, unlike English, lacks PG-constructions such as (44a,b). The answer lies partly with the fact, pointed out in section 5.3, that strong pronouns can cooccur with a clitic pronoun in MA. Shlonsky (1994) and Roberts and Shlonsky (1996) outline a number of properties of clitic pronouns in the Semitic languages, in particular Arabic and Hebrew, which turn out to radically distinguish them from clitic pronouns in Romance. The properties of Semitic so-called clitic pronouns are shown to be consistent with their being object agreement markers and arguably inconsistent with their being clitic pronouns of the Romance type. Semitic clitic pronouns are base-generated as inflection on their lexical hosts instead of as DPs in an argument position. Their function is to locally identify a null pronoun in the argument position they are related to. According to this analysis, Semitic clitic pronouns appear in contexts such as (45a), where X can be any lexical category as well as one of a limited number of functional categories. In contrast, Romance clitic pronouns appear in contexts such as (45b), prior to their movement by cliticization$_{SYN}$.

(45) a. X + CL [$_{DP}$ *pro*]    (Semitic)
     b. V [$_{DP}$ CL ]          (Romance)

It follows from the analysis of Semitic clitic pronouns outlined in (45a) that the MA examples corresponding to the PG-constructions discussed here include a null pronoun instead of an overt pronoun inside the adjunct phrase. In this particular respect, they are identical to PG-constructions, contrary to what was assumed. The difference lies in that the null pronoun is locally identified by overt object agreement inflection in the MA constructions, but not in the PG-constructions. It is precisely because the null pronoun can be locally identified by object agreement inflection in MA that the language lacks PG-constructions of the type in (44a,b).

Identification via overt movement of the null pronoun to C is available to both languages, indeed to all languages. MA has an alternative or an additional mechanism of identifying the null pronoun—namely, local identification by overt object agreement inflection. This mechanism is not

available to English because English lacks overt object agreement inflection. It follows that the null pronoun can only be identified via overt
movement in English PG-constructions. It is not implausible to assume
that identification of a null pronoun via overt movement is more costly
than local identification by overt agreement inflection and no movement.
Movement is a last resort operation, which only applies if the requirement
that triggers it cannot be satisfied otherwise (Chomsky 1995). Recall that
overt movement of the null pronoun in PG-constructions is motivated by
the need to place the null pronoun in a configuration where it can be
locally identified (by the *wh*-antecedent). Because the null pronoun in the
corresponding MA constructions can be identified in situ by overt object
agreement inflection, it does not undergo overt movement. Thus, (44a,b)
are excluded by economy considerations. In (44a,b), the null pronoun
must undergo overt movement to be identified, as in PG-constructions.
However, there is an alternative derivation for these constructions in MA
that does not require overt movement of the pronoun for identification.
The alternative derivation involves the Spell-out of object agreement to
identify the null pronoun.[14]

The only implication that the reanalysis of clitic pronouns as object
agreement inflection has for the analysis of the MA constructions in
question is that the pronoun inside the adjunct phrase is now considered
to be null instead of overt. The idea that the pronoun moves at LF instead
of at S-structure is not affected. A derivation for (46a) that incorporates
the revision introduced is outlined in (46b) (Spell-out) and (46c) (LF).

(46) a. Shmen maqal ntaqd      qblma yqra    h?
        which article he-criticized before reading it

    b. [$_{CP}$ shmen maqal [$_{C'}$ C [$_{IP}$ ntaqd          $t_{shmen\ maqal}$ [$_{Adjunct}$ qblma
        which article          he-criticized                              before
        yqra-h      [$_{DP}$ *pro*]] . . .
        reading-AGR

    c. [$_{CP}$ shmen maqal [$_{C'}$ [$_{D}$ *pro*]-C [$_{IP}$ ntaqd          $t_{shmen\ maqal}$
        which article          he-criticized
        [$_{Adjunct}$ [$_{DP}$ $t_{pro}$] qblma yqra-h          [$_{DP}$ $t_{pro}$]] . . .?
        before reading-AGR

## 5.6   Conclusion

The major concern of this chapter was to investigate the question whether
parasitic gaps, on the view that they are null pronouns, are or are not

instances of resumptive pronouns. A possible link is initially suggested by the fact that the null pronoun in PG-constructions resembles resumptive pronouns in that it has an obligatory bound reading. The question was resolved on the basis of a definition of resumptive pronouns and the contexts in which they are licensed, independently of PG-constructions. It turned out that parasitic gaps and PG-constructions are not only consistent with the definition reached but also with some of their major properties, including the so-called anti-c-command requirement. One of the defining properties of resumption discussed—in particular, the fact that it makes a distinction between weak and strong pronouns—was said to show that the interpretation of resumptive pronouns cannot be said to involve the mechanism of (free) indexing. Rather, it involves a mechanism that makes a natural and independent distinction between weak and strong pronouns, namely cliticization. An analysis which assumes that the null pronoun in PG-constructions undergoes movement to its *wh*-antecedent was shown to be consistent with other properties of PG-constructions, including the fact that they are sensitive to islands.

**Notes**

In preparing this chapter, I have benefited from extremely helpful comments by Joseph Aoun, Lina Choueiri, Abbas Benmamoun, Peter Culicover, and Paul Postal. I am grateful to them.

1. As is well known, parasitic gaps can also be found inside clausal subjects and relative subjects. The latter type is illustrated in (i) (Chomsky 1986b p. 58).

(i) He's a man that [anyone who talks to *e*] usually likes *t* . . . .

MA does not tolerate clausal subjects well. However, it is possible to construct an example with a relative subject along the lines of (i):

(ii) Hada huwwa l-seyyed lli    shkunma tlaqa h    kaybghi h.
     this  is      the-man that whoever  meets him likes     him
     'This is the man who [anyone who meets *e*] likes *t* . . . .'

A peculiar property of (ii) is that an overt pronoun is required not only in the position corresponding to the parasitic gap but also in the position corresponding to the trace. I have nothing significant to say about this fact except to point out that, as we will see later on, a similar pattern is also found in constructions with an adjunct phrase, though optionally.

2. The observation extends to the mechanism of interpretation suggested by Chomsky (1986b), namely chain composition. According to Chomsky (1986b), parasitic gaps are null operators that undergo local *wh*-movement (more on this later on). The Ā-chain derived by this particular movement merges with the Ā-chain derived by movement of the *wh*-operator in the root clause. Merger of the two Ā-chains derives a single Ā-chain whereby the *wh*-operator binds its variable trace in the root clause as well as the variable trace in the parasitic gap. Chain

composition is obviously an additional mechanism of interpretation designed to ensure that the parasitic gap is bound by the *wh*-operator in the root clause.

3. The possibility that resumptive pronouns may have a special property that requires them to be Ā-bound arises in analyses that take resumptive pronouns to be the spellout of traces. According to this analysis, resumptive pronouns have an obligatory bound reading for whatever reason variable traces have an obligatory bound reading. The analysis of resumption contexts such as (6a,b) I assume in this paper is one where they do not involve movement of the *wh*-operator out of the island that includes the resumptive pronoun. Both the *wh*-operator and the resumptive pronoun are base-generated in their respective surface positions. Resumptive pronouns have the interpretive features that characterize pronouns in general.

4. The reason a strong pronoun can cooccur with a clitic pronoun in MA is explained in section 5.5. Pending the explanation, I will assume that strong pronouns occupy the argument position they are associated with.

5. Chomsky (1986b:61–62) considers cases of PG-constructions where the trace of the *wh*-antecedent appears to c-command the parasitic gap—for example, *Which men did the police warn that they were about to arrest?*—and dismisses them on the grounds that that they "are not entirely persuasive as counterevidence to the anti-c-command requirement." Citing Rizzi, Chomsky goes on to point out that the example mentioned, among others, is consistent with an analysis whereby the "complement clause" is an adjunct of VP, in which case the gap it includes is outside the c-command domain of the trace of the *wh*-operator. Peter Culicover (personal communication) cites *Which senator did they learn was a spy only after bribing?* as another potential counterexample to the anti-c-command requirement. However, I believe that this example is consistent with an analysis whereby the adjunct phrase headed by *after* is adjoined to the root VP, on the grounds that it modifies (the VP headed by) *learn*. If this analysis is correct, the gap inside the adjunct phrase falls outside the c-command domain of the trace in the subject position of the complement clause.

6. I am excluding as unworkable the possibility that the trace of the *wh*-operator in the subject position does not c-command the pronoun in the adjunct phrase. This would be the case if the adjunct phrase were assumed to be adjoined to IP instead of to VP in the MA examples. This particular view implies that there is variation among languages, in this case MA and English, as to where the same type of adjunct phrase is adjoined. In principle, it is not unreasonable to exclude such variation.

7. The overt forms of strong pronouns are derived by "merger" (in the sense of Halle and Marantz 1993) at the level of Morphological Structure (MS) situated between Spell-out and PF. This process takes the two adjacent nodes, D and X in (25), and merges them into a single node under which strong pronouns are inserted. I do not know of any facts that motivate a derivation in terms of $X^0$-movement to D.

8. Cardinaletti and Starke (1994) assume a three-way distinction between pronouns—clitic pronouns, weak pronouns, and strong pronouns. Clitic pronouns

are heads whereas weak and strong pronouns are "full phrases." Weak and strong pronouns differ from each other in that strong pronouns include an extra layer in their structure. Cardinaletti and Starke's discussion of the null pronoun *pro* seems to indicate that it belongs to the weak class and therefore has a branching structure. This analysis of *pro* is obviously different from the one adopted here. It may be that null pronouns do not form a uniform class, but divide into two different classes, the clitic class and the weak class. Cardinaletti and Starke's classification could then be maintained if the null pronoun that occurs in resumption contexts is taken to belong to the clitic class and therefore has a nonbranching structure.

9. The claim put forward here—that resumptive pronouns undergo LF movement—is radically different from the claim put forward by Demirdache (1991) in relation to relatives and CLLD constructions. According to Demirdache's analysis, resumptive pronouns are disguised in-situ *wh*-operators that undergo *wh*-movement at LF, essentially the analysis outlined by Borer (1984) for Hebrew relatives.

10. The LF representation (34) involves a clitic cluster associated with C that includes a subject clitic and a nonsubject clitic moved from an adjunct phrase. Peter Culicover (personal communication) points out that such clusters are at best unfamiliar, and it is not clear if they are legitimate. Unfortunately, I have nothing significant to say about this particular problem. The fact that a nonsubject clitic can move across a subject clitic is, presumably, comparatively unproblematic. It can be seen in French examples such as *L'a-t-elle vu*? ('him-has-she seen?'). According to Kayne (1975), the subject clitic attaches to the complex under C (at PF) subsequent to movement of the auxiliary verb and the object clitic to C.

11. This question is worth addressing, regardless of one's theoretical framework. However, in a framework that does not recognize S-structure as a legitimate level of representation, such as the Minimalist Program, the question obviously acquires more significance. The licensing of parasitic gaps is one of those so-called S-structure effects that Chomsky (1995) points out have to be reinterpreted somehow in the context of the Minimalist Program.

12. The S-structure requirement on the licensing of resumptive pronouns was carried over from Sells's (1984) original definition, where it is implicit in the notion "operator binding." Sells's analysis is intended to account for resumption contexts as well as contexts where a pronoun is Ā-bound by a quantifier, as in *Every pupil thinks that the teacher likes him (best)*. The S-structure requirement is intended to exclude a resumptive interpretation for the pronoun in such examples, on the assumption that quantifiers undergo raising to an Ā-position at LF. However, once quantifiers are excluded from the picture, the S-structure requirement becomes irrelevant to overt pronouns bound by a *wh*-operator. The pronoun is still excluded from having a resumptive interpretation in examples like *Which pupil thinks that the teacher likes him (best)?* on the grounds that the pronoun is not directly Ā-bound at LF. The S-structure requirement was carried over into the definition adopted here because, as we will see shortly, it is crucially relevant to the licensing of resumptive pronouns that are null, situated in contexts not discussed by Sells (1984).

13.  The analysis of the movement of the pronoun outlined in (41b) and (41c) is similar in spirit to the analysis outlined in Baker 1988 of causatives of transitive verbs where the subject of the causativized verb has the properties of an indirect object. According to Baker (see also Chomsky 1995), the derivation of these causative constructions involves movement of VP to the specifier of the embedded CP (first step), followed by head movement of the verb out of the VP to the root V (second step). The first step derives a configuration that makes it possible for the verb to incorporate into the root verb. However, there is a potentially significant difference between the two contexts. In the causative constructions, the verb head-moves out of a complement clause, whereas in the constructions discussed in this paper, the pronoun head-moves out of an adjunct clause. I have nothing further to say about this problem here, except to refer the reader to Spencer 1995, where some cases of incorporation out of adjuncts are discussed (see also Baker 1996).

14.  There is a sense in which the explanation for why MA lacks PG-constructions predicts that languages with genuine clitic pronouns (e.g., the Romance languages) are expected to have PG-constructions in free variation with constructions containing a clitic pronoun in the position of the parasitic gap. In these languages, the two constructions do not share the same numeration. Their respective numerations differ with respect to whether they include a null pronoun or a clitic pronoun. The derivations of the two constructions are therefore not in competition. This is not the case in MA, where the numeration of both constructions includes a null pronoun. In MA, the two constructions differ with respect to whether the object agreement features on the verb are or are not spelled out. At least Italian appears to be consistent with the prediction. Example (i), with an optional clitic pronoun in the position of the parasitic gap, is cited and discussed by Cinque (1990:154).

(i)  ?Le carte   che Gianni ha  messo *t* via dopo aver   (le)     esaminate
      the papers that Gianni put away       after having (them) examined
      con  cura . . . .
      with care

# Chapter 6

| Parasitic Gaps in English: Some Overlooked Cases and Their Theoretical Implications | Robert D. Levine, Thomas E. Hukari, and Michael Calcagno |
|---|---|

## 6.1 Introduction

In the very first research we are aware of that called attention to the parasitic gap (P-gap) phenomenon, Ross 1967, two possibilities were entertained: (i) that P-gaps are essentially ordinary *wh*-type gaps, and (ii) that such gaps are null pronouns. Subsequent writers have for the most part lined up on behalf of one or the other of these alternatives.[1] We argue in section 6.2 that, contrary to common belief, P-gaps need not be nominal. We further present evidence that the distribution of such gaps is not congruent with that of weak definite pronominals. These findings remove what we take to be the chief empirical motivations for treating P-gaps as different in kind from canonical gaps. In section 6.3 we consider certain apparent instances of breakdown in case connectivity between the different gap sites in P-gap constructions. Such cases initially appear to constitute a major obstacle to treating P-gaps as formally identical to "normal" gaps. To overcome this difficulty, we outline an approach that allows all English P-gap constructions to be treated as completely case-consistent and that is, moreover, independently motivated by the behavior of syncretic forms not only in English but also in German, as discussed in Heinz and Matiasek 1994.

## 6.2 The Evidence Base for Null Pronominal P-gaps

The arguments for a null pronominal analysis of parasitic gaps are largely due to Cinque and Postal. In the following discussion, we reproduce their respective arguments, subsequently noting the empirical and/or analytic difficulties each of these arguments encounters.

### 6.2.1  Cinque's Proposals

**6.2.1.1  Putative Arguments for *pro* Gaps**   In Cinque 1990, P-gaps are identified as null resumptive pronouns—instances, that is, of *pro*.[2] Cinque's argument is actually twofold. First, he claims that missing object constructions and nonparasitic adjunct-island extractions form a single species with P-gaps, as attested by their common distributional idiosyncrasies. Second, he argues that these idiosyncrasies receive a unified treatment if both subtypes of construction are taken to be instances of *pro* rather than trace.[3]

In support of the first part of the argument, Cinque asserts that

(a) Missing object constructions such as *tough*, extraction from adjunct-islands such as

(1) Which papers did you go to England without signing *e*?

and P-gaps are all restricted to instances with NP fillers;

(b) All three constructions are barred from associating a filler with a gap in subject position of a finite clause, as in:

(2) a. *?Someone who John expected [*e* would be successful though
         believing [*e* is incompetent]] . . . .
    b. *?The student that Susan left because John said [*e* was
         intelligent] . . . .
    c. *?Mary is hard for me to believe [*e* kissed John]. (Cinque
         1990:105)

whereas ordinary *wh*-extraction can link fillers and finite clause subject position impeccably;

(c) In Italian and French, certain kinds of infinitival clauses that do not tolerate overt subjects do allow gaps in subject position. But such subject extraction is not possible when these clauses are the adverbial element in P-gap or adjunct-island constructions, or are the site of the gap in missing object constructions, in evident contrast to *wh*-extraction, which can apply to the subject positions of such clauses unproblematically.

(d) The second object of the dative construction, shown in boldface in (3a), is inaccessible to extraction in the family of constructions under consideration, though evidently accessible to normal *wh*-extraction:

(3) a.   We gave that man **the book**.
    b.   *?Books are not easy to give (even) that man *e*.
    c.   *?Those books are too boring to give even that man *e*.

d. *?the book that we filed instead of giving that man $e$.
e.   What did you give that man $e$?
(Cinque 1990:108)

(e) Finally, the class of extractions under discussion cannot extract an NP from an adjunct that itself occurs within an adjunct phrase:

(4) a.   the book that we left Russia after distributing $e$.
    b.   *the book that we left Russia without being arrested while distributing $e$.

and similarly for missing object and P-gap constructions. Thus again, all three constructions share a property which, Cinque argues, does not follow from a *wh*-extraction treatment.

On Cinque's account, all of the properties that group these three together in a natural class follow from the appearance of *pro*, rather than *t*, at the gap site at S-structure:

(a) *Only NP:* If, as Cinque (1990:115) asserts, "NP is the only category that has an empty pronominal form (*pro* or PRO)," then it follows that filler/gap constructions which necessarily take *pro* will have to be nominal.[4]

(b) *No Subject Gaps:* There is really nowhere *pro* can be as a finite subject that will give rise to a legal structure. By assumption, *pro* can only appear in syntactic contexts that allow it to be uniquely identified with respect to its φ-features. It cannot remain in finite subject position, because neither I nor C need be taken to be "proper licensors" in Cinque's terms, just as they are not proper head governors for purposes of the ECP. If *pro* moves to the Spec of its CP, it will no longer be in an A-position and hence cannot be interpreted at S-structure as a variable.

(c) *Romance Infinitival Subjects:* Cinque's account of his solution in French and Italian will be omitted here in the interests of conciseness; there is no English analog of the phenomenon in question.

(d) *Weak Pronominal Prohibition:* The prohibition on gaps in the second dative object position would follow if weak pronominals, such as *it*, and a fortiori *pro*, could not occupy the second dative position. According to Cinque, examples such as (5) show this to be a true generalization.

(5) *I gave that man it/them.

Hence the second dative object phenomenon receives a unified account on the assumption that *pro*, not *t*, is involved in the three constructions where extraction of this object is forbidden.

(e) *LF Pied-Piping:* The final datum—the effect of embedding in multiple island contexts—is the most complex part of Cinque's discussion. At issue is the sensitivity of parasitic, adjunct-island, and missing object gaps not only to iterated adjunct-island effects but to the full range of island effects as discussed at length in Chomsky 1986b. The prime piece of evidence here is the claim that parasitic and adjunct-island gaps, in common with missing object constructions, "seem able to violate one, but not more than one, island at a time" (Cinque 1990:133). A *wh*-movement analysis would putatively lead one to expect that an arbitrary number of island-violating extractions should be possible if a single one is. Cinque suggests that the nature of the island violation in such cases therefore involves not simple *wh*-extraction, but rather a form of pied-piping in which *wh*-properties attributed to *pro*, and subject to a set of conditions on pied-piping based on Kayne's (1983) connectedness proposal, give rise to the observed one-island-only effect.

What is relevant to Cinque's proposal is Kayne's hypothesis that the [+*wh*] feature also percolates from a *wh*-word to those elements which are its g-projections. Assume that the position occupied by a *wh*-phrase requires the [+*wh*] feature; then g-projections define a percolation path from the *wh*-word that launches the feature to the licensing $\bar{\text{A}}$ position. Suppose, as Cinque proposes, that the [+*wh*] feature attributed to *pro* percolates only to g-projections of *pro*. Add the requirement that being in a canonical government configuration is not enough, but that proper goverment of a maximal (g-) projection of $\alpha$ is necessary for the mother of the governor to be a g-projection of $\alpha$. Then only the lower adjunct acquires the [+*wh*] feature of the null pronominal.[5] Pied-piping of the internal adverb is ruled out by the absolute barrierhood of the larger adjunct phrase, under Cinque's adaptation of the *Barriers* framework.[6] Hence the duality of (4) is accounted for. On the other hand, the failure of, say, examples like:

(6) a.  *Which artist$_i$ did you invest heavily in $t_i$ after having talked with critics who$_j$ you had introduced $t_j$ to *pro*$_i$?
    b.  *Which artist$_i$ did you invest heavily in without wondering which critics$_j$ you should introduce $t_j$ to *pro*$_i$?

—that is, CNPC and *wh*-island effects—are straightforwardly attributable to the fact that there is no available $\bar{\text{A}}$-position from which the *pro* gap can be legally bound. Various other parallels between ordinary traces and *pro* in the class of constructions in question can be derived by reinterpreting the relevant constraints as restrictions on Ā-dependencies, re-gardless of the nature of the empty category involved.

**6.2.1.2  Empirical and Conceptual Flaws in Cinque's Account**  In this section we document the problems that, in our view, undermine every one of Cinque's categories of evidence. Consider first the claim that only NPs, and referential NPs at that, are eligible as gaps in the relevant con-structions that Cinque proposes the *pro* analysis to handle, in light of the following examples. (Note that small capitals indicate contrastive stress in examples throughout the chapter.)

(7) a. How harshly do you think we can treat THEM *e* without in turn
       being treated *e* OURSELVES? (adverbial P-gap)
    b. That's the kind of table ON WHICH it would be wrong to put
       expensive silverware *e* without also putting *e* a fancy centerpiece.
       (PP P-gap)[7]
    c. I wonder just how nasty you can PRETEND to be *e* without
       actually BECOMING. (AP P-gap)
    d. THAT DRUNK, it would be impossible for ME to get *e* without
       ROBIN getting *e* as well. (AP P-gap)[8]
    e. How drunk can you APPEAR (to be) *e* without actually BECOMING
       *e*?/How drunk can you APPEAR (to be) *e* without ACTUALLY being
       *e*? (AP parasitic gap)[9]
    f. That's exactly how strange we got them to act (after, of course,
       acting OURSELVES). (AP P-gap)
    g. A doctor, YOU could spend your whole life trying to be without
       ever becoming! (nonreferential NP P-gap)
    h. That Robin is a spy would naturally be difficult to refute *e*
       without (someone) having first conjectured *e*. (clausal P-gap)

It is worth noting that similar counterexamples are readily adduced for the other constructions that Cinque analyzes as instances of *pro*:

(8) a. There are certain developmental stages THROUGH which no one
       can reach true adulthood without first passing *e*. (PP adverbial
       island violation).
    b. It was one of those horrible situations FROM which you could go
       round in circles forever trying to extricate yourself. (PP adverbial
       island violation)
    c. I can tell you exactly how drunk an average guy can spend an
       hour in a bar without getting. (AP adverb island violation)

d. That Robin is a spy would be reasonable to conjecture at this point. (non-NP missing object construction)

e. Under the bed would be hard for me to consider to be a reasonable place to keep your beer. (PP missing object construction)

f. Proud (of themselves) is hard for me to picture ANY of them feeling, after what they've all done. (AP missing object construction)

These examples are precisely the kind of data which should not be well-formed on Cinque's hypothesis.[10]

Next, consider again Cinque's claim that subject position is uniformly barred as a site for the P-gap of the adjunct type and that the "identification" restrictions on *pro* can be shown to give rise to this effect. In contradiction to this claim, we find the following sentences to be essentially impeccable:

(9) a. Which people did you invite *e* to the party without thinking *e* would actually come? (finite subject P-gap)

b. Robin was the guru that critics of *e* traveled halfway round the world to PROVE *e* had been cheating young students out of their spring break money. (finite subject P-gap)

c. John is someone that Mary expects *e* will be successful though believing that to his dying day *e* will have the intelligence of a horsefly. (finite subject P-gap)

Interestingly, the construction of such finite-subject P-gap examples becomes extremely straightforward when the adjunct precedes the VP, rather than follows it, as in the following examples:

(10) a. Robin sold me a car, which after I discovered *e* wouldn't go more than forty miles an hour I sold *e* to an eccentric collector. (finite subject P-gap)

b. There go the Enroughity twins, who I after I learned *e* were coming here I decided not to see *e*. (finite subject P-gap)

c. Terry is someone who once you realize *e* is a flattery addict, you can get *e* to do anything you want. (finite subject P-gap)

On Cinque's account, none of these should be remotely as well formed as we find them, among many other similar examples.[11]

We turn now to the cases in which a gap in the second dative object position is blocked. Consider the following, where V̆ indicates an unstressed vowel and V́ indicates a stressed vowel:

(11) a. I can think of a couple of presents that would be really fun to
       give Róbin for his birthday.
     b. *We gave Róbin thĕm for his birthday.

(12) a. I found a really nice card that I decided to keep for myself
       instead of sending Róbin for his birthday.
     b. *I sent Róbin ĭt for his birthday.[12]

(13) a. There's certain evidence that we may have to go to trial
       without ever shówing Robin.
     b. There's certain evidence which I won't feel comfortable acting
       on without first shówing Robin.
     c. *We shówed Róbin ĭt.

(14) a. There was certain crucial news about the case that Robin went
       on holidays without ever télling her attorneys.
     b. *Robin tóld her attorneys ĭt.[13]

Once again, we conclude that the evidential basis required from English
to maintain Cinque's proposal simply does not exist. In fact, if Zwicky
(1986) is right about such constructions, as we believe, the failure of cases
with overt pronominals is a purely prosodic effect that should not arise
when the material corresponding to the second dative position is inaudible, so that the second dative object phenomenon is essentially irrelevant
to the argument.

    Finally we come to what Cinque calls the "selective" island sensitivity
of the gaps he analyzes as *pro*. Under his argument that where a single
instance of an island configuration seems violable but a double violation
involving an iteration of the same island within a large island is ruled out,
*wh*-movement has no explanation and therefore other analyses must be
pursued. We reject this argument entirely because it is has been proposed
numerous times in the literature that island effects display a cumulative
pattern and that it is precisely the iteration of such violations which
causes difficulties (for the processing mechanism, most probably) that result in a negative assessment of the data. Our first point, then, is that
Cinque's rejection of a conventional filler/trace link in the cases in question is unnecessary, given the existence of clear examples of the same sort
of pattern in uncontroversial *wh*-extractions, as we document directly. But
beyond this point, we observe that under Cinque's analysis, perfectly legal
P-gaps must be analyzed in English as instances of illegal movements
occurring at LF—an outcome that clearly contradicts his insistence on the
importance of the covariation between legal S-structure movements and
the possibility of LF pied-piping in Italian, as in his invocation of Lonzi

1988 (Cinque 1990:142); see our examples in (16) and (17) below. We also note below that Cinque's rationale for the LF pied-piping is in fact rather shaky. Together, these points gravely undermine the final empirical argument Cinque offers on behalf of the the null-pronominal treatment of P-gaps.

So far as we are aware, the first observation in print that simple iteration can result in an island effect was Fodor 1983, where the following example is given:

(15) a.    Who did you take a photograph of *e*?
     b.    *??Who did you take a photograph of a statue of *e*?

As Fodor notes, since extraction from a picture-noun PP complement is legal, there is presumably no island associated with such an NP, which then makes it exceedingly difficult to motivate (15b) in strictly syntactic terms. Along lines very reminiscent of Fodor's speculations, Chomsky (1986) suggested that subjacency should not be treated as an all-or-nothing effect, but rather that cumulative occurrences of 1-subjacency violations might be thought of as additive. More recently, Kluender (1998) proposed a model of island effects as the accumulation of processing burdens which, while still more qualitative than quantitative, presents a psycholinguistic architecture that makes cases such as Fodor's in (14) or the failure of iteration in adjunct island violations that Cinque finds so significant, an entirely straightforward matter calling for no special dichotomies in the classification of filler/gap dependencies. Kluender argues that there are a number of processing effects that can be independently established for well-formed sentences based on both functional criteria (e.g., differences in response times in experimental contexts) and neurophysiological measures (EPR potentials and related measures) which reveal certain real-time processing effects demonstrably relevant to island phenomena. Chief among these are both the greater persistence in processing memory—and the concommittant processing costs—of constituents in proportion to their lexical content (definite descriptions at the top end, weak pronouns at the bottom); the significant cost, in terms of processing resources, of linking elements across clause boundaries; and the relatively greater accessibility of more, versus less, referential elements. Kluender shows that in cases whose problematic nature seems closely associated with processing difficulties, these difficulties can be ameliorated by manipulating the processing factors just cited, and that precisely parallel manipulations tend to ameliorate both strong and weak island violations. If we further assume that adjunct clauses represent less accessible domains than complement clauses (for reasons possibly related to those factors making less referential constituents more vulnerable to elimination from real-time processes), then it is not difficult to see how a single transition into an adjunct domain might be viable but a second one could well cause the process to exceed the available resources and therefore halt. Thus, quite detailed psychological models exist which plausibly explain the facts in question in terms completely compatible with what is known about the cumulative effects of processing difficulties, making the elaborate pied-piping scenario Cinque posits unnecessary.

Beyond the issue of necessity, however, there is also excellent reason to reject Cinque's LF pied-piping hypothesis on strictly factual grounds. The basic data here are cases of uncontroversially well-formed parasitic and adjunct island gaps that do not correspond to legally pied-pipable constituents in English. Consider, for example, cases such as the following:

(16) a. Which papers$_i$ did you take $e_i$ without Robin discovering $e_i$?
     b. I wonder which papers$_i$ Leslie escaped to Bermuda without Robin ever discovering $e_i$.

Given the necessity for LF pied-piping that Cinque posits, we are apparently required to move the entire adjunct phrase, which is the maximum g-projection of the [+wh] feature originating in *pro*. But overt instances of such pied-piping are impossible:

(17) a. *[The papers$_i$ [without Robin discovering which$_i$] you took $e_i$] are on the table.
     b. *These are the papers Robin discovering which we must prevent.

In view of this widely acknowledged distributional fact about English (which, for a small minority of speakers, apparently contrasts somewhat with that of possessive gerundive phrases as in ??*These are the papers Robin's discovering which we must prevent*), it is difficult to see how Cinque's analysis can meet his own plausibility requirement, alluded to earlier, that claims of LF pied-piping need to be ratified by evidence that such pied-piping is possible in "overt" syntax.[14]

In summary, it appears to us that closer examination of Cinque's arguments reveals that the specific factual claims used to support the various arguments given for a *pro* rather than *wh*-extraction treatment of gaps in the three constructions in question are simply mistaken. We have given counterexamples to every one of them, and on these grounds alone, it seems unnecessary to abandon the default position that P-gaps (inter alia) are instances of the same mechanism as other filler/gap linkages.[15]

## 6.2.2 Postal's Proposals

### 6.2.2.1 Postal's Evidence for Null Resumptive Parasitic Gaps Postal's (1994b) argument takes essentially the following form:

First, there is evidence in English for two different kinds of extraction: one that can only occur in pronominal environments—roughly speaking, those environments where a pronoun can occur—and one that is not so restricted. One sort of extraction ("*B*-extraction"), according to Postal (1994b:162), comprises clefts, NP topicalization, and nonrestrictive relative extraction and is accounted for by positing an underlying null resumptive pronominal at the gap site. But although Postal introduces only the first three constructions as "basic" examples of this extraction type, he notes (p. 175) that "every context supporting the claim that *B*-extractions are excluded from antipronominal contexts supports a parallel claim for [missing object and P-gap] constructions." He also suggests (p. 181) that all left-extractions can be partitioned into "those which require R[esumptive] P[ronouns] in their extraction sites; these are the *B*-extractions of earlier discussion" on the one hand and "all others" on the other. This seems to imply that any construction that gives evidence of being tied strictly to pronoun-compatible extraction sites must be a *B*-extraction. Because the inability to appear in antipronominal contexts is what forces the RP analysis, in Postal's view, it follows that missing object and P-gap constructions must be further instances of *B*-extractions.[16]

On Postal's account, this null pronominal eventually undergoes movement, creating exactly the island effects associated with the the other type ("*A*-extraction") and thus helping to mask the essential difference between the two. NP topicalization, for example, is claimed to be *B*-extraction, on the basis of its putative restriction to pronominal contexts, where the relevant notion of pronominal is specifically that comprising weak definite pronouns, prototypically English *it*. This original dichotomy between extraction types is defended in Postal 1994b, where a large range of syntactic contexts is used to motivate it, including the following:[17]

(18) *Antipronominal Environments*
    a. Change of color environments:
        i.   *They painted their porch green, but I refused to paint mine it.
        ii.   They painted their porch green, but he never painted my car green.
        iii.   *Green/that color, he never painted the cart.

   b. Predicate nominal positions
      i. *Frank became it.
      ii. Frank became a bodyguard.
      iii. *A bodyguard, Frank became.
   c. Specialized spatial/locational contexts
      i. *Robin thinks the president was born in Argentina, but I
         know she wasn't born in it.
      ii. *Argentina, the President was born in.
      iii. *Mike didn't enter the Greek army, but Sam did enter it.
      iv. *What Mike criticized after entering was the Greek army.
   d. Extraposition contexts
      i. They published a scurrilous review of his book last year.
      ii. [No such scurrilous review of his book]$_i$ did they publish
         last year.
      iii. [No such scurrilous review]$_i$ did they publish $e_i$ of his book.
      iv. *[Such a scurrilous review]$_i$ they published $e_i$ last year of his
         book.
      v. *[Which review]$_i$ did they eventually publish $e_i$ after first
         rejecting of his book?[18]
   e. Existential *there* constructions
      i. He knew that there were such chemicals in the bottle.
      ii. *He knew that there were them in the bottle.
      iii. *[Such chemicals]$_i$ he knew that there were $e_i$ in the bottle.

In these and other example contexts, the starred forms given are taken to be representative of the behavior of the entire class of *B*-extraction types. Thus, in (18a–c) Postal's explicit intention is to show that *B*-extractions *as a class* are barred from antipronominal contexts.[19] Postal's proposal is that the overall simplest account of the large and diverse range of environments in which *B*-extraction is impossible is that *B*-extraction gap sites are initially occupied by null resumptive pronouns, and the demonstration that in all such cases, weak definite pronouns are inadmissible is intended as the primary empirical support for this claim. The logic is similar to that pursued by Cinque in connection with, for example, the second dative object position, although Postal (1994b) provides a broader range of evidence and argues in finer detail for his conclusions.

**6.2.2.2 Critique of Postal's Evidence** Two separate components of Postal's arguments need to be considered here: on the one hand, the position that PG=NP (i.e., that P-gaps must be nominal constituents), and on the other, the idea that null resumptive elements are the source of parasitic gaps. These claims are logically independent; it is conceivable that there could be nonnominal null resumptive proforms, in addition to what is typically designated as *pro* in the GB literature. If so, then we would expect to encounter nonnominal P-gaps even under the assumption that such gaps are in general linked to their antecedents by a fundamentally different connectivity mechanism from *wh*-question gaps. But reframing the argument in these terms places a severe burden of proof on the argument that P-gaps are actually (traces of) null proforms, for the following reason. We provided in (7) a number of P-gap examples in which the gap site is located in antinominal, hence antipronominal, contexts or in nominal contexts that are not referential (e.g., (7g)).[20] Consider another example of the same general class, involving an unexceptionable PP P-gap:

(19) a. This is a cause TO which many people are ATTRACTED without ever becoming seriously DEVOTED.
   b. On whom can you never foist your OWN troubles without foisting everyone ELSE'S as well?
   c. Robin is someone OF whom people are ENVIOUS without ever being really FOND.

Such examples directly counterexemplify Postal's claim that PG=NP, just as they do Cinque's. Therefore, if the null pronominal component of Postal's proposal is to be preserved, there must be at least one null resumptive pro-PP corresponding to *to whom* and *on him/her*. But no independent evidence for such a proform exists in English, where to our knowledge the only PP proforms are locative or temporal in nature (i.e., *there, here,* and *then*):

(20) a. *I noticed that many people were attracted to this cause, but that almost nobody wound up seriously devoted there.
   b. *Under the circumstances, it will be necessary for me not only to foist my troubles on Robin, but to foist yours there as well.

Hence, maintaining the null pronominal analysis of English P-gaps inevitably entails positing a proform that is not only inaudible but completely different in its distribution from any overt English proform.

Note also that the distribution of nonnominal P-gaps is not confined to the [VP VP XP] construction. The following examples, illustrating such gaps within subjects, strike us as unexceptionable:[21]

(21) a. This is a table [ON which]$_i$ anyone who puts some books $pg_i$ must subsequently put some magazines $t_i$ as well.

b. [On which table]$_i$ would you putting the BOOK $pg_i$ entail ME putting some MAGAZINES $t_i$?

c. This is the kind of table [ON which]$_i$ you(r) putting your feet $pg_i$ would allow me to put my elbows $t_i$.

d. This is cause [TO which]$_i$ anyone who becomes ATTRACTED $pg_i$ will wind up becoming totally DEVOTED $t_i$.

e. [that nasty]$_i$, someone who TRIES to be $pg_i$ may well wind up actually BECOMING $t_i$.

f. How harshly will our treating Robin $pg_i$ lead to our being treated ourselves $t_i$?[22]

These data strike us as fine so far as syntactic well-formedness is concerned and thus convincingly refute any effort to depict our claims about P-gaps as unrepresentative or restricted to isolated, sporadic cases. Moreover, the argument just formulated against PG=NP receives independent confirmation from a variety of antipronominal contexts, including those cited in (18). We argue that there is in fact no congruence of P-gaps and pronominal contexts. Note the following examples, in which *B*-extractions appear in the antipronominal contexts cited:

(22) *Second dative object* (= (12)–(14))[23]

a. I found a really nice card that I decided to keep for myself instead of sending Róbin for his birthday.

b. *I sent Róbin ĭt for his birthday.

c. There's certain evidence that we may have to go to trial without ever shówing Robin.

d. There's certain evidence which I won't feel comfortable acting on without first shówing Robin.

e. *We shówed Róbin ĭt.

f. There was certain crucial news about the case that Robin went on holidays without ever télling her attorneys.

g. *Robin tóld her attorneys ĭt.

(23) *Change of color contexts*

a. *We painted the walls it.

b. Mint green is a color that you might paint your CEILING without necessarily wanting to paint the surrounding WALLS.[24]

(24) *Predicate nominals*

a. *Robin wants to be a doctor but I don't think he'll ever become it.

b. Anybody can become a bureaucrat, but a doctor, one could spend one's whole life STUDYING to be without ever BECOMING![25]

(25) *Specialized spatial/locative contexts*
   a. *He talked a lot about the Greek Army but had never entered it.
   b. The Greek Army is one national service that I would certainly want to assess carefully before entering.
   c. *Robin thinks the president was born in Argentina, but I know she wasn't born in it.
   d. Which countries do you become a citizen of only if you were actually born in?
   e. Japan is a country that no one who wasn't born in can ever become a citizen of.

(26) *Existential* there *postcopula contexts*
   a. He knew that there had been discussions like that from time to time.
   b. *He denied that the research group had ever had such discussions, but I know that there have been them from time to time.
   c. Discussions like that there HAVE been, from time to time, but we don't generally broadcast the fact.

One may also note examples like the following:

(27) a. New York City is crowded and dirty, but it's also very exciting.
   b. New York$_j$ is one city that (the) citizens of (*it$_j$) find terrifically exciting.
   c. The Grand Canyon is vast, but it's also ecologically fragile.
   d. We flew over the Grand Canyon, but none of my pictures of it came out.
   e. The Grand Canyon$_j$ is a place that pictures of (*it$_j$) seem to inspire millions of people to pay a visit to.

Pronominals, including weak definite pronouns such as *it*, appear to be systematically blocked within subject position in relative clauses on the indicated coindexing with antecedents in the higher clause. Yet the data show that such positions readily display P-gaps. The generalization that P-gaps can only appear in nonantipronominal contexts, and therefore are most parsimoniously accounted for by analyzing them as null pronouns, thus seems to encounter a major factual challenge from examples such as (27).

Postal handles such challenges by what he terms the "wide/narrow pronominal ban distinction." Wide bans on pronouns hold in contexts where neither an overt nor covert pronoun can appear, whereas narrow bans apply only to overt pronominals. The story for (27) would then be that the subject-NP–internal position only supports a narrow ban on weak definite pronominals. An obvious question then is whether Postal's hypothesis can in principle be falsified. In a context where a *B*-gap can appear but a weak indefinite pronoun cannot, the weak-ban escape hatch is always available. Is there in principle any way of jeopardizing the claim that *B*-gaps can only appear where weak definite pronouns can? Significantly, Postal (1994b:176) acknowledges that the answer to this question "is, for the moment, negative," but he goes on to argue that the empirical nature of the claim is nonetheless supported by the fact that all *B*-construction gaps, across the board, can appear in the same set of antipronominal environments. The implicit argument seems to be that this convergence of behavior indicates some special property of the antipronominal contexts that allow *B*-constructions, setting them off from those that do not, and the wide/narrow ban distinction captures this dichotomy. But the examples given in (23)–(27) appear to show that contrary to Postal's claim that *B*-extractions reflect uniform behavior, P-gaps can indeed appear in environments where by his own account other *B*-extractions cannot. Since one group of pronominal-gap constructions can appear in (23)–(25) while others cannot, it is hard to see how the wide/narrow ban provides an account of the difference; on either account, the behavior of one or the other group of extractions is entirely mispredicted. The ban dichotomy in fact is simply a diacritic, taking Postal's hypothesis out of the realm of what can be empirically challenged.

### 6.2.3   A Critique of Some Challenges

**6.2.3.1   Adjectival P-gaps**   We believe that the foregoing observations establish that there are ample grounds for skepticism about the partitioning of extractions advocated in somewhat different forms by Cinque and Postal. But it should be evident that we are not claiming that the data they have claimed to be ill-formed in building their case are in all instances actually good. Our position is rather that there is a large amount of data which should not be good on their account which is in fact well-formed, and which thus—in the absence of some appropriate elaboration of their hypotheses—undermines their analyses. We also claim that certain of the ill-formed data that have been adduced become acceptable with only minor, structurally irrelevant lexical substitutions, while others turn out to be irrelevant to the claims being made.

The nature of adjectival P-gaps is a useful point of departure in this regard. Consider our claims that, in general, P-gapped predicate adjectives are grammatical, in light of the following examples from work by Lasnik and Saito (1992:147):

(28) a. *How angry$_i$ can John appear $e_i$ without becoming $e_i$?
    b. *How quickly did John solve the problem $e_i$ after proving the
        theorem $e_i$?

We agree that these P-gap examples are ungrammatical, and we do not
claim that all nonnominal P-gaps will be good. Therefore, examples of
ill-formed nonnominal P-gaps do not jeopardize our position. Crucially,
previous theories of P-gaps have been heavily based on the claim that there
are no systematically nonnominal P-gaps and that P-gaps cannot occur in
antipronominal contexts. The evidence we have adduced above—which
we think comprises more than a few examples and which can be expanded
without difficulty—directly challenges the factual basis of these hypotheses. We claim that, in the general case, nonnominal P-gaps are good, but
that in many instances they may be ill-formed—just as, for example, ATB
extractions from coordinate structures may be permissible in general but
bad in particular instances.

The data involving adjectival P-gaps from Lasnik and Saito (1992)
provide a useful case in point. We ourselves do not find the example *How
angry can one APPEAR without later BECOMING?* to be ill-formed, though
for some speakers it is unquestionably awkward. But we do claim that it is
no worse (or better) than:

(29) *??How angry$_i$ can John appear $e_i$ but not become $e_i$?

Particularly on the reading where the question corresponds to "for what
degree $x$ of anger can John appear $x$ angry but not become $x$ angry," this
example seems indistinguishable from (28). Postal (1993) has written a
detailed defense of the claim that P-gaps and ATB extraction are different
phenomena, and so would presumably take the shared awkwardness
of these two examples to reflect some property independent of the P-gap
status of one of member of the comparably ill-formed pair.[26] In fact, both
examples seem to us to improve markedly if one assumes that there is
some threshhold of anger such that, to convincingly appear angrier than
that maximum level of anger, a psychological effort is required that
inevitably leads one to becoming that angry.[27]

Consider now examples (7e–f). These data have important implications
for the status of sentences such as *How sick can you plausibly pretend to be
without actually being?*. Suppose that examples of AP P-gaps such as (7e)
were, instead, derived through AP-deletion, as in *Terry is drunk, and Bo is
also.* In support of this analysis, one might note an apparent correlation
between the AP-deletion class of constructions and such AP P-gaps. The
AP-deletion constructions corresponding to ill-formed AP P-gap constructions like the following are also ungrammatical:

(30) a. *How drunk is it possible to APPEAR (to be) $e$ without actually turning $e$?

 b. *It is possible to APPEAR to be very drunk without actually turning $e$.

But nonparasitic analogs of this extraction are extremely marginal at best:

(31) a. ??How drunk would you say Robin turned $e$ at the party?

 b. ??I wonder how drunk to turn $e$ at the party tonight.

Hence the data in (30) do not appear to have much bearing on the point at issue. Note also that (32a) is ungrammatical, despite the fact that the corresponding *wh*-construction is fine.

(32) a. *Mike appeared to be very drunk without being $e$.

 b.  How drunk did Mike APPEAR to be without actually being $e$?

By the same token, the presumed source of the second example in (7e) is bad as well:

(33) ?*It is possible to APPEAR to be totally drunk without ACTUALLY being.

Derivation of these AP examples by deletion is thus challenged by the fact that the presumed source is indeed ill-formed.[28]

We further note that VP deletion as a source for all AP parasitic gaps is in any case precluded by the existence of cases such as the first example in (7e), where the verb governing the parasitic gap site, *become/becoming*, does not tolerate AP-deletion under any circumstance. Moreover, AP P-gaps appear in contexts where AP-deletion is, to our knowledge, never possible, as in the case of P-gaps within subjects such as (21e,f), repeated here:

(21) e. THAT nasty$_i$, someone who TRIES to be $t_i$ may well wind up actually BECOMING $t_i$.

 f.  How harshly$_i$ will our treating Robin $t_i$ lead to our being treated ourselves $t_i$?

Thus, given the full range of facts, there seems to be no reason to suppose that examples like (7d,e) are anything other than AP P-gaps, in direct contradiction to Cinque's (1990) and Postal's (1994a) assertions that (true) P-gap constructions are restricted to NPs.

**6.2.3.2 Pseudoparasitic Gaps via RNR**    The examples in (7) are exactly what one would expect VP adjunct P-gaps to look like based on the properties of hitherto "canonical" NP P-gaps: they are multiple gap constructions with *wh*, topicalization, or missing-object construction fillers in which the gap in the adjunct is in some sense dependent on the existence of a gap in the main VP (cf. ??*How harshly do you think we can treat* THEM *well without our being treated ourselves?*). Our view therefore is that the burden of proof falls on the position that these are *not* P-gaps. In the preceding subsection we considered and rebutted an alternative derivation of our AP parasitic gap examples. Here we examine a second alternative source for examples such as those in (7), based on the possibility of combining Right Node Raising (RNR) with left extraction of the RNRed constituent. Our conclusion, again, is that this alternative derivation fails empirically and thus cannot challenge the status of (7) as true parasitic gaps.

Consider:

(34) This is the closet [INTO which]$_i$ I wouldn't want to put that box $e_i$ without also putting a lot of other things $e_i$.

Suppose that, rather than being derived in a fashion parallel to nominal parasitic gaps, (34) were licensed along the following lines:

(35) I wouldn't want to put that box into which without also putting a lot of other things into which →
[I wouldn't want to put that box $e_i$ without also putting a lot of other things $e_i$] [into which]$_i$ (by RNR) →
[into which]$_i$ [I wouldn't want to put that box $e_i$ without also putting a lot of other things $e_i$] (by *wh*-movement)

If we assume that RNRed constituents can serve as the locus for applications of leftward extraction, as in Postal 1998, then there is no reason why such a derivation should not occur, yielding the data in (7) and many others we have cited in this paper as nonnominal P-gap constructions. It then follows that such data cannot be invoked as counterevidence to the claim that only nominal categories can be genuine parasitic gaps.

This alternative derivational approach leads, however, to a major misprediction. It has been observed in much of the literature that RNR appears to violate syntactic constraints on leftward extraction (see, for example, Wexler and Culicover 1980). Postal himself (1998:102) suggests with respect to Subjacency and other major island restrictions that "although all extractions, including RNR, share many properties, the island types in question constrain only L[eft]-extractions." If apparent nonnominal P-gaps are derived as in (35), it should then follow that there is a derivational route available that yields pseudoparasitic gaps in which the island restrictions in question are acceptably violated. For example, the following derivation should be legal:

(36) You bought [a new book about homunculi]$_i$, without having met the man who you believe wrote [a new book about homunculi]$_i$ →
You bought $e_i$, without having met the man who you believe wrote $e_i$, [a new book about homunculi]$_i$ →
[Which new book about homunculi]$_i$ did you buy $e_i$ without having met the man who you believe wrote $e_i$

But the resulting form, *Which new book about homunculi did you buy without having met the man who you believe wrote?, seems to us ill-formed to the point of uninterpretability. Evidence that island constraints are respected by whatever linkage holds between P-gap fillers and their corresponding P-gaps has appeared in the literature at least since Chomsky 1986b. Postal takes this evidence into account in essentially the same fashion as in Chomsky 1986b by requiring that the null resumptive pronouns in the underlying position of parasitic gaps move to some higher position en route to the terminal stage in the derivation of P-gap sentences. But if the pseudoparasitic derivation in (36) is available, these island effects should not occur at all.

We therefore conclude that the alternative derivation source for (7) and comparable examples is not available. It follows that this source cannot be invoked to deny such examples the status of bona fide P-gaps. We conclude, then, that they must be regarded as authentic contraindications to Cinque's and Postal's respective analyses of the P-gap phenomenon.[29]

**6.2.3.3 Extraposition**  Postal (personal communication) cites the following data in support of his A/B-extraction distinction, asserting that it undermines a view of P-gaps as no different syntactically from ordinary wh-gaps:

(37) a. Jerome saw a woman/*her in Denver who had green hair.
b. What woman$_i$ did Jerome see $t_i$ in Denver who had green hair?
c. What woman$_i$ did Jerome call $t_i$ after meeting $t_i$ in Denver (*who had green hair)?
d. Jerome saw some other woman in Denver who had green hair.
e. Some other women $t_i$, Jerome saw in Denver ([*who had green hair]$_i$).

By hypothesis, P-gaps involve an underlying weak definite pronominal. Such pronominals do not form constituents with relative clauses. Hence, an extraposition from the moved wh-constituent will not be licensed, because the extraposed relative cannot be associated with a pronominal (*Which woman who had green hair did Jerome call after meeting her in Denver?* but *??Which woman did Jerome call after meeting her in Denver who had green hair?*). The unacceptability of (37c) in the relevant version would therefore be due to the pronominal character of parasitic gaps.[30] The problem is that extraposition of the relative clause from its site within the *wh*-phrase seems to force it to be interpreted as a modifier of the pronoun as well. But then it follows that ordinary *wh*-extraction from coordinate structures should show a markedly different acceptability pattern in the relevant examples. Furthermore, we should never find P-gap cases that comfortably allow the kind of extraposition exhibited in (37c).

These predictions are incorrect. In the first place, we find

(38)  ??Which women did Jerome meet in Denver and then call who had green hair?

to be about as ill-formed as the relevant version of (37c). More important, we have examples such as (39).

(39)  a.  How many people$_i$ did you interview $t_i$ without hiring $t_i$ for this job who could have done it much better than the guy you got?

  b.  How many people$_i$ did you interview $t_i$ and then not hire $t_i$ for this job who could have done it better than the guy you got?

Examples (39a,b), structurally identical to the ill-formed example in (37c), seem entirely acceptable. If Postal is indeed correct that extraposition compatibility is indicative of antipronominality, then examples such as (39), far from offering support, turn out to be crucial counterexamples: antipronominal contexts in which P-gaps nonetheless occur at least as freely as other kinds of multiple gap constructions.

**6.2.3.4  Other Cases**    Other challenges to the claim that P-gaps can be nonnominal fail because they turn out to have nothing to do with P-gaps per se. Consider, for example, the following paradigm suggesting that PP P-gaps derive from RNR, and therefore that where RNR fails such nonnominal P-gaps fail also:[31]

(40)  a.  Your being fond of Mike made Sally take pictures of Lou.
  b.  *Your being fond $e_i$ made Sally take pictures $e_i$ [of Mike]$_i$.
  c  *This is the guy [of whom]$_i$ your being fond $e_i$ made Sally take pictures $e_i$.

But the ungrammaticality of (40c) is independent of the P-gap nature of the construction. Compare:

(41) a. *Do you have any idea [of whom]$_i$ Bo was fond $e_i$ and Kelly
      took pictures $e_i$?
    b. *Robin$_i$ is the guy of whom Lee was fond and Kelly took
      pictures $e_i$.

We do not have an explicit account of extraction phenomena that would
correctly predict this pattern, but it is evident from (41) that such an
account, if correct, is unlikely to make the ungrammaticality of (40c)
a specific outcome of P-gap (as opposed to ordinary *wh*-extraction)
phenomena.

In challenging Postal's account of P-gaps, we wish to stress that we
do not regard the empirical base he has assembled as negligible. On the
contrary, it is formidable and deserves a far more detailed response than
space limitations allow us to provide here.[32] Nonetheless, the lesson we
draw from the examples we have adduced above is that a large number of
essentially unanalyzed negative examples of some phenomenon do not
and cannot by themselves confirm the nonexistence of that phenomenon,
particularly when there are many quite acceptable apparent instances of
the same phenomenon and when comparable ill-formedness seems to
arise in structurally parallel cases of other phenomena whose existence is
not at issue. The pseudoparasitic derivation hypothesis is, as we have
shown, an untenable alternative to our claim that many kinds of nonnominal P-gap phenomena exist, and, for the reasons we have stated, and
in the absence of a detailed and convincing demonstration that our data
are not in fact P-gaps, such phenomena must be taken seriously as effec-
tive counterexamples to the analysis of P-gaps as resumptive pronouns.

## 6.3  P-gaps as "Normal" Gaps

The foregoing observations, we believe, have established the claim that
the covert resumptive pronominal analysis of P-gaps remains fundamentally unmotivated. We propose that parasitic gaps, at least, are no different in kind from canonical instances of extraction, such as *wh*-question
gaps. This conclusion, however, is compatible with two quite distinct
alternative solutions.

One of these is the treatment of P-gaps due to Contreras (1984), where
such gaps are linked by Move α to Ā-position operators just as true gaps
are. The operators binding P-gaps are empty and acquire referential content only via a process of composition with the chain linking the overt
operator to the "true" gap under certain structural conditions. Thus the
overt filler binds only a single gap; the P-gap and its covert filler form a
separate chain, entailing at least the possibility that the P-gap and the

"true" gap will differ in terms of certain morphosyntactic features, sharing only an index.

A stronger version of this hypothesis requires that the overt filler bind both the parasitic and the "true"gap, so that the morphosyntactic content of the two gaps must be identical up to the point determined by the connectivity mechanism that links gaps and fillers. Such an analysis, though possible in principle within GB, is apparently precluded by the Bijection Principle proposed by Koopman and Sportiche (1981) and adopted in much subsequent work, at least under the assumption that the P-gap is a variable to the same extent as the "true" gap. But it is in fact the standard account of P-gaps in several analyses couched in various avatars of phrase structure grammar, begining with Gazdar 1981. Such analyses thus embody a particularly pure version of a research strategy in which extraction constructions are taken to instantiate a unitary syntactic phenomenon. This position is itself extremely strong, and as such should not, in our view, be abandoned in the absence of convincing counterevidence. As we hope to have established, the arguments offered by Cinque (1990) and Postal (1994a,b) do not incorporate such counterevidence, so it seems reasonable to explore the unitary treatment of P-gaps and consider what problems arise for such an account of unbounded dependencies.

We now sketch an account of P-gaps within the framework of Head-driven Phrase Structure Grammar.

### 6.3.1  P-gaps

Our account of P-gaps incorporates the hypothesis first stated in Gazdar 1981 and adhered to in Gazdar, Klein, Pullum, and Sag 1985 and later Pollard and Sag 1994 (hencefore P&S), according to which SLASH specifications may pass up from more than one daughter. When these specifications are identical, they simply merge by set union, as in P&S's Nonlocal Feature Principle (1994:164). Thus we predict the examples in (42) to be grammatical.

(42)  a. The article that we went to England without reading *e* ...
      b. The article that we filed *e* without reading *e* ...
      c. Which of those instructors did you repeat complaints about *e* to *e*?

The first of these examples exhibits extraction from an adjunct, and the second shows simultaneous extraction from a complement position in the main VP (i.e., a "licensing" gap) as well. The third demonstrates the possibility of multiple (but identical) extractions out of sister complements. The tree in example (43) makes the well-formedness of such examples more transparent.[33]

(43)

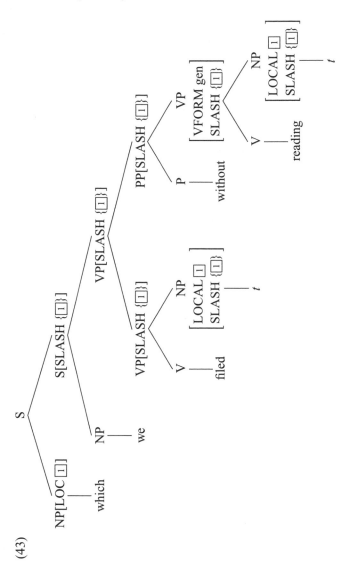

The VP *filed NP without reading NP* must, by the NFP, share its SLASH specification with at least one daughter, so that in principle any number of its descendants could bear the same SLASH value without running afoul of the NFP, as long as one of them does. If both the VP and the PP daughters share their mother's SLASH value, then we wind up with a tree like the one in (43), where the split in the instantiation path of SLASH on the mother VP yields two lower pathways for SLASH percolation, one terminating on the object of *reading* and the other on the object of *filed*. Example (43) displays in its essential form the PSG approach to P-gaps that has been followed since the mid 1980s.

Similarly, we predict that both of the following are well formed, although subjects are, we admit, recalcitrant extraction domains.

(44) a. It's the kind of policy statement that jokes about *e* are a dime a dozen.
   b. It's a tax initiative that only massive opposition to *e* will defeat *e*.

The same kind of analysis we have already given for adjunct parasitic gaps applies here: the SLASH on the clausal head licensed by the Filler-Head schema may be passed down to the subject daughter only, as in (44a), or it may, as in (44b), be passed down in addition to the head daughter (apart, of course, from the case where it is passed down solely to the VP head daughter). Nothing further need be added to the framework in order to get P-gaps, which therefore emerge as an almost trivial consequence of the fact that the NFP makes no stipulation as to the number of daughters that must share the mother's SLASH value.[34]

Consider now how the data adduced earlier fare under this analysis of P-gaps. Given that P-gaps are syntactically identical—both in internal content and in their connectivity relationship to the filler—to "true" gaps, and given that the evidence apparently suggests that no true parasitism is involved, it follows that any category of gap licensed under the Filler-Head schema will be able to appear within any nonhead constituent, whether or not there is an additional gap elsewhere in the structure linked to the same filler. On this approach, incorporating essential insights of GPSG and HPSG, the well-formedness of examples such as those we provided in (7) immediately follows, with no special extra requirements.

As well, the connectivity mechanism discussed in regard to normal extraction allows gaps, and therefore P-gaps, to appear essentially freely, so that the latter are not restricted just to sites where some other type of anaphoric element (e.g., a pronominal) can appear. If there were empirical warrant for such a restriction, it could in fact be captured in HPSG by restricting the type of the SLASH value to pronominal content values, as

P&S do in the case of *tough* gaps; but as we discussed in some detail in section 6.2, there is no basis for this move in the case of P-gaps.[35] Hence the HPSG treatment we have presented appears to license the possibilities exemplified in our data with an absolute minimum of machinery.

Nonetheless, the HPSG solution we have sketched is not unproblematic. The near-complete identity between the categorial content of the filler on the one hand and its associated SLASH values on the other, together with the nature of the HPSG feature-passing mechanism, jointly entail the near identity of the filler and all gap sites linked to it. Given HPSG feature architecture, this identity extends to the case specifications of all gaps in P-gap constructions. But it is easy to demonstrate case discrepancies among the gaps in such constructions. Consider the following kind of example, noted in Hukari and Levine 1996:

(45)  Robin is someone who$_i$ even [good friends of $e_i$] believe $e_i$ should be closely watched.

with the following partial analysis:

(46)

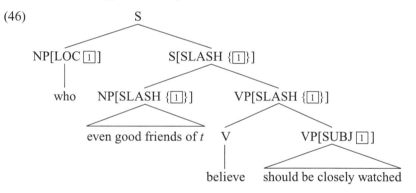

The problem, of course, is that the subjects of finite clauses are uniformly nominative in English. The standard PSG account of the relatively simple English case system assumes, in effect, that finite verbs select nominative subjects, with accusative case being either a default for all other verbs or explicitly specified in the lexical entries for such verbs. Regardless, it is clear that a case mismatch is unavoidable on the HPSG approach, because the value of SUBJ specified in the verb's valence must be nominative, whereas the LOC value tagged by ① must be accusative.[36]

However, this case mismatch problem is not an artifact of the HPSG framework itself. It arises inevitably in any hypothesis about P-gaps, regardless of the theoretical platform on which that hypothesis rests, which makes the same two assumptions that we make here: (i) that there is a single filler linked to multiple gap sites, and (ii) that there is a strong connectivity relation holding between this filler and its linked gaps which includes case information. HPSG need not make either of these assumptions, and other frameworks support hypotheses incorporating either or both of them.

Thus, it would be straightforward to state a version of HPSG that allowed only one gap per filler by changing the form of the Nonlocal Feature Principle (or, in more current versions of the theory, the Slash Amalgamation Principle; see Bouma, Malouf, and Sag 1998) so that only one daughter of a SLASH-bearing mother would be specified for SLASH. Thus, P-gaps would require a separate schema for introducing SLASH on an adjunct (or subject) just in case there is a nonnull SLASH specification on the (main) VP, and the relation between the two SLASH specifications could be stipulated to be no stronger than, say, index sharing. Such a solution would be a close analog of the treatment of P-gaps in Contreras 1984 and Chomsky 1986b; it would avoid the case conflict problem in precisely the same way as, and be comparably weaker than, the solution we present here. Conversely, a natural interpretation of Williams's (1978) ATB rule application format—which leaves a single *wh*-operator in COMP at S-structure linked to gap sites in each conjunct in a coordinate structure—would lead to a case-conflict problem within a transformational theory in precisely the way it does for the HPSG hypothesis just discussed, given data such as Goodall's example (1987:70) in (47).

(47)  This is [the man]$_i$ who Robin saw $e_i$ and thinks $e_i$ is handsome.

The first gap is accusative whereas the second is nominal. Thus, under the widespread assumption that case connectivity is a property of extraction, Williams's transformational analysis seems to encounter precisely the same challenge as the nonderivational HPSG analysis.

What is specific to the HPSG framework in the following discussion is not the problem, then, but the precise form of the solution. By showing that an approach to case assignment is possible which respects the formal ontology of types in HPSG's model theory, and which is as we note below independently required on empirical grounds, we show that it is possible to adopt a strong set of hypotheses about P-gaps without overlooking a glaring technical and empirical challenge.

### 6.3.2   Case Connectivity as a Nonproblem

Our solution to the "case connectivity" problem is in some ways independent of the treatment of P-gaps sketched here.[37] That is, the key to the proposal lies in the way that elements compatible with more than one case position (like proper names in English or the word *who*) are characterized in the theory.

The "standard" treatment of such elements in most unification-based proposals to date has been to simply underspecify their CASE feature in the lexicon, or to specify the value of their CASE feature as a disjunction of two or more possible cases. So, for example, the relevant part of a typical lexical entry for *who* might look like either (48a) or (48b).

(48)  a.  who[SYNSEM | LOC | HEAD | CASE *case*]
      b.  who[SYNSEM | LOC | HEAD | CASE *nom* $\vee$ *acc* $\vee$ *dat*]

It turns out, however, that this way of dealing with a syncretic form like *who* predicts that examples like (45) will be bad, which is incorrect. The reason is that, under HPSG's standard ontological assumptions, the disjunction we entered in the lexical entry for *who* must be resolved in the linguistic object in which *who* appears, rather than in a description of that object.[38] That is, in (45), the case value of the sign corresponding to *who* cannot remain underspecified but must resolve to either *nom* or *acc* or *dat*; underspecification is permitted only for descriptions of signs, not signs themselves. Thus the value of the SLASH feature terminating in the two different contexts must either fail to match either selectional requirement (by lacking a specific value for CASE) or, as before, match one of the requirements at the cost of failing to match the other.

We elect to solve the case mismatch problem in P-gap constructions by rejecting the disjunctive characterization of syncretism sketched above, and instead represent the fact that certain syncretic elements can appear in more than one case environment through the use of conjunction. Intuitively, this means that the CASE value for a syncretic element will look at first blush overspecified rather than underspecified (i.e., it will have CASE *nom* and *acc* and *dat*), and it will appear inconsistent. We will see, however, that we can make sense of such specifications and that this characterization gives us exactly what we want in the P-gap cases.

Making sense of overspecification involves changing the sort hierarchy. The sort hierarchy sketched here assumes a distinction between structural and lexical case.[39] The relevant changes all occur in the subsorts of *scase*.

(49)

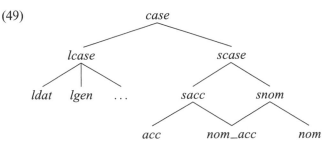

The maximal sort *nom_acc* is a subsort of both *snom* and *sacc*. The conjunction *snom* $\wedge$ *sacc* is thus no longer inconsistent but instead resolves to *nom_acc*. In effect, the revised type hierarchy provides for a third structural case value in English besides nominative and accusative, with the property that it satisfies any selectional requirement for either of these.

To implement this solution, we propose the following case values for various English NPs.

(50)  he       [CASE *nom*]
      him      [CASE *acc*]
      whom     [CASE *acc*]
      who      [CASE *nom_acc*]
      Robin    [CASE *nom_acc*]
      *t*       [CASE *scase*]

*He, him,* and *whom* work exactly as before. They can each appear in only one case environment. The syncretic forms, however, now bear the CASE value *nom_acc*, which means that they are specified for both *snom* and *sacc*; they are compatible with both. Finally, traces are underspecified for case in the same way that the syncretic forms used to be in the previous disjunctive-style approaches.

This solution gives us exactly what we want both in more typical examples (where there are constraints on case assignment but no case mismatches) and in the previously problematic examples like (45). Consider the following examples:

(51)  a.  Who(*m) likes him?
      b.  Who(m) does he like?

Here, assuming the case theory we have outlined, the selectional properties of *likes* assign *snom* to the subject of this verb in the first example, and *sacc* to its object in the second. However, on our proposal, *snom* is really just an abbreviation for either *nom* or *nom_acc*. The word *who* is, as specified in (50), *nom_acc* and is compatible with the case assignment *snom*, ensuring that the first example will be licensed when *who* is the filler. The word *whom*, however, is specified as a (pure) *acc* element, so it is not compatible with an *snom* case assignment. Therefore the first example is correctly ruled out when *whom* is the filler. Similarly, in (51b) *sacc* is just an abbreviation for *acc* or *nom_acc*. *Who* is *nom_acc*, compatible with the *sacc* specification of the object trace. *Whom* is *acc*, which is also compatible with *sacc*. Both variants of this example are therefore correctly predicted to be good.

On the account we have provided, the case connectivity problem in parasitic gap examples like (45) essentially disappears. The tree in example (52) illustrates the licensing of such sentences.[40]

(52)

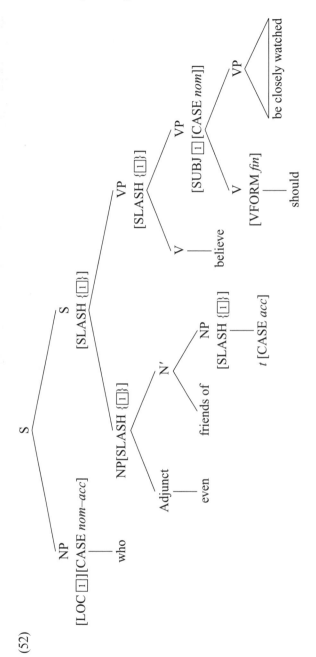

The case theory assigns *sacc* to *t* and *snom* to the SUBJ specification of the finite VP *should be closely watched*. Under our theory of P-gaps, both the trace and the SUBJ specification must have the same local value because both are structure-shared with the value of SLASH on the sister to the filler. Hence we end up with the requirement that the filler of the trace (which must also bear that same LOCAL value) be [CASE *snom* ∧ *sacc*]. Under traditional analyses, this would fail, and the sentence would be incorrectly ruled out. In our new type system, however, [CASE *snom* ∧ *sacc*] resolves uniquely to [CASE *nom_acc*], so the prediction, then, is that these values will be licensed as long as the filler is also CASE *nom_acc*. In fact, examples where the filler is syncretic for nominative and accusative are good (as with *who* or topicalized nonpronominal NPs), but examples where the filler is a pure nominative or a pure accusative fail, as in:

(53) a. *He, even friends of believe should be closely watched.
     b. *He is someone whom even friends of believe should be closely watched.

The elimination of the case connectivity problem removes from the HPSG treatment of P-gaps the one empirical misprediction that arises from the hypothesis of strict identity among the filler and the gaps in such constructions. Interestingly, categorial mismatches are correctly disallowed by the theory:

(54) *Running, Robin found she disliked *e* after she was *e* for an hour.

The proposal we offer permits the retention of a strong, well-defined ontological interpretation of the HPSG formalism and fits well into other proposals for the organization of the case-system subhierarchy. Indeed, the revisions we propose for the case system account for (47) in essentially the same way as for (45), with the seemingly case-discrepant multiple gaps appearing in coordinate structures rather than in a head-adjunct structure. Our hypothesis is thus compatible with the full range of phenomena and is fully explicit; it is therefore preferable to the treatments we considered previously.

It may be worth noting at this point that other phenomena which are problematic for the assumption of strong connectivity under various alternative assumptions do not, to our knowledge, constitute difficulties for the account presented above. Consider, for example, examples of the sort originally noted by Kearney (1983, cited in Chomsky 1986):

(55) [Which pictures of himself$_i$/*herself$_k$]$_j$ did John$_i$ hang $e_j$ on the wall without Mary$_k$ liking $e_j$ in the least?

Such examples are difficult to account for on the assumption that the filler is reconstructed into the position of both traces at LF, given the apparent Condition A violation of the GB binding theory which thereby results, with the false prediction that the version of (55) with *himself* is ill-formed. On the approach taken following Contreras 1984, of course, the problem does not arise, because the *wh*-phrase will only be reconstructed into the main VP gap site. This effect then apparently entails that the single-filler hypothesis is falsified, or at least strongly contraindicated, by such data. But in fact nothing of the sort follows once an argument-based version of the binding theory is selected in preference to a configuration-based one. Under the assumptions of the binding theory in Pollard and Sag 1994, for example, both traces in (55) structure-share the HEAD specification of the filler (since the LOC values, which contain the HEAD specifications, are structure-shared); therefore both of them are projections of the filler, in the sense of Pollard and Sag 1994 (p. 279). This conclusion entails in turn that *John* and *Mary* both o-command the filler and, given the definition of o-command, the anaphoric pronoun *himself* within the filler. But neither of these NPs *locally* o-commands the anaphor, which thus need not be coindexed with either NP and can be freely construed in its reference—a prediction that Pollard and Sag argue at length is the emprically correct one. Note, by contrast, that (56) is ill-formed and predicated to be so by the binding theory given in Pollard and Sag 1994:

(56) *Himself$_i$, John$_i$ admires $e_i$ without Mary$_j$ liking $e_i$ in the least.

Here, both NPs *locally* o-command the corresponding trace, which structure-shares its index with the filler; hence *himself* is not exempt and must be coindexed with both *John* and *Mary*—clearly impossible, hence (correctly) entailing the ill-formedness of (56). It follows, therefore, that examples like (56) in no respect count as challenges to the single-filler analysis we defend here.[41] It might be noted in passing, incidentally, that P-gaps by no means exhaust this particular effect; the ATB extraction (57) which we find perfectly well-formed, is quite parallel and receives an essentially identical account under our analysis:

(57) [Which pictures of himself$_i$/*herself$_i$]$_j$ does John$_i$ love $e_j$ and Mary$_k$, not surprisingly, hate $e_j$?
(Cf. *Himself, John loves and Mary hates)

Finally, it has been pointed out to us by Ivan Sag (personal communication) that (58a) is reasonably acceptable and apparently challenges our proposed solution, because an unequivocally accusative pronoun must be linked to a nominative gap site. We agree that the example is acceptable, but we do not believe that such data is problematic for our approach, because topicalized accusative pronouns can be linked to nominative contexts even in nonparasitic constructions, as evidenced by (58b). (Note that small capitals indicate contrastive stress, whereas large capitals represent strong, emphatic stress.)

(58) a. HIM$_i$, even friends of $t_i$ believe $t_i$ should be closely watched.

b. ..., but HIM$_i$, EVERYONE thinks $t_i$ should be closely watched.

Apparently, contrastive topicalization of the accusative pronoun has the effect of neutralizing its case specification. Although we do not claim to have a full account of this phenomenon, it is evident that whatever solution accounts for (58b) also accounts for (58a), so that such examples do not in themselves represent an actual contraindication to our approach.[42]

## 6.4 Conclusion

We have argued, in the preceding sections, that:

• contrary to apparently general belief, robust examples of nonnominal P-gaps exist;

• the distribution of P-gaps is in no sense congruent with that of weak indefinite pronouns;

• the apparently open categorial status of P-gaps and their fillers, and the fact that the content of parasitic and "true" gaps are the same, follows from the HPSG treatment of extraction phenomena without any further elaboration or extra conditions at all; and

• the one apparent empirical challenge to this treatment—the possibility of case mismatches between gaps in P-gap constructions—disappears once certain independently required modifications to the HPSG analysis of case assignment are instituted.

In short, insofar as we are interested in the licensing of the grammatical possibilities attested in robust examples of P-gap constructions, the HPSG story is maximally comprehensive and parsimonious, and therefore has, we maintain, a privileged status as an account of these constructions.

The foregoing account nonetheless raises certain questions deserving a detailed account that space limitations here preclude—in particular, the source of the fact that although well-formed non-NP P-gap constructions can be readily constructed, there is considerably more effort involved in doing so than in constructing nominal examples, or the explanation for the significant role apparently played by a heavily contrastive prosody linking the main VP and the adjunct clause in such cases.[43] We find it plausible that many of these effects can ultimately be shown to arise from an interaction of several factors.

First, consider online performance effects of the sort documented in Kluender 1998, involving the differential longevity in working memory of referential and nonreferential fillers, working in tandem with, on the one hand, the pressure on the processing mechanism to discharge fillers from storage, and on the other, the burden on processing resources of transporting such fillers across clausal (and similar) boundaries. We believe that the work reported in this paper indicates that the relative intractability of nonnominal P-gaps cannot be a function of the syntax itself. There is reason to suspect that the interaction of well-formed but complex filler/gap linkages with real-time processing limitations is at least partially responsible for this intractability, along the lines Kluender (1998) suggests as the source for both strong and weak island effects. Conceivably, the markedly greater ease we find in constructing finite-clause subject P-gaps in adjuncts preceding, rather than following, the main VP (though good examples of the latter are also available) is another instance of these processing effects. The fact that only the linear order of the constituents changes seems to us to strongly suggest such a conclusion.

Another factor to be considered is a property of P-gaps, in contrast to certain (but, importantly, not all) ATB extraction, which disallows a distributive reading of the filler's denotation across the multiplicity of extraction sites. We observed at several points in the preceding discussion that examples like *How harshly will our treating THEM lead to our being treated OURSELVES?* are strange because it seems necessary to take the question to be about a single degree of harshness that links the two situations. But notice that such an interpretation is not necessarily imposed on ATB extractions; thus in

(59) Tell me how harshly you think they will treat us *e* and Robin will treat them *e*?

it appears much easier to interpret the question as being about two possibly different, unrelated degrees of harshness, in the same way that *Tell me who you think Robin likes and Leslie hates* is easy to interpret as a request for two separate lists, one the list of the people whom Robin likes and the other the list of those whom Leslie hates. (This point is independently explored in Munn, this volume.) The distinction between P-gaps and coordinate structures just noted is not restricted to conventional P-gaps of the subject-internal or adjunct-internal variety. Consider the following:

(60) a. Which people$_i$ did you give pictures of $e_i$ to $e_i$?
     b. How worried$_i$ did YOU get $e_i$ about ROBIN getting $e_i$?

It seems quite impossible to interpret (60a) as a question whose answer could simply be the Cartesian product of two sets, one the set of people whose pictures were taken and the other the possibly disjoint set of people who were given those pictures. Rather, the answer must be a list of people each of whom received a picture of himself or herself. By the same token, (60b) seems peculiar, because it apparently requires that the respondent identify a degree of worry not only experienced in response to Robin's worrying, but whose extent must be just the same as Robin's: 'what is the degree $x$ of your worrying such that it was a response to Robin's worrying to exactly degree $x$?' The pragmatics here are fully as strange as in the parallel cases we adduced above for ordinary P-gaps.

In the absence of evidence that P-gaps genuinely covary in their distribution with pronominal contexts, we find no justification for taking the more problematic character of nonnominal P-gaps alluded to earlier to be a directly syntactic property. The pragmatic and processing considerations we have alluded to, on the other hand, typically allow for amelioration of worst-case unacceptability—which Cinque (1990) and Postal (1994a,b) restrict their attention to—by judicious manipulations of context and choice of lexica. These considerations thus seem to have the right sort of properties to explain the possibility, shown in our preceding discussion, of significantly improving the nonnominal P-gap data. This fact therefore constitutes excellent reason for theorists interested in P-gap phenomena to take such nonsyntactic factors into account in their own investigations.

**Notes**

The earliest ancestor of this chapter was presented by Hukari and Levine at the 1994 HPSG Conference in Copenhagen. We wish to thank a number of colleagues who assisted its evolution into its present form, especially our editors, whose meticulous scrutiny was largely responsible for the emergence of whatever coherence the current version possesses. Additionally, Peter Culicover provided critical scrutiny, constructive feedback, and a wealth of judgments and terrific data, often on a daily basis. To Paul Postal we owe a special debt: his counterexamples and suggestions for alternative interpretations of the facts forced us to examine our central hypothesis and its consequences from many angles and to develop new analyses to meet his objections. More generally, the enormous empirical base on which his own theory of extractions rests ensures that dissenters had better be comparably thorough in arguing their cases; we hope that we have at least partially succeeded in this respect. We also wish to thank Ivan Sag and his 1998–99 Stanford seminar on unbounded dependency constructions for very useful comments on an earlier draft, and the audience at the 1999 HPSG Conference at the

University of Edinburgh, where portions of this chapter were presented, for their informative and encouraging response. The Synners discussion group at Ohio State, in particular Martin Jansche and Nathan Vaillette, contributed important observations on much of the data we refer to. Carl Pollard has been an ever-patient source of acceptability judgments, analytic insights, and renewed morale for much of the life of this project. Finally, we acknowledge with gratitude the support for Hukari's work on this project provided by Social Sciences and Humanities Research Council of Canada grant 410-94-1676. None of those named should be assumed to agree with our conclusions, and, seeing no plausible way out, the authors accept full responsibility for whatever errors are contained in the present work.

1. Thus, although certain early work, such as Gazdar 1981, took the first view, other approaches (e.g., Chomsky 1982) argued for the second. The same dichotomy was played out somewhat later, with Contreras 1984 taking P-gaps to be traces of null operators, whereas Cinque 1990, discussed below, argues that the distributional anomalies such gaps (inter alia) reveal support an analysis of them as *pro* (possibly moved during the derivation). Still later, Pollard and Sag (1994) continue to take P-gaps to be manifestations of the same connectivity mechanism as ordinary gaps, although they seriously entertain the possibility, subsequently argued for at length in Sag and Fodor 1994 and Bouma, Malouf, and Sag 1998, that gaps in general correspond not to empty categories but rather to a reduction of valence consonant with constraints of various kinds on the form of lexical entries. Their view thus runs counter to that of Postal (1994a,b), also discussed below, who again finds what he takes to be convincing evidence in the distribution of parasitic and other adverbial gaps for a null pronoun analysis. Most of the work on P-gaps can ultimately be assigned to one or the other of these two general positions, whatever the particular framework assumed or the precise content of the hypothesis offered.

2. This treatment was first suggested in Chomsky 1982.

3. In this section, all notations of acceptability reflect Cinque's own judgments or those of his informants.

4. There are a number of important questions that this assertion leaves unanswered. As stated, Cinque's formulation appears to be predicting that *That Robin is a spy is tough to believe* e/*Robin getting control of Ostrogothia is frightening to imagine* e, are ill-formed, which is evidently not the case. It must be then that something else is involved, such as the *pro* object actually being homophonous, as it were, between an NP and a CP (and possibly IP) category memberships. Or perhaps *pro* is really exclusively an NP, but some kind of accommodation occurs that allows the CP subject in such cases to be anaphorically linked to this *pro*. Such a solution then raises the further question of why this accommodation could not extend to other maximal projections besides CP/IP and so on.

5. This extra stipulation, due to Longobardi, is as Cinque argues not sufficient to save Kayne's version of connectedness, because it rules out both examples in (4). However, applied to the percolation of [+*wh*], it allows at least the internal adjunct to qualify for this feature.

6. The movement of adverbial phrases, in Cinque's system, can only be accomplished through antecedent government, which is, in Cinque's (and Chomsky's) view of the *Barriers* system, a true relationship of government and therefore more easily blocked than the relationship of binding, which involves free coindexing with referential indices. Cinque claims that this option is unavailable to non-referential constituents such as adjuncts, which denote not individuals but something like properties of predicates. Adjunct extraction is blocked therefore not only by strong islands but by weak islands as well.

7. As this volume was going to press, Peter Culicover pointed out to us that similar examples, such as *The table on which I placed the book pg before carefully positioning the glass pg*, are given in Steedman 1996. Such examples are instances of the same kind as (7b), although their effectiveness is weakened somewhat by the fact that *position* only optionally takes a PP complement; therefore it could be claimed that Steedman's example does not actually exhibit a parasitic gap (though the location identified by the gap in the main VP can be inferred as the site of the positioning action in the adjunct). For (7b), however, no such explanation is possible.

8. To make this example pragmatically plausible, imagine the following discourse context: "Terry was telling us last night about the time she got so drunk she was seeing in color in a completely dark room. Can you believe it? . . . you know, when we go out to parties or bars, Robin insists on matching me shot for shot—so THAT drunk, it would be impossible for ME to get *e* without ROBIN getting *e* as well—and can you imagine *both* of us that plastered at one time???"

9. We address challenges to our interpretation of this data as true P-gap phenomena in section 6.2.3.2.

10. In the case of the P-gap and adjunct island violation cases, the verbs in question—verbs like *pass, conjecture, become*—are not readily interpretable in the absence of other material. A gap then must be present in each such adverb, and there seems no plausible way to take this gap to be an NP, of any kind, contrary to Cinque's analysis.

11. Note that we have not attempted to provide any parallel examples from missing object constructions; our judgment is that such examples, in contrast to those involving P-gaps and adjunct islands, are generally bad—along with all other instances where the missing object gap is located inside a finite clause—although certain isolated cases seem significantly better, such as ?*That particular argument is hard for me to believe would convince* ANYONE.

12. The (a) examples in (11) and (12) seem fine to us and many of our informants, but some speakers judge them to be marginal.

13. It might be objected that these examples are not valid as counterevidence because *tell* need not have a theme argument, as in *Robin left without telling us*, where the theme—the information that Robin had left—is implicit. But this objection is not tenable because, since there is a filler but no gap site in the main VP *go on holidays*, the only way in which the structure of (14a) can be well formed is if there indeed is a syntactic gap in the adjunct; otherwise, there is a relative clause with a filler but no gap site.

14. Kayne (1983) presents a few instances of pied-piped clauses which are alleged to be, if not exactly acceptable, then at least not as bad as certain other examples, at least for some speakers. In our view, such extremely attenuated versions of acceptability fail to support the complete acceptability of P-gaps in nonpossessive gerundive clauses such as those in (16). In fact, to the best of our knowledge, English speakers simply do not accept sentences such as (17), which indicates that LF pied-piping of the gerundive clauses in these examples is strongly contraindicated. Cinque's objective, of course, is to use the contrast in acceptability between pied-piping instances with the *wh*-phrase in subject position versus object position to bolster his argument that pied-piping correlates with parasitic and adjunct island gaps. However, as we showed, because there is no difficulty adducing well-formed examples of such gap constructions involving subject gaps, this line of argument seems beside the point.

15. One important issue that Cinque does not address is the motivation for the pied-piping of constituents at LF, including those that are barred from such movement en route to S-structure. Cinque relies on this movement to get the various island effects in P-gaps, but there is no obvious reason why it must occur in the first place. Thus the credibility of his overall analysis depends to some degree on an essentially undefended assumption.

16. Postal at one point seems to be distinguishing between *B*-extractions on the one hand and missing object and P-gap constructions on the other, as when he argues (p. 177) that "the antipronominal contexts cited earlier are incompatible *not only with B-extractions but with object raising, object deletion, P-gaps and several other constructions*" (emphasis added). But the contexts he is referring to are not incompatible with *A*-extraction constructions, and if *A*- and *B*-extractions are all there are, as Postal explicitly states, then it is hard to avoid the conclusion that P-gaps are part of the *B*-extraction class. This point becomes important in connection with the theoretical status of Postal's wide/narrow extraction ban distinction discussed below.

17. In the following inventory of examples, all judgments are Postal's.

18. We have here supplied what we take to be the kind of evidence Postal would adduce to show that P-gaps sort with topicalizations and missing-object constructions so far as extraposition contexts are concerned. We address the correctness of Postal's generalizations about these and the preceding contexts, inter alia, so far as compatibility with P-gaps is concerned. For the present, the reader should note that in spite of Postal's observation that "contrasts like that between [(18d,iii)] and [(18d,iv)], based on parallel NP types, seem quite remarkable," the contrast in question becomes a good deal less remarkable once the starred item is altered to make it strictly parallel to (18d,iii) so that an adjunct no longer intervenes between the verb governing the gap site and the extraposed PP. The reader is invited to compare the result—*Such a scurrilous review they published of his book*—with (18d,iii) and judge whether there is any discernible difference in acceptability that would motivate a deep dichotomy between the extraction mechanisms in the two cases.

19. Because P-gaps are taken to be instances of *B*-extraction, they have for Postal the essential property, long assumed in the literature, of being restricted to NPs

(the PG=NP claim of Postal 1994a). Postal (1994a) considers a particular wrinkle in the data which at first glance threatens this claim. In particular, he exhibits some apparent examples of clausal P-gaps and argues that these examples actually comprise two separate species: genuine P-gaps, involving the topicalization of clauses and therefore entailing the occurrence of a covert resumptive pronoun in both the "true" and the P-gap sites, on the one hand; and instances of non-coordinate Right Node Raising (RNR) which give the impression of being parasitic, but which display a completely different cluster of distributional properties with respect to pronominal contexts, island properties, and the like from true P-gaps. The core of Postal's claim, in fact, is that apparent P-gaps are disjoint with respect to this cluster of properties and that one subset shows the same properties independently attested for RNR. The other subset supposedly shows the distributional properties of *B*-extraction.

20. The latter contexts are antipronominal on Postal's assumption that the null definite pronouns require referential antecedents.

21. Our thanks to Peter Culicover for suggesting some of these examples and providing us with judgments of acceptability.

22. This example seems to us syntactically impeccable, but it is semantically very odd indeed; we suspect that this oddness is a symptom of why non-NP P-gaps, particularly those involving predicative categories, have struck some investigators as anomalous. The question corresponds to the pseudological translation, For what degree $x$ of harshness will our treating Robin $x$ harshly lead to our being treated $x$ harshly ourselves? The presupposition involved is pragmatically strange, involving as it does the background assumption that, at a particular unique degree of some gradable property, there is an exact reciprocation between action and reaction involving that property. Because P-gaps that involve predicative filler categories, such as [*wh*-degree] APs, necessarily require that a particular degree of some predicate hold in two different, linked situations, they provide ample opportunity for pragmatic anomaly of this kind.

23. Note again that if Zwicky's (1986) account of these effects is correct, then the second dative object construction doesn't have implications for the debate one way or another.

24. Postal has noted (personal communication) that this example can be interpreted so that the adjunct refers to the act of painting, without respect to color. Although this is of course true, we also find the alternative reading, where green is a color such that one might want to paint the walls but not the ceiling that specific color, completely available.

25. Postal (1994b) asserts that in examples such as *A good doctor, she isn't*, the phrase *a good doctor* is not really an NP but rather some other kind of constituent parallel to the AP *fond of Mike* in *Fond of Mike she isn't*. Presumably, then, in other examples of *B*-extraction gaps involving predicative rather than referring NPs, as in (24b), the same proposal must be invoked. It is difficult to assess this suggestion, which offers no indication of what kind of non-NP constituent *a (good) doctor* is or what its phrase structure consists of, but surely a more specific proposal is required. Moreover, if *a doctor* in (24b) were not an NP, it would necessarily be a nonnominal P-gap, and as we have discussed earlier, there would

have to be an appropriate kind of proform for this category that could appear in the indicated position—for example, *Terry wanted to be a doctor but was unable to become XP*, where $X \neq N$. No English proform we are aware of exhibits these properties; the only proform corresponding to XP here is *one*, which is clearly nominal.

26. Part of the difficulty may be due to the somewhat anomalous status of examples like *How angry did he appear?*, where there seems to be pressure among many speakers to use an infinitival complement for the raising verb: *How angry did he appear to be?* As far as the P-gap/ATB dichotomy is concerned, we suggest that much of the data in Postal 1993 has the same character as in Postal 1994a,b: a large number of negative examples are provided, without discussion of the fact that good examples can readily be found, so far as we can tell, for every single type alleged to be impossible. Again, space considerations preclude a detailed inventory of such examples, but for two of Postal's putative dichotomizing properties—restriction of parasitic gaps to NPs and their exclusion from finite subject position—we have provided robust counterexamples; for purposes of further illustration, we note the following counterevidence to Postal's assertion that P-gaps are not possible in contexts that block passivization:

(i)     I had my paycheck deposited.

(ii)    *That paycheck was had deposited.

(iii)   There was an entire paycheck that John FORGOT about *e* after having had *e* DEPOSITED in his bank account.

(iv)    Robin resembles Chris.

(v)     *Chris is resembled by Robin.

(vi)    Robin is someone whom$_i$ I'm often TAKEN for $e_i$ without my RESEMBLING $e_i$ in the slightest.

Similarly, Postal claims that *from* PPs block passivization of their objects and that this correlates with the lack of P-gaps in object position in such PPs, but we find the following unexceptionable:

(vii)   Terry is someone whom$_i$ the twins continually cheated $e_i$ without ever actually STEALING anything from $e_i$.

(viii)  Robin is the person$_i$ I can't imagine you dealing with $e_i$ after having stolen so much money from $e_i$.

Although Postal gives ill-formed examples involving *stealing from*, the grammaticality of the foregoing seems to show that there is in principle no problem with P-gaps in such contexts. A broad review of Postal's evidence base suggests to us that, in general, there are numerous good examples to match every one of the syntactic contexts for which he claims that no good examples are possible.

27. The other example from Lasnik and Saito 1992, (28b), has the general difficulty we noted earlier in note 22 of involving a bizarre implicit assumption that there is a specific degree of quickness *x* such that John solved the problem with quickness *x* after proving the theorem with quickness *x*. Given the availability of a reading in which the adverb does not have scope over the adjunct, it seems more natural to favor this reading over the bizarre reading just sketched. Again, we

believe that many instances of anomalous nonreferential P-gap extractions arise on the base of just this sort of semantic/pragmatic bizarreness.

28. It might be countered that in the case of undisputed parasitic gaps (e.g., *Which book did you buy without ever putting on your bookshelf?*) the "source" forms corresponding to cases such as (33) are also bad (*\*You bought this book without putting on my bookshelf*). The thrust of such an observation would be that just as the badness of the "source" form is correlated with the goodness of the corresponding form where there is a main VP extraction, so the badness of (33) may plausibly be correlated with the goodness of (7e). In both cases, extraction is required to license the missing element. On this argument, the ill-formedness of (33) is no obstacle to deriving our AP P-gap examples by AP-deletion.

But under Postal's assumptions about why examples such as *\*I bought this book without putting on my bookshelf* are bad—why, that is, P-gaps are in fact parasitic on "real" extractions—the counterargument just sketched has no force. Postal has made it clear (in, e.g., Postal 1993) that such examples are bad because P-gaps, like other instances of null pronominals, must be in a control relation with an *extracted* antecedent, and there is no such antecedent in the bad example given. This explanation cannot be extended to the case of AP-deletion, however, because the very point distinguishing the AP-deletion analysis from a parasitic gap analysis is that in the former, there is no null element present at the "gap" site. Hence, there is nothing to be "controlled." It follows, then, that the proposed parallelism between parasitic NP gaps and parasitic AP-deletion fails because, crucially, there is no common mechanism giving rise to the parasitism in the two separate constructions. Thus, there is no independent account for the badness of (33) vis-à-vis (7e), and our original argument stands.

29. Postal's chief argument for the resumptive pronoun analysis—the claimed exclusion of P-gaps from antipronominal contexts—would in fact be seriously undermined by the pseudoparasitic derivation we have considered and rejected above. For if this derivational source were admitted, we would predict that parasitic gaps should occur freely regardless of the (anti)pronominality of their context, so long as RNR were possible. But then, given the well-formedness of *Robin became, after being told he would never become, a particle-beam neurosurgeon*, we would expect ??*What kind of neurosurgeon did Robin become after being told he would never become?* to be just as good, whereas it is quite bad. Similarly for *Robin painted his house—without* TELLING *anyone that he was going to paint his house—a hideous malignant tropical green*, versus *\*What kind of green did Robin paint his house without telling anyone he was going to paint his house?*, on the relevant reading, where the judgment reported is Postal's for this class of P-gaps (personal communication). The problem is that these, and a number of other of Postal's antipronominal environments, support RNR, yet, according to Postal, do not give rise to felicitous parasitic gap constructions. Hence, admitting the RNR-based derivations we have alluded to leads to the prediction that antipronominality should be irrelevant over a large range of the cases that Postal seeks to explain by appeal to their antipronominality. The only way to eliminate the anomaly appears to be to reject the pseudoparasitic derivation, as indeed seems motivated on the independent grounds provided above.

30. This and all such statements in this paper are made with the implicit caveat that on Postal's account, the gap in the surface representation is not, strictly speaking, a pronominal, but the trace of this null pronominal, which has moved.

31. Brought to our attention by Paul Postal.

32. We hope to rectify this restriction on the scope of our critique in the near future. In the meantime, we note that the evidence base that Postal has assembled on behalf of his analysis of extractions is of a range that is difficult to parallel in the past two decades of syntactic theorizing, and any complete critique of it will necessarily be monograph-length.

33. We utilize P&S's trace mechanism, reflecting the classic phrase structure–theoretic analyis of the filler/gap connectivity mechanism. The traceless alternative proposed late in Pollard and Sag 1994 and in certain more recent work in HPSG could be used instead without any material changes in the analysis sketched.

34. The same mechanism yields multiple gap constructions of the form *Who did you give a picture of to?*, where, on the double-chain analysis in Chomsky 1986, it not evident which of the gaps is the "true" gap and which is bound by the empty operator, or indeed where the latter's landing site is.

35. By the same token, the existence of clear cases of nonnominal *tough* fillers and gaps, as in *That Robin had left the keys in the car would be logical for someone in Terry's position to find herself hoping e/*I guessed that Robin had left the keys in the car before any of the others even found themselves hoping it* suggests that this aspect of P&S's treatment of *tough* requires correction.

36. Note that if the LOC value of the filler is taken to be nominative, then the same problem appears in reverse at the gap site within the subject: the prepositional object of *of* must be accusative, yet the gap will, on this alternative treatment, be nominative. One way or the other, a case conflict inevitably arises.

37. For example, as we note below, our solution also extends to Goodall's (1987) datum (47), and so extends to multiple-gap constructions generally.

38. For a full treatment of this and other assumptions about the objects entering into the HPSG formalism, see King 1989, 1994 and Carpenter 1992.

39. This approach has been recently pursued independently by a number of researchers, including Heinz and Matiasek (1994), Przepiorkowski (1996), and Calcagno and Pollard (1997). It is independently motivated for English, because on the standard GPSG/HPSG account of case assignment, whereby all case is assigned via lexical selection, it turns out to be impossible to assign case correctly in simple sentences with auxiliaries or raising verbs. The problem is that if the subject specification of the main verb is shared with the subject of the auxiliary or raising verb, yet another instance of case conflict results; thus, in *He was sleeping*, the participle *sleeping* will assign accusative case, but the raising subject must have nominative case. Hence there is independent reason for the separation of case into lexical and structural subsorts.

40. In order to minimize extraneous complications, in the representation in (52) we follow the standard HPSG treatment of subject gaps as selection of a finite NP complement. However, see Hukari and Levine 1998 for arguments that this

analysis is inferior to one that treats subject and complement extraction as fully parallel, and Bouma, Malouf, and Sag 1998 for one implementation of this suggested revision to the theory.

41. What remains to be explained about (55), as well as the ATB extraction example (57) below, is the ill-formedness induced by the extraction of the picture NP containing the reflexive *herself*, coindexed with the subject of the adjunct clause/second conjunct rather than that of the main clause/first conjunct. Evidently, linear-order factors play an important role in how such sentences are processed, but space precludes a deeper discussion of the issues here. See Bresnan 1994 for discussion of the relevance of linear order in anaphora.

42. Our thanks to Arnold Zwicky for discussion of this point.

43. This prosodic pattern may also be present in other varieties of P-gaps, such as the subject-internal cases exemplified in section 6.2.2.2.

# Chapter 7

| Further Lacunae in the English Parasitic Gap Paradigm | Paul M. Postal |
|---|---|

## 7.1 Background

Noncoordinate, multiple gap structures like those in (1) have been extensively studied since the burst of interest stimulated by Engdahl (1983/this volume):

(1) a. [Not many dignitaries]$_1$ could they present carvings of $pg_1$ to $t_1$.
   b. That is the candidate who$_1$ they persuaded several neighbors of $pg_1$ to support $t_1$.
   c. [Which ship]$_1$ did everyone who saw $pg_1$ sinking think $t_1$ was carrying gold?
   d. It was an elderly grizzly that$_1$ they captured $t_1$ after chasing $pg_1$ for hours.

In such cases one gap, represented throughout as $pg$, is now commonly assumed to be in some sense parasitic on the other gap, indicated as $t$.[1] Widely cited views of such parasitic gap (P-gap) structures include Chomsky's (1986b) chain composition view, Kayne's (1984) connectedness approach, the slash category views of Sag (1983), Gazdar, Klein, Pullum, and Sag (1985) and Pollard and Sag (1994). Numerous other works deserving mention are cited by Culicover (this volume). These approaches all in effect take P-gaps to involve a relation between a pair of gaps, one viewed as the real or licensing gap (L-gap), the other as the P-gap, each occurring in an independently licit extraction gap position.[2]

The maximum class of P-gaps would exist if there were no further constraints, so that P-gaps were possible for any (at least lexical) category and regardless of the structural relations between L-gap/P-gap pairs. It has, of course, been known since at least Engdahl's (1983) work that this is far from the case. So, all the approaches cited above impose additional constraints to delineate that proper subset of such related gap pairs actually yielding well-formed P-gap structures.

Despite that, current treatments arguably sanction for English far too many P-gaps, along several dimensions.[3] First, most fail to systematically preclude non-DP gaps, although such are at best difficult to document for English and perhaps nonexistent; see Aoun and Clark 1985, Cinque 1990, Postal 1993b, 1994a, and references therein.[4] The question of non-DP P-gaps is addressed by Levine, Hukari, and Calcagno (this volume) and I will not comment on it further here.[5]

Second, even among DP positions, various illicit P-gaps are not properly blocked. So current views of P-gaps do not yield the sort of parallelisms between passivization and P-gap constraints for various DP positions noted in Postal 1993b. Examples (2a–f) illustrate the phenomenon with new data.

(2) a.   Their relations involved abuse.
    b.   *Abuse was involved by their relations.
    c.   [What kind of abuse]$_1$ did their relations involve $t_1$?
    d.   [What kind of abuse]$_1$ did his constantly discussing $pg_1$ suggest that their relations involved $t_1$?
    e.   *[What kind of abuse]$_1$ did your discovering that their relations involved $pg_1$ lead him to discuss $t_1$?
    f.   *[What kind of abuse]$_1$ did their relations lead to condemnation of $pg_1$ without involving $t_1$?

Here (2b,c) illustrate that the object of *involve*, though nonpassivizable, is not incompatible with ordinary extraction. Moreover, (2d) indicates that that object position can be an L-gap. However, in spite of these properties, (2e,f) show that the object position of *involve* cannot be a P-gap. No framework of P-gap description known to me offers a basis for the nonrandom sharing of passivization and P-gap restrictions which I claim that (2) illustrates.[6] Although of considerable interest, this topic is beyond the scope of the present paper.

Third, there are constraints on P-gap formation in positions corresponding to reflexives or reciprocals:[7]

(3) a.   Himself$_1$, Mike praised $t_1$ after describing himself$_1$/*$pg_1$ to Mary.
    b.   It was herself$_1$ that$_1$ studying herself$_1$/*$pg_1$ led Sonia$_1$ to appreciate $t_1$.
    c.   *Himself$_1$, I talked to John$_1$ about $t_1$ after describing him$_1$ to $pg_1$.

(4) a.  [Each other]$_1$, they$_1$ (never) praised $t_1$.
   b.  [Each other]$_1$, they$_1$ praised $t_1$ after describing each other$_1$/*$pg_1$ to Mary.
   c.  It was each other that$_1$ their$_1$ getting to know [each other]$_1$/*$pg_1$ led them$_1$ to respect $t_1$.

Since the L-gaps and P-gaps here seem to share all relevant features including that of being reflexive or reciprocal, past claims about required feature sharing between L-gap and P-gap (see, e.g., Kiss 1985/this volume; Barss 1986:278) fail to block the bad variants of (3a,b) or (4b), and nothing else in the literature seems to either. This issue also cannot be dealt with here.

Fourth, most current frameworks do not block P-gaps in positions that permit ordinary extraction gaps but are incompatible with weak definite pronouns (Wdps);[8] these are the antipronominal contexts (ACs) of Postal 1993b, 1994b, 1998. However, P-gaps are systematically precluded in ACs. Twelve supporting cases are given in (5)–(16).

(5) a.  It was *her(no stress)/HER that the drug helped.
   b.  *[Which child]$_1$ did everyone who believed it was $pg_1$ that the drug had helped see $t_1$ in the hospital?

(6) a.  Mirabelle dyed her sheets purple/*it.
   b.  *the color that everyone who dyed their sheets $pg_1$ praised $t_1$

(7) a.  The government contains/includes Valdez/HIM/*him.
   b.  What$_1$ the new government contains/includes $t_1$ is several spies.
   c.  *What$_1$ every government which contains/includes $pg_1$ needs to worry about $t_1$ is spies.

(8) a.  Mike doesn't mind [that you mistreated our gerbil]$_1$ but I do mind that$_1$/*it$_1$.
   b.  *[That you mistreated the gerbil]$_1$, many who would not have minded $pg_1$ still refused to admit $t_1$.

(9) a.  These facts may mean that he is guilty but those facts don't mean that/*it.
   b.  What$_1$ these facts mean $t_1$ is that he is guilty.
   c.  *What$_1$ several facts that meant $pg_1$ led Mary to claim $t_1$ is that he is guilty.

(10) a.  Maurice drove at that speed but I didn't drive at that speed/*it.
   b.  [What speed]$_1$ did you drive at $t_1$?
   c.  *[What speed]$_1$ did her driving at $t_1$ lead him to water ski at $pg_1$?

(11) a.  Joe couldn't determine/tell that Sam was a werewolf but Ethel could determine/*tell it.

   b.  What$_1$ everyone who could determine/*tell $pg_1$ later testified $t_1$ was that Sam was a werewolf.

(12) a.  That remark betrays [disregard for human rights]/THEM/ *them.

   b.  *It was disregard for human rights which$_1$ the UN criticized $t_1$ after the dictator's remarks betrayed $pg_1$.

   c.  *It is indifference to suffering which$_1$ every remark that betrays $pg_1$ creates more of $t_1$.

(13) a.  Tina remarked [that it was hot]/*it.

   b.  What$_1$ Tina remarked $t_1$ was that it was hot.

   c.  *What$_1$ everyone who remarked $pg_1$ later denied $t_1$ was that it was hot.

(14) a.  Nora spent/stayed that week in Bermuda.

   b.  Nora spent/*stayed it in Bermuda.

   c.  the week that$_1$ Nora spent/stayed $t_1$ in Bermuda

   d.  the week that$_1$ Nora's planning to spend/*stay $pg_1$ in Bermuda made Mike want to spend $t_1$ there

(15) a.  The Porsche cost $50,000/that much/*it.

   b.  What$_1$ the Porsche cost $t_1$ is amazing.

   c.  *What$_1$ your saying the Porsche cost $pg_1$ led them to try to sell the Jaguar for $t_1$ is amazing.

(16) a.  The concert lasted for the whole night/two hours/*it/*them.

   b.  the length of time which$_1$ the concert lasted $t_1$

   c.  *[How long a time]$_1$ did their saying the concert would last $pg_1$ make Quentin miss work for $t_1$?

Such facts can be initially explicated by—and, as far as I can see, only by—analyzing P-gaps as inherently pronominal. In other words, P-gaps need to be regarded minimally as invisible Wdps. Although this view was seen as a possibility in Ross 1967/1986:118–120,[9] was in effect transitorily adopted in Chomsky 1982 (then abandoned in Chomsky 1986b), was also a key feature of Aoun and Clark's (1985) proposal, and is advocated by Cinque (1990), Koster (1987) and Postal (1993b, 1994a), it remains very much a marginal position.[10] Moreover, rendering prevalent views consistent with this property may not be straightforward.[11]

## 7.2   Further Lacunae

This article focuses on further restrictions ultimately linked to ACs where popular approaches do not block impossible P-gaps and where mere identification of P-gaps with invisible Wdps (as in Cinque 1990, Postal 1993b, 1994a) does not suffice. A relevant example is the contrast between (17a,b):

(17) a.  [Which child]$_1$ did everyone who saw $pg_1$ believe the drug had helped $t_1$?

 b.  *[Which child]$_1$ did everyone who saw $pg_1$ believe it was $t_1$ that the drug had helped $t_1$?[12]

 c.  [Which child]$_1$ did everyone who saw Gail believe it was $t_1$ that the drug had helped $t_1$?

Example (17b) relates, of course, to (5b), which I took to support the claim that P-gaps and ACs do not intersect. Remarkably, (17b) is ill-formed although in contrast to (5b), its L-gap and not its P-gap is an AC. The difference between (17a,b) exists although the L-gap position in (17b) no more independently blocks extraction than it does in the grammatical (17a), as (17c) illustrates. Needing explanation is why cases like (17b) are ill-formed even though a P-gap does not appear in an AC and no standard P-gap constraint is violated.

The key factual generalization relevant to the needed explanation must, I believe, be based on an extension of the observation of previous work that English P-gaps are incompatible with ACs. For, as in the ill-formed (17b), it turns out that (18) holds.

(18)  No P-gap, even in an otherwise licit P-gap position, is licit if its L-gap is one of a large class of ACs, including all those of (5)–(16).[13]

Initial support for (18) was, in effect, already given in Postal 1993b:747, although the overall generalization was not explicit. Rather, I observed only that for the three specific AC constraints of (19), well-formed P-gap structures whose L-gaps occurred in one of the AC positions were impossible.

(19)  The L-gap for a P-gap cannot be:

 a. a PN position,

 b. the post-*be* DP position of an expletive *there* construction, or

 c. the color-designating DP of a change of color construction.

Relevant supporting data included:

(20) a. Tom turned into some kind of zombie/*it.
   b. Tom turned into [some kind of zombie]$_1$ after studying [that kind of zombie]$_1$/*it$_1$.
   c. the kind of zombie which$_1$ Tom praised/*turned into $t_1$ after studying $pg_1$

(21) a. There was some kind of soup/*it on the table.
   b. the kind of soup which$_1$ everyone who liked $pg_1$, said (*there) was $t_1$ on the table

(22) a. Ernestine painted her house yellow/*it.
   b. [What color]$_1$ did she criticize/*paint her house $t_1$ after discussing $pg_1$ with Abigail?[14]

I have already extended the support for (18) found in (20)–(22) via (17). Further strengthening derives from the fact that (18) correctly predicts that each AC type in (7)–(16) also yields ill-formed structures involving P-gaps which, although not ACs, have L-gaps that are. This is shown in (23)–(32), respectively.

(23) a. *[How many spies]$_1$ did the committee include $t_1$ before the secret police eliminated $pg_1$?
   b. *What$_1$ every government which fears $pg_1$ no doubt contains/includes $t_1$ is spies.

(24) a. What$_1$ he didn't mind $t_1$ after hearing $pg_1$ from Sally was that the gerbil had escaped.
   b. *What$_1$ someone who learned $pg_1$ did not mind $t_1$ was that you sold the gerbil.

(25) a. *What$_1$ those facts probably meant $t_1$ although no doubt not proving $pg_1$ was that she would resign.
   b. *What$_1$ everyone who claimed $pg_1$ interpreted those facts to mean $t_1$ was that he is guilty.

(26) a. *[What speed]$_1$ did he try to drive his Volvo at $t_1$ shortly after exceeding $pg_1$ in a helicopter?
   b. *the speed which$_1$ her exceeding $pg_1$ in a helicopter led her to drive her Volvo at $t_1$

(27) a. *What$_1$ was Sidney able to tell $t_1$ for sure only long after suspecting $pg_1$?
   b. What$_1$ everyone who at first only suspected $pg_1$ could later determine/*tell $t_1$ for sure was that Sam was a werewolf.

(28) a. [Which attitude]$_1$ did the dictator's remarks betray $t_1$ even while he was criticizing $pg_1$?

    b. *It was disregard for human rights which$_1$ the UN's criticizing $pg_1$ indicated that the dictator's remarks had betrayed $t_1$.

(29) a. *What$_1$ Tina remarked $t_1$ shortly after denying $pg_1$ in court was that she was Finnish.

    b. *What$_1$ your discovering $pg_1$ on Tuesday led Tina to remark $t_1$ on Thursday was that apples were toxic.

(30) a. *[What week]$_1$ did Carl stay $t_1$ in Rome despite first choosing to spend $pg_1$ in Hawaii?

    b. *the week that$_1$ Nora's planning to spend $pg_1$ in Rome made Mike want to stay $t_1$ there

(31) a. *What$_1$ he claimed the Jaguar would cost $t_1$ even before learning Mike offered $pg_1$ for it was outrageous.

    b. *What$_1$ their trying to sell the Jaguar for $pg_1$ led Irma to say the Porsche cost $t_1$ was outrageous.

(32) a. *[How much time]$_1$ did the concert last $t_1$ because the director wanted to fill up $pg_1$?

    b. *[How long a time]$_1$ did Quentin's missing work for $pg_1$ lead him to say the concert lasted $t_1$?

## 7.3 Two Approaches to the L-gap AC Property

To simplify discussion, I refer to the failure of P-gaps and ACs to intersect as the P-gap AC Property (PACP) and to the fact illustrated in (23)–(32) that L-gaps and ACs fail to intersect as the L-gap AC Property (LACP). As already touched on, the PACP is directly explicable by assuming (33).

(33) Each P-gap position contains an invisible Wdp.

For, if (33) holds, P-gaps fall under whatever constraints bar Wdps in the relevant ACs.[15]

However, (33) alone leaves the LACP with no basis. This feature is initially puzzling because it has not hitherto been claimed by anyone that L-gaps have any particular relation to Wdps. So, there is no standard ground for the observation in section 7.2 that L-gaps fail to intersect a broad class of ACs. Suppose, though, that one also assumed (34).

(34) P-gap structures (also) involve invisible Wdps in the L-gap position.

Principle (34) means that any extraction actually licensing a P-gap requires an invisible resumptive Wdp in its extraction site (L-gap), even if the same extraction type in other cases does not. If so, the LACP would be imposed exactly as the PACP is.

To put (34) in perspective, Postal 1994b, 1998 claims that English left extractions (of NPs) divide into two major types, called there *A*-extractions and *B*-extractions. The idea is that whereas the latter require invisible resumptive Wdps in extraction sites, the former do not. The basic evidence for this distinction is precisely that *B*-extraction sites, unlike *A*-extraction sites, are incompatible with ACs. The *B*-extractions recognized are (DP) topicalization, (DP) clefting, and (DP) nonrestrictive relative extraction. Examples (35) and (36) show that these are incompatible with the ACs documented in (7) and (16).

(35) a. *Pedro$_1$, the new cabinet includes $t_1$.
     b. *It was Pedro who$_1$ the new cabinet included $t_1$.
     c. *Pedro, who$_1$ the new government includes $t_1$, .... .

(36) a. *[The whole night]$_1$, the ball lasted $t_1$.
     b. *It was the whole night that$_1$ the ball lasted $t_1$.
     c. *The afternoon, which$_1$ the ball lasted $t_1$, was supposed to be spent in the lab.

Against the background of an independently motivated *A*/*B*-extraction distinction, principle (34) merely amounts to hypothesis (37).

(37) Any P-gap-licensing extraction (i.e., one from the L-gap position) is a *B*-extraction.

Accepting (37) of course precludes a merely elementary assignment of phenomena to the *A*/*B*-extraction types, so statements of the maximally general form "questioning is an *A*-extraction" would not be viable. For, according to (37), that proper subset of instances of, for example, question extraction which license P-gaps are *B*-extractions. But Postal 1994b, 1998 already rejected the adequacy of such elementary assignments on other grounds.

The informal proposal (37) could be executed in various ways and seems like a reasonable extension both of (33) and of the scope of the notion *B*-extraction. Despite that, there is good reason to doubt that (37) is the correct basis for the LACP.[16] Principle (37) makes an enormously strong claim: no L-gap should be able to intersect an AC that is incompatible with *B*-extraction sites. However, this claim is too general. There exist ACs, which, although definitely precluding previously recognized $B$-extraction gaps, nonetheless allow L-gaps. A clear example is seen in (38).

(38) a. That caused every student/someone else/*her to giggle other than Louise.
   b. Who$_1$ did that cause $t_1$ to giggle (other than Louise)?
   c. [Someone else]$_1$, that caused $t_1$ to giggle (*other than Louise).
   d. It was someone else who$_1$ that caused $t_1$ to giggle (*other than Louise).
   e. [Someone else]$_1$, who$_1$ that caused $t_1$ to giggle (*other than Louise) is outside.
   f. Who$_1$ did your tickling $pg_1$ cause $t_1$ to giggle (other than Louise)?
   g. The people who$_1$ your tickling $pg_1$ caused $t_1$ to giggle (other than Louise) are outside.

Here, (38a) shows that a DP position linked to an extraposed *other than* phrase is an AC; (38b) shows that the $t_1$ position is open to extraction. But (38c–e) illustrate that, as expected from the posit of $B$-extractions, this position is incompatible with the $B$-extractions recognized in Postal 1994b, 1998. But (38f,g) show that the same position can be an L-gap.

This pattern would be impossible if (37) were literally true. Moreover, no viable approach to these data can just deny that *other than* phrases yield ACs of the sort relevant to P-gap structures. For, as expected of an AC, such phrases do yield the PACP:

(39) a. Who$_1$ did your tickling $pg_1$ yesterday (*other than Louise) cause $t_1$ to giggle?
   b. The people who$_1$ your tickling $pg_1$ (*other than Louise) caused $t_1$ to giggle are outside.

Cases where the PACP occurs but the LACP does not are not restricted to paradigms involving ACs defined by extraposed *other than* phrases.[17] A similar pattern manifests with extraposed restrictive relative clauses:

(40) a. The police arrested someone/*him today who was waving a gun.
   b. Who$_1$ did the police arrest $t_1$ today who was waving a gun?
   c. *Kramer$_1$, the police arrested $t_1$ today who was waving a gun.
   d. *It was Kramer who$_1$ the police arrested $t_1$ today who was waving a gun.
   e. *Kramer, who$_1$ the police arrested $t_1$ today who was waving a gun, was insane.

   f.   Who$_1$ did their denouncing $pg_1$ lead the police to arrest $t_1$
today who was waving a gun?

   g.  the woman that$_1$ the police, despite respecting greatly $pg_1$,
arrested $t_1$ today who was waving a gun

   h.  Who$_1$ did their denouncing $pg_1$ today (*who was waving a gun)
lead the police to arrest $t_1$?

   i.  the woman that$_1$ the police, despite respecting greatly $pg_1$
(*who was waving a gun), arrested $t_1$ today

Here (40a,b) illustrate that the position of a nominal linked to an extraposed restrictive relative precludes a Wdp but is not incompatible with all types of L-extraction. But (40c–e) show that this position does bar the *B*-extractions of Postal 1994b, 1998. Examples (40f,g) reveal that the position can be an L-gap. But (40h,i) document that the PACP holds and that P-gaps in the position are barred.

Third, a similar pattern is seen with the extraposed variant of the curious form *exactly*:

(41)  a.   They tested exactly who/*someone/*her while interviewing her.

      b.  [Exactly who]$_1$ did they test $t_1$ today?

      c.  Who$_1$ did they test $t_1$ today exactly?

      d.  *Irma$_1$, they tested $t_1$ today exactly.

      e.  *It was Irma who$_1$ they tested $t_1$ today exactly.

      f.  *Irma, who$_1$ they tested $t_1$ today exactly, was unhappy.

      g.  Who$_1$ did your hiring $pg_1$ lead them to test $t_1$ today exactly?

      h.  Who$_1$ did their persuading friends of $pg_1$ to resign upset $t_1$
exactly?

      i.  Who$_1$ did your hiring $pg_1$ (*exactly) lead them to test $t_1$ today?

      j.  Who$_1$ did their persuading $pg_1$ of that (*exactly) lead $t_1$ to
resign?

Example (41a) shows that *exactly* combines with some nominals but not with Wdps. Examples (41b,c) jointly show that some L-extractions are compatible with *exactly*, extraposed or not. But (41d–f) indicate that *exactly* is incompatible with *B*-extractions. And, although (41g,h) show that *exactly* is not incompatible with L-gaps, (41i,j) reveal that it cannot directly link to a P-gap.

Overall, such data support three conclusions. First, (37) is erroneous. Second, the correct basis for the LACP involves a division of ACs. Members of one class, containing what one can call Type I ACs, determine both the PACP and the LACP. Elements of the other, containing

Type II ACs, determine only the PACP. Third, explanation of the LACP involves the proper statement of *the constraints determining Type I ACs.*

A few words are required here about the highlighted phrase. Past work treated the concept AC as purely descriptive. No account was offered of the features of a grammar that might impose these conditions on particular contexts.[18] Such an ultimately necessary theoretical account was, for many purposes, not required. These included appeal to ACs as factual motivation for *B*-extractions, as justification for the Wdp nature of P-gaps and other gaps, and as support for a resumptive Wdp-based account of extraction from selective islands (see Postal 1998).

However, purely descriptive appeal to ACs provides no insight into the contrast between those that induce the LACP for P-gaps and those that do not. Thus, current purposes demand at least some account of the principles imposing ACs.

Consider first the Type II ACs, which fail to yield the LACP. I suggest that these ACs do not reflect any grammatical conditions directly pertaining to the distribution of pronouns. Rather, recalling the cases with extraposed exceptive phrases, relative clauses, and *exactly*, one finds various forms that can combine with a certain restricted subset of DP structures to form more specified DP structures. This is, notably clear for the relevant use of *exactly*, which seems to combine only with interrogative DPs:[19]

(42) a. Ted saw exactly who/what/which cat/*that cat/ *some cat/*a cat/*every cat/*lots of cats/*few cats.
  b. Exactly who/what/which cat did Ted see?
  c. Who/What/Which cat did Ted see exactly?

If we assume that (42c) is in a sense I will not specify here an extraposed variant of (42b), it then follows, for the reasons given in (43), that the gap position in an extraposed *exactly* case like (42c) is an AC.

(43) a. Nonextraposed *exactly* combines only with DPs of the subcategory Q-DP = {interrogative}.[20]
  b. The categories Q and Wdp do not intersect.
  c. Extraposed *exactly* structures can exist only for those DP structures licensed by (43a).

So, the fact that the gap linked to extraposed *exactly* is an AC is not expressed by a direct statement to that effect in the grammar; rather, it is essentially a theorem of the restriction of *exactly* to DPs of the subcategory Q-DP.

Although the specific constraints on the other Type II ACs encoun-
tered earlier—with extraposed *other than* phrases and extraposed relative
clauses—differ from those in (43), the logic of their relation to Wdps is
the same. For each, the relevant forms combine with a restricted subset of
DP types not including Wdps. If so, in these cases also, the Type II ACs
are not a function of specific conditions referencing Wdps. Rather, a Type
II AC is a logical consequence of some other condition plus the fact that
the referenced DP subclass excludes Wdps, as in (44).

(44) a. Many people/Someone/Everyone/No one/*She/*They* other
        than Louise arrived late.
     b. Many people/Someone/Everyone/No one/*She/*They* who
        were/was from Peru arrived late.

These considerations suggest the following generalization:

(45) A Type II AC is induced via logical entailment from a grammatical
     condition that does not reference the distribution of Wdps.

Conclusion (45) then raises the possibility that a Type I AC does involve
such a condition.

Moreover, the idea that the Type I ACs considered earlier involve conditions that do reference Wdp distribution is plausible, because their
properties contrast with those of the Type II ACs just discussed. Consider,
for example, the AC in change of color contexts like (46).

(46) Estelle dyed her eyebrows purple/*it.

This constraint involves no independent restriction on the combination of
a form (like, e.g., *exactly*) with some restricted subtype of DP. Rather, the
particular argument position simply seems not to allow Wdps. If so, the
grammar must contain some statement to that effect, although the scope
and generality of the required condition is not immediately evident.

### 7.4   A Solution

I now argue that in the Metagraph Grammar (MGG) framework of
Johnson and Postal (1980), Postal (1986, 1989, 1990, 1991, 1992, 1996), a
basic hypothesis about the nature of P-gap structures combines with a
specific reconstruction of the nature of Type I ACs just sketched to yield
the LACP for P-gap structures (as well as the PACP).

The core of MGG lies in its appeal to objects called arcs. A priori, it
might seem that a typical Type I AC should be expressed in this frame-

work by picking out certain contexts, say for (8), the object context for the verb *mind*, and claiming something like (47).

(47) A 2-arc that cooccurs with a Predicate-arc headed by the V *mind* cannot be weak pronominal.

Abstracting away from its informality and various not directly relevant issues, (47) is adequate for (8) and, under the view that P-gaps are Wdps, also accounts for the PACP. But it says nothing about the LACP.

To overcome this limitation, I propose that (47) (and analogs for other Type I ACs) be reformulated in MGG terms via appeal to a relation between arcs that I refer to as Overstrike (defined in (53)). The key is that this is logically an ancestral, hence logically reflexive, relation. Hence, (47) can be generalized to:

(48) A 2-arc that cooccurs with a predicate-arc headed by the V *mind* cannot overstrike a weak pronominal arc.

Because Overstrike is a reflexive relation, (48) clearly entails (47). For if A is a weak pronominal arc, then A overstrikes such an arc. But (48) also prohibits cases where the 2-arc of *mind*, although not itself a weak pronominal arc, relates to one in a way covered by Overstrike.

I show briefly how one can describe P-gap structures in such a way that the arc whose head corresponds to the L-gap position overstrikes the arc corresponding to the P-gap position. Since the latter is, given (33), a weak pronominal arc in all cases, where the L-gap arc is either a 2-arc associated with *mind* or an arc subject to a distinct but parallel Type I AC condition, a violation must ensue; this then accounts for the LACP.

I explicate the account around the description of a single P-gap pattern like that in (49).

(49) a. [What situation]$_1$, did no one who foresaw/*minded $pg_1$ discuss $t_1$?

b. [What situation]$_1$ did no one who discussed $pg_1$ foresee/*mind $t_1$?

The *foresee* examples show that this is overall a viable P-gap configuration. The *mind* variant of (49a) is, however, ungrammatical because of the PACP, whereas the *mind* variant of (49b) is ill-formed because of the LACP.

I propose that a relevant MGG structure for (49a) with irrelevant simplifications and an appropriate level of detail is given by the figure in example (50).

(50)

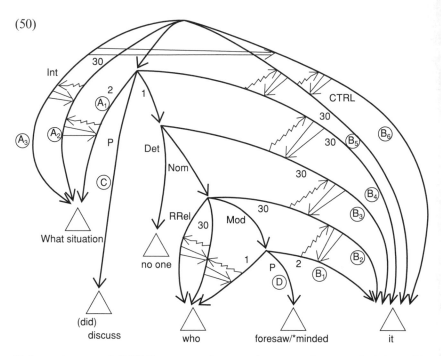

Relevant general MGG assumptions and conventions underlying this structure include those of (51). For more details, see the works cited earlier.

(51) a. Arcs are represented by single lines (arrows).
   b. The point of a line represents the arc's head node; the other extremity represents its tail node.
   c. Circled labels on arcs are meaningless tags to facilitate reference to pieces of structure.
   d. An uncircled label to the left of an arc represents a Relational Sign (R-sign), which is the name of the primitive grammatical relation represented by that arc. Each arc expresses the fact that the constituent defined by its head node bears the grammatical relation designated by its R-sign to the constituent defined by its tail node.
   e. Broken arrows denote the primitive Sponsor relation between arcs. Some arcs have no sponsors; none has more than one.
   f. Double arrows represent the primitive Erase relation between arcs. No arc has more than one Eraser. The surface form of a structure includes only arcs that are not erased—that is, arcs that, in diagrams, do not occur at the point of double arrows.

g. If one arc A sponsors another B, and A and B have the same head node (that is, overlap), then A is said to be a predecessor of B, B a successor of A.

h. The ancestral of any relation V between arcs is called R(emote)-V. So the ancestrals of Predecessor/Successor are R-Predecessor/R-Successor, respectively.

i. If neighboring arcs A, B stand in some relation W, one speaks of Local W. Otherwise, they stand in Foreign W. So a successor relation between nonneighboring arcs is a foreign successor relation.

In these terms, in (50) $B_1$ is a (foreign) predecessor of $B_2$, which is a (foreign) successor of $B_1$. $B_1$ is a (local) R-predecessor of itself, a (foreign) R-predecessor of $B_2$, $B_3$, $B_4$, $B_5$, and $B_6$. These are the only R-predecessor relations of $B_1$. Just so, $B_6$, $B_5$, $B_4$, $B_3$, $B_2$, and $B_1$ are all and only the R-successors of $B_1$.

Following the accepted wisdom embedded in almost all current approaches to P-gaps, I assume that such structures involve extraction and, somewhat parallel to Chomsky's (1986b) chain composition view, that there are at least two linked extractions involved. However, commensurate with the different theoretical frameworks, the extractions and the linkage between them are conceptualized quite differently.

In MGG terms, an extraction involves foreign successors for arcs representing certain basic relations like direct object (R-sign = 2). The extraction of the direct object of the verb *discuss* in (49a) is represented as follows. The object of that verb is indicated by the 2-arc $B_1$. If that object were not extracted, $B_1$ would have no foreign successor. Moreover, I assume that extractions involve two types of successors. There is a general extraction relation, here taken to involve R-sign 30, as well as an ultimate local successor relation between the last 30-arc in a chain of such foreign successors and some arc representing one of the so-called Overlay relations, each defining a distinct type of extraction (e.g., interrogative, topicalization). Int in (50) is then the R-sign naming the interrogative relation.

My basic assumptions about P-gap structures in particular can then be described as follows. As suggested informally in Postal 1993b:753, 1994a:93–95, such structures instantiate a kind of control relation. Here that relation is reconstructed as erasure of a specific type of arc by an Overlay arc. I posit a characteristic relation (R-sign: CTRL) to represent (at least) the control type at issue. CTRL-arcs can be assumed to have at least four properties imposed by MGG theory:

(52) a. A CTRL-arc must be a weak pronominal, which can be taken to mean that its head node represents a Wdp.
   b. Each CTRL-arc must have an eraser.
   c. Each erased CTRL-arc must be anaphorically paired with the arc that erases it.
   d. The erasure indicated in c is exclusively local.[21]

The basic current assumption about P-gaps can now be represented as follows. Such a gap exists only if an arc like $B_1$ in (49a)/(50) has a CTRL R-successor. Given (52), if it does, that CTRL-arc has to have a Wdp head and be anaphorically paired with some neighboring arc that erases it.[22] In effect, these conditions require the Wdp defining a P-gap to extract to the position of the filler of the L-gap. Because each P-gap corresponds to a CTRL-arc and each such arc is erased, (51f) determines the gap property of P-gap structures.

Assuming that $B_6$ is anaphorically paired with $A_3$, which is not formally justified in (50), the generally required P-gap conditions are met in both variants of (49a)/(50). Nonetheless, the version with *mind* is ungrammatical. But this follows from a clash between the requirement that a CTRL-arc's head be a weak pronominal, and condition (48). The latter references *mind* but not a V like *foresee*, and it bars a weak pronominal 2-arc. Thus the PACP is straightforwardly imposed.

To indicate how the present approach also imposes the LACP requires only two further steps. The first is to define Overstrike:

(53) *Overstrike*
   Arc A overstrikes arc B if and only if there exist arcs C and D such that C is an R-successor of A, D is an R-successor of B, and C R-erases D.

Given the ancestral character of the relation defined in (53), every arc overstrikes itself, but one arc, A, overstrikes a distinct arc B only if A has an R-successor that erases an R-successor of B.

Given that definition of overstrike, $B_1$ overstrikes itself in (49a)/(50), which is licit where the verb is *foresee* but violates (48) if the verb is *minded*. $A_1$ also overstrikes $B_1$, although this is not directly relevant to (49a)/(50), because the PACP is imposed by $B_1$ alone.

But nonreflexive instances of Overstrike are the key to the LACP, found in (49b), which has the structure shown in the figure in example (54).

(54)

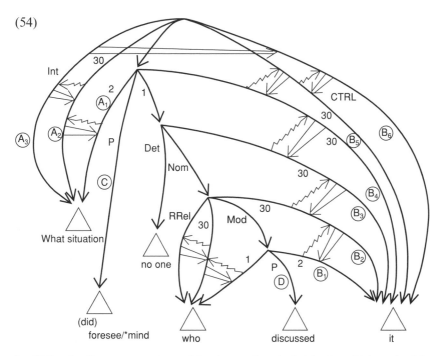

In (54), the 2-arc occurring with the verb *minded* is $A_1$. Although this arc overstrikes itself, that does not yield a violation of (48) because $A_1$ is not weak pronominal. However, $A_1$ also overstrikes $B_1$ because $A_1$ has an R-successor, $A_3$, which R-erases (since it erases) an R-successor of $B_1$, namely, $B_6$. But that violates (48).

Although the preceding discussion is restricted to the Type I AC involving the verb *mind*, one can generalize as follows. If a condition defining a Type I AC, K, is characterized in terms of Overstrike (as in (48)), present assumptions about P-gap structures entail that K will not only, like essentially all ACs, yield the PACP, but also that it will project the LACP. I conclude that the existence of the LACP in connection with Type I ACs is determined as follows. First, P-gaps are properly described in the arc erasure terms discussed around (52). Second, each Type I AC is defined by some grammatical constraint G (Type I $AC_x$) having the logical properties of (48). That is, each G (Type I $AC_x$) bars for a fixed arc environment not weak pronominal arcs, but, more generally, the overstriking in that environment of weak pronominal arcs.[23]

There is one major problem with the just-finished discussion, touched on in note 13. I have assumed that one can give a list of Type I ACs like those in (5)–(16) and claim that they systematically determine both the

PACP and LACP. However, there seems to be variation. Although the general claims hold for the author, for some speakers some of these ACs determine only the PACP. For example, Peter Culicover informs me that the AC in (6) does not determine the LACP. So, besides accepting (22b), he finds examples like (55a,b), which are not possible for me, to be "perfect."

(55) a. *the color which$_1$ she decided, despite really hating $pg_1$, to paint her dresser $t_1$

    b. *He likes the color that$_1$ everyone who praised $pg_1$ dyed their sheets $t_1$.

And he reports a similar absence of the LACP for several other cases in (5)–(16).

Although such variation might initially seem to undermine present proposals, as such they do not. Recall that the only grammatical assumption that in present terms yields the LACP for a particular AC is the formulation of the grammatical constraint underlying that AC in terms of Overstrike, that is, as an analog of (48). Given data like that in (55), one is then free to claim that contrary to what I implicitly assumed so far, for some speakers, some Type I ACs are in fact formulated without appeal to Overstrike, that is, in a way analogous to (47). This minor variation in the formulation of the grammatical conditions underlying certain Type I ACs would account for the observed speaker variation in the appearance of the LACP.

But, given the assumption that Type II ACs are never defined via appeal to Overstrike, but rather are theorems of constraints not referencing Wdps or weak pronominal arcs at all, it also follows that, although inducing the PACP, Type II ACs should never generate the LACP for any speakers.[24]

If the combination of the PACP and LACP, where it appears, is correctly treated by formulating Type I ACs in terms of Overstrike, one then expects the account to generalize beyond the domain of P-gaps to other structures limited by Type I ACs. Two cases of potential interest are the purposive and instruction-set constructions. Postal (1993b, 1994a) proposed that, like P-gap cases, these are control structures and argued that they manifest analogs of the PACP. This involved data like (56) and (57), where $p$ indicates a weak indefinite pronoun.

(56) a.   Irma painted that house that color/*it.
    b.   Irma painted it that color.
    c.   I chose [that house]$_1$ to paint $p_1$ that color.
    d.   *I chose [that color]$_1$ to paint that house $p_1$.

(57) a. ?Number [a prepared wing section]$_1$ after quickly painting $p_1$ green.

b. *Number [a dark color]$_1$ after quickly painting a prepared wing section $p_1$.

These constructions are highly restricted, and, as is clear, testing even for the PACP is difficult.

Although testing for the LACP is still more difficult, results are in the direction predicted by the view of Type I ACs proposed earlier, under the assumption that these constructions involve the same type of control (that is, CTRL-arcs) as P-gaps.[25]

(58) a. I painted [my house]$_1$ [that color]$_2$ to advertise ?$p_1$/*$p_2$ more easily.

b. Paint [a wall]$_1$ [a dark color]$_2$ and describe ?$p_1$/*$p_2$ to friends.

So, for me, the $p_1$ interpretations of (58a,b) are quite strained, but the $p_2$ interpretations are entirely impossible. And it is hard to see how this result can follow from any independent semantic or pragmatic considerations, given that (59a,b) seem perfect:

(59) a. They advertised that color more easily.

b. They described a dark color to friends.

Although much more work is clearly needed, there is thus some ground to conclude that an analog of the LACP holds for the purposive and instruction-set cases—a conclusion that supports the general assumptions made here.

## 7.5 Implications

The account developed in section 7.4 shows how, in the framework assumed, the grammatical constraints underlying Type I ACs, which exist independently of P-gaps, can be formulated in simple terms. It enables us to predict without additional stipulation that Type I ACs yield both the PACP and LACP. Moreover, under reasonable assumptions about the constraints underlying Type II ACs, it also follows that these induce only the PACP. Further, the account also permits a parallel approach to the purposive and instruction-set cases.

These results, if maintainable, provide support for the MGG framework that yields them by permitting an arc erasure view of P-gaps, grounding the definition of the key concept Overstrike, and so forth. The weight of this support can, however, only be appropriately evaluated by determining whether competing frameworks of P-gap description can adequately capture the generalizations at the end of the previous paragraph. Because most current views appear not even to recognize the Wdp character of P-gaps (purposive gaps or instruction set gaps), considerable doubt seems warranted on this score.

### 7.6    Appendix: Locality Condition

This section briefly motivates the locality condition given in (52d). This condition requires that in a figure like (50), the erased CTRL-arc, B6, has the same tail node as its eraser, A3. There are two types of motivation for such a condition. First, any theory of control must constrain the relation and, in an arc-based framework, (52d) represents an extremely strong (restrictive) constraint. This provides a "conceptual" motivation. Second, factual grounds exist in that this condition accounts for at least two general features of the class of constructions which Chomsky (1986a,b) claimed should be represented by so-called empty operators. These include P-gap, object deletion, object raising, and purposive structures. One feature involves the interaction of these constructions with island constraints; the other involves their relation to strong crossover violations.

To keep the discussion to manageable proportions, I illustrate the issues not only with P-gap constructions but partly with somewhat simpler object-deletion examples like (60).

(60) Jane$_1$ is too unpleasant for you to have Cynthia invite her$_1$/t$_1$.

This choice imposes no distortion because it is easy to determine that the problems focused on here do also arise in P-gap cases. Chomsky (1986a,b) claimed that the posit of empty operators, specifically for cases like (60), is supported by the fact that the movement of the posited operator obeys island constraints.[26] So he observed (1986a:110) that of the examples in (61), the null object variant is grammatical only in the first case. Here and in what follows, posited empty operators are represented as a subscripted $O$ and "$\langle\ \rangle$" mark island boundaries.

(61) a.  John is too stubborn $O_2$ to expect anyone to talk to Bill/$t_2$.
     b.  John is too stubborn $O_2$ to visit anyone $\langle$who talked to Bill/ *$t_2\rangle$.
     c.  John is too stubborn $O_2$ to ask $\langle$why Tom wondered who talked to Bill/*$t_2\rangle$.

Chomsky assumed that the ungrammaticality of the gap variants of (61b,c) reflects the requirement for the empty operator to extract. If the empty operator is forced to extract to the position of $O_2$ in (61a–c), then it must extract from at least one island in the latter two but not in the former. As desired, this accounts for the ungrammaticality under a variety of distinct assumptions as long as these determine that restrictive relative clauses and interrogative complements are islands. So far, this much is insightful, but a great deal is left open.[27] Critically from the present point of view, Chomsky does not seem to have indicated why it is necessary for the empty operator in the construction of (61) not only to move but to move as far as it must if all island violations associated with the construction are to be captured.

For instance, to guarantee the existence of the observed island violation in (62), it does not suffice that the empty operator object of the verb *consider* be forced to extract.

(62) Wayne$_1$ is too stubborn to ask ⟨why Jeanne would not persuade Sally to consider him$_1$/*$t_1$⟩.

Some principle must, further, force it to extract at least as far as a position external to the interrogative complement, which forms the first island between the object position and other possible derived loci for the empty operator. This case appears to be entirely typical. For all the constructions Chomsky analyzes as involving empty operators, the presence of any island between the base position of the empty operator and the element defining the construction (e.g., in (62) *too*) yields, with one exception, an island violation.[28] If so, then to account for the right class of island violations, a theory must incorporate principles that guarantee that empty operators or their analogs not only extract, but always extract "far enough." In (62), "far enough" is to the front of the infinitival complement of *too* but is not, for example, just to the initial position of the infinitival complement of *persuade*.

In the current framework, the locality principle given in (52d) fills this role. It requires that a controlled element head an arc that is a neighbor of an arc headed by its controller. In more standard terms, this says, informally, that an element to be controlled must extract to be a sister of its controller. So, in an example like (62), the controlled object of *consider* must extract to be a sister of *Wayne*. And the analog holds regardless of the complexity of the structure between these two positions. Hence if that structure contains an island, ungrammaticality will in general ensue (modulo the remarks of note 28) because two valid principles clash—one requires the controlled element to achieve a locus sister to its controller; the other forbids extraction from islands. These cannot both be satisfied.

Paul M. Postal

Considerations parallel to those just discussed for island violations also motivate principle (52d) from the domain of strong crossover violations. That is, such a violation ensues from the presence of a pronoun (in the proper structural configuration) linked to the controller of the relevant class of constructions anywhere along the path between the construction gap and the controller. This is illustrated for an object-deletion case in (63a) and for a P-gap case in (63b).

(63) a. Claire$_1$ is too shy for us to get *her$_1$/her$_2$ to admit that Jim was attractive to $t_1$.

    b. It was Claire who$_1$ they convinced $t_1$ that you would hire *her$_1$/her$_2$ despite your feeling that the job was too hard for $pg_1$.

If in (63a), the object of *to* extracted, say, only to the complementizer region of the complement of *admit*, there would be no way to reduce the violation in such a case to the principle independently needed for cases like (64).

(64) It was Claire who$_1$ we got *her$_1$/her$_2$ to admit that Jim was attractive to $t_1$.

Just so, unless the object of *for* in (63b) extracts to a position outside the *despite* adjunct, and at least as high as the object of *hire*, there is also no principled reason why (63b) manifests the same strong crossover constraint typical of cases like (64).

Thus a principle like (52d) can predict key facts about the interaction of the sort of control constructions at issue with both island constraints and strong crossover constraints. This substantive factual motivation well complements the "conceptual" restrictiveness of the principle.

**Notes**

I am grateful to Judith Aissen, Mark Baltin, and Peter Culicover, for extremely helpful comments on earlier versions of this study. Usual disclaimers are in effect.

1. However, as is well known (see, e.g., Sternefeld, 1991:79), decisions as to which of two linked gaps are parasitic remain arbitrary in certain cases, such as in (i):

(i) [Which emperor]$_1$ did they compare drawings of $t_1$ to carvings of $t_1$?

2. The phrase "licit position for extraction gaps" ignores island constraints. As has been much discussed, in certain cases, a P-gap can, as in (i), appear inside an island not containing its L-gap:

(i) the meteorite which$_1$ everyone who saw $pg_1$ wanted to videotape $t_1$

See also note 27.

3. The distinct question of whether they sanction too few P-gaps needs, no doubt, to be raised proposal by proposal.

4. Steedman (1996:98, n. 41) claims that cases like (i) "seem impeccable."

(i) the table [on which]$_1$ I placed the book $t_1$ before carefully positioning the glass $pg_1$

For the language of those who agree (I do not), such instances of multiple non-DP gaps appear to be evident instances of English non-DP P-gaps.

Although this hypothesis is possibly correct, there is an alternative. Postal (1994a/ this volume) argues for the existence of so-called pseudo-P-gaps. These denote multiple gaps, one of which might be (and has been) taken to be a P-gap but which can be argued instead to be a gap devolving on Right Node Raising (RNR). It is logically possible, and conceivably more, that examples like (i) also involve pseudo-P-gaps. Sustaining that view also requires analyzing (i) as manifesting left extraction of the RNR pivot constituent. Supporting such a highly abstract analysis would require showing that gaps like those in (i) manifest properties otherwise characteristic of RNR but not freely associated with gaps in general. I do not deal with this issue here.

A role for RNR in apparent P-gap cases was first suggested by Joan Bresnan, in oral remarks in 1981 (cited in Engdahl 1983/this volume:n. 11), a fact which, I regret, was overlooked in Postal 1994a. Bresnan hypothesized that all P-gaps might involve RNR, a proposal seemingly designed to explain certain incompatibilities between P-gaps and finite subject positions. This universal approach was argued against by Engdahl. The suggestion here, which would extend the claim in Postal 1994a that some assumed P-gaps are actually pseudo-P-gaps, is much more restricted.

5. Engdahl (1983/this volume:17) cited apparent Swedish prepositional phrase and adjectival phrase P-gaps. These may also be subject to the remarks of note 4.

6. The correlation between passivization constraints and P-gaps is a special case of broader links between the former and one type of control structure. So, for example, object raising and object deletion structures also manifest the constraint in (2):

(i) *Abuse was impossible for their relationship to involve.

(ii) *Abuse of that sort is too rare for their relationship to have involved.

7. At least for some speakers; Barss (1986:377) cites both (i) and (ii) as well-formed:

(i) It was himself$_1$ that$_1$ John$_1$ nominated $t_1$ before he$_1$ voted for $pg_1$.

(ii) It was himself$_1$ that$_1$ John$_1$ nominated $t_1$ before PRO$_1$ voting for $pg_1$.

For me, clearer cases include (iii) and (iv), which seem totally impossible:

(iii) *It was herself$_1$ that$_1$ everyone who described her$_1$ to $pg_1$ later criticized $t_1$.

(iv) *It was herself$_1$ that$_1$ they felt that your describing her$_1$ to $pg_1$ led her$_1$ to lose faith in $t_1$.

8. The reasons for only linking invisible pronouns to Wdps are discussed in Postal 1994b, 1998. Roughly, the claim is that only Wdps can be invisible. If so, strong pronoun distribution is in general irrelevant to posits of invisible pronouns, the major ground for talking about ACs.

9. Page references are to the published 1986 version. This is, to my knowledge, the earliest recognition of P-gaps in the generative literature

10. Frampton (1990:76) claims to have provided evidence against the view that P-gaps are null resumptive pronouns. But he does not treat any data like that in (5)–(16). Nor does Taraldsen (1981:491), who also seems to reject a pronominal view of P-gaps.

11. For example, under Chomsky's (1986b) composed chain approach, P-gaps are nonpronominal traces of so-called empty operators. To bring this view into compliance with the arguably Wdp character of P-gaps would require inter alia abandoning his Condition C account of the strong crossover effect (see Chomsky 1981:183f, 193f, 278–279; 1982:20, 23; 1986a:78, 109, 182, 207n; 1995:71–72). For, as is known, P-gaps regularly yield strong crossover violations in cases like (i).

(i) *the woman who$_1$ Emile concluded the agreement with $t_1$ in spite of your
    trying to persuade her$_1$ that I was trying to defraud $pg_1$

Under Chomsky's (1986b) proposal, the P-gap in (i) would not be a Wdp, but a "referring expression," consistent with a claim that (i) is blocked by Condition C (which only governs referring expressions). But the evidence indicating that P-gaps are Wdps renders Condition C irrelevant to cases like (i).

12. Examples like (i) are well-formed:

(i) [Which child]$_1$ did they believe it was $t_1$ that the doctor treated $t_1$ after
    rescuing $pg_1$?

I believe that this is the case because, unlike (17b), (i) has an analysis where both the L-gap and P-gap are internal to the relative-like part of the cleft, and hence on that analysis, neither is an AC.

13. Two caveats about (18) are required. First, the reasons for the hedged formulation "large class of ACs" are explicated in section 7.3. Second, the implication that (18) holds for all speakers for all the mentioned ACs is untenable, as discussed in section 7.4.

14. There is, for many speakers, an irrelevant grammatical reading of the starred variant of (22b) in which there is no gap after *house* and in which the gap after *discussing* is a non-P-gap representing extraction from a selective island.

15. As there are different kinds of Wdps—for example, resumptive and nonresumptive ones, expletive and nonexpletive ones—(33) is far from fully specifying the character of P-gaps. My current view is that each P-gap involves two distinct Wdps, each of which is nonexpletive. Of course, these distinct pronouns relate to a unique position at different levels of analysis. Take (i) as a typical case for concreteness.

(i) [Which vampire]$_1$ did your denouncing $pg_1$/him$_1$ lead people to revile $t_1$?

One of the pronouns associated with the $pg$ position is an ordinary "coreferential" one, the same type as the *him* found in the non-P-gap version of (i). The other pronoun is a resumptive associated with the fact that the nonresumptive just described extracts (an extraction having the characteristic of linking to a resumptive) as in the selective island extractions discussed in Postal 1998. I cannot attempt to justify this dual pronominal view of P-gaps here. The motivations involve parallels between properties of P-gaps and properties of a proper subset of other gaps that can be argued to involve resumptive pronouns, like the selective island gaps discussed in Postal 1998. The control account of P-gaps sketched in what follows is partial and treats only the invisibility of the "coreferential" pronoun. Note that the dual-pronoun claim is inherently no more obscure than standard claims that some position involves an underlying element (e.g., a then-moved *wh*-form) and a (distinct) trace of that moved *wh*-form.

16. A reason beyond that given in the text for rejecting (37) is derivable from the observation of Lasnik and Stowell (1991:695) that weak crossover (WCO) effects are not found in a parasitic domain. For example, the two variants of (i) are equally grammatical although the version with *his* seems to manifest a WCO configuration:

(i) Who$_1$ did his$_1$ son's/Mabel's stories about $pg_1$ annoy $t_1$?

If, as I have claimed, P-gaps represent Wdps, one would relate the lack of WCO effect precisely to the presence of the Wdp. This suggests that if (37) were valid, a similar absence of WCO effect would manifest in the licensing domain. But this does not seem to be the case:

(ii) *Who$_1$ did his$_1$ manager scold $t_1$ (while having lunch with $pg_1$)?

Even given the known subtlety of WCO judgments, I find it clear that addition of the parasitic domain fails to improve the antecedent/pronoun linkage in (ii).

17. Other exceptive phrases including *but/except* + DP behave in the same way.

18. A very limited partial exception is the distinction between wide versus narrow bans on Wdps drawn in Postal 1994b, 1998. The idea was that some contexts bar only surface Wdps. Such contexts would thus allow the variety of invisible controlled Wdps and would represent a restricted range of cases where the correlation between the distribution of, for example, P-gaps and selective island extraction gaps and the distribution of visible Wdps breaks down.

19. The form in question is distinct from a homophonous manner adverbial. Some sentences have both readings.

   The claim that the relevant use of *exactly* combines only with interrogative DPs ignores cases like:

(i) Herb saw exactly three/seven cats.

(ii) Exactly that was proved by Helen.

If this is the same use discussed in the text, the specification of the category Q in (43) needs to be expanded, in ways irrelevant to the present discussion.

20. Specifically interrogative forms and not *wh*-forms in general are relevant, as shown by the impossibility of combining the form with exclamatory *wh*-structures:

(i) a. [(*Exactly) what a great guy]$_1$ she is dating $t_1$!
   b. [What a great guy]$_1$ she is dating $t_1$ (*exactly)!

21. Motivation for the condition given in (52d) is briefly provided in the appendix.

22. As discussed at length by Johnson and Postal (1980), anaphoric pairing is a complex relation between arcs that depends on combined patterns of sponsoring and erasing. Specifically, to support the claim that B$_6$ in (50) is anaphorically

paired with $A_3$, it is necessary to recognize at least one further arc, G, with the same tail node as $B_2$ and the same head node as $A_1$. G is erased by $A_1$ and sponsors $B_1$. In terms of Johnson and Postal 1980 and relevant revisions, it would be said that G replaces $B_1$ and that $A_1$ seconds G. Anaphoric pairing then holds essentially between (all) R-successors of such replacee/seconder pairs.

23. The reader should be able to verify that the offered account encounters no difficulty with the fact that the LACP is also found in multiple P-gap cases, first noted by Ross (1967/1986:118–119).

(i) [What color]$_1$ did everyone who criticized/*painted their house $pg_1$ discuss $t_1$ with Abigail after choosing $pg_1$?

24. A description in terms of the overstriking of pronominal arcs is not at all equivalent to one in terms of binding. In fact, binding is generally well formed in environments where the LACP manifests, yielding contrasts like:

(i) a. the insulting remark which$_1$ Jane, even though hearing it$_1$/*$pg_1$ quite clearly, seemed not to mind $t_1$.

    b. the color which$_1$ Arthur painted his garage $t_1$ after seeing it$_1$/*$pg_1$ in an advertisement

25. Although these cases would share with P-gap structures the presence of CTRL-arcs, the erasing arcs would not be Overlay-arcs but Central-arcs (e.g., 2-arcs). The same point would hold for the object-raising and object-deletion constructions of note 6.

26. Specifically, (1986a:110): "Indeed, these structures do observe these general conditions on movement." Chomsky (1986a:111) also rightly observes that postulation of something (in his terms, an empty operator) which extracts in such cases is motivated by the fact that the constructions at issue yield proper L-gaps, as in:

(i) John is too charming to talk to $t_1$ [without liking $pg_1$].

The correctness of Chomsky's point is not undermined by the poor choice of a marginal example, with its adjunct-internal stative verb; any problems related to that are also found in non-P-gap cases like that in which $pg_1$ in (i) is replaced by $him_1$.

27. The facts cited merely support the existence of extracted elements; they do not as such indicate their nature. Chomsky's "operator" terminology with its connotations of logical operators is entirely unmotivated by any semantic properties. The semantics of the gaps in these constructions seems to be that of pronouns, as expected in current terms, where such gaps are taken to be a type of controlled pronoun.

28. The exception is illustrated by P-gap cases like (i).

(i) [Which aviator]$_1$ did ⟨your criticizing $pg_1$⟩ lead them to dismiss $t_1$?

Here in present terms, in order for an arc headed by $pg_1$ to be controlled, it must have a successor in the main clause. So, extraction must cross the subject island boundary, which makes the deleted object of *criticizing* a sister at the relevant level of the object of *dismiss*. This is a case, I suggest, of selective island extraction in the sense of Postal 1994b, 1998, and wherever that is possible, Chomsky's claim can fail to be strictly true. However, there are evidently many narrow but poorly understood constraints that prevent the possibility of selective island extraction from expanding the class of P-gaps as much as might be expected. Consider that cases like (ii) are not possible.

(ii) *[Which aviator]$_1$ did they persuade $t_1$ that ⟨your criticizing $pg_1$⟩ was illegal?

Although the issues mentioned in this note are important and deserve detailed discussion, I do not believe they affect the conclusions of this section. Hopefully, the same constraints can account for the failure of selective island extraction to permit, for example, object deletion cases like (iii).

(iii) *Pamela$_1$ is too cynical for your praising her$_1$/$t_1$ to accomplish much.

# PART III

## What Is Not a Parasitic Gap?

# Chapter 8

## Parasitic and Pseudoparasitic Gaps    Paul M. Postal

### 8.1  Background

What has been considered the English *parasitic gap* (P-gap) phenomenon is illustrated in (1).[1]

(1) a. [Which article]$_1$ did Ted copy $t_1$ without reading $pg_1$?
   b. the woman who$_2$ your attack on $pg_2$ enraged $t_2$
   c. It was Irving who$_3$ they proved associates of $pg_3$ to have bribed $t_3$.
   d. John offended $t_4$ by not recognizing $pg_4$_____[his favorite uncle from Cleveland]$_4$. (Engdahl 1983:12, crediting Tom Wasow)

In these and following examples P-gaps are marked *pg*, "true" gaps $t$.[2] A view about P-gaps that has gained some currency in recent years is expressed in (2).

(2) a. Cinque 1990:102[3]
      "Thus, parasitic gaps of a category other than NP are quite generally impossible."
   b. Koster 1987:156 (following Cinque's then unpublished work)
      "Parasitic gaps are always NPs, and non-NPs give a typically bad result ..."
   c. Emonds 1985:91
      "... the present analysis is compatible only with parasitic NP gaps, ..."
   d. Frampton 1990:56, fn. 17
      "... the fact that parasitic gaps are restricted to the category NP ..."

See also Aoun and Clark 1985:33–34 and Lasnik and Saito 1992:147. Hereafter, I refer to the doctrine that P-gaps can only be NPs as the *P-Gap NP Restriction* (PG = NP).[4]

PG = NP seems to explain the fact, noted by Pesetsky (1982:584), Chomsky (1982:55), and others, that in English P-gaps cannot be based on prepositional phrases (PPs); see also Kiss 1985:73, fn. 11. Emonds (1985:91) gives such data as (3a–d) in support of PG = NP.

(3) a. *[How sick]$_1$ did John say he felt $t_1$ before getting $pg_1$?
    b. *[How long]$_2$ does John drink $t_2$ before lecturing $pg_2$?
    c. This is a topic$_3$ you should think about $t_3$ before talking about $pg_3$.
    d. *This is a topic [about which]$_4$ you should think $t_4$ before talking $pg_4$.

Other English data supporting it are found in (4).

(4) a. *Tall$_1$ though Frank was $t_1$ without looking $pg_1$, he couldn't reach the shelf.
    b. *Unbearable$_2$, he is $t_2$ even when trying not to seem $pg_2$.
    c. *[Beaten by the guards]$_3$, she seems to have been $t_3$ while trying to avoid being $pg_3$.
    d. *[Abuse my ferret]$_4$, I refused to accept that he could $t_4$ even after seeing him $pg_4$.

On the basis of contrasts like (5a) versus (5b–c), it is generally accepted that a P-gap can appear in one domain only in the presence of an *extraction* in another.[5]

(5) a. [Which article]$_1$ did Ted copy $t_1$ without reading $pg_1$?
    b. *Ted copied that article$_2$ without reading $pg_2$.
    c. *Which spy copied [which article]$_3$ without reading $pg_3$?

I use *extraction* as an informal, theory-neutral term to refer to (for instance) the leftward positioning of elements in questions, relatives, and the like. Extractions are described by successive-cyclic movements to Ā-positions in Government-Binding (GB) work, by Slash categories in the Generalized Phrase Structure Grammar (GPSG) approach, and so on. It becomes important to distinguish those extractions in which the extracted phrase is to the left of its associated gap from those in which it is to the right of its gap; henceforth, these are called *L(eft)-extractions* and *R(ight)-extractions*, respectively.

Given contrasts like those in (5), data like (3) and (4), which motivate PG = NP, would in addition support two independent principles of English. One would require that the "licensing" gap associated with a P-gap be an NP; the other would determine that the extractee—for example, *which article* in (5a)—be an NP. I refer to the latter as the *P-Gap Licensing Restriction* (PLR). Under most views of extraction, the claim that extractees are restricted to some category is extensionally (though not logically) equivalent to the assertion that "licensing" gaps are so restricted. For present purposes, I regard the PLR as claiming that extractees "licensing" P-gaps are NPs, and I assume, except where specifically noted, that this entails the NP-hood of "licensing" gaps. Although the distinction between PG = NP and the PLR is evident once made explicit, it is unclear that advocates of the former have recognized the existence of the distinct claims involved in the latter. Given the general acceptance of the notion that P-gaps depend on some kind of extraction of the "licensing" category, the PLR entails that every genuine P-gap cooccurs with some *NP* extraction (outside of the parasitic domain). The conjunction of PG = NP and the PLR then claims that every bona fide English P-gap involves an NP P-gap "licensed" by an NP extractee linked to a "real" NP gap. Theories assuming that extractions are invariably linked to traces in the extraction site combine with the PLR to determine that each P-gap structure contains (at least) three linked NPs.

Both PG = NP and the PLR are, at least for English, plausible principles with considerable initial support. Data like (3a–d), which have been taken to support PG = NP, equally support the PLR. Moreover, in the context of other assumptions, PG = NP may well imply the PLR. For example, Chomsky 1986b:56 initiated a tradition of P-gap description that appeals to the notions "chain" and "chain composition." Although I can find no definition of "chain" in this work, in earlier work (1981:333) Chomsky defines "chain" such that its first element is an NP. The claim that P-gap description depends on "chain composition" then entails the PLR.

In the GPSG framework, "licensing" gap and P-gap are linked in that both correspond to so-called Slash categories with the same binder.[6] Although it is possible, as Gerald Gazdar (personal communication, 8/10/92) stresses, to formulate Slash descriptions under which a P-gap (any gap) represents one category—say, NP—but its binder does not, such analyses are not given by independently motivated extraction schemas. Rather, they depend on relatively ad hoc rules of, say, the form S → PP, S/NP, unnecessary if binders and gaps are of the same category, as they are in the case of P-gaps if the PLR holds.

So, although seemingly not previously made explicit in the literature, the PLR has nonetheless arguably been implicit in a considerable body of work.

The chief goal of these remarks is to explore the tenability of both PG = NP and the PLR *for English*. I show that if one adopts now standard views of the *extension* of the P-gap phenomenon, both principles would be falsified. However, I believe that this conclusion is incorrect. An attested clustering of properties instead supports the view that what have been called P-gaps actually represent at least two different phenomena. Although both PG = NP and the PLR are clearly false for one type, there is reason to believe that they remain free of known counterexamples for the other. In fact, data examined here extend the support for PG = NP *in the restricted domain*.

Surprising complications arise in assessing the status of the PLR. Several types of apparently unresolvable counterexamples are documented in section 8.2. Whereas one type of apparent difficulty for the PLR is relatively easily circumvented, the others are not. The initial problems for the PLR relate, directly or indirectly, to *that* clauses. Whereas earlier work, like Rosenbaum 1967, Ross 1967, and Postal 1971, had typically taken such clauses to be NPs in many contexts, since the arguments of Emonds 1970, 1972, 1976 (see also Emonds 1985), principle (6) has been widely accepted.[7]

(6) *That* clauses are non-NPs (in surface structure).

Given (6), the PLR entails that if there is any *that* clause extraction, it should not per se "license" P-gaps. Section 8.2 adduces material that seemingly shows, however, that some extracted *that* clauses and other constituents *of the same category* do "license" P-gaps. It is also shown that some constituents of that category can also apparently *be* P-gaps. It appears then that one must conclude that both PG = NP and the PLR are simply false for English, and it is shown that one cannot avoid this conclusion merely by abandoning principle (6).

However, section 8.3 reappraises that conclusion, suggesting that both PG = NP and the PLR are nonetheless true on the basis of a rather surprising discovery that leads to a distinction between *true P-gaps* and *pseudo-P-gaps*. It is then denied that those gaps taken in section 8.2 to be P-gaps threatening PG = NP and the PLR are actually P-gaps. Section 8.4 provides a brief characterization of pseudo-P-gaps and shows how it succeeds in regularizing otherwise anomalous properties of numerous pseudo-P-gaps. Together sections 8.3 and 8.4 justify the view that both PG = NP and the PLR actually cover only a proper subset of all those gaps that would have previously been characterized as P-gaps. Section 8.5 defends this conclusion against apparent anomalies found in the domain of parenthetical expressions. Section 8.6 summarizes the results and considers certain more general implications.

## 8.2 The Apparent Falsehood of PG = NP and the PLR

### 8.2.1 The Interaction of the PLR with Topicalization and "Object Raising"

The viability of the conjunction of the PLR and (6) is seemingly impacted by the truth of assertions (7a–b).

(7) a. Topicalized NPs "license" P-gaps.
   b. Topicalized *that* clauses "license" P-gaps.

These claims are supported by examples such as (8a–b).

(8) a. That$_1$, he asserted $t_1$ without verifying $pg_1$.
   b. [That the ruble is worthless]$_2$, he asserted $t_2$ without verifying $pg_2$.

Parallel points hold for "object-raising" constructions:

(9) a. "Object-raised" NPs "license" P-gaps.
   b. "Object-raised" *that* clauses "license" P-gaps.

Claims (9a–b) are illustrated in (10).

(10) a. That$_1$ is easy to assert $t_1$ without verifying $pg_1$.
    b. [That the ruble is worthless]$_2$ is easy to assert $t_2$ without verifying $pg_2$.

A parallel discussion could also be based on clefts, for those speakers who allow *that* clauses to be clefted. For me, though, clefts like (11) have a definite foreign (Irish) feeling about them.

(11) It's [that the pipes leak]$_1$ that he asserted $t_1$ without proving $pg_1$.

Although initially troubling for the PLR, more precisely for its conjunction with (6), the acceptable P-gaps in (8b) and (10b) are ultimately probably benign with respect to such a conjunction. The latter does not entail that the *that* clauses in (8) and (10) are NPs, even if they have been extracted. It only entails that *some* NP in (8b) and (10b) appropriately linked to the P-gap has been extracted, and this (weaker) position can be independently supported.[8]

Without going into great detail (see Postal 1993b, 1998), considerable evidence can be found for both the topicalization and "object-raising" constructions, supporting the view that an invisible (resumptive) pronoun exists in their complements.[9] Under the assumption that this pronoun has been extracted, (8b) and (10b) would not be incompatible with the conjunction of (6) and the PLR. The view I advocate is that NP and clausal topicalization constructions involve extraction both of the topic and of an invisible pronoun, which is a resumptive form associated with the first extraction.[10] Such extractions of resumptive elements appear to be independently attested. For instance, Koster (1987:63), citing work by Henk van Riemsdijk, gives the German example (12).

(12) Den Hans$_1$    den$_1$    mag ich $t_1$ nicht.
     the  Hans$_{ACC}$ him$_{ACC}$ like I      not
     'Hans, I don't like.'

Parallel sentences are common in Scandinavian, where they are sometimes referred to as *contrastive dislocation* sentences; see such works as Andersson 1982:35 for Swedish examples and Thráinsson 1986:189 for Icelandic ones. Sells (1984:91–94) cites parallel Hebrew (relative clause) cases and McCloskey (1979:94–97) discusses relevant Irish relative clause material. I suggest that English NP topicalizations parallel (12) except that an extracted English topicalization resumptive, unlike the *den* of (12), is always invisible. These considerations suggest a structure for, say, (8a) in which its main clause contains an NP extractee parallel to *den* in (12), as well as a "true" NP gap represented by $t_1$ linked to that extractee. In these terms, the PLR would be satisfied.

A similar analysis can be proposed for "object-raising" cases. It is known that cognate constructions in related languages (e.g., Spanish) manifest (optional) resumptive pronouns; it is then not a great step to claim that in English the relevant resumptives are extracted.[11]

Evidence for invisible pronouns in the cases of interest takes the form of showing that the constructions obey constraints independently holding for *explicit definite pronouns*. I give three examples, the first of which is illustrated by (13)–(14).

(13) a.  They named their son/him Ethelbert.
     b.  *They named their son/him it.
     c.  Their son, they named Ethelbert.
     d.  Their son$_1$ would be impossible for them to name $t_1$ Ethelbert.
     e.  *Ethelbert$_2$, I wouldn't name anybody $t_2$.
     f.  *Ethelbert$_3$, was impossible for them to name their son $t_3$.

(14) a.  They called your cousin/him an idiot (and an incompetent).
     b.  *They called him it/them.

c. Your cousin$_1$, they called $t_1$ an idiot and an incompetent.

d. Your cousin$_2$ would be impossible for them to call $t_2$ an incompetent.

e. *An idiot$_3$, they couldn't call your cousin $t_3$.

f. *An idiot$_4$ was impossible for them to call your cousin $t_4$.

These examples indicate that "name" positions preclude definite pronouns and that, correspondingly, such positions cannot be linked to topicalized or "object-raised" elements. This cannot follow from any *fully general* constraints on "name" extractions, since "name" elements are extractable, in (for example) questions and restrictive relatives:

(15) a. What$_1$ did they name their son $t_1$?

b. What$_2$ they named their son $t_2$ is unknown.

c. What$_3$ did they call you $t_3$?

d. The things which$_4$ they called him $t_4$ were obscene.

Second, the "focus" position of an *existential there* construction cannot be a definite pronoun, probably as a consequence of this position's general incompatibility with definites (see Heim 1988:22). Examples (16a–f) show that this constraint correlates with the impossibility of linking that position to topicalized or "object-raised" phrases.

(16) a. He allowed there to be (pictures of) nude dancers at the party.

b. He allowed there to be *(pictures of) them at the party.

c. [Nude dancers]$_1$, he allowed there to be *(pictures of) $t_1$ at the party.

d. [Nude dancers]$_2$ will be impossible to allow there to be *(pictures of) $t_2$ at the party.

e. [Such parties]$_3$, he allowed there to be (pictures of) nude dancers at $t_3$.

f. [Such parties]$_4$ were impossible to allow there to be (pictures of) nude dancers at $t_4$.

Again, as (17a–b) illustrate, the constraints in the starred versions of (16c–d) cannot follow from *general* restrictions on extraction from the focus position.

(17) a. [What kind of dancers]$_1$ were there $t_1$ at the party?

b. The dancers that$_2$ there were $t_2$ at the party were students.

Third, one type of inalienable possession construction precludes a body part from being represented by a definite pronoun:

(18) a. They shouldn't have touched his thumb$_1$ but they did touch it$_1$.
   b. They shouldn't have touched him on the/his thumb$_2$ (*but they did touch him on it$_2$).

The contrast in (18) projects to similar contrasts in both "object-raising" and topicalization structures:

(19) a. [His/The thumb]$_1$ is easy to touch $t_1$.
   b. *[His/The thumb]$_2$ is easy to touch him on $t_2$.

(20) a. [His/The thumb]$_1$, I never touched $t_1$.
   b. *[His/The thumb]$_2$, I never touched him on $t_2$.

Again, these restrictions cannot follow from general constraints on extraction:

(21) a. [What part of the/his body]$_1$ did you touch (him on) $t_1$?
   b. the part of the/his body that$_2$ I touched (him on) $t_2$

   More direct evidence that both topicalized and "object-raised" *that* clauses are associated with *NP* extraction is seen in (22) and (23), for example.

(22) a. I convinced Frank of/*∅ that.
   b. I convinced Frank *of/∅ that Sonia was very competent.
   c. That$_1$, I couldn't convince Frank of/*∅ $t_1$.
   d. [That Sonia was really quite competent]$_2$, I couldn't convince Frank of/*∅ $t_2$.
   e. That$_3$ was difficult to convince Frank of/*∅ $t_3$.
   f. [That Sonia was really quite competent]$_4$ was difficult to convince Frank of/*∅ $t_4$.

(23) a. I insisted on/*∅ that.
   b. I insisted *on/∅ that Sonia attend the interview.
   c. That$_1$, I couldn't insist on/*∅ $t_1$.
   d. [That Sonia attend the interview]$_2$, I couldn't insist on/*∅ $t_2$.
   e. That$_3$ was difficult to insist on/*∅ $t_3$.
   f. [That Sonia attend the interview]$_4$ was difficult to insist on/*∅ $t_4$.

These paradigms show that both topicalization and "object raising" with verbs like *convince* and *insist* have the following properties. They relate the seemingly extracted clause to a position in which surface *that* clauses cannot actually occur but surface NPs can; they cannot relate such clauses to positions in which *that* clauses can occur. That is, the cases with *that* clauses, just like those with unchallenged NPs, require stranded prepositions. In these respects, both topicalization and "object raising" of *that* clauses behave like NP extraction, not like simple *that* clause extraction; see Kaplan and Bresnan 1982:242.

Although postulation of an extracted invisible pronoun in such examples as (8b), (10b), (22d,f), and (23d,f) raises questions, including those about the status of the *that* clauses in such structures, it seems that as such, these examples provide no good reason to reject the conjunction of (6) and the PLR.

## 8.2.2 The Interaction of PG = NP, the PLR, and Complex NP Shift

However, an analog of the approach to maintaining the PLR sketched in section 8.2.1 for topicalization and "object raising" fails to extend to cases such as (24c).

(24) a. We suggest $t_1$ to our employees—[the sort of behavior in question]$_1$.

   b. We suggest $t_2$ to our employees without actually requiring $pg_2$ of them—[the sort of behavior in question]$_2$.

   c. We suggest $t_3$ to our employees without actually requiring $pg_3$ of them—[that they wear a tie]$_3$. (Authier 1989:21, 1991:731)

That is, Authier (1989, 1991) observes in effect that in certain contexts the *complex NP shift* (CXS) phenomenon seen in (24a–b) seems to involve a *that* clause and that in such cases the "shifted" clause can apparently "license" a P-gap; a similar conclusion is drawn by Rochemont and Culicover (1990:188–189, n. 18).

Actually, the assumption that (24c) involves CXS, that is, the same phenomenon as (24a), is far from obvious. There are even reasons to doubt that (24b) manifests CXS; see section 8.4.4. Obviously, it might be claimed that (24c) represents not CXS but *extraposition*. For current purposes, this issue is not paramount since, in any case, the "licensing" category for the P-gap is a *that* clause. But the question becomes relevant and is taken up in section 8.3.2. I will continue to refer to cases like (24c) as involving P-gaps "licensed" by CXS, though, chiefly as an expository convenience.

Example (24c) raises the same kind of prima facie problems for the conjunction of (6) and the PLR that (8b) and (10b) did. However, a solution parallel to the one I suggested for topicalization and "object-raising" structures appears unavailable. Such a treatment would have to claim that, regardless of whether it involves *that* clause extraction, (24c) manifests extraction of some (evidently invisible) NP. The difficulty is that the type of pronominal constraint evidence that supports the existence of an invisible pronoun in NP topicalization and "object-raising" clauses supports the nonexistence of such pronouns in CXS constructions:

(25) a.  They renamed him either Ethelbert or Throckmorton three days ago.
   b.  *They renamed him it/them three days ago.
   c.  They renamed him $t_1$ three days ago—[either Ethelbert or Throckmorton]$_1$.

(26) a.  They called her a liar, a cheat, a thief, and a perjurer right to her face.
   b.  *They called her them right to her face.
   c.  They called her $t_1$ right to her face—[a liar, a cheat, a thief, and a perjurer]$_1$.

Although the "name" position in (25) and (26) fails to accept pronominal NPs, CXS cases corresponding to that position seem quite acceptable.

The facts for existential *there* constructions also argue *against* the presence of invisible pronouns:

(27) a.  There are errors in that monograph.
   b.  *There are them in that monograph.
   c.  *There are $t_1$ in that monograph—errors$_1$.
   d.  There are $t_2$ in that monograph—[a number of surprisingly egregious errors]$_2$.

Evidence relevant to the presence of pronouns in CXS cases cannot, however, be derived from the inalienable construction because CXS independently cannot strand prepositions. Hence, (28) does not bear on the issue.

(28)  The doctor should never have touched (*Bill on) $t_1$ yesterday—[the arm which he broke while skiing]$_1$.

Overall, though, since CXS structures fail to reveal the sensitivity to pronominal constraints found in topicalization and "object-raising" cases, not only is there no independent evidence for an invisible pronoun in such structures, an assumption that there is one is contraindicated.

This conclusion can be strengthened by material that makes it irrelevant whether or not cases like (24c) really involve CXS. If they do not, then the pronominal evidence in (26) and (27) would be strictly irrelevant. That would leave open the possibility of an analysis of examples like (24c) parallel to the one I proposed for topicalizations, that is, one involving an invisible pronoun. However, consider the verbs in (29).

(29) boast, comment, complain, hold

These verbs take *that* clauses but not NP objects and hence, in particular, not object pronouns:

(30) a.   Albert boasted/commented/complained/held that his results were fantastic.
     b.   *Albert boasted/commented/complained/held something/that/it.

Given this, if the formation of structures like (24c) were truly only possible when the *pg* position is compatible with definite pronouns, it would be predicted that analogs of (24c) based on the verbs of (29) would be impossible. But this is incorrect:

(31) a.   Albert boasted at the office $t_1$ after boasting at home $pg_1$—[that his results were fantastic]$_1$.
     b.   Albert commented to the doctor $t_2$ without commenting to the nurse $pg_2$—[that his ears were swollen]$_2$.

These cases indicate that apparent violations of the PLR like (24c) cannot be circumvented by postulating invisible pronouns. In fact, they do more —for not only are (31a–b) prima facie counterexamples to the PLR that do not lend themselves to an appeal to invisible pronouns, they are also prima facie counterexamples to PG = NP.

Evidence parallel to (22)/(23) does not exist for CXS cases, because, as known since Ross 1967:139, CXS does not in general strand prepositions; see section 8.4.4.[12] The underlying distinctions in (22)–(23) are therefore not available to argue that cases like (24c) and (31a–b) "really" involve NP extraction.[13] Nonetheless, although maintaining the conjunction of (6) and the PLR seemingly requires treating (24c) and (31a–b) as involving some instance of NP extraction, no viable analysis of this sort is apparent. Consequently, the P-gaps in (24c) and (31a–b), unlike those in (8b) and (10b), appear genuinely threatening to the conjunction of (6), PG = NP, and the PLR.

### 8.2.3   The Interaction of PG = NP, the PLR, and Right Node Raising

An argument almost identical to that in section 8.2.2 can be based on *right node raising* (RNR) rather than CXS. Alongside (24) there are paradigms like (32).

(32) a.   We could suggest $t_1$ to our employees without actually requiring $pg_1$ of them, and should suggest $t_1$ to them without actually requiring $pg_1$ of them—[the sort of behavior in question]$_1$.

b. We could suggest $t_2$ to our employees without actually requiring
$pg_2$ of them and should suggest $t_2$ to them without actually
requiring $pg_2$ of them—[that they wear a tie]$_2$.

So RNR structures involving *that* clauses appear to "license" P-gaps just
as those I have decided to analyze as CXS structures do. And the same
arguments appealed to in section 8.2.2 to show that CXS is *not* linked to
invisible pronouns show this as well for RNR structures. Compare (26c)
and (27d) to (33a) and (33b), respectively.

(33) a. They might have called her $t_1$ right to her face and probably did
call her $t_1$ right to her face—[a liar, a cheat, a thief, and a
perjurer]$_1$.
b. There may be $t_2$ in that monograph, and there certainly are $t_2$ in
this monograph—[a number of surprisingly egregious errors]$_2$.

Further, RNR expressions parallel to (31a–b) also threaten both PG =
NP and the PLR:

(34) Albert might have boasted at the office $t_1$ after boasting $pg_1$ at
home and George certainly did boast at the office $t_1$ after boasting
$pg_1$ at home—[that his results were fantastic]$_1$.

Moreover, the conclusion from RNR can be strengthened in ways not
possible for the CXS argument in that RNR *can*, as observed by Ross
(1967:141), strand prepositions. This permits, first, evidence from the inalienable construction that RNR does not involve invisible pronouns:

(35) The doctor might have accidentally touched (him on) $t_1$ yesterday
and certainly did touch (him on) $t_1$ today—[his only properly
functioning arm]$_1$.

The grammaticality of RNR gaps in a position where definite pronouns
are impossible supports the view that RNR is not linked to the presence
of masked pronouns.

Second, when the phrase isolated by RNR is a *that* clause, preposition
stranding is impossible. That is, RNR in this circumstance does not behave
like NP extraction:

(36) a. I could have convinced Lois *$\emptyset$/of $t_1$, and should have
convinced Lois $\emptyset$/of $t_1$—[the fact that Greg was a scoundrel]$_1$.
b. I could have convinced Lois $\emptyset$/*of $t_2$, and should have
convinced Lois $\emptyset$/*of $t_2$—[that Greg was a scoundrel]$_2$.

The category isolated by RNR can thus seemingly "license" P-gaps, even
when that category is a *that* clause. But RNR shows no sign of the sensi-

tivity to pronominal constraints of the sort which would justify an invisible
NP analysis, and a *that* clause isolated by RNR manifests preposition-
stranding behavior which contrasts with that of NP extraction under RNR.
Thus, if (6) is accepted, RNR of *that* clauses also seems incompatible with
both PG = NP and the PLR.

### 8.2.4   PG = NP, the PLR, and Parentheticals
If assumption (6), which takes (surface) *that* clauses to be non-NPs, raises
direct difficulties for PG = NP and the PLR because of (8b), (10b), and,
much more seriously, (24c), (31a–b), (32b), and (34), it also creates potential conflicts in the case of various types of *parenthetical* expressions corresponding to *that* clauses. By *parentheticals*, I refer to the italicized
phrases in sentences like the following:

(37) a. Death rays should not, *as you apparently feel*, be illegal
       everywhere.

   b. Death rays should, *I feel*, be illegal everywhere.

(38) a. Death rays are not, *as Fred feared*, illegal everywhere.

   b. Death rays are, *Fred fears*, illegal everywhere.

I call the parenthetical type in (37a)/(38a) *as-parentheticals* (A-
parentheticals), and the type in (37b)/(38b) *null parentheticals* (N-
parentheticals). These forms have been studied relatively little; some
relevant works include Jackendoff 1972:94–100, Emonds 1976:43–60, and
especially Ross 1973, which are all mostly limited to N-parentheticals.

   Ross (1973) established, I think, that N-parentheticals in general correspond to main clauses containing *that* clause complements.[14] A similar
conclusion holds for A-parentheticals.[15] Grounds for these conclusions
are that both types of parenthetical can be formed from expressions that,
essentially, occur only with *that* clauses, such as those in (39).[16]

(39) a. It appears/seems/turns out that Glen married the nurse.

   b. Glen has, $\emptyset_1$ it appears/seems/turns out $t_1$, married the nurse.

   c. Glen did not, as$_2$ it first appeared/seemed $t_2$, marry the nurse.

   d. Glen has, as$_3$ it turns out $t_3$, married the nurse.

Given that in simple clauses almost nothing can appear in the contexts
*it appears/seems/turns out*—except *that* clauses, the conclusion that both
A-parentheticals and N-parentheticals correspond to such clauses seems
straightforward.[17] I assume that both types of parenthetical contain an
(invisible) category corresponding to a *that* clause, and I refer to such
categories as *T-projections* (of *that* clauses). Hereafter, I take both *that*

clauses and T-projections to belong to a grammatical category simply designated as *T*. It is left open how T relates to such categories as S, NP, and so on.

Moreover, the assumption implicit in the notation of (39) that T-projections in parentheticals have been L-extracted is supported by the observation that formation of both types of parenthetical is sensitive to island boundaries occurring between the front of the parenthetical and the putative extraction site:

(40) a. Most linguists are not, as$_1$ I am sure he (*IS ACQUAINTED WITH THE PHILOSOPHER WHO FIRST) claimed $t_1$, ignorant of set theory.

b. Most linguists should, $\emptyset_2$ I am sure he recognizes (*THE POSSIBILITY THAT IT IS NECESSARY) $t_2$, learn set theory.

(41) a. Most linguists are not, as$_1$ I am sure the director realizes $t_1$ (*AND THE SECRETARY IS GRATEFUL THAT THEY AREN'T (SUCH)), ignorant of set theory.

b. Most linguists should, $\emptyset_2$ I am sure the director recognizes $t_2$ (*AND THE SECRETARY IS GRATEFUL THAT THEY CAN (DO SO)), learn set theory.

Several authors have recently commented on A-parentheticals. Specifically, as part of an array of arguments sustaining the claim that adverbial (adjunct) extraction is more restricted in specific ways than that of NPs, Rizzi (1990:15) states:

(42) "*Wh*-movement of the adverbial element *as* is affected by the presence of negation, whereas movement of the argumental (proclausal) element *which* is not ..."

In support of this claimed adverbial status, he cites observations from a 1983 paper by Ross (published as Ross 1984), represented in (43); see also Ross 1973:151–152, n. 21, 1967:232.[18]

(43) a. Bill is here, which$_1$ they (don't) know $t_1$.

b. Bill is here, as$_2$ they (*don't) know $t_2$.

The idea that *as* is a non-NP is apparently also accepted by Cinque (1990:79–80). Similarly, Tellier (1988:134–135), representing proposals of Stowell (1987) (which I have not seen), claims that the gap in A-parentheticals (associated with what I have called extraction of a T-projection) is a movement trace of a null CP (*not* NP) operator. The same idea is adopted by Authier (1989, 1991). This follows in these authors' terms from the fact the *that* clauses are CPs and that A-parentheticals correspond to clauses containing "missing" *that* clauses. The consistency of this work with principle (6) is clear.

Thus, a body of recent claims in effect denies that those A-parentheticals corresponding to *that* clauses involve NP extraction. This view interacts with the conjunction of (6) and the PLR in an obvious way. If A-parenthetical structures do not involve NP extraction, then, even under the assumption that they involve extraction of T-projections, they should not "license" P-gaps, even NP P-gaps, in contrast, specifically, to parenthetical *which* clauses of the sort mentioned by Rizzi. But A-parenthetical structures seemingly *do* "license" P-gaps:

(44) a. Those forms are true clitics, which$_1$ Clyde had claimed $t_1$ without proving $pg_1$.

   b. Those forms are not, as$_2$ Clyde asserted $t_2$ without proving $pg_2$, true clitics.

(45) a. Ted is a foreigner, which$_1$ she believed $t_1$ even before verifying $pg_1$.

   b. Ted is a foreigner, as$_2$ I suspected $t_2$ even before proving $pg_2$.

There seems to be no difference in grammaticality in (44) and (45) between the P-gaps in A-parentheticals and those in parenthetical *which* clauses.

Moreover, the behavior of N-parentheticals parallels that of A-parentheticals in (44) and (45).

(46) Those rules were, $\emptyset_1$ many of us naively believed $t_1$ without ever trying to prove $pg_1$, capable of generating all the required forms.

(47) The secret of eternal life, $\emptyset_1$ many who long refused to accept $pg_1$ will probably now grant $t_1$, is broccoli.

Hence, to maintain the PLR for English, both A-parentheticals and N-parentheticals would apparently have to incorporate some form of NP extraction.

For A-parentheticals, this could involve taking *as* itself as an NP, contrary to the views of Rizzi and Tellier, or else recognizing some invisible NP extractee. But neither alternative seems viable. Inferences from the PLR aside, A-parentheticals do not manifest properties typical of NP extraction; rather, in specific cases A-parentheticals clearly contrast with NP extractions. First, the T-projections in A-parentheticals like (39c–d) correspond to positions where NPs are impossible. This property can, moreover, be taken as the basis for the ungrammaticality of corresponding parenthetical *which* clauses, whose distribution otherwise follows that of NPs, as Rizzi (1990) in effect notes:

(48) *They said Glen married the nurse, which$_1$ it appears/seems/turns out $t_1$.

Second, the A-parenthetical/NP extraction contrast can be seen by focusing on A-parentheticals parallel to paradigms like (22)/(23). Recall that with verbs such as *convince*, extraction of the second argument must strand a preposition in topicalization and "object-raising" cases, structures that can independently be shown to manifest a sensitivity to pronominal constraints. Then, if A-parentheticals involved *NP* extraction, either of *as* itself or of some invisible NP, A-parentheticals formed with *convince* would parallel in these respects the topicalization and "object-raising" structures in (22)/(23). But they do not:

(49) a. The beast was not, as$_1$ Everet tried to convince me *of/$\varnothing$ $t_1$, suffering from malnutrition.

   b. The beast was not, as$_2$ Everet had insisted *on/$\varnothing$ $t_2$, suffering from malnutrition.

The extracted T-projections in (49) contrast minimally with the extracted elements in (22d,f)/(23d,f) in precluding preposition stranding. Hence, it is difficult to see how (49a–b) can be analyzed as containing NP extractions. Moreover, A-parentheticals formed with such verbs, which resist analysis in terms of NP extraction of the "licensing" category, nonetheless appear to "license" P-gaps:

(50) a. Ted is not, as$_1$ many who believed $pg_1$ fervently tried to convince me $t_1$, a dope fiend and a swindler.

   b. Ted is not, as$_2$ many lawyers who claimed $pg_2$ on TV later insisted $t_2$ in court, a dope fiend and a swindler.

The points just made for A-parentheticals have strict analogs for N-parentheticals:

(51) a. The beast was not, $\varnothing_1$ I tried my best to convince him *of/$\varnothing$ $t_1$, suffering from malnutrition.

   b. The government, $\varnothing_2$ I suspect that many who now only propose $pg_2$ privately will soon try to convince us *of/$\varnothing$ $t_2$ publicly, could build a transatlantic tunnel.

Notice the contrast between (49)–(51) and cases with parenthetical *which* clauses:

(52) a. He forgot that the beast was suffering from malnutrition, which$_1$
I had tried my best to convince him of/*$\emptyset$ $t_1$.

b. He forgot that the beast was suffering from malnutrition, which$_2$
I had convinced his wife of $t_2$ before trying to convince him of
$t_2$.

Unlike A-parenthetical or N-parenthetical structures, the *which* clauses do
manifest the properties of NP extractions. This makes it even more difficult to formulate a treatment for A-parentheticals and N-parentheticals
that renders their P-gap properties consistent with the conjunction of (6)
and the PLR or even with the latter alone.

Further, seemingly grave problems for both PG = NP and the PLR are
derivable from parentheticals based on the verbs of (29). Such verbs,
which do not take NP objects, appear able both to cooccur with P-gaps
"licensed" by parenthetical extractions in other clauses and to "license"
P-gaps:

(53) a. Tony is not, as$_1$ those who believed $pg_1$ most strongly boasted $t_1$
in class, able to run a four-minute mile.

b. Tony is not, as$_2$ those who boasted $pg_2$ in class later claimed $t_2$
to the reporters, able to run a four-minute mile.

(54) a. Tony is now, $\emptyset_1$ those who believed $pg_1$ most strongly boasted
$t_1$ in class, able to run a four-minute mile.

b. Tony is now, $\emptyset_2$ those who boasted $pg_2$ in class later claimed $t_2$
to the reporters, able to run a four-minute mile.

Examples (53a) and (54a) show presumed P-gaps "licensed" by parenthetical extractions that apparently fail to satisfy the PLR. Examples
(53b) and (54b) manifest presumed P-gaps occurring in positions that
could not satisfy PG = NP.

### 8.2.5 The Status of PG = NP and the PLR

Sections 8.2.2–8.2.4 have argued as follows. First, CXS and RNR constructions seemingly containing only extracted *that* clauses and failing to
manifest evidence of invisible pronouns appear to "license" P-gaps; see
(24c), (31a–b), (32b), and (34). Second, the "missing" categories in both
A-parentheticals and N-parentheticals—that is, T-projections, which correspond to *that* clauses in an obvious sense and thus presumably are of the
same category as *that* clauses—also appear to "license" P-gaps. Moreover,
clausal patterns with both types of parenthetical contrast (in preposition-
stranding behavior) with those of topicalization and "object-raising"

paradigms, which are plausibly taken to involve extraction of invisible (pronominal) NPs. Further, these parentheticals correspond to subconstituents of constructions like those in (39), where NPs are impossible. This correlates with the fact that the internal properties of both types of parenthetical also contrast with *which* clauses, whose extracted elements systematically correspond to NP positions.

These facts are apparently flatly incompatible with the conjunction of principle (6), which denies that *that* clauses are NPs, and the PLR. Moreover, cases like (31), (34), (53), and (54) indicate that related problems arise for PG = NP. If the difficulties were limited to CXS and RNR data like (24c) and (25b), one might consider trying to save PG = NP and the PLR by abandoning only principle (6). However, this would leave unexplained the distributional contrasts that first led Emonds to reject the NP status of *that* clauses.

Worse, a solution that rejects principle (6) seems to have no genuine application to the parenthetical data. Focus for concreteness on, say, (50a), which contains an A-parenthetical whose "missing" element corresponds to the gap in (55).

(55) fervently tried to convince me *of/$\emptyset$ t

Trying to deal with the facts by taking *that* clauses to be NPs has an application to (55) only if the gap is also characterized as an NP. But the structure shows the *non*-NP behavior of (56a), not the NP behavior of (56b).

(56) a. He fervently tried to convince me *of/$\emptyset$ that Ellen was intelligent.
     b. He fervently tried to convince me of/*$\emptyset$ that.

Consequently, abandoning principle (6) offers no real help for the challenge to PG = NP and the PLR raised by the parenthetical data. These data seemingly demand that these principles themselves be abandoned, at least for English.

## 8.3   Salvaging PG = NP and the PLR

### 8.3.1   Parasitic Gaps versus Pseudoparasitic Gaps

Despite the arguments of section 8.2, I remain unconvinced that there are any genuine English counterexamples to either the PLR or PG = NP. Although nothing so far indicated offers any chance of grounding a successful defense of these principles, they are nonetheless defensible. This is true because the discussion of section 8.2 hinges on an assumption implicit in section 8.1, which, although both initially reasonable and entirely consistent with the past literature on P-gaps, is challengeable and, I will argue, wrong. This assumption is that those gaps I have hitherto taken to be P-gaps "licensed" by CXS- and RNR-isolated *that* clauses or by T-projections are actually P-gaps. I will argue that they are not.

Since the beginning of the burst of interest in P-gaps in the early 1980s, it has been assumed, as I did implicitly in (1), that both L-extractions and R-extractions—specifically for the latter, CXS—"license" P-gaps. The supporting cases involved, of course, NP extractions. Thus, it has been assumed that both (1d) = (57a) and, say, (57b) represent the same construction type, that is, the P-gap phenomenon.

(57) a. John offended $t_1$ by not recognizing $pg_1$—[his favorite uncle from Cleveland]$_1$.

    b. [Which uncle from Cleveland]$_2$ did John offend $t_2$ by not recognizing $pg_2$?

The idea that (57a) involves a P-gap in the same sense as, say, (57b) seems never to have been challenged and has been widely accepted since Engdahl 1983; see, for example, Chomsky 1982:47, Bennis and Hoekstra 1985a:80, 1985b:12, Browning 1987a:171, and Williams 1990. However, the agreement that (57a–b) instantiate the same phenomenon can be argued to represent a serious descriptive mistake and, moreover, the same mistake as the assumption in Authier 1989, 1991, and section 8.2 above that there are P-gaps "licensed" by CXS (or RNR) of *that* clauses.

I hereafter refer informally to anything that *seems* to be a P-gap as an *apparent-P-gap* (A-P-gap), a terminology highlighting the possibility that some A-P-gaps might not be P-gaps. I will argue that such A-P-gaps exist and refer to them informally as *pseudo-P-gaps*.[19] I will claim that *none* of the A-P-gaps "licensed" by T-projections or by *that* clauses isolated by CXS or RNR are genuine P-gaps, a concept to which I will try to lend further content. More generally, I will argue that *all* A-P-gaps seemingly "licensed" by either CXS or RNR, like the one in (57a), or by parenthetical extractions are pseudo-P-gaps. It follows (among other things) that, at least in English, *only L-extractions "license" genuine P-gaps*. The claim that some A-P-gaps are pseudo-P-gaps of course raises the issue of providing a (non-P-gap) analysis for pseudo-P-gaps, a question considered in section 8.4.

It is important to characterize the logic of an argument having a priori the possibility of showing that some A-P-gaps are not genuine P-gaps. First, one should specify more precisely what it means to be an A-P-gap. Informally, the literature on P-gaps suggests something like (58) as the defining feature of P-gaps, and I therefore take (58) to characterize A-P-gaps in general.

(58) *The Dependency Condition*
A gap is a P-gap only if its existence is dependent on that of another gap, which is a true extraction gap.[20]

In this relatively weak sense, all the dependent gaps cited so far are A-P-gaps. Unfortunately, it is also true that across-the-board (ATB) extraction gaps permitted in coordinate structures would also qualify. I presume that these are excluded, without specifying here how.

Given (58), it is logically possible to assemble a class of other principles characterizing those elements satisfying (58). There are several such principles, of which PG = NP and the PLR are only a *proper* subset. It can then be argued that certain A-P-gaps are not P-gaps by showing the following. Those cases argued in section 8.2 to contravene one or both of PG = NP and the PLR also fail to satisfy the other principles arguably taken to characterize P-gaps. One conclusion would then be that all of these principles are simply false. Alternatively, they might all be true, but only over some restricted domain. The latter view is supported by the existence of a genuine clustering of properties. Violations and nonviolations of the principles in question turn out to define two largely disjoint classes of A-P-gaps. One can then envisage taking one class to contain all genuine P-gaps, for which all the principles are true. The validity of this approach is supported because a *non-P-gap* analysis of pseudo-P-gaps can be justified. This accounts for their basic properties, including those under which they contrast with genuine P-gaps. In these terms, then, the fact that PG = NP and the PLR are not satisfied by a range of A-P-gaps, as in part previously documented, *shows nothing about P-gaps*, but merely reflects the existence of pseudo-P-gaps, which previous work on A-P-gaps has in effect confused with P-gaps.

Let us now make explicit constraints that have been, or can be, taken to hold of P-gaps, seen as defined by (58). Perhaps the most important of these is the one represented in (59); see, for example, Kayne 1984:chap. 8, Aoun and Clark 1985, Longobardi 1984, 1985a,b, Chomsky 1986b:55, Koster 1987:156, Browning 1987b:60, and Cinque 1990:100.

(59) *The Island Condition*
A P-gap "licensed" by a gap G cannot occur internal to an island $\Sigma$ not containing G unless $\Sigma$ is coextensive with the entire parasitic domain.

Thus, (59) allows, say, P-gaps in subjects, which are islands, but not in other islands inside subjects:

(60) a.   a woman who$_1$ your courting $pg_1$ would probably upset $t_1$
     b.   *a woman who$_2$ your opposing his courting $pg_2$ would probably upset $t_2$
     c.   *a woman who$_3$ your hiring the man who lives with $pg_3$ would upset $t_3$

A second principle noted in section 8.1 (see (2)) is, of course, that P-gaps are categorially limited:

(61)  $PG = NP$
      A P-gap is an NP.

Section 8.2.1 revealed what is in effect an important corollary of (61):

(62)  *The Preposition-Stranding Condition*
      A P-gap "licensed" by a T behaves with respect to preposition stranding like an NP-gap and hence, in particular, not like a T-gap.

A third property of P-gaps stressed in section 8.1 is, naturally, the PLR:

(63)  *PLR*
      The "licensing" category (the extractee from the position of the true gap) of a P-gap is an NP.

Fourth, it can be argued, as already in effect suggested by Cinque (1990), that there is a condition on P-gaps linking them to definite pronouns:[21]

(64)  *The Pronominal Condition*
      P-gaps cannot occur in positions incompatible with definite pronouns.[22]

Space precludes supporting claim (64) here in the detail it deserves.[23] I discuss only factors linked to the arguments seen in section 8.2.1 to be relevant to showing that topicalization and "object raising" are limited by a principle of pronominal compatibility. An analog of those arguments yields the same implications for P-gaps. Thus, as predicted by (64), P-gaps are incompatible with "name" positions, with the "focus" position of existential *there* structures, and with an inalienable possessor position preceded by (for example) *on*, since those positions preclude pronouns:[24]

(65) a.   He named his camel Ernie/*it.
     b.   *What$_1$ did he name his dog $t_1$ after naming his camel $pg_1$?

(66) a.  There are guns/*them in the cabinet.
   b.  *What$_1$ did he look for $t_1$ in the closet without knowing there
       were $pg_1$ on the table?

(67) a.  They touched (*him on) it.
   b.  [Which of his arms]$_1$ did they have to immobilize $t_1$ after
       accidentally touching (*him on) $pg_1$?

What can be considered a fifth condition on English P-gaps is uncovered in Postal 1990 and reviewed and extended in part in Postal 1993. In a
host of cases an NP can only alternate with a P-gap if it meets a condition
closely related to passivizability. Informally:

(68)  *The Passivizability Condition*
      If an NP$_x$ alternates with a P-gap, then NP$_x$ must not be inherently
      unpassivizable.

Principle (68) is quite vague and unclear; for clarification and greater detail, see the references just cited. The Passivizability Condition is intended
to account for such correlations as those in (69)–(71).

(69) a.  Jerome spoke (in) Serbian to the Turks.
   b.  Serbian should not be spoken (*in) to Turks.
   c.  [Which language]$_1$ did he sneer at $t_1$ shortly after speaking (*in)
       $pg_1$ for two hours?

(70) a.  Trolls died/frolicked under that bridge.
   b.  That bridge has been *died/frolicked under for years by trolls.
   c.  [Which bridge]$_1$ did they destroy $t_1$ after trolls began to *die/
       frolic under $pg_1$?

(71) a.  I watched Barbara faint.
   b.  *Barbara was watched faint.
   c.  *[Which dancer]$_1$ did they want to operate on $t_1$ after watching
       $pg_1$ faint?

That is, there is a strong tendency for unpassivizable NPs to resist alter-
nating with P-gaps.

   A sixth principle constraining P-gaps is represented in (72); see Postal
1993b.

(72)  *The Predicate Nominal Condition*
      Neither a P-gap nor its "licensing" category can be a *predicate
      nominal*.

Since predicate nominal positions are in general incompatible with definite pronouns, and not passivizable, the first part of the Predicate Nominal Condition (72) might be a theorem of the Pronominal Condition (64) or of the Passivizability Condition (68).[25] But, since "licensing" gaps are in general subject to neither of these restrictions, the second part is not. Therefore, the Predicate Nominal Condition (72) can be considered independent of the Pronominal Condition (64). Evidence supporting this principle includes the examples in (73) and (74).

(73) a. They turned into derelicts.
b. [What kind of derelicts]$_1$ did they turn into $t_1$?
c. *[What kind of derelicts]$_2$ did they analyze $t_2$ after their children turned into $pg_2$?
d. *[What kind of derelicts]$_3$ did they turn into $t_3$ after their children analyzed $pg_3$?

(74) a. Slaves make good cannibal snacks.
b. [What kind of cannibal snacks]$_1$ did those slaves make $t_1$?
c. *[What kind of cannibal snacks]$_2$ did the cannibal look for $t_2$ after hearing that young slaves made $pg_2$?
d. *[What kind of cannibal snacks]$_3$ were all those slaves who discussed $t_3$ expected to make $pg_3$?

Notable in (74) is that expressions of the form *make NP* are ambiguous with respect to the predicate nominal status of the NP. And the stars in (74) only hold for predicate nominal interpretations. If the verbs are interpreted to mean 'manufacture', with concomitant "referential" status for the NP, I believe both (74c–d) are grammatical.

Assume then that all of principles (59), (61)/(62), (63), (64), (68), and (72) are characteristic of uncontroversial English P-gaps. It might seem bizarre to list PG = NP and the PLR among these principles, since section 8.2 documented apparent counterexamples to these for a range of A-P-gaps. Citing them here might thus seem to beg questions. However, the logic exposed at the beginning of this section reveals that it is proper to include them; for the goal is to show that the cases that violate these two principles likewise fail to obey the other conditions characteristic of true P-gaps. Such documentation can thus be interpreted as showing not that PG = NP and the PLR are false for P-gaps but that the apparent counterexamples were not genuine instances of P-gaps; for, ultimately, P-gaps must be taken to be gaps that satisfy not merely the Dependency Condition (58) but the full set of principles.

### 8.3.2  Pseudoparasitic Gaps "Licensed" by Complex NP Shift

Recall Authier's example (24c), which could seem to suggest that *that* clauses (i.e., constituents of the category T $\neq$ NP) can both be P-gaps, falsifying PG = NP, and "license" P-gaps, falsifying the PLR. On closer examination, (24c) surely does not sustain the first claim. Both the "true" gap and the A-P-gap in (24c) arguably occur in positions open to NPs:

(75)  We suggest it/$t_1$ to our employees without actually requiring it$_1$ of them—[that they wear a tie]$_1$.

Given this, (24c) itself cannot show anything about PG = NP or the PLR. But the negative consequences for both principles are supported by cases linked to the verbs of (29), which preclude object NPs. Consider for instance (31), repeated here.

(31)  a.  Albert boasted at the office $t_1$ after boasting at home $pg_1$—[that his results were fantastic]$_1$.

     b.  Albert commented $t_2$ to the doctor without commenting $pg_2$ to the nurse—[that his ears were swollen]$_2$.

Observe how, say, (31a) contrasts with the corresponding topicalization structure:

(76)  *[That his results were fantastic]$_1$, Albert boasted $t_1$ at the office after boasting $pg_1$ at home.

Given the resumptive pronoun analysis of topicalization supported in section 8.2.1, one might conclude that (31) and its contrast with (76) falsify both PG = NP and the PLR. A resumptive analysis is hardly conceivable for (31), given that the main verb does not even permit nonpronominal NPs.

However, critically, the A-P-gaps in (31), unlike those in topicalization structures, for instance, also do not obey the Island Condition (59):

(77)  a.  Albert boasted at the office $t_1$ after firing the woman who had heard him boasting at home $pg_1$—[that his results were fantastic]$_1$.

     b.  *[That his results were fantastic]$_2$, Albert boasted at the office $t_2$ after firing the woman who had heard him boasting at home $pg_2$.

     c.  Albert commented to the doctor $t_3$ without thanking the patient who had commented to the nurse $pg_3$—[that his ears were swollen]$_3$.

d. *[That his ears were swollen]$_4$, Albert commented to the doctor $t_4$ without thanking the patient who had commented to the nurse $pg_4$.

See also:

(78) a. We told our employees $t_1$ without ever introducing them to the scientist who had just proved $pg_1$—[that the products were safe]$_1$.

b. *[That the products were safe]$_2$, we told our employees $t_2$ without ever introducing them to the scientist who had just proved $pg_2$.

The A-P-gap in (78b), "licensed" by an L-extraction defining in part the topicalization structure, is sensitive to the island constraints imposed by the restrictive relative clause, whereas the one in (78a), "licensed" by an R-extraction, is not. Thus, those A-P-gaps I took for argument to be "licensed" by CXS of *that* clauses, which were shown to violate PG = NP and the PLR, also contravene the Island Condition (59). Moreover, this is true in a stronger sense than illustrated in (77a) and (78a), where the island-forming nodes occur in the adjunct; for such nodes also fail to affect well-formedness even when the island-forming node is in the main clause. Again this yields a sharp contrast with topicalization:

(79) a. The police arrested the doctor who had refused to admit $t_1$ shortly after getting the nurse to confess $pg_1$—[that the baby had been poisoned]$_1$.

b. *[That the baby had been poisoned]$_2$, the police arrested the doctor who had refused to admit $t_2$ shortly after getting the nurse to confess $pg_2$.

Analogs of Authier's (24c) also do not obey the Preposition-Stranding Condition (62).

(80) We told our employees $t_1$ without/before really being convinced/ certain *of/$\emptyset$ $pg_1$ (ourselves)—[that the products were safe]$_1$.

If $pg_1$ in (80) were a genuine P-gap, then PG = NP and its corollary (62) would be seriously undermined. Again the putative CXS case contrasts with the corresponding topicalization structure:

(81) [That the products were safe]$_1$, we told our employees $t_1$ without/ before really being convinced/certain of/*$\emptyset$ $pg_1$ (ourselves).

These observations thus strengthen earlier conclusions that A-P-gaps involving CXS of *that* clauses violate PG = NP.

The conclusion that such A-P-gaps violate the PLR can also be strengthened:

(82) a.   It can seem to one policeman $t_1$ without seeming to another $pg_1$—[that a suspect is guilty]$_1$.

   b.   *[That a suspect is guilty]$_2$, it can seem to one policeman $t_2$ without seeming to another $pg_2$.

Since no NP can occur as a complement to a verb like *seem* in the positions of $t_1$, the "licensing" category for the A-P-gap in (82a) clearly cannot be an NP, violating the PLR if that A-P-gap is a P-gap. Moreover, the structural assumption that the A-P-gap is not an NP is supported since it explains (82b), under the view supported earlier that English NP topicalizations involve (among other things) extracted invisible resumptive NP pronouns.

Now, do A-P-gaps of the sort "licensed" by CXS of *that* clauses obey the Pronominal Condition (64)? Evidently, they do not, as already indicated by (82a), for example. See also:

(83) a.   *We repeatedly told our employees [that the products were safe]$_1$ without, however, apparently ever convincing them it$_1$.

   b.   We repeatedly told our employees $t_2$ without, however, apparently ever convincing them $pg_2$—[that the products were safe]$_2$.

(84) a.   *We knew for a long time [that the products were contaminated]$_1$ without, however, ever informing them it$_1$.

   b.   We knew for a long time $t_2$ without, however, ever informing them $pg_2$—[that the products were contaminated]$_2$.

Here, although the environment *convince/inform + pronoun + X* is incompatible with pronouns, an A-P-gap can occur there. Except for this property, (83b) and (84b) are essentially parallel to Authier's (24c).

So far in this section I have considered the clustering of violations of the Island Condition (59), PG = NP (61), and so on, while limiting attention to cases taken to exhibit CXS extraction of *that* clauses. But for the Passivizability Condition (68) and the Predicate Nominal Condition (72) this becomes difficult or impossible because of the nature of the principles themselves. For example, there are arguably no predicate nominal *that* clauses. Notably, though, CXS-"licensed" instances of A-P-gaps also fail the Island Condition (59) and the Pronominal Condition (64) when the extracted phrase *is an NP*. To see this for the Island Condition (59), consider analogs of an example "classically" taken to contain a P-gap "licensed" by CXS, for instance, Engdahl's (1d) = (57a):

(85) a. John offended $t_1$ by not recognizing THE PEOPLE WHO WERE SUPPORTING $pg_1$ AT THAT TIME—[his favorite uncle from Cleveland]$_1$.

b. Who$_2$ did John offend $t_2$ by not recognizing (*THE PEOPLE WHO WERE SUPPORTING) $pg_2$?

The addition of the capitalized island-forming material has no effect on the grammaticality of (57a); hence, the A-P-gaps "licensed" by CXS of uncontroversial NPs do not obey the Island Condition (59). But, as the starred variant of (85b) shows, the Island Condition (59) cannot be violated by A-P-gaps "licensed" by a corresponding L-extraction.

To show that CXS cases involving extracted NPs also fail the Pronominal Condition (64), it suffices to consider CXS correspondents of the starred variants of (65b), (66b), and (67b), which are grammatical:

(86) a. She named her youngest dog $t_1$ after naming her oldest camel $pg_1$—[exactly what she was told to name them]$_1$.

b. He looked for $t_2$ in the closet without knowing there were $pg_2$ on the table—[the kind of magazines you were told to hide]$_2$.

c. They had to immobilize $t_3$ for several weeks after the nurse had unintentionally touched him on $pg_3$—[the arm he hurt while skiing]$_3$.

So there is good reason to assert that A-P-gaps "licensed" by CXS violate all of the Island Condition (59), PG = NP/the Preposition-Stranding Condition (61)/(62), the PLR (63), and the Pronominal Condition (64), regardless of whether the extracted phrase is an NP or a T.

That the Passivizability Condition (68) also does not hold for CXS-type A-P-gaps is shown by analogs of the unacceptable variants of (69c), (70c), and (71c).

(87) a. Jerome sneered at $t_1$ immediately after she spoke (in) $pg_1$ for two hours—[the language you are studying]$_1$.

b. They decided to destroy $t_2$ immediately after trolls began to die/ frolic under $pg_2$—[the small bridge you see over there]$_2$.

c. They wanted to operate on $t_3$ after watching $pg_3$ faint—[the tall nurse next to the window]$_3$.

Finally, that CXS cases are not subject to the Predicate Nominal Condition (72) is shown by grammatical analogs of (73c–d) and (74c–d):

(88) a. They only determined to analyze $t_1$ right after their children turned into $pg_1$—[the sort of derelicts who cause such problems in our cities]$_1$.

b. They ended up turning into $t_2$ not long after their children analyzed $pg_2$—[the sort of derelicts who cause such problems in our cities]$_2$.

c. The cannibal only decided to consume $t_3$ after hearing from you that certain slaves made $pg_3$—[just that sort of high protein cannibal snack]$_3$.

d. Those slaves ending up making $t_4$ even though it had been denied that they ever would make $pg_4$—[just that sort of high protein cannibal snack]$_4$.

It has thus been argued that the failure of CXS-"licensed" A-P-gaps to satisfy PG = NP and the PLR correlates with their failure to satisfy several other principles arguably characteristic of P-gaps. Before considering implications of these correlations, I should point out another feature of examples involving A-P-gaps linked to CXS-shifted *that* clauses that shows they do not behave like true P-gaps. Example (89a) seems essentially as good as (24c), and (89b) essentially as good as (83b).

(89) a. We suggest it$_1$ to our employees without actually requiring $pg_1$ of them—[that they wear a tie]$_1$.

b. We repeatedly mentioned it$_2$ to our employees $t_2$ without apparently ever convincing them $t_2$—[that the products were safe]$_2$.

See also:

(90) a. We pointed it/$t_1$ out to our managers without ever informing our hourly workers $pg_1$—[that the products were radioactive]$_1$.

b. We took it/$t_2$ for granted $t_2$ (without ever proving $pg_2$)—[that that integer was larger than its successor]$_2$.

Expressions (89a–b) and the versions of (90a–b) containing *it* reveal that A-P-gaps occur in the adjuncts apparently even in the absence of "licensing" (NP) gaps. Given PG = NP, this seemingly even violates the Dependency Condition (58), generally taken to be the most distinctive (defining) property of P-gaps. Except for the A-P-gap containing adjuncts, these examples would appear to be simply extraposition structures in which the extraposition expletive occurs in object position. Though (89a–b) and (90a–b) may be a bit strained, that arguably only reflects the strain associated with object position nonnull extraposition expletives with most verbs. Note, moreover, that regardless of whether the pronoun *it* appears in the main clause of a case like (89a), a pronoun can appear with no loss of grammaticality in the subordinate phrase:

(91) We suggest (it$_1$) to our employees without actually requiring it$_1$ of them—[that they wear a tie]$_1$.

The considerations just adduced suggest rather clearly that the A-P-gaps I have taken to be "licensed" by CXS of *that* clauses are *not* P-gaps. Among other things, such gaps fail various key conditions otherwise holding for P-gaps. If, however, these A-P-gaps are not P-gaps, then they are, of course, strictly irrelevant to the truth of, among other principles, both PG = NP and the PLR, if these are considered to quantify exclusively over genuine P-gaps. Before pursuing this claim, I consider further supporting data.

### 8.3.3  Pseudoparasitic Gaps "Licensed" by Right Node Raising
The same points established in the preceding section for A-P-gaps "licensed" by CXS can, as I will very briefly illustrate, be made for A-P-gaps "licensed" by RNR. First, they violate the Island Condition (59):

(92) a.  I could have asserted $t_1$ even without consulting with the first genius who proved $pg_1$ and would have asserted $t_1$ even without consulting with the second genius who proved $pg_1$— [that 2 and 2 is 4]$_1$.

   b.  *[That 2 and 2 is 4]$_2$, I could have asserted $t_2$ even without consulting with the first genius who proved $pg_2$ and would have asserted $t_2$ even without consulting with the second genius who proved $pg_2$.

The presence of island-forming nodes in the main clause also fails to undermine grammaticality:

(93) The police might have arrested the doctor who had refused to admit $t_1$ shortly after getting the nurse to confess $pg_1$ and they probably did arrest the receptionist who had refused to admit $t_1$ shortly after preventing the guard from revealing $pg_1$—[that the baby had been poisoned]$_1$.

Second, such A-P-gaps do not satisfy the Preposition-Stranding Condition (62):

(94) Ed could have suggested $t_1$ to them without convincing them *of/ $\emptyset$ $pg_1$, and Mike did suggest $t_1$ to them without convincing them *of/$\emptyset$ $pg_1$—[that the products were safe]$_1$.

That is, in these cases the extractions in the parasitic domains behave like non-NP extractions, violating the Preposition-Stranding Condition (62) and PG = NP, of which the former is a corollary.

Third, (95) exemplifies that certain A-P-gaps involving RNR are also directly inconsistent with both PG = NP and the PLR.

(95) It could have seemed to the male officer $t_1$ without seeming to the female officer $pg_1$ and probably did seem to him $t_1$ without seeming to her $pg_1$—[that the suspect was guilty]$_1$.

Here the extracted T "licenses" A-P-gaps even though both the "true" gap and A-P-gap positions accept only Ts and not NPs.

As illustrated further by (96) and (97), (95) shows in addition that the relevant A-P-gaps are also inconsistent with the Pronominal Condition (64).

(96) We could have told our employees $t_1$ without ever convincing them $pg_1$ and they did tell their employees $t_1$ without ever convincing them $pg_1$—[that the products were safe]$_1$.

(97) Albert could have commented to the doctor $t_1$ without commenting to the nurse $pg_1$ and probably did comment to him $t_1$ without commenting to her $pg_1$—[that his ears were swollen]$_1$.

In both cases A-P-gaps appear in positions that preclude pronouns.

It can next be shown that, with respect to extracted *NPs*, RNR expressions fail to obey the Island Condition (59), the Pronominal Condition (64), the Passivizability Condition (68), and the Predicate Nominal Condition (72):

(98) John might have offended $t_1$ by not recognizing THE WOMEN WHO WERE SUPPORTING $pg_1$ AT THAT TIME and probably did offend $t_1$ by not recognizing THE MEN WHO WERE SUPPORTING $pg_1$—[his favorite uncle from Cleveland]$_1$.

(99) a. She might have named her youngest dog $t_1$ after naming her oldest camel $pg_1$ and probably did name her favorite cat $t_1$ after naming her least favorite monkey $pg_1$—[exactly what she was told to name them]$_1$.

   b. He might have looked for $t_2$ in the closet without knowing there were $pg_2$ on the table and probably did look for in the drawer $t_2$ without knowing there were $pg_2$ on the bookcase— [the kind of magazines you asked for]$_2$.

    c. They might have touched him on $t_3$ accidentally yesterday and probably did touch him on $t_3$ deliberately today—[the arm he hurt while skiing]$_3$.

(100) a. Jerome might have sneered at $t_1$ immediately after speaking (in) $pg_1$ and probably did sneer at $t_1$ immediately after speaking (in) $pg_1$—[the language you are studying]$_1$.

    b. They could have decided to destroy $t_2$ shortly after small trolls began to die/frolic under $pg_2$ and probably did decide to destroy $t_2$ shortly after large trolls began to die/frolic under $pg_2$—[the small bridge you see over there]$_2$.

    c. Herman might have wanted to operate on $t_3$ after watching $pg_3$ faint and probably did want to operate on $t_3$ after watching $pg_3$ faint—[the tall nurse standing over there]$_3$.

(101) a. They might have only determined to analyze $t_1$ right after their children turned into $pg_1$ and probably only did determine to analyze $t_1$ right after their children turned into $pg_1$—[the sort of derelicts who cause such problems in our cities]$_1$.

    b. They might have ended up turning into $t_2$ not long after their children analyzed $pg_2$ and no doubt did end up turning into $t_2$ not long after their children analyzed $pg_2$—[the sort of derelicts who cause such problems in our cities]$_2$.

Thus, it seems that RNR-"licensed" A-P-gaps systematically contravene the Island Condition (59), PG = NP (61), the PLR (63), the Pronominal Condition (64), the Passivizability Condition (68), and the Predicate Nominal Condition (72).

Finally, (102) shows that, if PG = NP is accepted, these A-P-gaps would even fail to satisfy the basic Dependency Condition (58).

(102) We could have pointed it out to our managers without convincing them $pg_1$ and we might have pointed it out to them without convincing them $pg_1$—[that the products were safe]$_1$.

That is, even when a *visible* extraposition expletive is present, A-P-gaps are still grammatical. This is parallel to facts involving CXS touched on earlier; see (92). Note that the topicalized correspondents of (92) and (102) are ungrammatical independently of questions of stranded prepositions.

### 8.3.4  Property Clustering

There is thus considerable English evidence to suggest that those A-P-gaps seemingly "licensed" by CXS or RNR of *that* clauses are not P-gaps but pseudo-P-gaps. A priori, the notion "A-P-gap" is defined by the Dependency Condition (58). Barring the appearance of anomalies, it is reasonable and proper to assume, as done up to now in work on A-P-gaps, that the collection of all those gaps satisfying (58) forms a single, essentially homogenous phenomenon. And, although the properties documented in previous sections suggest that such an assumption is incorrect, the known facts do seem to fall into patterns that are far from chaotic. Indeed, the data surveyed in sections 8.3.2 and 8.3.3 appear to manifest the systematic correlations tabulated in (103).

(103) Among all gaps satisfying the Dependency Condition (58), there are two distinct classes:

|  | $A$-gaps | $B$-gaps |
|---|---|---|
| a. Subject to the Island Condition (59) | yes | no |
| b. Satisfy PG = NP (61) | yes | no |
| c. Satisfy the PLR (63) | yes | no |
| d. Subject to the Pronominal Condition (64) | yes | no |
| e. Subject to the Passivizability Condition (68) | yes | no |
| f. Subject to the Predicate Nominal Condition (72) | yes | no |
| g. "Licensed" by L-extractions | yes | no |

Here the category of $A$-gaps covers all those dependent gaps previously taken to be P-gaps and "licensed" by L-extractions. The category of $B$-gaps designates those dependent gaps "licensed" by either CXS or RNR, that is, by R-extractions.

The key new information made explicit in (103) is that in (g). This brings out the fact largely left implicit up to this point that those A-P-gaps that are *correctly* characterized by the principles cited in (103a–f) are all "licensed" by L-extractions, whereas those that violate them are in general "licensed" by R-extractions. The latter claim might seem excessive, given that parenthetical instances of A-P-gaps were earlier apparently shown to violate both PG = NP and the PLR, and parenthetical structures were taken to instantiate L-extractions. I return to this matter in section 8.5.

Given the systematic patterning represented in (103), it is reasonable to conclude not that the properties of $B$-gaps falsify those principles whose satisfaction defines $A$-gaps, but rather that the $B$-gaps represent a different phenomenon. This allows PG = NP, the PLR, the Island Condition (59), the Pronominal Condition (64), the Passivizability Condition (68), and the Predicate Nominal Condition (72) all to be maintained as truths

characteristic of *one class* of dependent gaps, $A$-gaps = P-gaps. None
would hold of $B$-gaps, which are pseudo-P-gaps. Provided that a reasonable and justifiable analysis can be provided for the latter *distinct from
that of P-gaps*, such a reanalysis of apparently related phenomena is a
methodologically standard way of regularizing observed patternings of
data. Much further evidence of the correctness of the $A$-gap/$B$-gap distinction is presented below. However, maintaining this view requires further discussion of those A-P-gaps "licensed" by parenthetical extractions,
since these do not seem to fully satisfy the conditions on pseudo-P-gaps in
(103). That is, although they are indeed negative for the properties (b)–(e)
in (103), it turns out that they are positive for (a). But before attempting
to deal with parenthetical A-P-gaps, I offer a partial characterization of
pseudo-P-gaps.

## 8.4   What Are Pseudoparasitic Gaps?

### 8.4.1   Characterizing Parasitic Gaps
A defense of the validity of PG = NP and the PLR for true P-gaps has led
to the recognition of A-P-gaps that are not true P-gaps; these are the
pseudo-P-gaps. If the latter are not P-gaps, they are of course in general
not required to meet the conditions on P-gaps, such as the Island Condition (59) and PG = NP (61). The price of accepting this conclusion is the
requirement to provide two distinct theoretical analyses, one for P-gaps,
one for pseudo-P-gaps. I cannot say much about the analysis of true P-
gaps here, since this is a complicated matter and my views of the topic are
very nonstandard and depend on a poorly known theoretical framework.
In order to sharpen the contrast with pseudo-P-gaps, I will however
sketch certain outlines of a conception of P-gaps.

   Most fundamentally, I assume that P-gaps represent a *control* phenomenon, in the same sense as the well-known equi constructions with
verbs like *want*. Moreover, I interpret control as involving a mechanism
that determines the invisibility (equivalently, nonpresence in surface
forms) of ordinary definite pronouns. Critically, I assume that, universally, a pronoun is subject to control only if it is L-extracted. Thus, as in
Chomsky's (1986b) "chain composition" proposal about P-gaps, I take
each English P-gap case to involve at least two extractions, each of which
is an L-extraction. However, in the terms I would suggest, the fact that
the licensing NP is extracted reflects the assumption indicated in note 5,
namely, that control in general involves arc erasure. A theory of control
must then specify the types of arcs that can be erasers (and erasees). If one

assumes, crucially, that all extractions are characterized by a particular relation, call it Escape, then it can turn out that the licensing extraction defining P-gaps merely reflects the case where the eraser arc defining an instance of control is an Escape-arc. As a consequence of this view, P-gap structures can be interpreted as manifesting the same essential phenomenon as the nonsubject control variants of (104a–b); in the latter, the eraser arc would be a Direct Object-arc rather than an Escape-arc.

(104) a. Jack bought the cart$_1$ to move wood around in it$_1$/$p_1$.
      b. Baste the turkey$_2$ after placing it$_2$/$p_2$ on a greased tray. (recipe context)

Here the "licensing" NPs are, of course, not extracted.

It is also then possible to see P-gaps as representing the same sort of control structure as that in "complement object deletion" forms such as (105); see Lasnik and Fiengo 1974.

(105) The wood$_1$ is too heavy to transport g$_1$ in that cart.

This construction also exhibits a pattern quite similar to that of P-gap expressions, except that the control antecedent has not been extracted. Note for instance that constructions like (105) obey an analog of the Pronominal Condition (64) on P-gaps and hence are, for example, incompatible with complements of the "name," existential *there*, or inalienable *on* type:

(106) a. *Ethelbert$_1$ is too silly to name your son g$_1$.
      b. *[Such jewels]$_2$ are too rare for there to be g$_2$ in that drawer.
      c. [His arm]$_3$ is too sore for us to touch (*him on) $t_3$.

It can also be shown that they obey analogs of the Passivizability and Predicate Nominal Conditions. The inference is that these constraints are defined not for P-gaps in particular but for the type of control (basically nonsubject control) shared by P-gaps, "complement object deletion," and the like; see Postal 1990.

Although a control view of P-gaps is partially similar to Chomsky's (1986) "chain composition" approach, it differs in many ways. First, for Chomsky, the element extracted in the parasitic domain is not, as here, a pronoun, but rather an "empty operator." Its trace would be, in GB terms, a variable/R-expression. Hence, that view provides no ground for the Pronominal Condition (64).[26] Second, the "empty operator" view creates the problem of why "empty operator" structures cannot appear on their own, that is, why in Chomsky's terms they can only appear either in the noninitial element of a "composed chain" or in a structure where an "empty operator" chain is linked to an element in argument position (as in "complement object deletion" cases). At issue is why, given (107a), (107b) realizing structure (107c) is bad.

(107) a.  Who$_1$ did Frank promise $t_1$ (that) he would talk to $pg_1$?
      b.  *He would talk to.
      c.  $\emptyset_2$ (he would talk to $t_2$)

The analogous problem does not arise in the control view. The contrast between (107a) and (107b) follows from the nature of the control relation; for control is inherently a mechanism that determines the invisibility of a pronoun *depending on the existence in a structurally appropriate relation of some antecedent of that pronoun*, and no such antecedent exists in (107b).[27]

Sketchy and incomplete as the present control view of P-gaps is, it has as entailments the Island Condition (59) and the Pronominal Condition (64). The former follows from the claim that controlled elements must be extracted combined with a "locality" condition on the loci of controller and controllee. In the case of a *potential* controllee whose basic position is far from, and to the right of, its potential controller, the "locality" condition will force the controllee to L-extract, subjecting it to the island constraints governing L-extractions. The latter follows directly from the view that controlled elements are pronouns. The control view of P-gaps would also entail PG = NP if it is true that only NPs can be controlled.

A final point. It has been a persistent issue to explain why, in spite of the Island Condition (59), a P-gap can occur in an island not containing the "true" gap, for example, in a subject. To add plausibility to the non-standard view that P-gaps represent a control phenomenon, note that this property holds of uncontroversial control cases such as "backward" equi examples:

(108)  Unfortunately, $p_1$/his$_1$ tickling Gladys did not amuse Bob$_1$.

Such facts suggest, independently of the P-gap phenomenon, that control relations per se are *not sensitive to island boundaries*.

Although I would have preferred not to discuss the control conception of P-gaps at all in the present context, and I have not attempted to assemble serious factual support for this view, which merits a separate paper, I have been led to characterize P-gaps here essentially to lend some theoretical content to the claim that pseudo-P-gaps are *not* P-gaps. This denial can now be taken at least to mean that they fail to manifest those properties just sketched as characteristic of P-gaps under the control view. Specifically, it is then claimed (a) that pseudo-P-gaps are not a control phenomenon, hence need not, and do not, involve invisible pronouns and (b) that, unlike English P-gaps, they do not in general involve L-extractions (but see section 8.5).

Analysis of pseudo-P-gaps can be facilitated by focusing for concreteness on particular cases such as (24c) and (32b), repeated here.

(24) c.  We suggest $t_1$ to our employees without actually requiring $pg_1$ of them—[that they wear a tie]$_1$. (Authier 1989:21, 1991:731)

(32) b.  We could suggest $t_1$ to our employees without actually requiring $pg_1$ of them and should suggest $t_1$ to them without actually requiring $pg_1$ of them—[that they wear a tie]$_1$.

If, as has been concluded, the gaps marked $pg$ in these cases are not P-gaps, then what are they? I believe the correct answer is entailed by the general statement in (109).

(109) a.  All pseudo-P-gaps are RNR gaps.
         Or, somewhat more precisely:
      b.  In all pseudo-P-gap structures, both the "licensing" gaps and the pseudo-P-gaps are RNR gaps.

Since I have not given a theoretical account of RNR, (109) is quite vague. I cannot resolve most of this vagueness here. It will simply be specified that RNR is a type of R-extraction and that standard coordinate occurrences of it are instances of *across-the-board* (ATB) R-extraction. This means, among other things, that in effect an RNR structure with $n$ related gaps represents $n$ extractions. Clearly, though, to apply (109) to noncoordinate cases like (24c), one must assume (110).

(110) a.  There is noncoordinate RNR.
         Or, somewhat more precisely:
      b.  The maximal constituents containing related RNR gaps need not be linked by coordination.

It is important to neutralize a likely objection to (110). Postulation of RNR in *noncoordinate* structures might seem entirely ad hoc because it tends to be taken for granted that RNR is limited to *coordinate* structures, not found in cases like (24c). Thus, Huybregts and Van Riemsdijk (1985:175), for example, claim, "RNR is limited to conjoined structures,..." And Williams (1990) states, "... Right Node Raising extractions ... are ordinarily found only in coordinate structures." Fortunately, though, an objection along these lines has no force, because, as noted by Hudson (1976) and mentioned by McCawley (1988:545, n. 5), RNR is possible in certain noncoordinate structures. ((111a–b) are both from Hudson 1976:550.)

(111) a. Of the people questioned, those who liked $t_1$ outnumbered by two to one those who disliked $t_1$—[the way ... the devaluation of the pound had been handled]$_1$.

b. It's interesting to compare the people who like $t_2$ with the people who dislike $t_2$—[the power of the big unions]$_2$.

Any attempt to reduce (111a–b) to instances of RNR in coordinate structures would essentially eliminate the content of the notion "coordinate"; see Williams 1990 for such a proposal and Postal 1993b and below for criticisms.[28] Examples like (111a–b) then motivate recognition of noncoordinate RNR independently of the analysis of pseudo-P-gaps. Given that, a treatment of the latter that appeals to noncoordinate RNR cannot be rejected as ad hoc.

I am thus proposing that cases like (24c), so far described as containing a P-gap "licensed" by a CXS gap, actually involve two non-P-gaps, each of which is a gap of the sort associated with noncoordinate RNR. The situation in cases like (32b) is a bit more complicated. Previously, I took this to involve two P-gaps, each "licensed" by an RNR gap. I am now suggesting that all the gaps are RNR gaps, with the following being the most likely analysis. RNR exists independently in each of the two coordinated constituents, yielding two RNR gaps in each. This is noncoordinate RNR. In addition, the structure thereby determined is itself subject to RNR, of the coordinate variety. The kind of RNR "recursion" implicit in this description is independently attested for coordinate RNR; see Levine 1985 and Postal 1998:chap. 4.

As stressed above, recognition of the P-gap/pseudo-P-gap contrast requires independent theoretical accounts of the distinguished phenomena. This might seem a priori an undesirable complication. However, if (109) can be maintained, no such theoretical objection stands, for RNR must receive a theoretical characterization independently of the way pseudo-P-gaps are treated.

## 8.4.2 Properties of Right Node Raising Relevant to the Clustering in (103)

**8.4.2.1 Remarks** Whereas the previous section sketched a non-P-gap analysis of pseudo-P-gaps, and stressed its theoretical desirability, the present section tries to support it factually. The structure of this support is as follows. I survey properties of uncontroversial instances of RNR and try to show that the same properties characterize pseudo-P-gaps. In particular, I focus on the pseudo-P-gap properties tabulated in (103), that is, properties with respect to which P-gaps and pseudo-P-gaps clearly contrast. Specifically, I will show that coordinate RNR has some property P, then illustrate that what has been taken to be noncoordinate RNR (e.g., sentences parallel to Hudson's (111a–b)) also has P, and finally document that pseudo-P-gaps previously taken to be "licensed" by CXS or coordinate RNR also manifest P. Proceeding in this way justifies the reduction of pseudo-P-gaps to RNR gaps and thus the distinction between P-gaps and pseudo-P-gaps.

**8.4.2.2  Island Restrictions**   One well-documented property of *coordinate* RNR is that it is insensitive to those island constraints frequently designated by the term *subjacency*; see, for example, Wexler and Culicover 1980:299–303, McCawley 1982:100–101, 1988:530–532, Levine 1985, and Postal 1998:chap. 4. Thus, Levine (1985:492) observes, "... elements [i.e., those isolated by RNR] may be an unlimited number of bounding nodes removed from their associated gaps, representing massive violations of island constraints...." The latter include the ban against extracting from a restrictive relative clause (at least, one with a definite head). Notably, the previously observed property of coordinate RNR also holds for the noncoordinate variety in (111).

(112)  Of the people questioned, those WHO KNEW THE
       PROFESSOR who liked $t_1$ outnumbered by two to one those
       WHO KNEW THE DEAN who disliked $t_1$—[the way ... the
       devaluation of the pound had been handled]$_1$.

The addition of the capitalized island-forming material in (112) has no effect on the grammaticality of the result. If, though, noncoordinate RNR is not subject to the relevant island constraints, then principle (109) correctly predicts, under the reduction analysis, those of my earlier observations that were taken to show that nonparenthetical pseudo-P-gaps, regardless of category, are not, in contrast to true P-gaps, subject to the Island Condition (59).

Something further linked to island constraints can be said in support of principle (109). This relates to the need to clarify the yes/no contrast in (103) with respect to satisfaction of the Island Condition (59). Although the "yes" specification is straightforwardly valid for $A$-gaps, the "no" for $B$-gaps requires elaboration. Although it is true that $B$-gaps are not subject to "subjacency"-type island constraints, they are subject to the *Coordinate Structure Constraint* (CSC):

(113) a. Frank offended $t_1$ by not calling $pg_1$ (*or recognizing Glen)—[his favorite uncle from Cleveland]$_1$.

   b. Frank claimed $t_2$ without really proving $pg_2$ (*or believing that $2 + 2$ is 5)—[that $3 + 3$ is 7]$_2$.

This fact is, however, not anomalous under the present view. As observed by McCawley (1982:101, fn. 11) and Postal (1998) (coordinate) RNR in general also obeys the CSC:

(114) a. I argued for $t_1$ and Frank argued against (*both your proposal and) $t_1$—[the idea Shirley suggested]$_1$.

   b. I purchased pictures of $t_2$ (*and carvings of Zeus) and Mary purchased videos of $t_2$—[the divinity you are trying to pay respect to]$_2$.

Significantly, the same is true for the noncoordinate variety of RNR noted by Hudson:

(115) Everyone who (*lives near Sandra or) works with $t_1$ tends to end up disliking those who respect $t_1$—[the guy she is married to]$_1$.

These data further support (109), for the fact that RNR is controlled by the CSC then predicts correctly that pseudo-P-gaps, although unconstrained by "subjacency"-type island constraints, obey the CSC just as "true" P-gaps do:

(116) a. Edmond recognized (*that the products were too expensive and) $t_1$ without admitting publicly $pg_1$—[that the managers were too lazy]$_1$.

   b. Edmond recognized $t_2$ without criticizing his predecessor (*and without admitting publicly $pg_2$)—[that the managers were too lazy]$_2$.

One further point marginally linked to island constraints should be made in connection with the P-gap/pseudo-P-gap contrast. A much-remarked fact is that English allows P-gaps in a subject with the "licensing" gap outside of the subject island. However, it has been little discussed that analogs are often impossible with CXS, and the same is true of RNR, especially when the A-P-gap strands a preposition; see Williams 1990:267. Hence, contrasts such as the following are found:

(117) a. It was Amanda$_1$ that your criticism of $pg_1$ led Bill to introduce $t_1$ to Mary.

b. *Your criticism of $pg_2$ led Bill to introduce $t_2$ to Mary—[the new student who failed the exam]$_2$.

c. *Your criticism of $pg_3$ might have led Bill to introduce $t_3$ to Mary and probably did lead him to introduce $t_3$ to her—[the new student who failed the exam]$_3$.

The contrast between (117a) and (117b–c) seemingly further supports the view that P-gaps and pseudo-P-gaps are distinct phenomena. Moreover, one might well try to derive the ungrammaticality of the latter examples from the ill-formedness of RNR cases like (118a–b).

(118) a. *Your criticism of $t_1$ on Monday led Bill to discuss their criticism of $t_1$ on Tuesday—[the new student who failed the exam]$_1$.

b. *Your criticism of $t_2$ on Monday might have led Bill to discuss their criticism of $t_2$ on Tuesday and probably did lead him to discuss their criticism of $t_2$ on Wednesday—[the new student who failed the exam]$_2$.

That is, these data, which reveal the restriction in both coordinate and noncoordinate RNR structures, would seem to further strengthen an RNR analysis of pseudo-P-gaps.

However, certain problems may cloud this conclusion. The contrasts just uncovered correlate with the fact that unlike the relevant L-extraction in (117a), both CXS and RNR are arguably VP-level and not S-level phenomena, as observed in effect for CXS by (among others) Stowell (1981), Nakajima (1989), Rochemont and Culicover (1990), and Jayaseelan (1990:65):

(119) a. I have expected that he will confess to me all his faults, and [$_{VP}$ confess $t_1$ to me—[all his faults]$_1$] he will. (Nakajima 1989:328)

b. Ellen will explain $t_2$ to those students—[the nature of the problem]$_2$ and help them in other ways.

c. Ellen could explain $t_3$ to those students and should explain $t_3$ to them—[the nature of the problem]$_3$ and might help them in other ways as well.

In all these cases the NPs isolated by CXS or RNR clearly remain at some VP level. Given this fact, the subject contrasts in (117) might be predicted even if, contrary to present views, pseudo-P-gaps were P-gaps. That is, the structural conditions on control might be met in the S-level L-extraction cases but not in their VP-level R-extraction correspondents.

Against this objection, though, it can be noted that (120b), in which *all* gaps are VP-internal, is nonetheless ungrammatical:

(120) a.  It was [the TV announcer she met at Club Med]$_1$ that Francine sent neighbors of $t_1$ photos of $pg_1$ and (sent) colleagues of $t_1$ etchings of $pg_1$.

   b.  *Francine sent neighbors of $t_2$ photos of $pg_2$ and (sent) colleagues of $t_2$ etchings of $pg_2$—[the TV announcer she met at Club Med]$_2$.

In (120b) there is good reason to believe, especially given (120a), that any structural conditions relevant for control of the A-P-gaps by the VP-internal extracted phrase would be met. If so, there is no account of (120b) derivable from control considerations. Hence, in general, an analysis of (117b–c), (120b), and so on, as containing P-gaps turns their ungrammaticality and their respective contrasts with (117a) and (120a) into a mystery. On the contrary, treating the A-P-gaps in these examples as pseudo-P-gaps, analyzed as RNR gaps, would permit reducing their ungrammaticality to the RNR restrictions in (118), supporting an RNR analysis of pseudo-P-gaps. Given the importance of the issue and its complexity, this matter evidently merits much further research.

**8.4.2.3 Categorial Restrictions** English *coordinate* RNR is not limited to NPs but, in particular, takes Ts as arguments:

(121)  It appeared to the first officer $t_1$ but did not appear to the second officer $t_1$—[that the suspect was intoxicated]$_1$.

It also takes a variety of other constituent types, including PPs, VPs, Adjective Phrases, and Ss:

(122) a.  They tried to speak $t_1$ in person but ended up only writing $t_1$ (letters)—[to the official in charge of frankfurters]$_1$.

   b.  No one asserted that Bob $t_2$ or denied that Fred $t_2$—[had consumed more beer than was wise]$_2$.

   c.  Marsha claimed she had long been $t_3$ but certainly did not appear to me to be $t_3$—[over 5 feet tall]$_3$.

   d.  He might learn when $t_4$ and she might learn where $t_4$—[the victims will be buried]$_4$.

Given that coordinate RNR functions for the constituent types illustrated in (122), the simplest assumptions would allow noncoordinate RNR to have the same properties, which is the case:

(123) a. People who write letters $t_1$ tend to differ from people who send telegrams $t_1$—[to their favorite TV personalities]$_1$.

   b. Spies able to learn when $t_2$ can be more valuable than those able to learn where $t_2$—[major troop movements are going to occur]$_2$.

Given this feature of RNR, principle (109) correctly allows for the fact that there are pseudo-P-gaps of these categories as well:

(124) a. Helga mentioned the first problem $t_1$ without mentioning the second problem $pg_1$—[to the professor who taught Greek]$_1$.

   b. Helga didn't know he could $t_2$ before realizing he should $pg_2$—[help elderly tuberculosis victims]$_2$.

   c. Helga was determined to become $t_3$ even after being told she could never be $pg_3$—[extremely muscular]$_3$.

   d. Helga learned when $t_4$ before learning where $pg_4$—[the accident had occurred]$_4$.

In other terms, principle (109) combines with independently established features of RNR to explain why, as documented, neither PG = NP nor the PLR holds of the pseudo-P-gaps whose properties were summarized in (103).

Cases like those in (124) show that earlier demonstrations that pseudo-P-gaps violate PG = NP and the PLR merely touched the tip of an iceberg. Those discussions were essentially limited to extracted *that* clauses, where it seemed at least to make sense to search for ways to maintain such principles. But (124) indicates that any defense of PG = NP or the PLR interpreted to cover pseudo-P-gaps is quite out of the question. This reinforces the conclusion drawn originally on the basis of members of the category T, that those principles can only be salvaged by restricting their domain in such a way as to exclude pseudo-P-gaps.

**8.4.2.4 Pronominal Conditions**   Next, coordinate RNR is not subject to pronominalization conditions; see (33a–b), (35), and the following examples:

(125) a. They might have named their dog $t_1$ and certainly named their camel $t_1$—[something quite unusual]$_1$.

   b. There might be $t_2$ in the first drawer and there certainly are $t_2$ in the second drawer—[the sort of magazines you are looking for]$_2$.

c. The doctor might have touched him on $t_3$ accidentally and the nurse certainly did touch him on $t_3$ deliberately—[his injured but still functional right arm]$_3$.

These sentences are good although all the gaps appear in positions precluding pronouns. Parallel facts obtain for noncoordinate RNR:

(126) a. People who believe there may soon be $t_1$ on Venus tend to distrust those who believe there already are $t_1$ on Mars—[extraterrestrials capable of understanding parasitic gaps]$_1$.

b. Those who were careful not to touch him on $t_2$ accidentally may well resent those who touched him on $t_2$ deliberately—[his injured but still functional right arm]$_2$.

Therefore, principle (109) correctly predicts that pseudo-P-gaps need not obey the Pronominal Condition (64), which is correct:

(127) a. Albert might have cruelly nicknamed one student $t_1$ without nicknaming the other $pg_1$—[either Birdbrain or Airhead]$_1$.

b. There can exist $t_2$ in one department without existing $t_2$ in another—[the sort of hostile atmosphere which prevents serious work]$_2$.

c. They might have had to bandage $t_3$ after touching him on $pg_3$ quite accidentally—[the only arm he could still use]$_3$.

**8.4.2.5 Passivization Constraints** Additionally, no analog of the Passivizability Condition (68) holds for coordinate RNR:

(128) a. Engineers may speak (in) $t_1$ and scientists certainly can speak (in) $t_1$—[a variety of Western languages]$_1$.

b. Large trolls may die under $t_2$ and small trolls certainly do die under $t_2$—[the bridge which they built last year]$_2$.

The same insensitivity to passivization constraints holds for noncoordinate RNR:

(129) People who are learning to speak (in) $t_1$ may hate those who already can speak (in) $t_1$—[that little-known language]$_1$.

Thus, (109) correctly predicts that pseudo-P-gaps are not limited by the Passivizability Condition (68):

(130) a. Such a student may never be permitted to speak (in) $t_1$ even after repeatedly asking to be permitted to speak (in) $pg_1$—[that extremely demanding language]$_1$.

b. One can prove that large trolls are likely to die under $t_2$ without thereby proving that small trolls will die under $t_2$—[the sort of bridge you are talking about]$_2$.

**8.4.2.6 Predicate Nominal Conditions** The condition that neither "licensing" gap nor A-P-gap can be a predicate nominal, valid for P-gaps, is characteristic of neither coordinate nor noncoordinate RNR:

(131) a. Melvin may have become $t_1$ and Jerome certainly did become $t_1$—[a highly competent linguist]$_1$.
   b. She wanted to turn into $t_2$ and did turn into $t_2$—[a ruthless executive]$_2$.

(132) a. People who used to be $t_1$ are sometimes jealous of those who have recently become $t_1$—[major rock stars]$_1$.
   b. Men who currently are $t_2$ tend to outweigh those who used to be $t_2$—[professional sumo wrestlers]$_1$.

**8.4.2.7 Summary** It seems, then, that all those properties of pseudo-P-gaps tabulated in (103) that are anomalous under the assumption that they are P-gaps are predicted under the view in (109)/(110) that they are actually one or another type of RNR gap.

### 8.4.3 Other Features of Right Node Raising

English P-gaps and pseudo-P-gaps are both A-P-gaps, gaps satisfying the Dependency Condition (58). Under the assumption that pseudo-P-gaps are not P-gaps, one must ask why they satisfy (58). Happily, an analysis of pseudo-P-gaps as instances of RNR directly explains why they seem to involve a "licensing" gap. The latter just turns out to be one of the $>1$ gaps invariably associated with any instance of English RNR.

Further, the RNR view provides an account of cases like (133), which are exceptional under a P-gap treatment.

(133) We suggest it$_1$ to our employees without actually requiring it/$pg_1$ of them—[that they wear a tie]$_1$.

Under a P-gap view, such examples violate both PG = NP and the PLR. Under an RNR approach, (133) can be taken to involve noncoordinate RNR of the Ts independently occurring in (134).

(134) a. We suggest it to our employees that they wear a tie.
   b. We don't actually require (it) of them that they wear a tie.

Each clause contains an extraposed phrase of category T, and the non-coordinate RNR in (133) can be assumed to take these as its arguments. Hence, like every RNR structure, (133) has multiple gaps, in this case two T gaps in the position of extraposed clauses.

### 8.4.4 Williams's Observations
Although previous work has not challenged the P-gap character of pseudo-P-gaps, Williams (1990) does, contra Engdahl (1983), deny that any P-gaps are "licensed" by CXS. Instead, he takes cases like (57a) to involve RNR. Rather than recognizing, as done here, that in certain cases RNR gaps can appear in noncoordinated constituents, Williams claims that all P-gaps (in my terms, all A-P-gaps) occur in coordinate structures. This claim is maintained, though, only through appeal to a conception of "coordination" that is so unclear as to have, I believe, almost no current content. Given this extended view of "coordination," Williams attempts to reduce the P-gap phenomenon to the independently existing ATB phenomenon characteristic of extractions from true coordinate structures. This reduction cannot be maintained; see Postal 1993. A further argument against it is provided below.

Nonetheless, Williams does make several very important observations that bear on the present claim that A-P-gaps previously taken to be P-gaps "licensed" by CXS actually involve noncoordinate RNR. Williams notes that alongside (135a), which conforms to Ross's (1967) observation that CXS cannot strand prepositions, there is the well-formed (135b).

(135) a. *I talked to $t_1$ yesterday—[all the members who voted against Hinkly]$_1$.
   b. I talked to $t_2$ without actually meeting $pg_2$—[all the members who voted against Hinkly]$_2$. (Williams 1990:267)

Taking (135b) to involve a P-gap "licensed" by CXS, as does Engdahl (1983), then renders it anomalous in not manifesting the restriction of (135a).

But under the present view, which analyzes (135b) as instantiating non-coordinate RNR and not a P-gap, the anomaly disappears; for, as Ross (1967) notes, English RNR is like L-extractions in being compatible with preposition stranding. Note that Ross's observation, based on coordinate RNR, holds as well of the noncoordinate variety:

(136) Politicians who have fought for $t_1$ may well snub those who have fought against $t_1$—[chimpanzee rights]$_1$.

The contrast between (135a) and (135b) then devolves on their structural contrasts. The *multiple gap* R-extraction case in (135b) cannot represent a P-gap structure and must therefore instantiate noncoordinate RNR; so it is predictably not subject to constraints on CXS. But (135a), with only *one gap*, must involve CXS, and hence manifests all genuine constraints on that construction type.

Thus, in my view, two aspects of Williams's conclusion about cases like (57a) and (135b) are correct. First, they do not represent P-gaps "licensed" by CXS, since they do not contain P-gaps at all. Second, without adopting Williams's vastly extended view of "coordination," one leading to a treatment of (57a)/(135b) as P-gap examples manifesting ATB extraction from coordinate structures, it is possible to capture the insight that (57a)/(135b) partially resemble coordinate structures. The resemblance is that both can manifest RNR, because this exists in true coordinate structures and also in certain noncoordinate ones.[29]

The considerations appealed to in connection with (135) directly explain another observation made by Williams (1990:267), namely, the contrast in (137).

(137) a. I met $t_1$ yesterday without really having the chance to talk to $pg_1$—[all your friends]$_1$.
      b. I met $t_2$ yesterday—[all your friends]$_2$ without really having the chance to talk to them$_2$/*$pg_2$.

Williams takes this type of contrast as an argument that CXS cannot "license" P-gaps, since no P-gap is possible in (137b). In present terms, (137a–b) must be analyzed as involving noncoordinate RNR, as is imposed under the view that R-extractions cannot "license" true P-gaps. Then (137a) meets, but the starred variant of (137b) violates, the invariant property of all RNR structures, coordinate or not, that a phrase isolated by RNR never appears *between* any of the gaps determined by the extraction of that phrase. In general, it must appear to the right of all such gaps.[30] Hence, Williams's observations are accounted for with no need to stretch the concept "coordination."

I promised a new argument against Williams's claim that P-gaps instantiate ATB extraction out of coordinate structures. This can be based on an observation by Goodall (1987), who claims in passing and without argument that RNR occurs with noncoordinating conjunctions:

(138) John throws out $t_1$, whereas Mary eats $pg_1$—[anything that happens to be in the refrigerator]$_1$. (Goodall 1987:96)

I agree with Goodall that this is an instance of noncoordinate RNR; thus, in my terms, it does not instantiate a "true" P-gap. As evidence, note the insensitivity to specific island constraints, which has been shown to be characteristic of pseudo-P-gaps:

(139) John SCOLDS THE PEOPLE WHO throw out $t_1$, whereas Mary PRAISES THE INDIVIDUALS WHO eat $pg_1$—[those things which happen to be in the refrigerator]$_1$.

Moreover, *whereas* structures permit pseudo-P-gaps of categories other than NP:[31]

(140) Jane may still be $t_1$, whereas Lucille certainly no longer is $t_1$— [infatuated with Rodney]$_1$.

For Williams (1990), (138)–(140) would be cases of ATB extraction, with *whereas* exceptionally behaving as a "coordinator." In my terms, there is no coordination in such sentences, hence no possible ATB extraction. And, since English R-extractions do not "license" P-gaps, there can be no P-gaps in them either. Notably, these assumptions, unlike Williams's ATB/"coordination" view of (138)–(140), are consistent with the fact that genuine P-gaps are impossible in *whereas* constituents. That is, no L-extraction can "license" such a P-gap:

(141) a. *What$_1$ does John throw out $t_1$ whereas Mary eats $pg_1$?
      b. *the apples which$_2$ Melvin peeled $t_2$ whereas Louise cut up $pg_2$
      c. *It was Ferdinand who$_3$ Ernestine snubbed $t_3$ whereas Lydia insulted $pg_3$.

These facts are sharply anomalous under Williams's assumptions. If it were the ability of *whereas* to form "coordinate" structures that allowed putative ATB R-extraction, the assumed analysis of (138)–(140) in his terms, then the same "coordinate" structure should support ATB L-extractions. These are in general impossible. See also:

(142) [How long]$_1$ did he say that Sally yelled $t_1$ and/*whereas Lucy moaned $t_1$?

The contrast between (138) and (141a) and the badness of the *whereas* version of (142) thus count strongly against Williams's assumptions.

The former, contrastive pair of course further supports the fundamental claim of the present work, that P-gaps and pseudo-P-gaps are distinct phenomena. These examples show that although they share some domains (e.g., that of *without* phrases), they do not share others. In my terms, it is hardly surprising that some environments permit noncoordinate RNR but not the sort of *control* involved in true P-gaps. Observe in connection with the earlier claimed parallelism between P-gaps and "complement object deletion" that (143) resembles (141c).

(143)  Ferdinand$_1$ was too nice for me to believe Ernestine snubbed $t_1$
       (*whereas Lydia insulted $pg_1$).

Given that both "complement object deletion" and genuine P-gaps instantiate a type of control, (143) further supports the view that *whereas* expressions, though open to RNR, preclude that type of control.

The argument based on *whereas* was formulated with extracted NPs. But the same contrast between grammatical R-extractions and ungrammatical L-extractions can be illustrated with clear non-NPs:

(144)  a.  Betty may be $t_1$, whereas Carla certainly is not $pg_1$—[quite
           sympathetic to you]$_1$.
       b.  [Quite sympathetic to you]$_2$, Betty may be $t_2$ (*whereas Carla
           doesn't seem $pg_2$).

Again, Williams's ATB approach could only describe (144a) by positing a "coordinate" structure whose existence would wrongly predict the grammaticality of the long form of (144b) as an ATB structure.

## 8.5  Apparent Parasitic Gaps "Licensed" by Parenthetical Extractions

Sections 8.3.2–8.3.4 and 8.4 explored the possibility of salvaging both PG = NP and the PLR as true principles characterizing the English P-gap phenomenon. The logic of the defense was to suggest that those A-P-gaps that appear to violate these principles also fail to observe several others arguably characteristic of genuine P-gaps—namely, the Island Condition (59), the Pronominal Condition (64), the Passivizability Condition (68), and the Predicate Nominal Condition (72). This clustering of violations was taken to justify the proposal made explicit in section 8.3.4 to divide A-P-gaps into true P-gaps and pseudo-P-gaps; the latter would include all those A-P-gaps "licensed" by R-extractions, including whatever is involved in the positioning of Ts in nonobject positions ("extraposition"). This approach led to a critical observation represented graphically in (103): true P-gaps seem to be "licensed" by L-extractions, pseudo-P-gaps by R-extractions. If so, then one could claim that it is lawful for English that those A-P-gaps that are "licensed" by L-extractions obey all of conditions (59), PG = NP/Preposition-Stranding (61)/(62), the PLR (63), (64), (68), and (72). A-P-gaps "licensed" by R-extractions would not be subject to them. But such a rigid correlation seems to run afoul of the facts for parentheticals, where apparent counterexamples to PG = NP and the PLR involved T-projections. To complete a defense of these principles as well as the general idea of distinguishing P-gaps from pseudo-P-gaps in terms that include a basic contrast between L-extraction and R-extraction, it must be assumed that apparent P-gaps "licensed" by T-projections in parentheticals are not P-gaps. And, if they are to be treated as pseudo-P-gaps, maintaining the simple bifurcate analysis suggested by the correlations in (103), one must justify assignment of parenthetical A-P-gaps to the $B$-gap category.

The immediate problem with such an assignment is that parenthetical A-P-gaps, unlike all those assigned to the $B$-gap category in (103), seem to be associated with L-extractions. In this respect, they resemble P-gaps and not the $B$-gaps in (103). Significantly, correlated with their link to L-extractions is that, in contrast to the CXS and RNR varieties, parenthetical A-P-gaps *are* constrained by the Island Condition (59):

(145) a. *Gloria is not, as$_1$ they only learned $t_1$ long after interrogating THE DOCTOR WHO ASSERTED $pg_1$, incapable of having children.

   b. *Gloria is, $\emptyset_2$ he acknowledged $t_2$ only long after interviewing THE DOCTOR WHO DENIED $pg_2$, capable of having children.

Examples (145a–b) reveal the consequences of island-forming nodes in the subordinate constituent. The following cases show parallel effects when such nodes appear in the main clause:

(146) a. *Gloria is not, as$_1$ THE DOCTOR WHO WAS TOLD $pg_1$ at the conference later reported $t_1$ to Melvin, incapable of having children.

   b. *Gloria is, $\emptyset_2$ THE DOCTOR WHO ACKNOWLEDGED $pg_2$ in private later denied $t_2$ in public, capable of having children.

With respect to the correlations in (103), then, the A-P-gaps linked to parenthetical expressions have a mixed status. Condition (f) of (103) is apparently untestable. But, for the others, the pattern is as shown in (147).

(147) *A-P-gaps "licensed" by parenthetical extractions*
   a. Subject to the Island Condition (59)           yes
   b. Satisfy PG = NP (61)                            no
   c. Satisfy the PLR (63)                            no

Paul M. Postal

   d. Subject to the Pronominal Condition (64)          no
   e. Subject to the Passivizability Condition (68)     no
   f. Subject to the Predicate Nominal Condition (72)   (untestable)
   g. "Licensed" by L-extractions                       yes

I have just supported the entries for (147a); those for (147b) and (147c)
were supported in section 8.2.4. Note, for instance, that with respect to
preposition-stranding behavior, parenthetical A-P-gaps seem to violate
the Preposition-Stranding Condition (62) and hence PG = NP:

(148) a. He believes Sidney is living in Australia, which$_1$ I suspected $t_1$
         long before becoming certain of/*$\varnothing$ $pg_1$.
      b. He believes Sidney is living in Australia, as$_2$ I suspected $t_2$ long
         before becoming certain *of/$\varnothing$ $pg_2$.
      c. Sidney is, $\varnothing_3$ I suspected $t_3$ long before becoming certain *of/
         $\varnothing$ $pg_3$, living in Australia.

Although judgments are a bit subtle, it appears that preposition stranding
with A-P-gaps is impossible with both types of parentheticals, in contrast
to the situation with true NP extraction in (148a). By the same token,
since pronouns cannot alternate with $\varnothing$ in (148), the well-formed variants
of (148b–c) also violate the Pronominal Condition (64), supporting
(147d). for (147e), examples like (149a–d) indicate that unpassivizable Ts
of some of the verbs in (29) nonetheless yield viable parenthetical A-P-
gaps.

(149) a. Marvin holds that traces are lexical.
      b. *That traces are lexical is held by many scholars.
      c. Traces are not, as$_1$ some who unaccountably still hold $pg_1$
         would have us believe $t_1$, lexical in that sense.
      d. Traces are, $\varnothing_2$ some who have long held $pg_2$ have finally
         succeeded in convincing me $t_2$, lexical in that sense.

   Overall, then, the pattern manifested by parenthetical A-P-gaps is curiously mixed, showing some of the features associated with P-gaps and
some characteristic of pseudo-P-gaps. I see only one means of fully regularizing these facts. To account for properties (147b–e), one must take the
parenthetical A-P-gaps to be pseudo-P-gaps, that is, following section 8.4,
RNR gaps. To account for (147a,g), one must, as in section 8.2.4, posit L-
extractions in both A-parentheticals and N-parentheticals and claim that
the Island Condition (59) characteristic of P-gaps holds of parenthetical
A-P-gaps not because they are P-gaps but merely because they involve an
L-extraction.

The way to integrate these assumptions is to posit that the L-extraction characteristic of both types of parenthetical at least *can* extract a constituent isolated by RNR. In these terms, the parenthetical structures involving A-P-gaps would manifest *both* R-extractions and L-extractions, the former masked by the existence of the latter. Parenthetical A-P-gaps would then be "licensed" not by L-extractions but by R-extractions, just as in the cases earlier treated under the rubrics of CXS and RNR.

There is factual evidence for the claim that parenthetical A-P-gaps involve a masked form of (noncoordinate) RNR. Recall that *whereas* expressions were shown to preclude ordinary L-extraction-"licensed" P-gaps but to permit (noncoordinate) RNR. Then, if *parenthetical* A-P-gaps depend on RNR, such A-P-gaps should be compatible with *whereas* expressions. And they are:

(150) a.  We should not, as$_1$ Dave proposed $t_1$, whereas he really had no business proposing $pg_1$, hire college students.
      b.  The government, $\emptyset_2$ Dave was told $t_2$ whereas only Steve should have been told $pg_2$, will withdraw all support for the project.

Compare the ungrammatical true P-gap structures:

(151) a.  *What$_1$ Dave proposed $t_1$ whereas he had no real business proposing $pg_1$ was that we hire college students.
      b.  *That$_2$, Dave was apparently told $t_2$ whereas only Steve should have been told $pg_2$.

Although factually supportable and not inherently problematic, the assumption that the parenthetical A-P-gap cases involve L-extractions of constituents isolated by RNR does raise two technical difficulties. First, there must exist severe constraints on the possibility of L-extraction of phrases extracted by RNR. Otherwise, for example, many of the properties of P-gaps would not hold. In particular, for example, (151a–b) must indicate that neither the L-extraction defining pseudoclefts nor that involved in topicalization can extract a phrase that has been extracted from a *whereas* phrase by RNR. It seems then that the proposals that have been made require assuming for the L-extractions associated with parentheticals a freedom not typical of L-extractions. This property might be regarded as suspicious, and certainly suggests that the proposal in question deserves much greater scrutiny. In any event, it will be necessary to specify which L-extractions have the freedom to take as arguments phrases isolated by noncoordinate RNR. But I cannot consider that issue here.

Second, it has been shown that RNR is not sensitive to "subjacency"-type island constraints in any of the constituents containing RNR gaps, but that parenthetical A-P-gaps are sensitive to such constraints in both "licensing" and "parasitic" constituents, These facts combine with the proposal that parenthetical A-P-gaps involve L-extraction of RNR-extracted constituents to require a theory of island induction of a rather "global" sort. There are various ways this could be approached, but I cannot consider the matter in detail. I want to observe here only that this feature of the current approach is *not* ad hoc and thus cannot ground an argument against it; for what is true of the RNR I have posited in parenthetical A-P-gaps is, I would argue, essentially just a property noted long ago by Wexler and Culicover (1980:301) for standard (coordinate) RNR:

(152) "[A] raised [by RNR] node always behaves, vis-à-vis all constraints on analyzability, just as it would if it were in its original underlying position. Hence, whereas it is apparently possible to apply RNR to a constituent of a relative clause, if we then try to analyze this raised node, we find that it acts as though it were still within the relative clause."

This generalization was intended to cover cases like (153b).

(153) a. Mary buys $t_1$, and Bill knows a man who sells $t_1$—[pictures of Elvis Presley]$_1$.
      b. Who$_2$ does Mary buy $t_3$ and Bill (*know a man who) sells $t_3$— [pictures of $t_2$]$_3$?

Here, although RNR can yield a gap inside the relative clause, the RNR extractee acts with respect to L-extraction as if it had *not* been extracted by RNR. That is, (153b) instantiates generalization (154).

(154) With respect to island conditions on L-extractions, an RNR extractee behaves as if it were in the position of all of its associated RNR gaps.

Hence, in particular, in the ungrammatical long form of (153b), the L-extraction of *who* treats *pictures of $t_2$* as if it were inside the relative clause, inducing a "subjacency" violation.

Regardless of how (154) is ultimately built into an overall theory of extractions, it covers the situation found with parenthetical L-extractions as well. Thus, recall the island case (145a), repeated here.

(145) a. *Gloria is not, as$_1$ they only learned $t_1$ long after interrogating
THE DOCTOR WHO ASSERTED $pg_1$, incapable of having
children.

In terms of (154), this is ungrammatical even under my posit of masked
RNR, because the L-extractee—say, *as*—acts as if it were inside the relative clause *the doctor who asserted pg*, which induces "subjacency" violations on L-extractions. The bottom line then is that, given Wexler and
Culicover's (1980) generalization, positing RNR in parenthetical A-P-
gaps imposes no *new* complications on the formulation of the proper
theory of the relation between L-extraction and "subjacency" violations.

## 8.6 Conclusions

### 8.6.1 Results
The long and complicated discussion in the previous five sections leads, I
suggest, to the following conclusion. What was previously taken to be an
essentially homogenous English P-gap domain in fact divides into two
separate phenomena. Those A-P-gaps "licensed" by L-extractions other
than those in parenthetical cases are what I have called "true P-gaps" and
represent what I claim is a control phenomenon. But those A-P-gaps
"licensed" by R-extractions instantiate a distinct, noncontrol construction, which I have analyzed as a special case of noncoordinate RNR.
I also argued that the A-P-gaps "licensed" by the extractions linked to
parentheticals are not P-gaps but RNR cases, this property being masked
by the fact that parentheticals also involve "secondary" L-extractions.
The latter determine that these A-P-gaps, unlike those only linked to R-
extractions, obey "subjacency" requirements.

The fact that pseudo-P-gaps are not P-gaps eliminates a host of otherwise uneliminable counterexamples to a variety of principles otherwise
valid for English P-gaps: the Island Condition (59), PG = NP (61), the
PLR (63), the Pronominal Condition (64), the Passivizability Condition
(68), and the Predicate Nominal Condition (72). The fact that these hold
of P-gaps but not of pseudo-P-gaps supports the view that P-gaps are a
control phenomenon; for other control phenomena also essentially obey
them (e.g., the "complement objcet deletion" construction). Ultimately,
true P-gaps are far more like the control gaps in the latter construction
than they are like the pseudo-P-gaps, which are RNR gaps.

In summary, then, the bifurcate conception of A-P-gaps argued for here
is supported from two different directions. First, this view permits main-

tenance of a theory of P-gaps that incorporates restrictive and generally accepted principles only properly including PG = NP and the PLR, which would all be falsified if pseudo-P-gaps were P-gaps. Since they are not, these principles arguably remain free of known English counterexamples.

Second, the bifurcate approach permits an insightful view of pseudo-P-gaps as noncoordinate RNR gaps. This accounts for all their basic properties with hardly any need for specific assumptions, since the combination of Universal Grammar and English grammar must, independently, account for the properties of both coordinate and noncoordinate RNR structures.

### 8.6.2 New Questions

The conclusions just reached raise a number of new questions about A-P-gaps. First, one must ask whether there is any principle that determines that true P-gaps can only be linked to L-extracted antecedents.[32] Second, if it is true that English A-P-gaps represent two radically distinct phenomena, one must ask how to link what have been called P-gaps in other languages with the appropriate English cases. That is, one must determine to what extent A-P-gaps in other languages correspond to true English P-gaps, and to what extent they correspond to pseudo-P-gaps. Correct answers presuppose rich accounts of A-P-gaps in the languages in question. Such comparisons are in general obviously beyond the scope of this discussion. But it is important to make certain comments about Dutch, especially as described by Bennis (1986), Bennis and Hoekstra (1985b), and Huybregts and Van Riemsdijk (1985), for it is plausible that these authors, especially Huybregts and Van Riemsdijk, have already drawn a distinction parallel to the one made here between true P-gaps and pseudo-P-gaps.

Attempting to account for various contrasts between Dutch A-P-gaps and English A-P-gaps, Huybregts and Van Riemsdijk (1985) in fact conclude that Dutch A-P-gaps differ in nature from English P-gaps. They take Dutch A-P-gaps to be ATB gaps, based on assumptions parallel to those of Williams (1990) rejected earlier, that is, assumptions that take certain "subordinators" to have the possibility of functioning as "coordinators." Although I have rejected this idea for English and suspect that it is equally wrong for Dutch, Huybregts and Van Riemsdijk's conclusions are otherwise largely consistent in an interesting way with the distinction I have drawn between P-gaps and pseudo-P-gaps.[33]

Huybregts and Van Riemsdijk (1985) conclude that at least many Dutch A-P-gaps involve a phenomenon that is the "mirror image" of English RNR, which they call *left node raising* (LNR). This is invoked to account for such sentences as (155).

(155) Hij heeft deze artikelen [zonder PRO *pg* te lezen] opgeborgen.
      he has   these articles   without       to read  filed
      'He filed these articles without reading (them).'

Recalling the earlier claim that RNR yields VP-level extractees, we can see that it is quite plausible to take (155) to involve a mirror-image analog.[34] In that case, the conclusion seems apparent that Dutch A-P-gaps like (155), which Huybregts and Van Riemsdijk (1985) deny are the same sort of phenomenon as true English P-gaps, represent essentially the structure type I have taken to be pseudo-P-gaps. Whereas they take these to involve ATB extraction based on an extended notion of "coordination," as in Williams 1990, I would take them to involve an analog of English non-coordinate RNR, that is, noncoordinate LNR.

The similarity between Dutch A-P-gaps as analyzed by Huybregts and Van Riemsdijk (1985) and my analysis of English pseudo-P-gaps is made especially clear by certain parallels drawn by Bennis and Hoekstra (1985b) between specific Dutch instances of LNR and English pseudo-P-gap cases of the type in (51a). Bennis and Hoekstra explicitly compare a sentence exactly parallel to (155) (their (18a)) and one identical to my (57a) (their (23)) and claim (1985b:12), "The sentences in (18) are in fact the mirror image of constructions like (23)." Thus, the association of pseudo-P-gaps with Dutch A-P-gaps seems highly plausible.

To solidify this identification, it would be necessary, among other things, to uncover for Dutch analogs of the kind of conditions I have taken to characterize *true* P-gaps (PG = NP (61), the PLR (63), the Pronominal Condition (64), the Passivizability Condition (68), etc.) and to show that Dutch A-P-gaps do not satisfy these analogs. If that can be done, there would be overwhelming support for the view that Dutch A-P-gaps are pseudo-P-gaps, differing chiefly in ways linked to the difference between RNR and LNR. Unfortunately, I do not know enough about Dutch to say anything more about the matter.

The account of English A-P-gaps advocated here recognizes that English has both true P-gaps and pseudo-P-gaps. The question arises whether the same is true of Dutch. At issue would be, among other things, the proper treatment of cases like (156).

(156) [Welke artikelen]$_1$ heeft hij zonder  $pg_1$ te lezen opgeborgen $t_1$?
      which articles      has  he without       reading filed
      'Which articles has he filed without reading?' (Bennis 1986:86)

One analysis would take (156) to be parallel to a true English P-gap case, whatever the right treatment of those is. But another could analyze (156) as involving an L-extraction taking as an argument the NP extracted by LNR. In such an account, the parallelism between (156) and its English translation would be exactly as misleading as that between (57a) and (57b). A treatment of (156) positing LNR would raise the sort of questions that were mentioned in connection with the parallel analysis I proposed in section 8.5 for the A-P-gaps "licensed" by the structure of parentheticals.

A final remark. It is notable that the distinction that Huybregts and Van Riemsdijk made between P-gaps Dutch A-P-gaps and the one that I have drawn between true English P-gaps and English pseudo-P-gaps are based on quite different factual and theoretical assumptions. The parallelism of the results under these conditions therefore strongly suggests the existence of a single reality underlying them, that is, a sharp distinction in natural language between P-gaps and pseudo-P-gaps.

**Notes**

I am indebted to Guglielmo Cinque, Gerald Gazdar, Warren Plath, and two *LI* referees for useful criticisms of earlier versions of this article.

1. For discussions of this topic, see among others Taraldsen 1981; Chomsky 1982, 1986; Pesetsky 1982; Engdahl 1983, 1984, 1985; Kayne 1984; Kiss 1985; Bennis and Hoekstra 1985a,b; Bennis 1986; Stowell 1985; Browning 1987a,b; Koster 1987; Safir 1987; Sag 1983; Gazdar, Klein, Pullum, and Sag 1984, 1985; Hukari and Levine 1987; Sells 1986; Williams 1990; Tellier 1991; Pollard and Sag 1994; and Postal 1993.

2. These convenient notations need not, and here do not, represent any commitment to the linguistic reality of traces.

3. This idea was probably first expressed in unpublished work by Cinque in the early 1980s; see Cinque 1983.

4. None of the authors cited shows how their claims can, if interpreted as *universally relevant*, be made compatible with Engdahl's (1983:17) observations and explicit claims about Swedish to the effect that this language allows some P-gaps licensed by prepositional phrases. Cinque (1990:187, n. 9) recognizes the problem but essentially dismisses it.

5. Although I take it to be true that each English P-gap requires the occurrence of an independent extraction, as in (5a), I would account for this in a way that differs from the views defining current conventional wisdom. The proposal I would adopt

depends on a relational view of control as based on erasure of arcs standing in certain anaphoric relations; see section 8.4 for brief further discussion.

6. See Gazdar 1981, 1982; Gazdar, Klein, Pullum, and Sag 1984, 1985; Hukari and Levine 1987, 1989, 1991; Maling and Zaenen 1982; Sag 1982, 1983; Sag and Klein 1982; Sag, Gazdar, Wasow, and Weisler 1985; and Sells 1986.

7. Chomsky's writings reveal the evolution. In Chomsky 1965:200, n. 13, he claims that the *that* clause complement of *expect* is embedded in an NP. In Chomsky 1968:44 he claims that it is unclear whether the *that*-clause complements of *think* are NPs. And in Chomsky 1973 he gives several examples where *that* clause complements are represented only as Ss.

8. After completing this article, I became aware of Lasnik and Saito's (1992:148) claim, on the basis of (i), "that CP parasitic gaps are possible."

(i) [That John is here]$_1$, Mary claimed $t_1$ [without really believing $e_1$].

However, they then mention (p. 206, n. 2), without definitively accepting, an argument by Safir (1982) to the effect that the trace position in (i) is actually an NP. Only the latter view is consistent with the conclusions reached here.

9. In general terms, this conclusion is for the most part compatible with the overall position of Cinque (1983, 1990) that the constructions mentioned in (2) involve invisible pronominal elements. However, the present view differs (among other ways) in recognizing a pronominal aspect to a broader range of constructions including topicalization and clefting, not previously treated as involving resumptive pronouns; see Postal 1998. Thus, Cinque (1990:199, n. 59) states, "This requires a different treatment for the absence of weak crossover effects in topicalization and appositive relatives, which I regard as true movement constructions leaving a real variable." Moreover, it would not be trivial in Cinque's terms to view topicalization as involving invisible resumptive pronouns, since it does not manifest key properties taken by Cinque as diagnostics for this in English (e.g., compatibility of the posited pronoun with all finite subject positions). Note such contrasts as (ia) versus (ib).

(i) a.   Mary$_1$, they only recently proved $t_1$ had been with the victim.
    b.   *Mary$_2$ was difficult for them to prove $t_2$ had been with the victim.

10. I take no position on the character of *non-NP* topicalizations like those in (i).

(i) a.   [To Bob]$_1$, I was never able to speak $t_1$ in person.
    b.   [Fond of pickled grapes]$_2$, he no longer claims to be $t_2$.

That is, I know of no evidence indicating whether or not they manifest invisible resumptive elements.

11. The Spanish situation is illustrated by the following examples from Moore 1990:325:

(i) Esta carta es dificil de escribir(la) al presidente.
    this letter is difficult write (it)   to the president
    'This letter is difficult to write to the president.'

12. Here and elsewhere, page references to Ross 1967 are to the published 1986 version.

13. Williams (1990) denies that CXS "licenses" P-gaps. He claims that apparent cases of this are instead instances of right node raising; see section 8.4.

14. However, there are N-parentheticals that correspond to infinitives rather than to *that* clauses:

(i)  Do not, I beg you, eat the gerbil.

(ii) a.   I beg you not to eat the gerbil.
     b.   *I beg you that you not eat the gerbil.

15. A distinct *as* is a subordinating conjunction roughly equivalent to *since:*

(i)  As Kirk was sick, the play had to be canceled.

Another different *as* seems to function as a relativizer for manner adverbials, as illustrated in (ii).

(ii) I did it exactly as he told me to.

A third variant of *as* seems analogous to the one in (37a) and (38a), except that it corresponds to verbal phrase type constituents rather that to *that* clauses:

(iii) Mary could not, $as_1$ she wished to $t_1$, hire an archeologist.

(iv) We are trying, $as_2$ we must $t_2$, to develop healthier pork products.

Though it is hard to believe the correct account of these instances of *as* is unrelated to that of those linked to *that* clauses, I will not discuss them here.

16. Actually, this is a slight exaggeration. There are also structures such as (i).

(i) It appears/seems/turns out to be true that S.

But these have no bearing on the central point in the text.

17. Further hedging is required because of grammatical structures like (i) and (ii).

(i)  Is Frank ill? Yes, it seems so.

(ii) Frank is ill or so it seems.

18. The latter work credits the original observation to an unpublished paper by Katherine Gilbert.

19. For convenience, I will continue to mark all A-P-gaps, both P-gaps and pseudo-P-gaps, with the notation *pg*.

20. This claim is, evidently, far from obviously true in the case of those P-gaps "licensed" in "object-raising" or "object deletion" structures like (i) and (ii):

(i)  [That monograph]$_1$ will be hard to review $t_1$ without reading $pg_1$.

(ii) [That monograph]$_2$ is short enough to review $t_2$ without reading $pg_2$.

But I agree with GB work, such as Chomsky 1982:45, that the main clauses in such examples involve an extraction of an invisible element. In my terms, the invisible element is a resumptive pronoun associated with raising of the object; see Postal 1990.

21. The essence of this idea arguably originates in Ross 1967:120, the first generative work to attest P-gaps. Ross in effect outlined two distinct views of these. On one, they were regarded as "pure extraction" gaps, related to those in across-the-board extractions; on the other, they were viewed as resulting from a "rule of

pronoun deletion." Ross did not claim to be able to decide between these alternatives, and the literature on P-gaps since the early 1980s contains proposals of both the pronominal and nonpronominal types, the latter, however, clearly dominating.

22. This claim is slightly too strong and needs to be amended along the lines of Postal 1993b, 1999. Roughly, a P-gap *can* appear in a position incompatible with definite pronouns if the constraint barring those references exclusively *surface* pronouns; for even if, as I would argue, P-gaps are pronouns, they are evidently not surface pronouns.

23. One might ask whether the Pronominal Condition (64) entails PG = NP. It is doubtful that there is such a logical connection. For example, there are pronominal forms like *there*, which seem not to be NPs, at least in many occurrences. Notably, P-gaps cannot appear in positions that accept *there* but are incompatible with uncontroversial pronominal NPs:

(i) a. [Which room]$_1$ did they hang out in $t_1$ so the children could play in $pg_1$?
   b. *Where$_2$ did they hang out $t_2$ so the children could play $pg_2$?

I conclude that PG = NP and the Pronominal Condition (64) are independent.

24. The Pronominal Condition (64) also explains ill-formed "adjunct" P-gap examples like (i), which Stowell (1986) and Tellier (1991:40–44), among others, have sought to explain in terms of various GB principles:

(i) *This is the way$_1$ you presented it $t_1$ without having read it $pg_1$. (Tellier 1991:40)

That is, (i) cannot mean (ii).

(ii) This is the way$_1$ you presented it without having read it (in) that way$_1$.

In terms of the Pronominal Condition (64), (i) follows from the pronominalization restriction manifest in (iii).

(iii) *He told me to read them in that way$_1$ but I didn't read them (in) it$_1$.

That is, as is well known, manner phrases cannot be definite pronouns. The key point is that the Pronominal Condition (64), which can be taken to explain (i), also accounts for a host of facts like the unacceptable P-gaps of (65)–(67), which the GB principles appealed to by Stowell and Tellier would say nothing about.

25. After completing this work, I noticed that Lasnik and Saito (1992) make a claim equivalent to the first part of (72), which they support with (i).

(i) *[What (kind of teacher)]$_1$ did Mary become $t_1$ [without considering John $e_1$]? (Lasnik and Saito 1992:147)

26. The view I have suggested here should be compared with the claim of Aoun and Clark (1985) that P-gaps are "anaphors" internal to a certain interpretation of "binding theory." But space prohibits such a comparison here.

27. A control view of P-gaps and the other constructions taken to involve non-subject control also is relevant to explaining that what are, in GB terms, called "empty operator constructions" fail to manifest prepositional pied piping. Thus, although the preposition in (107a) can pied-pipe in other constructions, this is impossible in analogs of (107a), for example:

(i) *Who$_1$ did Frank promise $t_1$ (that) to he would talk $pg_1$?

Although I cannot develop the explanation of (i) here, in my terms it devolves on a kind of relational case condition on nonsubject control; see Postal 1990. I know of no GB account of facts like (i), which bear considerable resemblance to free relative facts taken by Bresnan and Grimshaw (1978:342–345) to count against an extraction analysis of free relative constructions.

28. One problem with taking examples like (111a–b) to be coordinate is that this makes false predictions about L-extractions, just as in the case of *whereas* structures discussed below. Thus, although there is noncoordinate RNR of adjective phrases, corresponding to (111a–b), the analogous L-extractions are impossible:

(i) a.   Those who want to be $t_1$ greatly outnumber those who already are $t_1$—
        [extremely slim]$_1$.

    b.  *[Extremely slim]$_2$ though those who want to be $t_2$ outnumber those who
        already are $t_2$.

    c.  *[Extremely slim]$_3$, those who want to certainly be $t_3$ outnumber those
        who already are $t_3$.

If (ia) were grammatical because of the ATB possibilities associated with coordination, there would be no basis for the failure of that coordination to permit ATB L-extractions of otherwise L-extractable English phrases. In other terms, though, the contrast between (ia) and (ib–c) is due to the previously known fact, documented in section 8.4.2, that RNR is not subject to certain ("subjacency") island constraints that limit L-extractions.

29. Of course, it is important to specify the overall conditions that group coordinate structures with *only some* noncoordinate ones. Although this matter is beyond the present discussion, a preliminary observation is that no member of a set of linked RNR gaps c-commands another. Thus, they occur in positions where an antecedent can link to an epithet. Compare (136) and (i).

(i) Politicians who have fought for Jones$_1$ may snub those who have fought
    against the idiot$_1$.

30. The restriction is necessary to allow for the case where an RNR extractee is L-extracted; see section 8.5.

31. An example rather parallel to (138) is cited by Huybregts and Van Riemsdijk (1985:177):

(i) John is, while sternly opposed to $pg_1$, nevertheless mighty interested in $t_1$—
    [censorship]$_1$.

Such *while* examples have the basic features of the *whereas* cases; for example, the extractee can be a non-NP:

(ii) John, while ostensibly claiming not to know where $t_1$, nevertheless admits to
    knowing when $t_1$—[the meeting will be held]$_1$.

32. This remark assumes that it has been shown that English R-extractions do not "license" true P-gaps. A more accurate statement would be that it has been shown that those A-P-gaps previously taken to be P-gaps have motivated analyses as RNR gaps. No case has been documented where allowing R-extractions to "license" P-gaps would make false predictions. An example like the starred form

of Williams's (137b) comes close; but this can be treated otherwise, as Williams suggests, by denying that CXS is an extraction phenomenon.

33. The ATB approach to Dutch A-P-gaps is criticized in Bennis 1986:sect. 1.7.3.

34. In a slightly different account, Bennis (1986:62) takes the NP extraction I have just called LNR to be formally identical to English CXS. But, given the similarities between CXS and RNR, which even raise the possibility of their reducing to manifestations of the same underlying phenomenon (that is, RNR might be, in spite of their contrasts with respect to preposition stranding, ATB CXS), it is doubtful that there is any factual conflict here.

# Chapter 9

## On the Nonexistence of True Parasitic Gaps in Standard German

Andreas Kathol

### 9.1 Introduction

Typical cases of English parasitic gap constructions discussed in the syntactic literature are given in (1), from Postal (1994a:63).

(1) a. [Which article]$_1$ did Ted copy $t_1$ [without reading $pg_1$]?
   b. the woman who$_2$ your attack on $pg_2$ encouraged $t_2$
   c. It was Irving who$_3$ they proved [associates of $pg_3$] to have bribed $t_3$.

It is standardly assumed that there is an asymmetric relationship between the different kinds of missing constituents in such constructions. Thus, the gaps in the adverbial phrase, subject, and raised object respectively, notated as $pg$, are dependent on the presence of another extraction site. Although there is no shortage of theoretical attempts to explain this phenomenon of English (see, for instance, the references in Postal 1994), relatively few studies have investigated putatively similar constructions in other languages, Dutch possibly exempted. With the widely accepted view of syntax concerned with crosslinguistically valid principles, the default assumption would appear to be that the explanatory mechanisms uncovered for English should also be of relevance for other languages exhibiting the phenomenon.

The aim of this chapter, however, is to show that this is in fact a mistaken assumption, at least as far as equating superficially similar constructions in standard German with "true" English parasitic gaps (in the sense of Postal 1994) is concerned.

### 9.2 Parasitic Gap Candidates in German

The possibility of parasitic gap (P-gap) constructions in standard varieties of German was first extensively discussed by Felix (1985:190), who cites examples such as (2).[1]

(2) a. Hans hat Maria$_i$ [ohne     $pg_i$ anzusehen] geküßt.
     Hans has Maria   without      to-look-at kissed
     'Hans kissed Maria without looking at her.'
   b. Man hat Hans$_i$ [ohne     $pg_i$ zu verständigen] entlassen.
     one has Hans  without      to notify       layed-off
     'They fired Hans without notifying him.'

Since then, their status in the syntactic description of German has had a
somewhat peculiar quality. It appears that some researchers take their
generally marginal status and significant variation of speakers' judgments
as indicating that these phenomena are only of limited interest in the syntactic description of German. For instance, no mention of German parasitic gaps is made in standard references for transformational German
syntax such as Grewendorf 1988 (see p. 189) or von Stechow and Sternefeld 1988.

The opposite strategy, occasionally advocated by adherents of the
principles-and-parameters approach to syntax, has been to take the marginal status of parasitic gaps as a particularly valuable feature of the
grammatical system.[2] This is because the putative poverty of parasitic gap
stimuli during language acquisition entails that intuitions in this area
must be the direct result of UG interacting with particular parameter-
setting triggers. Implicit in this way of thinking has been the assumption
that parasitic gaps across languages more or less constitute a coherent
class of phenomena requiring a rather similar set of devices for their
structural description.[3] Applied to the German construction in (2), this
entails that (2) should be expected to have essentially the same properties
that have been reported for their English—or Dutch—counterparts. In
particular, this means that the parasitic gap is licensed by means of an
operator in an Ā-position that c-commands both gaps, whereas no c-
command relationship can hold between the real and parasitic gaps.

One area where this approach, adopted for German by Felix (1985),
has often been taken as a testbed for different syntactic proposals is
scrambling. Thus, typical Ā-movement as in question and relative clause
formation can license P-gaps in German in a fashion analogous to the
situation in English.

(3) a. [Welches Mädchen]$_i$ hat Hans $t_i$ [ohne     $pg_i$ anzuschauen]
       which    girl          has Hans    without      to-look-at
       geküßt?
       kissed
       'Which girl did Hans kiss without looking at her?'

b.  das Mädchen welches$_i$ Hans $t_i$ [ohne     $pg_i$ anzusehen] küßte
    the girl     which  Hans  without    to-look-at  kissed
    'the girl that Hans kissed without looking at her'

Additionally, however, the well-formed examples in (2) show that the proper kind of structural configuration may also be effected by scrambling, for which there is no direct analogue in English. In fact, the set of candidate P-gap constructions that are licensed by ordinary Ā-movements appears to be exactly the same as those seen with scrambling. This has often been taken to mean that there is a fundamental similarity between both in terms of placing the Ā-operator in question into a structurally higher position. This idea is sketched in (4), which subsumes a number of positions adopted at one point or another in the literature regarding the categories involved.

(4)

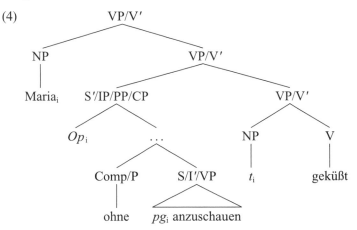

Although there have been proposals to analyze scrambling as A-movement (see Fanselow 1987), a competing position has been to simply equate scrambling with Ā-movement, as for instance by Müller (1993:191). Müller concludes on the basis of the unacceptability of (5) that A-movement, which is commonly assumed in the transformational literature to underly passive formation, cannot license parasitic gaps.[4]

(5) *daß dieses Buch$_i$ [ohne     $pg_i$ zu lesen] dem Jungen $t_i$ gegeben
    that this book    without    to read  the boy       given
    wurde
    was

Although Müller takes this fact to argue for the Ā-movement status of scrambling, a more cautious position is taken by Webelhuth (1989, 1992:209). Webelhuth shares the configurational view underlying the structures in (4), in particular, that the German *Mittelfeld* has a binary and right-branching structure. However, he argues that analyzing the landing site as an Ā-position fails to explain why in (6), an element which has moved into that position (e.g., *die Gäste*), is eligible for binding a reciprocal like *einander*.

(6) ?Peter hat die Gäste₁ [ohne      *pg*ᵢ anzuschauen] einanderᵢ  *t*ᵢ
     Peter has the guests  without       to-look-at     each other
     vorgestellt.
     introduced
     'Peter introduced the guests to each other without looking at
     (them).'

Webelhuth's conclusion is that (6) shows that the landing site for scrambling is neither an argument nor an operator position, and hence that scrambling must lie outside of the usual GB dichotomy of A-versus Ā-movement. Instead, scrambling is to be viewed as a third kind of movement so that "elements in such positions" are not "restricted in their binding potential" (Webelhuth 1992:209). If so, such an element can at the same time bind the anaphor *einander* as well as the parasitic gap.

Whether one adopts Webelhuth's proposal or tries to argue for a more conventional analysis of scrambling as Ā-movement, as Mahajan (1990) does, any movement-based theory of parasitic gap licensing poses a severe challenge to approaches to scrambling without dislocation, as for instance in much of the current unification-based literature. In particular, it is anything but clear how a landing site can be provided in theories (see Uszkoreit 1987, Pollard 1996) that assume a flat structure analysis for the German *Mittelfeld*. The same holds for propsals such as Reape 1996, in which constituent order is accounted for in terms of intermediate levels of structure, which then in effect become invisible in the course of the successive linearization of some involved constituents. Crucially, in none of these theories is there room for a general approach to *Mittelfeld* order variations in terms of true dislocations parallel to GB's Move α, which, on the transformational view, provide the necessary c-command relations for licensing parasitic gaps.

Of central importance in light of these opposing views of order variation, then, is a critical assessment of whether the putative analogues of English P-gap constructions are really syntactically identical to them, as has frequently been claimed—perhaps without sufficient reflection. For terminological convenience, I will continue to refer to examples as in (2) as parasitic gap (P-gap) constructions.

## 9.3 Challenges to Parasitic Gaps in German

It has often been observed that the range of P-gaps in German is significantly smaller than that in English. Although this is doubtless correct, it is not immediately clear whether it follows from the fact that German simply lacks particular structural properties that are involved in many of the English cases or whether deeper differences are at play.

A first challenge to the assumption that P-gap-licensing involves c-command relationships comes from data reported by Santorini (1991), who claims that some German speakers "detect no appreciable contrast between the two word order variants" given in (7).

(7) a. Leider      hat Maria [ohne     $pg_i$ zu beantworten] [alle drei
     unfortunately has Maria without     to answer       all    three
     Briefe]$_i$ weggeworfen.
     letters   thrown-away
     'Unfortunately, Maria threw away all three letters without
     answering them.'
   b. Leider      hat Maria [alle drei   Briefe]$_i$ [ohne     $pg_i$ zu
     unfortunately has Maria all    three letters    without      to
     beantworten] weggeworfen.
     answer       thrown-away
     'Unfortunately, Maria threw away all three letters without
     answering them.'

Given the widely accepted assumption that scrambling only affects arguments, whereas adverbial material stays put, it would seem that the phrase containing the P-gap in (7a), is in a structurally higher position than its understood antecedent, *alle drei Briefe*. Clearly, this presents a problem for those theories of binding that require a tree-configurational asymmetry between antecedent and gap. Therefore, this example seriously challenges the assumed need for a movement operation into a higher position and consequently drives a clear wedge between German and English in this regard. However, judgments on (7a) appear not to be too reliable. For instance, Müller (1993:192, n. 56) disputes Santorini's data, claiming that the contrast arising from the ordering differences "is real and [...] very strong for most speakers." Even though I disagree with this particular assessment, I will skirt issues regarding ordering altogether and concentrate on other evidence in the remainder of this paper.

Another fact that is peculiar from a movement perspective is the lack of P-gap-licensing into extraposed phrases.

(8) *Hans hat Maria$_i$ geküßt [ohne     $pg_i$ anzusehen].
    Hans has Maria   kissed   without      to-look-at

If the German cases are simply an application of the same mechanisms
that are responsible for the missing element in adjuncts in English, then
this is unexpected, especially because of the existence of phenomena such
as the *Third Construction*, in which it appears that an argument (here: *das
Fahrrad*) has been dislocated into the *Mittelfeld* from an extraposed VP:[5]

(9) daß Hans [das Fahrrad]$_i$ versucht [$t_i$ zu reparieren]
    that Hans the bicycle    tries       to repair
    'that Hans tries to repair the bicycle'

Once we consider other candidate dislocation environments for P-gap
in German versus English, it is clear that one will not be able to find a
grammatical German counterpart of the English subject P-gap in (1b)
because the language does not permit English-style preposition stranding,
as shown in (10).

(10) *die Frau,   welche$_i$ deine Attacke [auf $pg_i$] $t_i$ ermutigte
      the woman who    your attack   on         encouraged

A rather similar situation presents itself in Dutch, where extractions from
prepositional phrases is equally ruled out. Yet, Huybregts and van
Riemsdijk (1985:186) claim that if the subject gap is contained in a postpositional phrase, which in general allows extraction, "licit" cases parallel
to (1b) can indeed be found, as shown in (11).

(11) ?Dat   zijn incomplete systemen waar$_i$ [ieder onderzoek    [$pg_i$
      those are  incomplete systems   that     every investigation
      naar]] ernstig  $t_i$ door belemmerd wordt.
      into   seriously  by   impeded    is

However, even though German has corresponding cases in which a pronoun appears dislocated from a postpositional structure (see (12)),[6] P-gap
constructions analogous to the one in (11) appear to be significantly worse
in their acceptability. This is independent of whether the pronoun *da(r)*
occurs dislocated because of scrambling (13) or relative clause formation
(14).

(12) a.   weil    mich [ein Bild [davon]] [davor]       gewarnt hat
          because me   a picture there-of there-against warned  has
          'because a picture of it warned me of it'
     b.   weil    mich da$_i$  [ein Bild] [$t_i$ vor]  gewarnt hat
          because me   there a picture   against warned has
          'because a picture warned me of it'

c. weil mich da$_i$ [ein Bild [$t_i$ von]] gewarnt hat
because me there a picture of warned has
'because a picture of it warned me'

(13) a. *weil mich da$_i$ [ein Bild [$pg_i$ von]] [$t_i$ vor] gewarnt hat
because me there a picture of against warned has
b. *... [$t_i$ drüber] aufgeklärt hat
over enlightened has

(14) a. *Dies ist die Stadt wo$_i$ mich [ein Bild [$pg_i$ von]] [$t_i$ vor]
this is the city where me a picture of against
gewarnt hat.
warned has
b. *... [$t_i$ drüber] aufgeklärt hat
over enlightened has

Other candidate environments licensing P-gaps involve cooccurring gaps in complement clauses and matrix postpositional phrases. For instance, Huybregts and van Riemsdijk (1985:179) state that the Dutch example in (15) is "near perfect."

(15) ?Dit is een boek [waar$_i$ ik [$e_i'$ van] denk [dat Jan [$e_i$ naar] verlangt]]
this is a book which I of think that Jan for longs
'This is a book about which I think that Jan longs for it.'

Although there is disagreement in the literature over which of the gaps is parasitic and which is real, note that corresponding examples in German are strictly ungrammatical, as demonstrated in (16).

(16) *Dies ist ein Umstand [wo$_i$ ich [$e_i'$ von] denke, [daß Ede
this is a circumstance which I of think that Ede
nicht [$e_i$ mit] gerechnet hat]]
not with counted has

However, one area where Dutch and German do converge on a similar pattern—contrasting with English—is the unavailability of parasitic gaps in relative clauses, exemplified by the contrast in (17) ((17b) from Bennis 1987:46).

(17) a. This is the book that$_i$ [everyone [who reads $pg_i$]] becomes enthusiastic about $t_i$.
b. *Dit is het boek dat$_i$ [iedereen [die $pg_i$ leest]] $t_i$ bewondert.
c. *Dies ist das Buch welches$_i$ [jeder [der $pg_i$ liest]] $t_i$ bewundert.

The data in (18) show that extractions from postpositional phrases are similar in this respect.

(18) a. *Dit is een vraag    waar<sub>i</sub> [iedereen [die  [*pg*<sub>i</sub> over] denkt]] een
this is a    question which everyone  who      about thinks an
antwoord [*t*<sub>i</sub> op] weet.
answer       to  knows

   b. *Dies ist ein Umstand    wo/welcher<sub>i</sub> [jeder     [der [*pg*<sub>i</sub> von]
this is a   circumstance where/which everyone who      of
gehört hat]] [*t*<sub>i</sub> mit] rechnen muß.
heard has     with count   must

The explanation for this difference given in Bennis 1986 is that, in Dutch,
the relative clause, following its head noun, is not *canonically* governed,
where *canonical government* amounts to government to the left in an OV
language such as Dutch. Because German is similar to Dutch in this
respect, this explanation would then seem to carry over to the cases in
(17c) and (18b). However, it is unclear how gap licensing in terms of
canonical government can be made to work for German in general. As
has been observed, for instance, by Webelhuth (1992:107), certain finite
complement clauses in German may precede the matrix head, in addition
to the more common extraposed placement option after the verb cluster.

(19) a. weil     ich [daß Hans krank ist] nicht glauben kann
because I    that Hans sick  is  not   believe can
'because I can't believe that Hans is sick'

   b. weil     ich nicht glauben kann [daß Hans krank ist]
because I   not   believe can     that Hans sick  is

Bennis's account would thus predict that the verb *glauben* ('believe') canonically governs its complement clause only in (19a). This would lead us
to expect that in general, extraction is possible in this case, and not in the
(19b) example, hence mirroring the extraction asymmetries from PPs in
Dutch and German. Yet, we find exactly the opposite: extraction is only
possible where the complement follows the verb, as in (20b).

(20) a. *Wen<sub>i</sub> hast du  [daß Maria *t*<sub>i</sub> liebt] geglaubt?
who  have you  that Maria    loves believed

   b. Wen<sub>i</sub> hast du  geglaubt [daß Maria *t*<sub>i</sub> liebt]?
who  have you believed  that Maria    loves
'Who did you believe Maria loves?'

Following Webelhuth, we may, then, take these facts as indicating that
CP complements in German are base-generated to the right of their verbal
heads, which is also the direction of θ-government in this case.[7] If this
notion of government, rather than canonical government, is responsible
for licensing Ā-positions, as Bennis and Hoekstra (1985b:7) claim, it

becomes difficult to see what exactly prevents long-distance dependencies within the adjunct phrase. As demonstrated in (21b), such examples are ungrammatical in German even when the extraction from the complement clause is permitted, as shown in (21a) (see also Bennis 1986:54).[8]

(21) a.  Welche Bücher$_i$ hast du  gewußt [daß du  $t_i$ anschauen
         which  books   have you known  that you   look-at
         durftest]?
         could
         'Which books did you know that you were allowed to look at?'
     b. *Welche Bücher$_i$ hast du  [ohne    zu wissen [$t_i'$ [daß du  $pg_i$
         which  books   have you  without  to know          that you
         anschauen durftest]]] $t_i$ durchgeblättert?
         look-at   could        browsed-though

I take this discussion to show that the occurrence of candidate P-gap cases in German is significantly more limited than in Dutch, which in turn is more restrictive than English. Although the Dutch facts may still be subsumable under an approach based on filler-gap dependencies, the corresponding case for German is much more tenuous. This strongly suggests that explanations for putative parasitic-gap constructions such as in (2) ought to be sought without appealing to syntactic dislocation phenomena.

I now turn to evidence that argues for an approach that on the one hand recognizes the basic lexical basis of the phenomenon and on the other hand makes its relationship to coordinate constructions clear. First, let us survey the scope of potential German P-gap constructions.

## 9.4  Parasitic Gap Construction Candidates

The range of phenomena that remain as P-gap candidates consists of adverbial phrases with the verb in the form of a *zu*-infinitive. There are no more than three lexical items that can head such phrases: *ohne* ('without'), *(an)statt* ('instead'), and *um* ('in order to'). When these elements take a full VP complement without a gap, the phrases can occur either inside the *Mittelfeld* or extraposed, shown in (22) and (23).

(22) a. Hans hat Maria [ohne    sie anzusehen] geküßt.
        Hans has Maria  without her look-at    kissed
        'Hans kissed Maria without looking at her.'
     b. Lisa hat Hans [anstatt   ihn zu küssen] geohrfeigt.
        Lisa has Hans  instead-of him to kiss   slapped-in-the-face.
        'Lisa slapped Hans in the face instead of kissing him.'

   c. Lisa hat Hans [um       ihn  zu überzeugen] belogen.
      Lisa has Hans in-order-to him to convince    lied-to
      'Lisa lied to Hans in order to convince him.'

(23) a. Hans hat Maria geküßt [ohne     sie anzusehen].
       Hans has Maria kissed  without her to-look-at
       'Hans kissed Maria without looking at her.'
    b. Lisa hat Hans geohrfeigt       [anstatt   ihn zu küssen].
       Lisa has Hans slapped-in-the-face instead-of him to kiss
       'Lisa slapped Hans in the face instead of kissing him.'
    c. Lisa hat Hans belogen [um        ihn zu überzeugen].
       Lisa has Hans lied-to   in-order-to him to convince
       'Lisa lied to Hans in order to convince him.'

The pattern of grammaticality that emerges if any of the phrases in (22) contains a gap is that *anstatt*-phrases appear to enjoy widespread acceptance, whereas *um*-phrases are universally rejected, as shown in (24).[9]

(24) a.  Lisa hat Hans$_i$ [anstatt    $pg_i$ zu küssen] geohrfeigt.
       Lisa has Hans  instead-of   to kiss     slapped-in-the-face
    b.  *Lisa hat Hans$_i$ [um      $pg_i$ zu überzeugen] belogen.
       Lisa has Hans  in-order-to   to convince   lied-to

Judgments on *ohne*-phrases range greatly, but they appear to be better than marginally acceptable to many speakers.

   Again, if what licenses the missing constituent in the acceptable cases was truely syntactic in nature, analogous to genuine P-gap constructions in English, this pattern of variation would be surprising. Moreover, any attempt at deriving the badness of (24b) from some semantic factor would be hard put to explain why its English counterpart in (25) is impeccable.

(25) This is the man that$_i$ Lisa lied to $t_i$ [in order to convince $pg_i$]

This pattern suggests that the lexical involvement of the prepositional head plays a crucial role in the proper description of the construction. Before making a concrete proposal to that effect, I want to explore some of the ways in which P-gap constructions share properties with coordinate structures.

## 9.5  Pseudo Parasitic Gap Properties

An important insight to be pursued here is that on the basis of Postal's (1994a) typology distinguishing between genuine and pseudo-P-gap constructions, the German phenomenon patterns with the second class. In particular, Postal (1994a:113) in discussing the Dutch counterparts of (1) suggests that such cases should be taken to "involve an analog of English noncoordinate RNR [Right Node Raising], that is noncoordinate LNR [Left Node Raising]." The analogy between the Dutch and German P-gap constructions with coordination has been noted in the literature by Huybregts and van Riemsdijk (1985) and Yatabe (1993), among others.[10] In concrete terms, this means that (2a) should receive a treatment that puts it into a single class with coordinative constructions such as (26), in which the object *Maria* is shared among the two conjuncts *zuerst lange angesehen* and *dann leidenschaftlich geküßt*. Unlike in English RNR, the shared material has to precede, rather than follow the conjuncts, hence the reference to a leftward occurrence of the conjunct factor (here: *Maria*).

(26) Hans hat Maria$_i$ [zuerst lange $t_i$ angesehen] und [dann
     Hans has Maria  first   long    looked-at  and  then
     leidenschaftlich $t_i$ geküßt]
     passionately    kissed
     'Hans looked at Maria for a long time and then kissed her
     passionately.'

A number of properties of the German P-gap construction fall into place if such a proposal is adopted.

    First, LNR-like constructions involving different verbal heads with partially overlapping argument structure are only permitted if those heads occur in clause-final position—that is, either in subordinate contexts or as nonfinite dependents of auxiliaries. Therefore no sharing of any argument is possible if one of the predicates involved occurs fronted (i.e., in a root clause verb-first or verb-second structure).[11]

(27) a. *Hans sah    Maria [erst lange an] und [dann leidenschaftlich
       Hans looked Maria first long at  and  then  passionately
       geküßt hat]
       kissed has
  b. *Hans sah    Maria [erst lange an] und [küßte dann
       Hans looked Maria first long at  and  kissed then
       leidenschaftlich]
       passionately

The analogy with LNR constructions sheds new light on an observation that so far has not received any explanation in the literature, namely that German P-gap constructions in general seem significantly degraded in their acceptability if the finite main verb occurs fronted. In such structures, the finite verb precedes the shared *Mittelfeld* argument in contrast to the nonfinite verb within the adjunct phrase, which necessarily has to follow that argument:[12]

(28) a. ??Hans küßte Maria$_i$ [ohne     $pg_i$ anzusehen]
        Hans kissed Maria  without    to-look-at
     b. *Hans sah     Maria$_i$ [ohne     $pg_i$ zu küssen] lange an.
        Hans looked Maria  without    to kiss    long   at

If German P-gap constructions were a direct analogue of true P-gap constructions in English, this sensitivity to verb placement would be totally unexpected. Under that analysis, all that matters would be that the *ohne*-phrase be in the proper structural relationship with respect to the antecedent of the parasitic gap. But given that the finite verb in the main clause has no direct involvement in the licensing of the parasitic gap, its placement should be orthogonal to the well-formedness of the construction— contrary to fact.

Another virtue of the LNR-based approach is that it presents a straightforward solution to a challenge to Webelhuth's analysis, reported by Mahajan (1990:56). The question is why the sentence in (29), with both direct and indirect object before the PP adverbial, should be degraded.[13]

(29) a. ??Peter hat jeden Gast$_i$     seinem Nachbarn    [ohne    $pg_i$
        Peter has each  guest-ACC his      neighbor-DAT without
        anzuschauen] vorgestellt.
        to-look-at     introduced
     b.  Peter hat jeden Gast$_i$  [ohne    $pg_i$ anzuschauen] seinem
        Peter has each  guest-ACC without   to-look-at    his
        Nachbarn    vorgestellt.
        neighbor-DAT introduced
        'Peter introduced each guest to his neighbor without looking at
        him (= the guest).'

This pattern is completely analogous to the distribution of grammaticality judgments seen with the corresponding coordinate LNR constructions.[14]

(30) a. *Peter hat jeden Gast$_i$     seinem Nachbarn    [kurz $t_i$
        Peter has each  guest-ACC his      neighbor-DAT briefly
        angeredet] und [dann $t_i$ vorgestellt].
        addressed  and  then    introduced

b.  Peter hat jeden Gast$_i$      [kurz $t_i$ angeredet] und [dann $t_i$
    Peter has each  guest-ACC  briefly addressed and  then
    seinem Nachbarn      vorgestellt].
    his      neighbor-DAT introduced
    'Peter briefly addressed each guest and then introduced him
    (= the guest) to his neighbor.'

What this difference in grammaticality indicates is that any material that
only belongs to the second conjunct must not occur in a place where it
precedes both conjuncts. Similarly, in the P-gap cases, the occurrence of
an argument before the *ohne*-phrase strongly suggests that is has to be
construed not only with the modified predicate (here: *vorstellen*) but also
with the verbal head of the *ohne*-phrase. However, in the example at
hand, the monotransitive verb *anschauen* does not permit a dative complement. The ill-formedness of (29a) would be quite unexpected if the sole
factor determining grammaticality is whether the gap is matched with an
antecedent in the proper configurational relation. The intervention of
other arguments, such as the dative object *seinem Nachbarn* should not be
significant.

Next, note that dative objects can participate in the P-gap construction
just as much as accusatives:

(31) a.  Karl hat seiner Tochter$_i$      [ohne    $pg_i$ Geld   zu geben]
         Karl has his    daughter-DAT without     money to give
         helfen können.
         help  could
         'Karl was able to help his daughter without giving her money.'
     b.  Karl hat seiner Tochter$_i$      [anstatt    $pg_i$ zu helfen] einen
         Karl has his    daughter-DAT instead-of     to help    an
         Kündigungsbrief geschickt.
         eviction-letter     sent
         'Karl sent his daughter an eviction note instead of helping her.'

Not too surprisingly, the same also holds true of coordinate LNR
constructions.

(32)  Karl hat seiner Tochter$_i$      [erst nicht $t_i$ helfen wollen] aber [dann
      Karl has his    daughter-DAT first not    help  wanted but   then
      $t_i$ Geld   gegeben].
         money given
      'Karl did not want to help his daugher at first, but then sent her
      money.'

In general there exists a strict requirement of case matching between the missing argument of the adverbial phrase and the P-gap controller.[15] Thus, in (33a) a missing accusative object of *informieren* is illicitly matched against the dative phrase *seiner Tochter*, whereas in (33b) the distribution of missing and overt cases is reversed, resulting in ungrammaticality as well.

(33) a. ?*Hans hat seiner Tochter$_i$      [ohne $pg_i$ davon  zu
Hans has his     daughter-DAT without  thereof to
informieren] DM 100 überwiesen.
inform         DM 100 wired
Intended reading: 'Hans wired his daughter 100 DM without telling her of it.'

b.  *Hans hat seine  Tochter$_i$      [ohne $pg_i$ Geld   zu geben]
Hans has his    daughter-ACC without  money to give
unterstützen können.
support        could
Intended reading: 'Hans was able to help his daughter without sending her money.'

This matching of case requirements is also seen with coordinate LNR constructions.

(34) *Hans möchte      seine/seiner    Tochter$_i$ [Geld $t_i$ geben] und
Hans would-like his-ACC/his-DAT daughter  money give     and
[auch moralisch $t_i$ unterstützen]
also  morally      support

Coordinate LNR constructions also allow for situations in which more than one phrase is shared among both conjuncts (see (35)), in which both the accusative *den Käfer* as well as the dative *seiner Tochter* are construed with either predicate.

(35) Karl hat den Käfer$_i$      seiner Tochter$_j$     [erst     $t_i$ $t_j$ schenken
Karl has the VW Beetle his     daughter-DAT at-first      give
wollen] aber [dann $t_i$ $t_j$ teuer       verkauft].
wanted but   then        expensively sold
'Karl first wanted to give the VW Beetle to his daughter for free, but then he sold it to her for much money.'

An LNR-based approach to German straightforwardly predicts that multiple P-gap constructions should be possible in that language—a prediction that is indeed borne out by facts such as (36).

(36) ?Karl hat den Käfer$_i$          seiner Tochter$_j$     [anstatt
     Karl has the VW Beetle-ACC his    daughter-DAT instead-of
     $pg_i$ $pg_j$ zu schenken] teuer          verkauft.
                to give       expensively sold
     'Karl sold the VW Beetle to his daugher for much money instead of
     giving it to her.'

Analogous cases for English have been reported by Williams
(1990:277):[16]

(37) Which book$_i$ do you wonder who$_j$ [Bill told $t_j$ that Mary bought $t_i$]
     [before Sam persuaded $pg_j$ that Mary wanted $pg_i$]?

Williams observes that in such cases it is not possible to only replace one
parasitic gap with a pronoun. That is, the presence of one parasitic gap
requires that the other dependent element is also realized as a gap:

(38) a. *Which book$_i$ do you wonder who$_j$ [Bill told $t_j$ that Mary
        bought $t_i$] [before Sam persuaded $pg_j$ that Mary wanted it]?
     b. *Which book$_i$ do you wonder who$_j$ [Bill told $t_j$ that Mary
        bought $t_i$] [before Sam persuaded him that Mary wanted $pg_j$]?

No such constraint appears to apply in German; thus in the following
variant of (36) both the direct and indirect object putatively have been
dislocated (by topicalization or scrambling, respectively), yet, the *anstatt*-
phrase can contain a coreferential dative pronoun.

(39) Den Käfer$_i$          hat ihr Karl [anstatt     $pg_i$ ihr zu schenken]
     the  VW Beetle-ACC has her Karl  instead-of   her to give
     teuer          verkauft.
     expensively sold
     'Karl sold the VW Beetle to her for much money instead of giving
     it to her for free.'

    Another consequence of the coordinate LNR approach is the predic-
tion that the language should allow for P-gap controllers other than NPs.
As is illustrated in (40), PP complements are eligible coordinate factors in
LNR constructions. Quite significantly, data such as (40b) suggest that PP
complements can also marginally occur in P-gap constructions.[17]

(40) a. Unsere Firma     hat [mit  der Konkurrenz]$_i$ [lange $t_i$
        our     company has whit the competition    long
        verhandelt] und [schließlich $t_i$ einen Vertrag abgeschlossen]
        negotiated and  finally        a contract    signed
        'Our company negotiated with the competition for a long time
        and finally signed a contract with them.'

b. ?Unsere Firma    hat [mit  dem Vertreter]ᵢ    [ohne    lange
   our     company has  with the  representative without long
   *pg*ᵢ zu reden] einen Vertrag abgeschlossen.
       to talk   a     treaty    signed
   'Our company signed a treaty with the representative without
   talking to him for long.'

The relative well-formedness of (40) is significant in light of Postal's
(1994a) criteria, according to which non-NP gaps are precluded in genuine P-gap constructions whereas they are possible in pseudo-P-gap
constructions. Inasmuch as English-type genuine P-gap constructions
represent a phenomenon with properties that have crosslinguistic validity,
this strongly suggests that German P-gap constructions do not group with
English true P-gap cases.

## 9.6  Control Properties

Although a substantial subset of the properties of German P-gap constructions strongly suggests a close constructional relationship with LNR
structures, there nevertheless seems to be a residue that requires reference
to lexical relations mediated by the prepositional head.

In particular, infinitival PP constructions have control properties that
play a crucial role in explaining some facts that do not seem to be immediately derivable from the LNR status. For instance, consider again the
unacceptability of Müller's example in (5), repeated here:

(5) *daß dieses Buchᵢ [ohne      *pg*ᵢ zu lesen] dem Jungen *t*ᵢ gegeben
     that this   book   without       to read  the  boy       given
     wurde
     was

On the face of it, this sentence should be grammatical because the accusative NP *dieses Buch* is matched with the object of *zu lesen* as well as the
direct object of *geben*. However, what would be ignored is the fact that
the *ohne*-PP requires a controller for its understood subject and that this
controller must be in general clause-internal. The only NP meeting this
criterion is *dieses Buch*, but this phrase cannot be an eligible controller of
the *ohne*-phrase for semantic reasons. Thus, the unacceptability follows
from the failure to provide a controller for the adjunct phrase.[18] The
control-based explanation is clearly superior to Müller's because it naturally extends not only to the P-gap-less variants of (5) in (41), but also

to cases such as those in (42) where no passive is involved and hence no putative A-movement could have taken place. Rather, the badness of that example is due to the semantic anomaly arising from the required association of the inanimate noun *der Titel* with the agent role of *zu lesen*.

(41) a. *daß dieses Buch$_i$ [ohne     es$_i$ zu lesen] dem Jungen gegeben
         that this  book  without it  to read  the boy    given
         wurde
         was

     b. *daß dieses Buch$_i$ dem Jungen gegeben wurde [ohne    es$_i$ zu
         that this  book  the  boy    given   was   without it  to
         lesen]
         read

(42) a. *daß der Titel dieses Buch$_i$ [ohne     *pg*$_i$ zu lesen] in   die
         that the title this  book  without      to read  into the
         Bestsellerliste    katapultierte
         bestseller charts  tossed

     b. *daß der Titel dieses Buch$_i$ [ohne     es$_i$ zu lesen] in   die
         that the title this  book  without it  to read  into the
         Bestsellerliste    katapultierte
         bestseller charts  tossed

On the basis of structural considerations alone, these examples should be impeccable. Hence Müller's account of (5) in terms of movement types offers no explanation of the ill-formedness.

Next, consider again the boundedness of relations between the filler and the P-gap gap site. Although in general more restricted than in English, long-distance dependencies generally tend to be acceptable in German if they involve PP arguments. Example (43a) features the well-formed fronting of a PP which is construed with gaps in two conjuncts, the first gap occurring within a complement clause. But, like the related example in (21b), the corresponding P-gap example is ungrammatical.

(43) a. [Mit wem]$_i$ hat Hans vermutet    [daß wir lange $t_i$ verhandelt
         with whom has Hans conjectured  that we  long      negotiated
         hatten] und [deshalb  sofort       $t_i$ einen Vertrag
         had     and  therefore immediately      a    treaty
         geschlossen]?
         signed
         'Who did Hans think that we had been negotiating with and
         therefore sign a treaty with immediately?'

b. *[Mit wem]ᵢ hat Hans [ohne      zu vermuten  [daß wir lange *pg*ᵢ
with whom has Hans without to conjecture that we long
verhandelt hatten]] einen Vertrag *t*ᵢ geschlossen?
negotiated had    a       treaty    signed

Given that "pure" coordination constructions in general are not sensitive
to the structural complexity of the conjuncts involved, this pattern would
be unexpected if the P-gap cases were exhaustively described as LNR
constructions.

By contrast, the different behavior in (43) receives a natural explanation
if the argument structures in the P-gap cases are lexically linked together
by the head of the PP modifier. In particular, this means that prepositions
such as *ohne* and *(an)statt* should be thought of as fusing (parts of) their
argument structures with that of the V′ category they modify to form a
complex predicate of sorts. To make matters concrete, I adopt the framework of Head-driven Phrase Structure Grammar (HPSG; see Pollard and
Sag 1987, 1994) in displaying the lexical information involved, even
though other frameworks with a sufficiently articulated theory of lexical
information could serve for this purpose as well. In (44) I list a schematic
feature description for *ohne* and *(an)statt*.

(44)
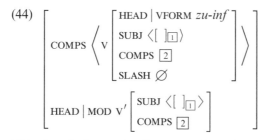

This description embodies a number of assumptions about the representation of lexical information assumed in recent versions of HPSG. Specifically, the infinitival complement of the preposition is given as the value
of the COMP(LEMENT)s attribute, and the value of the feature MOD(IFIED)
states what the whole PP modifies, that is, a verbal projection (which I
will here call "V′" for convenience). Note that the level of saturation of
the latter, again given by the COMPS attribute, is given as the tag [2]—that
is, a variable over lists including the empty list. Whatever the instantiation, the level of saturation of the PP adverbial is guaranteed to be exactly
the same as that of the modified V′ owing to structure sharing between
both COMPS values indicated by the coreference tag [2]. I will refer to this
characteristic (partial) unification of valence properties among modifier
and modifiee as *Valence Matching*.

There is also structure sharing involved between the understood subject of the PP-adverbial and the syntactically expressed subject of the V'. This provides an immediate explanation as for why structures such as (5), in which no appropriate controller for the *ohne*-phrase can be found, are bad. Yet, the information shared only consists of the *index*, not the entire syntactic category. Notationally this is reflected by the subscripted occurrence of the coreference tag ($\boxed{1}$). Structure sharing of index information is the canonical way in HPSG of analyzing control phenomena, and I propose to analyze the subject identification of infinitival PP adjuncts as an instance of lexically constrained control.

The analysis proposed here has a number of consequences. Given that the linkage between the subject of the adverbial clause and the modified V' is one of control, and not of part of Valence Matching proper, nonnominative NPs should be expected to serve as subjects for both predicates. This is so because according to the HPSG feature architecture, CASE is not an attribute borne by indices and can therefore vary across two coindexed elements. This prediction is indeed borne out when we consider cases such as the so-called AcI constructions. In these, like their English raising-to-object counterparts, the subject of the lower predicate (here: *ihren Bruder*) bears accusative case. Despite the accusative case marking, that phrase is construed as the subject for the adverbial phrase *ohne zu reparieren*.

(45) Maria ließ ihren Bruder      den alten Wagen [ohne   zu
     Maria let   her   brother-ACC the old   car     without to
     reparieren] nach Italien fahren.
     repair      to   Italy   drive
     'Maria let her brother drive the car to Italy without (him) repairing it.'

But it should not be possible in general to share complements if the predicates involved impose different requirements on those shared complements. In fact, this is precisely what was found earlier in the examples in (33).

The kind of structures licensed by the lexical description in (44) are outlined in (46). Note in particular that, in contrast to the structure in (4), no (analogue of) a filler-gap relation is involved between the shared constituent (here: the object *Maria*) and any putative extraction site within the V' (nor within the PP modifier, for that matter). As a consequence, no reference to tree configuration needs to be made.

(46)

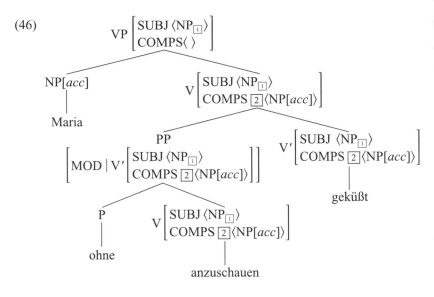

## 9.7    Conclusion

What I hope to have shown in the present study is that candidates for parasitic gap constructions in German must be distinguished from "true" P-gap constructions in English in the sense of Postal (1994a). A number of properties were identified that group those constructions with English pseudo-P-gap constructions, in particular, as "noncoordinate LNR," as initially suggested by Postal (1994a:113). Although this style of analysis offers an explanation for some of the striking conditions on linear par-ellelism, it does not appear that the construction can be accounted for in its entirety in those terms. In particular, the lack of any long-distance dependencies and the sensitivity to the choice of preposition suggest that the phenomenon is lexically mediated by the prepositional head of the adverbial phrase, which in turn is responsible for the matching of valence requirements of the verbal predicates involved.

### Notes

The present chapter is an substantially revised and extended version of earlier work (Kathol 1995), first presented at the Fifth Meeting of the Formal Linguistic Society of Midamerica (May, 1994), University of Illinois, Champaign–Urbana. For discussion I am grateful to Bob Levine, Carl Pollard, and Gert Webelhuth. I would also like to thank the editors of this volume for many helpful suggestions. I claim responsibility for all remaining errors.

1. Felix also discusses different P-gap-like constructions in Bavarian German, illustrated in (i) (similar cases are discussed in Lutz 1997).

(i) Das ist der Kerl, den$_i$ wenn ich $e_i$ erwisch, erschlag   ich $e_i$.
   that is the guy   who when I      catch   beat-dead I
   'That is the guy who I will beat to death when I catch him.'

Such constructions are utterly impossibly in standard varieties and hence will not be further considered here.

2. See, for instance, Bennis and Hoekstra (1985b:2):

Given the peripheral nature of the parasitic-gap construction and the methodology of GB-theory, grammars of particular languages should not contain any statements specific to the parasitic-gap phenomenon.

3. An underlying presupposition of this claim is that parasitic gaps also form a single class within English. However, as Postal (1994a) convincingly shows, the class is actually heterogeneous and it is necessary to distinguish pseudoparasitic gap constructions from "true" P-gap phenomena. Unless otherwise stated, the following comparison with English will reference the latter class only.

4. Müller (1993) rejects reducing the badness of (5) to a case conflict. Citing the example in (i) from Bayer (1988:420), he argues that case mismatches between the P-gap and the "real gap" are possible so long as the antecedent's morphology is nondistinct from either case specification (here: dative and genitive, respectively):

(i) Dieser Dame$_i$ hätte er sich [ohne      $pg$-D schon mal Geld    angeboten zu
   this   lady   had he self without      already   money offered    to
   haben] $t_i$-G niemals erinnern   können.
   have          never   remember could
   'He never could have remembered this lady if he hadn't offered her money once before.'

I find the grammaticality of this example highly dubious.
   Nevertheless, as I will argue in section 9.4, Müller's argument is still independently flawed because it overlooks important constraints regarding the control of the *ohne*-phrase.

5. For a movement-based analysis of the Third Construction, see Rambow 1994. For an example of a lexicalist alternative without scrambling, see Hinrichs and Nakazawa 1998.

6. Cases like these do not seem to qualify as giving rise to parasitic gap environments in the strict sense because, as (12b–c) show, either postpositional phrase appears to license extraction independently of the other. The ungrammaticality of the examples in (13)–(14) thus presents a puzzle for any analysis that appeals to a filler-gap dependency between *da* and its putative base position within the PP. See Oppenrieder 1991 for discussion of an alternative approach.

7. This would also be in line with Zwart's (1997) proposal of an underlying SVO order for Dutch and German or Kayne's (1994) suggestion that the underlying SVO order holds universally.

8. Interestingly, (Bennis 1986:52–54) does discuss the Dutch equivalent of (21b), which is also ungrammatical. He argues that the ungrammaticality is an ECP

effect induced by lack of canonical government under the assumption that parasitic gaps are licensed nonderivationally. This, however, is in contradiction to the position taken by Chomsky (1986b:56), who argues for a null operator, and hence derivational, theory of P-gap licensing.

9. It may not be insignificant that a search of the *Frankfurter Rundschau* corpus comprising 40 million words (2 million sentences) revealed no clear example of a P-gap construction with either preposition.

The overwhelming majority of occurrences of adverbial phrases with *ohne* or *(an)statt* occur extraposed, as in the examples in (23). Though much rarer, examples of the pattern in (22) can indeed be found—that is, examples with the adverbial phrase occurring in the *Mittelfeld* and containing a pronoun coreferential with a preceding case-identical NP:

(i) a. Dann habe der Täter [ ... ] den Afrikaner$_i$, [ohne ihn$_i$ mit dem [ ... ]
   Küchenmesser zu treffen], angegriffen [ ... ]
   'Then the perpetrator is supposed to have attacked the African without
   hitting him with the kitchen knife ...'

   b. wenn er die Liebhaber$_i$, [anstatt sie$_i$ drastisch mit eigener Hand zu töten],
   durch einen [ ... ] Riesenpfeil verscheuchen läßt
   'when he has the lovers be chased away by a huge arrow instead of killing
   them with his own hand'

10. See Postal 1993b for a critical assessment of Williams's (1990) proposal for an Across-the-Board extraction analysis of all P-gap phenomena in English.

11. This can be derived from the fact that the verb placement of each of the conjuncts has to be consistent with the syntactic environment in which the conjunction occurs—that is, either as root clauses (clause-initial) or as subordinate clauses (clause-final).

12. Further evidence for this sensitivity to linear relations comes from the fact that, at least in my judgment, *wh*-interrogative versions of (28) in which the shared object precedes the finite verb seem noticeably better.

(i) a. ?Wen$_i$ küßte Hans [ohne     pg$_i$ anzusehen] t$_i$?
      who   kissed Hans without      to-look-at
      'Who did Hans kiss without looking at?'

   b. ?Wen$_i$ sah    Hans [ohne     pg$_i$ zu küssen] t$_i$ lange an?
      who   looked Hans without      to kiss      long  at
      'Who did Hans look at for a long time without kissing?'

13. Similar examples are judged to be only slightly marginal by Lee and Santorini (1994:8), but for me the difference in grammaticality between (29a) and (29b) seems robust.

14. Moreover, as Yatabe (1993:207) points out, the distinction in question is observed independently of any anaphoric dependencies:

(i) a. ??Peter hat jeden Gast$_i$     dem Studenten [ohne     pg$_i$ anzuschauen]
      Peter has each  guest-ACC the  student-DAT without      to-look-at
      vorgestellt.
      introduced

b.  Peter hat jeden Gast$_i$    [ohne    $pg_i$ anzuschauen] dem Studenten
Peter has each  guest-ACC without    to-look-at    the student-DAT
vorgestellt.
introduced
'Peter introduced each guest to the student without looking at him
(= the guest).'

15. Bayer (1988:420) reports systematic exceptions to this constraint, cases in which the morphological realization of the different cases involved is not distinct. Thus, (ia) (repeated from note 5) is claimed to be better than expected given that the dative case of the object of *anbieten* does not seem to match the genitive complement of *entsinnen*. Whatever the operative constraints at work here, the same pattern can also be observed with coordinate LNR constructions, which seem no worse, as shown in (ib).

(i) a.  Dieser Dame$_i$ hätte er sich [ohne    $pg_i$ schon mal Geld    angeboten zu
this    lady    had he self without    already    money offered    to
haben] niemals entsinnen    können.
have    never    remembered could
'He never would have been able to remember this lady if he hadn't offered her money before.'

b.  Dieser Dame$_i$ hat sich Hans [zunächst nicht $t_i$ entsinnen  können] aber
this    lady    has self Hans at-first    not    remember could    but
[dann später $t_i$ DM 100 angeboten]
then later    DM 100 offered

'At first Hans couldn't remember this lady, but later he offered her
100 DM.'

16. Furthermore, as has been pointed out to me by Peter Culicover (personal communication), English also allows more than one shared constituent in coordinate and adverbial modification constructions in the case of reordering of complex constituents within the VP:

(i) a.  (?)Carl first wanted to give, but then sold (for a considerable sum), the
VW Beetle (that he had been driving) to his daughter.
b.  Carl first wanted to give, but then sold (for a considerable sum) to his
daughter the VW Beetle that he had been driving.

(ii)    ?Carl gave instead of selling (for a considerable sum) the VW that he
had been driving to his daughter.

17. However, additional factors, presumably semantic in origin, often render constructions with shared PP arguments rather unacceptable even when the same prepositional head is compatible with either predicate (see (ia)). Whatever the constraints at work, though, it appears that corresponding LNR cases are no better (see (ib)).

(i) a.  ??Hans hat [an Gott]$_i$ [ohne    wirklich $pg_i$ zu glauben] einen Brief
Hans has to God    without really    to believe a    letter
geschrieben.
written
'Hans wrote a letter to God without really believing in Him.'

  b.  *Hans hat [an Gott]ᵢ [weder $t_i$ geglaubt] noch [einen Brief $t_i$ geschrieben].
      Hans has to God    neither  believed  nor  a      letter   written

18.  The same explanation also covers examples such as in (i), which Grewendorf
(1988:305) adduces as indirect evidence for *pro*-subjects in German.

(i)  *ein Mann, derᵢ [ohne $pg_i$ zu kennen] eingeladen wurde
      a   man   who  without  to know    invited    was

Grewendorf claims that if the relative clause in (i) did not contain such an empty
subject element, there would be no way to rule out the sentence as a violation
of the anti-c-command constraint on parasitic gaps. But as with Müller's earlier
example, the sentence does not contain any eligible controller for the *ohne*-phrase.
Note that *der*, the subject of the passive phrase *eingeladen wurde*, could not act as
the controller because, notwithstanding semantic implausibility, *kennen* would be
deprived of an antecedent for its understood object. The fact that Grewendorf's
argument is undermined by the arguably simpler explanation offered here is in
accord with the generally highly dubious status of *pro*-subjects in German.

# PART IV
## Restrictions on Parasitic Gaps

# Chapter 10

## On Some Distinctive Properties of Parasitic Gaps in French

Christine Tellier

### 10.1 Introduction

Parasitic gaps (P-gaps) in English have been argued to exist with varying degrees of marginality in a variety of environments: within infinitival and gerundive adjunct clauses, within subjects, within relative clauses, within tensed complement clauses, and within tensed adjuncts. With respect to gerundive clauses, French (and more generally, Romance) patterns like English in allowing P-gaps. This is shown in (1); in all the examples, *t* is the real gap, and *e* is the P-gap.

(1) a. This is the book that you destroyed *t* while reading *e*.
    b. Voilà le livre que vous avez abîmé *t* en feuilletant *e*.

This paper focuses on four contexts where the distribution of P-gaps in French differs from that in English.

First, tensed adjuncts may host P-gaps in English but not in French:

(2) a. This is the report that you filed *t* after John had read *e*.
    b. *Voilà le rapport que tu as rangé *t* après que Jean ait lu *e*.

Secondly, P-gaps may occur within relatives in English; this is impossible in French:

(3) a. This is a boy who [everyone who has met *e*] thinks *t* is clever.
    b. *Voilà le garçon que [tous ceux qui ont rencontré *e*] trouvent *t* intelligent.

A third, related difference between English and French appears in the context of complement object deletion (COD) constructions. Strikingly, whereas the *easy-to-please* construction licenses PGs, its French counterpart does not:

(4) a.   These papers are difficult to evaluate *t* without having read *e* in
         detail.
    b.   *Ces articles sont difficiles à évaluer *t* sans avoir lus *e* en détail.

Finally, French and English both allow P-gaps within certain DPs. However, as Frampton (1990:60) points out, determiner choice has an effect
on the possibility of P-gaps in English:

(5) a.   A man who [friends of *e*] admire *t*.
    b.   *A man who [the friends of *e*] admire *t*.

(6) a.   Jack, who [everyone who likes *e*] visited *t* ...   = Frampton's (13)
    b.   ??Jack, who [the man who likes *e*] visited *t* ...

French behaves differently in this respect. In fact, DP-internal P-gaps are
more often found when the DP is headed by the definite determiner:[1]

(7) Un homme dont       l'honnêteté *t* se voit dans [les  yeux *e*]
    a   man    of-whom the-honesty is-seen in      the  eyes
    'A man whose honesty can be seen in his eyes.'

The analysis I propose of these contrasts relies on independent differences
in the agreement systems of French and English, with particular reference to the CP/DP layers. As will be shown, the proposed analysis
accounts for a further asymmetry manifested in the distribution of P-gaps
in French: though most nonfinite adjunct clauses may host PGs, not all of
them do:

(8) a.   Voilà les livres que tu   as   déchirés *t* au lieu de consulter *e*.
         here  the books that you have torn       instead of consult-INF
         'Here are the books that you tore instead of consulting.'
    b.   *Voilà les livres que tu   as   rangés *t*  de manière à
         here  the books that you have put away so-as     to
         retrouver *e* facilement.
         find-INF    easily
         'Here are the books that you put away so as to retrieve easily.'

The paper is organized as follows. Section 10.2 deals with the tense effect
in Romance and English P-gap constructions. Section 10.3 discusses the
licensing conditions on null operators and the role of tensed complementizers in this regard. Section 10.4 deals with French nonfinite adjunct
clauses; it presents an asymmetry in the distribution of P-gaps. The relation between P-gap occurrence and the type of nonfinite complementizer
is also discussed. Section 10.5 examines the properties of *easy-to-please*

constructions in French, with particular reference to their inability to license P-gaps. Finally, section 10.6 treats PGs within DPs in French and in English: it is argued that the observed differences can be traced back to independent differences in the agreement systems within DP.

## 10.2    Finite Adjunct Clauses

### 10.2.1    Tense Effects in English and Romance

As was mentioned in the introduction, P-gaps within tensed adjuncts are excluded in French; this is true of any type of adjunct (temporal, manner, purpose, etc.). What needs to be discussed is the extent of the contrast between French and English in this regard.

The existence of tense effects in P-gap constructions was pointed out by Engdahl (1983:9), who noted that tense domains are less accessible to P-gaps than untensed domains. However, she observes that there is no discernable tense effect in English temporal adjuncts: that is, there is no contrast between (9a,b) (= Engdahl's (8)/(2)).

(9) a. This is the kind of food you must cook *t* before eating *e*.

b. This is the kind of food you must cook *t* before you eat *e*.

The relative lack of tense effects with P-gaps in English apparently manifests in other types of adjunct clause as well. Barss (1986:377–378) gives the following examples:

(10) a. It was him that Mary recognized *t* because he had described *e* so well.

b. It was him that John claimed Mary liked *t* even though he knew she hated *e*.

Acceptable examples of P-gaps within tensed adjuncts are also given by Chomsky (1986b:54,57) and Lasnik and Stowell (1991:692), among others. According to Stowell (1986), in the case of object extraction, English P-gaps are immune to the tense effect. But Frampton (1990:71) finds that tense decreases grammaticality in P-gap constructions, although he evaluates its effect as mild compared to that induced in *wh*-island constructions. All in all, then, most authors agree that in English, adjunct-internal object P-gaps display rather weak tense effects for those speakers who detect them.[2]

In French, however, the tense effect is very robust: no speaker accepts (11b), the counterpart of (9b).

(11) a.  C'est le  genre de plat que tu  dois cuire *t* avant de
this-is the type  of dish that you must cook  before
consommer *e*.
eat-INF
'This is the type of dish that you must cook before eating.'
b. *C'est le  genre de plat que tu  dois cuire *t* avant que tu
this-is the type  of dish that you must cook  before that you
ne        consommes *e*.
EXPL-NEG eat

The same is true in Spanish (Bordelois 1985, García-Mayo and Kemp-chinsky 1994) and Catalan (García-Mayo 1993): as these authors report, P-gaps within tensed adjuncts are sharply ungrammatical.

How can this difference between French (more generally, Romance) and English be accounted for? On the assumption that P-gaps are derived by movement of a null operator to the [Spec,CP] position of the adjunct clause (Contreras 1984, Chomsky 1986b), a tense effect is unexpected to start with. On this analysis, the parasitic gap is a *wh*-trace, and the parasitic chain itself should be immune to tense effects. An explanation of tense effects in P-gap constructions could then be attributed to the requirements imposed on null operators. Given that variables must be assigned a range (or be "strongly bound" in the sense of Chomsky 1986a:85), the null operator must link to an overt antecedent. In the case of P-gaps, the antecedent is the overt *wh*-operator. Chomsky (1986b:56f) proposes that linking of the null operator to its antecedent is effected by chain composition, a process subject to the same locality constraints as real chains—namely, the null operator must be 1-subjacent to the foot of the real chain. In adjunct clauses, the CP node dominating the null operator is L-marked by P, hence only one barrier (PP) intervenes between the null operator and the real gap:

(12)  *Wh* ... *t* ... [$_{PP}$ [$_{CP}$ *Op* ... *t*]]

On this analysis, the difference between English and Romance could be related to a difference in the bounding nodes for Subjacency. For instance, one could suppose that the CP node, if tensed, counts as a barrier in Romance but not in English. However, this solution runs counter to the fact that, with respect to tensed *wh*-island violations, French patterns like English and unlike Spanish, Catalan, or Italian. In the core cases, the latter languages allow extraction out of tensed *wh*-islands, but French does not (see Sportiche 1981, Rizzi 1982, Torrego 1984), and English allows extraction only marginally.[3] For these cases, Chomsky (1986b:37) suggests that the parametric variation might lie in the barrier status of the tensed functional projections, CP or IP. For English and French, the most embedded tensed IP would constitute an extra barrier. For Italian (and Spanish), the most embedded tensed CP would be a barrier: in this case, because CP is already a barrier by inheritance, tense adds no barrier. The fact that French and, to a certain extent, English, pattern together against Italian, Spanish, and Catalan with respect to tensed *wh*-islands thus seems, on a Subjacency-based chain-composition analysis, difficult to reconcile with the fact that they pattern differently with respect to tense in P-gap constructions.

### 10.2.2   The Ā-bound *pro* Analysis of Parasitic Gaps

A different type of solution is advocated by Cinque (1990). He argues that, within the class of English and Romance constructions usually viewed as involving *wh*-movement, two subclasses must be recognized. The first class comprises pure variables created by *wh*-movement: it includes relatives, interrogatives, clefts, and topicalizations. The second subclass is represented by P-gap constructions, apparent (NP)-extraction from adjunct islands, and COD constructions (*easy-to-please*, degree adjectives, purposives). As Cinque shows, these two subclasses of constructions display different properties. For instance, in the second subclass, but not the first, the gap is restricted to the category NP, it cannot correspond to the dative object in the dative construction in English, and it cannot occur in positions that exclude overt pronominals.[4] Cinque argues that these differences can be captured if constructions of the second subclass are not derived by movement. He proposes, in a vein similar to Chomsky's (1982) analysis of P-gaps, that these constructions contain a base-generated null pronominal (*pro*), which is, however, Ā-bound at S-structure. One of the problems associated with nonmovement analyses of P-gaps is the fact that they do display some island sensitivity, as shown by Kayne (1984: chap. 8) and Longobardi (1985a). Cinque's analysis addresses the problem by positing that base-generated *pro*, though unmoved in the syntax, must move at LF, either alone or pied-piped as part of a larger constituent that constitutes a g-projection of it, in the sense of Kayne's (1984) Connectedness Condition, as revised by Longobardi (1985). For instance, in the case of a P-gap contained within an adjunct, the whole adjunct clause moves at LF to the [Spec,CP] position occupied by the "real binder," replacing it. If the adjunct clause containing the P-gap is itself embedded under an adjunct clause, such movement is impossible, owing to the intervention of an added barrier; this derives the fact, observed by Longobardi (1985a), that P-gaps cannot be embedded two adjunct islands down.

Cinque (1990:136ff) takes the view that tense renders the second subclass of constructions (but not the first) relatively unacceptable, and he proposes that the tense effect is attributable to pied-piping. Kayne (1984: chap. 8) proposes that (overt) pied-piping is constrained by the Connectedness Condition: in effect, only *wh*-phrases or g-projections of *wh*-phrases can occupy the [Spec,CP] position. Cinque extends this proposal to the LF pied-piping of *pro*, suggesting further that tensed I weakly blocks the upward percolation of features. If we assume that the larger constituent moved at LF to [Spec,CP] must bear the features of *pro*, this (weakly) rules out constructions where the P-gap or the COD gap is embedded in a tensed clause.

However, as I have shown, P-gaps within tensed adjuncts are sharply ungrammatical in French. Under Cinque's proposal, one might suggest that this is a matter of parametric variation, with tense strongly blocking feature percolation in French. But a look at further data suggests that this hypothesis is not viable. Consider the following contrast:

(13) a. *Voilà un livre  que tu   as      acheté *t* alors que tu   possédais *e*
         here  a    book  that you have   bought  while    you  owned
         déjà.
         already
         'This is a book that you bought although you already had.'

     b. ?Voilà un livre  que tu   as      acheté *t* sans    penser   que tu
         here  a    book  that you have   bought  without thinking that you
         possédais *e* déjà.
         owned          already
         'This is a book that you bought without thinking that you
         already had.'

For many speakers (myself included), the sentence in (13a) improves noticeably when the complement of the adjunct clause—rather than the adjunct clause itself—bears tense. This surprising contrast is unaccounted for under Cinque's proposal: in (13b), the presence of tense should block percolation of the features of *pro* just as it does in (13a).

In this paper, I suggest that the ungrammaticality of (13a) and the like is only indirectly linked to tense; rather, it arises from the conditions governing the identification and licensing of null operators. This analysis hinges on the presence of a null operator in the [Spec,CP] position of the adjunct clause. Unlike Cinque, I take the null operator, not the P-gap, to be *pro*. Accordingly, I will reject Cinque's Ā-bound *pro* analysis in favor of the null operator movement analysis proposed by Contreras (1984) and Chomsky (1986b).

## 10.3  Null Operators and Complementizers

### 10.3.1  Null Operators in Parasitic Gap Constructions

It has often been pointed out in the literature that P-gaps can only be NPs (see in particular Cinque 1990, Postal 1994a; but see Engdahl 1983, Hukari, Levine, and Calagno this volume, for a different view). If this is indeed a property of P-gaps, it can be made to follow in various ways. For Cinque (1990), this categorial restriction follows from his analysis of P-gaps as null pronouns (*pro*). I am assuming here that P-gaps are derived by movement of a null operator to the [Spec,CP] of the adjunct clause; thus, null operators (at least in P-gap constructions) are NPs. But the question arises as to what kind of NPs null operators are. I assume that they are analyzable in terms of the [±anaphoric] and [±pronominal] features, like other NPs within Chomsky's (1981) typology. Since null operators are not traces, they can only be *pro* or PRO. Browning (1987a:123ff), who addresses this issue, argues that null operators are *pro*; but unlike Cinque's proposal discussed above, she advocates a movement analysis, with $Op = pro$ moved in the syntax to a [Spec,CP] position. This is the analysis that I adopt here.

Rizzi (1986) proposed that the null pronominal that occurs in null subject languages must be both formally licensed and identified for its ϕ-features. Identification of the ϕ-features of *pro* requires an antecedent, such as a clitic; rich inflection can also fulfill this function. Formal licensing, a structural requirement, is fulfilled through government by a Case-assigning head; for Italian, Agr or V. Under a split-Infl structure such as proposed by Pollock (1989) and modified by Chomsky (1995), the government relation between Agr and the *pro* subject can be reinterpreted as a Spec-head relation between $Agr_S$ and [Spec,Agr$_S$P].[5] Now, if null operators in PG constructions are *pro*, they ought to be subject to similar requirements. Chain composition can be viewed as fulfilling the identification requirement, as it connects the null operator with an antecedent, the overt operator. But what about formal licensing? Operators are typically in [Spec,CP] positions; but in this position, they are not in a Spec-head configuration with a Case-assigning head. However, complementizers may display agreement features (see for instance Shlonsky 1994b; Rizzi 1990, 1997). I would like to suggest that null operators are, like subject *pro*, licensed by being in a Spec-head relation with Agr. Concretely, my proposal for P-gap constructions is that the null operator in [Spec,CP] must cooccur with an agreeing complementizer. I now turn to a brief survey of the complementizers that appear in tensed contexts in French and in English.

### 10.3.2  Tensed Complementizers in French and English

In French, as is well known, embedded declarative clauses are always headed by an overt complementizer, *que* (realized as *qui* when adjacent to an extracted subject; see Kayne 1976). Embedded tensed interrogative clauses may be headed by the *wh*-complementizer, *si* ('whether'); if the embedded interrogative contains a fronted *wh*-phrase, the complementizer is null (presumably deleted) or, in the varieties that allow it (such as Québec French), realized as *que*.

(14) a. Elle prétend que tu    savais que cet  homme viendrait.
         she claims   QUE you knew   QUE this man     would-come
         'She claims that you knew that this man would come.'
     b. Quel  homme prétend-elle que tu    savais qui viendrait?
         which man      claims-she   QUE you knew   QUI would-come
         'Which man does she claim that you knew would come?'
     c. Elle ne   sait    pas si tu    partiras.
         she NEG knows not if you will-go
         'She does not know whether you will go.'
     d. Je me demande à   qui  (que) Max a     prêté mon livre.
         I  wonder       to who (QUE) Max has lent   my    book
         'I wonder to whom Max has lent my book.'

Tensed relative clauses pattern like embedded interrogatives, except when the target of movement is the direct object: the object *wh*-constituent introduces the embedded interrogative, but the relative clause must be introduced by the complementizer *que*:

(15) a. Je me demande quel   homme tu  as     rencontré.
         I  wonder       which man    you have met
         'I wonder which man you met.'
     b. l'homme que tu   as     rencontré
         the-man QUE you have met
         'the man you met'

Thus, in all tensed contexts in French, either C or [Spec,CP] must be filled by overt material; in contrast, English allows a null complementizer in some declarative and relative clause positions.[6] As for the choice of overt complementizers in French, there are two: the [–wh] variant (*que*) and the [+wh] variant (*si*). In the case of embedded clauses, the choice of complementizer is indirectly imposed by the higher verb, which selects not a particular complementizer but a clause type. The complementizers are themselves associated with clause type (or Force, in the terminology of Chomsky 1995 and Rizzi 1997): that is, the complementizers signal whether the clause is a declarative, an interrogative, a relative, and so on. This is relevant because, as I discuss in section 10.4, complementizer selection is altogether different in nonfinite clauses.

To account for the *that*-trace effect in English (and for the *que/qui* alternation in French), Rizzi (1990) proposed that the tensed complementizers in French and English differ with respect to their features. In Rizzi's system, *that*-trace violations reflect a lack of lexical government from the complementizer. *that* and *que*, he argues, are inert for government. (I will assume that this is also true of *que* in Spanish and Catalan and *che* in Italian, though these languages show no complementizer-trace effects, presumably because of their *pro*-drop character; see Rizzi 1982). In contrast, the null complementizer in English can be viewed as Agr, and French *qui* is *que* + Agr. The presence of Agr in C endows this otherwise inert node with the features required for proper government: hence the absence of ECP violations with the null complementizer in English and with *qui* in French.[7]

Returning to P-gaps, observe that in English the tensed adjunct clauses are all headed by the null complementizer; but in French (also in Spanish and Catalan), they are headed by the complementizer *que*. Schematically, the representation in present terms of a tensed adjunct clause with a parasitic gap in English and French is as in (16) and (17), respectively.

(16) a.   This is the report that you filed *t* after John had read *e*.

   b.   ... after [CP *Op*ᵢ [C Agr [IP John had read *e*ᵢ]]]

(17) a.   *Voilà le  rapport que tu  as     rangé *t* après que Jean ait
      this-is the report    that you have filed     after    Jean had
      lu *e*.
      read

   b.   ... après [CP *Op*ᵢ [C que [IP Jean ait lu *e*ᵢ]]]

In (16), but not in (17), the null operator (= *pro*), is in a Spec-head relationship with Agr; it is therefore formally licensed in English but not in French (or Spanish). This accounts for the difference displayed by Romance versus English in tensed adjunct clauses.

The analysis proposed here is compatible with the fact that P-gaps within relative clauses are grammatical in English (see (18)) but not in French (see (19)).

(18) a.  Here is the boy who [everyone who has met *e*] thinks *t* is clever.
     b.  a person who I would never talk to [anyone who dislikes *e*] about *t*.

(19) a.  *Voilà  le   garçon que  [tous ceux qui  ont rencontré *e*]
         here-is the boy     who  everyone  who has met
         trouvent *t* intelligent.
         finds         clever
     b.  *une personne que j'ai demandé à [tous ceux qui
         a   person   that I  asked      everyone who
         fréquentent *e*]  de contacter *t*
         associates-with to contact

The contrast here appears to be another instance of the tense effect, operative in French but not in English; but once again, this contrast can be viewed in terms of differences in the complementizer systems. Chomsky (1986b:58f) proposes that cases like (18) involve the Vacuous Movement Hypothesis (George 1980): that is, the *wh*-constituent *who* remains in situ, and the parasitic null operator moves to the [Spec,CP] of the relative clause. Because this CP is presumably headed by the null complementizer (= Agr), the formal licensing condition on the null operator is fulfilled. Consider now the French case. As argued by Rizzi (1990:56ff), *qui* in French is *que* + Agr. But, as Rizzi points out, *qui* is a C that agrees both with its specifier and with its complement (IP): this can only arise if a constituent coindexed with the head of IP (i.e., a subject) is *wh*-moved to the specifier position of the CP headed by *qui*. In other words, although *qui* is an agreeing form of the complementizer, its specifier is necessarily filled. Therefore in (19), there is no landing site for a null operator within the relative clause; as a result, a parasitic gap is precluded.[8]

### 10.3.3  Some Apparent Problems
The proposal just outlined raises several questions. The first one concerns object relative clauses. These are generally assumed to involve movement of a null operator; yet in tensed object relatives, the complementizer is *que* in French, *that* in English. This apparent problem dissolves under any analysis that does not posit null operator movement for object relatives. In Tellier 1991:40f, I argued, on different grounds, that relatives lacking an overt *wh*-operator result from deletion of the moved *wh*-operator, as

originally proposed by Kayne (1976). Another analysis compatible with the proposal made here is raising, an account of relatives due to Vergnaud (1974) and recently revived by Kayne (1994). On this analysis, the nominal head raises from its base position within the relative clause to the specifier of the CP selected by the determiner; in this view, there is no operator at all in *que/that* object relatives.

Another problem posed by the analysis advocated here directly concerns parasitic gap constructions. It has generally been assumed in the literature that in a sentence like (20), though both positions are accessible for extraction, the second gap, $e_2$, is a P-gap.

(20) the man who you persuaded $e_1$ that you would hire $e_2$

This idea is inconsistent with the proposal in this paper: as I have claimed, a parasitic null operator is not formally licensed in the specifier position of a CP headed by *that*. But (20) can be reconciled with the analysis advocated here on the assumption that overt *wh*-movement takes place from the most embedded position, with $e_1$ as the parasitic gap. The null operator would then adjoin to *who*, creating by absorption the type of complex operator typical of multiple questions.

(21) The man who$_i$ + *Op* you persuaded $e$ [$t_i$ that you would hire $t_i$]

The fact that the overt operator and the null operator must have the same reference follows, given that a null operator requires an antecedent.[9]

To summarize, I have proposed that the null operator in P-gap constructions is *pro*, and that as such it must be formally licensed in a Spec-head configuration with Agr in C. The differences in tense effects between English and Romance have been attributed to the complementizers involved: *that* and *que/che* lack Agr, whereas the null complementizer in English has it. This analysis yields as a consequence that a null operator within a tensed adjunct may be formally licensed in English but not in Romance. I now turn to P-gaps within nonfinite adjunct clauses in French. Their distribution displays asymmetries which I argue stem from independent properties of the C-system in French.

### 10.4   Nonfinite Adjunct Clauses in French

#### 10.4.1   An Asymmetry in the Occurrence of Parasitic Gaps
Nonfinite adjunct clauses constitute the core domain of P-gap occurrence in English. This is also true to some extent in French, although P-gaps in this language occur more systematically DP-internally (see section 10.6).

Indeed, (22b), just like its English counterpart, is acceptable to many French speakers with the degree of marginality typical of parasitic gap constructions.

(22) a. This is the report that you filed *t* without having read *e*.
 b. Voilà le rapport que tu as rangé *t* sans avoir lu *e*.
    this-is the report that you have filed without have-INF read

Yet, a look at a wider array of nonfinite adjunct clauses reveals that the occurrence of P-gaps within French nonfinite adjuncts is not unrestricted. Consider the following examples:

(23) a. Voilà les documents que tu as rangés *t* avant de
    here the documents that you have filed before
    consulter *e*.
    consult-INF
    'Here are the documents that you filed before consulting.'
 b. ?Voilà les livres que tu as réparés *t* pour vendre *e* au
    here the books that you have repaired to sell-INF at-the
    marché.
    market
    'Here are the books that you fixed in order to sell at the market.'
 c. ?Voilà les livres que tu as emballés *t* de peur
    here the books that you have covered for fear
    d'abîmer *e*.
    of-damage-INF
    'Here are the books that you covered for fear of damaging.'
 d. *Voilà les livres que tu as rangés *t* de manière à
    here the books that you have put-away in a-manner to
    retrouver *e* facilement.
    find-INF easily
    'Here are the books that you put away so as to retrieve easily.'
 e. Voilà les livres que tu as mis de côté *t* afin de
    here the books that you have put-away in-order to
    vendre *e* au marché.
    sell-INF at-the market
    'Here are the books that you put away in order to sell at the market.'
 f. Voilà les livres que tu as déchirés *t* au lieu de consulter *e*.
    here the books that you have torn instead of consult-INF
    'Here are the books that you tore instead of consulting.'

g. *Voilà les documents que tu  as   rangés *t* quitte à
here the documents that you have put-away but   to
reprendre *e*   plus tard.
take-again-INF later
'Here are the documents that you put away on the chance of
taking them again later.'

It was noticed early on that not all adjunct clauses enjoy the same status with respect to hosting P-gaps. Engdahl (1983:9) points out that, in untensed domains, adjunct clauses can be classified according to the following decreasing hierarchy: manner adjuncts, temporal adjuncts, purpose clauses. Still, something else appears to be at stake in the above examples. Example (23d) arguably involves a manner adjunct, the highest on the accessibility hierarchy; yet, for many speakers, the example is ill-formed. Note also the contrast in grammaticality between (23c,f), on the one hand, and (23g), on the other: although the adjunct clause in these examples appears to fulfill a similar semantic function, (23g) is rejected by most speakers.[10]

The difference between these examples then appears to lie not in their semantic relation to the main clause but rather in their internal structure. A likely candidate is the material introducing the clause. In French, infinitive adjunct clauses are typically introduced by a (complex) preposition, which may be followed by *de* or *à*; it can also stand alone, as in example (23b). The examples in (23) show adjunct clauses introduced by *avant de* ('before'), *pour* ('in order to'), *de peur de* ('for fear of'), *de façon à* ('so as'), *afin de* ('in order to'), *au lieu de* ('instead of'), *quitte à* ('even if, but'). One common factor shared by the ungrammatical cases is that the preposition is followed by *à*. The fact that *à* prevents the occurrence of P-gaps suggests that it has properties making it incompatible with the demands of a null operator of the sort found in P-gap constructions. Example (24) suggests that *à* is incompatible with local construal with a null operator in a P-gap construction; it is not incompatible with a link within the parasitic chain.

(24) C'est le  genre de livre qu'il    faut lire *t* attentivement avant de
this-is the type  of book that-one must read carefully     before
commencer à  critiquer *e*.
starting      to criticize-INF
'This is the type of book that you must read carefully before starting to criticize.'

This obviously recalls the observation made with respect to *que* in connection with (13). In keeping with the proposal advocated here, I will suggest that *de*, like the null complementizer in English, may formally license *pro*, but that *à*, like *que* or *that*, cannot. To see why that should be the case, let us start by examining some of the properties of nonfinite *à* and *de*.

### 10.4.2   Some Properties of *à* and *de*

It is generally admitted that *de*, when preceding an infinitive clause, is a nonfinite complementizer (Kayne 1975, Huot 1981; this is also true of Italian *di*, see Rizzi 1982). A similar claim has been made for *à* (Kayne 1975:339, 1984: chap. 5). However, Huot (1981) defends the position that *à*, contrary to *de*, is a true preposition. This proposal poses some problems, as Huot acknowledges, because unlike PPs, *à*-infinitives do not block extraction:

(25) a. *le   traître de qui      nous avons assisté     [à la   reddition *t*]
        the traitor of whom we    have   witnessed  À the surrender
        'the traitor whose surrender we witnessed'

   b. l'ami        de qui      nous avons cherché [à modifier      le
      the friend   of whom we  have   tried       À change-INF the
      comportement *t*]
      behavior
      'the friend whose behavior we tried to change'

I adopt the view that nonfinite *à*, though not a preposition, categorially differs from *de*; but I suggest that the two are related in a manner reminiscent of the *be*/*have* alternation (see Freeze 1992; Kayne 1993, 1994).

Let us first look at the distribution of *à* and *de* in nonfinite contexts. Nonfinite declarative complements may be introduced by either *à* or *de*; there is also a complementizerless third option. However, unlike what was seen in tensed clauses, complementizer choice in infinitival complements is not a reflex of clause type or Force selection. Rather, it is a matter of lexical selection by the higher verb. The following examples illustrate this:

(26) a. Les voisins     ont   accepté   de/*à/*Ø partir.
        the neighbors have accepted DE/À/Ø        leave-INF
        'The neighbors agreed to leave.'

   b. Les voisins     ont   consenti   à/*de/*Ø partir.
      the neighbors have consented À/DE/Ø         leave-INF
      'The neighbors agreed to leave.'

c. Les voisins    ont   voulu    Ø/\*de/\*à partir.
the neighbors have wanted Ø/DE/À    leave-INF
'The neighbors wanted to leave.'

I will not be concerned with these cases, because they reflect lexical idiosyncrasies. However, there are cases where the choice of *à* or *de* seems to correlate with the semantic/aspectual properties of the main verbs. French displays a curious alternation between *à* and *de* that occurs with verbs having a pronominal counterpart. Consider the following:

(27) a. risquer de/\*à faire quelque chose
   to-risk DE/À to-do something
   'to risk doing something'

   b. se risquer à/\*de faire quelque chose
   SE risk    À/DE to-do something
   'to venture to do something'

(28) a. essayer de/\*à faire quelque chose
   to-try DE/À to-do something
   'to try doing something'

   b. s'essayer à/\*de faire quelque chose
   SE-try    À/DE to-do something
   'to try one's hand at doing something'

(29) a. décider   de/\*à faire quelque chose
   to-decide DE/À to-do something
   'to decide to do something'

   b. se décider à/\*de faire quelque chose
   SE decide À/DE to-do something
   'to make up one's mind to do something'

(30) a. résoudre de/\*à faire quelque chose
   to-resolve DE/À to-do something
   'to decide to do something'

   b. se résoudre à/\*de faire quelque chose
   SE resolve À/DE to-do something
   'to resolve to do something'

(31) a. attendre de/\*à faire quelque chose
   to-wait DE/À to-do something
   'to wait to do something'

   b. s'attendre à/\*de faire quelque chose
   SE-expect À/DE to-do something
   'to expect to do something'

Riegel, Pellat, and Rioul (1994:261) characterize the meaning change associated with pronominalization (in the (b) examples) as follows: pronominal verbs convey an internalization (of perception, etc.) that results in a change of psychological state. Note that the verbs in (b) also differ from the nonpronominal forms in (a) in that they take the *être* ('be') auxiliary. As has been observed for Italian by Levin and Rappaport (1989) and for Dutch by Hoekstra and Mulder (1990), auxiliary choice sometimes correlates with aspectual properties—for instance, the presence or absence of an endpoint with verbs of motion. The correspondence between pronominal verbs and the choice of *à* then makes sense if *à* is associated with clausal content. I thus propose that *à* is not in $C^0$; rather, it occupies the head position of the infinitive clause, $Agr^0$, which presumably hosts the modal and aspectual properties of the infinitive. This is further supported by the observation, due to Riegel, Pellat, and Rioul (1994:189), that *à* in infinitives often expresses modality (possibility or necessity). The representation of an infinitive with *à* is thus as in (32).[11]

(32) se décider [$_{CP}$ [$_C$ $\emptyset$] [$_{AgrP}$ [$_{Agr}$ à] (NEG) [$_{VP}$ PRO partir]]]

The representation in (32) assumes the presence of a CP layer with *à* infinitives. Support for this comes from Rizzi's (1997) observation that in Italian, left-dislocated phrases must follow the complementizer *che* but precede the complementizer *di*. A similar distribution holds in French:

(33) a. ??J'ai    pensé,    ton   livre, que Sylvain l'apprécierait.
          I-have thought your book that Sylvain would-appreciate-it
     b.  J'ai    pensé    que, ton   livre, Sylvain l'apprécierait.
          I-have thought that your book Sylvain would-appreciate-it
          'I thought that, your book, Sylvain would appreciate it.'

(34) a.  J'ai    essayé, ton   livre, de le trouver en magasin.
          I-have tried,  your book DE it find   in store
          'I tried, your book, to find it in the stores.'
     b. *J'ai    essayé de, ton   livre, le trouver en magasin.
          I-have tried   DE your book it find   in store

Rizzi argues, in a vein similar to Pollock's (1989) split-Infl hypothesis, that the CP layer is more articulated than is generally believed. He proposes that *che/que* occupies the topmost functional head (Force), whereas *di/de* occupies the lowest functional head within the CP layer (Finiteness). The data in (33)–(34) suggest that left-dislocated phrases occupy a position in the middle of the CP field. If this is correct, then the presence of left-dislocated phrases to the left of *à* may be taken as evidence that a CP layer is indeed activated:

(35) a.  Je cherche,  ton  livre, à l'acheter d'occasion.
         I  am-trying your book À buy-it    used
         'I am-trying, your book, to buy it used.'
     b. *Je cherche    à, ton  livre, l'acheter d'occasion.
         I  am-trying À your book buy-it    used

For simplicity's sake, I will continue to represent CP as a single node, abstracting from Rizzi's split-CP hypothesis. If infinitives with *à* have a CP layer, the question arises as to what the C node dominates. In tensed clauses, as I have shown, French does not have the English equivalent of the null complementizer. The simplest hypothesis is that this empty category is absent in all clauses, finite or nonfinite. I will then assume that C in (32) is radically empty.

### 10.4.3  Nonfinite Complementizers and Operator Licensing
With this in mind, consider the derivation of a P-gap construction within an infinitival adjunct introduced by *à*. The relevant portions of the structure are given here:

(36) [$_{PP}$ de manière [$_{CP}$ $Op_i$ [$_C$ $\varnothing$] [$_{AgrP}$ [$_{Agr}$ à] (NEG) [$_{VP}$ PRO retrouver
     $e_i$ ...]]]]

In this configuration, $Op = pro$ is not formally licensed, as the C head has no features at all. This accounts for the lack of P-gaps in these adjunct clauses.

But note that in general, the mood of the clause is closely associated with the C node, as is clear from the fact that the complementizers compatible with the indicative or subjunctive differ from those used in the infinitive. Furthermore, verbs select the mood of their complement clause: for instance, *vouloir* ('to want') requires the subjunctive, *dire* ('to say') selects the indicative, and *tenter* ('to try') selects the infinitive. Suppose further that these features must be licensed, either by being morphologically supported or by incorporating into a higher functional head. In a configuration like (36), where $Agr^0$ contains *à*, the mood features are morphologically supported, hence they need only raise covertly to $C^0$. But in a nonfinite clause where Agr contains no morphological material, the mood features must raise overtly to $C^0$.

I have already assumed that *de* is a complementizer in nonfinite clauses in French. If $Agr^0$ must raise overtly into $C^0$, then *de* is an agreeing complementizer.

In Hulk and Tellier 2000, we analyze the particle *de* in possessive constructions in a similar way: as we argue, *de* arises from incorporation of a null head into a higher functional head. This is in the spirit of Freeze's (1992) and Kayne's (1993) proposal concerning the relation between *have* and *be*, the former being the realization of the copula into which a preposition has incorporated. In nominals, as we propose, the possessive constructions that relate through incorporation are the following:

(37) a. un ami    à Julie
        a   friend À Julie
     b. un ami    de Julie
        a   friend DE Julie
        'a friend of Julie's.'

In the structure underlying these French possessives, the preposition is either *à* or null. A null preposition must, in order to be licensed, incorporate into the next functional head up: the feature-bearing functional head so created must lexicalize, and surfaces as *de*. As we show, this analysis extends to *de* in other nominal constructions as well (see Hulk and Tellier 1999, 2000 for details).

I now propose that a similar analysis applies to complementizer *de*: it is a functional head (a complementizer) endowed with features as a result of the incorporation of a lower functional head ($Agr^0$).[12] Following incorporation of $Agr^0$ into C hosting *de*, C can be viewed as an agreeing head. Like French *qui*, it agrees with its complement—here, AgrP (this time, by virtue of acquiring the index of the head of its complement). Because C is an agreeing head, *pro* in its specifier position is formally licensed.

Now, if $C^0$ does not host *de*, $Agr^0$ will have to raise overtly for the reasons indicated. In this case, the C node will remain covert but will nonetheless inherit the agreement features necessary for licensing the operator in its specifier. This will account for the complementizerless nonfinite adjunct clauses in French and in English, which all allow P-gaps.

We are now in a position to explain the puzzling contrasts displayed by P-gaps in adjunct clauses with respect to tense effects (see (13)), repeated below with the relevant structure added):

(38) a. *Voilà un livre que tu   as      acheté *t* alors [$_{CP}$ $Op_i$ [$_C$ que] tu
         here   a   book that you have bought      while                          you
         possédais $e_i$ déjà]
         owned           already
         'This is a book that you bought although you already had.'

b. ?Voilà un livre que tu  as    acheté *t* sans [$_{CP}$ *Op*$_i$ [$_C$ Agr$^0$]
here  a  book that you have bought  without
penser *t*$_i$ que tu    possédais *e*$_i$ déjà]
thinking that you owned    already
'This is a book that you bought without remembering that you
already had.'

The null operator in (38a) is not formally licensed, for the reasons I
have already indicated. But in (38b), following incorporation of Agr into
C, the operator is in a Spec-head relation with Agr, as required. One issue
that I have not yet addressed concerns the effect of incorporation on
the subject of the embedded clause. Given that an Agr complementizer
properly governs the subject in tensed clauses, the question arises whether
the same situation obtains in (38b), with adverse effects on PRO. Note
that infinitive Agr is not, in any event, a proper governor for PRO. Its
raising to C does not change that property; nor does it turn an otherwise
C into a proper governor. There are independent reasons to believe that
the process of incorporation does not endow a head with the ability to be
a proper governor. A similar case is discussed by Rizzi and Roberts
(1989), concerning subject-auxiliary inversion in English. As they show,
inversion does not help license a subject trace, showing that Infl movement to C does not endow the latter with the property of being a proper
governor (see also Rizzi 1990).

In this section, I explored the distribution and properties of *à* and *de*, as
well as their role in the licensing of null operators and the distribution of
P-gaps. As I will argue in the following section, the alternation between *à*
and *de* also plays a part in the behavior of the *easy-to-please* construction
in French.

## 10.5   *Easy-to-please* Constructions and Parasitic Gaps

Canac Marquis (1990) has observed that *easy-to-please* constructions in
French differ from their English counterpart in two important respects.
First, the infinitive is obligatorily introduced by *à*, whereas the corre-
sponding impersonal construction requires *de*. Compare:

(39) a. It is difficult to summarize this book.
     b. This book is difficult to summarize.

(40) a. Il est difficile de/*à résumer ce livre.
     b. Ce livre est difficile à/*de résumer.

Second, *easy-to-please* constructions license P-gaps in English but not in French:

(41) a.  This book is difficult to summarize without having read *e* carefully.
     b.  *Ce livre est difficile à résumer      sans      avoir  lu *e*
         this book is  difficult À summarize without having read attentivement.
         carefully

Canac Marquis (1990) proposes that the adjectives in (40a) and (40b) have a different subcategorization frame: the complement is a CP in (40a) but a PP selecting a bare VP in (40b). That the subcategorization frame is different appears, in view of the following contrast, to be an inescapable conclusion:

(42) a.  Il sera     difficile, durant la  semaine, de rencontrer Max
         it will-be difficult during the week    DE meet        Max
         seul à seul.
         alone
         'It will be difficult, during the week, to meet Max alone.'
     b.  *Max sera    difficile, durant la  semaine, à rencontrer
         Max will-be difficult during the week    À meet
         seul à seul.
         alone
     c.  Max sera    enclin, durant la  semaine, à mieux travailler.
         Max will-be prone  during the week   À better work
         'Max will be prone, during the week, to work better.'

Preposed adverbs, like dislocated phrases, necessarily precede *de* (see (42a)) and *à* (see (42c)). They also follow *que*, which constitutes for Rizzi (1997) an indication that they occupy a position in the middle of the CP field. But in the *easy-to-please* construction in (42b), adverb preposing between the adjective and *à* is precluded. This suggests that the infinitive clause does not have a CP layer. I argued earlier that infinitival *à* is under Agr; it is then natural to suppose that the infinitive in (42b) is AgrP.

The fact that *easy-to-please* constructions in French do not license P-gaps can now be envisioned as a consequence of the lack of CP layer. Assuming a null operator movement analysis, the derivation of a construction like (40b) would be as follows:

(43)  Ce livre est difficile [$_{AgrP}$ $Op_i$ [$_{Agr}$ à] ... [$_{VP}$ PRO résumer $t_i$]]

The only landing site available for the operator is [Spec,AgrP]. If $Op = pro$, it is correctly licensed by being in a Spec-head relationship with Agr. Identification for the features of $Op = pro$ is effected through coin-dexation with the matrix subject. By all accounts, [Spec,AgrP] is an A-position: hence the chain, not being an Ā-chain, cannot license a P-gap.[13]

Indirect support for the analysis proposed here is provided by *easy-to-please* constructions in Spanish. Montalbetti and Saito (1983) report that these constructions feature the same complementizer as the impersonal construction and that, furthermore, they license P-gaps. The relevant examples thus contrast with the French cases in (40b) and (41b):

(44)  a.  Es fácil de convencer a Juan.
          is easy DE convince      John
          'It is easy to convince John.'

      b.  Juan es fácil de convencer.
          John is easy DE convince
          'John is easy to convince.'

(45)     Esta teoría es difícil    de explicar *t* sin         conocer *e*.
         this theory is difficult DE explain      without know-INF
         'This theory is difficult to explain without knowing.'

Assuming that Spanish *de*, like its French counterpart, is a complemen-tizer, the complement of the adjective in (44b) must be a CP. Assuming that the incorporation analysis I have proposed for French *de* extends to Spanish, the difference between Spanish and French with respect to P-gap licensing follows: in (45), *de* in $C^0$ may license a null operator in its spec-ifier (by virtue of Agr incorporation). Furthermore, because in Spanish the CP layer is present, the null operator may land in [Spec,CP], an Ā-position; this allows it to license P-gaps.

## 10.6 Parasitic Gaps in DPs

English allows P-gaps within DPs. However, as was mentioned in the in-troduction, the occurrence of DP-internal P-gaps is sensitive to determiner type. This is illustrated in (5) and (6), from Frampton (1990), repeated here:

(46)  a.   a man who [friends of *e*] admire *t*.
      b.  *a man who [the friends of *e*] admire *t*.

(47)  a.   Jack, who [everyone who likes *e*] visited *t*
      b.  ??Jack, who [the man who likes *e*] visited *t*

The corresponding French examples exhibit different properties, since, unlike English, the subject constitutes in some cases a possible site for relativization (only with *dont,* however; see Tellier 1990). Still, other examples can be constructed where a DP-internal gap is clearly parasitic, as its position prohibits extraction. This is the case when the DP is complement of a preposition.

(48) a.  un homme dont      l'honnêteté *t* se voit [dans les  yeux *e*]
         a  man     of-whom the-honesty is-seen in     the eyes
         'a man whose honesty can be seen in his eyes'
     b.  un enfant dont      le  père *t* ne    parle   plus [à  la  mère *e*]
         a  child   of-whom the father NEG speaks not    to the mother
         'a child whose father no longer speaks to the mother'

Such examples are discussed at length in Tellier 1991. It is shown that the bracketed constituent indeed contains an empty category corresponding to the genitive complement; this empty category, analyzed as an NP, has all the properties of P-gaps. As the examples in (48) show, French, unlike English, allows P-gaps in definite DPs. This difference clearly correlates with the contrast in (49).

(49) a.  *Who did you see the picture of *t*?
     b.  De qui     as-tu    vu   la  photo *t*?
         of whom have-you seen the photo

English does not allow *wh*-extraction out of definite DPs, a fact that is usually referred to as the specificity effect (see Fiengo and Higginbotham 1981). By contrast in French, and more generally in Romance, definite DPs are transparent for extraction. In fact, the correlation between P-gap occurrence and extraction possibilities is even more obvious if we consider the class of DPs with definite determiners that do allow *wh*-extraction in English. This class includes, for instance, superlative DPs (Szabolcsi 1986) and DPs with process deverbal nominals:

(50) a.  Who did you see the best picture of *t*?
     b.  The man that you witnessed the execution of *t* had been on
         death row for years.

Strikingly, DPs of this type can also host P-gaps:

(51) a.  a man who even the closest associates of *e* could not defend *t*
     b.  the man that you interviewed *t* before witnessing the execution
         of *e*

This correlation is at first glance surprising because in the P-gap construction, the null operator must land within DP; in subjects like (51a), for instance, any extraction out of DP is precluded in English. In what follows I will propose that the common ground between *wh*-extraction and P-gap occurrence lies in the properties of [Spec,DP]. More precisely, I will propose that being in a Spec-head relationship with an agreeing head D is a requirement on both null operator licensing and on *wh*-extraction.

The questions to be answered in connection with these facts are:

(52) a. What accounts for the contrast between French and English regarding the occurrence of P-gaps in (certain) definite DPs?
   b. How is this difference tied to the difference in specificity effects with definite DPs?
   c. How is the null operator in DP-internal P-gaps formally licensed in French and in English?

I would like to propose that these three questions receive the same answer and that these differences can be traced back to agreement differences in the determiner system of French and English.

Let us start with the specificity effects illustrated in (49). Tellier and Valois (1996) propose that extraction out of DPs is dependent on agreement. I will not go into the details of this analysis; suffice it to say that the presence of agreement features on the determiner forces movement of the complement NP to a position where both sets of features can be checked in a Spec-head relation (let us suppose for convenience that NP moves to [Spec,DP]). The presence of the NP in this position is then viewed as essential for *wh*-extraction of a subconstituent of the NP out of DP. Now, in French, both the definite and the indefinite determiner display number and gender features. But the English definite determiner *the* shows no agreement at all, whereas the indefinite determiner varies for number: *a* in the singular, null in the plural. It follows that, in English, only those NPs that are complements of indefinite determiners may move to [Spec,DP] and subsequently extract.

This proposal, however, is insufficient, as it does not straightforwardly account for the extractability out of superlative DPs and DPs with process nominals (see (50)). One crucial observation concerning those DPs is that the determiner *the* is obligatory in these contexts: in superlatives, it arguably forms a discontinuous constituent with the *-est* suffix; and in process nominals, it is the only determiner allowed, as Grimshaw (1990:54f) pointed out:[14]

(53) a. *(The) closest associates of this man cannot defend him.
     b.   They witnessed *a/the slow execution of the prisoners.

The obligatory character of *the* in these DPs suggests that it is an instance of the expletive determiner, in the sense of Vergnaud and Zubizarreta (1992) and Longobardi (1994): that is, a determiner which does not single out a unique object (but a property; see (53a)), and that is consequently nonspecific. According to Longobardi, the expletive determiner in English only occurs as a last resort, to fulfill the requirements imposed by restrictive modifiers, generics, superlative suffixes, and so forth, whereas the expletive determiner in Romance arises as a need to realize agreement features in argument DPs. However, given that English does have (number) agreement in DPs, I will assume that the expletive determiner is Agr, although it does not overtly agree with the head noun. The distinction between the definite determiner *the* and the expletive *the* lies in their semantic and grammatical features: +specific, −Agr for the former; −specific, +Agr for the latter. The extraction possibilities with expletives determiners then follow, under an agreement-based analysis of *wh*-extraction: [Spec,DP] is in a Spec-head relationship with an agreeing head.

This distinction provides an immediate answer to questions (52b) and (52c). I have proposed that the null operator in P-gap constructions is formally licensed in a Spec-head configuration with Agr. We can suppose that Agr in D has a morphological reflex: if the determiner displays agreement features (gender, number), then Agr is present. In French, the definite determiner shows agreement and can therefore formally identify the null operator (=*pro*) in its specifier position. In English, the indefinite determiner contains Agr (as shown by the alternation), but the definite determiner does not: thus the former, but not the latter, constitutes a formal licenser for the null operator. It follows that P-gaps may occur DP-internally in English if the DP is indefinite, but not if it is definite. The expletive determiner, however, will fulfill the requirements on $Op = pro$, hence the possibility of superlatives and the like to host P-gaps.

## 10.7   Conclusion

In this chapter, I have examined four properties associated to P-gaps in French that distinguish them from P-gaps in English. I have argued that these properties are all tied, directly or not, to independent differences in the agreement systems of French and English, either at the C level or at the D level. Building on the idea that null operators, just like *pro*, must be licensed in a Spec-head configuration with an agreeing head, the tense effects with P-gaps in adjunct clauses in French (and their relative absence in English) are linked to complementizer differences, and specifically the absence of a null (Agr) complementizer in French. The lack of P-gaps within relatives in French is also linked to the nature of the complementizer that introduces relatives. The fact that *easy-to-please* constructions license P-gaps in English, but not in French, can be viewed as arising from differences in the infinitive complementizer systems. Finally, the lack of DP-internal P-gaps with (certain) definite DPs in English—and their occurrence in French—correlates with agreement differences between the determiner and the head noun.

**Notes**

I wish to thank the editors of this volume for their helpful comments. All remaining shortcomings are mine. Financial support from the Social Sciences and Humanities Research Council of Canada (grant #410-95-0886) is gratefully acknowledged.

1. Not all DPs may host P-gaps in French, and there are cases in English where P-gaps may be found in the presence of a definite determiner, for instance in superlatives. See section 10.6 for discussion.

2. One subcase where English displays a strong tense effect is when the parasitic gap occupies the subject position of a tensed complement in the adjunct clause. As originally proposed by Taraldsen (1981), this can be viewed an ECP effect; I leave the question aside here. See Chomsky 1982:55 and Cinque 1990:105 for discussion.

3. Judgments vary for English. Chomsky (1986b:37) notes that for many speakers, tense decreases the acceptability of *wh*-island violations. However, some speakers do accept extraction over tensed *wh*-islands, especially with object relatives and D-linked interrogatives.

4. Paul Postal points out to me that this last restriction actually holds of other constructions as well (e.g., instruction sets). See Postal 1994a for related discussion.

5. This extends to (arbitrary) object *pro*, which is licensed by V in Italian (also in French; see Roberge 1990). Under the view that all Case is assigned in a Spec-head configuration (Sportiche 1996), the verb and its object must move to the head and specifier position of a functional projection.

6. Kayne (1984: chap. 3) notes that the null complementizer option in English is available only when the clause is properly governed (see also Stowell 1981:396ff). The contrasts in (i)–(iii) thus support the view that the null complementizer is an empty category, subject to the ECP.

(i)    I believe (that) time will tell.

(ii)   [That time will tell] is likely.

(iii)  *[Time will tell] is likely.

The impossibility of omitting *that* in complements of nouns follows if Ns are not structural governors, hence cannot govern across CP:

(iv)  the belief *(that) time will tell

This leaves relative clauses, which allow the null complementizer, as a problem. For one solution, see Rizzi 1990.

7. As Bresnan (1977) and Culicover (1992, 1993) discuss, the intervention of certain adverbials in English alleviate *that*-trace violations:

(i)    *an amendment which they say that $t$ will be law next year

(ii)   an amendment which they say that, next year, $t$ will be law

For an analysis of (ii) compatible with an ECP approach to *that*-trace violations and developed in the context of a more articulated CP-layer, see Rizzi 1997; see Culicover 1993 for a different view.

8. Paul Postal (personal communication) suggests that the difference between French and English with respect to P-gaps within relatives might instead be tied to the fact that English allows extraction out of some relatives, an option precluded in French:

(i)    It is that spy that they will arrest everyone who contacted $t$.

(ii)   *C'est l'espion qu'ils      arrêteront tous ceux qui   ont contacté $t$.
       it-is  the-spy that-they will-arrest everyone  who has contacted

However, in some cases there is no correspondence between extraction and P-gap occurrence—that is, extraction out of a relative is excluded, yet a P-gap within the same relative is allowed. Frampton (1990:58) gives the following contrast:

(iii)  Jack, who [everyone who likes $e$] visited $t$ . . .

(iv)   *Jack, who I met [everyone who likes $t$] . . .

9. One argument that has been adduced in favor of a null operator movement analysis of P-gaps is the relative unacceptability of (i), from Chomsky 1986b:62.

(i)  Who did you ask $t$ [why you should visit $e$]

This example is ruled out on the assumption that a null operator cannot land in the filled [Spec,CP] of the embedded clause. However, the ill-formedness of (i) is also compatible with an analysis where the first gap is the P-gap. On this analysis, (i) is a *wh*-island violation.

(ii)  Who + $Op$ did you ask $e$ [why you should visit $t$]

The proposal made here has consequences for the conditions on chain composition, because plainly the null operator is not 1-subjacent to the foot of the real chain. I leave this question aside.

10. Contrastive judgments were obtained from twelve native speakers of French; the examples were presented in written form and in the order given here. Examples (23d) and (23g) were judged ungrammatical by six of the speakers and somewhat deviant by five. By contrast, example (23f) was judged perfect by nine speakers, deviant by two, and ungrammatical by one. Examples (22b) and (23a,b,c) were judged perfect or slightly marginal by every informant. All the speakers accept the counterparts of these examples with the parasitic gap removed

and replaced by a clitic pronoun. As is typical of judgments on P-gaps, there is some measure of speaker variation, yet the contrasts indicated in the text emerge clearly.

11. Though infinitival *à*, like English infinitival *to*, derives historically from a locative preposition, they occupy different positions within the clause: *to* may follow the negation marker *not*, whereas *à* must precede the negation *pas*:

(i) I agree not to smoke.

(ii) a. Je consens à ne pas fumer.
       I  agree  À NEG not smoke
       'I agree not to smoke.'
    b. *Je consens ne pas à fumer.
       I  agree  NEG not À smoke

This suggests that *to* is lower down than Neg, presumably in $T^0$.

12. There is, however, one important difference between nominals and nonfinite clauses: whereas the particle must surface as either *de* or *à* in nominals, nonfinite clauses need not be introduced by *à* or *de*, as there is a null third option. Thus for nonfinite clauses the idea that *de* is a feature-bearing functional head can be maintained; but a feature-bearing functional head will not necessarily surface as *de*.

13. The A-chain is well formed under Rizzi's (1990) Relativized Minimality: PRO within VP is either not an A-position, or, in Koopman and Sportiche's (1991) view, it does not occupy the [Spec,VP] position but rather a position adjoined to VP.

14. DPs like *a most beautiful picture of Julie* are irrelevantly grammatical, as they are not superlatives, "most" here being equivalent to "very."

# Chapter 11

## Explaining Parasitic Gap Restrictions     Alan Munn

## 11.1 Introduction

Among the differences between "real" gaps and parasitic gaps (P-gaps) that have been noted in the literature, two kinds of asymmetries have received much attention: (i) P-gaps, unlike real gaps, are restricted to (certain kinds of) NPs (Cinque 1990, Postal 1993b) and (ii) P-gaps, unlike real gaps, do not show weak crossover (WCO) effects (Lasnik and Stowell 1991). An implicit assumption of these works is that both asymmetries are properties of the same underlying phenomenon, usually cashed out in terms of properties of the gap itself. There is reasonable factual justification for this assumption, since a number of other *wh*-movement structures including *tough*-constructions and nonrestrictive relative clauses show similar effects.

In this chapter I argue that although the restriction of P-gaps to NPs can explain the lack of WCO effects in the parasitic domain, lack of WCO effects in a domain does not entail NP restrictions in that domain. The argument is based on a comparison between across-the-board (ATB) gaps (Williams 1978, 1990) and P-gaps. Postal (1993b) showed that ATB gaps do not exhibit category restrictions. If what underlies the category restrictions also accounts for the lack of WCO effects, then ATB gaps should show WCO effects in all gaps. However, I will show that only some ATB gaps exhibit WCO effects, and they do so in a way that parallels P-gaps. I will attribute the lack of WCO to the presence of a null resumptive pronoun and then argue that whereas the parasitic domain *requires* the use of the resumptive pronoun strategy, the ATB domain merely *allows*, but does not require, the use of it. I argue that independent differences in the two domains can account for the obligatoriness of the resumptive strategy in the parasitic domain and its optionality in the ATB domain.

## 11.2   Parasitic Gaps and ATB Gaps

Various researchers have proposed that ATB gaps and P-gaps be given an identical analysis—in particular, see Munn 1992, Williams 1990, Huybregts and van Riemsdijk 1985, Haïk 1985, and Pesetsky 1982. Logically, there are two ways a reduction of the two phenomena can proceed: either P-gaps can be taken as instances of ATB gaps, or ATB gaps can be treated as instances of P-gaps. The two approaches are quite different in spirit and in execution. The first approach takes ATB movement for granted and tries to treat the parasitic domain as coordinated in some way, whereas the second approach tries to eliminate ATB movement from the grammar entirely and to use existing devices to derive the properties of all multiple-gap structures.

The fact that there are asymmetries between P-gaps and "real" gaps makes it difficult to reduce P-gaps to ATB movement, because most formalizations of ATB movement have no way of representing the differences between gaps and would not even predict such asymmetries to arise. This point is made explicitly (and I think convincingly) by Postal (1993b), who shows that there is a clustering of properties that P-gaps share (following Cinque 1990) that are not found in ATB gaps. For Postal and Cinque, an important part of the argument is that these same properties also hold of other single-gap constructions such as *tough*-constructions. This adds to the implausibility of treating P-gaps as ATB gaps because the similarities between P-gaps and single-gap constructions would be accidental. As I will show, this correlation is not as iron-clad as it might first appear, and the actual situation provides evidence that a monolithic account of P-gap restrictions is likely to be wrong.

Postal assumes that ATB movement is independently needed. In this paper I argue that one nonetheless can (and in fact must) dispense with a separate mechanism for ATB movement. The reason is that although the Postal/Cinque restrictions on P-gaps are not shared by ATB gaps, WCO effects only arise in the first gap of an ATB extraction but not in subsequent gaps. Given that lack of weak crossover also manifests itself in single-gap constructions, it cannot be reduced to properties of multiple-gap constructions either. It will become clear, however, that the range of single-gap constructions that exhibit one set of restrictions is not the same as the range of single-gap constructions that exhibit the Postal/Cinque effects, which provides further evidence against a monolithic account of P-gap restrictions.

## 11.2.1 Similarities between Parasitic Gaps and ATB Gaps

**11.2.1.1 Island Effects** This section reviews some of the original arguments for treating ATB gaps and P-gaps alike.[1] Consider the following cases of both P-gaps and ATB extraction:

(1) a. Which paper did John file *t* before Mary read *e*?
    b. Which paper did John file *t* and Mary read *e*?

The basic data that support the claim that ATB extraction and P-gaps are the same lies in the arguments that both exhibit movement-like behavior, as shown originally by Kayne (1983) and used by Chomsky (1986b) as evidence for the null operator hypothesis. Both yield subjacency effects as the examples in (2) show (adapted from Chomsky 1986b:55, (126)–(127), which give comparable examples with P-gaps).

(2) Which man did John interview *t* and ...
    a.  expect us to hire *e*
    b.  expect us to give the job to *e*
    c.  *expect us to ask which job to give to *e*
    d.  *wonder who to ask which job to give to *e*
    e.  tell you that you should give the job to *e*
    f.  *read the book you gave to *e*
    g.  *hear about the plan you proposed to *e*
    h.  ?*announce the plan to speak to *e*
    i.  ?*hear about the plan to speak to *e*
    j.  *expect you to leave without meeting *e*
    k.  *meet the man in the office near *e*

As in P-gap sentences, island violations of various types in ATB structures produce the same degree of unacceptability as their canonical (i.e., single gap) counterparts, thus (2c,d) are comparable with single-gap *wh*-island violations; similarly the contrast between noun complement CNPC violations as in (2h,i) and the relative clause type in (2f,g) is maintained in the ATB structures.

A P-gap inside the subject of an adjunct is disallowed, as is the comparable ATB gap:

(3) a.  Who did John describe *t* without examining any pictures of *e*?
    b.  *Who did John describe *t* without any pictures of *e* being on file?
    c.  Who did John describe *t* and Mary examine pictures of *e*?
    d.  *Who did John describe *t* and pictures of *e* upset Mary?

Browning (1987) and Weinberg (1988) showed that a P-gap in the highest subject position in an adjunct is unacceptable, as shown in (4).

(4) *Who did John support *t* after *e* said would run for Governor?

However, if the subject is more deeply embedded in the adjunct, the gap becomes acceptable. This fact mirrors the original examples pointed out for ATB gaps by Williams (1978). We thus find the following comparable sets of P-gaps (5a,c,e) and ATB structures (5b,d,f) involving embedded subjects of various types.[2]

(5) a. Who did John support *t* after Mary said *e* would win?
    b. Who did John support *t* and Mary say *e* would win?
    c. Who did John hire *t* after Mary found out *e* was fired from his old job?
    d. Who did John hire *t* and Mary find out *e* was fired from his old job?
    e. Who did John meet with *t* after Mary claimed *e* had left?
    f. Who did John meet with *t* but Mary claim *e* had left?

**11.2.1.2 Anti-c-command**  Another property that P-gaps manifest is that the real gap may not c-command the P-gap (Chomsky 1982). This means that a subject gap in the matrix clause will not license a P-gap in an adjunct clause it c-commands (6a,b). This fact is mirrored in ATB extraction as well: A subject ATB gap cannot license an object gap as in (6c), nor can it license an embedded subject gap (ruling out some sort of parallelism constraint) as in (6d).

(6) a. *Who *t* filed the paper before [*e* read it]
    b. *Who *t* read the paper before [John talked to *e*]
    c. *Who *t* read the paper but [John didn't reply to *e*]
    d. *Who *t* read the paper but [John thought *e* was biased]

The only kind of apparent ATB subject extraction arises in cases such as (7a). These can be accounted for by analyzing them as instances of VP coordination rather than IP coordination; thus the proper structure for (7a) is (7b), involving a single extraction. The fact that (6c) is unacceptable showed that when IPs are coordinated a subject gap cannot license the second gap. Thus if (7a) were the correct structure, there would be no explanation for the contrast between it and (6c,d).[3]

(7) a. Who *t* read the paper and [*e* filed it]
    b. Who *t* [VP read the paper] and [VP filed it]

The data above do not show that P-gaps are instances of ATB gaps, nor do they show that ATB gaps are instances of P-gaps, since both approaches would presumably predict movement-type effects.[4]

There is one major difference between the two analyses, however. Under an ATB analysis, there is no such thing as a "parasitic" gap, as Williams states, "... it should be clear that the 'pg' in these structures is not really parasitic on the 'real' gap; in fact both gaps have equal status" (1990:271). This is a direct consequence of Williams's ATB formalism, which derives ATB gaps by a single application of *wh*-movement from all conjuncts simultaneously.[5] If, on the other hand, we adopt some form of the null operator analysis for P-gaps (e.g., Chomsky 1986b, Lasnik and Stowell 1991, Cinque 1990, Postal 1998), there is a distinction between the two gaps in that the chain of the P-gap must in some way be licensed by the chain of the real gap. If null operator constructions manifest differences in their distribution compared to overt operator constructions, then such differences constitute evidence against the ATB analysis.

There are, in fact, a number of ways that P-gaps differ from real gaps, and many of these differences show up in ATB gaps as well.

## 11.2.2 Crossover Effects

Crossover effects constitute an important set of criteria for distinguishing properties of gaps generally, and ATB gaps and P-gaps exhibit identical effects with respect to both strong and weak crossover.[6]

**11.2.2.1 Strong Crossover** Williams (1990) showed that P-gaps and ATB gaps show strong crossover (SCO) effects in the parasitic domain, as in (8).

(8) a. *Whose$_i$ mother did we talk to $t_j$ after he$_i$ saw $e_j$?
    b. *Whose$_i$ mother did we talk to $t_j$ and he never visit $e_j$?
    c. *Whose$_i$ mother did we talk to $t_j$ after he$_i$ said Mary saw $e_j$?
    d. *Whose$_i$ mother did we talk to $t_j$ but he$_i$ not think that we saw $e_j$?

These examples show that the gap in both an ATB construction and a P-gap behaves like a *wh*-trace and not some other empty category. Strong crossover does not distinguish between real and parasitic gaps, however.

**11.2.2.2 Weak Crossover** Whereas strong crossover does not distinguish between real gaps and P-gaps, weak crossover clearly does. Lasnik and Stowell (1991) showed that a number of constructions do not show weak crossover effects, despite having other hallmarks of being *wh*-

movement constructions (island effects, strong crossover, etc.) Included in this set are *tough*-constructions, topicalization, clefts, and P-gaps. Lasnik and Stowell call this absence of WCO "weakest crossover."

P-gaps do not exhibit weak crossover effects, as the examples in (9) illustrate. What is important here is that there is an asymmetry between the real gap, which induces a weak crossover effect, and the P-gap, which does not. We thus find a contrast between (9a,b) and (9c,d), in which the WCO-inducing element is in the main clause rather than in the adjunct.

(9) a.   Who$_i$ did you gossip about $t_i$ despite his$_i$ mother's having vouched for $e_i$?
    b.   Which man$_i$ did you visit $t_i$ just before his$_i$ boss fired $e_i$?
    c.   *Who$_i$ did his$_i$ mother gossip about $t_i$ despite you(r) having vouched for $e_i$?
    d.   *Which man$_i$ did his$_i$ boss fire $t_i$ just after you visited $e_i$?

These same contrasts show up in ATB extraction:

(10) a.   Who$_i$ did you gossip about $t_i$ but his$_i$ mother vouch for $e_i$?
     b.   Which man$_i$ did you hire $t_i$ and his$_i$ boss fire $e_i$?
     c.   *Who$_i$ did his$_i$ mother gossip about $t_i$ but you vouch for $e_i$?
     d.   *Which man$_i$ did his$_i$ boss fire $t_i$ and you hire $e_i$?

Importantly, the relevant contrast (see note 1) is that WCO arises in the first conjunct of an ATB extraction but not in any subsequent conjunct, as the data in (11) show.

(11) a.   Which man$_i$ did you hire $t_i$, his$_i$ boss fire $e_i$, and his$_i$ sister vouch for $e_i$?
     b.   Which man did you hire $t_i$, Bill fire $e_i$, and his$_i$ sister vouch for $e_i$?
     c.   *Which man$_i$ did his$_i$ boss fire $t_i$, you hire $e_i$, and his$_i$ sister recommend $e_i$?

In addition to the lack of weak crossover in P-gaps, Postal (1993a) showed that there is a correlation between the lack of weak crossover and the lack of what he calls secondary strong crossover. Unlike a regular strong crossover effect, as in (12a) (see also (8) above), a secondary strong crossover effect arises when a *wh*-element embedded in another phrase crosses over a coreferential pronoun.

(12) a.   *Who$_i$ did they inform him$_i$ that Joan would call $t_i$?
     b.   *[Whose$_i$ sister]$_j$ did they inform him$_i$ that Joan would call $t_j$?

In P-gaps, whenever the weak crossover effect does not appear, the secondary strong crossover effect does not appear. There is a crucial asymmetry between the P-gap and the real gap. Thus, whereas (13a) shows the secondary strong crossover effect when the bound pronoun is in the main clause, similar to (12b), if the bound pronoun is in the adjunct clause, no effect appears, as (13b) shows.[7]

(13) a. *[Whose$_i$ sister]$_j$ did you inform him$_i$ that you were going to fire $t_j$ after insulting $e_j$?

b. [Whose$_i$ sister]$_j$ did you insult $t_j$ after informing him$_i$ that you were going to fire $e_j$?

Exactly the same contrast holds in an ATB extraction: the secondary strong crossover effect shows up in the first conjunct, but not in the second.

(14) a. *[Whose$_i$ sister]$_j$ did you inform him$_i$ that you were going to fire $t_j$ and also insult $e_j$?

b. [Whose$_i$ sister]$_j$ did you insult $t_j$ and inform him$_i$ that you were going to fire $e_j$?

The lack of weak crossover effects found in P-gap constructions is not restricted to multiple gap constructions. Instead, as Lasnik and Stowell (1991) argued, it seems to be sensitive to the nature of either the element binding the gap or the gap itself. Given that weakest crossover is also found in topicalization constructions, *tough*-constructions, and nonrestrictive relatives, it cannot be attributed to characteristics of multiple gaps per se.

### 11.2.3 Resumptive Pronouns

A second asymmetry found in ATB movement arises in languages with resumptive pronouns, as shown by Hebrew data from Sells 1984. Resumptive pronouns are generally allowed in Hebrew relative clauses. However, in ATB extraction, there is a first conjunct asymmetry: if a second or subsequent conjunct contains a gap, then the first conjunct must not contain a resumptive pronoun. If the first conjunct contains a gap, the second conjunct may be either a gap or a resumptive pronoun. These facts are illustrated by the contrasts between (15) and (16).

(15) a. ha ʔiš še Rina roca ve ʔohevet ʔoto yoter mikulam
the man that Rina wants and loves him more-than anyone
'the man that Rina wants and loves more than anyone'

b. kol profesor še Dani roce lehazmin ʔaval lo maarix
every professor that Dani wants to-invite but not esteems
ʔoto maspik
him enough
'every professor that Dani wants to invite but doesn't esteem enough'

(16) a. *ha ʔiš še Rina roca ʔoto ve ʔohevet yoter mikulam
the man that Rina wants him and loves more-than anyone
'the man that Rina wants and loves more than anyone'

b. *kol profesor še Dani roce lehazmin ʔoto ʔaval lo
every professor that Dani wants to-invite him but not
maarix maspik
esteems enough
'every professor that Dani wants to invite but doesn't esteem enough'

The same facts hold in P-gap constructions, as shown in (17), further supporting the idea that ATB gaps and P-gaps are closely related constructions.

(17) a. ha mʔamar še karati lifnei še tiyakti ʔoto
the article that read-I before that filed-I it
'the article that I read before I filed it'

b. *ha mʔamar še karati ʔoto lifnei še tiyakti
the article that read-I it before that filed-I
'the article that I read it before I filed'

(18) a. ha ʔiš še Rina hikta kedey lifgoa bo
the man that Rina hit so-as to-hurt at-him
'the man that Rina hit in order to hurt him'

b. *ha ʔiš še Rina hikta ʔoto kedey lifgoa
the man that Rina hit him so-as to-hurt
'the man that Rina hit him in order to hurt'

The data above show that there are a number of ways in which ATB gaps and P-gaps behave alike. What is important about these properties is that they are asymmetric with respect to real gap properties. Given that the ATB formalism does not distinguish between gaps, these data constitute a strong argument in favor of reducing ATB movement to whatever mechanism underlies P-gaps.

## 11.3 Resumptive Pronouns and Crossover

The fact that resumptive pronouns in Hebrew show up in P-gaps when there is a real gap in the main extraction site suggests that P-gaps in English may be given a similar analysis. As Postal (1998) points out, the idea that null resumptive pronouns may be involved in certain kinds of extractions goes back to Perlmutter 1972, and has been adopted in various guises by Obenauer (1984), Koster (1987), Cinque (1990), and Postal (1993b, 1998). If P-gaps involve null resumptive pronouns, the lack of WCO effects would follow, because resumptive pronouns do not exhibit WCO effects (Sells 1984, May 1985; see also Safir 1996).

It is beyond the scope of this chapter to present a theory of WCO and its absence. However, there is considerable convergence with respect to the relationship between resumptive pronouns, lack of WCO, and P-gaps. Since ATB gaps and P-gaps behave similarly in these respects, then ATB movement may also take place using the resumptive-pronoun strategy. However, the fact that both P-gaps and ATB gaps show island effects and obey strong crossover leads to a significant complication in any account that posits null resumptive pronouns in the gap site.

The movement-like properties of P-gaps leads Chomsky (1986b) to propose the null operator analysis of P-gaps. There are a number of varieties of this kind of analysis in the literature: Lasnik and Stowell (1991) argue that the operator is not quantificational and, further, that the empty category it binds is a null name. Browning (1987) argues that the operator is *pro*. Postal (1998) takes the element to be a null pronoun, while Weinberg (1988) argues that it is PRO. Not all of these accounts are consistent with both the strong and weak crossover facts, however. They all agree that there is movement, and that this movement should capture the island and strong-crossover effects.

Safir (1996) suggests a way of capturing the difference between strong and weak crossover. Given that weakest crossover effects in single-gap constructions only arise when the element extracted is not a quantifier (Lasnik and Stowell 1991, Postal 1993a), Safir proposes to allow non-quantificationally bound traces to be converted to resumptive pronouns at LF. This captures the distinction between WCO and SCO in terms of the level of representation at which it applies: SCO is a constraint on movement, whereas WCO is a constraint on LF representations. Crucially, the moved element in the parasitic domain must be taken to be nonquantificational if this account of WCO is to be adopted. This can be done by assuming that the operator is in fact a null pronoun, as suggested by Browning and Postal.

In what follows, I assume the following basic analysis of P-gaps:

(19) a. A P-gap involves movement of a null pronoun to the edge of its domain.
     b. Movement is constrained by SCO and islandhood.

I will further adopt Safir's principle stated in (20).

(20) A derivational variable *v* is converted to a resumptive pronoun at LF iff it is not bound by a true quantifier.

### 11.4  Restrictions on Parasitic Gaps

The data above show consistent asymmetries between first and subsequent gaps in both ATB and P-gaps. It is important to note also that, with respect to WCO, the lack of WCO is found in single-gap constructions as well as multiple-gap constructions. However, Postal (1993b) argues convincingly that there are restrictions which P-gaps display that are not displayed by ATB gaps, and he argues that different analyses for each construction are required, with ATB extraction being analyzed as an instance of "real" extraction.

Postal identifies four major properties (listed in (21)) that distinguish parasitic extraction from real extraction.

(21) a. The P-gap and the licensing gap must be NPs.
     b. P-gaps are disallowed where definite pronouns are disallowed.
     c. A P-gap must not be in a position that is inherently unpassivizable.
     d. Neither the P-gap nor the licensing gap can be a predicate nominal.

Data exemplifying the properties in (21) are given here:

(22) a. *How sick did John look *t* without actually feeling *pg*?
     b.  They painted their house green/*it.
     c. *What color did they criticize *t* after painting their house *pg*?
     d. *What did John turn into *t* after Bill became *e*?

Postal claims that these restrictions are also found in other constructions, including the same kind of single-gap constructions that Lasnik and Stowell (1991) argued not to show WCO effects: *tough*-constructions and nonrestrictive relatives.[8]

Lasnik and Stowell, as well as Postal, implicitly assume that the particular properties they describe (weakest crossover and P-gap restrictions) are derivable from a single property that all the above constructions have in common. The fact that ATB gaps and P-gaps diverge on the two sets of properties shows that these implicit assumptions cannot be entirely correct. Whatever accounts for the lack of WCO cannot account entirely for the gap restrictions, and vice versa.

## 11.4.1   Semantic Constraints on Pronominalization

Postal (1993b) leaves the restrictions in (21) as descriptive statements. Property (21b) by itself, which refers to what Postal (1998) calls Anti-pronominal Contexts (AC), covers almost all of the other restrictions except (21c): non-NPs cannot be pronominalized with definite pronouns, and predicate nominals cannot generally be pronominal either.

Proforms are generally sensitive to semantic categories. The interrogative proforms *what, how*, and *when*, for example, select semantic categories (predicates, manners, times) rather than syntactic categories, as shown in (23).

(23) a. What did John do?          Eat the cake.              VP
     b. What is John?              A doctor/very happy.       NP/AP
     c. How did John fix the car?  Carefully/with a wrench.   AdvP/PP
     d. When did John leave?       Yesterday/On Tuesday.      NP/PP

It would not be surprising, therefore, that if a certain position bars a definite pronoun, the position is one that requires a semantic type different from the type that definite pronouns can be anaphoric to.

Postal (this volume) gives twelve examples of ACs, all of which disallow P-gaps. It is beyond the scope of this chapter to present analyses of all of these constructions, but I believe there is a common semantic thread that connects them: all involve positions which require semantic types that are not individual denoting. I have organized Postal's examples below and divided them into three groups, because I believe that they form a heterogeneous set.

Consider first the ACs in (24). Szabolcsi and Zwarts (1997) argue that one property distinguishing individuals from other semantic types is the former's ability to be collected into unordered sets. Unordered sets form Boolean algebras, which, by definition, are closed under all Boolean operations (intersection, union, and complementation). Non-individuals, on the other hand, can range over partially ordered domains upon which not all Boolean operations are defined. Colors, speeds, durations, and amounts are gradable with respect to some scale, and thus are partially ordered. All of the contexts in (24) are thus nonindividual denoting.

(24) a. Mirabelle dyed her sheets purple/that/*it.
     b. Maurice drove his car at that speed, but I didn't drive at that speed/*it.
     c. Tina stayed that week/*it in Bermuda.
     d. The Porsche cost $50,000/that/*it.
     e. The concert lasted the whole night/two hours/*it/*them.

A second kind of AC arises with certain kinds of sentential complements, as shown in (25). The simplest observation one can make about these cases is that sentential complements denote propositions, and propositions are not individual denoting. One must be careful, however, because not all sentential complements behave the same way. Anaphora to the sentential complements in (25a,b) uses the demonstrative *that*. *That* can also be used for anaphora to colors and amounts as in (24a,d) and is also the proform for predicates. The choice of *that* in (25a,b) therefore suggests that these complements are also nonindividual denoting.

(25) a. Mike doesn't mind [that you mistreated our gerbil], but I mind that/*it.
     b. These facts mean [that he is guilty] but those facts don't mean that/*it.
     c. Joe couldn't tell [that Sam was a werewolf], but Ethel could tell *it.
     d. Tina remarked [that it was hot]/*it.

A third type of antipronominal context involves the distinction between weak versus focused pronominal forms, as in (26). These cases certainly appear to be individual denoting; however, there is some evidence that suggests that they are in fact predicative.

(26) a. It was (only) HER/*her that the drug helped.
     b. The government contains (only) HIM/*him.
     c. That remark betrays [disregard for human rights]/(only) THEM/*them.

Bayer (1990) argued that focus-associating particles such as *only* combine with an XP to form a quantificational expression that raises at LF to some scope position. Since focused pronouns can combine with *only*, a focused pronoun must denote a predicate, according to Bayer, because only then could it combine with *only*.

It is beyond the scope of this chapter to present analyses for each of these types of constructions, but the connection between pronominalization constraints and semantic type seems to be quite clear. It is now possible to make a connection between the resumptive pronoun strategy used in parasitic gaps and the antipronominal effects. It is well known that null pronominal subjects in pro-drop languages must be definite. For example, although (27a) (data from Portuguese) is felicitous, (27b) is not (nor is its English counterpart). Instead, an overt indefinite pronoun must be used, as in (27c). This shows that *pro* cannot be indefinite.

(27) a. Um homem entrou na     sala. Usava           um terno escuro.
        a    man    entered in-the room wore-3SG-IMP a    suit  dark
        'A man entered the room. He was wearing a dark suit.'
     b. Dois homens entraram na     sala. #Usava          um terno
        two    men   entered   in-the room wore-3SG-IMP a    suit
        escuro.
        dark
        'Two men entered the room. He was wearing a dark suit.'
     c. Dois homens entraram na     sala. Um usava         um terno
        two    men   entered   in-the room One wore-3SG-IMP a    suit
        escuro.
        dark
        'Two men entered the room. One was wearing a dark suit.'

If parasitic gaps involve movement of a null pronominal, as the crossover data suggest, then parasitic gaps are necessarily restricted to positions where definite pronouns are allowed. Further, if the relationship
sketched above between pronominalization and semantic type is correct,
then Postal's generalization about parasitic-gap restrictions can be recast
in terms of semantic type:

(28) a. A null resumptive pronoun denotes an element of type $\langle e \rangle$.
     b. The semantic element represented by a P-gap must be a variable
        of type $\langle e \rangle$.

The statement in (28b) simply follows from (28a), provided that parasitic gaps *must* use the resumptive-pronoun strategy. I will return to this
below but will first present some more evidence in favor of (28b).

### 11.4.2  Lack of Functional Readings

Independent evidence for (28b) comes from two further restrictions on
P-gaps: lack of both functional readings and amount readings. Haïk
(1985) observed that P-gaps do not license sloppy identity of reflexives.
Thus (29) cannot be answered with *John$_i$ destroyed that picture of himself$_i$
after Bill$_j$ criticized this picture of himself$_j$*.

(29) Which picture of himself did John destroy after Bill criticized?

One can use this fact to show that P-gaps do not allow functional readings of *wh*-questions, a notion introduced by Engdahl (1986) to account for
examples such as (30).

(30) Q: Which poem does every poet hate?
     A: His first.

For concreteness, I adopt the analysis of functional readings outlined in Chierchia 1993. Under Chierchia's analysis, functions are higher order variables containing one (or more) arguments that are bound by a c-commanding element. Thus in (30), *every poet* binds the argument of the function, in this case, a function that maps poets into poems. A rough logical form for (30) is given in (31a), and a corresponding LF in (31b).

(31) a. For which $f$ : every poet$_x$ [x hates $f(x)$]
     b. [$_{CP}$ which poem$_i$ did [$_{IP}$ every poet$_j$ [$_{IP}$ $t_j$ hate $t_i^j$]]]

Functional answers to P-gap questions are obviously possible, given examples such as (32).

(32) Q: Which poem did every poet throw out $t$ without reading *pg*?
     A: Her first.

Crucially, however, this example does not really show that the P-gap itself can denote a function. If the P-gap itself were a function, then we would expect sloppy identity of the function argument to be possible, as shown in (33). But the only possible interpretation for (33) is (33a). It cannot mean (33b), which would be a possible interpretation if sloppy identity were allowed. Interpretation (33b) would arise from the LF in (34).

(33) Which poem did every poet throw out $t$ before her agent read *pg*?
     a.   Every poet threw out her first poem before her agent could
          read it.
     b.   *Every poet threw out her first poem before her agent read his
          first poem.

(34) [$_{CP}$ which poem$_i$ did [$_{IP}$ every poet$_j$ [$_{IP}$ $t_j$ throw out $t_i^j$ [before her agent$_k$ read $pg_i^k$]]]

The impossibility of sloppy identity of the functional argument is predicted if the P-gap is subject to (28b). If the P-gap is restricted to an individual, then the sloppy functional reading will never be licensed. Importantly, even though the P-gap is clearly anaphoric to the *value* of the function, this is consistent with (28b), given that the function is a mapping from individuals into individuals.[9]

Importantly, ATB gaps allow a sloppy reading of the function, as shown in Munn 1998, 1999b. Consider the example in (35) in the context of the following situation: Bill and Fred are both restaurant critics, and each have a respective list of restaurants to review. A good answer to

(35) can clearly be given in terms of the lists that Bill and Fred have. For example, we might answer *Bill reviewed his first restaurant and Fred reviewed his second.* I will call this the "paired reading."

(35) Which restaurant did Bill review on Tuesday and Fred review on Wednesday?

The LF of (35) (given in (36)) is essentially identical to that in (34), which thus shows that sloppy identity of function arguments is independently possible.

(36) [Which restaurant]$_i$ did Bill$_x$ review $t_i^x$ on Tuesday and Fred$_y$ review $t_i^y$ on Wednesday?

We can see that sloppy identity of the function is indeed the explanation for the felicitous answer to (35), because if there is no c-commanding binder for the argument, the sloppy reading disappears. For example, if the coordination is of VPs, the sloppy reading is not possible:

(37)  #Which restaurant did John review on Monday and criticize on Tuesday?

Although John could have reviewed two different restaurants, (37) only has the infelicitous reading where he reviews the same restaurant twice. Similarly, in the passive corresponding to (35), as in (38), the paired reading is absent. This is predicted because the NPs in the *by*-phrase do not c-command the traces in object position.

(38) a.   Which restaurant *t* was reviewed *t* by Bill and criticized *t* by Fred?

   b.   *His first restaurant was reviewed by Bill and his second restaurant was criticized by Fred.

The fact that ATB gaps allow functional answers with sloppy identity while P-gaps do not lends support to Postal's claim that ATB gaps are not restricted by the properties in (22). This amounts to saying that ATB gaps are not subject to any analog of (28b).

## 11.4.3   Lack of Amount Readings
A second independent piece of evidence for (28b) comes from the fact that amount relatives (Carlson 1977, Heim 1987, Grosu and Landman 1998) cannot form P-gaps, as in (39a), which only has the reading in which the wine Bill drank is that which was spilled. This is not the case of non-parasitic extraction as in (39b).[10]

(39) a. It was amazing the wine Bill drank *t* after Fred spilled *e* on the floor.

   b. It was amazing the wine we drank *t* that night.

Amount relatives are standardly analyzed as involving quantification over degrees, which are not individual denoting; the inability of amount relative P-gaps thus follows directly from (28b). Again, this restriction does not hold of ATB gaps; examples such as (40) are perfectly fine with an amount interpretation.

(40) It would take us weeks to drink the wine that John drank and Bill spilled.

The data above yet again support Postal's (1993b) claim that ATB gaps differ in nature from P-gaps. We can thus state the following generalization about ATB gaps and semantic type:

(41) An ATB gap may range over any semantic type.

**11.4.4   Resumptive Pronouns and Category Restrictions**
I noted earlier that generalization (28b) would follow from the idea that the extraction in P-gaps involves a null resumptive pronoun. The resumptive-pronoun strategy would therefore be able to capture the category restrictions of P-gaps correctly. However, here we reach an apparent paradox: I have argued that the lack of WCO effects follow from treating the gap as a variable converted to a resumptive pronoun at LF. The lack of WCO in noninitial ATB gaps clearly shows that ATB extraction is able to use the null resumptive strategy. However, since ATB gaps are unrestricted in their semantic type, they must only optionally use the null resumptive strategy. P-gaps, on the other hand, *must* use the resumptive-pronoun strategy. Provided the resumptive-pronoun strategy is *possible* in ATB extractions, the weakest crossover facts follow. If it is optional, however, no category restrictions will arise.

   The optionality of the resumptive strategy in ATB extraction makes the surprising prediction that WCO effects should arise in second conjunct ATB extractions which *require* sloppy identity. This prediction is borne out. Compare (35) (repeated here as (42a)) with (42b). Although (42a) allows the paired reading, (42b) does not. It can only have the interpretation in which Fred thinks his partner reviewed the same restaurant that Bill reviewed. Here the WCO-inducing element is incompatible with a nonresumptive strategy, and sloppy identity is blocked.

(42) a. Which restaurant did Bill review on Tuesday and Fred review on Wednesday?

  b. Which restaurant did Bill review on Tuesday and Fred$_i$ think his$_i$ partner reviewed on Wednesday?

The optionality of the resumptive strategy in ATB movement, however, raises two new questions: why is the resumptive strategy obligatory in P-gaps, and why is it optional in ATB extractions? This latter question is important, because if the resumptive strategy is not constrained in some way, it might always be available and WCO effects should never arise in simple questions and restrictive relative clauses, for example.

To answer the first question, I would like to pursue the idea that the obligatory nature of the resumptive strategy in P-gaps is due to properties inherent to the parasitic domain, which forces the use of the resumptive strategy, since no other kind of extraction will be possible. In ATB gaps, these properties are absent, and the use of the resumptive strategy is optional. This amounts to saying that coordinate structures do not constitute selective islands whereas parasitic-gap domains do.

Parasitic-gap domains can be divided roughly into two sorts: adverbial adjunct domains and NP domains. These are exemplified in (43) and (44), respectively.[11]

(43) a. Which paper did you read before/after filing?

  b. Which paper did you file without reading?

  c. Which paper did you read because Bill recommended?

(44) a. Which paper did everyone who read like?

  b. Which man did you discuss friends of with relatives of?

  c. Which man did you compare Fred's picture of with Bill's picture of?

I will treat the two cases separately, since it may not be possible to account for the islandhood of NPs in the same way as the islandhood of adverbial clauses.

## 11.5 Relativized Minimality Effects

Rizzi (1990) showed that relativized minimality effects arise when adjuncts and "nonreferential" arguments are extracted over other $\bar{\text{A}}$-elements. Referential arguments are not as sensitive to this restriction, although the data is more variable for them. The basic facts are given in (45).

(45) a.  What do you know how to fix?
     b.  *How do you know what to fix?
     c.  What didn't you fix?
     d.  *How didn't you fix the car?
     e.  What did John frequently say that Bill bought?
     f.  *Why did John frequently say that Bill bought books?

Examples (45a,b) show that referential arguments can extract over wh-islands but adjuncts cannot. Examples (45c,d) show that negation blocks extraction of adjuncts but not referential arguments, and (45e,f) show that intervening adverbial elements can also block extraction of adjuncts but not of referential arguments.

Szabolcsi and Zwarts (1993, 1997) make the connection between referentiality and semantic type by noting that the nonreferential elements for Rizzi (measure phrases, adverbials, predicates) are of semantically higher types than individuals. (See also Cresti 1995 for a similar suggestion.) In this sense, the relativized minimality effects in (45) show a restriction similar to (28b): only individuals can escape selective islands. Significantly, the effects in (45) are independent of whether there is another movement involved—that is, negation and adverbial elements plausibly do not involve movement, but block the extraction nonetheless.

Szabolcsi and Zwarts characterize individuals as denoting Boolean algebras, which are closed under intersection, union, and complementation. They treat selective island phenomena in terms of scope, as in (46). Individuals are always able to take wide scope over any other Boolean operator, because they are closed under all Boolean operations.

(46)  *Scope and operations*
      Each scopal element SE is associated with certain operations (e.g., *not* with complements). For a *wh*-phrase to take wide scope over some SE means that the operations associated with SE need to be performed in the *wh*'s denotation domain. If the *wh*-phrase denotes in a domain for which the requisite operation is not defined, it cannot scope over SE. (1997:232)

For adverbial adjunct P-gaps, there is substantial evidence that the parasitic domain involves the presence of independent scopal elements similar to negation and adverbials. If P-gap movement is to a scopal position wider than these elements, it will be restricted to individuals, as (28b) requires. In what follows, I informally treat these effects as relativized minimality effects, with the understanding that they are in fact derivable from (46).

**11.5.1  Temporal Adjuncts**

Temporal adjuncts provide clear evidence of the presence of another operator in the parasitic domain. Larson (1990), following Geis (1970), argued that temporal adjuncts such as *before* and *after* involve movement of a null temporal operator similar to *when*, which accounts for the ambiguity of examples such as (47).

(47)  a.  I saw Mary in New York before [$_{S1}$ she claimed [$_{S2}$ that she would arrive]]

   b.  I saw Mary in New York after [$_{S1}$ she swore [$_{S2}$ that she had left]]

   c.  I couldn't leave until [$_{S1}$ John said [$_{S2}$ I could leave]]

   d.  I haven't been there since [$_{S1}$ I told you [$_{S2}$ I was there]]

Each example in (47) is ambiguous with respect to the interpretation of the temporal preposition—the main clause in each sentence can be interpreted as relating either to the time of the clause marked S1 or to the clause marked S2. So, (47d), for example, can be interpreted as *I haven't been there since the time of my telling you* or *I haven't been there since the last time I was there*.

Supporting this analysis is the fact that the ambiguity is sensitive to islands, as the examples in (48) show. In neither case is the lower clause reading available.

(48)  a.  I haven't been there since I made the claim that I was there.

   b.  I haven't been there since you asked whether I was there.

The fact that P-gaps are allowed inside temporal adjuncts means that there must be two landing sites for the relevant null operators. It is not obvious where each operator lands, however. The issue depends partially on what assumptions are made about the structure of the adjunct, and what conditions allow the temporal operator or the parasitic operator to be interpreted. For concreteness, I will therefore make the following assumptions. Following Larson 1990 (see also Munn 1991), I assume that the temporal preposition selects a CP which hosts the null temporal operator. I also assume that the null element of the P-gap moves to the [Spec,PP] position. This yields the schematic structure in (49).

(49)  [$_{PP}$ $Op_{pg}$ before [$_{CP}$ $Op_{temp}$ [$_{IP}$ ... $t_{pg}$ ... $t_{temp}$]]]

In these cases, just as in the examples in (45) above, if the P-gap were a variable denoting a nonindividual (i.e., if *Op* in (49) were not *pro*), there would be a Relativized Minimality violation induced by the temporal operator. If the P-gap is individual denoting (i.e., *pro*), then the Relativized Minimality violation will not arise.[12]

### 11.5.2  Negative Islands

In addition to temporal adjuncts, the clausal preposition *without* can be treated as a negative element, and thus is expected to induce selective island effects. Evidence for this comes from the fact that clauses headed by *without* yield unacceptable sentences with overt negation in its immediate scope:

(50)  a.  *John left without no one hearing.
      b.  *John left without seeing no one.

In the semantic account of selective islands that I am adopting here, we can simply extend the analysis given for temporal adjuncts. The schematic configuration in (51) is sufficient to induce the relevant relativized minimality effects:

(51)  [$_{PP}$ $Op_{pg}$ [$_{P'}$ without [$_{IP}$ ... $pg$]]]

The two cases above show that the presence of other operators in adjunct P-gaps could account for the obligatory use of the resumptive-pronoun strategy.

### 11.5.3  Parasitic Gaps in NPs

Whereas the islandhood of adverbial adjuncts can be easily ascribed to the presence of interveners that block nonindividuals from taking scope over them, NPs do not obviously contain such interveners. I have nothing further to add on this issue. It may be possible that there is a purely syntactic account of these cases. One possibility is that the [Spec, DP] position can only host operators of a particular sort. It is not clear what such a restriction would follow from, however. I leave these cases for future research.

### 11.6  ATB Extraction

To account for the possibility of the resumptive-pronoun strategy in ATB extraction it is necessary to show both that the conditions under which the strategy is possible are met in coordinate structures, and, if the results of the previous section are correct, that there are no intervening operators.

Munn 1992 proposed that (syntactic) coordination is an instance of adjunction of a conjunction phrase to the initial conjunct of a set of conjuncts. Conjoined VPs, for example, would have the structure shown in (52), where B is the head of a Boolean phrase headed by a conjunction.

(52)

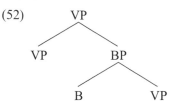

There are a number of independent arguments for the structure in (52), stemming particularly from the analysis of first/second conjunct asymmetries (see Munn 1993, 1999a, 2000 for details).

Treating coordinate structures as adjunction structures, we can immediately account for the fact that ATB gaps and adjunct P-gaps are similar: they arise in similar syntactic configurations. The structure in (52) is the same structure as a VP-adjoined adverbial clause. This allows one to treat ATB movement as an instance of "real" extraction from the first conjunct and parasitic extraction from subsequent conjuncts. An ATB extraction such as *Who did John see and Bill talk to* would thus have the structure given in (53).

(53)  Who$_i$ did [[$_{IP}$ John see $t_i$][$_{BP}$ Op$_i$ [$_{B'}$ and [$_{IP}$ and Bill talk to $e_i$]]]]]

The crucial ingredients for using the resumptive extraction strategy are thus in place: rather than "real" ATB movement, there is a second (independent) movement within the ATB structure which allows the resumptive strategy to be used if necessary. This allows WCO to be avoided in noninitial conjuncts, as shown in 11.2.2.2.

It is also clear that there is no intervening operator in an ATB structure that would induce a Relativized Minimality violation in the structure in (53). Thus, movement of a null operator that binds a trace of a higher semantic type will not be ruled out. Now, the second question raised above, concerning the optionality of the resumptive strategy in ATB gaps, can be addressed. The fact that P-gaps show category restrictions is simply because "real" movement is blocked. This means that the resumptive strategy is not attributable to null operator movement per se. We know independently that null operators must be allowed to range over nonindividuals, given that we can form restrictive relative clauses using them (for example, the amount relatives discussed in 11.4.3). This fact, combined with the fact that there are no intervening operators in a coordinate structure, will allow the operator in an ATB gap to range over nonindividuals.

We must, however, still constrain the system somehow; restrictive relative clauses in English yield WCO effects for many (but not all) speakers, and thus the resumptive strategy must be blocked. Because the relative clause in a restrictive relative must be semantically a predicate, the resumptive strategy may not be permitted semantically, although this would not account for the variation among speakers. The fact that the second conjunct in an ATB extraction is an adjunct may be sufficient to allow the resumptive strategy.

**11.7  Conclusion**

In this chapter I have argued that ATB gaps are similar to adjunct P-gaps with respect to crossover effects, particularly WCO. The lack of WCO effects in noninitial conjuncts of an ATB extraction are plausibly attributable to a resumptive-pronoun strategy within the noninitial conjunct. ATB gaps, however, do not show the category restrictions that P-gaps do, and thus must also be able to allow "real" (i.e., nonresumptive) extraction in their noninitial conjuncts. If the category restrictions also follow from the resumptive-pronoun strategy, then ATB gaps must only use this strategy optionally, whereas P-gaps must use it obligatorily. I have tried to reduce the category restrictions to the semantic distinction between individual-denoting variables and variables of higher semantic type. Null resumptive pronouns are only able to refer to individuals. The obligatory use of the resumptive strategy in the parasitic domain but not in the ATB extraction then follows naturally from independent differences between the two types of domains: real extraction of a nonindividual-denoting null operator in the adjunct parasitic domain will always be blocked by the presence of an intervening operator independently needed by the semantics of the adjunct clause. Such operators are not present in the coordinate structures, and thus ATB extraction does not show category restrictions. The question of NP-domain parasitic gaps remains open, however, but I hope that a direction in which an answer may be found is now clearer.

**Notes**

An early version of this chapter was presented at ZAS in Berlin in 1998. I thank Peter Culicover and Paul Postal for their comments and encouragement. Thanks are also due to Danny Fox, Norbert Hornstein, Sabine Iatridou, Chris Kennedy, Howard Lasnik, Winnie Lechner, Jon Nissenbaum, David Pesetsky, Cristina Schmitt, Satoshi Tomioka, and Chris Wilder for helpful discussion.

1. In this section I mainly restrict myself to cases of binary coordination, as the data begin to complicate quite quickly with more conjuncts. This is of course an arbitrary distinction (as it is with P-gaps, which are similarly unrestricted). For

simplicity I will refer to the "first" and "second" gaps in an ATB construction. Throughout, however, the correct distinction is between "first" and "subsequent" gaps.

2. Judgments seem to vary on these data, especially in the P-gap examples. Both Weinberg (1988) and Browning (1987) report the P-gaps to be acceptable, but others (e.g., Cinque 1990, Postal 1993b) have reported them to be unacceptable.

3. Peter Culicover points out that examples such as (i) indicate that something larger than VP coordination may be required. The issue then depends on whether $e$ in the second conjunct is the trace of the subject moved ATB fashion or not. But this sort of gap can appear independently of $wh$-movement, as in (ii), in which case $e$ in one may not be a ($wh$)-trace. See Munn 1993 for discussion of similar cases.

(i)  Who $t$ has just read the paper and tomorrow $e$ will file it.

(ii)  John has read the paper and tomorrow $e$ will file it.

4. Relative clauses seem to show a different pattern, as in (i).

(i)  the man who $e$ read the paper and Bob said $e$ understood it

Here however, it is possible that this case involves CP coordination with a null relative pronoun in the second conjunct, as in (ii), in which case no ATB subject movement is involved.

(ii)  the man [CP who $e$ read the paper] and [CP (who) [IP Bob said $e$ understood it]]

5. It is also a problem for most other accounts of ATB movement that appeal to parallel structures (e.g., Goodall 1987, Wilder 1998). See Munn, 2000, for discussion.

6. One property that distinguishes adjunct P-gaps from real gaps is their inability to license anaphor reconstruction in the parasitic domain (Kearny 1983), as shown by the contrast in (i).

(i)  a.  Which pictures of himself$_i$ did John$_i$ paint $t$ before Mary bought $e$?
     b.  *Which pictures of herself$_i$ did John paint before Mary$_i$ bought $e$?

The same contrast appears in ATB structures, as noted in Munn 1987, 1992:

(ii)  a.  Which pictures of himself did John buy and Mary criticize?
      b.  *Which pictures of herself did John buy and Mary criticize?

However, the reconstruction facts that hold for adjunct P-gaps are reversed for subject P-gaps, as in (iii), and the lack of reconstruction does not extend to single-gap extractions such as *tough*-constructions. This means that anaphor reconstruction per se is not prohibited into a P-gap, but rather that the second gap of a multigap structure is unavailable for anaphor reconstruction. See Munn 1994 for a discussion of these cases.

(iii)  a.  *Which picture of herself did every boy who saw say Mary liked?
       b.  Which picture of himself did every boy who saw say Mary liked?

7. Judgments seem to vary on examples such as (13b). Williams (1990) finds similar examples unacceptable, although I find them acceptable. Paul Postal (personal communication) points out that the judgment improves with possessives such as *which manager's* instead of *whose*, as in (i)

(i) a. *[Which manager's$_i$ sister]$_j$ did you inform him$_i$ that you were going to fire $t_j$ after insulting $e_j$?

    b. [Which manager's$_i$ sister]$_j$ did you insult $t_j$ after informing him$_i$ that you were going to fire $e_j$?

8. Topicalization constructions present a puzzle in this respect. Postal (1998) argues that NP topicalization exhibits properties (21b) and (21d), but topicalization per se does not seem to be restricted only to NPs. Topicalization of nonquantificational NPs does not show WCO effects, so it can clearly exploit the null resumptive strategy, but because it obeys the antipronominal contexts, it appears that use of the pronominal strategy is obligatory.

9. Cases like (i) suggested to me by Paul Postal (personal communication), do not pose a problem for (28b).

(i) It is every part of every Acura that they will X-ray $t$ before installing $pg$.

Although *every part of every Acura* denotes a function from Acuras to their parts, an LF of (i) (abstracting away from the syntax of the cleft) requires only individual denoting variables, as shown in (ii).

(ii) [$_{IP}$ [$_{DP}$ every Acura$_i$ [$_{DP}$ every part$_j$ of $t_i$]] [$_{IP}$ they will X-ray $t_j$ before installing $t_j$]]

More complex cases such as (iii) seem to require the value of the function to be a function, but I believe these cases still denote individuals in the semantics. The notion of a functional reading of a *wh* must therefore be distinguished somehow from that of a function in the (mathematical) real world.

(iii) [Which third-order functions of which second-order functions]$_i$ did they find the first-order function components of $t_i$ before studying the inverses of $pg_i$?

10. Example (39b) also has a individual variable reading in which the wine itself was amazing. This reading is not relevant here.

11. A third class may exist that includes cases such as (i) which appear to violate the anti-c-command requirement on P-gaps.

(i) Which man did you warn $t$ that Bill would visit $pg$?

I do not find these cases very acceptable, and they seem to arise with verbs that allow an implicit direct object argument in the "real" gap position as in (ii).

(ii) I warned that Bill would visit Mary.

To my ear, and to other speakers I have talked to, the examples degrade significantly with verbs that do not license an implicit argument in the real gap position, as in (iii) and (iv), although the judgment in (iv) is not shared by all speakers.

(iii) *I persuaded that Bill would visit Mary.

(iv) *Which man did you persuade that Bill would visit?

12. In Szabolcsi and Zwarts's terms, we must identify a Boolean operation associated with the temporal prepositions. *Before, after,* and *when* can be treated as quantification over times (Higginbotham 1988, also Larson 1990). *While* can be given a similar analysis in terms of durations rather than moments of time (Munn 1991).

# Chapter 12

## VP-Deletion and "Nonparasitic" Gaps

Christopher Kennedy

### 12.1 VP-Deletion, Parasitic Gaps, and Islands

Kim and Lyle (1995, 1996) discuss a very interesting set of facts involving parasitic gaps and VP-deletion (see also Rooth 1981 and Kehler 1993). They observe that apparent parasitic gap constructions do not show island effects when the gap is contained in a deleted VP, as demonstrated by the contrast between the (a) and (b) examples in (1)–(4) (in which the extraction islands are enclosed in brackets). In each set, the (a) example illustrates the well-known fact that parasitic gaps are sensitive to islands, and the (b) example shows that when the gap is contained in a deleted VP, the island effect disappears. (1)–(3) make this point for *wh*-islands, extraction from an adjunct, and complex NPs, respectively, and (4) shows that deletion even saves violations of the Coordinate Structure Constraint.[1]

(1) Wh-*islands*
   a. *Which article$_i$ did you read $t_i$ after Jim asked [who would be willing to summarize $pg_i$]?
   b. Which article$_i$ did you read $t_i$ after Jim asked [who would be willing to _____]?

(2) *Adjuncts*
   a. *Which movie$_i$ did you see $t_i$ because Polly was so excited [after going to $pg_i$]?
   b. Which movie$_i$ did you see $t_i$ because Polly was so excited [after she did _____]?

(3) *Complex NPs*
   a. *Dick Dale$_i$, who we attempt to emulate $t_i$ despite the admonitions of [many people who say we shouldn't try to sound like $pg_i$], is performing tonight at the Catalyst.

b. Dick Dale$_i$, who we attempt to emulate $t_i$ despite the
   admonitions of [many people who say we shouldn't _____ ], is
   performing tonight at the Catalyst.

(4) *Coordinate structures*
   a. *Which books$_i$ did you read $t_i$ after learning that Erik [read $pg_i$
      and found them$_i$ interesting]?
   b. Which books$_i$ did you read $t_i$ after learning that Erik
      [did _____ and found them$_i$ interesting]?

Kim and Lyle conclude from these facts that at least some parasitic
gaps must be licensed at LF. This analysis is very important, because the
traditional analysis of parasitic gaps—that they are licensed at S-structure
(Chomsky 1986b; see also Engdahl 1983, 1984, Chomsky 1982)—
constitutes a significant challenge to the hypothesis put forth in Chomsky
1993, 1995 that all grammatical constraints are enforced at the interface
levels LF and PF. If Kim and Lyle's analysis is correct, however, the
status of parasitic gaps as an argument against Chomsky's recent proposals must be called into question.

Kim and Lyle's argument runs as follows. Assume first that Subjacency
is a constraint on movement, and second that a deleted VP is devoid of
structure prior to LF, at which point its structure is built in by a copying
operation of some sort (see May 1985, Haïk 1987, Kitagawa 1991,
Chung, Ladusaw, and McCloskey 1995). If a deleted VP has no structure
prior to LF, then there is no parasitic gap chain in examples like the (b)
cases of (1)–(4) at S-structure. The chain cannot be created until after the
antecedent VP has been copied into the position of the elided one, introducing an empty category. Kim and Lyle suggest that a null operator is
then inserted into the structure, creating the parasitic gap chain (cf. Contreras 1984). Because this operation does not involve actual movement,
sentences of this type do not show Subjacency effects. Moreover, since the
parasitic gap chain is not instantiated until after the deleted VP has been
rebuilt, it must be the case that some parasitic gap chains are licensed at
LF.

My intention in this chapter is to present an alternative explanation of
the grammaticality of the (b) examples in (1)–(4). Specifically, I will argue
that sentences like the (b) cases of (1)–(4) do not show Subjacency effects
because they do not contain parasitic gap chains at all. Instead, I will
claim that the "gap" in the deleted VP is actually a pronoun, which is
interpreted as a variable bound by the overt *wh*-operator. That is, I will
argue that the actual LF representations of the (b) examples of (1)–(4) are

(5)–(8) (in which the content of the deleted VP is shown in boldface). Like their counterparts that do not involve VP-deletion, these LF representations are perfectly well formed.

(5) Which article$_i$ did you read $t_i$ after Jim asked who would be willing to **read it**$_i$?

(6) Which movie$_i$ did you see $t_i$ because Polly was so excited after she **saw it**$_i$?

(7) Dick Dale, who$_i$ we attempt to emulate $t_i$ despite the admonitions of many people who say we shouldn't **attempt to emulate him**$_i$, is performing tonight at the Catalyst.

(8) Which books$_i$ did you read $t_i$ after learning that Erik **read them**$_i$ and found them$_i$ interesting?

I will support this proposal by showing that the "gap" in the deleted VP in sentences like these is not sensitive to strong crossover (Condition C), which should be the case if it were a true parasitic gap, but is instead sensitive to Condition B, as expected if it is a pronoun. A result of this analysis is that "nonparasitic" gap structures like the (b) cases of (1)–(4) provide additional empirical evidence for the operation of *vehicle change* proposed by Fiengo and May (1994), which (among other things) establishes identity between a coindexed pronoun and Ā-trace in the context of VP-deletion.

## 12.2   Vehicle Change

Since at least the appearance of Sag 1976 and Williams 1977, it has been accepted that VP-deletion is licensed by some kind of identity relation between logical representations. Following Fiengo and May (1994), I will assume that this relation is stated in terms of *reconstruction*: formal identity between representations at LF (see Wasow 1972, Williams 1977, May 1985, Haïk 1987, Kitagawa 1991, and Chung, Ladusaw, and McCloskey 1995 for related approaches).

A number of facts indicate that reconstruction cannot require strict syntactic identity. Those of relevance here are exemplified by sentences like (9) and (10), discussed by Fiengo and May (1994) (sentences like (10) were originally discussed by Webber (1978)).

(9)   Achtenberg supports Brown$_i$, and he$_i$ thinks Alioto does, too.

(10)  Albert named a country that he wants to visit, and given the amount of traveling he does, I'm sure that he will.

(9) shows that VP-deletion eliminates Condition C effects. If (11) were the LF representation of (9), as we would expect if deletion required strict identity, then (9) would violate Condition C.

(11)  *Achtenberg supports Brown$_i$, and he$_i$ thinks Alioto **supports Brown$_i$** too.

Similarly, (10) indicates that VP-deletion can eliminate at least some Empty Category Principle (ECP) effects. If the LF representation of (10) were (12), then this sentence would violate the ECP, because the trace in the elided VP is not antecedent-governed.

(12)  *Albert named a country $Op_i$ that he wants to visit $t_i$, and given the amount of traveling he does, I'm sure that he will **visit $t_i$**.

To explain facts like these, Fiengo and May (1994) propose an operation of *vehicle change*, which in effect states that certain features are non-distinct with respect to reconstruction. The aspect of vehicle change that is relevant to the current discussion is that it establishes identity between coindexed elements with different values of the pronominal feature, as stated in (13) (cf. Fiengo and May 1994:218).[2]

(13)  *Vehicle change*
      $X_{[+\text{pro}]i}$ is a reconstruction of $Y_{[-\text{pro}]i}$.

With vehicle change, the LF representation (14), in which the name *Brown* is replaced by a coindexed pronoun, licenses deletion in (9), because the LF representation of the deleted VP is a reconstruction of the VP in the first conjunct.

(14)  Achtenberg supports Brown$_i$, and he$_i$ thinks Alioto **supports him$_i$** too.

Likewise, in (15) vehicle change establishes identity between the pronoun $it_i$ and the trace $t_i$ in the antecedent VP, licensing deletion in (10).[3]

(15)  Albert named a country $Op_i$ that he wants to visit $t_i$, and given the amount of traveling he does, I'm sure that he will **visit it$_i$**.

Although vehicle change bleeds Condition C in the context of VP-deletion, because it establishes identity between a referring expression or Ā-trace and a pronoun, it licenses deletions that are sensitive to Condition B (see the discussion of this point in Fiengo and May 1991, 1994). This is illustrated by the contrast between (16) and (17).

(16)  Rachel nominated Geoff$_i$ because he$_i$ asked her to.

(17) *Rachel nominated Geoff$_i$ because he$_i$ couldn't.

With vehicle change, the LF representation of (16) is (18), which is well formed with respect to both Conditions B and C.

(18) Rachel nominated Geoff$_i$ because he$_i$ asked her to **nominate him$_i$**.

The LF representation of (17), however, is (19), which satisfies Condition C, but violates Condition B because the pronoun in the elided VP is bound in its minimal governing category.

(19) *Rachel nominated Geoff$_i$ because he$_i$ couldn't **nominate him$_i$**.

The importance of these facts is that they show that Condition B effects can be used as a test to determine whether a particular deletion involves vehicle change. Before applying this test to the sentences under investigation here, I should not that if vehicle change is a general component of the grammar of ellipsis, as claimed by Fiengo and May, its effects should be apparent in a variety of contexts. In particular, vehicle change entails that (5)–(8) are *possible* LF representations of the (b) cases of (1)–(4). If it can also be shown that (5)–(8) are the *actual* LF representations of these sentences, the analysis that I have proposed here will be confirmed: namely, that sentences of this type do not show Subjacency effects because they do not contain parasitic gaps.

### 12.3 (Non)parasitic Gaps, Strong Crossover, and Condition B

In order to present the argument, I must establish a fact about parasitic gaps. Like other types of constructions involving Ā-movement, parasitic gap constructions show strong crossover effects. This is illustrated by the contrast between (20) and (21) (see Cinque 1990:150, Postal 1993b, n. 14).

(20) *This is the guy who$_i$ they arrested before he$_i$ realized they suspected.

(21) This is the guy who they arrested before anyone realized they suspected.

The ungrammaticality of (20) is expected: like other Ā-bound empty categories, a parasitic gap must not be bound by an expression in an argument position. In this sentence, however, it is A-bound by the pronoun *he*, as shown in (22).

(22) *This is the guy [who$_i$ they arrested $t_i$ [$Op_i$ before he$_i$ realized they suspected $pg_i$]]

Because parasitic gaps are sensitive to strong crossover, and assuming that strong crossover is calculated at LF (with respect to Condition C, which Chomsky (1993, 1995) has argued applies only at LF), the analysis of the (b) cases of (1)–(4) presented by Kim and Lyle and the one I have proposed here make very different predictions. If the deleted VPs in these examples contain true parasitic gaps, then sentences of this type should show strong crossover effects. If the deleted VPs contain pronouns licensed by vehicle change, however, then sentences of this type should not show strong crossover effects, but they should be sensitive to Condition B. Two sets of facts support the vehicle change analysis.

First, (23)–(25) show that sentences of this type are not sensitive to strong crossover.

(23) Which candidate$_i$ did Maureen vote for because he$_i$ asked her to?

(24) Who$_i$ did you nominate without him$_i$ knowing that you did?

(25) Who$_i$ did Marcus recommend after she$_i$ asked him to?

Each sentence is grammatical on the reading indicated by the coindexing, which is expected if their LF representations are (26)–(28), in which the elided VPs contain a pronoun instead of a parasitic gap.

(26) Which candidate$_i$ did Maureen vote for $t_i$ because he$_i$ asked her to **vote for him$_i$**?

(27) Who$_i$ did you nominate $t_i$ without him$_i$ knowing that you did **nominate him$_i$**?

(28) Who$_i$ did Marcus recommend $t_i$ after she$_i$ asked him to **recommend her$_i$**?

True parasitic gap constructions in the same contexts are not grammatical.

(29) *Which candidate$_i$ did Maureen vote for because he$_i$ asked her to support?

(30) *Who$_i$ did you nominate without him$_i$ knowing that you backed?

(31) *Who$_i$ did Marcus recommend after she$_i$ said he owed a favor?

(29)–(31) contrast with examples in which the offending pronoun is replaced with an expression that is not bound by the $wh$-operator, which are acceptable.[4]

(32) Which candidate did Maureen vote for because the mayor asked her to support?

(33) Who did you nominate without anyone knowing that you backed?

(34) Who did Marcus recommend after remembering he owed a favor?

Second, (35)–(37) demonstrate that sentences like the (b) cases of (1)–(4) *are* sensitive to Condition B.

(35) *Which candidate$_i$ did Maureen vote for because he$_i$ wouldn't?

(36) *Who$_i$ did you nominate at the same time that he$_i$ did?

(37) *Who$_i$ did Marcus recommend without realizing that she$_i$ already had?

Each of these examples is ungrammatical on the intended reading, in which the overt pronoun in the adjunct is coindexed with the *wh*-phrase. This is expected if their LF representations are as shown in (38)–(40), which violate Condition B.

(38) *Which candidate$_i$ did Maureen vote for $t_i$ because he$_i$ wouldn't **vote for him$_i$**?

(39) *Who$_i$ did you nominate $t_i$ at the same time that he$_i$ did **nominate him$_i$**?

(40) *Who$_i$ did Marcus recommend $t_i$ without realizing that she$_i$ already had **recommended her$_i$**?

If the pronoun is replaced by an expression that is not interpreted as coreferential with the object of the deleted VP, then the examples become perfectly acceptable, as expected.

(41) Which candidate did Maureen vote for because Louis wouldn't?

(42) Who did you nominate at the same time that Willie did?

(43) Who did Marcus recommend without realizing that Charles already had?

The conclusion to be drawn from these facts is that the "gap" in sentences like the (b) cases of (1)–(4) is not a gap at all, but rather a pronoun, licensed by vehicle change. An important potential objection to this analysis is raised by Kim and Lyle (1995). They point out that changing the featural content of an Ā-trace from [−pro] to [+pro] generates a [+pro] empty category—that is, *pro*—yet *pro* is otherwise unattested in English. Even allowing for the possibility of *pro* in English (see Cinque 1990), this would be an undesirable result. *Pro* is a syntactic variable; therefore, we would incorrectly predict that nonparasitic gaps should show strong crossover effects (Cinque 1990, McCloskey 1990).

In fact, within the set of assumptions I have adopted here, the vehicle change analysis does not require the introduction of *pro* into the LF representations of these constructions. This is because reconstruction—the relation that licenses VP-deletion—is a formal identity relation between phrase markers, not a derivational, structure-building procedure (see Fiengo and May 1994:288). Vehicle change should be understood not as a type of coercion operation that transforms a [−pro] empty category into a [+pro] empty category, but rather as a relation that establishes identity between two expressions in a syntactic representation that differ in featural content but agree in indexical value. Within this framework, the reconstructed pronouns in LF representations like (5)–(8) are lexically nondistinct from their overt counterparts and, as verified by the data discussed in this section, are subject to exactly the same distributional constraints.

## 12.4   Conclusion

Supporting my claims with evidence from strong crossover and Condition B effects, I have argued that the absence of Subjacency violations in the (b) cases of (1)–(4) indicates that the deleted VPs in sentences of this type do not contain parasitic gaps, but rather pronouns that are interpreted as bound variables. These are not variables in the syntax (i.e., resumptive pronouns, as suggested in Fiengo and May 1994); if they were, they would exhibit strong crossover effects, as shown by McCloskey's (1990) work on Irish. The pronouns in the LF representations of the (b) cases of (1)–(4) are ordinary English pronouns, equivalent in all relevant respects to the pronouns in their nonelided counterparts.

If sentences like the (b) cases of (1)–(4) do not contain parasitic gaps, however, then they do not support the conclusion that some parasitic gap chains must be licensed at LF, and so do not remove the challenge presented by parasitic gaps to the hypothesis that grammatical constraints are imposed only at the interface levels. Although there might be arguments in favor of LF licensing of parasitic gaps (see, e.g., Kim and Lyle's (1995, 1996) discussion of multiple *wh*-questions), nonparasitic gaps do not provide one of them.

Finally, nonparasitic gaps provide additional empirical support for an operation of vehicle change. The fact that these sentences do not exhibit strong crossover effects, but are sensitive to Condition B, shows that a pronoun and a coindexed Ā-trace must count as identical with respect to licensing VP-deletion, as argued by Fiengo and May (1991, 1994). More generally, if Condition B is a constraint on the distribution of pronominal expressions in an LF representation, then nonparasitic gaps provide additional support for the position that an elided VP is fully syntactically represented at LF.

## Notes

An earlier version of this squib was presented at the annual meeting of the Linguistic Society of America in San Diego, California, January 1996, and I am grateful to audiences there and at the University of California, Santa Cruz, for useful comments. In addition, I would like to thank Dan Hardt and Sandy Chung for helpful discussion of these issues, and two *LI* referees for detailed comments on an earlier draft. Any inconsistencies, errors, or omissions that remain in the current version are my responsibility.

1. Similar examples are also discussed by Lappin (1992, 1996), who presents sentences like (i)–(ii) in support of the position that VP-deletion does not ameliorate island effects in parasitic gaps (though Lappin (1996, no. 6) observes that not all speakers find these sentences unacceptable). The judgments shown here are those given in Lappin 1996.

(i)   ??This is the book which Max read before hearing the claim that Lucy did.

(ii)  *This is the play which John saw before Bill went because he wanted to.

Although these examples are clearly degraded, there are at least two reasons to believe that their awkwardness is due to factors independent of the parasitic gap issue. First, (iii)–(iv), although not ungrammatical, are only marginally better than (i)–(ii). Neither of these examples involves extraction out of either the antecedent or deleted VP, however.

(iii) Max read this book before hearing the claim that Lucy did.

(iv)  John saw this play before Bill went because he wanted to.

Second, (v)–(vi), in which the deleted VPs are in positions structurally identical to those in (i)–(ii), are significantly more acceptable (see also (2b) and (3b)).

(v)   This is the book that Max reviewed before hearing the news that Lucy already had.

(vi)  This is the play that John decided to see only after we criticized him because he hadn't.

These facts, along with the clear contrasts between the (a) and (b) sentences in (1)–(4), suggest that the awkwardness of (i)–(ii) stems from a difficulty in identifying the antecedent VP in these particular examples, not from illicit parasitic gap configurations.

2. Vehicle change is also involved in establishing identity between featurally distinct but referentially identical indexical expressions, licensing deletion in examples like (i) (from Sag and Hankamer 1984; see the discussion of this point in Fiengo and May 1994:218).

(i)   A:  Do you think they'll like me?
      B:  Yes, I'm sure they will. (**like you**)

3. See Hardt 1993 for an alternative, semantic approach to examples like (10). Observing the ill-formedness of LF representations like (12), Hardt argues that

"deleted" VPs are actually proforms and that the interpretation of VP-deletion involves recovering a VP meaning dynamically from context, rather than establishing syntactic identity at LF. Sentences like (10) are acceptable because the expression in the recovered VP meaning that corresponds to the trace in the antecedent is a free variable whose interpretation is contextually determined. An important difference between this type of approach to VP-deletion and the one I have adopted here, which relies on establishing identity between LF representations, is that it does not provide a direct explanation for the sensitivity of a deleted VP to syntactic constraints. As I will show, the gaps in the deleted VPs in examples like the (a) cases of (1)–(4) *are* sensitive to Condition B. If Condition B is a constraint on syntactic representations, as traditionally assumed, then cases such as these raise questions for a purely semantic account of ellipsis such as the one developed by Hardt (as well as those discussed in, e.g., Rooth 1981, Dalrymple, Shieber, and Pereira 1991, and Jacobson 1992).

4. An *LI* referee questions the strength of the contrast between (29)–(31) and their counterparts in (32)–(34), claiming that the two sets of examples are equally unacceptable. Although my own research has indicated that speakers consistently detect a contrast between these examples (and, crucially, (29)–(31) are invariably rejected), it is not surprising that some speakers may find (32)–(34) degraded: constructions in which parasitic gaps are contained in tensed adjuncts are generally considered marked in comparison with constructions in which parasitic gaps occur in nonfinite adjuncts. This fact actually provides another argument against analyzing sentences like the (b) cases of (1)–(4) as parasitic gap structures. The "gaps" in these examples are contained in tensed adjuncts, yet the sentences do not show the same degree of markedness as (32)–(34).

# Chapter 13

| Missing Parasitic Gaps | Paul M. Postal |
| --- | --- |

## 13.1 Background

Kennedy (1997) analyzes claims of Kim and Lyle (1995, 1996) to the effect that there are real instances of English parasitic gaps (P-gaps) which are, as it were, "inside" VPs elided in VP-deletion structures. Examples of the sentence types at issue are provided in (1) (= Kennedy's (2b)/(4b)).[1]

(1) a. [Which movie]$_1$ did you see $t_1$ because Polly was so excited [after she did _____]?
   b. [Which books]$_1$ did you read $t_1$ after learning that Erik [did _____] and found them$_1$ interesting?

Under the proposal that Kennedy criticizes and rejects, a case like (2a) would be regarded as a VP-deletion form of the P-gap-containing structure (2b):

(2) a. [Which movie]$_1$ did you see $t_1$ after Polly did _____?
   b. [Which movie]$_1$ did you see $t_1$ after Polly saw $pg_1$?

In an unformalized but intuitively clear sense then, the P-gap would be obscured by the presence of the VP ellipsis.

Advancing an impressive and persuasive argumentation based on pronominal antecedence facts, strong crossover effects, and island violations, Kennedy (1997:705) concludes inter alia that "the deleted VPs in *sentences of this type* (emphasis mine: PMP) do not contain P-gaps, but rather pronouns that are interpreted as bound variables." This would give (2a) a structure more like (3).

(3) [Which movie]$_1$ did you see $t_1$ after Polly did [see it$_1$]?

I regard the quoted part of Kennedy's conclusion about cases like (1) as both essentially correct and important. However, I will here challenge an inference one might easily (but as it turns out unjustifiably) draw from Kennedy's results because it is a natural generalization of them and he does not address the question explicitly and thus does not exclude it. This conclusion would be to the effect that Kennedy's results about "sentences of this type" are completely general, at least for English. Taking "sentences of this type" to mean "sentences with P-gaps inside of VP elisions," and referring to such P-gaps as "missing P-gaps,"[2] this inference would thus be the powerful universally quantified negative claim in (4a):

(4) a. There are no instances of missing P-gaps in English.
   b. There are no instances of missing P-gaps in any natural language.

Principle (4a) would be a logical consequence of, and weakly suggestive of the truth of, (4b).

The burden of this chapter is to argue that (4a) is false, and hence that (4b) is as well. I will try to show that this burden can be met not only without challenging Kennedy's results for the particular sentence class he dealt with but in part by using inter alia his patterns of argument. That is, I argue that in partially different sentence patterns, the same factual assumptions and logic that Kennedy applied quite effectively to show that sentences like (1) and (2a) do not contain missing P-gaps show that other (not too different) sentences do contain them.

## 13.2 An Earlier Observation

Material relevant to arguing the falsehood of (4a) had appeared in the literature before Kennedy 1997. Engdahl (1985:41, note 19) cited paradigm (5).

(5) a. ?a person who$_1$ you admire $t_1$ because you know close friends of $pg_1$
   b. *a person who$_1$ you admire $t_1$ because close friends of $pg_1$ become famous
   c. ?a person who$_1$ you admire $t_1$ because close friends of $pg_1$ seem to

Engdahl observed that the key factor rendering (5c) much improved compared to (5b) was the presence of the instance of VP deletion.[3] Clearly, (5c) is a priori interpretable as a case of a missing P-gap; this would be to treat it as the VP-deletion form of (6).

(6) ?a person who$_1$ you admire $t_1$ because close friends $pg_1$ of seem to admire $pg_1$

Recalling Kennedy's (1997) line of argument, it might seem that (5c) should be related rather to the non-P-gap structure of (7).

(7) *a person who$_1$ you admire $t_1$ because close friends $pg_1$ of seem to admire him$_1$

But an immediately visible problem is the initial clue underlying the entire argument of this chapter. Unlike (6) and (5c), (7) is, like (5b), ungrammatical, and moreover for the same relatively well understood reason, although one which has received a variety of distinct theoretical explications. Namely, it contains a subject P-gap whose licensing gap (L-gap) is structurally rather remote from it in specifiable ways.[4] In (6), on the contrary, the analogous subject-internal P-gap can be taken to have as its L-gap the P-gap in the direct object position, an independently attestable licit L-gap/P-gap configuration:

(8) ?a person who$_1$ close friends of $pg_1$ seem to admire $t_1$

These facts provide an initial indication that cases like (5c) do involve missing P-gaps, as in effect assumed by Engdahl; this analysis can explain why (5c) shares the relevant subject P-gap property of (6) and not, for example, that of (7). This earlier evidence for (4a) is, though real and suggestive, limited. And it now faces the apparent strong evidence to the contrary, provided by Kennedy.[5]

## 13.3   Applying Kennedy's Tests

### 13.3.1   The Island Test
For ease of discussion, it is useful to distinguish the cases Kennedy (1997) dealt with from those like that cited by Engdahl. Given that the key property of the latter involves a subject-internal P-gap whose putative local L-gap (critically, also itself a P-gap) is missing inside an elided VP, I refer to such cases as *subject missing P-gap cases* (SMP-gap cases) and to those putative missing P-gap structures that lack this feature, like those studied by Kennedy (1997), as *neutral missing P-gap structures* (NMP-gap cases). In this section, it will be argued that application of the very tests advanced by Kennedy yields contrasting results. Where Kennedy (1997) showed that NMP-gap cases do not involve missing P-gaps, the tests he utilized support the claim that SMP-gap structures do.

Kennedy's first argument is that NMP-gap structures do not manifest island violations, whereas their putative (under a missing P-gap analysis) P-gap-containing source structures do. A typical contrasting pair (from Kennedy 1997, (4)) is:

(9) a. *[Which books]$_1$ did you read $t_1$ after learning that Erik [read $pg_1$
       and found them$_1$ interesting]?
    b. [Which books]$_1$ did you read $t_1$ after learning that Erik
       [did _____ and found them$_1$ interesting]?

This contrast is taken by Kennedy, and no doubt rightly so, to show that
NMP-gap structures do not obey the Coordinate Structure Constraint;
this conflicts with the claim derivable from a missing P-gap analysis of
such structures that they should, given that the source without VP deletion does.

Kennedy gives parallel evidence for other island constraints, including
*wh*-islands, adjunct islands, and complex NP islands. It all consistently
shows that NMP-gaps do not yield island violations and provides a strong
initial basis for his conclusion that NMP-gaps do not manifest representations containing actual P-gap structures.

Remarkably though, when one applies the parallel assumptions and
logic to SMP-gap cases, partially different results are found. Contrary
to pairs like (9), in which the version with VP deletion is grammatical
and that with a visible P-gap is ill-formed, in the SMP-gap domain, both
members of the pair manifest violations. I show this for three island types:

(10) *Complex NP island*
    a. *[Which author]$_1$ did they defend $t_1$ despite the fact that friends
       of $pg_1$ didn't want to defend $pg_1$?
    b. *[Which author]$_1$ did they defend $t_1$ despite the fact that friends
       of $pg_1$ didn't want to?

A key point is the contrast between (10b) and the otherwise similar NMP-
gap case (11):

(11) Which author$_1$ did they defend $t_1$ despite the fact that Sally didn't
     want to?

(12) *Coordinate island*
    a. *That is the report which$_1$ Arlene copied $t_1$ after critics of $pg_1$
       read $pg_1$ and found it$_1$ interesting.
    b. *That is the report which$_1$ Arlene read $t_1$ after critics of $pg_1$ did
       and found it$_1$ interesting.

Again there is a relevant contrast with a corresponding NMP-gap
structure:

(13) That is the report which$_1$ Arlene read $t_1$ after Nick did and found
     it$_1$ interesting.

(14) wh-*island*
    a. *the one who$_1$ they hired $t_1$ after friends of $pg_1$ said it was unknown why Myron wouldn't hire $pg_1$
    b. *the one who$_1$ they hired $t_1$ after friends of $pg_1$ said it was unknown why Myron wouldn't $pg_1$

Again, comparison with a relevant NMP-gap structure reveals a contrast:

(15) the woman who$_1$ they hired $t_1$ after saying it was unknown why Myron wouldn't

One could construct further island cases, but I believe the data is quite consistent. The relevant island violations appear as well in the putative SMP-gap cases, which further supports the hypothesis that these examples actually do involve missing P-gaps.

### 13.3.2 The Strong Crossover Test

Kennedy's (1997) second test is based on the observation due to Barss (1986) (see also Cinque 1990:150, Postal 1993a:752, note 14) that P-gap structures manifest strong crossover effects. More precisely but still informally, it is not possible to have the path leading from a P-gap to its L-gap contain a weak definite pronoun anteceded by the L-gap. Hence the ill-formedness of the anaphoric linkages in (16b):

(16)  a.  the guy who$_1$ they convinced $t_1$ that you could get Mary to help $pg_1$
      b.  *the guy who$_1$ they convinced $t_1$ that he$_1$ could get Mary to help $pg_1$

Kennedy insightfully shows that putative NMP-gap cases contrast with parallel uncontroversial real P-gap structures in not manifesting strong crossover effects (= Kennedy's (26)/(29)):

(17)  a.  [Which candidate]$_1$ did Maureen vote for $t_1$ because he$_1$ asked her to?
      b.  *[Which candidate]$_1$ did Maureen vote for $t_1$ because he$_1$ asked her to support $pg_1$?

Kennedy rightly concludes that such contrasts counter an analysis that provides cases like (17a) with structures involving real P-gaps and provides an alternative analysis which appeals to Fiengo and May's (1994) notions of reconstruction and vehicle change.

However, the facts for SMP-gap structures are different:

(18) a. *[Which candidate]$_1$ did the linguist union support $t_1$ because
        friends of $pg_1$ claimed he$_1$ could get philosophers to support
        $pg_1$?
    b. *[Which candidate]$_1$ did the linguist union support $t_1$ because
        friends of $pg_1$ claimed he$_1$ could get philosophers to?

As in the case of island violations, there is again a sharp contrast for the
strong effect case in (18b) with an otherwise parallel NMP-gap form:

(19) [Which candidate]$_1$ did the linguist union support $t_1$ because they
      said he$_1$ could get philosophers to?

Thus I hope to have shown that the key arguments and assumptions
Kennedy used to show that NMP-gap cases do not involve true P-gaps
argue to the contrary that, as apparently first glimpsed by Engdahl (1985),
SMP-gap cases do.

## 13.4  Arguments for Missing P-gaps from Previously Argued Features of P-gaps

### 13.4.1  Antipronominal Contexts
Certain features appealed to in Postal 1993a, 1994a to characterize
English P-gaps in general can be used to formulate arguments with the
same outcome as those developed by Kennedy. That is, these features
seemingly argue that NMP-gap cases do not involve missing P-gaps but
that SMP-gap cases do.

The foremost such property is the incompatibility between P-gaps
and what are called by Postal (1993a, 1994a,b, 1998, this volume) antipronominal contexts (ACs), contexts precluding the occurrence of weak
definite pronouns. At issue then are a wide array of facts that pattern
like (20).

(20) a.  Otto dyed his rugs red/*it.
    b.  [What color]$_1$ did Otto dye his rugs $t_1$?
    c.  *That is the color that$_1$ Otto grew to hate $t_1$ after dyeing his
        rugs $pg_1$.

Example (20c) and other parallel ones below, are irrelevantly grammatical on a reading where the adjunct contains no P-gap and in fact no gap
at all and hence fails to specify that the rugs were dyed the same color that
Otto grew to hate.

A similar situation is illustrated in (21):

(21) a.  Adolph died in Berlin$_1$ and Eva died in Berlin/*it too.
     b.  the city which$_1$ Eva died in $t_1$
     c.  *the city which Eva died in $t_1$ because Adolph died in $pg_1$

Patterns like those in (20) and (21) can directly yield a test rather parallel to those tests utilized by Kennedy (1997), and the contrasts revealed further support his line of argument for NMP-gap cases:

(22) a.  *[What color]$_1$ did you dye your rugs $t_1$ before Albert dyed his rugs $pg_1$?[6]
     b.  [What color]$_1$ did you dye your rugs $t_1$ before Albert did?

However, remarkably, once again the same test yields opposite results for SMP-gap structures, arguing that they do contain P-gaps:

(23) a.  *[What trendy color]$_1$ did those women dye their hair $t_1$ just after certain partisans of $pg_1$ dyed their hair $pg_1$?
     b.  *[What trendy color]$_1$ did those women dye their hair $t_1$ just after certain partisans of $pg_1$ did?

(24) a.  *[What city]$_1$ did Eva die in $t_1$ because Adolph died in $pg_1$?
     b.  [What city]$_1$ did Eva die in $t_1$ because Adolph did?

(25) a.  *[What city]$_1$ did Eva die in $t_1$ because critics of $pg_1$ lived in $pg_1$?
     b.  *[What city]$_1$ did Eva die in $t_1$ because critics of $pg_1$ did?

The overall argument from ACs can also be based on the predicate nominal AC discussed in Postal 1993a; see also Lasnik and Saito 1992:147:

(26) Marsha became a vampire/*it/*her.

(27) a.  *[What kind of vampire]$_1$ did Marsha become $t_1$ (*shortly after Sylvia became $pg_1$)?
     b.  [What kind of vampire]$_1$ did Marsha become $t_1$ shortly after Sylvia did?

(28) a.  *[What kind of vampire]$_1$ did Marsha become $t_1$ shortly after several experts on $pg_1$ became $pg_1$?
     b.  *[What kind of vampire]$_1$ did Marsha become $t_1$ shortly after several experts on $pg_1$ did?

### 13.4.2  P-gaps in Passive Clauses

As observed in slightly different terms in Postal 1993a, it does not seem possible to have an English P-gap directly within a passive clause. One can distinguish two cases: (i) the P-gap is the object of the passive *by*-phrase; and (ii) the P-gap is some other object. Consider first case (i):

(29) a.   Who$_1$ was Sam convinced by $t_1$ that the director was a vampire
          (*just after Sandra was convinced by $pg_1$ that he was a
          werewolf)?
     b.   Who$_1$ was Sam convinced by $t_1$ that the director was a vampire
          just after Sandra was?

(30) a.   *Who$_1$ was Sam convinced by $t_1$ that the director was a vampire
          just after associates of $pg_1$ were convinced by $pg_1$ that he was a
          werewolf?
     b.   *Who$_1$ was Sam convinced by $t_1$ that the director was a vampire
          just after associates of $pg_1$ were?

The now familiar pattern obtains. Apparently missing P-gaps are possible in the NMP-gap structures but not in SMP-gap structures, in the case of P-gaps in passive *by*-phrases.

The same regularity holds in case (ii), where the P-gap is a non-*by*-phrase object of some sort:

(31) a.   Who$_1$ was Jane convinced to consult $t_1$ by the director
          (*shortly after Betty was convinced to consult $pg_1$)?
     b.   Who$_1$ was Jane convinced to consult $t_1$ by the director shortly
          after Betty was?

(32) a.   *Who$_1$ was Jane convinced to consult $t_1$ by the director shortly
          after relatives of $pg_1$ were convinced to consult $pg_1$?
     b.   *Who$_1$ was Jane convinced to consult $t_1$ by the director shortly
          after relatives of $pg_1$ were?

### 13.4.3   Unpassivizable Objects

Postal (1993a) observed that there are a range of unpassivizable objects that also systematically fail to be licit P-gaps. One can divide such cases into two classes: (i) the nominal in question is not part of a PP and hence is a priori subject to regular passivization; and (ii) the object is head of a PP and hence is a priori subject to pseudopassivization. As in previous sections, it turns out both types of restriction are maintained in SMP-gap cases but not in NMP-gap ones.

I start with case (i):

(33) a.   That book reached Mike yesterday.
     b.   *Mike was reached by that book yesterday.

(34) a.  the guy who$_1$ your book reached $t_1$ (*before my article reached $pg_1$)

b.  the guy who$_1$ your book reached $t_1$ before my article did

c.  *the guy who$_1$ your book reached $t_1$ before reviews of $pg_1$ reached $pg_1$

d.  *the guy who$_1$ your book reached $t_1$ before reviews of $pg_1$ did

Another instance of case (i) can be based on the observation of Postal (1993a) that unpassivizable objects of verbs taking bare infinitives do not permit P-gaps:

(35) a.  the pyramid which$_1$ Mike felt $t_1$ vibrate (*long before Arturo felt $pg_1$ vibrate)

b.  the pyramid which$_1$ Mike felt $t_1$ vibrate long before Arturo did

(36) a.  *the pyramid which$_1$ Mike felt $t_1$ vibrate long before other students of $pg_1$ felt $pg_1$ vibrate

b.  *the pyramid which$_1$ Mike felt $t_1$ vibrate long before other students of $pg_1$ did

For case (ii), consider:

(37) a.  Myron swore to that goddess to avenge the gerbil.

b.  *That goddess was sworn to by Myron to avenge the gerbil.

(38) a.  [Which goddess]$_1$ did they swear to $t_1$ to avenge the gerbil (*(only) after you swore to $pg_1$ to avenge the cat)?

b.  [Which goddess]$_1$ did they swear to $t_1$ to avenge the gerbil (only) after you did?

(39) a.  *[Which goddess]$_1$ did they swear to $t_1$ to avenge the gerbil (only) after friends of $pg_1$ swore to $pg_1$ to avenge the cat?

b.  *[Which goddess]$_1$ did they swear to $t_1$ to avenge the gerbil (only) after friends of $pg_1$ did?

Another instance of case (ii) is seen in:

(40) a.  Osmond left from that station.

b.  *That station was left from by Osmond.

(41) a.  [Which station]$_1$ did Osmond leave from $t_1$ (*before Greta left from $pg_1$)?

b.  [Which station]$_1$ did Osmond leave from $t_1$ before Greta did?

(42) a.  *[Which station]$_1$ did Osmond leave from $t_1$ before critics of $pg_1$ left from $pg_1$?

   b.  *[Which station]$_1$ did Osmond leave from $t_1$ before critics of $pg_1$
      did?

## 13.5  Arguments for the Missing P-gaps Based on Previously Unattested Features of P-gaps

### 13.5.1  A2 Extractions

There is a class of extractions, called A2s in Postal 1994b, 1998, which cannot form the L-gap for certain types of P-gaps. For instance, comparative extraction is of the A2 type:

(43)  a.  [Which lawyer]$_1$ did associates of $pg_1$ try to help $t_1$?
      b.  *Frank criticized more lawyers than$_1$ associates of $pg_1$ tried to
         help $t_1$.

And so is question extraction when the extractee is a nominal of the form [*How* adjective . . .].

(44)  a.  [What type of gorilla]$_1$ did stories about $pg_1$ enrage $t_1$?
      b.  [How ferocious a gorilla]$_1$ did stories about Sandra/*$pg_1$ enrage
         $t_1$?

Notably, these P-gap restrictions are maintained in SMP-gap structures:

(45)  a.  *Carla criticized more lawyers than$_1$ Tom defended $t_1$ shortly
         after associates of $pg_1$ criticized more lawyers than$_1$ Tom
         defended $pg_1$.
      b.  *Carla criticized more lawyers than$_1$ Tom defended $t_1$ shortly
         after associates of $pg_1$ did.

(46)  a.  [What type of gorilla]$_1$ did your story about $pg_1$ enrage $t_1$
         shortly after Bob's story about $pg_1$ enraged $pg_1$?
      b.  [What type of gorilla]$_1$ did your story about $pg_1$ enrage $t_1$
         shortly after Bob's story about $pg_1$ did?

(47)  a.  *[How ferocious a gorilla]$_1$ did your story about $pg_1$ enrage $t_1$
         shortly after Bob's story about $pg_1$ enraged $pg_1$?
      b.  *[How ferocious a gorilla]$_1$ did your story about $pg_1$ enrage $t_1$
         shortly after Bob's story about $pg_1$ did?

### 13.5.2  Objects of W-Verbs

It may not have been previously noted that the pre-infinitival objects of what were called W-verbs in Postal 1974 cannot be P-gaps. Again, it can be shown that this constraint does not hold for the NMP-gaps studied by Kennedy (1997) but does hold for SMP-gaps.

(48) a.  the guy who$_1$ I want/wish $t_1$ to resign (*although the boss doesn't want/wish $pg_1$ to resign)

b.  the guy who$_1$ I want/wish $t_1$ to resign although the boss doesn't

(49) a.  *the guy who I want/wish $t_1$ to resign although friends of $pg_1$ don't want/wish $pg_1$ to resign

b.  *the guy who I want/wish $t_1$ to resign although friends of $pg_1$ don't

## 13.6   An Unreal Air of Paradox

Combination of Kennedy's (1997) conclusions with those of the previous sections might at first seem to yield a paradoxical result. Considerable evidence shows that, for example, (50a) does not contain a missing P-gap whereas (50b) does.

(50) a.  [What book]$_1$ did Dorothy read $t_1$ before Gladys did?

b.  [What book]$_1$ did Dorothy read $t_1$ before most friends of $pg_1$ did?

Although there is of course no logical inconsistency in such joint conclusions, one might well conclude that no reasonable theory of P-gaps could permit them in (50b) while blocking them in (50a). Or, alternatively, if one tries to locate the problem in the conditions for VP deletion, one might conclude in a parallel way that no reasonable theory of VP deletion could make that incompatible with a missing P-gap in (50b) but not so incompatible in (50a).

However, any sense that the combined conclusions about missing P-gap distribution require some sort of special complication in either a correct theory of P-gaps or a correct theory of VP deletion is illusory. What one can and should say, I suggest, is that no special theoretical or descriptive complications ensue because missing P-gaps are allowed as much in the subset of sentences Kennedy studied, those called here NMP-gap cases, as in the subset focused on here, the SMP-gap cases. To maintain this view, all that is necessary is to explain why the evidence, including Kennedy's tests and the additional ones introduced here, fail to reveal the presence of missing P-gaps in NMP-gap structures but do reveal them in SMP-gap ones. But this is really straightforward. It involves one maximally simple assumption and then two quite uncontroversial observations that differentiate the NMP-gap and SMP-gap cases.

The assumption is that every potential missing P-gap case has at least one alternative analysis not involving a missing P-gap, namely, an analysis of exactly the sort which Kennedy argues for, one involving a pronoun not a P-gap in the relevant site. To be concrete, focus on (1a), repeated here as (51):

(51)  [Which movie]$_1$ did you see $t_1$ because Polly was so excited [after she did _____]?

All that I am assuming is that (51) realizes indifferently two modestly distinct structures for the elided structure, namely:

(52)  a.  after she did ⟨see it$_1$⟩
       b.  after she did ⟨see $pg_1$⟩

Call these the pronominal and parasitic analyses. Under the assumption that both exist, the reason that the sort of tests at issue fail to reveal the presence of a P-gap in sentences related to (51) is simply that those tests are only sensitive to parasitic structures like (52b). Hence the analogous VP-deletion cases can be good even when some constraint on P-gaps involving islands, strong crossover, and so forth would block a parasitic structure because these constraints fail to block a pronominal one like (52a). So, all the constraints at issue do is eliminate one of the two analyses, leaving the other to provide a grammatical structure for the NMP-gap cases.

When one turns to SMP-gap cases, however, say for concreteness (53), the situation contrasts:

(53)  *[Which movie]$_1$ did you see $t_1$ because Polly was so excited [after several critics of $pg_1$ did?

Although it is possible here to maintain the general posit that the VP deletion could involve either a pronominal or parasitic base, in every case parallel to (53) the former is independently excluded because it would have a form like:

(54)  $t_1$ ... [after several critics of $pg_1$ saw it$_1$]

That is, there is a violation of same constraint seen in (7). The upshot is that every SMP-gap case must actually have a parasitic base. Inevitably then, every constraint that distinguishes P-gaps from nonextracted pronouns, including every one appealed to by Kennedy and in previous sections of this paper, will have to be met. When they are not, ungrammaticality results, because unlike the situation with NMP-gap cases, there is no well-formed pronominal base for VP deletion.

Thus there is no hint of paradox nor any problem of providing a uniform treatment of both NMP-gap and SMP-gap structures, if one accepts the hypothesis of dual bases, one containing a P-gap, the other an ordinary pronoun.[7,8]

## 13.7 Conclusions

Kennedy (1997) in part takes his apparent demonstration of the nonexistence of missing P-gaps to bear on issues concerning the level at which P-gap "licensing" holds. Specifically, he takes his work to have undermined Kim and Lyle's argument from missing P-gap structures that P-gap "licensing" must be regarded as localized at a Chomskyan level of LF.

Present results alter the basis of his conclusions, which I will not consider further as they involve theoretical views I do not share. The following more general implications seem to me to be relatively unavoidable though:

(55) a. There are English P-gap sites that are "inside" constituents elided under VP deletion, that is, there are missing P-gaps.
b. Conclusion (a) provides further support for the view argued in Grinder and Postal 1971 and more recently in entirely different terms in Fiengo and May 1994 that an elided VP has a full syntactic structure.
c. It follows that a correct grammatical theory must allow the phenomenon of VP deletion and the phenomenon of P-gaps to interact in such a way that the latter forms structures relevant to the description of the former.[9]
d. One implication of (c) is, evidently, that, as also concluded by Fiengo and May (1994), theories of VP deletion based on purely semantic equivalences cannot be correct.

**Notes**

1. Here and below I normalize the notational conventions of quoted examples to those introduced in Postal, this volume.

2. The terminology of "missing P-gaps" is meant to recall the notion of "missing antecedents" of Grinder and Postal 1971. That work argued for the claim that elided VPs had full syntactic structures by invoking inter alia paradigms of the form:

(i) a. Mike didn't eat [any corn]$_1$ but Joe did because it$_1$ was healthy.
b. Mike didn't eat [any lima beans]$_1$ but Joe did because they$_1$ were healthy.
c. *Mike didn't eat [any oats]$_1$ but Joe did because it$_1$/they$_1$ was/were healthy.

The idea was that arguably the pronouns in (ia,b) need antecedents "inside" the elided VPs, since the constraint in (ii) shows that the overt indefinite under the scope of negation cannot provide one.

(ii) *Mike didn't eat [any corn]$_1$ because it$_1$ was unhealthy.

If so, the ungrammaticality of (ic) supports the existence of a richly specified syntactic structure for the elided phrase, given that the covert nominal inside the elision obeys the syntactic constraint on antecedence seen in (iii):

(iii) *Mike likes [oats]$_1$ but Joe doesn't like it$_1$/them$_1$.

The issue of missing P-gaps is in part parallel to that of missing antecedents. Both involve the question of whether syntactic evidence can be found for positing a particular kind of syntactic element inside a VP elision site.

3. Engdahl's marking of certain examples with question marks must be seen as having no relevant consequences for the present discussion, for it is part of a tradition that apparently sees most P-gap structures as marginal. If one ignores that view, which I do not share at all (I am grateful to Joseph Emonds for useful discussion on this matter), then (5a,c) would be treated, correctly I think, as simply grammatical. That is, I believe the tradition at issue here obscures the sharp distinction between (5b) and (5c).

4. There are many accounts of this restriction. The most often cited is probably that of Kayne 1984.

5. The hedge "apparent" here is explicated below. Just to keep things clear while proceeding however, my claim is that Kennedy's conclusions are quite unassailable as far as the particular class of data he dealt with. Implicitly at issue though is the extent to which those conclusions generalize to other related sentence types.

6. Again, (22) has an irrelevant reading where the adjunct contains no P-gap.

7. The idea that potentially missing P-gap structures have in general either parasitic or pronominal bases seems entirely consistent with the views of Fiengo and May (1994). For these authors need to and do allow reconstructions in which an extraction gap in one member of a reconstruction is equivalent to an extraction gap in another and in which an extraction gap is equivalent to a pronoun.

8. However, a problem for that view is pointed out to me by Christopher Potts (personal communication). Consider example (22b), repeated here as (i):

(i) [What color]$_1$ did you dye your rugs $t_1$ before Albert did?

Potts observes that, since (22a) shows that (i) does not have a grammatical parasitic analysis and the fact that the DP in the context $[dye + DP+\_\_]$ is an AC means (i) cannot have a grammatical pronominal analysis, it seems to be left with no analysis at all in current terms, and thus, contrary to fact, should be ill-formed.

In part following a suggestion by Potts, I believe the right way to avoid this unhappy conclusion is to generalize the notion of "pronominal analysis" to something better designated an "anaphoric analysis." The claim would be that the VP deletion in (i) involves an analysis of the invisible VP as involving the same anaphoric elements found in (ii).

(ii) Anthony dyed his rug purple$_1$ before Albert dyed his rug [that color]$_1$.

Required then is that the notion of equivalence relevant for the antecedence conditions for VP deletion treat the anaphoric device in (ii) in the same way that it treats the device of pronominalization. With respect to (i) in particular, note that (iii) is well-formed.

(iii) [What color]$_1$ did you dye your rugs $t_1$ before Albert dyed his rugs [that color]$_1$?

At issue here is, in large part, a question of the conditions governing what Fiengo and May (1994) call "vehicle change."

9. The argument for a full syntactic structure for elided VPs based on missing P-gaps is in effect just a special case of a more general line of argument which can be based on extractions not involving P-gaps. For instance, a whole set of such arguments can be formed on the basis of VP-deletion structures of type (i).

(i) Claudia respects Edgar but Marshall she doesn't [  ].

In such cases, the topic can only link to a gap inside of the elided VP. That it is correct to take such examples to be true instances of topicalization is supported by observing that forms like (i) obey a host of constraints on extraction manifest in cases where the gap is, in contrast to (i), overt. Some examples:

(ii)   a. *Maureen$_1$, I gave $t_1$ books.
       b. *I gave Peter magazines but Maureen, I didn't [_____].

(iii)  a. *[Green]$_1$, I would paint my car $t_1$.
       b. *Fred would paint his truck blue but green$_1$ he wouldn't [_____]

(iv)   a. *Harry$_1$ I should have called everyone except $t_1$.
       b. *Gloria should have called everyone except Sandra but Paula, she shouldn't have [_____].

(v)    a. *Quentin('s)$_1$, I contemplated $t_1$ riding the sled.
       b. *I contemplated Quentin('s) riding the sled but Arthur('s) I didn't [_____].

(vi)   a. *You$_1$, the person most likely to win is $t_1$.
       b. *The person most likely to win is Sheila so you, the person most likely to win isn't [_____].

(vii)  a. *[Those men]$_1$, Deirdre distrusts some of $t_1$.
       b. *Marsha distrusts some of those men but these men she doesn't [_____].

Example (viib) is ill-formed on the relevant reading "doesn't distrust some of" but well-formed on the irrelevant reading "doesn't distrust."

# References

Andersson, Lars-Gunnar. 1974. Topicalization and relative clause formation. *Gothenburg Papers in Theoretical Linguistics* 25.

Andersson, Lars-Gunnar. 1982. What is Swedish an exception to? Extractions and island constraints. In *Readings on unbounded dependencies in Scandinavian languages*, ed. Elisabet Engdahl and Eva Ejerhed, 33–45. Stockholm: Almqvist and Wiksell.

Aoun, Joseph, and Robin Clark. 1985. On non-overt operators. In *Southern California occasional papers in linguistics 10*, 17–36. Department of Linguistics, University of Southern California, Los Angeles.

Aoun, Joseph, and Yen-Huí Audrey Li. 1990. Minimal disjointness. *Linguistics* 28:189–203.

Authier, J.-Marc. 1989. V-governed pro, Case theory, and the Projection Principle. In *Proceedings of the West Coast Conference on Formal Linguistics 8*, 14–28. Stanford Linguistics Association, Stanford University, Stanford, Calif.

Authier, J.-Marc. 1991. V-governed expletives, Case theory, and the Projection Principle. *Linguistic Inquiry* 22:721–740.

Bach, Emmon. 1982. Purpose clauses and control. In *The nature of syntactic representation*, ed. Pauline Jacobson and Geoffrey K. Pullum, 35–57. Dordrecht: Reidel.

Bach, Emmon, and Barbara Partee. 1980. Anaphora and semantic structure. In *Proceedings of CLS Parasession on Pronouns and Anaphora*, 1–28. Chicago: Chicago Linguistic Society.

Baker, Mark C. 1988. *Incorporation: A theory of grammatical function changing.* Chicago: University of Chicago Press.

Baker, Mark C. 1996. *The polysynthesis parameter.* Oxford: Oxford University Press.

Barss, Andrew. 1984. Local binding, proper government, parasitic gaps: The role of VP-Spec. Ms., MIT, Cambridge, Mass.

Barss, Andrew. 1986. Chains and anaphoric dependence. Doctoral dissertation, MIT, Cambridge, Mass.

Barwise, Jon, and Robin Cooper. 1981. Generalized quantifiers and natural language. *Linguistics and Philosophy* 4:159–219.

Bayer, Josef. 1988. Fortschritte der Syntaxtheory. *Linguistische Berichte* 117:410–426.

Bayer, Josef. 1990. *Directionality of government and logical form: A study of focusing particles and* wh-*scope*. Dordrecht: Kluwer.

Bayer, Josef, and Jaklyn Kornfilt. 1990. Against scrambling as move-alpha. In *Proceedings of NELS 21*, 1–5. GLSA, University of Massachusetts, Amherst.

Bayer, Josef, and Jaklyn Kornfilt. 1994. Against scrambling as an instance of move-alpha. In *Studies on scrambling: Movement and non-movement approaches to free word-order phenomena*, ed. Norbert Corver and Henk van Riemsdijk, 17–60. Berlin: Mouton de Gruyter.

Bennis, Hans, and Teun Hoekstra. 1985a. Gaps and parasitic gaps. *The Linguistic Review* 4:29–87.

Bennis, Hans, and Teun Hoekstra. 1985b. Parasitic gaps in Dutch. In *Proceedings of NELS 15*, 1–14. GLSA, University of Massachusetts, Amherst.

Bennis, Hans. 1986. *Gaps and dummies*. Dordrecht: Foris.

Bever, Thomas, and David Townsend. 1979. Perceptual mechanisms and formal properties of main and subordinate clauses. In *Sentence processing*. ed. W. Cooper and E. Walker, 159–226. Hillsdale, N.J.: Lawrence Erlbaum.

Bordelois, Ivonne. 1985. Parasitic gaps: Extensions of restructuring. In *Generative studies in Spanish syntax*, ed. Ivonne Bordelois, Heles Contreras, and Karen Zagona, 1–24. Dordrecht: Foris.

Borer, Hagit. 1981. Parametric variation in clitic constructions, Doctoral dissertation, MIT, Cambridge, Mass.

Borer, Hagit. 1984. Restrictive relatives in Modern Hebrew. *Natural Language & Linguistic Theory* 2:219–260.

Bouma, Gosse, Rob Malouf, and Ivan Sag. 1998. Satisfying constraints on extraction and adjunction. Ms., Stanford University and Universität Tübingen.

Bresnan, Joan. 1977. Variables in the theory of transformations. In *Formal syntax*, ed. Peter W. Culicover, Thomas Wasow, and Adrian Akmajian, 157–196. New York: Academic Press.

Bresnan, Joan. 1994. Linear order and syntactic rank: Evidence from weak crossover. In *Papers from the Thirtieth Regional Meeting of the Chicago Linguistic Society*, 57–89. Chicago: Chicago Linguistic Society.

Bresnan, Joan, and Jane Grimshaw. 1978. The syntax of free relatives in English. *Linguistic Inquiry* 9:331–391.

Brody, Michael. 1984. On contextual definitions and the role of chains. *Linguistic Inquiry* 15:355–380.

Brody, Michael. 1990. Remarks on the order of elements in the Hungarian focus field. In *Approaches to Hungarian, Vol. 3*, ed. I. Kenesei, 95–122. Szeged: József Attila University.

Brody, Michael. 1995. *Lexico-logical form*. Cambridge, Mass.: MIT Press.

Browning, Marguerite A. 1987a. Null operator constructions. Doctoral dissertation, MIT, Cambridge, Mass.

Browning, Marguerite A. 1987b. Null operators and their antecedents. In *Proceedings of NELS 17*, 59–78. GLSA, University of Massachusetts, Amherst.

Browning, Marguerite A., and Ezat Karimi. 1994. Scrambling to object position in Persian. In *Studies on scrambling: Movement and non-movement approaches to free word-order phenomena*, ed. Norbert Corver and Henk van Riemsdijk, 61–100. Berlin: Mouton de Gruyter.

Calcagno, Michael, and Carl Pollard. 1997. Argument structure, structural case, and French causatives. Paper presented at the International Conference on HPSG, Ithaca, N.Y.

Campos, Hector. 1991. Silent objects and subjects in Spanish. In *Current studies in Spanish linguistics*, ed. Hector Campos and Fernando Martinez-Gil, 117–141. Washington D.C.: Georgetown University Press.

Canac Marquis, Réjean. 1995. The distribution of *à* and *de* in *tough*-constructions in French. In *Grammatical theory and Romance languages*, ed. Karen Zagona, 35–46. Amsterdam: John Benjamins.

Cardinaletti, Anna, and Michael Starke 1994. The typology of structural deficiency: On the three grammatical classes. Ms., University of Venice and University of Geneva.

Carlson, Greg. 1977. Amount relatives. *Language* 53:520–542.

Carpenter, Robert. 1992. *The logic of typed feature structures*. Cambridge: Cambridge University Press.

Chao, Wynn, and Peter Sells. 1983. On the interpretation of resumptive pronouns. In *Proceedings of NELS 13*, 47–61.

Chierchia, Gennaro. 1993. Questions with quantifiers. *Natural Language Semantics* 1:181–234.

Chomsky, Noam. 1965. *Aspects of the theory of syntax*. Cambridge, Mass.: MIT Press.

Chomsky, Noam. 1968. *Language and mind*. New York: Harcourt, Brace, and World.

Chomsky, Noam. 1973. Conditions on transformations. In *A festschrift for Morris Halle*, ed. Stephen R. Anderson and Paul Kiparsky, 232–286. New York: Holt, Rinehart, and Winston.

Chomsky, Noam. 1977. On *wh*-movement. In *Formal syntax*, ed. Peter W. Culicover, Thomas Wasow, and Adrian Akmajian, 71–132. New York: Academic Press.

Chomsky, Noam. 1980. On binding. *Linguistic Inquiry* 11:1–46.

Chomsky, Noam. 1981. *Lectures on government and binding*. Dordrecht: Foris.

Chomsky, Noam. 1982. *Some concepts and consequences of the theory of government and binding*. Cambridge, Mass.: MIT Press.

Chomsky, Noam. 1986a. *Knowledge of language.* New York: Praeger.

Chomsky, Noam. 1986b. *Barriers.* Cambridge, Mass.: MIT Press.

Chomsky, Noam. 1995. *The Minimalist Program.* Cambridge, Mass.: MIT Press.

Chomsky, Noam, and Howard Lasnik. 1977. Filters and control. *Linguistic Inquiry* 8:425–504.

Chung, Sandra, William Ladusaw, and James McCloskey. 1995. Sluicing and logical form. *Natural Language Semantics* 3:239–82.

Cinque, Guglielmo. 1983. Island effects, subjacency, ECP/connectedness, and reconstruction. Ms., University of Venice.

Cinque, Guglielmo. 1990. *Types of Ā-dependencies.* Cambridge Mass.: MIT Press.

Cole, Peter. 1974. Backward pronominalization and analogy. *Linguistic Inquiry* 5:425–443.

Contreras, Heles. 1984. A note on parasitic gaps. *Linguistic Inquiry* 15:698–701.

Contreras, Heles. 1987. Parasitic chains and binding. In *Studies in Romance Languages,* ed. Carol Neidle and R. A. Cedeno, 61–78. Dordrecht: Foris.

Contreras, Heles. 1993. On null operator structures. *Natural Language & Linguistic Theory* 11:1–30.

Corver, Norbert, and Henk van Riemsdijk, eds. 1994. *Studies on scrambling: Movement and non-movement approaches to free word-order phenomena.* Berlin: Mouton de Gruyter.

Cowper, Elizabeth. 1985. Parasitic gaps, coordinate structures, and the subjacency condition. In *Proceedings of NELS 15,* 75–86. GLSA, University of Massachusetts, Amherst.

Cresti, Diana. 1995. Extraction and reconstruction. *Natural Language Semantics* 3:79–122.

Culicover, Peter W. 1992. Topicalisation, inversion, and complementizers in English. In *Going Romance and beyond,* ed. Denis Delfitto, Martin Everaert, Arnold Evers, and Frits Stuurman, 1–43. OTS Working Papers, University of Utrecht.

Culicover, Peter W. 1993. The adverb effect: Evidence against ECP accounts of the *that*-t effect. In *Proceedings of NELS 23,* 97–110. GLSA, University of Massachusetts, Amherst.

Dalrymple, Mary, Stuart Schieber, and Fernando Pereira 1991. Ellipsis and higher order unification. *Linguistics and Philosophy* 14:399–452.

Demirdache, Hamida. 1991. Resumptive chains in restrictive relatives, appositives, and dislocation structures. Doctoral dissertation, MIT, Cambridge, Mass.

Déprez, Viviane. 1989. On the typology of positions and chains. Doctoral dissertation, MIT, Cambridge, Mass.

Déprez, Viviane. 1994. Parameters of object movement. In *Studies on scrambling: Movement and non-movement approaches to free word-order phenomena,* ed. Norbert Corver and Henk van Riemsdijk, 101–152. Berlin: Mouton de Gruyter.

Dowty, David. 1980. Comments on Bach and Partee. In *Proceedings of CLS Parasession on Pronouns and Anaphora*. Chicago: Chicago Linguistic Society.

Dowty, David. 1988. Type raising, functional composition, and non-constituent conjunction. In *categorial grammars and natural language structures*, ed. Richard T. Oehrle, Emmon Bach, and Diedre Wheeler, 153–197. Dordrecht: Reidel.

Emonds, Joseph. 1970. Root and structure-preserving transformations. Doctoral dissertation, MIT, Cambridge, Mass.

Emonds, Joseph. 1972. A reformulation of certain syntactic transformations. In *Goals of linguistic theory*, ed. Stanley Peters, 21–62. Englewood Cliffs, N.J.: Prentice-Hall.

Emonds, Joseph. 1976. A *transformational approach to English syntax*. New York: Academic Press.

Emonds, Joseph. 1985. A *unified theory of syntactic categories*. Dordrecht: Foris.

Engdahl, Elisabet. 1979. The nested dependency constraint as a parsing principle. In *Papers presented to Emmon Bach by his students*, ed. Elisabet Engdahl and M. Stein. Department of Linguistics, University of Massachusetts, Amherst.

Engdahl, Elisabet. 1980. The syntax and semantics of questions with special reference to Swedish. Doctoral dissertation, University of Massachusetts, Amherst.

Engdahl, Elisabet. 1981. Interpreting sentences with multiple filler-gap dependencies. Ms., Nijmegen: Max-Planck-Institute für Psycholinguistik.

Engdahl, Elisabet. 1982. Restrictions on unbounded dependencies in Swedish. In *Readings on unbounded dependencies in Scandinavian Languages*, ed. Elisabet Engdahl and Eva Ejerhed, 151–174. Stockholm: Almquist and Wiksell.

Engdahl, Elisabet. 1983. Parasitic gaps. *Linguistics and Philosophy* 6:5–34. Reprinted in this volume.

Engdahl, Elisabet. 1984. Why some empty subjects don't license parasitic gaps. In *Proceedings of the West Coast Conference on Formal Linguistics 3*, 91–104. Stanford Linguistics Association, Stanford University, Stanford, Calif.

Engdahl, Elisabet. 1985. Parasitic gaps, resumptive pronouns, and subject extractions. *Linguistics* 23:3–44.

Engdahl, Elisabet. 1986. *Constituent questions*. Dordrecht: Kluwer.

Engdahl, Elisabet. 1997. Relative clause extraction in contexts. *Working Papers in Scandinavian Syntax* 60:51–79. Instituten för nordiska språk, Lunds Universitet, Sweden.

Engdahl, Elisabet, and Eva Ejerhed, eds. 1982. *Readings on unbounded dependencies in Scandinavian Languages*. Stockholm: Almquist and Wiksell.

Erteschik-Shir, Nomi, and Shalom Lappin. 1979. Dominance and the functional explanation of island phenomena. *Theoretical Linguistics* 6:43–88.

Evans, Gareth. 1980. Pronouns. *Linguistic Inquiry* 11:337–362.

Fanselow, Gisbert. 1987. Konfigurationalität. Tübingen: Gunter Narr.

Felix, Sascha. 1985. Parasitic gaps in German. In *Erklärende Syntax des Deutschen*, ed. Werner Abraham, 173–201. Tübingen: Niemeyer.

Fiengo, Robert, and James Higginbotham. 1981. Opacity in NP. *Linguistic Analysis* 4:395–421.

Fiengo, Robert, and Robert May. 1991. Anaphora and ellipsis. Ms., City University of New York and University of California, Irvine.

Fiengo, Robert, and Robert May. 1994. *Indices and identity.* Cambridge, Mass.: MIT Press.

Fodor, Jerry A., and Janet D. Fodor. 1980. Functional structure, quantifiers, and meaning postulates. *Linguistic Inquiry* 11:759–770.

Fodor, Janet D. 1978. Parsing strategies and constraints on transformations. *Linguistic Inquiry* 9:427–474.

Fodor, Janet D. 1980. Parsing, constraints, and the freedom of expression. Ditto, University of Connecticut, Storrs.

Fodor, Janet D. 1983. Phrase structure parsing and the island constraints. *Linguistics and Philosophy* 6:163–223.

Frampton, John. 1990. Parasitic gaps and the theory of *wh*-chains. *Linguistic Inquiry* 21:49–77.

Franks, Steven. 1992. A prominence constraint on null operator constructions. *Lingua* 88:1–20.

Frazier, Lyn, Charles Clifton, and Janet Randall. 1981. Filling gaps: Decision principles and structure in sentence comprehension. Ms., University of Massachusetts, Amherst.

Freeze, Ray. 1992. Existentials and other locatives. *Language* 68:553–595.

García-Mayo, Pilar. 1992. *Pro* as parasitic gap licenser. In *Proceedings of the 1992 Mid-America Linguistics Conference and Conference on Siouan-Caddoan Languages*, ed. E. Smith and F. Zephir, 15–24. University of Missouri, Columbia.

García-Mayo, Pilar. 1993. A new look at parasitic gaps. In *Linguistic perspectives on the Romance languages*, ed. William J. Ashby, Marianne Mithun, Giorgio Perissinotto, and Eduardo Raposo, 250–258. Amsterdam: John Benjamins.

García-Mayo, Pilar, and Paula Kempchinsky. 1994. Finiteness in Romance versus English parasitic gap constructions. In *Issues and theory in Romance linguistics*, ed. Michael L. Mazzola, 303–316. Washington, D.C.: Georgetown University Press.

Gazdar, Gerald. 1981. Unbounded dependencies and coordinate structure. *Linguistic Inquiry* 12:155–184.

Gazdar, Gerald. 1982. Phrase structure grammar. In *The nature of syntactic representation*, ed. Pauline Jacobson and Geoffrey K. Pullum, 131–186. Dordrecht: Reidel.

Gazdar, Gerald, Ewan Klein, Geoffrey K. Pullum, and Ivan A. Sag. 1984. Foot features and parasitic gaps. In *Sentential complementation*, ed. Wim de Geest and Yvan Putseys, 83–94. Dordrecht: Foris.

Gazdar, Gerald, Ewan Klein, Geoffrey K. Pullum, and Ivan A. Sag. 1985. *Generalized phrase structure grammar.* Oxford: Blackwell.

Geis, Michael. 1970. Adverbial subordinate clauses in english. Doctoral dissertation, MIT, Cambridge, Mass.

George, Leland. 1980. Analogical generalization in natural language. Doctoral dissertation, MIT, Cambridge, Mass.

Goodall, Grant. 1987. *Parallel structures in syntax.* Cambridge: Cambridge University Press.

Grewendorf, Günter. 1988. Aspekte der Deutschen syntax. Tübingen: Gunter Narr.

Grimshaw, Jane. 1990. *Argument structure.* Cambridge, Mass.: MIT Press.

Grinder John, and Paul M. Postal. 1971. Missing antecedents. *Linguistic Inquiry* 11:269–312.

Groos, Anneke, and Henk van Riemsdijk. 1981. Matching effects in free relatives: A parameter of core grammar. In *Theory of markedness in generative grammar,* ed. Adriana Belletti, Luciana Brandi, and Luigi Rizzi, 171–216. Pisa: Scuola Normale Superiorie.

Grosu, Alexander, 1980. On the analogical extension of rule domains. *Theoretical Linguistics* 7:1–55.

Grosu, Alexander, and Fred Landman. 1998. Strange relatives of the third kind. *Natural Language Semantics* 6:125–170.

Haegeman, Liliane. 1984. Parasitic gaps and adverbial clauses. *Journal of Linguistics* 20:229–232.

Haïk, Isabelle. 1984. Indirect binding. *Linguistic Inquiry* 15:185–224.

Haïk, Isabelle. 1985. The syntax of operators. Doctoral dissertation, MIT, Cambridge, Mass.

Haïk, Isabelle. 1987. Bound VPs that need to be. *Linguistics and Philosophy* 10:535–565.

Halle, Morris, and Alec Marantz. 1993. Distributed morphology and the pieces of inflection. *The view from Building 20,* ed. Kenneth Hale and Samuel Jay Keyser, 111–176. Cambridge, Mass.: MIT Press.

Hardt, Daniel. 1993. Verb phrase ellipsis: Form, meaning, and processing. Doctoral dissertation, University of Pennsylvania, Philadelphia.

Haverkort, Marco. 1993. Romance and Germanic clitics: A comparison of their syntactic behavior. In *The Berkeley Conference on Dutch Linguistics 1993,* ed. T. J. Shannon and J. P. Snapper, 131–150. Lanham, Md.: University Press of America.

Heim, Irene. 1987. Where does the Definiteness Restriction apply? Evidence from the definiteness of variables. In *The representation of (in)definiteness,* ed. Eric J. Reuland and Alice G. B. ter Meulen, 21–42. Cambridge, Mass.: MIT Press.

Heinz, Wolfgang, and Johannes Matiasek. 1994. Argument structure and case assignment. In *German in Head-Driven Phrase Structure Grammar,* ed. Klaus Netter, John Nerbonne, and Carl Pollard. Stanford, Calif.: CSLI Publications.

Hellan, Lars. 1980. On anaphora in Norwegian. In *Proceedings of the CLS Parasession on Pronouns and Anaphora*. Chicago: Chicago Linguistic Society.

Hestvik, Arild. 1992. LF movement of pronouns and antisubject orientation. *Linguistic Inquiry* 23:557–594.

Higginbotham, James. 1988. Is semantics necessary? In *Proceedings of the Aristotelean Society*. London.

Higginbotham, James, and Robert May. 1981. Questions, quantifiers, and crossing. *The Linguistic Review* 1:41–80.

Hinrichs, Erhard, and Tsuneko Nakazawa. 1998. Third construction and VP extraposition in German: An HPSG analysis. In *Complex predicates in nonderivational syntax*, Syntax and Semantics 30, ed. Erhard Hinrichs, Andreas Kathol, and Tsuneko Nakazawa, 115–157. New York: Academic Press.

Hoekstra, Teun, and René Mulder. 1990. Unergatives as copular verbs: Locational and existential predication. *The Linguistic Review* 7:1–79.

Hornstein, Norbert. 1995. *Logical Form: From GB to minimalism*. Oxford: Blackwell.

Horvath, Julia. 1992. The anti-c-command and case-compatibility in the licensing of parasitic chains. *The Linguistic Review* 9:183–218.

Huang, C.-T. James. 1982. Logical relations in Chinese and the theory of grammar. Doctoral dissertation, MIT, Cambridge, Mass.

Huckabay, H. 1989. The closed licensing domain. In *Papers from the 25th Annual Regional Meeting of the Chicago Linguistic Society*, Vol. 1, ed. C. Wiltshire, R. Graczyk, and B. Music, 213–226. Chicago: Chicago Linguistic Society.

Hudson, Richard A. 1976. Conjunction reduction, gapping, and right node raising. *Language* 52:535–562.

Hukari, Thomas E., and Robert D. Levine. 1989. Category antirecursion: Paradoxical consequences of gap-within-filler constructions. In *Proceedings of the Eighth West Coast Conference on Formal Linguistics*, 192–206. Stanford Linguistics Association, Stanford University, Stanford, Calif.

Hukari, Thomas E., and Robert D. Levine 1987. Parasitic gaps, slash termination, and the c-command condition. *Natural Language & Linguistic Theory* 5:197–222.

Hukari, Thomas E., and Robert D. Levine. 1991. On the disunity of unbounded dependency constructions. *Natural Language & Linguistic Theory* 9:97–144.

Hukari, Thomas E., and Robert D. Levine. 1996. Phrase structure grammar: The next generation. *Journal of Linguistics* 32:465–496.

Hukari, Thomas E., and Robert D. Levine. 1998. Subject extraction. Ms., University of Victoria and Ohio State University. Originally presented at the 1996 International Conference on HPSG, Marseilles.

Hulk, Aafke, and Christine Tellier. 1999. Conflictual agreement in Romance nominals. In *Formal perspectives on Romance linguistics*, ed. J.-Marc Authier, Barbara E. Bullock, and Lisa A. Reed, 179–195. Amsterdam: John Benjamins.

Hulk, Aafke, and Christine Tellier. 2000. Mismatches. *Probus* 12.

Huot, Hélène. 1981. *Constructions infinitives du français: Le subordonnant* de. Geneva: Librairie Droz.

Huybregts, Riny, and Henk van Riemsdijk. 1985. Parasitic gaps and ATB. In *Proceedings of NELS 15*, 168–187. GLSA, University of Massachusetts, Amherst.

Jackendoff, Ray. 1972. *Semantic interpretation in generative grammar.* Cambridge, Mass.: MIT Press.

Jacobson, Pauline. 1977. The syntax of crossing coreference sentences. Doctoral dissertation, University of California, Berkeley.

Jacobson, Pauline. 1992. ACD in a variable free semantics. In *Proceedings of SALT 2*, 193–213. Department of Linguistics, The Ohio State University, Columbus.

Jayaseelan, K. A. 1990. Incomplete VP deletion and gapping. *Linguistic Analysis* 20:64–81.

Johnson, David E., and Paul M. Postal 1980. *Arc pair grammar.* Princeton, N.J.: Princeton University Press.

Jones, Charles. 1987. Empty operators and parasitic gaps. In *Proceedings of NELS 18*, Vol. 1, 254–270. GLSA, University of Massachusetts, Amherst.

Källgren, Gunnel, and Ellen F. Prince. 1989. Swedish VP-topicalization and Yiddish verb-topicalization. *Nordic Journal of Linguistics* 12:47–58.

Kaplan, Ronald M., and Joan Bresnan. 1982. Lexical-Functional Grammar: A formal system for grammatical representation. In *The mental representation of grammatical relations*, ed. Joan Bresnan, 173–281. Cambridge, Mass.: MIT Press.

Kardela, H. 1990. Paths. An analysis of parasitic gap phenomena in English and Polish. In *Further insights into contrastive analysis*, ed. J. Fisiak, 389–410. Amsterdam: John Benjamins.

Karimi, Simin. 1999. A note on parasitic gaps and specificity. *Linguistic Inquiry* 30:704–713.

Kathol, Andreas. 1995. Another look at parasitic gaps in German. In *Proceedings of the Fifth Meeting of the Formal Linguistic Society of Midamerica*, 303–315.

Kayne, Richard S. 1975. *French syntax: The transformational cycle.* Cambridge, Mass.: MIT Press.

Kayne, Richard S. 1976. French relative *que*. In *Current studies in Romance linguistics*, ed. F. Hensey and M. Luján, 255–299. Washington, D.C.: Georgetown University Press.

Kayne, Richard S. 1980. Extensions of binding and case-marking. *Linguistic Inquiry* 20:75–96.

Kayne, Richard S. 1981. On certain differences between English and French. *Linguistic Inquiry* 2:349–371.

Kayne, Richard S. 1983. Connectedness. *Linguistic Inquiry* 14:223–250.

Kayne, Richard S. 1984. *Connectedness and binary branching.* Dordrecht: Foris.

Kayne, Richard S. 1989. Null subjects and clitic climbing. In *The null subject parameter*, ed. Osvaldo Jaeggli and Ken Safir, 239–262. Dordrecht: Reidel.

Kayne, Richard S. 1991. Romance clitics, verb movement, and PRO. *Linguistic Inquiry* 22:647–686.

Kayne, Richard S. 1993. Toward a modular theory of auxiliary selection. *Studia Linguistica* 47:3–31.

Kayne, Richard S. 1994. *The antisymmetry of syntax.* Cambridge, Mass. MIT Press.

Kearney, K. 1983. Governing categories. Ms., University of Connecticut, Storrs.

Keenan, Edward. 1975. Logical expressive power and syntactic variation in natural language. In *Formal semantics of natural language*, ed. Edward Keenan, 406–421. Cambridge: Cambridge University Press.

Keenan, Edward, and Bernard Comrie: 1977. Noun phrase accessibility and grammar. *Linguistic Inquiry* 8:63–99.

Kehler, Andrew. 1993. The effect of establishing coherence in ellipsis and anaphora resolution. In *Proceedings of the Thirty-first Annual Meeting of the Association for Computational Linguistics*, 62–69. Association for Computational Linguistics.

Kennedy, Christopher. 1997. VP-deletion and nonparasitic gaps, *Linguistic Inquiry* 28:697–707. Reprinted in this volume.

Kim, Soowon, and James Lyle. 1995. Chain composition and logical form. Ms., University of Washington, Seattle.

Kim, Soowon, and James Lyle. 1996. Parasitic gaps, multiple questions, and VP ellipsis. *The Proceedings of the Fourteenth West Coast Conference on Formal Linguistics*, ed. Jose Camacho, Lina Choueiri, and Maki Watanabe, 287–301. Stanford, Calif.: CSLI Publications. Distributed by Cambridge University Press.

King, Paul. 1989. A logical formalism for Head-driven Phrase Structure Grammar. Doctoral dissertation, Manchester University.

King, Paul. 1994. An expanded logical formalism for head-driven phrase structure grammar. Arbeitspapiere des SFB 340, No. 59, Universität Tübingen.

Kiss, Katalin É. 1985. Parasitic chains. *The Linguistic Review* 5:41–74. Reprinted in this volume.

Kiss, Katalin É. 1987a. *Configurationality in Hungarian.* Dordrecht: Reidel.

Kiss, Katalin É. 1987b. Is the VP universal? In *approaches to Hungarian 2*, ed. I. Kenesei, 13–86. Szeged: József Attila University.

Kiss, Katalin É. 1988. An answer to Nakajima. *The Linguistic Review* 6:59–70.

Kiss, Katalin É. 1991. An argument for movement. In *Representation and derivation in the theory of grammar*, ed. Hubert Haider and Klaus Netter. Dordrecht: Kluwer.

Kiss, Katalin É. 1994. Sentence structure and word order. In *The syntactic structure of Hungarian*, ed. Ferenc Kiefer and Katalin É. Kiss, 1–90. New York: Academic Press.

Kitagawa, Yoshihisa. 1986. Subjects in Japanese and English. Doctoral dissertation, University of Massachusetts, Amherst.

Kitagawa, Yoshihisa. 1991. Copying identity. *Natural Language & Linguistic Theory* 9:497–536.

Kluender, Robert. 1998. On the distinction between strong and weak islands: A processing perspective. In *The limits of syntax*, 241–279. New York: Academic Press.

Koopman, Hilda, and Dominque Sportiche. 1981. Variables and the Bijection Principle. *The Linguistic Review* 2:139–160.

Koopman, Hilda, and Dominque Sportiche. 1986. A note on long extraction in Vata and the ECP. *Natural Language & Linguistic Theory* 4:357–374.

Koopman, Hilda, and Dominique Sportiche. 1991. The position of subjects. *Lingua* 85:211–258.

Koster, Jan. 1982. Do syntactic representations contain variables? Ms., Tilburg University, The Netherlands.

Koster, Jan. 1987. *Domains and dynasties.* Dordrecht: Foris.

Lappin, Shalom. 1992. The syntactic basis of ellipsis. In *Proceedings of the Stuttgart Ellipsis Workshop.* Arbeitspapiere des Sonder-forschungsbereichs 340, 29, IBM Germany, Heidelberg.

Lappin, Shalom. 1996. The interpretation of ellipsis. In *The handbook of contemporary semantic theory*, ed. Shalom Lappin, 143–175. Oxford: Blackwell.

Larson, Richard. 1990. Extraction and multiple selection in PP. The *Linguistic Review* 7:169–182.

Larson, Richard. 1990. Double objects revisited: Reply to Jackendoff. *Linguistic Inquiry* 21:589–632.

Lasnik, Howard. 1976. Remarks on coreference. *Linguistic Analysis* 2:1–22.

Lasnik, Howard, and Robert Fiengo. 1974. Complement object deletion. *Linguistic Inquiry* 5:535–571.

Lasnik, Howard, and Mamoru Saito. 1984. On the nature of proper government. *Linguistic Inquiry* 5:235–289.

Lasnik, Howard, and Mamoru Saito. 1992. *Move α.* Cambridge, Mass.: MIT Press.

Lasnik, Howard, and Tim Stowell. 1991. Weakest crossover. *Linguistic Inquiry* 22:647–686.

Lebeaux, David. 1983. A distributional difference between reciprocals and reflexives. *Linguistic Inquiry* 14:723–730.

Lee, Y.-S., and B. Santorini. 1994. Towards resolving Webelhuth's paradox: Evidence from German and Korean. In *Studies on scrambling: Movement and non-movement approaches to free word-order phenomena*, ed. Norbert Corver and Henk van Riemsdijk, 257–300. Berlin: Mouton de Gruyter.

Levin, Beth, and Malka Rappaport. 1989. An approach to unaccusative mismatches. In *Proceedings of NELS 19*, 314–328. GLSA, University of Massachusetts, Amherst.

Levine, Robert D. 1985. Right node non-raising. *Linguistic Inquiry* 16:492–497.

Longobardi, Giuseppe. 1984. Some remarks on connectedness and c-command. In *Sentential complementation: Proceedings of the International Conference held at UFSAL, Brussels, June 1983*, ed. W de Geest, and Y. Putseys, 151–163. Dordrecht: Foris.

Longobardi, Giuseppe. 1985a. Connectedness and island constraints. In *Grammatical representation*, ed. Jacqueline Guéron, Hans-Georg Obenauer, and Jean-Yves Pollock, 169–185. Dordrecht: Foris.

Longobardi, Giuseppe. 1985b. Connectedness, scope, and c-command. *Linguistic Inquiry* 16:163–192.

Longobardi, Giuseppe. 1994. Reference and proper names: A theory of N-movement in syntax and logical form. *Linguistic Inquiry* 25:609–665.

Lonzi, Lidia. 1988. Tipi di gerundio. *Rivista di Grammatica Generativa* 13:59–80.

Lutz, Uli. 1997. Parasitic gaps und vorfeldstruktur. In *Zur Satzstruktur im Deutschen*, Arbeitsberichte des SFB 340, No. 90, 55–80. Universität Tübingen.

Mahajan, Anoop. 1990. The A/Ā distinction and movement theory. Doctoral dissertation, MIT, Cambridge, Mass.

Mahajan, Anoop. 1991. Operator movement, agreement, and referentiality. In *More papers on* Wh-*movement: MITWPL, Vol. 15*, ed. Lisa Cheng and Hamida Demirdache, 77–96. MIT Working Papers in Linguistics, MIT, Cambridge, Mass.

Mahajan, Anoop. 1994. Toward an unified theory of scrambling. In *Studies on scrambling: Movement and non-movement approaches to free word-order phenomena*, ed. Norbert Corver and Henk van Riemsdijk, 301–330. Berlin: Mouton de Gruyter.

Maling, Joan, and Annie Zaenen. 1982. A phrase structure account of Scandinavian extraction phenomena. In *The nature of syntactic representation*, ed. Pauline Jacobson and Geoffrey K. Pullum, 229–282. Dordrecht: Reidel.

Manzini, M. Rita. 1983. Restructuring and reanalysis. Doctoral dissertation, MIT, Cambridge, Mass.

Manzini, M. Rita. 1994. Locality, minimalism, and parasitic gaps. *Linguistic Inquiry* 25:481–508.

May, Robert. 1985. *Logical form: Its structure and derivation*. Cambridge, Mass.: MIT Press.

McCawley, James D. 1982. Parentheticals and discontinuous constituent structure. *Linguistic Inquiry* 13:91–106.

McCawley, James D. 1988. *The syntactic phenomena of English. Vols. 1 and 2*. Chicago: University of Chicago Press.

McCloskey, James. 1979. *Transformational syntax and model theoretic semantics*. Dordrecht: Reidel.

McCloskey, James. 1990. Resumptive pronouns, Ā-binding, and levels of representation in Irish. In *The syntax and semantics of modern Celtic languages*, ed. Randall Hendrick, 199–248. New York: Academic Press.

Montalbetti, Mario. 1984. After binding: On the interpretation of pronouns. Doctoral dissertation, MIT, Cambridge, Mass.

Montalbetti, Mario, and Mamoru Saito. 1983. On certain tough differences between Spanish and English. In *Proceedings of NELS* 13, 191–198. GLSA, University of Massachusetts, Amherst.

Moore, John. 1990. Spanish clause reduction with downstairs cliticization. In *Grammatical relations: A cross-theoretical perspective*, ed. Katarzyna Dziwirek, Patrick Farrell, and Errapel Mejias-Bikandi, 319–333. Stanford, Calif.: CSLI Publications.

Müller, Gereon. 1993. On deriving movement type asymmetries. Doctoral dissertation, Universität Tübingen.

Müller, Gereon, and Wolfgang Sternefeld. 1994. Scrambling as Ā movement. In *Studies on scrambling: Movement and non-movement approaches to free word-order phenomena*, ed. Norbert Corver and Henk van Riemsdijk, 331–385. Berlin: Mouton de Gruyter.

Munn, Alan. 1987. Coordinate structure X̄ theory and PGaps. Honors thesis, Department of Linguistics, McGill University, Montreal.

Munn, Alan. 1991. Clausal adjuncts and temporal ambiguity. In *Proceedings of ESCOL 91*, ed. Germàn Westphal, Benjamin Ao, and Hee-Rahk Chae, 265–276. Ithaca, N.Y.: CLC Publications.

Munn, Alan. 1992. A null operator analysis of ATB gaps. *The Linguistic Review* 9:1–26

Munn, Alan. 1993. Topics in the syntax and semantics of coordinate structures. Doctoral dissertation, University of Maryland, College Park.

Munn, Alan. 1994. A minimalist account of reconstruction asymmetries. In *Proceedings of NELS 24*, 397–410. GLSA, University of Massachusetts, Amherst.

Munn, Alan. 1998. ATB movement without identity. In *Proceedings of ESCOL 97*, ed. Jennifer Austin and Aaron Lawson. Ithaca, N.Y., CLC Publications.

Munn, Alan. 1999a. First conjunct agreement: Against a clausal analysis. *Linguistic Inquiry* 30:

Munn, Alan. 1999b. On the identity requirement of ATB movement. *Natural Language Semantics* 7:421–425.

Munn, Alan. 2000. Three types of coordination asymmetries. In *Ellipsis in conjunction*, ed. Kerstin Schwabe and Nina Zhang. Tübingen: Niemeyer.

Nakajima, Heizo. 1985–1986. Kiss's case transmittance approach and the binding path approach to parasitic gaps. *The Linguistic Review* 5:335–344.

Nakajima, Heizo. 1989. Bounding of rightward movements. *Linguistic Inquiry* 20:328–334.

Nakajima, Heizo. 1990. Another response to Kiss. *The Linguistic Review* 7:365–374.

Neeleman, Ad. 1994. Scrambling as a D-structure phenomenon. In *Studies on scrambling: Movement and non-movement approaches to free word-order phenomena*, ed. Norbert Corver and Henk van Riemsdijk, 387–429. Berlin: Mouton de Gruyter.

Obenauer, Hans-Georg. 1984. On the identification of empty categories. *The Linguistic Review* 4:153–202.

Oppenrieder, Wilhelm. 1991. Prepositionstranding im Deutschen? Da will ich nichts von horen! In *Strukturen und Merkmale syntaktischer Kategorien*, ed. Gisbert Fanselow and Sascha Felix, 159–173. Tübingen: Gunter Narr.

Perlmutter, David M. 1971. *Deep and surface structure constraints in syntax*. New York: Holt, Rinehart, and Winston.

Perlmutter, David M. 1977. Evidence for shadow pronouns in French relativization. In *The Chicago which hunt: Papers from the Relative Clause Festival*, ed. Paul M. Peranteau, Judith N. Levi, and Gloria C. Phares, 73–105. Chicago: Chicago Linguistic Society.

Pesetsky, David. 1982. Paths and categories. Doctoral dissertation, MIT, Cambridge, Mass.

Pesetsky, David. 1987. *Wh*-in-situ: Movement and unselective binding. In *The representation of (in)definiteness.* ed. Eric Reuland and Alice ter Meulen, 98–129. Cambridge, Mass.: MIT Press.

Pollard, Carl J. 1996. On head non-movement. In *Discontinuous constituency*, ed. Harry Bunt and Arthur van Horck, 279–305. Berlin: Mouton de Gruyter.

Pollard, Carl J., and Ivan A. Sag. 1987. Information-based syntax and semantics. Vol. 1, CSLI Lecture Notes Series No. 13. Stanford, Calif.: CSLI Publications.

Pollard, Carl J., and Ivan Sag. 1994. *Head-driven phrase structure grammar.* Chicago: University of Chicago Press.

Pollock, Jean-Yves. 1989. Verb movement, Universal Grammar, and the structure of IP. *Linguistic Inquiry* 20:365–424.

Postal, Paul M. 1966. On so-called pronouns in English. In *Report on the Seventeenth Annual Round Table Meeting on Linguistics and Language Studies.* ed. F. P. Dineen. Washington, D.C.: Georgetown University Press.

Postal, Paul M. 1971. *Cross-over phenomena.* New York: Holt, Rinehart, and Winston.

Postal, Paul M. 1972. A global constraint on pronominalization. *Linguistic Inquiry* 3:35–60.

Postal, Paul M. 1974. *On raising*. Cambridge, Mass.: MIT Press.

Postal, Paul M. 1986. *Studies of passive clauses*. Albany: State University of New York Press.

Postal, Paul M. 1989. *Masked inversion in French*. Chicago: University of Chicago Press.

Postal, Paul M. 1990a. French indirect object demotion. In *Studies in relational grammar 3*, ed. Paul M. Postal and Brian Joseph, 104–200. Chicago: University of Chicago Press.

Postal, Paul M. 1990b. Some unexpected English restrictions. In *Grammatical relations: A cross-theoretical perspective*, ed. Katarzyna Dziwirek, Patrick Farrell, and Errapel Mejfas-Bikandi, 365–385. Stanford, Calif.: CSLI Publications.

Postal, Paul M. 1991. Phantom successors and the French *faire par* construction. In *The joy of grammar: A festschrift for James D. McCawley*, ed. Diane Brentari, Gary Larson, and Lynn MacLeod. Chicago: University of Chicago Press.

Postal, Paul M. 1993a. Remarks on weak crossover effects. *Linguistic Inquiry* 24:539–556.

Postal, Paul M. 1993b. Parasitic gaps and the across-the-board phenomenon. *Linguistic Inquiry* 24:735–754.

Postal, Paul M. 1993c. Some defective paradigms. *Linguistic Inquiry* 24:347–364.

Postal, Paul M. 1994a. Parasitic and pseudo-parasitic gaps. *Linguistic Inquiry* 25:63–117. Reprinted in this volume.

Postal, Paul M. 1994b. Contrasting extraction types. *Journal of Linguistics* 30:159–186.

Postal, Paul M. 1994c. A novel extraction typology. *Journal of Linguistics* 30:159–186.

Postal, Paul M. 1996. A glance at French pseudo-passives. In *Grammatical relations: Theoretical approaches to empirical questions*, ed. C. Burgess, K. Dziwirek, and D. B. Gerdts. Cambridge: Cambridge University Press.

Postal, Paul M. 1997. Strong crossover violations and binding principles. Presented at the annual meeting of ESCOL, Yale University, New Haven, Conn.

Postal, Paul M. 1998. *Three investigations of extraction.* Cambridge, Mass.: MIT Press.

Postal, Paul M. 1999. Overlooked extraction distinctions. In *Function and structure: In honor of Susumu Kuno*, ed. Akio Kamio and Ken-ichi Takami. Amsterdam: John Benjamins.

Postal, Paul M. This volume a. Further lacunae in the English parasitic gap paradigm.

Postal, Paul M. This volume b. Missing parasitic gaps.

Przepiorkowski, Adam. 1996. Nonconfigurational case assignment. Paper presented at the International Conference on HPSG, Marseilles.

Reape, Mike. 1996. Getting things in order. In *Discontinuous constituency*, ed. by Harry Bunt and Arthur van Horck, 209–254. Berlin: Mouton de Gruyter.

Reinhart, Tanya. 1976. The syntactic domain of anaphora. Doctoral dissertation, MIT, Cambridge, Mass.

Reinhart, Tanya. 1983. Coreference and bound anaphora: A restatement of the anaphora questions. *Linguistics and Philosophy* 6:47–88.

Riegel, Martin, Jean-Christophe Pellat, and René Rioul. 1994. *Grammaire méthodique du français.* Paris: Presses Universitaires de France.

Riemsdijk, Henk van, and Edwin Williams. 1980. NP-structure and a linear model of core grammar. Paper presented at the GLOW Meeting, Nijmegen.

Rizzi, Luigi. 1982. *Issues in Italian syntax.* Dordrecht: Foris.

Rizzi, Luigi 1986. Null objects in Italian and the theory of *pro. Linguistic Inquiry* 17:501–557.

Rizzi, Luigi. 1990. *Relativized minimality.* Cambridge, Mass.: MIT Press.

Rizzi, Luigi. 1997. The fine structure of the left periphery. In *Elements of grammar*, ed. Liliane Haegeman, 281–337. Dordrecht: Kluwer.

Rizzi, Luigi, and Ian Roberts. 1989. Complex inversion in French. *Probus* 1:1–30.

Roberge, Yves. 1990. On the recoverability of null objects. In *New analyses in Romance linguistics*, ed. Dieter Wanner and D. A. Kibbee, 299–312. Amsterdam: John Benjamins.

Roberts, Ian, and Ur Shlonsky. 1996. Pronominal enclisis in VSO languages. In *The syntax of the Celtic languages*, ed. Robert D. Borsley and Ian Roberts, 171–199. Cambridge: Cambridge University Press.

Rochemont, Michael S., and Peter W. Culicover. 1990. *English focus constructions and the theory of grammar.* Cambridge: Cambridge University Press.

Rooth, Mats. 1981. A comparison of three theories of verb phrase ellipsis. In *University of Massachusetts occasional papers in linguistics 7*, 212–224. GLSA, University of Massachusetts, Amherst.

Rosenbaum, Peter S. 1967. *The grammar of English predicate complement constructions.* Cambridge, Mass.: MIT Press.

Ross, John Robert. 1967. Constraints on variables in syntax. Doctoral dissertation, MIT, Cambridge, Mass. Published as *Infinite syntax.* Norwood, N.J.: Ablex (1986).

Ross, John Robert. 1969. Guess who. In *Proceedings of the Fifth Annual Meeting of the Chicago Linguistic Society*, eds. Robert I. Binnick, Alice Davison, Georgia M. Green, and Jerry L. Morgan, 252–286. Chicago: Chicago Linguistics Society.

Ross, John Robert. 1971. Variable strength. Handout, MIT, Cambridge, Mass.

Ross, John Robert. 1973. Slifting. In *The formal analysis of natural languages*, ed. Maurice Gross, Morris Halle, and Marcel-Paul Schützenberger, 133–169. The Hague: Mouton.

Ross, John Robert. 1984. Inner islands. In *Proceedings of the Tenth Annual Meeting of the Berkeley Linguistics Society*, 258–273. Berkeley Linguistics Society, University of California, Berkeley.

Safir, Ken. 1982. Syntactic chains and the definiteness effect. Doctoral dissertation, MIT, Cambridge, Mass.

Safir, Ken. 1984. Multiple variable binding. *Linguistic Inquiry* 5:603–638.

Safir, Ken. 1987. The anti-c-command condition on parasitic gaps. *Linguistic Inquiry* 18:678–683.

Safir, Ken. 1996. Derivation, representation, and resumption: The domain of weak crossover. *Linguistic Inquiry* 27:313–339.

Sag, Ivan A. 1976. Deletion and logical form. Doctoral dissertation, MIT, Cambridge, Mass.

Sag, Ivan A. 1982a. Coordination, extraction, and generalized phrase structure grammar. *Linguistic Inquiry* 13:329–336.

Sag, Ivan A. 1982b. On parasitic gaps. In *Proceedings of the First West Coast Conference on Formal Linguistics*, ed. Dan P. Flickinger, M. Macken, and N. Wiegand, 35–46. Stanford Linguistics Association, Stanford University, Stanford, Calif.

Sag, Ivan A. 1983. On parasitic gaps. *Linguistics and Philosophy* 6:35–45.

Sag, Ivan A., and Janet D. Fodor. 1994. Extraction without traces. In *Proceedings of the Thirteenth Annual Meeting of the West Coast Conference on Formal Linguistics*, 365–384. Stanford, Calif.: CSLI Publications.

Sag, Ivan A., Gerald Gazdar, Thomas Wasow, and Steven Weisler. 1985. Coordination and how to distinguish categories. *Natural Language & Linguistic Theory* 3:117–171.

Sag, Ivan A., and Jorge Hankamer. 1984. Toward a theory of anaphoric processing. *Linguistics and Philosophy* 7:325–345.

Sag, Ivan A., and Ewan Klein. 1982. The syntax and semantics of English expletive pronoun constructions. In *Developments in generalized phrase structure grammar: Stanford working papers in grammatical theory, Vol. 2*, 95–139. Indiana University Linguistics Club, Indiana University, Bloomington.

Saito, Mamoru. 1991. Extraposition and parasitic gaps. In *Interdisciplinary approaches to language: Essays in honor of S.-Y. Kuroda*, ed. Carol Georgopoulos and Roberta Ishihara, 467–486. Dordrecht: Kluwer.

Santorini, Beatrice. 1991. Scrambling and Infl in German. Ms., University of Pennsylvania, Philadelphia.

Seely, T. Daniel. 1991. On weak parasitic gaps. *Linguistic Inquiry* 22:218–224.

Sells, Peter. 1986. Resumptive pronouns in generalized phrase structure grammar. In *University of Massachusetts occasional papers in linguistics 10*, 59–79. GLSA, University of Massachusetts, Amherst.

Sells, Peter. 1984. Syntax and semantics of resumptive pronouns. Doctoral dissertation, University of Massachusetts, Amherst.

Shlonsky, Ur. 1986. Donkey-parasites. In *Proceedings of NELS 17, Vol. 2*, 569–579. GLSA, University of Massachusetts, Amherst.

Shlonsky, Ur. 1994a. Semitic clitics. *Geneva Generative Papers 2*, 1–11. University of Geneva.

Shlonsky, Ur. 1994b. Agreement in Comp. *The Linguistic Review* 11:351–375.

Spencer, Andrew. 1995. Incorporation in Chukchee. *Language* 71:439–489.

Sportiche, Dominique. 1981. Bounding nodes in French. *The Linguistic Review* 1:219–246.

Sportiche, Dominique. 1983. Structural invariance and symmetry in syntax. Doctoral dissertation, MIT, Cambridge, Mass.

Sportiche, Dominique. 1996. Clitic constructions. In *Phrase structure and the lexicon*, ed. Laurie Zaring and Johan Rooryck, 213–275. Dordrecht: Kluwer.

Stechow, Arnim von, and Wolfgang Sternefeld. 1988. *Bausteine syntaktischen Wissens*. Opladen: Westdeutscher Verlag.

Steedman, Mark. 1987. Combinatory grammars and parasitic gaps. *Natural Language & Linguistic Theory* 5:403–439.

Steedman, Mark. 1996. *Surface structure and interpretation*. Cambridge, Mass.: MIT Press.

Sternfeld, Wolfgang 1991. Chain formation, reanalysis, and the economy of levels. In *Representation and derivation in the theory of grammar*, ed. Hubert Haider and Klaus Netter. Dordrecht: Kluwer.

Stowell, Tim. 1981. Origins of phrase structure. Doctoral dissertation, MIT, Cambridge, Mass.

Stowell, Tim. 1985. Licensing conditions on null operators. In *Proceedings of the West Coast Conference on Formal Linguistics 4*, 314–326. Stanford Linguistics Association, Stanford University, Stanford, Calif.

Stowell, Tim. 1986. Null antecedents and proper government. In *Proceedings of NELS* 16, 476–493. GLSA, University of Massachusetts, Amherst.

Stowell, Tim. 1987. *As*-clauses and the D-structure ECP. Ms., University of California, Los Angeles.

Suñer, Margarita, and Maria Yépez. 1988. Null definite objects in Quiteño. *Linguistic Inquiry* 19:511–519.

Szabolcsi, Anna. 1986. Comparative superlatives. *MIT Working Papers in Linguistics 8*, 245–265. MIT, Cambridge, Mass.

Szabolcsi, Anna, and Frans Zwarts. 1993. Weak islands and an algebraic semantics for scope taking. *Natural Language Semantics* 1:235–284.

Szabolcsi, Anna, and Frans Zwarts. 1997. Weak islands and an algebraic semantics for scope taking. In *Ways of scope taking*, ed. Anna Szabolcsi, 217–262. Dordrecht: Kluwer.

Taraldsen, Knut Tarald. 1980. The theoretical interpretation of a class of marked extractions. In *Proceedings of the Third GLOW Conference*, 475–516. Pisa: Annali della Scuola Normale Superiore.

Taraldsen, Knut Tarald. 1981. The theoretical interpretation of a class of marked extractions. In *Theory of markedness in generative grammar*, ed. Adriana Belletti, Luciana Brandi, and Luigi Rizzi, 475–516. Pisa: Scuola Normale Superiore.

Taraldsen, Knut Tarald. 1982. Case-marking and parasitic gaps in Finnish. Ms., Tromsoe University.

Tellier, Christine. 1988. Universal licensing: Implications for parasitic gap constructions. Doctoral dissertation, McGill University, Montreal.

Tellier, Christine. 1989. Head-internal relatives and parasitic gaps in Mooré. In *Current approaches to African linguistics, Vol. 6*, ed. Isabelle Haïk and Lauri Tuller 298–318. Dordrecht: Foris.

Tellier, Christine. 1990. Subjacency and Subject Condition violations in French. *Linguistic Inquiry* 21:306–311.

Tellier, Christine. 1991. *Licensing theory and French parasitic gaps.* Dordrecht: Kluwer.

Tellier, Christine, and Daniel Valois. 1996. Agreement and extraction out of DPs. In *Proceedings of the Fourteenth West Coast Conference on Formal Linguistics 14*, 525–540. Stanford Linguistics Association, Stanford University, Stanford, Calif.

Thraínsson, Hoskuldur. 1986. V1, V2, V3 in Icelandic. In *Verb second phenomena in Germanic languages*, ed. Hubert Haider and Martin Prinzhorn, 169–194. Dordrecht: Foris.

Torrego, Esther. 1984. On inversion in Spanish and some of its effects. *Linguistic Inquiry* 15:103–129.

Uszkoreit, Hans. 1987. Word order and constituent structure in German. CSLI Lecture Note Series No. 8. Stanford, Calif.: CSLI Publications.

Vergnaud, Jean-Roger. 1974. French relative clauses. Doctoral dissertation, MIT, Cambridge, Mass.

Vergnaud, Jean-Roger, and Maria-Luisa Zubizarreta. 1992. The definite determiner and the inalienable possession construction in French and in English. *Linguistic Inquiry* 23:595–652.

Vikner, Sten. 1990. Verb movement and the licensing of NP-positions in the Germanic languages. Doctoral dissertation, Université de Genève.

Wahba, W. B. 1995. Parasitic gaps in Arabic. In *Perspectives on Arabic linguistics 4: Papers from the Seventh Annual Symposium on Arabic Linguistics*, ed. M. Eid, 59–68. Amsterdam: John Benjamins.

Wasow, Thomas. 1972. Anaphoric relations in English. Doctoral dissertation, MIT, Cambridge, Mass.

Webber, Bonnie. 1978. A formal approach to discourse anaphora. Doctoral dissertation, Harvard University, Cambridge, Mass.

Webelhuth, Gert. 1989. Syntactic saturation phenomena and the modern Germanic languages. Doctoral dissertation, University of Massachusetts, Amherst.

Webelhuth, Gert. 1992. *Principles and parameters of syntactic saturation*. Oxford: Oxford University Press.

Weinberg, Amy. 1988. Locality principles in syntax and parsing. Doctoral dissertation, MIT, Cambridge, Mass.

Wexler, Kenneth, and Peter W. Culicover. 1980. *Formal principles of language acquisition*. Cambridge, Mass.: MIT Press.

Wilder, Chris. 1999. Right node raising and the LCA. In Proceedings of West Coast Conference on Formal Linguistics 18. Tucson, Az.: Cascadilla Press.

Williams, Edwin. 1977. Discourse and logical form. *Linguistic Inquiry* 8:101–139.

Williams, Edwin. 1978. Across-the-board rule application. *Linguistic Inquiry* 9:31–44.

Williams, Edwin. 1990. The ATB theory of parasitic gaps. *The Linguistic Review* 6:265–79.

Yatabe, Shuichi. 1993. Scrambling and Japanese phrase structure. Doctoral dissertation, Stanford University, Stanford, Calif.

Zwart, C. Jan-Wouter. 1992. SOV languages are head initial. Paper presented at the Eighth Comparative Germanic Syntax Workshop, Tromso.

Zwart, Jan-Wouter. 1997. *Morphosyntax of verb movement.* Dordrecht: Kluwer.

Zolnay, Gy. 1926. Mondatátszövôdés, In *Értekezések a Magyar Tudományos Akadémia Nyelv- és Széptudományi Osztálya Körébôl* 23.

Zwicky, Arnold. 1986. The unaccented pronoun constraint in English. In *Interfaces.* Ohio State University Working Papers in Linguistics 42. Department of Linguistics, The Ohio State University, Columbus.

# Author Index

Andersson, Lars-Gunnar, 258
Aoun, Joseph, 41, 154, 226, 253, 272
Authier, J.-Marc, 266, 271, 276

Barss, Andrew, 113, 119, 407
Barwise, Jon, 140
Bayer, Josef, 380
Bennis, Hans, 19, 24, 271, 306, 321
Bever, Thomas, 83
Bordelois, Ivonne, 32, 55–56, 344
Bresnan, Joan, 4, 89, 261
Brody, Michael, 45
Browning, Marguerite, 19, 22, 272, 347,
    372, 377

Calagno, Michael, 6, 13
Campos, Hector, 15
Canac Marquis, Réjean, 359
Carlson, Greg, 383
Chao, Wynn, 81, 137
Chierchia, Gennaro, 382
Chomsky, Noam, 3, 18, 27, 32–35, 51, 70,
    119, 162, 172, 223, 254
Chung, Sandra, 395
Cinque, Gugliemo, 11, 17, 29, 32, 127, 150,
    181, 186, 192, 195, 214, 226, 272, 266,
    345, 377, 399
Clark, Robin, 41, 226, 253, 272
Comrie, Bernard, 7, 73
Contreras, Heles, 11, 32, 44, 59, 201, 211, 344
Cooper, Robin, 140
Corver, Norbert, 14
Cowper, Elizabeth, 62
Culicover, Peter W., 261, 290, 292, 304

Déprez, Viviane, 22
Dowty, David, 26

Emonds, Joseph, 148, 254, 256, 265
Engdahl, Elisabet, 3–4, 6, 23, 39–40, 54,
    115, 128, 144, 223, 297, 343, 353, 381,
    404, 408

Felix, Sascha, 19, 24, 57, 315–316
Fiengo, Robert, 53, 286, 395, 400, 407, 415
Fodor, Janet, 81, 85, 92
Frampton, John, 28, 342, 361
Franks, Steven, 37

García-Mayo, Pilar, 17, 56, 344
Gazdar, Gerald, 61, 70, 202
Geis, Michael, 56, 387
George, Leland, 350
Goodall, Grant, 298
Grewendorf, Günter, 316
Grimshaw, Jane, 363
Grinder, John, 415
Groos, Anneke, 106
Grosu, Alexander, 383

Haegeman, Liliane, 36, 39
Haïk, Isabelle, 47, 370, 395
Haverkort, Marco, 18
Heim, Irene, 259, 383
Heinz, Wolfgang, 181
Hestvik, Arild, 162
Hoekstra, Teun, 19, 24, 271, 306, 356
Hornstein, Norbert, 31
Horvath, Julia, 36–37, 44
Huang, C.-T. James, 171
Hudson, Richard A., 288
Hukari, Thomas E., 6, 13, 61, 205
Huot, Hélène, 354
Huybregts, Riny, 20, 24, 58, 288, 306, 320–
    321, 325, 370

Jackendoff, Ray, 265
Jacobson, Pauline, 81
Jayaseelan, K. A., 292
Johnson, David E., 234

Kaplan, Ronald M., 261
Kardela, H., 39
Karimi, Ezat, 19, 22
Karimi, Simin, 138

Kathol, Andreas, 24, 26
Kayne, Richard S., 17, 32, 41, 60, 101, 116,
    162, 184, 223, 272, 345, 351
Kearney, K., 29, 113, 210
Keenan, Edward, 7, 73
Kempchinsky, Paula, 56, 344
Kennedy, Christopher, 403–405, 412, 415
Kim, Soowon, 52, 393, 403
Kiss, Katalin É., 35–37, 41, 102, 106,
    254
Kitagawa, Yoshihisa, 45, 395
Klein, Ewan, 61, 202
Kluender, Robert, 188
Koopman, Hilda, 31–32, 43, 45, 202
Koster, Jan, 113, 226, 258, 272, 377

Ladusaw, William, 395
Landman, Fred, 383
Larson, Richard, 387
Lasnik, Howard, 32, 44–45, 70, 84, 89, 131,
    195, 253, 286, 343, 369, 373, 377, 409
Lebeaux, David, 162
Levine, Robert D., 6, 13, 61, 205, 289, 290,
    356
Li, Yen-Huí Audrey Li, 154
Longobardi, Giuseppe, 41, 59, 101, 272,
    345, 364
Lonzi, Lidia, 187
Lyle, James, 52, 393, 403

Mahajan, Anoop, 20–21, 318, 326
Manzini, M. Rita, 45
Matiasek, Johannes, 181
May, Robert, 53, 395, 400, 407, 415
McCawley, James D., 288, 290
McCloskey, James, 154, 258, 395, 399
Montalbetti, Mario, 138, 154, 361
Mooré, John, 48
Mulder, René, 356
Müller, Gereon, 20, 317, 319, 330
Munn, Alan, 28, 64, 370, 382

Nakajima, Heizo, 36, 39, 292
Neeleman, Ad, 21

Obenauer, Hans-Georg, 377

Pellat, Jean-Christophe, 356
Perlmutter, David M., 29, 376
Pesetsky, David, 254, 370
Pollard, Carl J., 202, 211, 223, 332
Pollock, Jean-Yves, 347, 356
Postal, Paul M., 6, 13, 24, 30, 33, 63, 127,
    131, 141, 171–172, 181, 190, 192, 195,
    214, 225–226, 234, 256, 289–290, 315,
    324, 330, 334, 377, 408, 415
Pullum, Geoffrey K., 61, 202

Rappaport, Malka, 356
Reape, Mike, 318
Reinhart, Tanya, 70, 84
Riegel, Martin, 356
Rioul, René, 356
Rizzi, Luigi, 17–18, 134, 266–267, 344, 347,
    350, 354, 356–357, 359, 385
Roberts, Ian, 359
Roberts, Yves, 174
Rochemont, Michael S., 261, 292
Rosenbaum, Peter S., 256
Ross, John Robert, 4, 73, 181, 226, 256, 263,
    297

Safir, Ken, 34, 43, 50, 377
Sag, Ivan A., 60, 61, 202, 211, 223, 332, 395
Saito, Mamoru, 43, 45, 131, 195, 253, 361,
    409
Santorini, Beatrice, 20, 319
Sells, Peter, 46–47, 137, 258, 377
Shlonsky, Ur, 47, 158, 174, 347
Sportiche, Dominique, 18, 31–32, 43, 45,
    202, 344
Steedman, Mark, 26–27, 54
Sternefeld, Wolfgang, 20, 316
Stowell, Tim, 32, 44, 266, 292, 343, 369,
    373, 377
Suñer, Margarita, 16
Szabolcsi, Anna, 362, 379, 386

Taraldsen, Knut Tarald, 4
Tellier, Christine, 14, 17, 28, 48, 54, 58,
    266–267, 350, 362–363
Thráinsson, Hoskuldur, 258
Torrego, Esther, 46, 344
Townsend, David, 83

Valois, Daniel, 363
van Riemsdijk, Henk, 20, 24, 58, 106, 288,
    306, 320–321, 325, 370
Vergnaud, Jean-Roger, 364

Wahba, W. B., 49
Wasow, Thomas, 76, 395
Webber, Bonnie, 395
Webelhuth, Gert, 19, 23, 317, 322
Weinberg, Amy, 372
Wexler, Kenneth, 290, 304
Williams, Edwin, 63, 71, 289, 297, 329, 370,
    394

Yatabe, Shuichi, 325

Zolnay, Gy, 106
Zubizarreta, Maria-Luisa, 364
Zwarts, Frans, 379, 386
Zwicky, Arnold, 187

# Subject Index

θ-criterion, 28, 34, 42
θ-government, 322
θ-marked, 102
θ-role, 34, 37, 107, 116, 134
  θ-role assignment, 107
θ-theory, 107

A-bound, 21, 34
A-movement, 5, 14, 19, 23, 317, 331
A-position, 11, 24, 33–34, 152
A-specifier, 165
A'-anaphor, 41
A'-antecedent, 29, 41, 46
A'-binding, 150, 153, 155, 158–159, 161, 163, 166
A'-bound, 33–34, 345
A'-chain, 99, 113, 121
  casemarking in, 108
A'-movement, 5, 14, 19–20, 23–24, 172– 173, 316
A'-operator, 317
A'-position, 13–15, 17, 19–20, 22–24, 41, 49, 100, 152, 254, 316, 318, 322
A'-specifier, 165
A'-trace, 399–400
Accessibility hierarchy, 73
Accusative, 36–37, 39, 58, 104–106, 109, 121, 205, 208, 328
Across-the-board (ATB) extraction, 37, 60– 64, 196, 211, 213, 272, 288, 298, 307, 371– 372, 374, 384, 388
Across-the-board (ATB) movement, 64, 370, 389
  deletion, 90
  dependency, 71
Adjunct clause, 351
  finite, 343
  nonfinite, 351–352
  tensed, 349
Adjunct island construction, 182

Adjunct island. *See* Island
Adjunct, 13, 32–35, 39, 42–43, 45, 55–56, 58–59, 112, 116, 135, 149, 158, 169, 244, 323, 330, 353
  clausal, 42, 142
  temporal, 56, 343
  untensed, 56
Adjunction, 23
  to IP, 52
Adverb preposing, 360
Adverb, manner, 8, 132
Adverbial
  clause, 55, 70, 74, 89, 92
  phrase, 86, 315, 328
  untensed, 55
Agr, 108, 112, 347, 356–357, 361
Agreement, 29–30, 155, 342, 347, 358
  case, 37
  object, 174–175
  subject, 159
American English, 110
Anaphor, 27, 32, 39, 42, 56, 83, 114
  empty, 32, 93
Anaphora, 86, 380
  backwards, 84
  bound, 88–89, 92
Anaphora question. *See* Question
Antecedent, 36, 40, 44, 109, 319, 326
  CP-, 53
  government, 40–41
  L-extracted, 306
  Non-NP, 5
  NP, 54, 63
  *wh-*, 23, 148, 158, 160, 167
Anti-c-command, 8, 11, 13, 16, 36–37, 39– 42, 45, 59, 61, 65, 99, 101–102, 111, 116, 147, 156, 159, 176, 372
Antipronominal contexts (Acs), 225, 227– 229, 231, 233, 240, 379, 408
AP-deletion, 196

AP, 5, 54, 293
Arabic
  Jeddah, 49–50, 65
  Moroccan, 31, 147
  Standard, 49–50
Arc, 234–236
  weak pronominal, 235
Argument, 89, 103, 328, 332
Attribute, 333
Auxiliary, 325

Bare phrase structure (BPS), 160, 162
Barrier, 11, 58, 62, 105, 119, 184, 345
Bijection Principle, 32–33, 43, 202
Binary branching, 61, 318
Binding, 319
  anaphoric, 152
  domain, 32
  into adjuncts, 43
Binding Theory, 11, 13, 32, 39, 39, 41, 211
Blocking category, 165
Boolean
  operation, 379
  phrase, 389
Bound anaphora. See Anaphora
Bounding node, 63, 290, 344
British English, 110

c-command, 7, 10, 13, 33–34, 36, 38, 43, 49,
    84, 86–88, 114, 153, 158, 161, 167, 316,
    318–319
  mutual, 102
CASE, 207–208
Case, 22–23, 35
  assignment, 35, 106, 111
  connectivity, 181, 206
  filter, 105, 108
  identity, 108
  inheritance, 107, 112
  lexical, 207
  marking, 36, 105, 106–109
  matching, 99, 104
  mismatch, 207, 212
  structural, 207–208
  theory, 106, 208
  transmittance, 99
Catalan, 17, 345, 349
Categorial grammar, 26
Chain, 5, 34–37, 47, 58, 101, 255, 286
  A-, 102
  antecedent, 13
  condition, 102
  CP, 52
  head of, 35
  null operator, 21
  wh-, 51
Cleft, 141, 190, 345, 374

Clitic, 17–18, 32, 162, 347
  argument, 14
  climbing, 56
  Germanic, 18–19
  object, 15
  pronominal, 19, 163
  reflexive, 163
  Romance, 18–19
Cliticization, 161, 163–164, 167, 169, 172
Clitic pronoun. See Pronoun
Coindexing, 83, 128, 153, 194, 398
Comparative, 89–91
Complement, 24–25, 34, 206
  clausal, 58
  noun, 81
  PP, 81
  sentential, 43
Complementizer (C), 10, 34, 84
  overt, 348
  wh-, 348
Complement object deletion (COD), 341
Complex NP. See NP
Complex NP shift, 276
Condition A, 32, 39, 44, 56, 114, 211
Condition B, 32, 39, 53, 117, 396, 399–400
Condition C, 11, 13, 33, 39, 41–42, 44–45,
    101–103, 395–396
Condition on extraction domain (CED), 60
Conjunct, 91, 325, 327, 331, 374
Conjunction, 72
  subordinate, 58
Connectedness Condition, 41–42, 101, 345
Coordinate structure, 63, 70, 200, 288–289,
    297
  constraint (CSC), 72, 291, 393, 406
Coordination, 63
Covert movement, 171, 173
Covert pronoun. See Pronoun
CP, 345, 351
  topicalized, 54
Crossover, 70, 81, 373
  strong, 53, 83, 242, 244, 373, 375, 377, 395,
    397, 399–400, 403, 407
  weak, 7, 20, 32–34, 82, 102, 369–370, 373–
    374, 377, 384, 390

Danish, 22–23
Dative, 25, 38, 58, 107, 327
  construction, 182
  movement, 97
  object, 183, 186, 191, 193, 345
Declarative clause, 348–349
Deep structure, 70
Deictic pronoun. See Pronoun
Demonstrative, 135, 380
Dependency
  condition, 275, 280, 284, 296

filler-gap, 69, 76, 83–84, 92, 94, 188, 323
leftward, 93
local, 77
long-distance, 323, 331, 334
non-local, 77, 90
rightward, 93
unbounded, 5, 93, 202
Determiner (D), 160, 351
definite, 363–364
indefinite, 363–364
Direct object, 40, 43, 71, 91, 153, 237, 348, 405
Do-support, 130
Doubly filled Comp filter, 53
Dutch, 18–21, 25, 58, 306–307, 315, 320–321, 325

Economy, 175
Empty category, 9–10, 27, 33, 43, 60–61, 185, 357, 377, 394, 399
Empty category principle (ECP), 9, 10, 28, 102, 183, 349, 396
Empty operator, 7, 59, 242, 287. See also Null operator
-in-situ, 16
movement, 64, 347
Empty pronoun, 27, 147, 150, 152, 156, 165, 181
Equi, 77
Escape, 286
arc, 286
Expletive, 280, 283
Extraction, 3, 36, 46, 92–93, 143, 182, 197, 201, 224, 231, 254, 260, 351, 393
adjunct, 266
adjunct island, 182, 345
AP, 128
coordinate, 7, 70
from adjunct island, 60
from coordinate structure, 30
from PP, 320
gap, 7
hierarchy, 7
island, 52, 78, 82, 90
left, 190, 230, 254, 271, 277, 284, 297, 300, 303, 305
leftward, 198
multiple, 202
NP, 128, 260, 263, 267, 302
object, 343
out of DP, 363
out of subject, 92
parenthetical, 301
PP, 128
question, 412
relative, 190
right, 254, 271, 277, 284, 292, 300, 303, 305

RNR, 288
that clause, 256, 261
through Comp, 39
VP, 128
wh-, 183, 187, 189, 362
Extraposition, 43, 199, 261, 280

Feature description, 332
Feature-matching condition, 115
Filler
covert, 201
gap-controlling, 92
nonreferential, 213
NP, 182
overt, 201
referential, 213
Filler-gap construction, 183
Filler-gap dependency. See Dependency
Filter, 3, 69, 89
long distance, 92
Focus, 100, 102
movement, 130
Free indexing. See Index
French, 14–17, 54, 58, 105, 161, 182, 341, 344, 346, 352, 361
Québec, 348
Full interpretation, 52
Functional
category, 58, 161, 174
head, 356–357
projection, 345

Generalized binding theory, 41
principle A of, 41
Generalized phrase structure grammar (GPSG), 40, 94, 204, 254–255
Genitive, 37–38, 55, 102, 362
German, 14, 18–21, 24–25, 57, 181, 258, 315, 318–319, 321, 325
Bavarian, 57
Standard, 57
Swiss, 18
Germanic, 18
Gerund, 81
Gerundive phrase, 189, 341
Governing category, 41, 56, 114, 397
Government-binding theory, 90, 94, 202, 254
Greek
Classical, 106–107

HEAD, 211
Head-adjunct structure, 210
Head-driven phrase structure grammar (HPSG), 24, 61, 202, 204–207, 212, 332
Head movement, 163
Head node, 236

Heavy NP shift, 4–5, 14, 23–24, 76
Hebrew, 46, 174, 258, 376
Hindi, 14, 21
Human parser, 92, 94
Hungarian, 35, 37, 41, 44, 99–100, 102, 104, 106, 108, 115

Icelandic, 22–23, 258
Impersonal construction, 361
Inalienable construction, 262
Inalienable possession construction, 259
Index(ing), 34, 101, 147, 333
  free, 161–162, 176
Indirect object, 71
Infinitive, 58
Infl., 49, 162, 359
Inflection, 174, 347
  agreement, 175
  subject agreement, 159
Inheritance, 111, 114, 345
Interrogative, 345, 348
Interrogative phrase, 70
Intonation, 76
IP, 19, 105, 345, 350, 372
Irish, 257
Island, 29, 49, 116, 119, 127, 140, 142, 176, 187–188, 233, 243, 266, 377, 387, 393
  adjunct, 164, 184, 188, 406
  complex NP, 172, 406
  condition, 141, 272, 276, 279, 281–282, 285, 290
  constraint, 242, 290, 299, 305, 406
  effect, 32, 213, 371
  multiple, 184
  restriction, 198
  subject, 291
  violation, 244, 403
Italian, 11–13, 17–18, 128–129, 136, 182, 187, 344, 354, 356

Japanese, 69, 75

L-marking, 60
Landing site, 23
Language acquisition, 316
Left-extraction. See Extraction
Left node raising (LNR), 26, 307, 325, 330, 332
  coordinate, 326–328
  noncoordinate, 334
Leftmost constraint, 81
Lexical case. See Case
Lexical category, 161, 174
Lexical functional grammar, 94
Lexical government, 41, 349
LF, 51–53, 155–156, 162, 166, 184, 187, 211, 377, 380, 382, 394, 396, 399–400, 415

movement, 49
pied-piping, 184
LOC(AL), 205, 210
Locality, 118
  condition, 242, 287
  constraint, 120, 344
  principle, 243
Locative adverbial, 128
Long distance dependency. See Dependency
Long operator movement, 106

m-command, 44
Maximal projection, 160–162, 168, 173
Metagraph Grammar (MGG), 234–235, 237
Missing object construction, 182, 190, 198
MOD(IFIED), 332
Montague grammar, 71, 94
Move-α, 201, 318

No-ambiguity constraint, 82
Nominalization, 21
Nominative, 36, 39, 104, 106, 109, 121, 205, 208, 211
Non-local dependency. See Dependency
Noncoreference, 86, 88, 94
  rule, 83
Nonderivational, 206
Nonlocal feature principle, 202
Norwegian, 88, 162
NP, 5–6, 11–13, 19, 26, 29, 47, 53, 74, 82, 88, 108, 134, 185, 197, 230, 253, 255, 257, 287, 292, 329
  complex, 52, 141, 393
  definite, 58, 136
  indefinite, 138–139
  movement, 5
  pronominal, 129
NP-type movement, 77
Null epithet, 33
Null operator, 11, 16–17, 21, 27, 32–34, 41–42, 45, 53, 56, 101, 120, 344, 346, 389. See also Empty operator
Null operator hypothesis, 371, 373
Null pronoun. See Empty pronoun
Null resumptive pronoun. See Resumptive pronoun
Null subject, 16
  language, 159, 347

o-command, 211
Object
  raising, 4–5, 64, 242, 257–258, 260–261, 268–269, 273
  deletion, 4, 64, 242, 244
  movement, 22–23
Object control, 88
Oblique, 106–107

Opacity, 56
Operator, 23, 29, 35, 58, 118
A'-position, 201
binding, 152
-in-situ, 34
movement, 47
nonreferential, 136
temporal, 56, 387
*wh-*, 46
Overlay relation, 237
Overstrike, 235, 238–239, 241
Overt pronoun. *See* Pronoun

Parenthetical
*as-*, 265
*null-*, 265
Passive, 5, 21, 63–64, 77, 317, 331, 409
Passivizability condition, 274–275, 278,
  282–284, 286, 300, 305, 307
Passivization, 224, 410
constraint, 295
Persian, 14, 19, 22, 138
Personal pronoun. *See* Pronoun
Pesetsky problem, 111
PF, 394
Phrase structure grammar (PSG), 60, 202
Pied-piping, 184, 187–189, 346
Polish, 37, 39
Portugese, 75
Possessive, 83
French, 358
Postpositional phrase, 321
PP, 5, 54, 88, 192, 254
Predicate nominal condition, 274–275, 278,
  282–284, 286, 296, 300, 305
Preposition, 55, 58, 264
Preposition stranding, 264–265, 268–269,
  273, 300, 320
condition, 277, 281, 302
Principles-and-parameters approach, 316
*pro*, 16–17, 50, 56, 116, 128, 160, 182–183,
  185, 189, 192, 345, 347, 351, 354, 357,
  380, 399
drop, 69, 349, 380
PRO, 8, 22, 33, 100, 183, 347, 359
Processing, 188–189
Proform, 13, 133, 143, 379
English, 192
interrogative, 379
locative, 129
null, 192
PP, 192
resumptive, 192
Pronominal, 30
condition, 131, 133, 273, 275, 278, 282–
  284, 286–287, 294–295, 300, 302, 305, 307
Pronominalization, 44, 356, 379, 381

Pronoun, 22, 27, 31–34, 41, 53, 80, 84, 87,
  167, 233, 281, 320
anaphoric, 211
clitic, 157–158, 160–161, 164, 173
coreferent, 76, 82, 374
covert, 194
dative, 329
definite, 190–191, 273, 285, 379, 381
deictic, 69
deletion rule, 69, 74, 90
indefinite, 380
Norwegian, 162
null, 13
overt, 194
personal, 81, 84
reflexive, 84
resumptive clitic, 167
Semitic clitic, 174
strong, 153–154, 160, 163, 168, 174, 176
weak, 153–154, 160, 163, 168, 173, 176, 188
weak definite (Wdp), 195, 225–227, 229,
  232, 238, 408
weak indefinite, 195, 212, 240
Prosofic effect, 187
Pseudopassivization, 410
Purposive, 64

Quantifier, 41, 100, 136, 140, 377
existential, 63
nonreferential, 137
phrase, 33, 47
raising, 52, 102
Question, 31
anaphora, 86
constituent, 76
echo, 78
indirect, 8
multiple, 78, 351

R-expression, 11, 33, 39, 42, 44, 286
Raising, 77
to subject, 5
Reciprocal, 224–225
Reconstruction, 30, 395, 400, 407
Recoverability, 170
Reflexive pronoun. *See* Pronoun
Reflexive, 21, 27, 29–30, 88, 224–225, 381
English, 162
long distance, 162
Relational sign (R-sign), 236
Relative clause, 8, 31, 48, 57–58, 70, 129,
  139, 142, 194, 199, 231, 243, 277, 290,
  320, 341, 350, 369
Hebrew, 375
Irish, 258
object, 350
tensed, 348

Relative, 345
  infinitival, 64
  nonrestrictive, 378
  pronoun, 38, 51, 57
  restrictive, 259, 385, 389
Relativization, 76, 362
Relativized minimality, 153, 165, 168, 173, 385, 389
Resumption, 154, 163
Resumptive pronoun, 5, 31, 46–49, 82, 137, 147, 151–152, 154, 158–159, 163, 166, 170, 172, 176, 190, 201, 257–258, 276, 375–376, 380, 384, 388
  Hebrew, 46
  null, 155–156, 164, 167–168, 170, 182, 199, 369, 376, 381, 390
  overt, 168, 170
Right-branching, 318
Right node raising (RNR), 20, 24, 26–27, 96, 198, 200, 263, 265, 269, 281, 288, 296
  coordinate, 290, 292–293, 296–297, 304, 306
  English, 307
  noncoordinate, 290, 292–293, 295–296, 298–299, 303, 305–306, 325
Romance language, 14, 18, 138, 162, 174, 183, 341, 344–345
Russian, 37–38

S-structure, 13, 16, 24, 34, 41, 51, 59, 100, 148, 170, 394
Scandinavian, 81, 95, 258
Scope, 388
Scope-indexing, 47
Scrambling, 14, 19–20, 24–25, 65, 317, 319, 329
  Dutch, 22
  German, 22
Selectional property, 208
Semitic language, 174
SLASH, 40, 60–61, 202–207, 210, 223, 254–255
Slavic, 37
Small clause, 40
Sort hierarchy, 207
Spanish, 15, 17, 32, 46, 55–56, 258, 344, 349, 361
Spec-head relation, 347–349, 351, 359, 361, 363–364
Spell-out, 175
Split-CP hypothesis, 357
Split-infl
  hypothesis, 356
  structure, 347
Stress, 135
Strong crossover. See Crossover
Strong pronoun. See Pronoun

Structural case. See Case
Structure-sharing, 210–211, 332–333
Subcategorization, 75–76, 360
SUBJ, 205, 210
Subjacency, 9, 27–28, 47, 50, 56, 62–63, 112, 118, 171, 188, 198, 290, 304–305, 344, 371, 394, 400
Subject, 32, 40, 315
Subject-auxiliary inversion, 359
Subject-object asymmetry, 41, 85, 102
Subjunctive, 117, 357
Subsort, 207
Successive-cyclic movement, 254
Superlative, 362–363
Swedish, 5, 12–13, 46, 69, 75, 81, 85, 87–88, 127–128, 132, 135, 138, 140, 142, 258
Syncretism, 207

Tag, coreference, 333
Tail node, 236, 242
that-t, 29, 34–35, 349
there, 30, 259, 262
Topic, 135
Topicalization, 20, 76, 102, 198, 257, 260–261, 268–269, 273, 276, 329, 345, 374
  clausal, 258
  interrogative, 237
  NP, 190, 258
tough construction, 76, 369–370, 374, 378
Trace, 27–28, 34–35, 90, 114, 153, 159, 396
  caseless, 78
  case-marked, 78, 90
  c-commanding, 163, 165, 173
  intermediate, 62
  non-c-commanding, 165
  NP, 33
  of NP movement, 27
  subject, 37, 44
  wh-, 156, 344
Turkish, 69, 75
Type hierarchy, 208

Unbounded dependency. See Dependency
Uniformity condition, 52
Universal grammar (UG), 13, 121, 306, 316

Vacuous movement hypothesis, 350
Vacuous quantification, 151
Valence, 205, 333–334
Vehicle change, 396–398, 400, 407
VP, 23, 28, 45, 52, 56, 60–61, 86, 89, 102, 292
  adjunct, 197
  bare, 360
  deletion, 132, 197, 393, 395, 403–404, 413, 415
  ellipsis, 403

extraposed, 320
fronting, 130
VP-scrambling
  in Dutch, 23
  in German, 23

Weak island, 29
Weak pronoun. *See* Pronoun
West Flemish, 18
*Wh*-antecedent. *See* Antecedent
*Wh*-extraction. *See* Extraction
  from coordinate structure, 200
*Wh*-in-situ, 15–16, 48–50, 156, 169
*Wh*-island, 165–166, 172, 184, 343–344,
    371, 393, 406
*Wh*-movement, 48–50, 77–78, 90, 118, 128,
    149, 171, 184, 266, 345, 351, 369, 373
*Wh*-operator, 46, 100, 121, 147–148, 151,
    155–156, 159, 161, 163–164, 167, 344, 398
*Wh*-phrase, 22–23, 28, 30, 34, 40, 49, 62, 82,
    136, 346
  fronted, 63
  in situ, 5
*Wh*-pronoun, 57
*Wh*-question, 31, 192, 381
  embedded, 52
  multiple, 51–53
Word order, 319

## Current Studies in Linguistics
Samuel Jay Keyser, general editor

1. *A Reader on the Sanskrit Grammarians*, J. F. Staal, editor
2. *Semantic Interpretation in Generative Grammar*, Ray Jackendoff
3. *The Structure of the Japanese Language*, Susumu Kuno
4. *Speech Sounds and Features*, Gunnar Fant
5. *On Raising: One Rule of English Grammar and Its Theoretical Implications*, Paul M. Postal
6. *French Syntax: The Transformational Cycle*, Richard S. Kayne
7. *Pāṇini as a Variationist*, Paul Kiparsky, S. D. Joshi, editor
8. *Semantics and Cognition*, Ray Jackendoff
9. *Modularity in Syntax: A Study of Japanese and English*, Ann Kathleen Farmer
10. *Phonology and Syntax: The Relation between Sound and Structure*, Elisabeth O. Selkirk
11. *The Grammatical Basis of Linguistic Performance: Language Use and Acquisition*, Robert C. Berwick and Amy S. Weinberg
12. *Introduction to the Theory of Grammar*, Henk van Riemsdijk and Edwin Williams
13. *Word and Sentence Prosody in Serbocroatian*, Ilse Lehiste and Pavle Ivić
14. *The Representation of (In)definiteness*, Eric J. Reuland and Alice G. B. ter Meulen, editors
15. *An Essay on Stress*, Morris Halle and Jean-Roger Vergnaud
16. *Language and Problems of Knowledge: The Managua Lectures*, Noam Chomsky
17. *A Course in GB Syntax: Lectures on Binding and Empty Categories*, Howard Lasnik and Juan Uriagereka
18. *Semantic Structures*, Ray Jackendoff
19. *Events in the Semantics of English: A Study in Subatomic Semantics*, Terence Parsons
20. *Principles and Parameters in Comparative Grammar*, Robert Freidin, editor
21. *Foundations of Generative Syntax*, Robert Freidin
22. *Move α: Conditions on Its Application and Output*, Howard Lasnik and Mamoru Saito
23. *Plurals and Events*, Barry Schein
24. *The View from Building 20: Essays in Linguistics in Honor of Sylvain Bromberger*, Kenneth Hale and Samuel Jay Keyser, editors
25. *Grounded Phonology*, Diana Archangeli and Douglas Pulleyblank
26. *The Magic of a Common Language: Jakobson, Mathesius, Trubetzkoy, and the Prague Linguistic Circle*, Jindřich Toman
27. *Zero Syntax: Experiencers and Cascades*, David Pesetsky
28. *The Minimalist Program*, Noam Chomsky
29. *Three Investigations of Extraction*, Paul M. Postal
30. *Acoustic Phonetics*, Kenneth N. Stevens

31. *Principle B, VP Ellipsis, and Interpretation in Child Grammar*, Rosalind Thornton and Kenneth Wexler
32. *Working Minimalism*, Samuel Epstein and Norbert Hornstein, editors
33. *Syntactic Structures Revisited: Contemporary Lectures on Classic Transformational Theory*, Howard Lasnik with Marcela Depiante and Arthur Stepanov
34. *Verbal Complexes*, Hilda Koopman and Anna Szabolcsi
35. *Parasitic Gaps*, Peter W. Culicover and Paul M. Postal, editors